AMERICAN PRIMACY
AND
MULTILATERAL COOPERATION

American Primacy

and

Multilateral Cooperation

Richard S. Williamson

Prairie Institute for Economic Growth & Freedom

Chicago

2006

ISBN: 0-9639022-5-3

Printed in the United States of America

Books by Richard S. Williamson

Human Rights, Democracy and Restorative Justice

The United States and U.N. Peacekeeping
A View From The U.N. Security Council

Seeking Firm Footing
America's Role in the World in the New Century

Disorder in the New World

United States Foreign Policy and the United Nations
(Co-Editor with William Charles Maynes)

Trade and Economic Growth
(Editor)

The United Nations
A Place of Promise and of Mischief

Reagan's Federalism
His Efforts to Decentralize Government

Conservatives View the 80's From the U.S. Senate
(Co-Editor with Paul Laxalt)

ACKNOWLEDGEMENTS

Off and on for the past 25 years I have been engaged in multilateral diplomacy in behalf of the United States. During that time countless people have helped me with these assignments. To all of them I am indebted. I do want to single out a few for special thanks: Ambassador Steve Minikes, Dan Russell, David Kostelancik, Richard Prosen, Father Paul A. Holmes, Dean Courtney Smith, Ambassador William Luers and Suzanne DiMaggio.

Also, I wish to acknowledge and thank my assistant Diane Stephensen. Her advice, organizational talents, skill and patience have been invaluable aids to this work. She's the most able right hand women anyone could ever wish to have as an assistant.

Rich Williamson
December, 2006

DEDICATION

To my family: Jane, Elisabeth, Craig and Ricky
who challenge me and enrich my life.

TABLE OF CONTENTS

SECTION III: THE UNITED NATIONS

Section IV: Democracy

Section V: Human Rights

SECTION VI: SECURITY

SECTION VII. REGIONAL

SECTION VIII. MISCELLANEOUS

INTRODUCTION

We live in an era of American Primacy. As Michael Mandelbaum writes in his book *The Case for Goliath*, "The enormous power and persuasive influence of the United States (is) universally acknowledged to be the defining feature of world affairs."

America has uncontested military might, economic strength and cultural reach. The United States economy produces about 29% of world output; larger than the combined output of the next three largest economies (Japan, Germany, and Britain). United States military spending is nearly 50% of total global defense spending. America accounts for an even higher share of world spending on military research and development. From laser guided "smart weapons" to undetectable stealth aircraft, America is generations ahead in the race for military technology. No other country has a "super carrier" battle group at sea, while America has nine. The United States is the leader in information technology and higher education. Eighteen of the world's top 20 universities are in America. America's culture is all-pervasive from its food, to clothes, to music, to movies. CNN is ubiquitous. English is the international language. The dollar is the global currency. The American dominated Western civilization value-system casts an enormous shadow worldwide. As Professor Paul Kennedy has written, "Nothing has ever existed like this disparity of power, nothing."

Unquestionably, American swagger, mismanagement, and the on-going struggle in Iraq have diminished United States power and influence. America's fidelity to its own values and competence have been questioned. A sense that America's approach to other countries too often is "our way or the highway" has brought into question its predictability and created unease about its power. Occasional unnecessarily brash unilateralism has strained other countries' acceptance of American leadership.

Nonetheless, American preeminence remains unchallenged. American primacy gives the United States greater freedom of action and greater influence over global issues. No other country approaches America's capacity to project its power to any corner of the globe.

America also has a wider range of preferences, desires, interests, and strategic requirements around the world than any other country. American economic activity is worldwide. Reliable trade, international financial stability, the free flow of information, and market opportunities all are critical to the welfare of America's economy. United States citizens live abroad in every country in the world. Projecting American values of personal liberty, the rule of law, democracy, human rights and market economies is a basic part of the great American Experiment. The list goes on. And, while America has greater might, strength and reach to advance and protect our preferences, desires, interests and requirements, there are real limits in America's capacity to do so.

1

American Primacy does not mean absolute dominance. There are legitimate limits to the willingness of Americans to sacrifice blood and treasury. There are threats, challenges and opportunities that exceed America's capacity to act effectively. Furthermore, many threats such as global terrorist networks, the spread of weapons of mass destruction, environmental degradation and pandemic disease do not lend themselves to unilateral answers.

Clearly, America has the ability to act alone, arguably on a wider range of issues than any other nation. Just as clearly, America should reserve its right to act alone if it must to protect vital interests, especially vital security interests. But history, logic and common sense suggest just as clearly that it is often in America's interest to work with others to protect our security, advance our interests and project our values. In other words, even in this time of American Primacy, multilateral cooperation is important.

Unilateral action, bilateral partnerships and multilateral cooperation are all important means to advance U.S. interests. For each of these approaches there are many implements in America's large foreign policy toolbox.

Critics of multilateralism call attention to the failures of the League of Nations and the United Nations. They emphasize the limits, frustrations and unreliability of multilateral diplomacy. They stress history's repeated rejection of judicial restraint on power and war. They scoff at the double standards, waste and abuse of international institutions. They accentuate the value of self reliance, freedom of action, and ultimately the necessity of being able to act alone to safeguard vital interests and respond to imminent threats to America's national security.

As Ivo Daalder and James Lindsay write in their volume *America Unbound*, some have "a deep skepticism of traditional Wilsonianism's commitment to the rule of law and its belief in the relevance of international institutions. They placed their faith not in diplomacy and treaties, but in power and resolve." While power and resolve are important, indeed fundamental, to protecting United States security and the other interests, often they are not enough. Working with others is required. Multilateral cooperation is necessary.

In each of these areas, critics of multilateralism raise legitimate concerns. Indeed the failure to acknowledge these limitations by proponents of multilateral cooperation ultimately weakens their cause. For example, fervent supporters of the United Nations contribute to its problems by failing to recognize the U.N.'s limitations and advocating that it do more than it is equipped to handle. Multilateral cooperation is not the answer to international relations, it is *an* answer. It is a valuable tool in America's foreign policy toolbox, but fortunately it is not the only one.

It has been my experience during Ambassadorial postings to the United Nations in New York, Geneva and Vienna that America's views do not automatically carry the day. But on issues of importance, the United States can prevail if it respects the interests of others, is practical, patient, persistent, and is willing to lead. It's not always easy. It takes time. It can be very frustrating. But generally it can be done. And the broad acceptance of others, the common responsibility, and the burden sharing can be very helpful and, sometimes, critical to success on the ground. Furthermore, the process provides comfort to the less mighty, less strong and those with less reach that America is not a rogue state interested only in its perception of its own self-interests. It demonstrates that America respects the views of others and accepts rules of the road.

While America has the capacity to act alone and from time to time may do so, it seeks to work with others when feasible.

My experience is that countries do not want to oppose the United States. They do not want to break with America. Most want to align with the world's greatest power. They seek to embrace its values of democracy, human rights, opportunity and market economies rhetorically, if not always in practice. Some suggest recent events have changed that paradigm. They suggest today many seek political gain by crossing and opposing America. Perhaps that is true for some at this moment in history. But over time America's power, and, even more important, the attraction of American values will transcend whatever impediments, real or imagined, that may exist today.

Similarly champions of American unilateralism tend to exaggerate the advantages of acting alone and hold too preciously its benefits while too easily dismissing its costs and limitations. During the Cold War, America followed policies that recognized that its power could be sustained and enhanced through multilateral cooperation. In the post-Cold War world that also is true.

The selections in this book look at a large range of post-Cold War issues in which America is engaged and a wide variety of ways and means for multilateral cooperation. Collectively they make the case for the value of multilateral cooperation during this era of American Primacy while, nonetheless, acknowledging its limitations and the requirement for America to retain the right and the capacity to act alone when it must.

SECTION I:
TERRORISM

THE UNITED NATIONS:
AN IMPORTANT INSTRUMENT
IN THE WAR AGAINST TERRORISM

The evil acts waged against America on September 11th horrified the entire civilized world. As President Bush has said, "It is always and everywhere wrong to target and kill the innocent." And that is precisely what Osama bin Laden and the Al Qaeda did. Nearly 3,000 innocent Americans, as well as citizens of 80 other nations died.

Immediately, President Bush declared war on terrorism of global reach beginning with the far-flung Al Qaeda network. An important part of the president's strategy is to engage the United Nations as an instrument to successfully wage this war. As President Bush has said, "My attitude all along was, if we have to go it alone, we'll go it alone; but I'd rather not."

While some terrorist acts are indigenous, such as Timothy McVeigh's bombing of the Federal Building in Oklahoma City, there are many terrorist networks not limited to one nation or one region. These killers know no boundaries. They are transnational in recruiting misguided souls, establishing training camps, devising their plans, financing their activities, and targeting their victims.

To win the war against terrorism we cannot attack just the Taliban in Afghanistan. That was a beginning, but only a beginning. It is a global threat. And a multilateral response, in many areas, is the best response.

At the same time, the Administration has kept its focus on the ultimate goal: to wipe out terrorism. Any international coalition, any actions within the U.N. or elsewhere, are only a means to that end, not an end in itself. As a number of senior Administration officials have said, "The mission should define the coalition, not the other way around." Building a coalition is an important part of the strategy, but other nations will not dictate the terms of battle.

The United Nations' greatest contribution to fight terrorism has been developing international norms and legal instruments for cooperation against terrorists. Prior to September 11th, there were 12 major international conventions in the emerging international regime against terrorism. These conventions criminalized specific acts of terror such as taking hostages, hijacking airplanes, and bombings. Signatories to these conventions must have domestic laws criminalizing these acts. When a person suspected of committing one of these terrorist acts is found, the state has a legal obligation to extradite or prosecute the accused.

National Strategy Forum, Spring, 2002, Vol. 11, Issue 3.

This legal framework has made it more difficult for terrorists to find safe haven – unfortunately not impossible, but more difficult. Between 1993 and 1998, the United States relied on these legal instruments to bring 12 foreign nationals to America for prosecution, including Ramzi Ahmed Yousef, the mastermind of the 1993 World Trade Center bombings.

The U.N. Security Council did set up sanction regimes three times against states protecting terrorists: against Libya following the 1998 bombing of Pan Am flight 103, against Sudan following a 1995 assassination attempt against Egyptian President Mubarak and in 1998 against the Taliban government until it turned over Osama bin Laden. In all of these actions, the United States was a major advocate for U.N. Security Council action. The United States was using the authority of the U.N. Security Council to strengthen sanction regimes that Washington had imposed unilaterally.

Prior to September 11, 2001, the U.N. Security Council had never authorized military action against terrorists. The devastating evil acts of September changed that.

The day after the September 11th attacks, the U.N. Security Council unanimously passed Resolution 1368. This resolution states that terrorist attacks pose a "threat to international peace and security." And it said that nations have an obligation to help "bring to justice" the organizers of terrorist acts. Most importantly, this resolution recognized "the inherent right of individual or collective self-defense in accordance with the Charter." For the first time the U.N. Security Council recognized military action as a legitimate act of "self-defense" against non-state terrorist actors. This new international law further legitimized Washington's long-standing position that a military response to terrorist attacks was a proper exercise of self-defense.

That same day, September 12th, the U.N. General Assembly, without a dissenting vote, passed Resolution 56/1 that condemned the terrorist attacks in the United States and called states to cooperate to "bring to justice the perpetrators, organizers and sponsors of the outrages of 11 September 2001."

These two U.N. actions were invaluable in helping enlist countries whose cooperation was required to wage war against the Al Qaeda. Pakistan, Iran and China are but three of the many countries who cited these two U.N. resolutions to justify their support of the war against Al Qaeda.

On September 28th, the U.N. Security Council unanimously adopted Resolution 1373, another key instrument in the war against terrorism. This resolution requires Member States to take specific steps in their domestic legislation to combat terrorism: requiring states to criminalize the transfer of money to terrorist networks and freeze those assets, requiring states to exchange information about investigations or proceedings against terrorists, and mandating that states stop the supply of weapons to terrorist groups.

To implement Resolution 1373, the Security Council created a Counter-Terrorism Committee to monitor implementation of this resolution. In the first 90 days, well over 100 nations have filed detailed reports on their compliance with this resolution.

Then in November, the U.N. Security Council passed Resolution 1377 which reiterated the need for "all States to take urgent steps to implement fully Resolution 1373," and "invites the Counter-Terrorism Committee to explore ways in which States can be assisted" in implementing "all the requirements of Resolution 1373."

This emerging anti-terrorist regime is supporting the United States war against global terrorism by establishing international law that explicitly states that a nation's military actions against terrorists is an appropriate exercise of self-defense. Thereby it has been easier to create a broad, more effective international coalition in the war against Al Qaeda. It has forced countries to review their own domestic laws to effectively fight terrorism, report on their status, and gain assistance in strengthening them. It has created a vehicle to freeze terrorist funds. Within the first four months after September 11th, 168 institutions or individuals were placed on the U.N. counter-terrorism sanctions list and over $110 million in terrorist assets were frozen worldwide.

Furthermore, a lesson from Al Qaeda is that failed states are fertile ground for terrorists to hide, to train, and from which to launch attacks against the United States and other countries. The U.N. is playing a critical role in supporting the transfer of power from the defeated Taliban to a new legitimate government in Kabul. And the U.N. will continue to play a role in helping Afghanistan work toward stability by training police, training the military, helping establish schools, and assisting economic development.

As stated earlier, President Bush said to wage the war against global terrorism, the United States will go it alone if we must, but he'd rather not. The United Nations is helping insure that this war is not the United States' alone, but a war that must be fought and won by the entire international community.

EFFORTS AT THE UNITED NATIONS TO FIGHT TERRORISM

I appreciate the invitation to participate in this Naval War College Current Strategy Forum on "Transforming American National Security in the 21st Century." I especially look forward to the question and answer period following my remarks.

As this year began, President Bush, in his first State of the Union address said, "Our war against terror is only beginning. We will win this war, we will protect our homeland."

The President went on to say that United States intelligence agents searching terrorist bases in Afghanistan found maps of U.S. cities, diagrams of nuclear power plants and water facilities, and instructions for making chemical weapons, as well as new evidence that "thousands of dangerous killers" are still at large.

The President warned that hostile countries, an "axis of evil," Iraq, Iran and North Korea, "pose a grave and growing danger by building chemical, biological or nuclear weapons." President Bush said, "I will not wait on events while dangers gather. …The United States of America will not permit the world's most dangerous regimes to threaten us with the world's most destructive weapons."

That was in January, words spoken as the ashes from the World Trade Center's destruction continued to darken America's horizon. Now it is June. While the tragic events of September 11th continue to tug at America's heart, a semblance of normalcy has returned to America. Other issues dominate the daily news.

But, just the other day, in his graduation speech at West Point, President Bush continued to talk about the war on terror and to signal new directions that this war might take.

He said, "In defending the peace, we face a threat with no precedent. Enemies in the past needed great armies and great industrial capacities to endanger the American people and our nation. The attacks of September the 11th required a few hundred thousand dollars in the hands of a few dozen evil and deluded men. All of the chaos and suffering they caused came at much less than the cost of a single tank. The dangers have not passed. This government and the American people are on watch, we are ready, because we know the terrorists have more money and more men and more plans." America's concerted counter-terrorism campaign still is in its early stages. But it is not too early to assess what we have accomplished and what we need to do; and how we can go about it.

U.S. Naval War College, Newport, Rhode Island, June 11, 2002.

The first battlefield was Afghanistan, the largest sanctuary of terrorism, the home base for Osama bin Laden and the al-Qaeda network. Afghanistan had become not a state that sponsored terrorists, but a terrorist sponsored state. And the United States did what it does well. It successfully engaged in a large campaign to defeat the Taliban regime and root out the al-Qaeda terrorist network.

Pentagon planners, superb logistics, advanced technology, brave soldiers, men and women, from flying planes to stealth special operations, engaged the enemy and defeated the enemy. As President Bush said the other day, "Our war on terror is only begun, but in Afghanistan it was begun well."

But there are other battlefields on which the war on terrorism must be waged; some of these also are areas in which America does well, but some are areas where America does not do well.

Rebuilding collapsed states (fertile ground for terrorist organizations); coalition-building; developing other countries' legal capacity; developing "best practices" for control of financial flow, immigration, customs and arms traffic; and establishing norms of international behavior are all areas where collective action and coalitions can better wage the war on terrorism than the United States can do it alone. The war on terrorism is a collective enterprise. A neighbor's failure or inability to make itself inhospitable to terrorists and those who aid and abet them threaten other states.

I hasten to add that the United States cannot and will not let any international coalition or multinational organization imbed its ability to prosecute the war on terrorism. Other nations cannot dictate the terms of battle. The mission should define the coalition, or the preferred multilateral organization, not the other way around. But in the war on terrorism, a coalition is central to success.

That is why, in his recent trip to Europe, President Bush worked to strengthen the U.S./European coalition against terrorism. That is why, in his address to the Bundestag, he reminded our allies that "[t]hose who seek missiles and terrible weapons are also familiar with the map of Europe."

A recognition of the value of multilateralism in the war against terrorism was behind the work of the United States with the 32 other member countries of the Organization of American States (OAS), to achieve the new Inter-American Convention Against Terrorism to enhance security cooperation in the Western Hemisphere that was signed by Secretary of State Colin Powell last week in Barbados. The Convention is designed to improve regional cooperation in cutting terrorist finances, improving border and customs control, and investigating terrorist acts.

A recognition of the important role of multilateralism in fighting terrorism is why Secretary of Defense Donald Rumsfeld traveled to Brussels last week to give our NATO partners a classified briefing describing the spread of biological, chemical and nuclear weapons and the links between terrorist networks and hostile states believed to possess those weapons. He called upon NATO to expand its definition of collective self-defense.

Secretary Rumsfeld challenged NATO. He said, "If a terrorist can attack at any time, at any place, using any technique, and it's physically impossible to defend in every place, at every time, against every technique, then one needs to calibrate the definition of defense.

"The only defense is to take the effort to find those global networks and to deal with them, as the United States did in Afghanistan," he said. "Now, is that defensive, or is it offensive? I personally think of it as defensive."

NATO Secretary-General Lord Robinson reinforced Secretary Rumsfeld's message by saying, "We must be ready to deal with threats whenever they occur and wherever the occur."

OAS, NATO, the G-8, and the United Nations are all important multilateral I in which an anti-terror coalition can act against terrorists of global reach.

Among multilateral organizations, the United Nations has *unique assets* that give it some comparative advantages in certain areas in the fight against terrorism. It is a *universal organization* with 189 Member States, soon to grow to 190 when East Timor completes its application process. This gives the United Nations a reach to every corner of the globe. The United Nations has a special moral authority and acceptance, which has been built over many years. Its charter is rooted in the same transcendent values as the United States Declaration of Independence and Constitution. The UN Declaration on Human Rights is embraced rhetorically, if not always in fact, throughout the world as the proper, civilized standard of behavior, of respect, of decency, of limits on state power. The United Nations has been the invaluable midwife for the birth of scores of new nations from colonialism, earning it a special high regard in villages and capitals throughout the third world. The United Nations is the venue where every nation, no matter how weak, how poor or how small can have a voice. It is an organization in which burdens are shared and through which the needy gain assistance.

These characteristics, this history, those assets make the United Nations an extremely helpful venue to fight terrorism through setting norms, building a counter-terrorism infrastructure of "best practices", battling proliferation of weapons of mass destruction and burden sharing (including burden sharing to rebuild failed states such as in Afghanistan).

President Bush has said, "Moral truth is the same in every culture, in every time, and in every place. Targeting innocent civilians for murder is always and everywhere wrong." That call of moral clarity is important to the war against terrorist networks of global reach. Ultimately, it is the foundation upon which we build the counter-terrorism infrastructure. And the United Nations helps transform that simple, clear moral truth into an international norm, an agreed upon standard for the entire international community, an accepted loadstone on which to build a counter-terror infrastructure of laws and actions to force terrorists out of their comfort zone, to root them out, and to destroy them.

Immediately after September 11, the United Nations Security Council adopted three important Resolutions, 1368, 1373 and 1377 which affirmed the right of self-defense, found terrorism to be a threat to international peace and security, stressed the accountability of the supporter, as well as the perpetrator of terrorist acts, obliged

Member States to limit the ability of terrorists and terrorist organizations to operate internationally by freezing assets of terrorist-affiliated persons and organizations and denying them safe haven, among other things, and set forth a Ministerial Declaration on International Terrorism.

United Nations Secretary-General Kofi Annan has used his position of global moral authority, a position strengthened when he received the Nobel Peace Prize last year, to condemn terrorist acts. In a speech the day after the evil acts of 11 September, Kofi Annan said, "All nations of the world must be united in their solidarity with the victims of terrorism, and in their determination to take action, both against the terrorists themselves and against all those who give them any kind of shelter, assistance or encouragement."

The United Nations General Assembly adopted two anti-terrorism resolutions that condemned the "heinous acts of terrorism" in Washington, Pennsylvania, and New York City. The U.N. General Assembly also continued its work on the negotiation of international terrorism conventions. Twelve such conventions have been adopted to date.

Through Security Council resolutions, General Assembly resolutions, negotiating international terrorism conventions, and statements by Secretary-General Kofi Annan, the United Nations has helped establish important international norms against terrorism, both terrorist acts and those who aid or harbor them.

A second area where the United Nations helps in the fight against terrorism is in helping build counter-terrorism capacity around the world. Assistance is one element in building effective collective security against terrorism. States differ in their capacity to fight terror. Even countries with substantial counter-terrorism capacity need help, if only in the area of understanding vulnerabilities. Some states have a great capacity to teach others. And, quite frankly, as the world's sole superpower, the United States demands respect but also engenders resentment. For many countries it is easier to accept counter-terror assistance and advice under the United Nations umbrella than bilaterally from the United States. And while the United States has substantial assistance capabilities, they are not infinite. We need to target our counter-terror help. And we need to work with others to help where we cannot.

Last fall, the UN Security Council established a "Counter-Terrorism Committee" (CTC) to oversee implementation of UN Security Council Resolution 1373. This UN Counter-Terrorism Committee is chaired by United Kingdom Permanent Representative Sir Jeremy Greenstock. Its goal is to improve worldwide counter-terrorism capacity. The Counter-Terrorism Committee is seeking to inventory each country's counter-terrorism capabilities and helps to match countries that need assistance with assistance providers. It is a switchboard of sorts.

It is important to note that counter-terrorism assistance is completely separate from development assistance and will have no impact on it.

In November 2001, as part of its effort to oversee implementation of Resolution 1373, the Committee invited all states with the capacity to do so to contribute to the compilation of a database of sources of advice and expertise in the areas of legislative and administrative practice. The Counter-Terrorism Committee subsequently created a web-based directory listing eight categories corresponding broadly with areas of activity covered by Resolution 1373 (drafting of counter-terrorism legislation, financial law and practice, extradition law and practice, police and law enforcement work, and illegal arms trafficking) and those countries and organizations that have offered assistance in the respective categories.

Also, the Counter-Terrorism Committee sought and Member States have sent reports in on the steps they are taking to fight terrorism in seven critical areas: legislation, financial asset controls, customs, immigration, extradition, law enforcement and arms traffic. The Committee is now following up with Member States to help them gain advice and assistance on how to strengthen their counter-terrorism capabilities. This effort to create "best practices" and to strengthen national capacities in these areas should prove to be very helpful to the global fight against terrorism.

A third area where the UN can help in the fight against terrorism is to curb the proliferation of weapons of mass destruction – especially to protect against acts of nuclear terrorism. The International Atomic Energy Agency, a UN specialized agency headquartered in Vienna, has various safeguards on nuclear power plants around the world to protect against diversion of nuclear material that could be used either to develop nuclear weapons or a so-called terrorist dirty nuclear devise.

The International Atomic Energy Agency also has adopted a resolution addressing measures to protect against acts of nuclear terrorism and is developing a program to coordinate assistance to Member States to improve security of nuclear facilities and of nuclear and radioactive materials.

Finally, Secretary-General Kofi Annan is engaged in negotiations with Iraq to return arms inspectors to the land of Saddam Hussein. Hard lessons were learned from the failures of UNSCOM. Hopefully, these negotiations will result in tough, intrusive, and reliably effective arms inspections. Saddam Hussein's efforts to acquire weapons of mass destruction have not stopped. We know this.

Yesterday in Kuwait, Secretary Rumsfeld talked about Iraq's program for weapons of mass destruction. "They have them, and they continue to develop them, and they have weaponized chemical weapons," he said. "They've had an active program to develop nuclear weapons. It's also clear that they are actively developing biological weapons. I don't know what other kinds of weapons would fall under the rubric of weapons of mass destruction, but if there are more, I suspect they're working on them, as well."

If, in the end, Saddam Hussein does not accept tough intrusive UN arms inspections, the world will know why. If he does, the UN arms inspections will (1) force Saddam to stop his efforts to acquire and stockpile weapons of mass destruction, or (2) result in evidence for the entire world of his WMD programs, or (3) he will again kick out UN arms inspectors and, thereby, say to the world that he does have a WMD program. In any case, either Saddam stops his weapons of mass destruction programs or the table is set for more forceful action to change the regime in Baghdad.

A fourth area where the U.N. can help in the fight against terrorism is to facilitate burden sharing, especially in the job of helping rebuild failed states, prime harbors for terrorists of global reach.

As noted earlier, the United States military might is unchallenged. Not only is our standing military large, but our technology is generations ahead of others. This is a result of many things, among them the United States willingness to spend a high percent of our GNP on the military. Other nations, including our NATO allies, notwithstanding muscular rhetoric, have made decisions to spend far lower percents of GNP on their military. Consequently, these other countries fall further and further behind the United States in their military strength and in their ability to project what military might they have to protect their interests. Frankly, they become more dependent upon the United States military whether it is to calm destabilizing ethnic unrest in their backyard such as the Balkans or to root out terrorists of global reach "familiar with the map of Europe" such as al-Qaeda. Therefore, it is not unreasonable to expect other countries to pick up more of the cost for nation building. And the United Nations can serve as a coordinator and facilitator of such collective action.

We see this in Afghanistan. While the United States military works to complete the mop up of al-Qaeda pockets in the Afghan countryside, ISAF (the Interim Security Assistance Force) keeps order and security in Kabul and its environs. The British have led ISAF and the Turks soon will take over that leadership role. Meanwhile, the Germans have taken the lead to train the Afghan police, the Italians have taken the lead to help train and build an Afghan judicial system, and the British have taken the lead in the important counter-narcotics program. The United States is taking the lead in training a new, professional Afghan army. And other countries, through the UN Tokyo Donors Conference last winter and the Geneva Donors Conference this spring, have made large financial commitments to support a wide variety of activities to rebuild a new Afghanistan from the Loya Jirga, to schools, to hospitals, to the economy.

The UN Secretary-General's Special Representative Lakhdar Brahimi has helped coordinate these efforts and he has been especially crucial in moving along the Loya Jirga process.

In a press conference on October 11, 2001, President Bush said, "It would be a useful function for the United Nations to take over the so-called 'nation-building', -- I would call it the stabilization of a future government – after our military mission is complete. We'll participate, other countries will participate…[to make] sure that the post-operations Afghanistan is one that is stable, and one that doesn't become yet again a haven for terrorist criminals." And in the ways I've outlined, the United Nations is working to do that.

In conclusion, the United Nations efforts to fight terrorism falls into 4 categories: Norm setting, helping other countries to build counter-terrorism capabilities, working to curb the proliferation of weapons of mass destruction (with particular attention to Iraq), and in burden sharing (as in getting other countries to participate to rebuild Afghanistan and other failed states).

As President Bush has said, the war on terrorism is difficult and it will take time. Just this past weekend Homeland Security Director Tom Ridge said, "Literally you have thousands and thousands of people probably located in 40 or 50 countries around the world, who look at the United States of America as the primary target."

This long, difficult war on terror can only be won with U.S. leadership. But a valuable mechanism to help us prevail, to help ensure that we triumph over terrorism, will be the United Nations.

Thank you.

COUNTERING TERRORISM, INTERNATIONAL EXPERIENCE, THE ROLE OF THE UNITED NATIONS

I applaud the leadership of the Government of Bulgaria for calling this international conference on terrorism, I thank the sponsors for inviting me to participate. And I applaud the remarks of President Parvanov as he opened our discussions this morning.

On September 11, 2001 history pivoted. Nearly 3000 innocent civilians were killed by an evil act committed by evil men.[1] People from nearly 80 countries perished in the World Trade Center.

As President George Bush said in a joint address to Congress a few days after the event, "On September the 11th , enemies of freedom committed an act of war against our country....night fell on a different world, a world where freedom itself is under attack."[2]

Unfortunately, this was not the first terrorist attack against the United States, it was not the first time American lives were lost due to terrorist acts committed by evil men.

There was the attack on the U.S.S. Cole off the Yemen coast; the bombings of U.S. Embassies in Kenya and Tanzania; the explosion of the U.S. housing complex in Saudi Arabia; and there have been many others.[3]

Nor, unfortunately, was the World Trade Center the last terrorist attack against the United States. Just last week, unknown assailants fired at least two rockets in the vicinity of the U.S. Embassy in Kabul. Also last week, a car bomb exploded outside the U.S. consulate in Karachi, Pakistan, killing 11 Pakistanis and injuring 45 other people, including one U.S. Marine.

And, as you know, terrorists also are familiar with the map of Europe.[4] In recent days I have been in Croatia, Bosnia-Herzegovina and Kosovo where too many innocent civilians have been killed in the past decade. Yes, the Balkans too have suffered at the hands of terrorists.

Just after September 11th, President Bush said, "These terrorists kill not merely to end lives, but to disrupt and end a way of life. With every atrocity, they hope that (we) grow fearful, retreating from the world and forsaking our friends. They stand against us, because we stand in their way.

Regional Policy Forum of the South East Europe Countries, Sofia, Bulgaria, June 27, 2002.

17

"...We have seen their kind before. They are the heirs of all the murderous ideologies of the 20th century. By sacrificing human life to serve their radical visions– by abandoning every value except the will to power -- they follow in the path of fascism, and Nazism and totalitarianism. And they will follow that path all the way, to where it ends: in histories unmarked grave of discarded lies."[5]

President Bush went on to say, "This is not...just America's fight. And what is at stake is not just America's freedom. This is the world's fight. This is civilization's fight. This is the fight of all who believe in progress and pluralism, tolerance and freedom. We ask every nation to join us. We will ask, and we will need, the help of police force, intelligence services, and banking systems around the world."[6]

That was the plea of President Bush days after the al-Queda terrorist attacks against Washington, Pennsylvania and New York City. And the world community has responded. No nation, not even the world's sole superpower, can win this war against terrorism of global reach alone. We need partners. We need coalitions. And we need multilateral organizations, including the United Nations.

Among the first stages for the counter terror war was to bring down the Taliban regime in Afghanistan. The State of Afghanistan did not sponsor terrorism so much as terrorists sponsored the state. The safe-haven of Osama bin Laden. The training base and launching pad of al-Qaeda. The Taliban regime became the target of the awesome military might of America. But even in Afghanistan a coalition of nations has been important.

British forces and others fought beside American Special Operations forces. Two-thirds of the NATO countries have forces directly involved in the war. More than half have forces on the ground in Afghanistan. And there have been other ways and means in which other nations have helped in Afghanistan.

In remarks last Friday, Secretary of Defense Donald Rumsfeld said, "Some 69 countries are contributing direct support to Operation Enduring Freedom. Thirty-three countries have representatives down at the combatant commander's headquarters, CENTCOM in Tampa, Florida"[7]

Coalition force have supplied a vast amount of humanitarian assistance and medical assistance, including more than a million pounds of wheat and assorted food.

The war in Afghanistan has gone well. Quickly the Taliban regime fell at the hands of coalition forces. America and others are engaged in the military mop up in the countryside. A broad based, multi-ethnic, participatory, political process has gone on in recent months in Afghanistan culminating in a grand Loya Jirga in Kabul which, last week selected Hamid Karzai to a two year term as President of the Afghanistan transition government. And, for the first, time Afghan women participated in the Loya Jirga.

The international community, led by the UN and Ambassador Brahemi, are there to insure that this new representative government takes root. For we have learned that failed states are fertile ground for the terrorists we must defeat.

As President Bush said in a graduation address at West Point earlier this month, "Our war on terror is only begun, but in Afghanistan it was begun well."[8]

Another critical phase in the war against terrorism is intelligence: the gathering of information, analyzing it and sharing it. Here once again cooperation among countries is important. Since September, 2001, the development of information and sharing of intelligence has resulted in "more than 90 countries (having) arrested or detained some 2,400 individuals, terrorists and their supporters."[9]

Lord Robertson, Secretary General of NATO, has underscored the continued relevance of NATO in the war against terrorism. He has said that NATO was in the midst of "major transformations" to build up its capabilities for the new era. "NATO is prepared to act as the focus of the international communities military preparations for defense against terrorism."[10]

Recognizing the vital role other nations must play to defeat terrorism of global reach, the United States has worked with our friends to rally important multilateral institutions to play their parts in this campaign. Immediately after 9/11, NATO declare those terrorist attacks against America as an attack against all NATO members.[11]

In May, the thirty-three member countries of the Organization of American States signed the new Inter-American Convention Against Terrorism to enhance security cooperation in the Western Hemisphere.

The Convention is designed to improve regional cooperation in cutting terrorist finances, improving border and customs control, and investigating terrorist acts.

Recognizing the importance of multilateral institutions, last month Secretary of Defense Rumsfeld traveled to Brussels to give our NATO partners a classified briefing describing the spread of biological, chemical and nuclear weapons and the links between terrorist networks and hostile states believed to possess those weapons. He challenged NATO to expand its definition of collective self-defense.

This week the G-8 is meeting in Whistler, Canada. And terrorism is central to the topics being discussed by those heads of state of the most industrial nations.[12]

OAS, NATO, the G-8 and other multilateral institutions have important roles to play in the war against terrorists of global reach. And so does the United Nations. Indeed the United Nations has a number of unique assets that give it a comparative advantage in certain areas in the fight against terrorists.

The United Nations is a universal organization with a reach to every corner of the globe. The United Nations has a special legitimacy and moral authority drawn from the transcendent values of its charter and the UN Declaration on Human Rights; from its role as a midwife for the birth of so many new nations emerging from colonialism; and from the fact that it is an organization in which burdens are shared and through which the needy gain assistance. And today, the United Nations' moral authority is strengthened by the stature and decency of its leader Secretary-General Kofi Annan.

The United Nations' long history and these unique assets make the UN extremely helpful in the fight against terrorism through setting norms, battling the proliferation of weapons of mass destruction, burden sharing (including burden sharing to rebuild failed states such as Afghanistan), and developing "best practices" and country's capacity to fight terrorism—especially in the area of impeding terrorist financing.

NORMS

Immediately after September 11, the United Nations Security Council adopted three important resolutions, 1368, 1373 and 1377, which affirmed the right of self-defense, found terrorism to be a threat to international peace and security, stressed the accountability of the supporter as well as the perpetrator of terrorist acts, obliged member states to limit the ability of terrorists and terrorist organizations to operate internationally by freezing assets of terrorist-affiliated persons and organizations and denying them safe-haven, among other things, and set forth a Ministerial Declaration on International Terrorism.

The United Nations General Assembly adopted two antiterrorism resolutions that condemned the "heinous acts of terrorism" in Washington, Pennsylvania, and New York City. The U.N. General Assembly also continued its work on the negotiation of international terrorism conventions. Twelve such conventions have been adopted to date. This week, President Bush signed two more of those international terrorism conventions.

Through Security Council Resolutions, General Assembly Resolutions, negotiating international terrorism conventions, and statements by Secretary-General Kofi Annan, the United Nations has helped establish important international norms against terrorism, both terrorist acts and those who aid or harbor them.

NON-PROLIFERATION

A second area where the UN can help in the fight against terrorism is to curb the proliferation of weapons of mass destruction-especially to protect against acts of nuclear terrorism. As Secretary of Defense Donald Rumsfeld has said terrorist networks "are aggressively trying to get nuclear weapons….and they would not hesitate one minute in using them."[13] The International Atomic Energy Agency, a UN specialized agency headquartered in Vienna, has various safeguards on nuclear power plants around the world to protect against diversion of nuclear material that could be use either to develop nuclear weapons or a so-called terrorist dirty nuclear devise.

The International Atomic Energy Agency also has adopted a resolution addressing measures to protect against acts of nuclear terrorism and developing a program to coordinate assistance to member states to improve security of nuclear facilities and of nuclear and radioactive materials.

Finally, Secretary General Kofi Annan is engaged in negotiations with Iraq to return arms inspectors to the land of Saddam Hussein. Hard lessens were learned form the failures of UNSCOM. Hopefully these negotiations will result in tough, intrusive, and reliably effective arms inspection.

A third area where the UN can help in the fight against terrorism is to facilitate burden sharing, especially in the job of helping rebuild failed states; prime harbors for terrorists of global reach.

We see this in Afghanistan. While the United States military works to complete the mop up of al-Qaeda pockets in the Afghan countryside, ISAF (the Interim Security Assistance Force) keeps order and security in Kabul and its environs. The British have led ISAF and the Turks took over that leadership role last week. Meanwhile the Germans have taken the lead to train the Afghan police, the Italians have taken the lead to help train and build an Afghan judicial system, and the British have taken the lead in the important counter-narcotics program. The United States is taking the lead in training a new, professional Afghan army. And other countries, through the UN Tokyo donors conference last winter and the Geneva donors conferences this spring, have made large financial commitments to support a wide variety of activities to rebuild a new Afghanistan from the Loya Jirga, to schools, to hospitals, to the economy.

In a press conference on October 11, 2001, President Bush said, "It would be a useful function for the United Nations to take over the so-called 'nation-building', -- I would call it the stabilization of a future government – after our military mission is complete. We'll participate, other countries will participate.....[to make] sure that the post-operations Afghanistan is one that is stable, and one that doesn't become yet again a haven for terrorist criminals." And in the ways I've outlined, the United Nations is working to do that.

CAPACITY BUILDING

A fourth area where the United Nations plays a crucial role in the fight against terrorism is in helping country's around the world build their counter-terrorism capacity. Sir Jeremy Greenstock, chairman of the United Nations Counter Terrorism Committee (CTC) has observed that a country with little counter-terror capability is a danger to neighbor states.

Just weeks after the attacks on the World Trade Center, the UN Security Council adopted Resolution 1373[14] imposing binding obligations on all States to suppress and prevent terrorism. The average level of government performance against terrorism around the world must be raised. This means upgrading the capacity of each nation's legislation and executive machinery to fight terrorism. And the process of counter-terrorism capacity building is being undertaken by the UN's Counter-Terrorism Committee.

UN Security Council Resolution 1373 is wide ranging. It covers all aspects of preventing and suppressing terrorism, from cutting off the funds to preventing access to weapons and building judicial cooperation. Each state was required by the resolution to report to the CTC on the steps taken to implement it.

The members of the Committee decided to be proactive, transparent, cooperative and eve-handed in this task. In order to be successful, the CTC must build cooperation internationally and at the regional level exchanging information about terrorism. We must share as widely as possible expertise and assistance on counter-terrorism. Quite frankly, that is why regional conferences such as this one are so important.

Since autumn, the CTC issued guidance to States on the submission of reports. The Committee published a directory of contact points to promote international cooperation including listing the contact details of those in UN Missions and capitals responsible for the implementation of 1373.

From January 2002, the CTC has been reviewing the reports submitted. In response to each report, the CTC is writing, in confidence, to the government concerned offering its comments. In the first round, the comments largely have been seeking more information, or specific clarification. The comments also begin to probe areas where implementation may not be full enough.

As of June 7th, 155 reports had been submitted form UN members and others. This is member state engagement unprecedented for a UN operation. Those member states who have not submitted a report are almost without exception those with little experience in the area and unsophisticated law and order systems.

Since June 7th, the CTC has engaged in a second review as the second round of reports have begun to arrive in response to the CTC letters. The Committee intends to be more direct in the second phase in identifying potential gaps and asking states what action they intend to take to address the issues of concern. The Committee may outline areas in which the Committee believes that legislation or further executive measures are needed to upgrade the State's capacity against terrorism in line with 1373. The Committee also will make recommendations on assistance.

The CTC does not plan to declare any member state compliant, because resolution 1373 is open-ended, and the threats posed by various forms of terrorism will evolve. But the CTC hopes to reach the point with increasing numbers of states that the Committee will have no comments, for now, on what they have done. Of course, even when we get to that point, there will be ways in which the state can improve; for example on regional cooperation, or exchange of information. But the Counter Terrorism Committee needs to be focused on the number one priority, the real gaps in global capacity.

To be successful in what we are trying to do, the CTC must promote the sharing of expertise and assistance on counter-terrorism. Governments share a common goal, but differ in their preparedness to act. A number of states have no experience with terrorism. But they are beginning to recognize that terrorism will migrate, and that a vacuum is dangerous. Therefore, they are trying to improve; starting from a lower basic capacity than a country which has been tackling terrorism for years. They will look to those with experience to help.

The coordination of effort between organizations and States with experience is key to ensuring that global anti-terrorist capacity is raised effectively and quickly. The CTC has set up a Directory of available help, and has invited all states and organizations in a position to offer assistance and expertise to contribute to it. This is designed to be a one-stop-shop for states looking for help.

The CTC intends to deepen its contact with regional organizations. States have an individual interest in upgrading their own capacity to ensure terrorists cannot operate on or from their territory. But they also have a collective interest with their neighbors to ensure that their region is not abused by terrorists.

Regional organizations have a key role to play in ensuring that action is taken across the region. They also may have a role in coordinating assistance on a regional level if the needs of their members have similar characteristics. As NATO Secretary General Lord Robertson said just the other day at a conference on regional stability, "The future stability and security of South-East Europe will depend critically on the willingness of the governments in the region to deepen and broaden cooperation with their neighbors."[15]

It is worth noting what the CTC is not. It is not a tribunal for judging States. It will not trespass on areas of competence of other parts of the UN system. It is not going to define terrorism in a legal sense, although we will have a fair idea of what is blatant terrorism. It has no plans to issue lists of terrorist organizations.

If member states cannot settle matters of political controversy, the CTC will refer them back to the Security Council.

FINANCING

Finally let me turn to the terrorism financing problem which has a number of facets.

One comes from the use of lawfully obtained assets to support terrorism; that is profits of legitimate businesses. Even sophisticated banking and financial regulatory systems are not designed to track lawful transactions. Their goal is to facilitate lawful economic enterprise. Methods are needed to find and stop the use of honestly obtained assets to support terrorism.[16]

A second area is "money laundering." The phenomenon of cleaning illegally obtained assets through investment in, and then extraction from, lawful enterprises is a familiar police problem. It has long been a feature of narcotics trafficking and therefore is familiar to almost every government and police force in the world.[17] That fact does not make the phenomenon easier to track and stop. It does mean that the international community has considerable competence, experience and resources in fighting laundering. And it means, through the UN Counter-Terrorism Committee, there are resources available to help less well-equipped countries in this area.

Finally, asset freezes. Most countries that recognize economic crimes, or even narcotics trafficking as crimes, and that have a system of enforcing contracts, have the capability to freeze assets.

The mechanism is familiar in the civil law area, when ownership of assets is disputed. For example, in the American system, Party A can ask a Court to enjoin Party B from using or removing assets until legal rights are established.[18] Absent such a freeze, Party A would find its rights nullified without a day in court. The same system is applied to asset freezes.

In the UN context, the mechanism of a single country is internationalized. For example, State A concludes that Party B needs to show cause that it is not engaged in terrorist activity and pending such a showing freezes Party B's assets. Party B has the right to go into court or, in the first instance, at least apply to the regulatory body for administrative relief by demonstrating that it is entitle to the property and not engaged in unlawful activity.

Under UN Security Council Resolution 1390,[19] the Security Council sanctions committee can adopt state A's determination as its own and order all countries not only to respect State A's asset freeze but to join State A in freezing any of Party B's assets that might be in their country. The result is to internationalize a local asset freeze to make it harder, if not impossible, for a terrorist to access financial support in its name.

To date, 161 countries have taken concrete action to block assets valued at U.S. dollar 116 million of 210 terrorist entities.

So you can see that the United Nations is playing an important role in countering terrorism.

President Bush spoke for all of us in his State of the Union Address when he said, "Our enemies send other people's children on missions of suicide and murder. They embrace tyranny and death as a cause and a creed. We stand for a different choice, made long ago, on the day of our founding. We affirm it again today. We choose freedom and the dignity of every life. Steadfast in our purpose, we press on. We have known freedom's price. We have shown freedom's power. And in this great conflict, my fellow Americans we will see freedom's victory."[20] Thank you.

---

1.   See Caleb Carr, *The Lessons of Terror: A History of Warfare against Civilians: Why it has always failed and why it will fail again* (New York, Random House 2002) in which he argues that warfare against civilians should always be viewed as terrorism.

2.   President George W. Bush, Address to Joint Session of Congress, September 20, 2001.

3.   "Foreign terrorists attacked American citizens, facilities or interests more than 2,400 times between 1983 and 1998." Fernando Reinares, "The Empire Rarely Strikes Back," *Foreign Policy*, January/February 2002, p.92.

4.   Unfortunately, the rate of terrorist attacks worldwide is accelerating. "During the 1970s, 8,114 terrorist incidents were reported around the world, resulting in 4,798 deaths and 6,902 injuries. During the 1980s the number of incidents increased nearly four-fold to 31,426 with 70,859 deaths and 47,849 injuries. From 1990 to 1996 there were 27,086 incidents, causing 51,797 deaths and 58,814 injuries. The number of deaths due to acts of terrorism varies from year to year, but there is a clearly increasing trend. Between 1970 and 1995, on average, each year brought 206 more incidents and 441 more fatalities. "Jessica Stern, *The Ultimate Terrorists* (Cambridge, Harvard University Press, 1999) p.6.

5.   President George W. Bush remarks to a Joint Session of Congress, September 20, 2001.

6.   Ibid. For interesting discussions on the role of intelligence in the counter terror effort see, John Deutch and Jeffrey H. Smith, "Smarter Intelligence," *Foreign Policy*, January/February, 2002, pp. 64-69, and Phillip B. Heyman, Terrorism and America: A Common sense Strategy for a Democratic Society (Cambridge, MIT Press, 1998).

7.   Secretary of Defense Donald Rumsfeld, Remarks at Foreign Press Center, Washington, D.C., June 21, 2001.

8.   President Bush's West Point Address, June 3, 2002.

9.   Rumsfeld, *ibid*.

10.   Speech by NATO Secretary General Lord Robertson at the International Conference on "Regional Stability and Cooperation: NATO, Croatia and South-East Europe," Zagreb, Croatia, June 24, 2002.

11.   Richard Wolffe and Edward Alden, "Bush Plans Strategy for War on Terror," *Financial Times*, June 21, 2002.

12.   Karen Deyoung, "Mideast Worries Impinge on G-8 Summit," *Washington Post*, June 26, 2002; David R. Sands, "Bush to Seek G-8's Support for War on Terror," *Washington Times*, June 24, 2002.

13.   Mortimer B. Zuckerman, "With the Urgency of War, *U.S. News and World Report*, p.64, June 17, 2002. More generally, see Richard A. Falkenrath, Robert D. Newman, and Bradley A. Thayer, *America's Achilles' Heel: Nuclear, Biological and Chemical Terrorism and Covert Attack*, (Cambridge; MIT Press; 1998). "Five interrelated developments have increased the risk that terrorists will use nuclear, chemical or biological weapons against civilian targets. First, such weapons are especially valuable to terrorist seeking to conjure a sense of divine retribution.... Second, terrorist motives are changing. A new breed of terrorists appears more likely than the terrorists of the past to commit acts of extreme violence.... Third, with the break up of the Soviet Union, the black market now offers weapons, components, and know how.... Fourth, chemical and biological weapons are proliferating, even in states known to sponsor terrorism...Fifth, advances in technology have made terrorism with weapons of mass destruction easier to carry out." Jessica Stern, *Ibid*., pp. 8-10.

14.   Adopted 9/28/01.

15.   Speech by NATO Secretary General Lord Robertson at the International Conference on "Regional Stability and Cooperation: NATO, Croatia and South-East Europe," Zagreb, Croatia, June 24, 2002.

16.   Stopping terrorist financing is very difficult. See Michael M. Phillips and Lan Johnson, "U.S. – Europe Divisions Hinder Drive to Block Terrorists Assets; Some Countries Identify Few Targets Except those that are of Local Interest," *The Wall Street Journal*, April 11, 2002; Steven Erlanger, "Germany Steps Up Probe of Businessman with Qaeda Ties," *International Herald Tribune*, June 21, 2002; and Karen DeYoung and Douglas Farah, "Al Qaeda Shifts Assets to Gold U.S. Agency Turf Battles Hampers Hunt for Untraceable Commodities," *Washington Post*, June 18, 2002.

17.   There is growing evidence that illicit drugs often help fund terror activities. See Rachel Ehrenfeld, "Narco-Terrorism; How Drugs Fund Terrorism," *The Journal of International Security Affairs*, No. 2, Winter 2002, pp. 87-92.

18.   Such rights might include ownership or rights to proceeds.

19.   And UNSC Resolution 1390's forerunners UNSC Resolutions 1267 and 1333.

20.   President George W. Bush, State of the Union Address, January 29, 2002.

TERRORISM FINANCE

On behalf of the United States, I want to praise the work of the 1267 Committee and the leadership of our chairman, Ambassador Alfonso Valdivieso.

I am attending this meeting to emphasize how important we view the work of this Committee.

Next week, on September 11th, we will mark the anniversary of the evil acts against America in Washington, DC, Pennsylvania and here in New York City. On that day, al Qaeda terrorists attached innocent men, women and children. In destroying the World Trade Center alone, they killed some 3,000 people from over 90 nations around the world.

The international community has responded to these acts of horror. A coalition, sanctioned by the United Nations and led by the United States, attacked the Taliban. With military might ad moral purpose the coalition quickly brought down the Taliban. In Afghanistan, the international community has responded by helping bring humanitarian aid to the victims of that vicious regime, by helping secure Kabul, by helping the people participate in a peaceful political process culminating in a Loya Jurga to select their new leadership, and by helping to train police, an afghan army, and a new judiciary.

But the international war against terrorism is far broader than the Taliban in Afghanistan. As President Bush has said, "In Afghanistan the war against terrorism was begun well, but it was just begun." The United States is dedicated to this cause. There are many battlefields on which this war must be waged. And among the most important battlefields is to cut off the financing terrorists depend upon to execute their evil deeds.

One of the most important developments in the counter-terrorism effort has been the transition of this UN Security Council Sanctions Committee, initially established pursuant to Resolution 1267, from sanctions on the Taliban to create a global regime against terrorism. This global regime, established by UN Security Council Resolution 1390, requires specific acts against terrorists including asset freeze, travel ban and arms embargo.

Since September 11th, the United States has been working very closely with the international community and this 1267 Committee on targeting sanctions to freeze the assets of terrorists and their networks.

Remarks at UN Security Council Committee Established Pursuant to Resolution 1267 (1999), September, 4, 2002.

The United Nations and this Committee have taken this fight seriously, and it is again encouraging to see the UN focus on the threat al Qaeda poses to the international community of civilized nations. We agree with this sense of urgency and call on all countries, as we have done consistently since September 11th, to take preventative, proactive steps to attack the financial network of al Qaeda and other terrorist groups.

International cooperation in the effort to freeze the assets of terrorist groups has been strong and consistent. Since September 11th, the United States and other countries have frozen more than $112 million in terrorist-related assets. As a result of this Committee's good work, 234 individuals and entities are currently designated as financiers of terror and their access to the international financial system is blocked. Over 160 countries have blocking orders in force, hundreds of accounts worth more than $70 million outside the United States have been blocked, and foreign law enforcement have acted swiftly to shut down terrorist financing networks and arrest financiers.

Now I would like to turn to the independent Monitoring Group's excellent second report. The report is limited in scope because it bases its analysis in large part on the reports submitted by countries pursuant to UN Security Council Resolution 1373 and on research done by the five members of that Committee. Nonetheless, the report is an important contribution to our efforts and the United States would like to commend Chairman Chandler and his colleague for their work product.

It is important to note that this report covers not only the past four months work, but builds on the information and knowledge which the Group had previously gathered for its first report. This report provides a lot of extremely useful information. This report correctly points out that a great deal has been accomplished to interrupt the flow of money to al Qaeda, to move the terrorist network out of its "comfort zone." However, this report also points out weaknesses in this regime where Member States should and must do more.

This first part of the report which is a brief narrative of the "Al Qaeda Phenomenon", its organization and modus operandi, is helpful. It provides useful information, especially for States that may lack expertise and intelligence on al Qaeda organization specifics. As Chairman Chandler has said, it is "important to present this image of al Qaeda, as concisely as possible, in order to emphasize the nature of the beast with which we are all having to deal and why it continues to pose such a significant threat to international peace and security."

A linchpin of international efforts to interrupt terrorist financing is the UN List. As the Monitoring Group correctly points out, we need to ensure that the United Nations List is maintained as a key and authoritative document and that it contains the name of as many members and operatives of al Qaeda and its financial and logistical supporters as possible.

The Monitoring Group has pointed out some problems with the List that may undermine its need to be authoritative and a key reference document supporting sanctions. Some states have indicated a reticence to submit to this Committee names of additional individuals or entities to be incorporated in the List. The List has fallen behind the actions of States in identifying, monitoring, detaining and arresting individuals believed to be associated with al Qaeda or the Taliban. Some States have expressed a concern about a perceived "lack of clarity for the process and procedures for submitting to this Committee names to be added to the List, or for identifying or clarifying information regarding persons or entities already on the List. They also noted a lack of established guidelines or evidentiary criteria for determining which names should be added to the List."

To respond to these problems and concerns with the UN list, the Monitoring Group has made eight recommendations, all of which the United States supports. [1]

Again, this Committee and the international community has had many successes in freezing assets. Considerable efforts have been taken by many governments to disrupt al Qaeda's ability, financially and logistically, to support its operations. Great inroads have been made into al Qaeda's financial structure and this has curbed its access to funding. These efforts have made it increasingly difficult for al Qaeda to operate. However, the Monitoring Group has properly pointed out that simultaneously, there has been "the apparent and consequential diversification of funding for, and by, al Qaeda." A crippling financial blow has not been dealt to al Qaeda. And there are many complex tasks that remain in cutting off its funding.

Some delegations have expressed frustration that more has not been achieved. Some delegations have raised concerns about where they may have been named by the report in discussing weaknesses in the system. Some delegations have questioned the process through which the Monitoring Group collected information and drafted its report. These reservations should be taken into account and inform the Monitoring Group's activities going forward and its future interim reports.

However, the Committee should not lose sight of the big picture. Despite specific claims in the report and possible misstatements in the report raised by some delegations today, if individual Committee members seek to amend the report they will compromise the credibility and independence of the Monitoring Group. Our important goal is to interrupt the flow of money to al Qaeda, money that is used to support terrorists' evil deeds against innocent people. No country has a perfect airtight system. To strengthen our collective efforts it is important to bring weakness to light. And it is important for us to learn from the Monitoring Group's observation and recommendations and, where appropriate, act to improve our efforts to interrupt the financial flow to al Qaeda.

Mr. Chairman, let me reiterate that the United States supports this Committee and its mission. We must continue to make strides in cutting off al Qaeda's economic resources, freezing their assets, rounding up their operations and preventing terrorist attacks. Towards that end, my delegation welcomes the Monitoring Group's Report as very useful and constructive. It helps point the way to how we can and must do better.

Thank you.

---

1. The following are the Monitoring Group's recommendations regarding the United Nations List:

1. The List should be used by all States as an authoritative and key reference document for the implementation of the measures contained in paragraph 2 of resolution 1390 (i.e. the blocking of financial and economic resources, the travel ban, and an arms embargo). It should be disseminated as widely as possible to all competent authorities including but not limited to

financial institutions, border control authorities, arms control authorities and administrative and judicial departments responsible for identification of individuals including changing of names.

2. Implementation of the measures contained in paragraph 2 of resolution 1390 should be carried out within the context of other Security Council resolutions, including 1373, to ensure that all appropriate measures are taken to freeze the assets, halt the travel, and inhibit access to arms and munitions, by al Qaeda, the Taliban and those associated with them.

3. The List must be updated regularly by the Committee on the basis of specific and reliable information on all individuals or entities that have identified as members of, or associated with al Qaeda or the Taliban. All States should submit to the Committee for possible addition to the List, the names, and identifying information, of all persons States have identified as members of, or associated with Al-Qaeda or the Taliban, including, at a minimum, those persons arrested or detained by States on the basis of "due cause" to believe they are members of, or associated with al Qaeda or the Taliban.

4. Names of persons or entities whose assets have been frozen by States on the basis of their membership or association with al Qaeda or the Taliban which currently do not appear on the List, should also be submitted to the Committee for its consideration regarding their addition to the List.

5. States should seek to assist the Committee in better identifying individuals or entities already on the List and to provide to the Committee any additional identifying information at their disposal regarding such individuals or entities, particularly where insufficient identifying information is included in the List. This should include confirmation of the name as it appears on passport or travel documents, cases of dual nationality; date and place of birth; passport numbers for all known nationalities; and physical description or any other remarks which could help to identify the listed individuals.

6. The Committee should establish an appropriate mechanism capable of responding on a 24 hour basis to inquiries presented to the Committee concerning the identification of persons being detained as suspected members, or associates of, al Qaeda or the Taliban.

7. The Committee should ensure that all member governments are aware of its guidelines for de-listing individuals and entities whose names should be removed from the List. The List should be reviewed by the Committee on a regular basis to ensure that it remains current.

8. All States should ensure that a sufficient legal basis is in place to at with the urgency required to carry out their obligations under paragraph 2 of resolution 1390 (2002).

(Second report of Monitoring Group pursuant to S/Res/1390 (2002), August 22, 2002.)

CURBING MONEY FLOW TO TERRORISTS

The events of recent years, most emphatically the tragedy of September 11, 2001, have sensitized us to the new realities, the disturbing new realities where the threat to innocent civilians from terrorist attacks confront us everyday.

The importance of the fight against terrorism is enormous. It is never right to target and kill innocent civilians, never.

There are three key battlefields of the war against terrorism where the United Nations plays a critical role. The UN has the ability to set international norms and standards. On terrorism, the General Assembly and the Security Council have worked to do that. Notably, after the evil attacks on America last September, the United Nations recognized as part of the right of self-defense that a state can use force to go after terrorists and those who harbor terrorists.

A second key area for the United Nations is to help build the capacity of countries to combat the threat of terrorism. The Counter Terrorism Committee, ably chaired by Ambassador Jeremy Greenstock, is meeting this challenge. Countries current capacity to safeguard borders, to control the flow of money, to control the flow of arms. Etc.

And the third area where the United Nations can make an invaluable contribution to the war against terrorism is to disrupt and curb the financial flow to terrorists. We must drive the terrorists out of their comfort zone, force them to make mistakes so that their evil plans can be discovered and they can be apprehended, and curb their activities.

My delegation would like to thank Ambassador Alfonso Valdivieso[1] for his able leadership of the 1267 Committee.[2] And, we would like to thank the work of Committee experts and the independent Monitoring Group.[3] The Monitoring Group has performed yeoman service. Their report is extremely helpful.

The al Qaeda/Taliban sanctions regime remains a top priority of the United States Government. We are pleased that it remains an important priority for the Security Council. And we look forward to further close cooperation with other governments in addressing the continued terrorist threat.

The global nature of this particular sanctions regime poses some unique challenges. However, my delegation believes that an appropriate balance has been struck between respecting individual rights and effective sanctions enforcement.

Remarks at UN Security Council Informal Consultations, September 30, 2002.

In the rush after September 11th, the United States moved quickly to put forward names of individuals and entities whom we felt sanctions were applicable and appropriate. While few in number, some mistakes were made. Since that initial rush, the United States Government has improved the procedures and safeguards to determine individuals and entities that we recommend the Committee add to the sanctions list. And, importantly, we have ensured that foreign nationals put on the sanctions list by the U.S. Government have all of the same protections as United States citizens to appeal that determination if they so desire.

In this regard, my delegation expects to reach agreement soon on the technical resolution allowing for humanitarian exceptions to the Security Council-imposed asset freeze. This will be an important step as has been highlighted by many of the previous interventions today.

The Monitoring Group's recent report[4] provides some important insights into the international community's ongoing efforts to freeze assets, ban travel and embargo arms to al Qaeda and associated individuals and entities.

Regarding the asset freeze area, the United States is pleased to note that approximately 112 million U.S. dollars in terrorist assets have been frozen to date, two-thirds of this amount outside the United States.[5] Most of those funds were frozen in the aftermath of September 11th. However, while the pace of freezing actions has slowed, additional asset freezes continue. And, as the Monitoring Group reports, "the financial needs of al Qaeda also have been greatly reduced with the collapse of the Taliban Government and the destruction of any of their training camps in Afghanistan."[6]

Continued international cooperation in following and freezing terrorist assets will be crucial to the fight against terrorism. My delegation recognizes that more needs to be done. We welcome the independent Monitoring Group report's recommendations that additional names be added to the United Nations list, especially since many of these targeted individuals already have been charged in national courts. The German Government's recent submission of four names to the list represents a pro-active step that we welcome and encourage other governments to consider as well.[7]

In freezing terrorist assets much has been accomplished, but much more needs to be done. There are new terrorist financial flows that must be addressed, including controls to regulate the hawala and other alternative transfer systems that lack transparency and accountability and operate in the absence of governmental regulations.[8] We have reason to believe that terrorists have diverted money into precious metals to transfer financing. In the coming months, my delegation is confident that the international community can strengthen its effectiveness in these areas.

The 1267 Committee also is making a valuable contribution to the travel ban.[9] My delegation notes that information on names and identifiers could be improved, which would make enforcement at borders easier. However, it is important to stress, in this regard, that the 1267 Committee's list will never be "perfect" with "perfect information."

Since the horrible events of September 11th, the United States Government has recognized the inherent challenges in monitoring movement through our own borders. The U.S. Government, like other governments, welcomes concrete steps toward improvement, some of which are outlined in the Monitoring Group's report. In this connection, my delegation is particularly interested in better understanding how the 1390 travel ban requirement meshes with the European Union's Schengen framework.

The United States also welcomes efforts to identify and build upon synergies between the work of the 1267 Committee and the Counter Terrorism Committee.

In conclusion, I'd like to reiterate our belief that the United Nations plays a central role in the fight against terrorism. The United States encourages Member States to remain vigilant in this important task; a job that is both far from over and without a prescribed end date.

---

1.   Colombian Permanent Representative to the United Nations.

2.   The Security Council 1267 Committee is so named because it was originally created as a result of Security Council Resolution 1267(1999).

3.   The Monitoring Group was established pursuant to Security Council Resolution 1390(2002) and is charged with monitoring, reporting on and making recommendations concerning the implementation of the measures that the Security Council decided States shall take against Osama bin Laden, the Taliban, and associated individuals and entities.

4.   S/2002/1050.

5.   "In paragraph 2(a) of its Resolution 1390(2002), the Security Council decided that States shall freeze without delay the funds and other financial assets or economic resources of the individuals whose names appear on the list, as well as the funds and other financial assets or economic resources of" entities whose names appear on the list. S/2002/1050.

6.   S/2002/1050.

7.   On September 30, 2002, the 1267 Committee approved the addition of four individuals, members of the notorious "Hamburg cell" linked directly to the September 11, 2001 plot, submitted by Germany: Mounir E. Montassadeq (Morocco), Ramzi Mohamed Abdullah Binal Shibh (Yemen), Said Bahaji (Germany) and Zakarya Essabar (Morocco). It is important to note that in the request submitted to the Committee, Germany not only provided the arrest warrants of each individual, but also extensive backgrounds of each linking them to the al Qaeda network and their involvement in and support for the terrorist acts of September 11, 2001. Germany submitted the names in response to the Monitoring Group's recommendation that governments be more pro-active in this regard.

8.   The hawala is an internal, paperless transfer of funds found within the Islamic world. On May 15 and 16, 2002, the International Hawala Conference was hosted by the Government of the United Arab Emirates in Abu Dhabi. More than 300 government officials, bankers, lawyers, representatives of law enforcement agencies and customs officials from 58 countries attended the Conference to address ways to ensure that money launderers and financiers of terrorism do not abuse those systems. S/2002/1050.

9.   "In paragraph 2(b) of Resolution 1390(2002), the Security Council decided that States shall take measures to "prevent the entry into or the transit through their territories" of individuals on the United Nations list. All individuals whose names appear on the list are barred from traveling to and through States." *Ibid*.

Combating Terrorism Through Treaty Implementation

As the former U.S. Ambassador to the UN Offices in Vienna, it is a particular pleasure for me to be back in Vienna and to be visiting the UN Office of Drug Control and Crime Prevention Programs. Your role in helping implement the 12 international terrorism conventions is very important. It reflects the increased attention that has been given to the connection between organized crime, drug trafficking, money laundering and terrorism. The United States supports your global program against money laundering, providing technical assistance and mentoring to states so that they are better able to trace and seize illicit funds, as well as track criminals, traffickers and terrorists.

The September 11, 2001 attacks against America were evil deeds. Fanatics used civilian airplanes to kill innocent men, women and children. To advance their perverse vision they tried to hijack a great religion and reign terror and destruction on America. Nearly 3,000 innocent people died. But America and the civilized world have risen up to say we will not let these evil acts defeat us. In the UN Security Council, we have rededicated ourselves to work together toward this end. And your work here in Vienna is important in this enterprise.

Back in December, 1994, the United Nations General Assembly passed a Resolution[1] on measures to eliminate international terrorism, which called for four practical steps to enhance international cooperation: collection of data on the status of existing multinational, regional and bilateral agreements; a compendium of national laws and regulations aimed at preventing and suppressing terrorisms; an analytical review of existing international legal instruments relating to international terrorism; to help identify matters which have not yet been covered, and a review of possibilities within the UN system for helping states organize workshops and training courses on combating terrorist crimes.[2] While the legal aspects of these matters are dealt with by the UN Office of Legal Affairs in New York, it is here in Vienna that the Terrorism Prevention Branch focused on the important work of research and assistance. By collecting "lessons learned" from Member States, the Terrorism Prevention Branch is identifying "best practices" in preventing and combating terrorism. And the United States supports plans for issuing a biennial Global Terrorism Survey. Such information can be a further tool in the war against terrorism of global reach.

Overall, the United States has dedicated more than $140 million to ODCCP programs.[3] We recognize the importance of your efforts. We will continue to

---

Remarks at The United Nations Office of Drug Control and Crime Prevention Programs, Vienna, Austria, December 9, 2002.

support your programs. And, together with the Security Council Counter-Terrorism Committee, we will increase the capacity of Member States to fight the evil of terrorism.

In Resolution 1373 of September 28, 2001, the Security Council declared that "...acts, methods and practices of terrorism are contrary to the purposes and principles of the United Nations and that knowingly financing, planning and inciting terrorist acts are also contrary to the purposes and principles of the United Nations." This resolution expressed a number of Security Council decisions requiring anti-terrorism actions by Member States, particularly in the area of cooperation with the Counter-Terrorism Committee formed by the Security Council.[4]

Among the mandatory decisions taken in Resolution 1373 are that states shall deny safe haven to those who finance, plan, support, or commit terrorist acts, or provide safe havens; and ensure that any person who participates in the financing, planning, preparation or perpetration of terrorist acts or in supporting terrorist acts is brought to justice. States must ensure that, in addition to any other measures against them, that terrorist acts are established as serious criminal offenses in domestic laws and regulations and that the punishment reflects the seriousness of such terrorist acts. And, in Resolution 1373, states are required to provide one another assistance in connection with criminal investigations and criminal proceedings related to the financing or support of terrorist acts.

In elaborating the means to accomplish these mandatory obligations, Resolution 1373 calls upon all states to become parties to the relevant international conventions and protocols related to terrorism,[5] and to increase cooperation.[6]

The United States has joined with others in supporting intensified efforts to promote universal adherence to, and implementation of, all existing universal legal instruments dealing with the prevention and suppression of terrorism. Promoting ratification of these instruments is important. The speedy entry into force and implementation of these instruments will improve collective action against terrorism. The work of the Centre for International Crime Prevention to help realize these goals is appreciated.

The Centre for International Crime Prevention should prepare guidance notes and implementation kits to help states to ratify the universal instruments against terrorism. The Centre also can provide guidance to countries on how to use domestic legislation against international terrorism. And the Centre should play a role in assisting states in their efforts to establish mechanisms for international cooperation, whether judicial assistance or in the form of police cooperation and early warning.[7]

The United States is pleased to have contributed $240,000 to the Centre's project on "Strengthening the Legal Regime Against Terrorism." We believe that this project will complement the activities of the Counter-Terrorism Committee. The objectives of this project are the right ones: a strategy to promote ratification and implementation of the international instruments against terrorism; developing advanced draft legislative guidelines; preparing draft implementation kits; and creating a methodology for technical assistance to build counter-terrorism capacities in selected countries.[8]

The war against terrorism is extremely important. In Vienna, you are playing a large role in this effort. And the United States appreciates your contribution and supports it.

---

1.   A/Res/49/60.

2.   When the 1972 Munich Olympic Games were disrupted by a Palestinian group's attempt to take Israeli athletes hostage and resulting in the group killing Israelis, the then UN Secretary-General Kurt Waldheim asked that terrorism be placed on the General Assembly's agenda under the heading "measures to prevent terrorism and other forms of violence which endanger or take innocent people or jeopardize fundamental freedoms." In the debate that followed, the General Assembly amended this title to add "and study of the underlying causes of those forms of terrorism and acts of violence which lied in misery, frustration, grievance and despair and which cause some people to sacrifice human lives, including their own, in an attempt to affect radical changes." This item was then assigned to the Assembly's Legal Committee, which subsequently passed several resolutions on terrorism.

3.   The United Nations Office of Drug Control and Crime Prevention.

4.   Under Article 25 of Chapter V of the Charter, Member Sates agree to accept and carry out such decisions.

5.   The universal instruments related to the prevention and suppression of international terrorism include the International Convention Against the Taking of Hostages, adopted by the UN General Assembly on December 17, 1979; the International Convention for the Suppression of Terrorist Bombings, adopted by the UN General Assembly on December 15, 1997; the International Convention for the Suppression of the Financing of Terrorism, adopted by the UN General Assembly on December 9, 1999; the Convention on Offences and Certain Other Acts Committed on Board Aircraft, signed at Tokyo on September 14, 1963; the Convention for the Suppression of Unlawful Seizure of Aircraft, signed at The Hague on December 16, 1970; the Convention for the Suppression of Unlawful Acts Against the Safety of Civilian Aviation, signed at Montreal on September 23, 1971; the Convention on the Physical Protection of Nuclear Material, signed at Vienna on March 3, 1980; the Protocol on the Suppression of Unlawful Actions of Violence at Airports Serving International Civil Aviation, supplementary to the Convention of the Suppression of Unlawful Actions Against the Safety of Civil Aviation, signed at Montreal on February 24, 1988; the Convention for the Suppression of Unlawful Acts Against the Safety of Maritime Navigation, done at Rome on March 10, 1988; the Protocol for the Suppression of Unlawful Acts Against the Safety of Fixed Platforms Located on the Continental Shelf, done at Rome on March 10, 1988; the Convention on the Marking of Plastic Explosives for the Purpose of Detection, signed at Montreal on March 1, 1991, and the International Convention for the Suppression of the Financing of Terrorism, adopted by the UN General Assembly on December 9, 1999.

6.   In addition to relevant international conventions and protocols related to terrorism, there is reference to Security Council resolutions 1269(1999) and 1368(2001).

7.   See the report of the Centre for International Crime Prevention (CICP/ODCCP) of its symposium on "Combating International Terrorism; the Contribution of the UN" held in Vienna, Austria, on June 3-4, 2002.

8.   The proposal calls for the methodology to be tested in one country, to be selected in consultation with the Counter-Terrorism Committee.

SANCTIONS AGAINST THOSE BELONGING TO OR ASSOCIATED WITH TERRORISTS

The United States appreciates the briefing by Ambassador Valdes, Chairman of the 1267 Committee[1] and Mr. Michael Chandler, who chairs the Independent Monitoring Group.[2] We welcome increased transparency in the work of this body, particularly as the Committee begins to move in some important new directions this year. We would welcome more frequent meetings of this type, in line with the constructive precedent established by Ambassador Greenstock[3] and the Counter Terrorism Committee. Under the leadership of Colombian Ambassador Valdivieso and now under the leadership of Ambassador Valdes, this Committee has become an important body that is doing good work in the war against terrorists of global reach.

The measures under the Taliban/Al Qaeda sanctions regime require that all States freeze financial assets and economic resources of the individuals and entities belonging to or associated with Osama bin Laden, Al Qaeda and the Taliban and apply the arms embargo and travel ban against them.4 And I certainly agree with our Chairman that effective cooperation between Member States of the United Nations, the 1267 Committee and the Independent Monitoring Group is critical to improving the implementation of the sanctions measures. Only through Member States' concerted efforts can we eradicate terrorism networks and neutralize their activities and their supporters.

Mr. Chairman, the United States applauds the past contributions of the 1267 Committee. Already as a result of this work some of the financial flow to terrorists has been curbed. Terrorists have been forced out of their comfort zone. Some terrorist acts may well have been prevented. Yet, we know that terrorists continue to commit their evil acts. Terrorists continue to target innocent civilians. And in Bali, Kenya and as recently as yesterday in Pakistan, the civilized world has been brutally attacked and victimized by terrorist acts.[5] We can do better in our war against terrorists, we must. Therefore, the United States believes it is time to rachet up the rigors of our efforts in the 1267 Committee.

The Security Council agreed with this when it passed Resolution 1455[6], the successor to Resolution 1390, which extends the sanction measures already in place with a view to improving their implementation. Resolution 1455 is a demanding resolution for the 1267 Committee, for the Independent Monitoring Group and for

---

Remarks at UN Security Council 1267 Committee Open Briefing, United Nations, Trusteeship Council Chamber, New York, N.Y., February 28, 2003

all United Nations Member States. Resolution 1445 puts a greater focus on States' implementation of the sanction measures. Its expectations are high, with a focus on improving the implementation of the Al Qaeda/Taliban sanctions regime by all States, including my own.

In 1455, the Security Council has called on all Member States to submit an updated report no later than 90 days from its adoption on all steps taken to implement the measures under the Taliban/Al Qaeda sanctions regime.[7] The information provided in States' reports must be clear, precise and complete.[8] My delegation is pleased that 1267 Chair, Ambassador Valdes, will transmit guidelines to Member States and relevant international organizations next week.[9] The 1267 Committee list is the key instrument for the implementation of all sanction measures established by the Security Council against these individuals and entities. It is important to know if Member States have incorporated the list into their legal and administrative system. It will be valuable to know if Member State authorities have identified within their territory any designated individuals or entities. And it will be very helpful for the 1267 Committee to know precisely what kind of action each Member State has taken to prevent individuals and entities under its jurisdiction from recruiting or supporting Al Qaeda members.

The United States strongly believes that expectations for Member States should be set high, not low. We all can, and should, do more to meet the challenges posed by terrorists who continue to seek to destroy the very fabric that binds us together. Shared vigilance must remain our watchword now, and for a long time to come.

Also under Resolution 1455, this Committee will provide periodic reports to the Security Council on the progress achieved. A regular dialogue in the Security Council, approximately every 90 days, will help us identify those areas in which States are lacking the capacity to build on anti-terror infrastructure and may need assistance.

The Counter Terrorism Committee (CTC) already has made significant strides in this area.[10] The United States expects to build on the good work of the CTC and to complement its work through the efforts of the 1267 Committee and its Monitoring Group.

The United States also would like to recognize the continued importance of the independent Monitoring Group, ably led by Chairman Michael Chandler.[11] We agree with our Chairman, Ambassador Valdes, that "the Monitoring Group established pursuant to Resolution 1363(2001), has become indispensable to the effective discharging of the Committee's mandate." The Monitoring Group has properly identified key themes and geographic areas that deserve greater attention by the 1267 Committee and the Security Council. The United States intends to follow-up closely on those topics and themes, including on a bilateral basis as appropriate.

During its first year, we have learned a great deal about how the Monitoring Group most effectively can make its visits. It has targeted in on such matters a Member States capabilities to electronically search "watch lists" and so forth at border controls. The Monitoring Group is seeking factual, concise and complete information for its reports. Member States' cooperation is important for that work to be done. Therefore, the United States hopes that all States will continue to strongly support the work of the Monitoring Group throughout its mandate.

A close analysis of Member State reports constitutes a core function of the Monitoring Group's expanded responsibilities. It is a very valuable contribution. We appreciate the hard work of the Monitoring Group, Secretariat and 1267 Committee members over the last several weeks in reaching agreement on detailed guidance for Member States regarding their 1455 reports.

The international community's counter-terrorism efforts remain incomplete. Shared attention and commitment will be needed for years to come. To that end, the United States Government strongly encourages willing and able States to do more, my government included. For example, the United States can learn and can do more to control our own borders. Second, the United States remains committed to helping unable but willing States achieve greater counter-terrorism success. Increased assistance to improve Member States' capacity remains a key to this shared effort. Finally, the United States emphasizes that unwilling States, whatever their reasons, must be encouraged, and, if necessary, pressured to do more. UN Security Council Resolution 1455 is not about pointing fingers, but rather it is about pointing to deficiencies that can be better addressed. We cannot tolerate unwilling States to remain the weak link that undermines the international community's counter-terrorism campaign. The United Nations and the international community cannot afford to fail in our counter-terrorism effort. Too much is at stake, not just for Americans but for all of us.

The United States again would like to thank Ambassador Valdes, his staff at the Mission of Chile, the UN Secretariat and 1267 Committee members for their good work. More work lies ahead, but my delegation is fully confident that all are up to the task.

Thank you, Mr. Chairman.

---

1.   The 1267 Committee was established by S/Res/1390(2002).

2.   The Independent Monitoring Group was established by S/Res/1390(2002).

3.   United Kingdom Permanent Representative, Ambassador Jeremy Greenstock chaired the Security Council's Counter Terrorism Committee and periodically held Open Briefings on CTC activities for non-Security Council member States.

4.   The 1267 Committee was established in 1999 in order to eradicate terrorism by the UN Security Council, S/Res/1267(1999). After September 11, 2001, and the attacks on the World Trade Center and the Pentagon, Security Council Resolution 1390 (Ss/sRes/1390(2002) expanded the counter terrorist measures beyond the territory of Afghanistan, formerly controlled by the Taliban, to include individuals and entities designated by the Committee, regardless of their location.

5.   On October 12, 2002, terrorists affiliated with the militant Islamic group Jemaah Islamiyah bombed a disco on the Indonesian island of Bali. According to the most recent tally, 202 people were killed, most of whom were Australian citizens, although two Americans were killed as well. The terrorists said they had targeted the discos hoping to kill "more Americans."

On November 28, 2002, terrorists attacked an Israeli-owned Paradiso Hotel in Mombasa, Kenya, and unsuccessfully targeted an Israeli-bound jet with a rocket-launched grenade. 10 Kenyans, 3 Israelis and the 3 bombers died as a result of the attack. The attack has been linked to Al Qaeda. Syria voted against the resolution introduced in the UN Security Council following that incident, because of the reference to Israel.

On February 28, 2003, gunmen opened fire on a police post guarding the United States Consulate in Karachi. No Americans were killed, but two Pakistani guards were killed in the attack. The assailants are suspected to be Al Qaeda. One gunman was identified as Aghani.

6.   S/Res/1455(2003).

7.   SC/Res/1455(2003), para 6. The due date for the updated report is April 17, 2003.

8.   The information already submitted to the Counter Terrorism Committee and the 1267 Committee pursuant to Security Council Resolution 1390 (200) need not be duplicated. States should provide precise relevant inferences to the reports already submitted.

9.   The 1267 Committee expects detailed replies regarding the asset freeze, travel ban and arms embargo measures. The guideline highlights are as follows:

Consolidated List

--inquires if there have been problems with implementation (lacking identifiers, e.g., addresses, dob/pob, etc.)

--whether lawsuits have been brought before governments (such as Somali-Swedes)

Asset Freeze

--defines assets using a broad definition (we were surprised we got this expansive definition in because it is considered "controlling" for governments).

--question about "know your customer" regulations, if any;

--summary of frozen assets (have States really implemented?); we know where entities are located so States will have a hard time skipping this question.

--unblocking of assets pursuant to UNSCR 1452 (exceptions based on rent, legal fees, etc); we have yet to receive a request from a government but expect some in the coming months.

--questions on "hawala" (informal money transfer systems), precious objects, etc. (this will put the Saudis, Pakistanis, others more on-the-spot – and could frame for us possible language in a future UNSCR)

Travel Ban

--do States have "stop lists" that include listed individuals?

--has a listed terrorist ever been stopped at a border? (so far, we do not have a case-in-point)

--are border officials using electronic means or much less?

Arms Embargo

--possible WMD acquisition by the Taliban (how are States controlling such components)?

--information is sought on arms brokers/broker licensing systems;

Assistance

--each State is asked if they'd be willing to put their money/resources where their mouths are regarding capacity/assistance. (I would like to know what Washington's answer will be – or should be. Again, States will be focused on if we take a lead and offer proposals.)

10.   The Counter Terrorism Committee does not issue formal reports on its activities. The CTC relates its activities to the Security Council through CTC Chairman, Ambassador Jeremy Greenstock's statements in open briefings and through submission of work programs every 90 days. The Counter Terrorism Committee does not issue formal reports on its activities. The CTC relates its activities to the Security Council through CTC Chairman, Ambassador Jeremy Greenstock's statements in open briefings and through submission of work programs every 90 days.

11.   The Monitoring Group (MG) is charged with overseeing Member State implementation of the Al Qaeda/Taliban sanctions regime. Under Security Council Resolution 1455 of January 17, 2003, their mandate was strengthened to include following up on "relevant leads" regarding any incomplete implementation. The MG will issue two reports to the 1267 Committee in 2003, one in June and the other in November. The three prior reports of the MG are S/2002/1338, December 17, 2002, S/2002/1050, September 20, 2002, and S/2002/541, May 15, 2002.

BUILDING CAPACITY
TO FIGHT TERRORISM

Mr. President, we, too, look forward to a productive month under your leadership. We join others in thanking our Guinean colleagues for his leadership as Council President in March.

Eighteen months after the establishment of the Counter-Terrorism Committee (CTC), the United States joins others in paying tribute to the work of the CTC Chairman, Ambassador Jeremy Greenstock, as he passes the baton to Ambassador Arias. Ambassador Greenstock's vision and vigorous and committed leadership has helped put the CTC at the center of the international community's efforts to combat terrorism. His chairmanship was an outstanding success. I also take this opportunity to thank the United Kingdom delegation for all of the hard work and creative work that was necessary to keep up with such an energetic ambassador, and translating his vision into reality. In particular, I mention Anna Clunes, who was Ambassador Greenstock's indispensable right-hand person throughout his chairmanship, and his legal counsel, Iain MacLeod. They have done exceptional work. I also want to join in thanking the Vice-Chairman of the CTC and the CTC experts.

Unfortunately, terrorism remains a clear and present danger, an ongoing threat to international peace and security. It is a violent outrage that must be dealt with. In the last year, there have been major terrorist attacks in Bali and Kenya. Earlier this year, there was a terrorist attack against the United States consulate in Karachi, killing 2 Pakistani guards. Recently, there was an attack in the Philippines. Unfortunately, there continue to be frequent terrorist attacks in the Middle East and elsewhere.

It is not acceptable to intentionally target innocent civilians for violent attacks. The United Nations Security Council must continue our work to fight terrorism. This threat must be met. The United Nations has made a valuable contribution in setting norms against terrorism. The United Nations is doing important work through the 1267 Committee to interrupt the financial flow to terrorists, to force them out of their comfort zone, to diminish the capacity of terrorists to do their evil acts. And the United Nations is in a unique position to help build the capacity of the international community to fight terrorism. And through the Counter-Terrorism Committee, under the leadership of Ambassador Greenstock, the United Nations has begun to make this important contribution to the fight against terrorism.

As President Bush has said, the world is threatened by the risk of the world's most destructive weapons getting into the hands of the world's most vicious predators:

United Nations Security Council Open Session, April 4, 2003.

terrorists of the world. Fighting terrorism and stopping the spread of weapons of mass destruction are critical to a safer, more secure world.

The Counter-Terrorism Committee's task is to increase the capability of every Member State to deal with terrorism. All Governments must take effective steps to ensure that there is no support, active or passive, for terrorism anywhere. Chairman Greenstock saw early on that the Counter-Terrorism Committee could not accomplish this task alone. It needs the help of others. These include donors of assistance in the different substantive areas covered by resolution 1373 (2001) and international, regional and subregional organizations, enhancing the effectiveness of action against terrorism by their member States.

The special meeting of 6 March, which brought more than 65 other organizations together, will not only help solidify these relationships and raise the counter-terrorism profile in these organizations, but it will also reinforce the central role that the CTC plays in the international effort to increase capacity.

The United States is pleased that the Organization of American States (OAS) has agreed to hold a follow-up conference in Washington for regional and subregional organizations, and we look forward to providing support to the OAS on this initiative.

In its review of more than 300 reports from Member States to date, the Counter-Terrorism Committee is focused on identifying legislative gaps in States' capacity to fight terrorism and working with States and assistance providers to ensure that those gaps can be filled. This approach is paying dividends, but in order for the CTC to be effective, to remain credible, this work must translate into on-the-ground results.

As Ambassador Greenstock said at the Security Council in January, it is time for the Counter-Terrorism Committee to move up a notch. The CTC will soon be focusing on whether States are actually implementing the legal and political measures necessary to prevent terrorism, so that we can name and shame those States that fail to meet their responsibilities. Effective monitoring of Member States' actual on-the-ground efforts to implement resolution 1373 (2001) is necessary for the full global implementation of the resolution and for the continuing efficacy of the CTC. The CTC enjoys a strong mandate to monitor implementation, and this effort should be given high priority.

As the CTC begins to focus on effectiveness, it will need to go beyond the review of written reports. For example, we will have to determine whether States' police, intelligence, judicial, customs and immigration institutions are operating effectively. The United States believes that the Committee must expand its tool kit in order to conduct a credible review of these issues. For example, each CTC member should direct its overseas missions to analyze the written reports against the reality of implementation and share this analysis with the CTC and its experts. Moreover, the Counter-Terrorism Committee should request international, regional and subregional organizations to undertake such assessments, which can complement the work of the CTC without duplicating it. Organizations such as the World Bank, the World Customs Organizations and the International Civil Aviation Organization are well placed to conduct these assessments. Such an approach would be an appropriate result of the 6 March Counter-Terrorism Committee special meeting.

In addition, we believe that some form of site visits might be necessary to ascertain the truth on the ground in certain instances. We look forward to discussing these and to hear ideas for enhancing the effectiveness of the Counter-Terrorism Committee during the early period of Ambassador Arias's chairmanship.

The work of the Committee established under resolution 1267 (1999) under the able leadership of Ambassador Valdés should also be noted. It, too, constituted a key part of the United Nations resolution 1455 (2003) rightly focuses on improved Member State implementation of the Al Qaeda Taliban sanctions regime.

The United States believes strongly that the counter-terrorism expectations for Member States should be set high. We all can and should do more to meet the challenged posed by terrorists, who continue to seek to destroy the very fabric that binds us together. We must remain ever vigilant in our effort to end the plague of terrorism and to protect our freedom. The United States strongly encourages willing and able States to do more, my own Government included. The United States can do better. We are still learning how to deal better with our ongoing threats at our own borders, in our skies and across our land.

The United States remains strongly committed to helping unable but willing States to achieve greater counter-terrorism successes. Increased assistance and capacity are key in this shared effort. The Counter-Terrorism Committee has made important strides that will require follow-up, both multilaterally and bilaterally.

Finally, the United States emphasizes that unwilling States, whatever the reason, must be encouraged and, indeed, pressured, as necessary, to do more. We cannot tolerate unwilling States to be the weak link that undermines the international community's shared counter-terrorism effort. These States must accept their obligation to the world at large. Ultimately, each Member State bears a special responsibility to fight terrorism. Those that harbour and support terrorists must be held accountable. They must be exposed, named and shamed. Shared vigilance must remain our watchword. Increased expectations, we believe, will result in increased accountability.

Although important progress has been achieved, the international community's counter-terrorism efforts remain incomplete. Shared attention and commitment will be needed for years to come. We cannot become complacent, not afford to fail in our long-term counter-terrorism efforts. Too much is at stake, not just for America, but for all of us.

Before closing, allow me once again to thank Ambassador Greenstock for all of his efforts. We are confident that he has left the chairmanship in good hands, and pledge our full support to Ambassador Arias and his delegation during the coming period.

SECTION II:

THE ORGANIZATION FOR SECURITY AND COOPERATION IN EUROPE (OSCE)

PANEL OF EMINENT PERSONS ON STRENGTHENING THE EFFECTIVENESS OF THE OSCE

I salute Foreign Minister Dimitrij Rupel for his leadership as this year's Chairman in Office for the Organization for Security and Cooperation in Europe (OSCE). It is a big job that he has undertaken with energy, enthusiasm and a willingness to confront the serious challenges that face the organization.

OSCE's challenges come from the historic trends that have changed the political landscape of the region: altering old paradigms, reordering past priorities, straining old assumptions, and fracturing historically fragile consensus. This has manifest itself in the OSCE most dramatically in the last two Ministerial meetings in which consensus could not be reached in a final document and in Russia's unwillingness to join consensus on an OSCE budget; thereby creating the current OSCE fiscal crisis. These developments certainly are consequential. And for those of us who believe in the values and mission of the OSCE, it is well worth the effort to address these developments, explore ways and means to heal the hemorrhage, and seek to reinvigorate an organization founded upon noble principles with a record of achievement in helping to advance human rights, democracy and enhancing the security thereby derived.

When the Helsinki Agreement was signed 30 years ago, Europe was a very different place. By then the Cold War had been waged for almost 30 years. The United States and the Soviet Union were the world's two great superpowers locked in a great confrontation. Europe was divided by the Iron Curtain. Soldiers, tanks, aircraft and nuclear weapons were at the ready. The threat of confrontation was real. The spector of possible nuclear annihilation hung over Europe. And political, military and academic experts foresaw the Cold War continuing as far as the eye could see. Containing your adversary while avoiding direct superpower confrontation was the preferred strategy.

In this climate, both sides sought a venue in which to speak with the other on a routine basis in hopes of finding common ground, easing tensions, and bridging the menacing divide. One consequence of this effort was the Helsinki Agreement that bound the nations of Europe, East and West, and North America to various fundamental human rights standards and created a venue in which to discuss security matters through a more routine process than the episodic Washington/Moscow bilateral summits. There would be an ongoing series of conferences at which NATO countries could talk with Warsaw Pact countries.

Remarks at Ljubljana, Slovenia, February 17, 2005.

Most in the West doubted that Moscow was truly committed to the human rights standards to which they had subscribed in the Helsinki Agreement. The Soviets treatment of their own citizens and of the people in their satellite countries certainly demonstrated no commitment to basic human rights. It was felt that Moscow nonetheless signed the Helsinki Agreements because these Agreements acknowledged (and Moscow believed it signaled acceptance) of the Soviet Union's sphere of influence in central and eastern Europe. Also, Moscow saw benefit in this new venue for security talks. It was felt that Moscow envisioned that this new security mechanism would become an umbrella in the European architecture under which NATO and the Warsaw Pact would operate. So, like most diplomatic minuets, the Helsinki Agreements had trade offs. They offered Moscow some benefits while obligating it only to some oratorical human rights standards that were relatively harmless since Moscow could continue to claim fidelity to them while violating them in practice.

During the next 14 years, the Helsinki Agreements and their progeny continued. The security mechanisms never realized the potential Moscow had envisioned. Moscow continued to ignore the human rights standards with impunity while other venues to discuss security issues developed. But then that paradigm ended and new realities immerged.

In 1989, the Soviet Empire imploded as the Berlin Wall fell. Then, in 1991, the Russian Empire collapsed. The Cold War was over. Democracy and free markets had prevailed over totalitarian communism. A much diminished Russia sought to retrench and adapt to the new realities. Within the OSCE context, new and far reaching agreements were made. Among them was the 1991 Moscow Declaration in which all member states not only reiterated prior commitments to human rights and democracy, but also explicitly agreed that every OSCE member state had a legitimate right to be concerned with the internal human rights practices of every other state since, OSCE agreements recognized, respect for human rights supported stability and a more pacific Europe.

Not only had the Warsaw Pact disappeared, but NATO relentlessly expanded eastward. Central and much of eastern Europe no longer were auxiliaries of the Kremlin. They aligned with the West. Understandably, notwithstanding assurances from Washington, Moscow saw these developments as very menacing indeed.

The competition Moscow saw themselves engaged in with the West no longer was a checkmate of vast military might. Russia was in retreat in that arena while the West continued to surge forward. True, Russia continued to have a vast nuclear arsenal but their soldiers went unpaid, equipment deteriorated and fear of Russian loose nukes eclipsed concerns of nuclear confrontation. The new field on which competition raged was the political battle for the hearts and minds of people so long subjected to Moscow's totalitarianism now free to choose their own way. And the failed communist ideology now adjusted to authoritarian rule in Russia has provided little attraction to these people newly freed.

In this battle of ideas, the OSCE agreements on human rights and democracy, to which Moscow had subscribed, grew from inconvenient to intolerable. Moscow's sphere of influence had shrunk from central and eastern Europe to the Near Abroad, those new states that had been part of the Soviet Union during the Cold War. Then in December, 2003 came the Rose Revolution through which rigged elections were discarded with the help of the OSCE. In a new vote the people of Georgia elected a new leader, Mikheil Saakashvili, who is pro-West. Then in November and December, 2004, a similar series of events supported by the OSCE occurred in Ukraine. Again rigged elections blessed by Moscow selected a man that leaned to Moscow, Victor Yanukovych. Again international election observers, including the OSCE, exposed the fraudulent vote. And then, the Orange Revolution resulted in the election of a new pro-West President, Victor Yushchenko.

So for Moscow, the OSCE no longer is benign. It is an instrument through which past human rights and democracy commitments are weakening Moscow's fragile status. The OSCE is contributing to the erosion of legitimacy of authoritarian regimes friendly to Moscow that abut Russia. The OSCE is a mechanism through which radical reform movements are disrupting the status quo in Russia's backyard. For Moscow this is absolutely unacceptable.

So in the months ahead, the Panel of Eminent Persons to Strengthen the Effectiveness of the OSCE on which I sit will try to address Russian concerns about too much autonomy of OSCE Field Missions; voluntary contributions; East/ West imbalance of OSCE activities; increasing OSCE security activities in areas of terrorism, tolerance and trafficking; OSCE election standards; increased authority for the OSCE Security-General and so on. I certainly hope we can agree on proposals in these areas that will be helpful. But the fundamental problem within OSCE will remain. Russia finds certain OSCE human rights and democracy commitments harmful to its interests. It seeks to impede OSCE's work in this area.

The Panel of Eminent Persons cannot be complicit in the Russian efforts in this regard. As the OSCE agreements attest, human rights and democracy do contribute to stability, peace and security. They are integral to a comprehensive approach to security. And the degree to which the OSCE reaffirms these core values and reinvigorates its work program to advance them is the degree to which the OSCE will remain a vital organization that deserves our support.

Thank you.

The other members of the Panel of Eminent Persons on Strengthening the Effectiveness of the OSCE were Nikolai Afanasjevski (Russian Federation), Hans van den Broek (Netherlands), Wilhelm Hoeynck (Federal Republic of Germany); Kuanysh Sultanov (Republic of Kazakhstan), Knut Vollebaek (Norway) and Miomir Zuzul (Republic of Croatia).

KYRGYZSTAN:
FREEDOM'S UNCERTAIN MOMENT

The countries of central Asia present one of the greatest challenges for the march of freedom and for the Organization of Security and Cooperation in Europe (OSCE). The events in Kyrgyzstan are consequential not only for the Kyrgyz but for the entire region. An authoritarian leader has been driven from office. But whether Kyrgyzstan is on a path toward freedom, democracy and human rights is not yet known. The events of the coming months will determine this story and there is a great deal of work to be done.

Askar Akayev came to power in Kyrgyzstan on the back of the "silk revolution" in 1990. He initiated important economic changes and allowed more freedom than his neighbors. But in recent years, Mr. Akayev became increasingly autocratic. With a poor economy, growing poverty created unrest and resentment. Economic corruption and sweetheart deals enriched the elite, including Akayev's family, but created few opportunities for normal people. To many President Akayev seemed increasingly disconnected from the people.

Then last month Kyrgyz parliamentary elections were held. Pro-government deputies were overwhelmingly elected. Concerns arose that the newly elected parliament would extend Mr. Akayev's term in office beyond the constitutionally mandated limit of October. International Election Observers, including those from the Organization for Security and Cooperation in Europe, declared that the election failed international standards for a free and fair election. It had been rigged.

Events moved rapidly. In the south of Kyrgyzstan after clashes with police, opposition forces seized the two key cities of Osh and Jalalabad. Within days people gathered under yellow and pink banners on the edge of Bishkek, many of the people were from the south. They marched to the central square of Bishkek, assembling before the large Soviet-era building known as the White House. And as had happened in Georgia sixteen months ago and in Ukraine just four months ago, the police and military stood down. They did not use force or shoot their weapons to try to repel their fellow citizens moving against the government.

Kyrgyz General Abolulgami Tokchayer was quoted as saying, "For the sake of security for both sides, I decided to take the soldiers out of the building." A military guard Eugentii Razinkin said, "We have enough bullets here to kill thousands. But we gave our oath to the people, to the constitution, not to the president."

Remarks at OSCE Center, Tashkent, Uzbekistan, April 5, 2005.

Unfortunately, however, opposition supporters and pro-presidential backers did clash. There was looting that went on for several nights and there was gunfire. People were hurt, but none killed. And Mr. Akayev fled to Russia where, the other day, he officially resigned as president of Kyrgyzstan. Akayev's 15 year authoritarian presidency was brought down in less than a week.

In the span of just 16 months, three former Soviet Republics, now independent, pushed pro-Moscow governments from power after fraudulent elections. The least likely of these was in Kyrgyzstan, the mountainous nation of just over five million people, in a neighborhood of strong authoritarian governments. What does the upheaval mean? If ever there was evidence that freedom is not secured in a single day, it is in Kyrgyzstan. For many questions will have to be addressed and many challenges overcome in the days ahead if these events are to be the start of a free society.

Unlike in Georgia and Ukraine, Kyrgyzstan does not have a unified opposition. Kormanbek Bakiyeu, a former prime minister who joined the opposition to Akayev, has been appointed interim prime minister and president. A post-putsch crisis arose in a parliamentary struggle as members from the old and newly elected Parliament vied for power. The Kyrgyzstan Supreme Court refused to register parliamentary members elected in the March 13th fraudulent elections. Felix Kulov, the popular former vice-president and ex-mayor of Bishkek, was jailed in 2000 for challenging Akayev for president. Kulov has been released. After initially agreeing to be coordinator of Kyrgystan's security services and thereby giving legitimacy to the new government, reportedly he abruptly resigned the other day. This has added to the confusion and raised concerns of a split between northern Kyrgyzstan where Kulov hails from and the south, the home of Mr. Bakiyev.

Clearly a priority must be to establish some order and stability in Kyrgyzstan. All factions must pull together to realize this elementary objective. And then the new government, different factions of the opposition and civil society must come together to organize and execute a "free and fair" election for the new president which has been scheduled for June 26th*. And there is an opportunity for the OSCE to play a critical role in helping realize this objective.

Last Thursday Slovenian Foreign Minister Dimitrij Ruppel, the OSCE Chairman in Office, went to Bishkek and met with Bakiyev and other new leaders of Kyrgyzstan's transitional government. Ruppel urged the various factions to avoid infighting that could lead to new unrest at this delicate time. And, quite appropriately, Ruppel has urged the various potential presidential candidates "against taking the elections to the street."

It is critical that the run up to election day and the voting be transparent and beyond reproach. It must be fair and it must be seen as being fair. The new elected president will need the legitimacy and stature that can only be conferred by the people through a free and fair election. The OSCE has the expertise, experience and credibility to provide technical help, provide forums for civil society and candidates to freely and frankly exchange views, monitor media access and media coverage to ensure a level playing field, and otherwise assist Kyrgyzstan, an OSCE member state, to successfully work through this process under these challenging circumstances.

The Organization for Security and Cooperation in Europe, working with international NGOs that have election expertise such as the International Republican Institute and the National Democratic Institute, along with Kyrgyzstan's new political leaders, civil society and the Kyrgyz people can help establish a foundation for the Kyrgyzstan to move from their authoritarian past to a democratic future.

The OSCE was founded upon the simple and self-evident principle that real security and sustainable peace requires respect for human rights and personal freedom. During the 30 year history of the OSCE the soundness of that fundamental principle has been proven time and again. And during these years freedom has spread.

The situation in Kyrgyzstan is difficult. The challenges are substantial. Success is not assured. But the Kyrgyz deserve the very best efforts of the OSCE and the entire international community to help them in this journey. For if they succeed it will bring a better life to those impoverished people and be a beacon of hope in central Asia. It is a struggle well worth the fighting for.

---

* The Kyrgyzstan presidential election was rescheduled for July 10, 2005.

HUMAN RIGHTS AND SECURITY

It is important that "The Panel of Eminent Persons on Strengthening the Effectiveness of the Organization for Security and Cooperation in Europe," on which I sit, be fully familiar with the work of the Office for Democratic Institutions and Human Rights (ODIHR) because the core commitment of OSCE member states and the unique value of OSCE is a recognition that respect for human rights is a precondition for stability and security. The development of a comprehensive security concept that goes beyond the classic politico-military area by including human rights was a momentous innovation. The link between human rights and security has animated the work of OSCE since its founding in 1975. And during these past thirty years the understanding and protection of human rights has deepened within OSCE and its member states. Democracy has advanced. And our common security has been strengthened.

The Helsinki process began in the early 1970's. Then called the conference for Security and Cooperation in Europe (OSCE), it began as a forum for East-West contacts and a loose series of conferences. It has evolved into a security organization that deals with preventing conflicts and restoring peace and stability in a region from North America to Europe to Central Asia; from Vancouver to Vladivostok. And human rights, democracy and the rule of law have been central considerations in the Helsinki process and the OSCE conflict prevention and resolution efforts. The political and social changes since the collapse of the Soviet Empire have demonstrated the wisdom of the OSCE core values: namely, human rights, functioning democratic institutions and the rule of law are fundamental preconditions for stability and for both internal and external security.

The Helsinki Final Act is the first multilateral security agreement containing provisions on the protection of human rights at the same level as traditional international law principles such as non-interference in internal affairs or respect for territorial integrity.[1] Since the signing of the Helsinki Final Act in 1975, the OSCE has accumulated a large body of commitments in the fields of human rights, democracy, rule of law and national minorities. Perhaps most important, these commitments include making human rights an issue of legitimate concern between states.

The OSCE's comprehensive concept of security is not limited to traditional issues of military security, disarmament or border issues. It deals equally with human rights. The OSCE concept is that a free society that allows everyone to fully

---

Remarks at Office for Democratic Instituions and Human Rights Organization for Security and Coopertion in Europe, Warsaw, Poland, April 6, 2005

participate in public life is a safeguard against conflict and instability. The exclusion of individuals or certain groups from society, often on ethnic grounds, can lead to tensions and even armed conflict. Massive human rights abuses that cause large scale refugee crisis also are destabilizing and can lead to conflict.

The OSCE is not another structure that just sets out human rights norms. While it does that, importantly it links human rights with the institutional and political system of a state. Through their OSCE commitments, all 55 OSCE member states have agreed that pluralistic democracy based on the rule of law is the only system of government that effectively guarantees human rights. The member states, through their OSCE commitments, have made a political promise to comply with these standards.

And, as I have noted, a fundamental aspect within the OSCE is that human rights and pluralistic democracy are not merely an internal affair of a state. The member states have agreed that human rights, fundamental freedoms, democracy and the rule of law are of international concern. Respect for these enumerated rights and freedoms constitutes a pillar of international, peace and security. Member states have "categorically and irrevocably" declared that the "commitments undertaken in the field of the human dimension of the OSCE (i.e., human rights) are matters of direct and legitimate concern to all participating states and do not belong exclusively to the internal affairs of the state concerned."[2] Therefore, OSCE member states cannot invoke the principle of non-intervention to avoid scrutiny of the human rights situation within their borders. The OSCE is not only a "community of values," but also a "community of responsibility."

Let me quickly touch upon some of the fundamental human rights commitments made by OSCE members. Human rights are birth rights derived from the inherent dignity of the human person.[3] Human rights are universal.[4] The participating States "recognize that pluralistic democracy and the rule of law are essential for ensuring respect for all human rights and fundamental freedoms, the development of human contacts and the resolution of other issues of a related humanitarian character. They therefore welcome the commitment expressed by all participating States to the ideals of democracy and political pluralism as well as their common determination to build democratic societies based on free elections and the rule of law.

"The participating States express their conviction that full respect for human rights and fundamental freedom and the development of societies based on pluralistic democracy and the rule of law are prerequisites for progress in setting up the lasting order of peace, security, justice and cooperation that they seek to establish in Europe."[5]

Protection and promotion of human rights is a basic purpose of government.[6] And member states have an obligation to implement these OSCE commitments.[7] "All OSCE commitments, without exception, apply to each participating State. Their implementation in good faith is essential for relations between States, between governments and their peoples, as well as between the organization of which they are members. Participating States are accountable to their citizens and responsible to each other for their implementation of their OSCE commitments."[8]

Indeed, the OSCE is a "community of values" and a "community of responsibility." The OSCE work in the human dimension on human rights, democracy and the rule of law is the heart and soul of this organization. It is the value added. And is an essential contribution to the advance of human dignity and freedom, and of stability and security.[9]

---

1.   Final Act of the Conference on Security and Cooperation in Europe, Helsinki, August 1, 1975.

2.   Document of the Moscow Meeting of the Conference on the Human Dimension of the OSCE, October 3, 1991.

3.   The participating states "will promote and encourage the effective exercise of civil, political, economic, social, culture and other rights and freedoms all of which derive from the inherent dignity of the human person and are essential to his free and full development." Declaration on Principles Guiding Relations between Participating States, principle VII, para. 2, Helsinki 1975. "Human rights and fundamental freedoms are the birthright of all human beings, are inalienable and are guaranteed by law. Their protection and promotion is the first responsibility of government. Respect for them is an essential safeguard against an over-mighty state. Their observance and full exercise are the foundation of freedom, justice and peace." Human Rights, Democracy and Rule of Law, para. 2, Charter of Paris for a New Europe/Supplementary Document to give effect to certain provisions contained in the Charter of Paris for a New Europe, Paris, November 21, 1990 (Paris 1990).

4.   "The participating States recognize the universal significance of human rights and fundamental freedoms, respect for which is an essential factor for the peace, justice and well-being necessary to ensure the development of friendly relations and cooperation among themselves as among all states. They will constantly respect these rights and freedoms in their mutual   relations and will endeavor jointly and separately, including in cooperation with the United Nations, to promote universal and effective respect for them." Declaration of Principles Guiding Relations between Participating States, principle VII, par. 5 and 6, Helsinki (1975).

5.   Preamble, par. 9 and 11, Document of the Copenhagen Meeting of the Conference on the Human Dimension of the OSCE, June 29, 1990 (Copenhagen 1990). "Respect for human rights and fundamental freedoms, democracy and the rule of law is an essential component of security and cooperation in the CSCE region. It must remain a primary goal of CSCE action." Summit Declaration, par. 14, Concluding Document of Budapest, December 6, 1994 (Budapest 1994). "Human rights and fundamental freedoms, the rule of law and democratic institutions are the foundation of peace and security, representing a crucial contribution to conflict prevention within a concept of security. The protection of human rights... is an essential foundation of democratic civil society." Chapter VIII, par. 2, Budapest 1994.

6.   The participating States express their conviction that the protection and promotion of human rights and fundamental freedoms is one of the basic purposes of government, and reaffirm that the recognition of these rights and freedoms constitutes the foundation of freedom, justice and peace." Copenhagen 1990, Par. 1.

7.   The participating States... reaffirm their commitment to implement fully all provisions of the Final Act and of the other CSCE documents relating to the human dimension (human rights) and undertake to build on the progress they have made." Copenhagen, 1990, Preamble, par. 11. "We declare our respect for human rights and fundamental freedoms to be irrevocable. We will fully implement and build upon the provisions of the human dimension of CSCE." Paris, 1990, "Human Dimensions," par. 1.

8.   Charter for European Security, par. 7, Istanbul Document, November 19, 1999.

9.   Significant portions of these remarks were taken from two publications of the OSCE Office for Democratic Institutions and Human Rights (ODIHR): *Ten Years of ODIHR Working for Human Rights and Democracy (1991-2001)*. (Warsaw, Poland," ODIHR; 2001), and *OSCE Human Dimension Commitments: A Reference Guide,* (Warsaw, Poland; ODIHR; 2001).

THE ORGANIZATION OF SECURITY AND COOPERATION IN EUROPE: ITS VISION AND ITS VALUE

It is a pleasure for me to be in Brussels and have this opportunity to talk about the Organization of Security and Cooperation in Europe, the OSCE.

With the end of the Cold War, the movement of NATO eastward and the enlargement of the European Community, there have been significant changes in the European architecture. Former institutions such as the Warsaw Pact have disappeared while others have grown. Some European institutions now have acted "out of area." NATO has played a central role in Afghanistan and is now training Iraqi soldiers while the OSCE sent election monitors to Afghanistan last October for that country's Presidential election.

The sorting out and rationalization of these various institutions will take time. Slovenian Foreign Minister Dimitrij Ruppel currently is serving as the OSCE Chairman in Office. In response to these changing circumstances and the current budget impasse at the OSCE, Chairman Ruppel established a seven person "Panel of Eminent Persons on Strengthening the Effectiveness of the OSCE" on which I sit.[1]

We have been working since February. We have met with OSCE Secretary General Kubis and other senior OSCE officials, with the Director General of ODHIR (the Office of Democracy and Human Rights), various heads of OSCE field missions, senior officials from NATO, the European Community, various diplomats and leaders of civil society familiar with OSCE activities, academics and other experts. We are trying to understand the mission and mechanisms of this complex organization. And we are trying to develop agreement on some reform proposals to strengthen the organization by providing focus, mechanisms and procedures to make the OSCE more effective in those areas in which the organization can bring added value.

While we have begun preliminary drafting of our report, it would be premature for me to share possible recommendations. However, it might be useful if I share my view on the central mission of the OSCE and the general role that this enables the OSCE to play in this new and changing environment.

The initial Conference for Security and Cooperation in Europe was held in Helsinki in 1975. The Cold War had been going on for nearly 30 years. Both sides found merit in trying to create a process for dialogue.

Brussels, Belgium, May 5, 2005.

Moscow wanted the conference to provide a more or less formal recognition or ratification of its domination of the Warsaw Pact countries and to create a mechanism to discuss East-West security issues that might serve as an umbrella over NATO and the Warsaw Pact. The United States negotiators, led by Ambassador Max Kampelman, wanted a means to raise important human rights issues with the Soviet Union. The entire exercise was viewed with great skepticism, if not open hostility, by many hard line conservatives in Washington.

In the end the Helsinki Conference agreed to ten principles of human rights, self-determination and the relations of the participating states.[2] It became a forum for dialogue, and a series of meetings followed. Eventually a number of agreements came out of this process including the treaty on the reduction of conventional forces in Europe (MBFR) and a declaration by the participating governments that they no longer were adversaries.

Participating states renounced the use of force to alter the territorial integrity or political independence of any states. And a system of confidence-building measures was established.[3] At the time most political/military strategic thinkers tended to regard this dialogue as marginal to the real issues of the East/West confrontation. But events proved them wrong. The power of ideas proved mighty indeed in the defeat of totalitarian communism.

In 1983, President Ronald Reagan said, "The ultimate determination in the struggle now going on for the world will not be bombs and rockets, but a test of wills and ideas – a trial of spiritual resolve: the values we hold, the beliefs we cherish, the ideas to which we are dedicated …the great civilized ideas: individual liberty, representative government, and the rule of law under God."[4]

President Reagan was right. Ideas have consequences. The idea of freedom prevailed. And OSCE helped.

The unique contribution of the OSCE when it was founded was the idea of a "comprehensive security strategy." That is the notion that human rights and democracy are integral to security and stability. Over the past thirty years this concept has gained wide currency. And that is a good thing. Respect for fundamental human rights and the machinery, checks and balances and protections of democratic institutions and the rule of law create more stable societies. Democracies are less likely to engage in foreign adventure. A Community of Democracies is more stable and more secure. And the broader recognition of this principle and its embrace by other international organizations contribute to a safer more secure world.

But what distinguishes the OSCE today is its comprehensive agreements. The OSCE process has resulted in a series of political agreements to which all 55 member states subscribe. These binding obligations cover a wide range of human rights concerns. Furthermore, the Final Act of the 1975 Helsinki Conference that launched the OSCE process contains the principle that the internal conduct and respect for human rights of a national government are subject to legitimate concern by other states.

This agreement was set forth with even more clarity and power in the "Document of the Moscow Meeting of the Conference on the Human Dimension of the OSCE, 3 October 1991" to which all OSCE member states agreed to be bound. This agreement reads in part:

> ... full respect for human rights and fundamental freedoms
> and the development of societies based on pluralistic democracy
> and the rule of law are prerequisites for a lasting order of peace,
> security, justice and cooperation in Europe. ...
>
> The participating States emphasize that issues relating to
> human rights, fundamental freedoms, democracy and the rule of
> law are of international concern, as respect for these rights and
> freedoms constitutes one of the foundations of the international
> order. They categorically and irrevocably declare that the
> commitments undertaken in the field of the human dimension of
> the CSCE (that is, the human rights commitments) are matters of
> direct and legitimate concern to all participating States and do not
> belong exclusively to the internal affairs of the State concerned.[5]

What further distinguishes the OSCE and gives it particular value is the organization's unique reach; its membership of 55 countries that span Europe, North America and Central Asia; from Vancouver to Vladivostock.

And today in Russia's Near Abroad, those CIS countries once part of the Russian empire but now independent countries, the value of these OSCE commitments and their reach are proving exceedingly helpful for the march of freedom. In the past 17 months we have seen authoritarian regimes overthrown and freely elected democratic governments sworn into office in Georgia and Ukraine. And the authoritarian leader of Kygyrzstan Askar Akayev, has been driven from office and the country is preparing for Presidential Elections on July 10th. So the march of freedom can be heard even in Central Asia. And in each of these cases, the OSCE commitments and OSCE assistance have proven invaluable to democratic transitions.

It is precisely this success which concerns Moscow and contributes to the current crisis in the OSCE. Where we see demonstrators demanding free and fair elections in the streets of Tiblisi or Kiev as the march of freedom, Moscow sees chaos and disintegration.[6] We see these emerging democracies as making the world safer and more secure, Moscow sees its sphere of influence diminish and feels threatened.

As Georgian President Mikhail Saakashvili wrote just last week, "[E]ven the peoples of the former Soviet Union who for the last 15 years have enjoyed independence without true freedom can choose their path to liberty. Clearly, no authoritarian regime, when confronted by the will of its people can hold back the forces of freedom in this period of history."[7]

So while Russia's refusal to agree to a budget for the OSCE may be the participating event that created the current crisis, it is not the cause.[8] The root cause is a fundamental divergence of views on human rights, democracy and the agreements made through the OSCE process over 30 years.[9]

Daan Everts, Dutch ambassador to the OSCE, was quoted recently as saying, "Russia is using the 2005 budget not because the issue is about money as such. Russia wants to make a point. It wants less human rights and human security."[10]

And Alexey Burudavkin, Russia's ambassador to the OSCE has said, "We are ready to pay. But this is not only a financial problem. It is a problem of principle. If the parties expect us to pay a large amount into the OSCE budget, then Russia's interests and concerns should also be taken into consideration."[11] And those "interests and concerns" are the Russian's view that the OSCE is playing too prominent and too effective a role in supporting human rights, the rule of law and election monitoring in countries that Russia seeks to keep under its tight sphere of influence, or rather its sphere of "control."

For now we agree to disagree. The European Union, the United States and others are deeply committed to the OSCE values and agreements on human rights and democracy. On April 16, at the end of a European Union Foreign Ministers meeting, Jean Asselborn, the foreign minister of the current EU presidency, Luxembourg, "forcefully underlined the bloc's commitment to the very OSCE priorities Russia is contesting." "I would like to recall the EU's commitment to the activities of the OSCE in the field [of political and human rights], in particular electoral observation missions, missions on the ground, and border – monitoring missions. All three are for us extremely important." Asselborn said.[12]

And en route to Moscow last month, Secretary of State Condoleezza Rice said about another CIS country, "Nobody benefits from the kind of last dictatorship in Europe which is the Lukashenka government in Belarus."[13]

In Russia, Dr. Rice reiterated "American concerns about authoritarian trends in the Kremlin" and reminded the Russians about their obligations to democracy.[14] Then, after a meeting with Russian President Vladimir Putin in Moscow, Secretary Rice traveled to Lithuania. And while in Vilnius, she met with seven Belarusian dissidents and "expressed admiration for their courage as they seek an end to what she called 'the last dictatorship in the center of Europe'."[15] These comments, of course, echo the sentiments expressed by President Bush when he last met with President Putin in Bratislava, Slovakia, in February.[16]

So there are fundamental disagreements. They will not be solved by changing machinery or process in the OSCE. Our Panel will make some suggestions for reforms. If adopted, hopefully they will help. But on the central issue of existing OSCE agreements to which all member states have agreed and the continued pursuit of human rights and democracy as guaranteed in those agreements, there is no room for compromise. I, for one, will never agree to retreat on that front.

I believe deeply in the OSCE comprehensive security strategy. The OSCE region, the entire world, is safer and more secure the freer and more democratic it is. As President Bush said last month in dedicating a new Library and Museum devoted to America's Great Emancipator, President Abraham Lincoln, "Whenever freedom is challenged, the proper response is to go forward with confidence in freedom's power."[17]

That is our responsibility. It is the mission of the Organization for Security and Cooperation in Europe. And any so-called reforms, any adjustments, in the OSCE's agreements or the implementation of these agreements that trim its sails would be to break faith with the spirit of the organization. It would diminish the OSCE's distinctive value. It would betray those people within its area who still seek freedom and respect for their human rights. And so it will not happen. It cannot.

As President Bush said the other day, "Freedom is the birthright and deep desire of every human soul, and spreading freedom's blessings is the calling of our time."[18]

Thank you.

1. The other members of the "Panel of Eminent Persons on Strengthening the Effectiveness of the OSCE" were Nikolai Afanasjevski, (Russian Federation); Hans van den Broek, (Netherlands); Wilhelm Hoeynck, (Federal Republic of Germany); Kuanysh Sultanov, (Republic of Kazakhstan); Knut Vollebaek, (Norway); and Miomir Zuzul (Republic of Croatia).

2. An Overview of the Human Dimension Commitments of the Organization for Security and Cooperation in Europe 1975-2003.

General Human Dimension Commitments:

- Government responsibility for human rights: The government has primary responsibility for the protection and promotion of civil, political, economic, social, cultural and other rights and freedoms, all of which derive from the inherent dignity of the human person.
- Universality of human rights: Participating states recognize the universal significance of human rights and fundamental freedoms.
- Human rights, democracy and rule of law: Participating states recognize that pluralistic democracy and the rule of law are essential for ensuring respect for all human rights and fundamental freedoms.
- Human dimension as "international concern": Participating states agree to fulfill in good faith their obligations under international law, whether such obligations arise under customary international law or through treaties.
- Human rights treaties: Participating states will act in conformity with the U.N. Charter and the Universal Declaration of Human Rights. They will also fulfill their obligations under other human rights agreements, including the International Covenants on Human Rights.
- Commitment to implement: Participating states affirm their commitment to implement the U.N. Charter, the Helsinki Final Act, the Charter of Paris, and all other OSCE documents to which they have agreed.
- Derogations and states of emergency: Any derogations from obligations relating to human rights and fundamental freedoms during a public emergency must be limited to the extent required by the situation. The imposition of a state of public emergency must be proclaimed officially, publicly, and in accordance with the provisions laid down by law.
- Terrorism and human rights: Participating states undertake to conduct all counter-terrorism measures and cooperation in accordance with the rule of law, the United Nations Charter and relevant provisions of international law, international standards of human rights and, where applicable, international humanitarian law. Participating states reaffirm their commitment to protect human rights and fundamental freedoms against terrorist acts.
- International humanitarian law: Participating states will in all circumstances respect and ensure respect for humanitarian law, including protection of the civilian population.

Democracy and Rule of Law

- Rule of Law: Rule of law is not merely a formal legality that assures regularity and consistency in the achievement and enforcement of democratic order, but justice based on the recognition and full acceptance of the supreme value of the human personality and guaranteed by institutions providing a framework for its fullest expression. Democracy is an inherent element of the rule of law.
- Free elections: Participating states should hold elections at regular intervals and through procedures, such as secret ballot, that ensure in practice that electors may freely elect their representatives. Participating states should guarantee universal and equal suffrage to adult citizens.
- Representative government: Governments should be representative in character, and the executive should be accountable to the elected legislature or the electorate. All seats in at least one chamber of the national legislature should be freely contested in a popular vote.
- Political parties: Participating states should respect the right of citizens to organize political parties and organizations and provide them with the necessary legal guarantees to compete equally in elections. There should be a clear separation between political parties and the state.
- Independence of the judiciary: The impartial operation of the public judicial service should be

assured. In addition, the independence of legal practitioners should be protected.

- Power of the prosecution: Criminal procedure laws should clearly define the powers of the prosecutor and prosecutorial procedures.
- Adherence to the law: Government and public authorities, including the judiciary, must adhere to the constitution and the law.
- Citizen control of military: The military and police should be controlled by and accountable to civil authorities.
- Human rights institutions: Participating states agree to facilitate the establishment and strengthening of independent national human rights institutions, such as ombudsmen offices.
- Access to legislation: Legislation and regulations should be published and made accessible to citizens.
- Equality: All persons are entitled to equal protection under the law.
- Remedies: Citizens should hae effective means of redress for infringement of their rights by the state, including by law enforcement officials.
- Corruption: Participating states pledge to strengthen their efforts to combat corruption and to promote a positive framework for good government practices and public integrity.

Civil and Political Rights

- Self-determination of peoples: Participating states will respect the equal rights of peoples and their right to self-determination.
- Right to life and capital punishment: Participating states note that capital punishment has been abolished in a number of countries and that in participating states where it has not been abolished, it may be imposed only for the most serious crimes and in accordance with international law. The participating states agree to keep the question of capital punishment under consideration.
- Torture and other cruel, inhuman or degrading punishment or treatment: Participating states agree to prohibit torture and other cruel, inhuman or degrading treatment or punishment and take effective legislative, administrative, judicial and other measures to prevent and punish such practices.
- Trafficking in human beings: Participating states affirm that trafficking in human beings is an abhorrent human rights abuse and a serious crime that demands a more comprehensive and coordinated response from participating states and the international community.
- Arbitrary arrest or detention and pre-trial detention: Participating states will ensure that no one will be subjected to arbitrary arrest, detention or exile.
- Fair trial: Individuals shall have the right to a fair and public hearing within a reasonable time before an independent and impartial tribunal, including the right to present legal arguments and to be represented by the legal counsel of one's choice. No one shall be tried for any offense not stipulated by law, and everyone shall be presumed innocent until proven guilty.
- Effective remedies: Participating states should ensure that individuals who claim that the state has violated their human rights and fundamental freedoms are aware of and have access to effective remedies.
- Freedom of thought, conscience, religion or belief: Participating states agree to respect the freedom of thought, conscience, religion or belief for all without distinction as to race, sex, language or religion.
- Freedom of expression, free media and information: Participating states recognize the right of individuals to freedom of expression without state interference. Participating states also affirm the right of the media to collect, report and disseminate information, news, and opinions
- Freedom of association, including human rights defenders and nongovernmental organizations: Participating states agree to ensure that individuals are permitted to exercise the right to association, including the right to form political parties, trade unions, and nongovernmental organizations. Nongovernmental organizations that seek to promote and protect human rights shall have unhindered access to similar bodies within and outside their own countries.
- Right of assembly: Everyone shall have the right of peaceful assembly and demonstration.
- Freedom of movement: Participating states agree to recognize the rights of individuals to freedom of movement within the borders of each state and to leave any country, including their own, and to return to their countries.
- Private and family life: Participating states reaffirm the right to the protection of private and family life, domicile, correspondence and electronic communications. Searches and seizures of persons and private premises and property will take place only in accordance with standards that are judicially enforceable.

- Rights of the child: Participating states agree to accord particular attention to the rights of the child.
- Persons with disabilities: Participating states decide to ensure protection of persons with disabilities and to take steps to ensure their full participation in society.
- Nationality: Participating states recognize the right to nationality and agree to take measures not to increase statelessness.
- Property rights: No one way may be deprived of property except in the public interest, subject to law, and consistent with international commitments and obligations.

Economic, Social and Cultural Rights

- Economic and social rights: Participating states will promote and encourage the effective exercise of economic and social rights, paying particular attention to the areas of employment, housing, social security, and health.
- Workers' rights: Participating states will ensure the right of workers to establish and join trade unions, as well as the right of trade unions to exercise their rights freely, including the right to strike.
- Cultural rights and heritage: Participating states will promote the effective exercise of cultural rights.
- Right to education: Participating states will pay attention to education.
- Human rights education: Participating states agree that human rights education is essential and will encourage their competent authorities to design effective human rights related curricula and courses for students at all levels.

Tolerance and Non-Discrimination

- Equality and non-discrimination, including equal rights of women and men: Participating states will ensure human rights and fundamental freedoms to everyone within their territory, without distinction of any kind, such as race, color, sex, language, religion, political or other opinions, nationa or social origin, property, birth or other status. Participating states will take all measures necessary, including legislative measures, to promote equally effective participation or men and women in political, economic, social and cultural life.
- Aggressive nationalism, racism, chauvinism, xenophobia, anti-semitism and ethnic cleansing: The participating states clearly and unequivocally condemn these phenomena and declare their intention to intensify their efforts to combat them. They draw particular attention to the problems of the Roma and Sinti.
- Migration, refugees, displaced persons and returnees, and migrant workers: Participating states express concern over the problem of refugees and displaced persons and pledge to refrain from any policy of "ethnic cleansing" or mass expulsion. Participating states will allow all refugees who so desire to return safely to their homelands. Participating states invite host countries and countries of origin to make efforts to improve further the economic, social, cultural and other conditions of life for migrant workers and their families legally residing in the host countries.

(This overview was drawn from a December 2003 paper prepared by Professor Douglass Cassel of Northwestern University Law School, which in turn summarized a 2001 OSCE compilation of human dimension commitments through 2000 and added references to OSCE documents from 2001 to 2003. The purpose of this overview is to provide a rough guide to the substance of the human dimension commitments made through the Helsinki process. It does not purport to be an exhaustive description of these commitments, which would require many more pages.)

3. This was taken as superseding the Brezhnev Doctrine which had asserted the non-reversibility of communism in the Soviet Union bloc.

4. President Ronald Reagan, Address to the British Parliament, London, England, June 8, 1982.

5.   The entire text of the opening section of the Document of the Moscow Meeting of the Conference on the Human Dimension of the OSCE, 3 October 1991, reads as follows:

The participating States renew their commitment to implement fully all the principles and provisions of the Final Act of the Conference on Security and Co-operation in Europe, of the Charter of Paris for a New Europe and of the other CSCE documents relating to the human dimension, including, in particular, the Document of the Copenhagen Meeting of the progress in the implementation of these provisions, as full respect for human rights and fundamental freedoms and the development of societies based on pluralistic democracy and the rule of law are prerequisites for a lasting order of peace, security, justice and co-operation in Europe.

In this context, the participating States underlined that, in accordance with the Final Act of the Conference on Security and Co-operation in Europe and the Charter of Paris for a New Europe, the equal rights of peoples and their right to self-determination are to be respected in conformity with the Charter of the United Nations and the relevant norms of international law, including those relating to territorial integrity of States.

At the Moscow meeting views were expressed by the participating States on the implementation of their commitments in the field of the human dimension. They considered that the degree of their commitments contained in the relevant provisions of the CSCE documents had shown further substantial improvement since the Copenhagen Meeting. They also considered that, in spite of the significant progress made, serious threats to and violations of CSCE principles and provisions continue to exist and have a sobering effect on the assessment of the over all situation in Europe. In particular, they deplored acts of discrimination, hostility and violence against persons or groups on national, ethnic or religious grounds. The participating States therefore expressed the view that, for the full realization of their commitments relating to the human dimension, continued efforts are still required which should benefit substantially from the profound political changes that have occurred.

The participating States emphasize that issues relating to human rights, fundamental freedoms, democracy and the rule of law are of international concern, as respect for these rights and freedoms constitutes one of the foundations of the international order. They categorically and irrevocably declare that the commitments undertaken in the field o the human dimension of the CSCE are matters of direct and legitimate concern to all participating States and do not belong exclusively to the internal affairs of the State concerned. They express their determination to fulfill all of their human dimension commitments and to resolve by peaceful means any related issue, individually and collectively, on the basis of mutual respect and cooperation. In this context they recognize that the active involvement of persons, groups, organizations and institutions is essential to ensure continuing progress in this direction.

The participating States express their collective determination to further safeguard human rights and fundamental freedoms and to consolidate democratic advances to their territories. They also recognize a compelling need to increase the CSCE's effectiveness in addressing human rights concerns that arise in their territories at this time of profound change in Europe.

In order to strengthen and expand the human dimension mechanism described in the section on the human dimension of the CSCE in the Concluding Document of the Vienna Meeting and to build upon and deepen the commitments set forth in the Document of the Copenhagen Meeting of the Conference on the Human Dimension of the CSCE, the participating States adopt the following.

6.   See Alex Rodriguez, "Creeping Revolts Alarm Moscow: Kyrgyzstan Uprising has Russia Nervous About Tilt to West," *Chicago Tribune*, March 27, 2005; Steven Lee Myers "Contagion: Popular Risings in Ex-Soviet Zone," *New York Times*, March 25, 2005; Peter Finn, "Another Russian Revolution? Youth Movement Adopts Spirit of Uprisings Nearby," *Washington Post*, April 9, 2005; and Steven Lee Myers, "What Would Happen If Russia Exploded in Protest," *New York Times*, April 3, 2005.

7.   Mikheil Saakashvili, "Principled Democracy," *Wall Street Journal*, April 29, 2005.

8.   Also in December 2004, Russia vetoed the extension of an OSCE border monitoring mission in Georgia.

9.   "Condoleezza Rice and Foreign Minister Sergei Lavrov discussed the problems of reforming the OSCE. It became clear that the USA and Russia have a different perception of the role that the organization plays in the world. Russia criticized OSCE's pro-Western stance in regulating conflicts in the countries of the former Soviet Union, as well as its approach to the estimation of democratic elections in the Commonwealth of Independent States ...The attitude of revolutions on the post-Soviet space and the freedom of mass media became the central subject of Condoleezza Rice's negotiations with Sergei Lavrov." Tatiana Stanovaya, "U.S.-Russian Relations: Lost in Translation," *Pravda*, April 28, 2005.

10. Judy Dempsey, "Russia Puts Pressure on OSCE Monitors," *International Herald Tribune*, March 29, 2005.

11. *Ibid.*

12. Alito Labyakas, "Europe: Russia, EU Look Set to Clash Over Putin of OSCE," *RFE/RL Article*, April 17, 2005. See also, Alexander Mineyev, "EU Intends to Strengthen OSCE Role in Europe," *ITAR-TASS World Service*, April 16, 2005.

13. George Gedda, "Calling for Change in Belarus, Rice Meets With Dissidents," *Associated Press*, April 21, 2005.

14. Steven R. Weisman, "Rice Reminds the Russians of Obligations to Democracy," *New York Times*, April 20, 2005; Neil Buckley, "Rice Outlines Fears Over Kremlin's Strong Grip on Power and Media," *Financial Times*, April 20, 2005; and Alex Rodriguez, "Russia Receives Democratic Pitch: U.S. Worries About Kremlin Grabbing Power," *Chicago Tribune*, April 21, 2005. See also, Tyler Marshall, "Belarus Dictatorship Can't Last, Rice Assures Opposition," *Chicago Tribune*, April 21, 2005.

15. George Gedda, "Calling for Change in Belarus, Rice Meets With Dissidents," *Associated Press*, April 21, 2005. It is noteworthy that while in Moscow, Secretary Rice both pushed for economic and political reform and sought to assure President Putin that the United States is no threat to Russia in the region. See, Steven R. Weisman, "Rice Tells Putin U.S. Is No Threat in Region," *New York Times*, April 21, 2005. See also, Yochi J. Dreazen, "Russia Criticizes U.S. for Backing Democratic Change in Belarus," *Wall Street Journal*, April 22, 2005.

16. "Strong countries are built by developing strong democracy," Bush said he told Putin. "I think Vladimir heard me loud and clear." Terrence Hunt, "Bush Challenges Putin on Democracy," *Chicago Sun-Times*, February 25, 2005. See also, Elizabeth Bumiller, "For Bush and Putin, a Romance With Signs of Rockiness," *New York Times*, February 28, 2005.

17. President George W. Bush, Remarks Dedicating Abraham Lincoln Presidential Library and Museum, Springfield, Illinois, April 19, 2005.

18. President George W. Bush, President Discusses Freedom and Democracy, The Rose Garden, Washington, D.C., March 29, 2005.

PROPPING UP AN
OLD PILLAR OF DEMOCRACY

The United States needs a strong, integrated Europe, not as a counterweight to U.S. power, but as a proactive partner.

Therefore, it has been disquieting to witness the turmoil in the European Union caused by the French and Dutch "No" votes on the EU constitution, followed by the failed EU summit earlier this month. It will take time for the European Union to sort out this wreckage.

Fortunately, while the EU works through this crisis, another important European institution seems to have weathered a storm created by Russian obstruction.

Thirty years ago during the height of the Cold War, East and West found common ground in signing the Helsinki Final Act. It dealt with security and economic issues, as well as important commitments to fundamental principles of democracy and human rights. This ground-breaking agreement has led to others in the Helsinki process and the creation of the Organization of Security and Cooperation in Europe (OSCE).

The OSCE membership has grown to 55 member states. Every European country is an OSCE member as well as North America and the central Asian countries that had been part of the former Soviet Union. The OSCE's geographic span goes from Vancouver to Vladivastock. This geographic footprint gives the OSCE, as a regional organization, a unique global reach.

More important, the OSCE has a series of commitments made by every member state over the past 30 years. They include agreements that "comprehensive security" is not only a consequence of military might and treaty alliances; but that security comes from a stability sustainable only in societies in which basic human rights are protected and democratic institutions and the rule of law guarantee free and fair elections.

And the OSCE established another key principle in the so-called Moscow Declaration. OSCE countries agreed that each member has a legitimate interest in every other members' adherence to their human rights and democracy commitments.

Appeared in *Tech Central Station*, July, 1, 2005

For years Moscow found their OSCE human rights commitments inconvenient. More recently they became intolerable. In both the Rose Revolution in Georgia and the Orange Revolution in Ukraine, the OSCE contributed to the advance of freedom.

In these neighboring states, Russia sought to certify elections to prop up regimes friendly to Moscow. In both cases, the OSCE joined others in declaring the elections fraudulent. That's right, an organization in which Russia was a member joined in exposing the fraud in which Moscow had been complicit. In both cases, the international community led by the OSCE emboldened the citizens to peacefully protest the rigged votes and force new elections which were "free and fair" and in which opposition parties won office.

In response, Russia has tried to eviscerate the OSCE. Moscow created a crisis by withholding its support for an OSCE budget and demanding a number of institutional changes that would have enhanced Russia's control over the OSCE and weakened the organization's capacity to effectively advance human rights and democracy.

The OSCE's current Chairman in Office, Slovenian Foreign Minister Dimitrij Rupel, responded by creating a Panel of international personalities charged to develop reforms to strengthen the effectiveness of the OSCE. Former Norwegian Foreign Minister Knut Vollebaek chaired this group. I served as one of the Panel's seven members, Russian Ambassador NikoliayAfanasievsky was another.

Over five months our group met in various European capitals, traveled to various OSCE Field Missions in Central Asia and elsewhere, and heard from many experts. Then we set about trying to negotiate a report to which we all could agree.

There were many conflicting views. We had spirited discussions. However, in the end, we reached consensus on our report.

The many structural matters and particular proposals to which we agreed are less important than the report's explicit reaffirmation of the centrality of OSCE human rights commitments. The values that have animated the OSCE for thirty years and the instruments to advance them have been sustained.

Later this month our report will be formally presented to the OSCE Permanent Council in Vienna. It will provide a platform for the OSCE to move beyond recent divisions and confrontation and continue its important work to build a sustainable peace through advancing human rights and democracy.

In this continuing mission Europe benefits as do we.

30 YEARS OF THE HELSINKI PROCESS: THE CONTRIBUTION OF THE OSCE IN A CHANGING WORLD

The Organization for Security and Cooperation in Europe has been active in building security through cooperation since 1975. I appreciate having this opportunity to join in this examination of the OSCE's contribution to a changing world on this, the 30th anniversary of the Helsinki Final Act.[1] And it's a particular pleasure to be on a program with Austrian Foreign Minister Usula Plassnik; the OSCE Chairman in Office, Slovenian Foreign Minister Dimitrij Rupel and Polish Foreign Minister Rotfeld.

For me it always is a particular pleasure to be back in Vienna. In the mid-80's, while Ambassador to the U.N. offices in Vienna, my family and I enjoyed living here immensely. I have a son who was born here. So I hold fond memories of and warm feelings toward this magnificent city.

Many global events have marked the past 30 years: many good, some not so good, and some horrific. The Killing Fields of Cambodia, Rwanda and ethnic cleansing in the Balkans are but some of the gravestones marking man's inhumanity to man during this period.[2] And the current genocide in Darfur, Sudan and the terrorist bombings in London earlier this month demonstrate that evil still walks among us.[3] But these years also have been a period of unprecedented expansion of democracy and freedom. These years have been a period of advancing hope and opportunity. And in this great transition, the OSCE has made a real contribution.

Thirty years into the Cold War, new mechanisms were sought for a regular dialogue between the East and the West rather than continuing to rely solely on episodic summits. In November, 1972, informal preparatory talks inaugurated the Helsinki process.[4] The signing of the OSCE Helsinki Final Act on August 1, 1975, marked the culmination of intense negotiations.[5] The OSCE dialogue would be inclusive.[6] It would proceed with a cooperative approach. The Helsinki process embraced the principle of equality among the states. A consensus rule in decision-making was agreed to.[7] And, most significantly, the Helsinki Final Act developed the concept of "comprehensive security" that includes political-military, economic, environmental, human rights and democracy; and which links international and domestic security. While such a comprehensive approach to security has become common; back in 1975 it was unprecedented.[8]

Remarks at PSCE Conference, The Federal Ministry of Foreign Affairs of the Republic of Austria, Vienna, Austria, July 20, 2005

Of course, from the outset certain countries had greater interest in certain aspects of the comprehensive security equation than others. There always was some tension. However, throughout the Cold War, the transition period from 1989 to 1992, and into the post-Cold War era, members found broad common ground, the OSCE remained flexible and adapted to new challenges and new circumstances, and the core principles of the OSCE were maintained. The entire membership benefited. But now one nation has created a crisis in the OSCE.[9]

In 2003 in Maastricht and in 2004 in Sofia, the Ministerial Councils were unable to agree on final communiques. And the same dissident member State created a financial crisis for many months this year by refusing to join consensus on an OSCE budget and threatening to repeat this obstruction unless its concerns are taken into account and adopted by the OSCE.

Some of the issues raised about the ways and means by which the OSCE operates deserve serious consideration. Parts of the OSCE structures and mechanisms should be re-examined. But most of the operational concerns raised and the structural reforms that have been proposed are just symptoms of a more fundamental rejection by some members of the core values of the Organization for Security and Cooperation in Europe, and their desire to eviscerate the effectiveness of this Organization to advance those values.

Therefore, any deliberations on OSCE reform should begin with some reflection on the unique assets of the organization, the value added. And any adjustments or reforms should not be adopted if they would circumscribe those assets or hinder the organizations capacity to pursue its mission.

There are two fundamental assets at the heart of the OSCE. They are the twin pillars that enable the organization to contribute to a safer, more secure world. The first pillar is the reach of its membership: 55 nations from Europe, North America and Central Asia.[10] The OSCE has a unique footprint stretching from Vladivostok to Vancouver. Within the reach of this regional organization are mature democracies with the deep habits and strong ramparts to protect individual rights; there are transitional states that need time and nurturing for democratic practices and values to take root and become sturdy so they can withstand the inevitable storms that will come; and there are some that still cling to the old ways of authoritarian rule. So the OSCE has a vast geographic reach within which there is much work yet to be done.

The other OSCE pillar is its Comprehensive Security Strategy and the series of commitments made by each and every member to achieve sustainable peace and security. At its core is agreement that respect for human rights in a democracy is integral to stability and security. That is the essence of the OSCE, its heart. And, critically, all OSCE participating states have agreed that compliance to accepted human rights and democracy standards by each member state is the legitimate interest of every other OSCE member state.

Today at this conference we again have heard criticism that when the OSCE advances human rights standards and democratic practices that it is interfering in the internal affairs of participating states.[11] Such a position is a rejection of prior OSCE agreements. As Secretary of State Colin Powell said at the Sofia Ministerial meeting last December, "Some countries have recently argued that the OSCE's field work constitutes interference in internal affairs, that the OSCE has 'double standards' and that the OSCE has concentrated its efforts in the former Soviet republic and has done it for political reasons. I categorically disagree. All OSCE participating states signed up to the proposition that fundamental freedoms, democracy and the rule of law are of legitimate concern to us all."[12]

This founding principle of the OSCE was reaffirmed forcefully in the 1991 Moscow Declaration to which all OSCE member states subscribed. It reads: "The participating States emphasize that issues relating to human rights, fundamental freedoms, democracy and the rule of law are of international concern, as respect for these rights and freedoms constitutes one of the foundations of the international order. They categorically and irrevocably declare that the commitments undertaken in the field of the human dimension of the OSCE are matters of direct and legitimate concern to all participating States and do not belong exclusively to the internal affairs of the State concerned. They express their determination to fulfill all of their human dimension commitments and to resolve by peaceful means any related issue, individually and collectively, on the basis of mutual respect and cooperation."[13]

The recognition of human rights and democracy as linchpins to sustainable security is fundamental in the OSCE. These values animate the work of the OSCE. And the many OSCE commitments made by participating States over the past 30 years, empower the OSCE to act to secure human rights and democracy from Vladivostok to Vancouver.

The world has changed profoundly over the past 30 years since the OSCE was founded in Helsinki, Finland. Freedom has been on the march, and the OSCE has helped that advance: most recently in the Balkans, Georgia, Ukraine and Kyrgyzstan. The world has been made anew.

Before we tinker with the structures and mechanisms of the OSCE let's recall why democracy matters. Every human being has inherent dignity and worth. Self-determination is a fundamental human right recognized in the U.N. Universal Declaration on Human Rights and by common sense. Furthermore, democracy is the best way to secure sustainable respect for other human rights. It is a rampart against state encroachment on individual rights and liberty. If you can participate in choosing your government through a democratic process, you can protect your interests and rights from abuse by government. Democracy fosters greater political equality.

Democracy is the surest path to a just society because it gives people the opportunity to live under laws of their own choosing. It provides restraints and accountability.

A democracy provides its citizens the freedom to follow their dreams, develop their talents and reap the reward of their labor. It helps create growth and opportunity.[14]

Among other things, today our security is threatened by global terrorism. The carnage in London the other day is but one of the recent testaments to this evil menace.[15] Dictatorships and authoritarian governments where there is no hope nor opportunity provide fertile soil to grow terrorists frustrated and bitter by their impotent lot in life, attracted to fanaticism, and willing to strike out in vile senseless violence against innocent civilians. Democracy, by empowering its citizens, encouraging personal responsibility, providing opportunity and allowing hope to flourish crowds out the despair upon which terrorism relies.

And democratic societies, with their capacity to adjust and adapt to changing circumstances at home and abroad, are inherently more stable than dictatorships unresponsive to the will of the people. Democracy leads to compromise, cooperation and coalitions.

Furthermore, democracies are most reluctant to engage in foreign adventurism and begin wars of aggression because they must build and sustain popular support. Whereas dictatorships often invade neighbors for the vain glory of its ruler such as Saddam Hussein's invasions of Iran and Kuwait.

So promoting democracy is not just some ideological preference or passing fashion. Promoting democracy helps protect human rights, create more just societies, helps in the war on terrorism, creates more stable societies and is a restraint on wars of aggression. Promoting democracy not only benefits those people long living under tyranny who will now live in freedom. Promoting democracy helps us all by making us all more secure. That is one important benefit from the march of freedom. That is the core value that has animated the OSCE for 30 years. And that is what we cannot diminish if the OSCE is to play a vibrant role that contributes to a changing world.

And it is important to note that when we speak of democracy and we look at the OSCE's priorities and work programs that we understand that democracy is not just about mechanics on election day. Democracy requires regular elections so that those out of power know that on a future day they again can compete for power, and those in power know they will be held accountable. There are no final victories. Democracy requires free speech and freedom of the press; the ability to exchange ideas, criticize and propose new approaches. There must be freedom to assemble and access to the media . A vibrant civil society is required. The rule of law must govern and be seen to govern. And every vote must be counted. These practices and institutions of democracy take time to build. The habits of democracy must be nurtured to take root. The OSCE can play a role. We all have some shortcomings. We all can do better.

It also is important to realize that democracy is not just some abstract idea, some sterile political procedure. Democracy is flesh and blood. It is hope and dreams and aspirations. It is real people gaining a measure of control of their own destiny.

I recall a conference in Gdansk, Poland, at which the President of Latvia spoke about the dark days before independence. He said that at night when he returned to his small one room apartment, he would walk from one end to the other with his small transistor radio trying to pick up the scratchy transmission of Radio Free Europe. On those nights when the broadcast came through he often heard stories of the Solidarity Trade Union standing up for freedom in the Gdansk shipyard and words of fidelity to freedom and to freedom fighters such as himself. He said those broadcasts gave him strength when there was little reason for hope. They inspired him to hold onto his dreams of freedom when so much of his life's experience could have driven him to despair. So the OSCE commitments matter not only to us, but to those not yet living in liberty.

As Secretary of State Condoleezza Rice said earlier this month, "Eastern and Central European citizens seized on the Helsinki agreement as an instrument with which to press for human rights and peaceful change. …[T]hey never stopped believing in the power of the Helsinki principles to advance the cause of freedom."[16]

In 1996, I was an international election observer in Veronezh during Russia's first presidential election.[17] I remember visiting polling stations in the countryside. People were so happy to finally have a say in choosing their leader. At almost every polling station there was music, dancing and refreshments. The Russian people were celebrating their empowerment. They were joyful in their new liberty. I recall seeing one peasant woman going into the small voting booth and crowding her six small children into the voting booth with here. When she emerged I asked her why she had taken her children into the small voting booth. She had a large smile on her face and tears in her eyes as she told me that this was the greatest day in her life and she had to share it with her children. She was casting her first vote ever in a free and fair election, this was important, this was monumental, and her children had to be part of it. For, she said, "this vote is about my children. It is about their future."

In 1999, I was an election observer in Nigeria's first free and fair election. It was in March. The weather was hot. And up in Minna, where I observed the voting, the land was a little desolate, dusty and I found the sun oppressive. Yet I witnessed men and women, some quite old, some having walked great distances barefoot, stand in line for hours waiting to vote without complaint. They had waited their entire lives to have a say in choosing their leader. A few more hours were not going to deter them.

Cambodia has witnessed some of the worst atrocities in modern history.[18] During Pol Pot's reign of terror one in four Cambodians died. Torture chambers and mass graves were the instruments of his viciousness. The screams of Cambodia's Killing Fields still echo in the villages, in the towns and in the streets of Phnom Penh. In 1998, I was an observer in Cambodia's first election after the U.N. peace process. I met Moeung Sem, a small woman who looked much older than her years. As we visited atop a building in the city of Siem Reip, her two young daughters lay asleep on straw mats in the hot sun. She told me about the night a week earlier when strangers with arms entered her home in the remote Chik Keak village. They rustled her husband out of bed, shouted questions at him and then took him outside and shot him dead. She believed it was because her husband was supporting one of the opposition candidates. Her eyes were so sad. Her small frame bent over as if she was weary from the weight of the world. I asked her about the next day's election. First she said she would do anything to have her husband back. She missed him. He was a good man. She was scared for herself and worried for her two children. And then her back stiffened a little and, for the first time, she stared directly into my eyes. She said that tomorrow she would vote. She would vote with hope for a better Cambodia, for change. Then she added, "Also I will vote for my husband. He lost his life so we could have a choice." Then she pointed to her sleeping daughters who had so recently lost their father and she said, "And I will cast a vote for them. It may not matter tomorrow. The election may be stolen. But someday it will matter, someday we will have change. Then it will be better for my daughters. Then they will not have to worry that someday their husbands will be taken out into the night and killed."

Last October I was in Afghanistan for the first presidential election in that nation's 5,000 year history. Afghanistan had been brutalized for 25 years: first by Soviet occupiers and then by the Taliban. Leading up to election day there had been substantial violence and intimidation. Eighteen Afghans were killed just for having voter cards. The day before I arrived a rocket was launched and landed just 75 yards from the American embassy compound. A tanker was discovered with five tons of explosives on the streets of Kabul the day before the voting. So many were asking would there be sufficient turn out to give the election legitimacy.

The Taliban and al-Qaeda understood the great threat to their ideology of hate and destruction poised by the advance of democracy. But the people of Afghanistan understood the promise and hope provided by the ballot box. They would not be intimidated. They would not be deterred. They came out to vote by the millions in Kabul, in rival villages and in the rugged mountains accessible only by foot or on horseback. They tolerated some technical problems. They voted and they felt empowered.

For me, the transformative power of the Afghan election and of democracy was captured in a story told to me by one of my election observer colleagues, Lena Auerbach. Under the Taliban girls could not go to school, most women were not allowed to get medical attention, and some were seldom even allowed to leave their homes. In a society where everyone was oppressed, women suffered the greatest.

It was late morning on election day in a village in the mountains outside Kabul. Lena was in a women's polling center. She watched women come into the voting place in small groups of three to five. Once inside, protected from male eyes, they lifted their burkas and talked and laughed with excitement as one by one they cast their vote. After voting, one woman came over near Lena and leaned against the wall. She had a soft smile on her face. Through a translator, Lena told the woman, "Today is a good day for your daughter." The woman's smile grew to a large grin and tears flowed down her cheeks.

Yes, democracy is about the mechanics of election day. It is about the environment in which votes are cast and the institutions erected to sustain it. But more fundamentally it is about the women in Russia casting her first vote surrounded by her family, the Nigerians waiting for hours in the hot sun to cast their ballot, the Cambodian widow voting for a better and safer life for her daughters, and the Afghan woman crying tears of pride and hope that democracy will provide the opportunities for her daughters she so long was denied. Democracy is about people's dreams, their hopes and about a better future in freedom.

So, on the 30th anniversary of the Helsinki Final Act it is appropriate to reflect, reform and reinvigorate the OSCE. There are improvements to be made. Chairman in Office Rupel has engaged the issue. He convened our Panel on Strengthening the Effectiveness of the OSCE.[19] The Panel took its task seriously because we believe the OSCE matters. It has contributed to making the world more secure. And there is more work to be done.

Our seven member panel, by consensus, has came up with a number of recommendations on strengthening the OSCE's identity and profile, improving consultative and decision-making processes, strengthening the Secretary-General, clarifying the role of the Chairman in Office, enhancing field operations, strengthening operational capacities, and so on.[20]

Hopefully these suggestions will be helpful. Now it lies with the Permanent Council to advance the process. And ultimately Ministers will make judgments to adopt the proposals they deemed appropriate. Hopefully the consequences will be a stronger, more focused, more effective OSCE.

But the real issue, the fundamental challenge to the OSCE is not the mechanics or structures of the organization. The threat to the OSCE will not be resolved by adjusting the organization's architecture or improving its procedures. The challenge is more fundamental.[21] The danger for the organization today is that some Participating States are less committed to the OSCE core values of human rights and democracy. Some Participating States have long felt that their OSCE commitments on human rights and democracy were inconvenient. Following the developments in Georgia and Ukraine, these Participating States now find those commitments intolerable. In the name of reform, efficiency and balance, they seek to create impediments to the OSCE continuing to fulfill its important mission. They seek to eviscerate the effectiveness of the OSCE to project the values that have animated its work for 30 years. They seek to discount their commitments by circumscribing OSCE activities, constraining its flexibility, and centralizing control in Vienna where, they believe, they are better able to contain Field Mission's activities.

Yes, there are areas in which the operations of the OSCE can improve. There are reforms that should be adopted. But beware.

We live in a time of an historic tide of freedom. It is a tide the OSCE has helped nurture and helped promote. Will the OSCE continue to be on the side of history, or will it not? Will the OSCE be faithful to the values that have animated its work for 30 years? If the answer is "Yes," the OSCE can contribute substantially to a changing world that is safer, more secure and freer. It will remain a relevant and consequential organization.

I hope and expect the answer will be "yes." Time will tell. If we all rededicate ourselves to these essential OSCE values and reaffirm our OSCE commitments, then the reforms can be achieved and the march of freedom will continue with the OSCE helping to advance the cause. For, as President Bush has said, "Free societies are peaceful societies. And by extending liberty to millions who have not known it, we will advance the cause of freedom, and we will advance the cause of peace."[22]

Thank you.

---

1.   See, http://www.hri.org/docs/Helsinki75.html.

2 .   For descriptions of and analysis about these terrible atrocities of the recent past see, Elizabeth Neuffer, *The Key to My Neighbor's House: Seeking Justice in Bosnia and Rwanda* (New York, N.Y.; Picador USA; 2001); Philip Gourevitch, *We Wish to Inform You That Tomorrow We Will Be Killed With Our Familie: Stories From Rwanda* (New York, N.Y.; Picador USA; 1998); Linda Polman, *We Did Nothing: Why the Truth Doesn't Always Come Out When the U.N. Goes In* (New York, N.Y.; Viking; 2003); Romeo Dallaire, *Shake Hands With the Devil: The Failure of Humanity in Rwanda* (Toronto, Canada; Random House Canada; 2003); Samantha Power, *A Problem From Hell: America and the Age of Genocide* (New York, N.Y.; Basic Books; 2002); Nicholaus Mills and Kira Brunner, eds., *The New Killing Fields: Massacre and the Politics of Intervention* (New York, N.Y.; Basic Books; 2002); Eric D. Weitz, *A Century of Genocide: Utopias of Race and Nation* (Princeton, N.J.; Princeton University Press; 2003); and Benjamin A. Valentino, *Final Solutions: Mass Killing and Gnocide in the 20th Century* (Ithaca, N.Y.; Cornell University Press; 2004).

3.   See. Richard Williamson, "Sudan Genocide in the UNCHR," *Chicago Sun-Times*, April 11, 2004; Richard Williamson, "Sudan Out of Africa, A Plea for World's Help," *Chicago Sun-Times*, June 15, 2004; and Richard Williamson, "Sudan Genocide Tests International Community," *Chicago Sun-Times*, August 6, 2004. See also, Wikipedia, "7 July 2005 London Bombings," http://en.wikipedia.org/wiki/7_July_2005_London_bombings.

4.   At the time when the Helsinki process began in 1972, the United States and the Soviet Union had just adopted a first interim agreement on the limitation of strategic nuclear weapons and had put into force the Anti-Ballistic Missile Treaty. With the signing of the Quadripartite Agreement on the status of Berlin and the treaties between the Federal Republic of Germany and the Soviet Union, Poland, and the German Democratic Republic, West Germany's policy of reapproachment with the Eastern Bloc (Ostpolitik) had gained momentum. "Preventing nuclear war by defusing the East-West military confrontation centered on Europe remained the overriding priority. And this was increasingly accompanied by a desire to at least partially overcome the confrontation by means of coexistence and cooperation." *The Culture of Dialogue: The OSCE Acquis 30 Years After Helsinki* (Hamburg, Germany; Institute for Peace Research and Security Policy at the University of Hamburg; 2005).

5.   CSCE stood for the Conference on Security and Cooperation in Europe. In 1995, the CSCE was transformed into the OSCE. "This reflected the growing permanence and institutional character of what had once been nothing more than a series of conferences." Dimitrij Rupel (OSCE Chairman in Office), Forward, *The Culture of Dialogue: The OSCE Acquis 30 Years after Helsinki*, (Hamburg, Germany; Institute for Peace Research and Security Policy at the University of Hamburg; 2005).

6.   "All European States, the United States and Canada shall be entitled to take part in the Conference on Security and Cooperation in Europe." Final Recommendations of the Helsinki Consultations, 1973.

7.   "Decisions of the Conference shall be taken by consensus. Consensus shall be understood to mean the absence of any objection expressed by a Representative and submitted by him as constituting an obstacle to the taking of the decision in question." Final Recommendations of the Helsinki Consultations, 1973.

8.   The "Declaration of Principles Guiding Relations between Participating States" enumerated in the 1975 Helsinki Final Acts read as follows: (I) Sovereign equality, respect for the rights inherent in sovereignty, (II) Refraining from the threat or use of force, (III) Inviolability of frontiers, (IV) Territorial integrity of States, (V) Peaceful settlement of disputes, (VI) Non-intervention in internal affairs, (VII) Respect for human rights and fundamental freedoms, including the freedom of thought, conscience, religion or belief, (IX) Cooperation among States, and (X) Fulfillment in good faith of obligations under international law.

9.   The Russian Federal Republic.

10.   The 55 OSCE Participating State are Albania, Armenia, Austria, Azerbaijan, Belarus, Belgium, Bosnia and Herzegovina, Bulgaria, Canada, Croatia, Cyprus, Czech Republic, Denmark, Estonia, Finland, France, Georgia, Germany, Greece, Holy See, Hungary, Iceland, Ireland, Italy, Kazakhstan, Kyrgyzstan, Latvia, Liechtenstein, Lithuania,   Luxembourg, Malta, Moldova, Monaco, Netherlands, Norway, Poland, Portugal, Romania, Russian Federation, San Marino, Serbia and Montenegro, Slovak Republic, Slovenia, Spain, Sweden, Switzerland, Tajikistan, the former Yugoslavia Republic of Macedonia, Turkey, Turkmenistan, Ukraine, United Kingdom, United States of America.

11.   Russian deputy foreign minister Vladimir Chizhov repeated this Russian position at this conference.

12.   Remarks by Secretary of State Colin L. Powell to the Ministerial Meeting of the OSCE, Sofia, Bulgaria, December 7, 2004.

13.   Declaration of the Moscow Meeting of the Conference on the Human Dimension of the CSCE, Moscow, 1991.

14.   See, Amartya Sen, *Development as Freedom* (New York, N.Y.; Anchor Books; 1999).

15.   On July 7, 2005, there was a coordinated bomb attack on three of London's underground trains and a double-decker bus. There were 700 to 800 people on each of the trains at the time of the explosions. The bombings killed more than 50 people.

16.   Remarks by Secretary of State Condoleezza Rice at OSCE Parliamentary Assembly's 14th Annual Session, Washington, D.C., July 1, 2005.

17.   See, Michael McPaul, *Russia's 1996 Presidential Election: The End of Polarized Politics* (Stanford, California; Hoover Institution Press; 1997).   For an interesting volume with a broader perspective on this topic see, Michael McPaul and Sergei Markov, *The Troubled Birth of Russian Democracy: Parties, Personalities, and Programs* (Stanford, California; Hoover Institution Press; 1993).

18.   See, Eric D. Weitz, *A Century of Genocide: Utopias of Race and Nation* (Princeton, N.J.; Princeton University Press; 2003), pp. 144-189.

19.   I served on the "Panel of Eminent Persons on Strengthening the Effectiveness of the OSCE." Other members of the Panel were Nikolay Afanasievsky/Vladimir Shustor (Russia), Hans van den Broek (Netherlands), Wilhelm Hoynck (Germany), Kuanysh Sultanov (Kazakhstan), Knut Vollebaek (Norway) and Miomir Zuzul (Croatia).

20.   Final Report and Recommendations of the Panel of Eminent Persons On Strengthening the Effectiveness of the OSCE, *Common Purpose: Toward a More Effective OSCE*, June 27, 2005.

21.   See Alito Labyakas, "Europe: Russia, EU Look Set to Clash Over Putin on OSCE," *RFE/RL Article*, April 17, 2005. Se also, Alexander Mineyev, "EU Intends to Strengthen OSCE Role in Europe," *ITAR-TASS World Sevice*, April 16, 2005.

22.   President George W. Bush, Addresses and Thanks Citizens of Tblisi, Georgia, Freedom Square, Tblisi, Georgia, May 10, 2005.

OSCE: Promises Made and Promises To Keep

Professor Raimo Vayrnen, thank you for that kind introduction. It's a pleasure to be here in Finlandia Hall to join others in this celebration of the Helsinki Final Act 30 years after its signing.

I appreciated the opportunity to listen to the speeches of President Halonen,[1] Chairman-in-Office Rupel,[2] and Foreign Minister Tuomioja.[3] Also I want to acknowledge three of my colleagues from the Panel of Eminent Persons who are here today: Ambassador Wilhelm Hoynck, Ambassador Vladimir Shustov and Minister Kuanysh Sultanov. All three brought experience, knowledge and wisdom to our deliberations. It is good to be with them again today.

The United States' Helsinki Commission is very active. Led by Senator Sam Brownbeck and Congressman Christopher Smith, the Commission ensures sustained interest in and active involvement with the OSCE by a broad spectrum of members of Congress.[4] The other day it hosted an event on Capitol Hill to celebrate the 30th anniversary of the Helsinki Final Act. Of particular note were the remarks of former Secretary of State Henry Kissinger.

Dr. Kissinger recalled that "when the Soviet Union first proposed a conference for security . . . we thought it was a Soviet maneuver following the occupation of Czechoslovakia by Soviet troops to make themselves acceptable again or more legitimate again. And, also, we thought it was a maneuver to undermine NATO. And so (America's) first attitude toward the security conference was essentially defensive."[5]

But as the talks progressed, gradually the United States became more interested in the possibilities. Kissinger recalled that out of the Helsinki discussions "came a really novel idea, which was the so-called Basket III, namely to try to implement an acceptance of certain human rights principles as part of an international agreement. That was . . . an absolutely novel approach." And Kissinger noted, "A lot of credit for this has to go to our European allies who were very committed to it."

So the Helsinki Final Act was ground-breaking. It was important at the time. But, I suspect Dr. Kissinger was not alone when he recalls that at the time "I did not expect . . . these provisions would reach the scope and the impact that they now have."

Remarks at Conference: Helsinki Final Act 30 Years, Helsinki, Finland, August 1, 2005.

When 35 nations gathered here in Helsinki to sign the Final Act, it was the largest gathering of European heads of state since the Congress of Vienna in 1815.[6] Among them was United States President Gerald Ford.

Late in the afternoon of August 1, 1975, it was President Ford's turn to speak. He said, "To my country these principles are not clichés or empty phrases. We take this work and these words very seriously. We will spare no effort to ease tensions and to solve problems between us, but it is important that you realize the deep devotion of the American people and their government to human rights and fundamental freedoms and thus to the pledges that this conference has made regarding the freer movement of people, ideas, information. History will judge this conference not by what we say here today but by what we do tomorrow – not by the promises we make but by the promises we keep."[7]

The value of establishing broadly accepted standards of behavior is very important. Standards of human rights. Standards of the rule of law. Standards of free and fair elections; of accountability to the people. And the Helsinki Final Act made a profound contribution to establishing the international standards on human rights and democracy so widely accepted today. The commitments made through the Helsinki Process, by some commitments initially made more in form then substance, helped set a platform on which champions of freedom could stand to seek accountability, to seek change, to seek the fundamental dignity that was their birthright. And standards that all OSCE participating states could and did require of one another.

The world has been remade. The Cold War ended. The East/West confrontation is over. Millions of people were liberated and now live in freedom. The Community of Democracies has grown. And the world is safer and more secure as a result.

A new optimism rose up. Some even proclaimed the end of history.[8] Liberal democracy and human rights had prevailed. Totalitarian communism had lost. Freedom, democracy and human rights have been on the march.

The front line of heroes in this advance of freedom were the brave men and women long subjected to authoritarian rule who had the imagination and courage to envision a life in liberty, dignity and justice. Names such as Sakharov, Walesa, Havel and millions more who are less renowned but no less brave and consequential.[9] They kept hope alive. They made the world anew.

The Organization for Security and Cooperation in Europe also played a role. Among other things, the OSCE commitments on human rights and democracy empowered champions of freedom in authoritarian countries to take these provisions not just as values of foreigners, but as principles to which their own government had subscribed.

When the Cold War ended, freedom spread like a prairie fire. The old dichotomy was gone.

But, of course, it was not so simple, it never is. The threat of nuclear Armageddon may have receded, but man's capacity for inhumanity remains. Some authoritarian governments stubbornly hold on to power.[10] Some new democracies struggle to establish the institutions and habits to sustain freedom.[11] Some fledgling democracies backslide.[12] And even as the Community of Democracies has grown providing broader stability and improved security, new threats have emerged. 30 years after the Helsinki Final Act, the challenges and opportunities for the OSCE remain considerable.

Today the OSCE has an active work program. In the area of economic development, the OSCE promotes good governance and helps countries put systems in place to fight corruption. In the political-military areas the OSCE is contributing to the fight against terrorism, border security, shipping container security, small arms and light weapons, policing, and destruction of excess stockpiles of ammunition and weapons, among other things. The OSCE is in the forefront of combating intolerance and anti-trafficking efforts.[13] The OSCE promotes human rights, democracy and provides election observers who work from well-established and publicly available standards.[14] And the OSCE has proven to be an effective diplomatic tool that complements participating states' bilateral diplomacy. All of these endeavors benefit all OSCE participating states.

And like any process that has gone on for 30 years, especially during a time of revolutionary change such as took place these past 30 years, the Helsinki process can be retooled and improved. Some reforms already have been implemented. For example, systems have been put in place to track budget allocations and expenditures more efficiently, providing more transparency and accountability. The Panel of Eminent Persons on Strengthening the Effectiveness of the OSCE, on which I sat, examined the organization to develop other ideas. Our report, "Common Purpose: Towards a More Effective OSCE," outlines many other suggestions dealing with strengthening the OSCE's identity and profile, improving consultations and decision-making processes, clarifying the roles of the Chairman-in-Office and Secretary General, enhancing field operations, strengthening operational capacities and other matters.[15]

I'm confident a number of reforms will be adopted and the OSCE will be better as a result.

But more important for the OSCE going forward than any particular work program is the participating states' fidelity to the core principles of the Helsinki Final Act.

In a seminal speech on democracy delivered at Westminster Hall London, in June, 1982, President Ronald Reagan said, "Freedom is not the sole prerogative of a lucky few but the inalienable and universal right of all human beings."

President Reagan went on to say, "The ultimate determination in the struggle now going on for the world will not be bombs and rockets, but a test of wills and ideas – a trial of spiritual resolve, the values we hold, the beliefs we cherish, the ideals to which we are dedicated . . . the great civilized ideas: individual liberty, representative government, and the rule of law under God." [16]

The struggles now going on in the world also will test our wills, our resolve and our values. And going forward we must remain dedicated to the great civilized ideas: ideas that the OSCE commitments bind us to, ideas and values that animate OSCE's work.

Today the Cold War is over, but we are still engaged in a great struggle. In the war on terror, there are those blinded by hopelessness, fanaticism and hate who target innocent civilians to advance their extremist cause.[17] The hope and opportunity that comes from freedom crowds out these evil-doers. And the struggle continues between the few who benefit from authoritarian rule and the many who long to live in freedom; with dignity, liberty and under the rule of law.

The OSCE's core mission remains helping to foster democratic change. By helping strengthen democratic institutions and civil society, the OSCE helps to defeat the underlying causes of instability. That was the OSCE's novel idea, the concept of comprehensive security. While far more widely understood and more broadly accepted today than 30 years ago when the Helsinki Final Act was signed, there still are millions of people who do not know freedom.

Among these numbers are heroes like Sakharov, Walesa and Havel who dare to dream that they too can someday live in freedom with dignity. They too hope that OSCE participating states will keep fidelity to its core values.

Some OSCE members now claim that political dialogue on human rights and democracy are internal affairs of concerned states.[18] That is factually inaccurate. All participating states have joined in commitments that are clear and unequivocal. The Moscow Document states, "The participating states emphasize that issues relating to human rights, fundamental freedoms, democracy and the rule of law are of international concern, as respect for these rights and freedoms constitutes one of the foundations of the international order. They categorically and irrevocably declare that the commitments undertaken in the field of the human dimension of the OSCE are matters of direct and legitimate concern to all participating states and do not belong exclusively to the internal affairs of the State concerned."[19]

The core value of the Helsinki Process has been the recognition that human rights and democracy are fundamental to stability and the security stability brings. This core value has animated the work of the OSCE for 30 years. Much has been achieved. More remains to be done.[20] But by allowing this core value to animate the work of the OSCE going forward, we will ensure the continuing relevance of the Helsinki Final Act.

Allow me to touch upon a few areas where the OSCE has been active and must remain engaged going forward.

Frozen Conflicts

In parts of the OSCE, troublesome frozen conflicts still remain frozen sixteen years after the end of the Cold War. The OSCE has responsibility for mediating three of the conflicts in the former Soviet Union: the Transnistria dispute in Moldova,[21] the South Ossetia dispute in Georgia,[22] and the Nagorno-Karabakh dispute between Armedia and Azerbaijan.[23] The OSCE also is involved in supporting U.N. efforts to resolve the conflict between Georgia and Abkhazia.[24] There has been little headway made toward resolving the situation in Nagono-Korabakh or in the breakaway regions of Moldova and Georgia.

Russia's commitments to withdraw its military forces from Moldova, and to agree with Georgia on the duration of the Russian military presence there, remains unfulfilled. A core principle of the CFE Treaty is host country agreement to the stationing of forces.[25]

It is important that the OSCE remain actively engaged in seeking peaceful resolutions for these frozen conflicts, urging all sides to work transparently to make concrete progress towards political settlements.

Elections

As I already have said, the OSCE comprehensive concept of security is extremely valuable. It recognizes the link between respect for human rights and democracy to stability and security. The participating states relevant commitments to this concept are the core value of the OSCE. Therefore the work of ODHIR in this area, including but not limited to election observer missions, is invaluable.[26]

ODIHR's election observation methodology is based on sound, standardized criteria applied in an objective fashion. Criticisms raised by some participating states is a consequence of their frustration with various election results, not due to legitimate critiques of ODIHR's standards and methodology. The work of ODHIR election observation missions is important to establishing the legitimacy of the vote for the citizens of the country where the balloting took place and for the international community. These missions contribute to the fairness of elections.

Freedom is on the march in Central Asia. In this area, in particular, OSCE involvement will be invaluable in the years ahead in promoting civil society, a free press, the rule of law, and democratic institutions and practices. Just days ago, the ODHIR election observer mission played a valuable role in the first free and fair election in Kyrgyzstan.[27] All efforts to limit, circumscribe, or diminished election observer missions must be resisted. This activity should have the full and active support of all participating states. And out of area election observer missions such as the recent OSCE observer mission to the presidential election in Afghanistan last October also deserve careful consideration and deployment when possible.[28]

Terrorism and Intolerance

The OSCE has a role to play in combating terrorism. OSCE programs on border security and shipping container security are good examples. But more fundamentally, the war on terror is a battle of ideas.[29] It is about freedom, opportunity and choice versus fanaticism, hopelessness and rage. The march of freedom, respect for human rights, the protections of the rule of law, the opportunities afforded by good governance and market economies all deny room for the apostles of hate to take root. The battle between freedom and terror, between opportunity and hatred, between civilization and fanaticism is a struggle of ideas.[30] The OSCE has been in the vanguard of the values of liberal democracy, human rights and progress. By further advancing those values, the OSCE can help us confront the threat of terror and help deny terrorists ground on which to stand.

Kosovo

The tragic events in the Balkans in the 1990's scared Europe. Centuries old devisions of faith and forefathers broke out in flames of war fanned by ethnic hatreds.[31] Atrocities were committed. Systematic campaigns of ethnic cleansing took place. Efforts to contain these conflicts initially failed. Now torn societies seek restorative justice, reconciliation and rebirth.[32]

In the Balkans on many fronts progress has been made. Slovenia is a member of the European Union. Croatia is on track to membership. Large OSCE Field Missions operate there. OSCE continued engagement, assistance and cooperation is required throughout the region. And one area warrants special attention: Kosovo.

NATO bombing stopped Serbian ethnic cleansing of the Muslim community in Kosovo.[33] After the war, the OSCE and NATO flooded the zone. Large contingents from the international community set up shop in Kosovo to help. The OSCE work in Kosovar police training is noteworthy. But the war ended many years ago. While functionally autonomous, Kosovo's final states remains unresolved. This situation is not sustainable. The international community, including the OSCE, must come to terms with this untenable situation.[34] Decisions must be made and actions taken in Kosovo. And this should happen sooner, not later.

Out of Area Activities

The OSCE has a large footprint, 55 participating states from Vladovostok to Vancouver. This wide reach is an OSCE strength. Yet, as we are reminded daily, we live in an increasingly interconnected world. Peace and security for OSCE participating states is not solely dependent upon events within the region. Therefore, I would note that going forward the OSCE should be mindful of the possibilities of activities out of area whether that means election observer missions such as the one last fall in Afghanistan or enhanced activities with OSCE's Mediterranean Partners.[35]

In Closing

We will build on the sterling legacy already achieved by the Helsinki Final Act. We will further project human rights, democracy and freedom.

Human rights and Democracy do bring stability. Advancing these values will ensure that 30 years from today more people will live in freedom and the world will be safer and more secure.

In this way we will have kept our promise, the promise of the Helsinki Final Act.

Thank you.

---

1.   President of the Republic of Finland Tarja Halonen.

2.   Chairman-in-Office of the OSCE, Minister of Foreign Affairs of Slovinia Dimitrij Rupel.

3.   Minister of Foreign Affairs of Finland Erkki Tuomioja.

4.   The event was held on July 28, 2005.

5.   Dr. Henry Kissinger, remarks at the "30th Anniversary of the Helsinki Final Act" event held by the United Commission on Security and Cooperation in Europe (Helsinki Commission), Washington, D.C., July 28, 2005.

6.   For a concise history of the OSCE's first 30 years, see, Frank Evers, Martin Kahl and Wolfgang Zellner, *The Culture of Dialogue: The OSCE Acquis 30 Years After Helsinki* (Hamburg, Germany; Institute for Peace Research and Security Policy at the University of Hamburg; 2005).

7.   Gerald R. Ford, *A Time to Heal: The Autobiography of Gerald R. Ford* (New York, N.Y.; Harper and Row Publishers; 1979), p. 305.

8.   Francis Fukuyama, *The End of History and the Last Man* (New York, N.Y.; Free Press; 1992).

9.   For example, "when General Wojciech Jaruzelski imposed martial law in Poland in December 1981, most of the male leaders of the trade union Solidarity were imprisoned. It was women who kept the organization going. They dodged the secret police, forged papers, gave underground seminars and produced a clandestine mass-circulation newspaper, which the authorities repeatedly, but vainly, tried to suppress." For their story see, Shana Penn, *Solidarity's Secret: The Women Who Defeated Communism in Poland* (Ann Arbor, Mich.; University of Michigan Press; 2005).

10. For example, see, Rustam Nazarov, "Tajik: Paper Suffers New Closure Blow," *Institute of War and Peace*, July 18, 2005. See also, Judy Dempsey, "Poland Recalls Envoy to Protest Belarus Raid," *International Herald Tribune*, July 29, 2005; "OSCE Office in Belarus Fails To Achieve Its Objectives," *Itar Tass*, July 27, 2005; Mark Lenzi, "Poland and Belarus: Poles Deserve the West's Support," *International Herald* Tribune, July 30-31, 2005; C. J. Chivers, "Polish-Belarusian Tensions Increase," *New York* Times, July 28, 2005; and Ileana Ros-Lehtinen, "New Reality in Uzbekistan," *Washington Times*, July 21, 2005.

11. For example, see, "OSCE's Croatia Report Highlights Both Successes and Needs for Further Efforts," *Southeast Europe Times*, July 12, 2005. See also, Judy Dempsey, "Bulgaria and Romania Urged to Speed Reforms," *International Herald Tribune*, July 13, 2005; and Mikheil Saadashvili, "It Takes a Cultural Revolution," *Wall Street Journal*, August 18, 2005..

President Bush has pointed out, "Almost every new democracy has gone through a period of challenge and confusion. In Slovakia, the Velvet Revolution was followed by a period of neo-authorian rule before freedom firmly took hold. In Romania, the communist regime was toppled in 1989 – and today the post-communist leadership is still dealing with the legacy of corruption they inherited, as they work to build a vibrant democracy. In Ukraine, citizens waited 13 years after independence for the Orange Revolution that solidified the democratic gains. All these countries still have much work to do, but their people are courageous, and their leaders are determined. …No nation in history has made the transition from tyranny to a free society without setbacks and false starts. What separates those nations that succeed from these that falter is their progress in establishing free institutions." President George W. Bush, President's Remarks at International Republican Institute Dinner, Renaissance Hotel, Washington, D.C., May 18, 2005.

12. "Mr. Putin and his ex-KGB allies seem intent on making sure democracy fails to put down roots." Editorial, "The Color Gray," *The Wall Street Journal*, July 27, 2005. See also, Masha Lipman, "Preempting Politics in Russia," *Washington Post*, July 25, 2005.

13. Regarding the scourge of trafficking in persons, President George W. Bush has said, "There is a spiritual evil in the abuse and exploitation of the most innocent, the most vulnerable of our fellow human beings. . . . And governments that tolerate this trade are tolerating a form of slavery." President George W. Bush, Remarks at the United Nations General Assembly, New York, N.Y., September 23, 2003.

14. Final Report and Recommendations of the Panel of Eminent Persons On Strengthening the Effectiveness of the OSCE, *Common Purpose: Towards a More Effective OSCE*, June 27, 2005. The other members of the Panel were Nikolay Afanasievsky/Vladimir Shustov (Russia), Hans vandon Broek (Netherlands), Wilhelm Hoynck (Germany), Kuanysh Sultanov (Kazakhstan), Knut Vollebaek (Norway), and Miormir Zuzul (Croatia).

For another analysis of OSCE activities and reform proposals see, Wolfgang Zellner, et al., *Managing Change in Europe: Evaluating the OSCE and Its Future Role: Competencies, Capabilities, and Mission* (Hamburg, Germany; Institute for Peace Research and Security Policy at the University of Hamburg; 2005).

15. Final Report and Recommendations of the Panel of Eminent Persons on Strengthening the Effectiveness of the OSCE, *Common Purpose: Towards a More Effective OSCE*, June 27, 2005.

16. Ronald Reagan, Address to the British Parliament, London, England, June 8, 1982.

17. "The Bush administration is retooling its slogan for the fight against Al-Queda and other terrorist groups, pushing the idea that the long-term struggle is as much an ideological battle as a military mission. …'It is more than just a military war on terror,' Steven J. Hadley, the national security advisor, said … 'it's broader than that. It's a global struggle against extremism. We need to dispute both the gloomy vision and offer a positive alternative." Eric Schmitt and Thon Shanker, "Hearts and Minds: New Name for War on Terror Reflects Wider U.S. Campaign," *New York Times*, July 26, 2005. See also, Thomas L. Friedman, "A Poverty of Dignity and a Wealth of Rage," *New York Times*, July 15, 2005; Editorial, "Reframing the Global War on Terror," *Financial Times*, August 2, 2005. Note also President Bush's remark, "Terrorists know that there is no room for them as freedom takes root in the broader Middle East, so they are fighting to stop its progress." President George W. Bush, Radio Address of the President to the Nation, May 21, 2005. See also, Jim VandeHei, "Bush Calls Democracy Terror's Antidote," *Washington Post*, March 9,

2005. (At the National Defense University at Fort McNair, President Bush said, "It should be clear that the advance of democracy leads to peace because governments that respect the rights o their people also respect the rights of their neighbors. It should be clear the best antidote to radicalism and terror is the tolerance kindled in free societies.").

18.   See, for example, Transcript of Remarks and Replies to Media Questions by Russian Minister of Foreign Affairs Sergey Lavrov Following Talks with Netherlands Minister of Foreign Affairs Bernard Bot, The Hague, June 28, 2005. Released by Ministry of Foreign Affairs of the Russian Federation. See also, Aleksandr Yakovenko (Russian MFA Representative), "Why Reform of OSCE is Needed," *Rossiyskaya Gazeta*, July 20, 2005. "There has also been a departure from one of the fundamental Helsinki principles -- non-interference in domestic affairs."

German political analyst Hanna Dietrich told RFE/RL the most important issue under study in the review is OSCE's role in supporting human rights, the rule of law and free elections in countries which Russia is considered to be within its sphere of influence. "Russia perceives the organization as acting against its interests," she said, "It wants less emphasis on human rights. . . ." In April, the Chairman of Russia's Central Election Commission, Alexander Veshnyakov, rejected the OSCE's custom of issuing a public statement about elections soon after the results are announced. He said OSCE election observer missions should not deliver what is called 'political judgments' immediately after elections are held." Ronald Eggelston, "Europe: OSCE Begins Talks About Proposed Reforms," *Radio Free Europe*, June 30, 2005.

19.   Document of the Moscow Meeting of the Conference on the Human Dimension of the CSCE, Moscow 1991.

20.   For example, the International Helsinki Federation for Human Rights, a Vienna-based nongovernment organization, issued a 500-page report covering human rights developments in 2004 in 38 member states of the OSCE which identifies areas of human rights concerns. Antoine Blua, "OSCE: Helsinki Report Finds Human Rights Problems Plague Entire Region," *Radio Free Europe*, June 27, 2005.

21.   Transnistria is a breakaway region of Moldova. The United States supports efforts to find a peaceful resolution which respects the sovereignty and territorial integrity of Moldova. From time to time the Tiraspol authorities have forcibly closed and harassed Latin-script-language schools. Also they have denied the OSCE Mission freedom of movement and refused to allow the OSCE and UNICEF to deliver supplies to orphanages. The precariousness of the situation was evidenced in late July when the Moldovan delegation, Ukraine and the OSCE boycotted an emergency meeting of the United Control Commission. See, *ITAR-TASS* "Moldovan Delegation, Ukraine and the OSCE Boycott United Control Commission meeting," July 28, 2005.

22.   South Ossetia had been a smuggler's paradise with an open border into the North Ossetian Autonomous Republic of the Russian Federation. Goods flowed freely, smuggling and black-market activities formed the basis of South Ossetia's economy. In June 2004, Georgian President Saakashvili took measures to shut down the black market and smuggling routes. Tensions rose. Two Russian Ministry of Defense trucks on route from Russia to the South Ossetian capital of Tskhinvali were confiscated by Georgian Interior Ministry troops in July, 2004. 180 air-to-ground non-guided missiles were discovered on the two trucks. Build ups led to nightly exchanges. Partly to avoid further casualties and partly to reduce tensions, Georgian troops were withdrawn in mid-August. A tentative cease-fire has held since then while talks continue through a mechanism known as the Joint Control Commission consisting of the OSCE, Georgia, South Ossetia, North Ossetia and Russia. Shootings, kidnappings and other violence have continued in the Zone of Conflict. An agreement by both sides to demilitarize the Zone, reached in October 2004, is unfulfilled by either side.

23.   Nargorno-Karabakh is an area that both Armenia and Azerbaijan claim. Azerbaijan and Armenia fought a war for the mainly ethnic-Armenian Nagorno Karabakh enclave in the early 1990's. Armenian forces took control of the region and seven others by the war's end in 1994. Some 25,000 people were killed and about one million people were displaced as a result of the Karabakh war. Some experts believe that this conflict is only a single firefight away from returning to a shooting war. Last month Azerbaijan's President Ilham Aliyeu said, "This year defense spending has grown by 76 percent, we will create a powerful army and will be able to liberate our lands at any time." "Military Spending Increase Could Finance New Karabakh War," *Agence France Press*, July 25, 2005. The OSCE has sought to keep periodic discussions on this dispute going between the respective leaders.

24.   In 1992, factions in Abkhazia began a conflict to secure independence from Georgia. Since the end of fighting, Abkhazia has retained a precarious autonomy from Tiblisi and continues to demand independence. The OSCE has a very limited role in this tense situation, deferring to the U.N. Special Representative and the U.N. Observer Mission in Georgia (UNOMIG). The zone of conflict is patrolled by

Russian peacekeepers, who in reality serve as border guards for the Abkhaz. The Abkhaz and Georgians harbor a deep distrust of one another. The population of Abkhazia now is roughly 70,000 ethnic Abkhaz and a similar number of others (Russians, Armenians and Ukrainians). Something over 200,000 ethnic Georgian Internally Displaced Persons, forced out during the war, have been unable to return to their homes. The Abkhaz claim that nearly 90% of their population now hold Russian passports.

25. The Adapted Treaty on Conventional Forces in Europe agreed to at the OSCE's Istanbul Summit in 1999. The Russian Duma has ratified the CFE, however Russia has not fulfilled its Istanbul commitments to withdraw its forces from Georgia and Moldovia. The United States has remained committed to moving ahead with ratification of the Adapted CFE Treaty, but has said it will do so only after all the Istanbul commitments on Georgia and Moldovia have been met.

26. ODHIR is the OSCE's Office for Democratic Institutions and Human Rights based in Warsaw, Poland.

27. See, Ambassador Jacques Reuter (Permanent Representative of Luxemburg at the OSCE), speech "OSCE, Permanent Council No. 561:EU Statement on Kyrgyzstan," June 30, 2005. See also, "Russia Picking a Fight Over Kyrgyzstan," *BBC*, March 22, 2005.

28. Afghanistan is an OSCE Partner in Cooperation. Three OSCE participating states share a border with Afghanistan. In response to requests from the Afghan authorities and the U.N., the OSCE sent an election observer mission to the October, 2004 Afghan Presidential Election, the first "free and fair" election in Afghanistan's 5,000 year history. See generally, Richard S. Williamson, "Forward Strategy Against the Apostles of Hate," *Tech Central Station*, October 13, 2004, and Richard S. Williamson, "Afghanistan Votes Triumph Over Excuses," *Chicago Sun-Times*, November 6, 2004.

29. See, for example, Phillip Blond and Adrian Pabst, "Fundamentalism and Fascism: The Roots of Islamic Terrorism," *International Herald Tribune*, July 28, 2005.

30. See, for example, Jim Hoagland, "The True War: Within, and for, Islam," *Washington Post*, July 14, 2005. See also, Phillip Blond and Adrian Pabst, "Fundamentalism and Fascism: The Roots of Islamic Terrorism," *International Herald Tribune*, July 28, 2005; Craig S. Smith, "Muslim Group In France Is Fertile Soil for Militancy," *New York Times,* April 28, 2005; Olivier Roy, "Why Do They Hate Us? Not Because of Iraq," *New York Times*, July 22, 2005; Hassan M. Fattah, "Jordan Is Preparing to Tone Down the Islamic Bombast in Textbooks," *New York Times*, June 12, 2005; Thomas L. Friedman, "All Fall Down," *New York Times*, July 29, 2005.

"[W]hat we call the 'war on terrorism' is in fact a small part of a larger intellectual and religious struggle within Islam, between countries, and radicals who want to impose their extreme interpretation of Sharia, or religious law." Anne Applebaum, "Think Again, Karen Hughes," *Washington Post*, July 27, 2005.

31. See generally, Robert D. Kaplan, *Balkan Ghosts: A Journey Through History* (New York, N.Y.; St. Martin's Press; 1993); David Halberstam, *War in a Time of Peace* (New York, N.Y.; Scribner; 2001); Richard Holbrooke, *To End a War* (New York, N.Y.; Random House; 1998); and David D. Kaplan, "In the Balkans, No Wars Are Local," *New York Times*, April 7, 1999.

32. See for example, David Rohde, "Bosnian Muslims Retrace Steps of Those Killed in 1995," *New York Times*, July 11, 2005.

33. For an interesting collection of essays on NATO's intervention in Kosovo see Aleksander Jokic, *Lessons of Kosovo: The Dangers of Humanitarian Intervention* (Toronto, Ontario; Broadview Press; 2003).

34. See, for example, Nicholas Wood, "Seeing Past the Hate: Kosovo's Factions Imagine a Future," *New York Times*, July 25, 2005. See also, Philip Shishkin, "Kosovo, Already Riff with Ethnicities, Discovers New Ones," *Wall Street Journal*, August 9, 2005.

35. The OSCE maintains special relations with six Mediterranean Partners for Cooperation (MPC): Algeria, Egypt, Israel, Jordan, Morocco, and Tunisia. This involves regular meetings of a Contact Group and Seminars dedicated to Mediterranean issues. Some even have suggested expanding OSCE membership to this group of six Mediterranean countries. At the 1999 Istanbul Summit Meeting of OSCE Heads of State and Government, the participating States reiterated their commitment to strengthening relations with the Mediterranean Partners.

RUSSIAN RULE-OUT

As Russia's power declines, influence wanes and reach recedes, its misbehavior rises. At the December Ministerial Meeting of the Organization for Security and Cooperation in Europe (OSCE), a valuable instrument to advance human rights and democracy standards, Russia will seek to eviscerate OSCE election monitoring. This challenge must be met and defeated.

Russia's problems are real and growing.

At home, Russia continues to experience lowering life expectancy, declining birthrates and social unrest. Crony capitalism reigns. Except for resource extraction, the Russian economy is stagnant. Unemployment is high. Pensioner benefits are meager forcing millions to live in desperate conditions. And the insurgency in Chechnya remains unchecked.

Russia's influence is waning in the various "frozen conflicts" in areas of the former Soviet Union. Russian mediation is being rejected in South Ossetia, Abkhazia and the Dniester Region. And Russian Peacekeepers face being driven out of these Conflict Zones.

Also, new nations, once part of the Soviet Union and now independent states, have joined the march of freedom: the Rose Revolution in Georgia, the Orange Revolution in Ukraine, and the Yellow Revolution in Kyrgyzstan. In each of these country's Moscow and its chosen instrument, the Commonwealth of Independent States (CIS), initially certified rigged elections. In each case international election observers, including the OSCE, declared the votes fraudulent emboldening people to demonstrate and force new elections. And, in each case, "free and fair" elections resulted that voted out Soviet-era bosses and elected new democratic leaders. From reliable allies firmly within Moscow's sphere of influence, these new democracies look to the West for support and inspiration.

Facing rebuffs in the Near Abroad and disquiet at home, Russian President Vladimir Putin is intent on holding on tightly to what he has. Within Russia there has been a rise in undemocratic behavior, tighter control of the media, and increased state interference in the economy. Where Moscow retains a foothold in the Near Abroad, Putin seeks to support Soviet-era bosses in power and thwart institutions that support the spread of pluralism and democracy. For example, Moscow supported Belarus closing the offices in Minsk of various non-governmental groups promoting democracy.

Appeared in *Tech Central Station*, December 1, 2005.

In the election earlier this month in Azerbaijan, international election observers from the OSCE and the Parliamentary Assembly of the Council of Europe found the vote tainted by fraud and abuse. It failed to meet democratic standards. However the Commonwealth of Independent States (CIS) observers dominated by Moscow found the vote "protected the electoral rights of the (Azerbaijan) citizens."

The skullduggery in Azerbaijan is important not only because the people were denied a free and fair election. Most of the country's 8 million people are Muslims, a group for whom the march of freedom is vital in order to create opportunity and crowd out potential terrorists. It has oil and gas. It is located strategically between Dagestan to the north, an anarchic region of Russia, and Iran to the south. Furthermore, in an act of jujitsu, Russia is using its endorsement of the fraudulent election results and the OSCE's report of irregularities as another reason to attack OSCE democracy standards.

Igor Borisov, chairman of the Russian Public Institute of Electoral Rights, has compared the work of the OSCE mission to the Azerbaijani elections to a "witch hunt." Russian Foreign Minister Sergei Lavrov has said that Russia "doubts the objectiveness of the (OSCE) assessment" in Azerbaijan. He said further, "The OSCE bias shows once again the need to sort out the matter of monitoring elections."

Russia has a litany of so-called reform proposals for OSCE monitoring. All are aimed at increasing Moscow's control over OSCE monitoring practices, limiting the independence of election monitoring missions, and delaying their reports to diminish their impact. Thereby Russia hopes to contain the contagion of the colored revolutions.

The United States has equities and shared interests with Russia. Moscow has been a partner in certain fronts of the war on terror. Russia can be helpful with the threat of nuclear breakout in North Korea and Iran. It is in the interest of both Washington and Moscow to secure Russia's loose nukes. Russia has become a principal supplier of oil and gas to our European allies.

We should, we must continue to cooperate with Russia on all these issues and more. But that need not prevent us from standing up for the values we cherish and the rights to which everyone everywhere is entitled.

Just as a constructive relationship with Russia is in our interest, so is the march of freedom. The spread of democracy benefits the people who gain self-determination and it benefits us because democracies are our natural friends and allies. Democracies are more stable and less likely to start wars. And democracies are not fertile soil for terrorists.

The OSCE is but one of many tools in the march of freedom. In the end people must select freedom and democracy for themselves. It cannot be imposed from outside. However when people are prepared to stand up and challenge entrenched power and seek the rights to which they are entitled but have long been denied, we should be prepared to help them.

At the upcoming OSCE Ministerial Meeting in Ljubljana, Slovenia, it is important that Moscow's proposals to weaken OSCE Election Monitoring be defeated. The United States should take a lead role in this effort.

SECTION III:
THE UNITED NATIONS

PRIORITIES OF THE
UNITED STATES AT
THE UNITED NATIONS

It's great to be in my hometown of Chicago. And I want to congratulate the Chicago Council on Foreign Relations for its new President, Marshall Bouton. You are especially fortunate to have Marshall here at this time. An expert on India, I'm sure he has been sharing with you his valuable insights on the current crisis in Kashmir.

We meet at an interesting time. Today, the United States is the world's sole superpower. The United States military might, economic power and cultural reach dominate the globe. Yale Professor Paul Kennedy has said that the world has never known such a disparity in power, never. Paradoxically, however, the United States needs multilateralism more in this unipolar world than we did during the long cold war.

During the cold war, there were two superpowers, Washington and Moscow, that balanced one another. Other countries picked sides based on ideology, or geography, or economic and security interests. Few nations were large enough or so small and insignificant that they could resist this gravitational pull. This created a bipolar ballast for world affairs.

Over the long cold war, rules of the game developed. Each superpower protected its sphere of influence. Wars were regional and controlled, usually waged by surrogates. They were contained. Rarely did either superpower get directly involved in an armed conflict. When this did happen in Vietnam and Afghanistan, a disaster took place.

But today the bipolar ballast is gone. The United States stands supreme. The old "rules of the game" don't apply. Other countries are finding their way in a world where they are less important, where their old patron is either gone, if it had been Moscow, or where in the case of Washington, their old patron does not need them as centrally as when they helped balance the global scales between democracy and communism. Other countries untethered by cold war logic are freer to seek their own national interests.

As Bismarck determined 125 years ago with the rise of unchallenged German power in Europe, as the sole superpower we must work to avoid having other countries

Remarks to the Chicago Committee of the Chicago Council on Foreign Reltaions, June 10, 2002.

join together against us. We must engage them. We must take their interests and concerns into account. When possible, we must work with them in concert to achieve shared objectives and to protect mutual interests. This means working together in coalitions, in multilateral venues.

Also, many of the issues that the United States must deal with today do not lend themselves to unilateral or bilateral action. Many environmental issues, HIV-AIDS, the proliferation of weapons of mass destruction and counter-terrorism are items better managed through multilateral venues.

At the same time, I hasten to add, Secretary of Defense Rumsfeld is certainly correct to point out that the mission must define the coalition, not the other way around. Certain multilateral I will have relative comparative advantages depending on the issue at hand, or the mission. No multilateral forum is best for all issues.

So in the unipolar world the United States can turn to the G-8 OAS, WTO, NATO and the United Nations to name a few.

A side point on NATO. The mission of any given multilateral organization can change over time. The NATO alliance was created in response to the perceived and the real threat to Europe from the Soviet Union. Today the Soviet Union is gone. Russia is struggling with a declining standard of living, a declining life expectancy, a military that often goes unpaid and an arsenal, nuclear and otherwise, in disrepair. The enemy is gone, the threat a thing of the past. NATO is transforming itself from a military/political organization into primarily a political institution. Therefore, as we seek to integrate Russia into the democratic and market economy community of nations, it is fully appropriate and useful to engage Moscow in NATO.

Regarding the United Nations, it does have certain assets that equip it with comparative advantages in some areas of concern and interest to the United States. The United Nations is a universal organization. It has 189 Member States, soon to rise to 190 when the world's newest nation, East Timor, completes its application process. This gives the UN the furthest reach of any multilateral organization.

For most of the world, the United Nations also has a unique and powerful moral and political authority. The United Nations' Charter draws upon the same transcending values as our own Declaration of Independence and Constitution. The UN Declaration of Human Rights set forth standards of decency, individual rights and limits on state power now broadly accepted throughout the world, rhetorically if not always in practice. The UN has a long history so other countries have experience and comfort with the institution. The UN served as midwife to scores of countries in the move from colony to independent, free states. And, in Secretary-General Kofi Annan, the United Nations as an institution benefits from his stature as an international civil servant of unusual decency and fairness.

This is a considerable list of UN assets. Of course the United Nations has weaknesses too. But it is this list of assets that have resulted in the United States' priorities in the UN.

Today, our first priority is to engage the United Nations to advance the war against terrorism. And there are four areas in the counter-terrorism effort where the UN has been particularly helpful in this campaign.

The United Nations can be very effective in norm setting. I already have noted its role with the UN Declaration on Human Rights, and that is only one example. And in our war on terror, clear well-established international norms are helpful.

President Bush has said, "Moral truth is the same in every culture, in every time, and in every place. Targeting innocent civilians for murder is always and everywhere wrong."

Immediately after 9/11, the United Nations Security Council adopted three important Resolutions, 1368, 1373, and 1377 which affirmed the rights of self-defense against terrorists, found terrorism to be a threat to international peace and security, stressed the accountability of the supporter as well as the perpetrator of terrorist acts, obliged Member States to limit the ability of terrorists and terrorist organizations to operate internationally for freezing assets of terrorist-affiliated persons and organizations and denying them safe haven, among other things, and set forth a Ministerial Declaration on International Terrorism. The UN General Assembly adopted two anti-terrorism resolutions that condemned the "heinous acts of terrorism" in Washington, Pennsylvania and New York City.

A second area where the United Nations helps in the fight against terrorism is in helping build counter-terrorism capacity around the world. A neighbor's failure or inability to make itself inhospitable to terrorists and those who aid and abet them, threaten other neighboring states. The UN is developing "best practices" to counter-terrorism. The UN is providing assistance for countries to develop their counter-terrorism capabilities; acting as a switchboard to match countries that need assistance with assistance providers.

And the UN can help rebuild failed states such as Afghanistan. As President Bush said last fall, "It would be a useful function for the United Nations to take over the so-called nation-building, – I would call it the stabilization of a future government." While the United States is completing its mop of al-Qaeda in the Afghan countryside, we also are training the new Afghanistan army. The Interim Security Armed Forces that keep security in Kabul and its immediate area has been led by the British and soon will be led by the Turks. The Germans are taking the lead in police training. The Italians are taking the lead in establishing a judiciary. The Brits are taking the lead in the counter-narcotics effort. And many other countries are assisting the Afghanistan rebuilding effort through the Tokyo Donors Conference last winter and the Geneva meetings this spring.

A second U.S. priority in the United Nations is in curbing the spread of weapons of mass destruction. The Vienna-based International Atomic Energy Agency provides safeguards on nuclear facilities throughout the world to deter diversion of nuclear materials and technology. And the UN is working to get arms inspectors back into Iraq.

There are negotiations going on between Secretary-General Kofi Annan and Iraq to establish the terms in which arms inspectors could return to Iraq. As you know, the United States believes that Saddam Hussein continues his various programs to acquire and stockpile weapons of mass destruction: chemical, biological and nuclear. A tough, intrusive arms inspection regime will force Saddam to end his WMD programs, or reveal further evidence to prove the existence of his WMD programs. If Saddam refuses inspectors or, as in the past, kicks them out of Iraq when they get close to the evidence, that too will make clear Saddam Hussein's intent and his danger. It will help set the table, if necessary, for the other actions to achieve the U.S. policy of changing the regime in Baghdad.

A third United States priority in the United Nations is effective, successful peacekeeping. There are conflicts around the world that are inflicting a terrible human toll. There are ethnic wars and border conflicts that threaten regional security. While the United Nations lacks the capacity on its own to impose peace, it can be a valuable mechanism in peacekeeping. Today, there are UN peacekeeping forces in Bosnia, Kosovo, the Democratic Republic of the Congo, Ethiopia and Eritrea, and elsewhere around the world. In East Timor and Sierra Leone there have been two UN peacekeeping success stories this year. The United States believes these efforts to save lives and bring peace and stability are important. We are the largest financial contributor to these UN peacekeeping missions and we provide logistical help, technical assistance and, sometime, personnel. In the first five months of this year, I have traveled to fourteen countries visiting UN peacekeeping operations.

A fourth priority at the United Nations is to advance human rights. Eleanor Roosevelt chaired the UN committee that drafted the UN Declaration on Human Rights and John Foster Dulles served on it. Since its adoption in 1948, the United States has been a leading supporter for recognition of its standards and their adoption everywhere. It is the right thing. Furthermore, history teaches us that a state that respects its own citizens' human rights is much less likely to start armed conflicts with their neighbors.

Unfortunately, from our perspective, the United Nations' record on human rights over the past year is none too good. This year, for the first time ever, the United States was denied a seat at the UN Human Rights Commission in Geneva. While that body did adopt a resolution addressing the continued denial of human rights in Castro's Cuba, the Human Rights Commission failed to address serious human rights abuses in Zimbabwe, Chechnya, China and elsewhere. The United States has been re-elected to the Commission for next year. Hopefully we and the UN will do better.

A fifth priority in the United Nations is helping to advance economic development in the third world where hundreds of millions of people barely subsist and where today too many of the world's poorest people see little reason for hope. Quite frankly, over the years most foreign aid has failed to help lift the poorest of the poor to move out of poverty. Too much aid money has been siphoned off by corrupt governments or static economies. Too much aid has been sent to controlled economies that stifle personal initiative and resist innovation. Some progress was made in this area at the United Nations Conference on Financing for Development, which took place in Monterrey, Mexico, this past March.

In part due to U.S. leadership, the discussions centered on what really works to promote development. The emphasis was on outcomes rather than inputs and there was broad agreement on the need to increase the effectiveness of all available resources, particularly private resources, which is the largest financial reservoir for development.

The Monterrey consensus stressed the primary responsibility of countries to advance their own development coupled with international support for developing countries to:

Practice good governance and establish sound institutions and market-oriented economic policies;

Create investment-friendly environments, increase trade, and improve productivity;

Encourage private enterprise as an important means to generate economic growth and development;

Increase human capacity by improving the health and education achievements of people;

Build capacity to trade and to attract investments.

This was a step forward. President Bush announced a "New Development Compact" and established a "Millennium Challenge Account," whereby the United States will increase its annual baseline aid levels by $5 billion over the next three budget years, with the new fund allocated strictly on developing countries' demonstrated development progress. This represents a fifty percent increase in United States current annual aid levels.

Our approach to development, President Bush stated, "unleashes the potential of those who are poor, instead of locking them into a cycle of dependence. [It] looks beyond arbitrary inputs from the rich, and demands tangible outcome for the poor."

President Bush has made it clear that "countries that live by these three broad standards – ruling justly, investing in their people and encouraging economic freedom – will receive more aid from America. And, more importantly, over time, they will really no longer need it."

A sixth priority for the United States in the United Nations is in the area of humanitarian assistance. The United Nations has a number of ways and means through which it provides needed humanitarian assistance to people desperately in need of help. Let me mention a few. The UN has become our partner in battling the awful HIV-AIDS epidemic in Africa where the rate of those infected in some countries has risen to over one-third of all adults. The UN High Commissioner For Refugees is another area of particular importance that we actively support. Since the end of the cold war there has been an increase of ethnic eruptions and civil wars. There are millions of refugees and internally displaced persons barely surviving day to day. The United Nations provides help with food, health and shelter to allow these people to sustain themselves until conditions change so they can return home. A final example of effective UN humanitarian assistance is the World Food Program. Many of you know Chicago native Catherine Bertini who just completed a 10-year tenure as the Director-General of this UN specialized agency. She did a marvelous job of bringing management reforms, broadening WFP's reach and effectiveness, and substantially increasing its voluntary donations, including from the United States.

A final priority for the United States in the United Nations is to push management reforms. As I have outlined, there are many substantive areas where the United Nations can and does help advance U.S. interests. And we benefit when it is a more effective institution. The United States also is the largest financial contributor to the UN. We want our money to be spent well. Over the past twenty years, the United States has pushed for UN reform. Over time we gained support for our reform efforts and we have accomplished a lot. But there is much more to be done. Any large organization with entrenched bureaucracies has inefficiencies and waste. The UN is no different. As an international organization it faces a wide range of claimants with a wide range of different and sometimes conflicting, interests. This too creates waste, inefficiencies and excess. So the United States will continue to push a reform agenda at the UN.

So there is a lot for us to do at the U.S. Mission to the United Nations. There are many challenges. There are often frustrations. But there also is satisfaction in pursuing U.S. priorities in the UN, because through the United Nations we can and often do help protect U.S. interests and advance U.S. priorities.

Thank you.

SELLING THE SECURITY COUNCIL ON U.S. SECURITY GOALS: CHALLENGES FOR AMERICAN LEADERSHIP AT THE UN

It's a pleasure for me to be back at Princeton University. I have fond memories of my years here as an undergraduate.

The United Nations is an important institution. It has unique assets due to its universality, the values in its charter, the Declaration on Human Rights, its role helping colonies move to independence, its help to refugees and the other vast humanitarian assistance that it provides. The United Nations is helping counter-terrorism by setting standards, helping nations build their capacity to fight terrorism, and helping curb the financial flow to terrorists. The United Nations peacekeeping operations are making a real difference in Timor Leste, Ethiopia/Eritrea, Sierra Leone, Bosnia and Kosovo. And early this month, the UN Security Council unanimously adopted a strong resolution calling on Saddam Hussein to fully disarm or face serious consequences. This was a great victory for the United States and for President Bush.

For many countries, the United Nations is their preferred instrument for implementing their foreign policy. It is not as central to the United States. Nonetheless, even for us, the UN can be very useful from time to time. And to sell the UN Security Council on U.S. security goals, it is important to understand the U.S. role in the world today. It is much different than when I served as Assistant Secretary of State for international organization affairs in the closing days of the cold war.

The bipolar ballast of the cold war is gone. The world is no longer balanced by the Washington orbit on one side and that of Moscow on the other. It is a unipolar moment with the United States standing as the world's sole superpower, unchallenged in military might, economic power or cultural reach. Some have said that at no time in the history of the world has any one nation so dominated the world, at no time in history has any one country had power so much greater than all others. And the United States has corresponding global interests and responsibilities. Yet, understandably, there are limits in treasury and blood to the support the American people will give to safeguard these interests. And some global problems such as the proliferation of weapons of mass destruction and environmental dangers are better addressed with others and not alone. Burden sharing is important.

There are a variety of vehicles to work with others. There are bilateral relations and ad hoc coalitions. There also are multilateral institutions such as the G-8, NATO, OAS, WTO, ASEAN and the United Nations. Each such organization has its own

Remarks at Woodrow Wilson School of Public and Internatioinal Affairs. Princeton University, November 19, 2002

strengths and weaknesses. And those assets and liabilities have different values to different countries depending on their particular circumstances in the world and their own interests. In the end, given the United States' great strength, it can afford to be more selective than others, less dependant on multilateralism. But, in any event, each country including the United States should let the mission define the coalition, and not let the coalition define the mission. And there are missions of interest to us best worked through the U.N. Security Council.

The Security Council has 15 members; five permanent members with power to veto any Security Council resolution and ten elected members serving two-year terms with five rotating each year. In 1945, the five permanent members were seen as the five most powerful countries at the end of World War II: the United States, the Soviet Union, China, the United Kingdom and France. Their special status on the Security Council mirrored their special status and superior power in the real world.

The ten elected Security Council seats are allocated to regional groups and rotate often in an established pattern and sometimes through contested elections. The five elected members whose terms expire this December 31st are Singapore, Ireland, Norway, Colombia and Mauritius. The five elected members whose terms run to the end of 2003 are Syria, Bulgaria, Mexico, Cameroon and Guinea. Obviously, the elected members vary in size, strategic interest and power. Of the ten elected members on the Security Council right now, none are global powers and most are not even regional powers. Tiny Mauritius is an island nation 600 kilometers east of Madagascar with a population of slightly over one million people. Its major industries are tourism and financial services. Mauritius has no army, navy or air force. Order is kept by 10,000 policemen. Obviously, its reach and strategic interests are much different than the United States. Yet, like us, it has a vote on the UN Security Council.

Professor Jeane Kirkpatrick, a former United States Permanent Representative to the United Nations, has written, "The multilateral approach has not only procedural consequences but also important substantive consequences because it redistributes power and affects the accountability of decision-makers and the culture in which they can take action."[1]

In the UN Security Council, states that lack military might, have little economic power and lack cultural reach are elevated in status and power. While major global powers are constrained not only by having but one vote among fifteen, but also by the culture of the Security Council that dictates on most issues that the Council must act by consensus. So on issues as varied as a $500 million per year UN peacekeeping operation in the Democratic Republic of the Congo to economic sanctions on Iraq, mighty Mauritius potentially has the power to block action as assuredly as does the United States. And, it might be argued that precisely because Mauritius is so small and so little constrained by international interests, obligations and entanglements that might constrain its freedom to act, the Mauritius delegate has more potential to impact Security Council action than representatives of other major countries who have many such encumbrances. Smaller states' approach to many issues in the Security Council are untethered to the real world precisely because most issues that are deliberated in the Council are outside that country's sphere of interest or influence. In my opinion, that is one reason the UN Security Council's actions on the Middle East problem so often are unhelpful or even harmful. The consequence of political posturing that exacerbates and does not ameliorate the Israeli/Palestinian issue has no real consequence to many Security Council members. This breeds a certain irresponsibility around the Security Council table on some issues.

Another significant dynamic in the Security Council is the five permanent members versus the elected ten. As I've already noted, the zone of national interests (security, economic and cultural) are more extensive for the larger powers, the P-5, than the smaller countries, most of the elected ten. Being a permanent member of the Security Council also means that the P-5 has extensive and entrenched bureaucracies in their UN missions in New York and in their capitals to deal with the enormous volume of work in the Security Council. Most of the elected ten lack the resources to have corresponding staffing even if they were to want to. And even large countries such as Germany, Japan or India must try to create an adequate bureaucracy from scratch each time they rejoin the Security Council. Therefore, the practical and intellectual capacity to analyze Secretariat reports, gather independent information, consult other member states, and so forth is not comparable. Many of the elected ten therefore are less well equipped to independently form positions. They sometimes have little choice but to defer to the P-5. Of course, this can build resentment and strain. The United States must try to be very sensitive to this.

But on the big issues, the ones of greatest interest to the United States and the ones where not consensus but a vote will determine the outcome, the dominant dynamic in the Security Council is not between the P-5 and the elected ten but rather between the five permanent members themselves, each with veto power. In such situations, the diplomatic minuet often is not gentle but a robust contact sport; and the outcome often not inconsequential but of great significance. That was the case with the Iraq resolution adopted earlier this month.

The Chinese have observed that the P-5 is composed of one great power, an emerging power and three declining powers. There is some truth to that. If the question were who are the five greatest powers in the world, it is doubtful today that anyone would pick the existing line-up of UN Security Council permanent members. What about Japan, Germany, India, Brazil and other large, powerful countries? What about a representative from Africa such as Nigeria or South Africa? The disconnect between the current Security Council structure and the real world is self-evident to everyone, especially France, Russia and the United Kingdom.

It is their permanent seat on the Security Council that gives those three nations a claim that they still are great powers. It is a vestige of a fading past yet a very important one. To the extent that global issues go through the Security Council is the extent to which these not-so-great powers retain an important role. Their power to wield a "veto" compels them to be taken seriously by the rest of the world. It is not that their military or economy is utterly irrelevant. They are not. But they also are not dominant nor even, in most cases, compelling. Their spheres of interest are not global and their spheres of influence are even more circumspect. However, by right of their veto power in the Security Council, at least on issues in that venue, they are great powers. Therefore, quite understandably, for them, their P-5 status is very precious. They are most attentive to protecting their P-5 status and to strengthening the centrality of the Security Council and opposing any challenge to the Security Council. In my opinion, this dynamic defines a great deal of Security Council debate, negotiation and resolution. And on important matters, it is this consideration more than most that the United States must confront in trying to sell U.S. interests to the Security Council. That certainly was true in passing Resolution 1441 on Iraq.

When President Bush addressed the UN General Assembly on September 12, he made clear that on Iraq it would not be business as usual. Iraq's failure to comply with 16 past UN resolutions was unacceptable. Iraq's continuing acquisition of weapons of mass destruction is a growing threat. Saddam Hussein's continued dealings with terrorists coupled with its WMD capability possess a clear and present danger. Therefore, the UN must take its own resolutions seriously and force Saddam Hussein to disarm. And, if the UN Security Council did not act, the United States would lead an international coalition and force him to disarm. It was this final element, the threat of force that would be exercised outside of any UN Security Council sanction, that drove the negotiations on Resolution 1441.

The UN community: the Secretary-General and the Secretariat, the UN member states, the UN Security Council members, and in particular permanent UN Security Council members France, Russia, China, and the United Kingdom, desperately wanted the use of force against Iraq to go through the Security Council. They want the Security Council to exercise the authority to "legitimize" the use of force. To the extent the Security Council is the sole authority empowered to legitimize the use of force is the extent to which they remain central to issues of war and peace. The extent to which the world's sole superpower bypasses the Security Council is the extent to which they are marginalized. That is what happened in Kosovo when the Security Council was unable to act. The United States with the United Kingdom led an international coalition to bomb Kosovo and stop the genocide. The UN community and particularly France, Russia, China and the United Kingdom did not want to see a repeat of that.

The negotiations on an Iraqi resolution had many considerations. Would the Security Council reiterate that Iraq was in "material breach" of past resolutions, and if so, on human rights, POW's, terrorism and WMD, or just WMD? What would the modalities be for UN inspections to verify Iraqi disarmament? Would Iraq be required to issue a declaration of all WMD capabilities? Could witnesses and their families be taken out of Iraq to be interviewed about what they knew? These were not simple issues. They would take time and require give and take to resolve. But it quickly became apparent that none of these matters, however important they might be, were "deal breakers." The heavy lifting would be on the consequences of non-compliance.

France, Russia, China and the United Kingdom wanted a so-called "two step approach." This resolution would reiterate that the Iraqi regime is in material breach, it must disarm, and it must comply with intrusive inspections to verify compliance. But it also would state that the matter must return to the Security Council for a separate, subsequent authorization of the use of force. In other words, this initial Iraqi resolution would bind member states to a subsequent determination by the Security Council on whether or not force could be used (with international legitimacy) to disarm Saddam Hussein. And, of course, the other fourteen members of the Security Council and in particular the other permanent members with veto power – France, Russia, China and the UK, would be empowered to restrain the United States.

President Bush made it clear from the outset that the United States would not accept any resolution limiting his power to defend America. If the UN did not act to disarm Saddam, the United States would. Through his rhetoric and his action in building up our military presence around Iraq, President Bush drove that point home.

Early on it was evident that a "diplomatic ambiguity" would bridge the gap. But a process was required to get there in which the United States listened to others' concerns, cajoled, tinkered with language and generally demonstrated that we took seriously the views of our Security Council colleagues; and in which we kept reiterating we would let no Iraq resolution pass that sought to limit our inherent right to self defense to disarm Saddam with force. Others pressed their case, the French most effectively, and the UK tried to bridge the gap.

The final product was a resolution that calls on the UN inspectors to report back on their findings and the Security Council to meet and consider those findings, but there is no suggestion that the Security Council must again act before a member state can act.

The Security Council remains seized with the issue. The U.S. in voting for the resolution recognizes continued multilateral involvement in trying to disarm Saddam. The Security Council demonstrated the relevance, if not the determinate centrality, of the Security Council to the issue of war and peace in Iraq. And in securing a unanimous vote for Resolution 1441, Saddam Hussein is given a clear, unambiguous requirement by the international community that he must disarm and that he must allow penetrating UN inspections anywhere, anytime, by anyone to verify his disarmament. A further moral and legal platform is constructed for the forcible disarmament of the Iraqi regime if required.

Upon passage of Resolution 1441, President Bush said, "With the resolution just passed, the United Nations Security Council has met important responsibilities, upheld its principles, and given clear and fair notice that Saddam Hussein must fully disclose and destroy his weapons of mass destruction. He must submit to any and all methods to verify his compliance. His cooperation must be prompt and unconditional, or he will face the severest consequences. The world has now come together to say that the outlaw regime in Iraq will not be permitted to build or possess chemical, biological or nuclear weapons."[2] Selling the Security Council on the U.S. security goals in Iraq in order to pass Resolution 1441 was not easy. But it was in the interest of the Security Council members, and in particular in the interest of France, Russia, China and the United Kingdom to successfully reach consensus. The particulars will change depending on the issue and its relative importance to the United States and to our colleagues. On issues that matter to us, we generally should be able to prevail. But looking down the road 5, 10 or 20 years, I suspect that the greater the disconnect between power in the Security Council and power in the real world, the less central the UN Security Council will be to advance our security goals.

---

1.   Jeane Kirkpatrick, "The Shackles of Consensus," *Foreign Policy*, September/October 2002, p. 36.

2.   President George W. Bush, Remarks on the United Nations Security Council Resolution on Iraq, the Rose Garden, November 8, 2002. President George W. Bush, Remarks on the United Nations Security Council Resolution on Iraq, the Rose Garden, November 8, 2002.

THE UN SECURITY COUNCIL: A REVIEW OF 2002

I am delighted to be back in Sofia and to be participating in this conference about the United Nations Security Council and Bulgaria's role in the Security Council during the past year.

First I want to congratulate Bulgaria and Foreign Minister Solomon Passy for the extraordinary year you have had in foreign affairs: NATO entry, an agreed target date for entry into the European Union, election to chair the OSCE in 2004, and serving in the UN Security Council. Mr. Minister, you and your team have been very busy indeed.

Recognizing that the Atlantic Club of Bulgaria was originally founded to promote Bulgaria's entry into NATO, at the time a visionary aspiration, which has been realized thanks to reform in Bulgaria and the strong leadership of many, including Minister Passy, I would like to share a story with you. In September 1999, I participated in a conference in Gdansk, Poland, titled "1989 – 10 years later." The conference was composed predominantly of center/right political and government leaders from central and eastern Europe. It was held in Gdansk as a symbolic tribute to the Solidarity Trade Union. For me it was a fascinating few days of exchanging ideas with the dynamic leaders of these nations newly independent from Soviet domination.

On the last night, the Polish Prime Minister hosted a small dinner party. Near the end of the evening, the President of Latvia stood to give a toast. He turned to the President of the Solidarity Trade Union and said that while he was a freedom fighter in his home country and there was little reason for hope, he remembered many evenings when he would take his battery operated radio and walk from one corner to another of his small one room apartment to try to pick up reception from Radio Free Europe. He said he would listen to the story of the brave members of Solidarity at the Gdansk shipyard standing up to the totalitarian boot of the Soviet Union, and it gave him hope. It inspired him and it inspired others. So he wished to toast Solidarity.

When the glasses had been lifted, the President of Solidarity rose. Knowing that I had served on President Ronald Reagan's White House staff, he turned toward me. He said that during those early days of their struggle for freedom, neither he nor his colleagues knew whether they would prevail. Often the prospects seemed dim. But, he said, he too listened to Radio Free Europe. And he heard the words of President determination in the struggle now going on for the world will not be bombs and rockets, but a test of will and ideas – a trial of spiritual resolve: the values we hold,

---

Remarks at The Atlantic Club of Bulgaria, Sofia, Bulgaria, December 18, 2002.

the beliefs we cherish, the ideals to which we are dedicated…the great civilized ideas: individual liberty, representative government, and the rule of law under God."[1]

Minister Passy, Ambassador Tafrov, and other members of the Atlantic Club of Bulgaria, it is those ideas, those transcendent values that binds us. It is those beliefs we cherish that guide us. It is an honor and a privilege to work with Bulgaria in the UN Security Council and I appreciate this opportunity to exchange views with you today about the Security Council.

Today, the United States has a unique status as the world's sole superpower. It is a "unipolar moment" in world affairs. But even for America there are limits to our reach. There are limits in treasury and blood. And there are challenges of environmental degradation, the proliferation of weapons (both small arms and weapons of mass destruction), and other challenges that demand multilateral solutions. And, while there are a variety of multilateral venues such as NATO, the G-8, the OAS, and WTO, the United Nations has unique attributes.

The United Nations' universality, its role in decolonization, its Declaration on Human Rights and the values enshrined in its charter earn it a respect and acceptance in every corner of the globe. The United Nations is a unique institution and within the UN the Security Council is its vital center, especially on issues of international peace and security.

In the Security Council, delegations are seated alphabetically. Consequently, this past year it has been my privilege to sit next to the Bulgarian delegation. Your Permanent Representative, Ambassador Stefan Tafrov, is an experienced and knowledgeable diplomat. He is highly intelligent and always well briefed. His interventions invariably are constructive. He effectively represents the interests of Bulgaria.

As you know, there are five permanent members of the UN Security Council: China, France, Russia, the United Kingdom and the United States. And there are ten elected members of the Council serving two-year terms. The elected members, the so-called E-10, fill a special role. They are elected by geographic groups. Therefore, in the Council each elected member represents its geographic group in addition to its primary responsibility of representing its national interest.

Among the E-10, certain delegations distinguish themselves over time for their thoughtfulness, their constructive participation, and, on occasion, serving as honest brokers among the 15 Security Council members. Over this past year, Bulgaria has so distinguished itself. They are more than just one of the E-10. Bulgaria has earned a position of trust and leadership within the Security Council.

In the Council, Bulgaria is among those delegations that seek to uphold the values of the UN charter. Of course, our principle attention is on issues of international peace and security. But the Security Council also must never forget our obligation to try to help those with no hope in the villages of Africa, those caught in bloody intractable conflicts, those trying to rebuild broken societies, those seeking justice after the killing stops.

There have been many UN peacekeeping operations this year. In Afghanistan, the UN is trying to help a society rebuild itself after the Taliban's reign of terror. Schools must be rebuilt. Women must be empowered. Political structures must be constructed. Health and safety services must be established. Infrastructures must be built. An indigenous Army must be recruited and trained. Hope and opportunity must be returned. All this must be accomplished while pockets of Al Qaeda terrorists continue to operate in the countryside. The international community is making an unprecedented commitment in Afghanistan. The UN is playing a crucial coordinating role. And Bulgaria has contributed money and personnel on the ground, as well as support within the Security Council.

In East Timor, the UN monitored the referendum for independence. The UN provided peacekeepers to monitor a potentially explosive security situation. And the UN has helped build and train a new civil service, schools and teachers, and police. The UN monitored the election of East Timor's first parliament and president. In May 2000, Secretary-General Kofi Annan was in East Timor to celebrate their independence. And in September, we welcomed East Timor as the newest member of the United Nations; the 191st member country.

In Ethiopia/Eritrea, a bloody border war quickly killed 80,000 people. The United Nations has deployed peacekeepers to monitor a ceasefire in the buffer security zone and provided humanitarian assistance to hundreds of thousands of displaced persons. The UN has conducted landmine removal efforts. And UN peacekeepers are now helping the demarcation of a new borderline determined by an international border commission. Last February, Ambassador Tafrov and I traveled on a UN Security Council mission to Ethiopia and to Eritrea to impress upon both capitals the expectations of the international community that they peacefully implement the new border and allow the internally displaced people to return home.

In the Democratic Republic of the Congo, there has been a bloody conflict over the past four years. Three million people have died as a result of this war. The United Nations peacekeepers are trying to monitor a ceasefire and promote a sustainable peace agreement. In May, Ambassador Tafrov and I traveled to the Great Lakes Region of Africa in an effort to bolster the fledgling peace talks. That UN Security Council Mission met with leaders in South Africa, Zimbabwe, the DRC, Angola, Uganda, Tanzania, Burundi and Rwanda to explore opportunities and to demonstrate the international community's commitment to support efforts to end the killing.

As all of you are very familiar, the UN has played a major role here in the Balkans. At the end of this month, the UN will close its mission in Bosnia and Herzegovina where the UN has taken the lead in training and integrating the Bosnia police force and in initiating necessary judicial reforms. Progress was achieved and at the end of this month the remaining work will be transferred to the European Union. In Kosovo, the scars of war still tear at society. The past few days, Ambassador Tafrov and I were part of a Security Council Mission to Kosovo where we had meetings in Pristina and then Belgrade. A great deal needs to be done to rebuild the institutions in Kosovo and create an integrated society where Kosovars and Croats live together and work together. Bulgaria, as the only Balkan state on the Security Council, plays a particularly important role in these discussions.

There are many other UN peacekeeping missions. Among those that the Security Council worked on this year include peacekeeping efforts in the Middle East, Georgia, Bouganville, Somalia, Prevlaka, the Western Sahara and the Central African Republic. In all these, Bulgaria is engaged, contributes to Security Council deliberations, and often plays an important leadership role.

This past year, the Security Council also addressed issues related to the new International Criminal Court. The United States has not signed the Rome Statute. We have serious reservations about the court, which forced my delegation to raise issues pertaining to ICC jurisdiction over UN peacekeepers. The divergent and deeply held views on this issue resulted in prolonged, difficult negotiations. Bulgaria was among the E-10 countries that helped steer the discussions toward an eventual resolution that achieved unanimity in the Security Council, satisfying the diverse interests within the Council.

This fall an enormous amount of Security Council time and attention went to Iraq and its weapons of mass destruction. On September 12, President Bush called upon the United Nations to deal with Saddam Hussein's challenge to the international community and his growing threat to international peace and security. Some in the Security Council wanted to avoid their responsibility. At stake was whether Iraq, or any country, could violate 16 United Nations resolutions with impunity; and whether Iraq could continue to develop and stockpile weapons of mass destruction. Tensions rose quickly within a badly divided Security Council. At that time, in September, the rotating Council Presidency was in the hands of Bulgaria. The skill of the Bulgarian delegation was important in establishing a climate conducive to dialogue and accommodation on the Iraq issue. There were eight weeks of intense, tough negotiations.

Last month, the UN Security Council unanimously adopted resolution 1441. It reiterates that Iraq is in material breach of existing UN resolutions. It states that the Iraqi regime must disarm; it must dismantle its program to produce weapons of mass destruction and forfeit its stockpiles of WMD. It creates an intrusive inspection regime to verify Iraqi compliance that inspectors can go anyplace, anytime, by anyone. UN Security Council Resolution 1441 gives Iraq its last, best chance to avoid war. Let's hope the Iraqi regime turns from its past policies of deceit and defiance and, this time, adopts a course of cooperation and compliance.

Another important topic that commanded Security Council attention this year has been the ongoing war against terrorism of global reach. The United Nations is playing an important role in setting counter-terror standards, helping countries develop their own capacity to fight terrorism and curb the financial flow to terrorists. In all these endeavors, Bulgaria is an active participant, including drafting the Security Council statement on terrorism issued on September 11, 2002, the anniversary of the terrorists' evil attack on America.

Let me note that Bulgaria also chairs the Security Council's Somalia Sanctions Committee. In that committee, more has been accomplished in this one year than had been accomplished since the Somalia arms embargo was established in 1991. These sanctions are important tools of the Security Council.

I could go on. It has been a very active year in the United Nations Security Council. The point, however, is simple. The UN matters. The UN Security Council is very important. And for me it is an honor to work with Bulgaria on the Security Council's extensive and varied work program.

Thank you.

---

1. Ronald Reagan, Address to the British Parliament, London, England, June 8, 1982.

THE U.N. AND POST-CONFLICT SITUATIONS

Mr. President, I want to thank you for convening this Security Council wrap-up session on post-conflict situations, which is a good way to continue to elaborate on the discussion that we have had in the special committee on peacekeeping several weeks ago. I thank the Secretary General for his interesting remarks. The Brahimi reforms still are not fully implemented, and if this discussion can help to push some of those proposals forward, then this would have been a very useful Security Council session. The Brahimi reforms are a good place to start the discussion because they drew on the United Nations' long and varied experience in various peacekeeping efforts over the years.

For obvious reasons, that exercise has been careful not to infringe on the role of the Security Council in making political decisions. In the nearly 58 years since the United Nations Charter was signed, there have been, by our count, 202 armed conflicts involving 114 nations. Over 27 million people have been killed in these conflicts. The United Nations has played a post-conflict role in only a small number of these conflicts, and has met with varying degrees of success. One need examine only a few of these conflicts to understand that the United Nations role varies significantly from one post-conflict environment to the next.

Mr. President, in your useful non-paper circulated last Thursday, you suggested that we look at the United Nations role in Afghanistan, Kosovo, Timor-Leste, and Sierra Leone. Before considering the United Nations role subsequent to these conflicts, I would like to make a point about conflicts themselves. My delegation agrees with Secretary General Annan that every conflict is unique. As a corollary to that axiom, I would add that the role of the United Nations and other international and regional organizations also varies case to case.

If we compare the baseline conditions in Afghanistan – a nation of 25 million people with a wide range of ethnic and linguistic backgrounds – with those in Timor-Leste – a nation of less than one million people without significant tribal or ethnic divisions – we quickly understand why the conflict in Afghanistan was far different from that in Timor-Leste, and why the post-conflict structures the United Nations established were distinct as well.

These differences point to the need for the United Nations to tailor its involvement on a case-by-case basis. Former Secretary General Dag Hammarskjold once said, in conflict situations, the U.N. must go to a tailor and tailor make the suit

---

Statement at U.N. Security Council Formal Meeting, April 30, 2003.

needed for the occasion. This flexibility has been institutionalized in the Brahimi reform process; it is not a weakness, but rather a strength of the dynamic nature of the United Nations itself, which encompasses and is affected by the national interests of United Nations members.

By virtue of having been involved in more than 60 conflicts, the United Nations has developed an ever-larger number of post-conflict experiences as well as lessons learned. This cumulative experience provides a toolbox, if you will, of solutions that it can bring to bear when faced with specific problems.

Part of our flexibility is understanding what the United Nations can and cannot do. We neither strengthen the United Nations, the Security Council, nor help bring peace to any conflict by over-promising, raising unrealistic expectations, or over-extending the capacity of the United Nations to deliver on the ground.

My delegation takes away several lessons from the United Nations role in Sierra Leone and other post-conflict situations in Africa. For example, one lesson is the need to find a mechanism for donor group coordination and follow-up on the reintegration element of any disarmament, demobilization and resettlement, any DDR program, undertaken as past of a post-conflict peace process.

Second, there is a need for effective coordination of humanitarian assistance between peacekeeping operations, international aid agencies, and humanitarian groups as a situation moves from peacekeeping to post-conflict reconstruction and renewal.

The United Nations is uniquely qualified to provide this coordination in a post-conflict environment, taking policy guidance from the Security Council or the lead security force on the ground – in Sierra Leone's case the British military, which provided umbrella security in the immediate post-conflict environment.

Sierra Leone offers insight on the United Nations role in a post-conflict environment, taking policy guidance from the Security Council or the lead security force on the ground – in Sierra Leone's case the British military, which provided umbrella security in the immediate post-conflict environment.

Sierra Leone offers insight on the United Nations role in a post-conflict environment in coordinating key humanitarian issues as well. How the United Nations and the United Nations Mission in Sierra Leone responded to the humanitarian needs of refugees and internally displaced persons in Sierra Leone offers valuable lessons.

In the case of United Nations Mission in Sierra Leone, its assistance was focused, responsive, and limited to its mandate. This is the way it should be – the primary task of a peacekeeping mission is to support a political process, even in the post-conflict period. The Council acted to authorize UNAMSIL to participate in the international humanitarian response in Sierra Leone only after a clear explanation of the role UNAMSIL would play and after it was clear UNAMSIL had unique capabilities that could not be duplicated by any other organization.

Another lesson on the humanitarian side of the ledger is the importance of disseminating explicit guidelines on the role of the various United Nations agencies and non-Governmental Organizations. It is also important to have clear mechanisms in place to address concerns over overlapping mandates between the activities of NGO's and U.N. agencies. We saw the benefit of such guidelines in the agreement between the Office of the High Commissioner for Refugees with United Nations Mission in Sierra Leone on the use of peacekeeping operation resources to move refugees.

In the area of transitional justice, critical to post-conflict societies, movement to peaceful, sustainable societies, Sierra Leone is providing a very important lesson. The Truth and Reconciliation Commission is doing its interviews, allowing the truth to be told. This is necessary to allow victims to come to terms with the atrocities of the past and move on. And, the Special Court has now handed down its first indictments against those who allegedly committed the worst crimes against humanity. If these two institutions of transitional justice are successful, there will be important lessons for the United Nations Security Council moving forward in the critical area of transitional justice.

In Timor Leste, a nation small in territory and modest in population, Australia was the indispensable lead nation in moving the country from conflict to peace and independence. The United Nations played the central role in organizing elections. And the donor community, working with the United Nations, was generous. In Timor Leste, to build a sustainable society, it was necessary to build the institutions of civil society; from building government buildings to constructing schools, from training teachers to building a police force with adequate numbers that are properly trained. The United Nations central role has been extremely important in all phases of that post-conflict situation and, aided by the United Nations and the donor community, the success of the Timor Leste people is significant and very promising.

In Kosovo, after NATO employed armed force to end the genocide of Albanian Kosovars, the United Nations has played a major role in the post-conflict society with invaluable assistance from the European Union and the larger donor community.

The Security Council met on Kosovo just a few days ago. The United Nations has helped this post-conflict situation. The goal of a stable, multi-ethnic Kosovo is a worthy and important aspiration. As laid out in the Security General's most recent report on Kosovo and as discussed around the Security Council table, major challenges in Kosovo remain. Devolution tempered by the realities on the ground must continue. Development of the Provisional Institutions of Self-government must progress. The human rights of all ethnic groups, including freedom of movement, must be achieved. In Kosovo the work is not done, but the United States is confident that the United Nations Mission in Kosovo will be successful, but Security Council continued attention and involvement in post-conflict Kosovo will be required.

In Afghanistan, the coalition forces ended the reign of the Taliban. Afghanistan had become not a state that sponsored terrorists, but a place where terrorists supported the state. Those days are over.

The United Nations has been the key coordinator as different nations have taken the lead in important areas to reconstruct the post-conflict Afghanistan: Italians in judicial reform, the United Kingdom in illicit drug irradiation, Germany in police training, Japan in DDR, the United States in training the Afghan National Army with help and support from the French. This is a much different model than Kosovo, and thanks to the leadership of Secretary-General Kofi Annan and the great talent and skill of the Special Representative of the Secretary-General, Ambassador Lakhdar Brahimi, the post-conflict Afghanistan reconstruction is on a clear path to success politically, reconstruction and otherwise.

Given that some of my colleagues have raised the topic of Iraq, I would like to reiterate some of the key principles of United States policy on this issue. Saddam Hussein's weapons of mass destruction no longer threaten international peace and security. The region and the world are safer and more secure. The Coalition has liberated the Iraqi people from the brutal tyranny of Saddam Hussein's regime. The days of thousands of unaccounted for disappearances in Iraq are over. The days of torture are behind the Iraqi people. The days of using chemical weapons against Iraqi Kurds and the days of genocide against the Iraqi Shiites in the south are over. The days of human rights travesties and abuse are over. The Coalition is working on the ground to ensure that the Iraqi people receive supplies for the essentials of daily life, including food, water and medical supplies, for the essentials of daily life, including food, water and medical supplies, until Iraq's return to a self-sustaining member of the global community.

As President Bush has said, the United Nations can play a "vital" role in the post-conflict Iraq. Fortunately, predictions of humanitarian catastrophe, even predictions of a humanitarian crisis, have proven inaccurate.

The Coalition also is working with the people of Iraq to facilitate their recovery. We are committed to the sovereignty and territorial integrity of Iraq as well as an Iraq free of weapons of mass destruction living in peace with its neighbors. The Coalition will not remain in Iraq longer than required. An Iraqi government chosen by the Iraqi people and serving the Iraqi people is a goal of the United States and its partners in this Coalition.

I would like to conclude my remarks with one other point that I often see omitted in public debate – the will of the governed.

We must not lose sight o the fact that the wants and needs of the people in a post-conflict environment are best defined by those people.

As the international community reaches out to help a population in need, one of its first tasks must seek to provide that population with a voice – a voice with which to articulate their own desires regarding what comes next.

Helping the people find their voice is especially important in cases where a new governmental model is being instituted, as is the case in all of the models that have been cited today, Mr. President, in your non-paper and in the discussion which we have had.

Thank you.

IS THE U.N. RELEVANT?

I have been asked to address the question: Is the United Nations relevant? The simple answer is yes; but it is not as central as many of the UN's strongest supporters would like to think.

I assume this topic was chosen because of events in Iraq over the past nine months; both the activities within the United Nations and developments on the ground.

Let me begin by saying that I believe the members of the UN Security Council failed to meet their responsibilities. Unquestionably, Saddam Hussein was in material breach of 17 UN resolutions. Saddam was a gathering threat to international peace and security. The Security Council Member States discounted their own resolutions by failing to enforce them. They raised questions about their resolve and, yes, they raised questions about the relevance of the United Nations. I believe their failure to meet the responsibilities has diminished the United Nations. The UN's failures in Rwanda, Kosovo and now Iraq raise serious questions about the institution.

Nonetheless, the United Nations is playing an important role on many matters, including in Iraq. Later this week, I believe the Security Council will adopt with overwhelming support a resolution that will lift the sanctions on Iraqi oil, phase out the Oil for Food program, and authorize the UN to play a "vital role" in Iraqi humanitarian assistance. The United Nations is uniquely well equipped to help deal with the real humanitarian needs of Iraq; a nation whose natural resources for too long were devoted to Saddam's palaces and his tyrannical control and not the needs of the Iraqi people. UN specialized agencies such as the World Food Program and UNESCO can provide immediate relief to the people and their culture. A UN coordinator for humanitarian assistance in Iraq can work with the Occupying Power and non-government organizations to appeal to the donor community for adequate support, to coordinate and direct assistance where it is most needed, and to help rebuild the institutions of a free Iraq liberated from Saddam's reign of terror.

But beyond Iraq, I'd like to raise two other trouble spots where the United Nations is playing a very important role. In both examples, the United States Government is deeply engaged. And in both cases, we are working very closely with France to mitigate a crisis situation and alleviate the suffering of innocent people. That's right, even as we are deeply disappointed by France's role in Iraq and in President Jacques Chirac's threat of a pre-emptive, unilateral veto of an 18th UN Security Council

---

Remarks to United Nations Association/USA, New York, N.Y., May 18, 2003.

resolution on Iraq, here at the UN we are working with France to help address problems in Cote d'Ivoire and in the Democratic Republic of the Congo. Because, whatever problems Washington must sort out with Paris in the wake of Iraq, we remain committed to help others where we can. And in both Cote d'Ivoire and the Congo, the United Nations is the best instrument through which we can provide the needed assistance.

Last September, fighting broke out in Cote d'Ivoire. Within days the Muslim north was controlled by rebels while the Christian south remained in government control. Some fierce fighting took place. Normal trade routes were interrupted. Since Abidjan and San Pedro are the ports used by Cote d'Ivoire to export its cocoa and the principle port used by neighboring states to export their goods, when these ports were interrupted due to the fighting, it had a devastating impact not only on the Cote d'Ivoire economy but also on the entire region. Human rights abuses were common, ethnic tensions were inflamed, and a climate of impunity took hold. Mercenaries from neighboring west African countries moved in and made the situation worse. This local conflict was bad and it risked creating larger regional instability.

The French have large commercial interests in Cote d'Ivoire that were threatened by this fighting. Also, there are about 20,000 French citizens in Cote d'Ivoire who were in danger. Therefore, relying upon a French/Cote d'Ivoire bilateral agreement, last fall the French quickly deployed troops to this west African country to help secure their interests and stabilize the situation.

Meanwhile, the Economic Community of West Africa, ECOWAS, worked on finding a political solution to this conflict that threatened the entire region. The efforts of ECOWAS last fall helped broker a cease-fire agreement. The French helped midwife a more comprehensive deal in January, the Linas Marcousis Agreement, in which the parties agreed to a transitional government that will lead to elections and a new government. And ECOWAS agreed to deploy a multinational peacekeeping force to Cote d'Ivoire.

ECOWAS and France sought a blessing for this process from the larger international community, so they came to the UN Security Council. The United States worked closely with the African states and with France to craft a resolution that could be adopted by the Security Council. This UN action has given further momentum to the peace process.

The United States Government also is the largest contributor to the ECOWAS peacekeeping force in Cote d'Ivoire. It now numbers 1200 soldiers. The United States has contributed $9 million to the ECOWAS multinational force and is supplying the communications capabilities for it.

Unfortunately, even as there has been progress politically on the transition government, some fighting has continued; especially in the east near the Cote d'Ivoire/Liberian border. Tragically, not only combatants but also scores of innocent civilians have been killed. In April, ECOWAS and France pushed for a new UN political office in Abidjan, Cote d'Ivoire and some UN military observers along the demilitarized zone.

While the United States believes the regional ECOWAS force should be the principal peacekeepers in Cote d'Ivoire, and while we will continue to provide substantial financial and other support to the ECOWAS force; we were persuaded by west African countries and by France that a UN political office in Abidjan and some limited UN military observers could usefully contribute to improving the situation. Therefore, we worked closely with the UN Department of Peacekeeping Operations and with colleagues on the Security Council over a period of weeks to draft a UN resolution that would address the needs of the people of Cote d'Ivoire. The resolution was adopted earlier this month.

The conflict in Cote d'Ivoire receives little attention in the West. United States national interests in Cote d'Ivoire exist, but they are not so central as to warrant unilateral U.S. action. But for hundreds of thousands of people in Cote d'Ivoire, this conflict's devastation is overwhelming. Many people have been killed. Hundreds of thousands of people have fled their homes. Ethnic unrest has been inflamed. Human rights have been abused. And the conflict in Cote d'Ivoire threatens regional stability in western Africa, an area already suffering due to the brutal Sierra Leone civil war and fighting in Liberia that continues to this day.

In this situation, the United Nations plays a valuable role. The prospects for stabilizing Cote d'Ivoire are better because of the UN. And the possibility of a better day for the victims of the fighting in Cote d'Ivoire is improved due to the UN.

Turning to the Democratic Republic of the Congo, the situation is even more desperate. For 4 ½ years that country has been caught in the cauldron of war. Many neighboring states and over a dozen local rebel groups, many of them proxies for various neighboring countries, have fought a devastating war. It is estimated that over 3 million people have been killed as a consequence of this war in the Congo. The suffering is staggering.

The efforts to end this conflict have been multifaceted. The UN Mission on the Congo, MONUC, has been large, the most expensive of any peacekeeping mission anywhere in the world. The Secretary-General's Special Representative to the Congo has worked to push the warring parties to a peaceful resolution. The United States and other major countries have worked hard on a bilateral basis to keep a peace process on track. African countries, particularly South Africa, have led a negotiation process called the Inter Congolese Dialogue, which has been the principal mechanism to develop agreements for a transition government.

Fortunately, in most of the Democratic Republic of the Congo, the political progress is encouraging. Foreign troops have left the Congo. Progress on forming a transitional government continues with almost all factions now having a stake in its success. It is accurate to say that the success so far is due to the Congolese parties themselves. But it also is fair to say that the United Nations has made an important contribution to this progress.

Unfortunately, in one district things are bad and threaten to get much worse. In the Ituri district in northeastern Congo, there are militias who do not have a stake in the success of the transition process. Also, in Ituri province there have been Ugandan troops who have benefited due to resource exploitation during the fighting and who have worked against a peaceful settlement in the region. Even as they exit, some Ugandans have worked through proxy militias to prolong the fighting. And, extremely troubling given the history in the area, there is combustible ethnic dimension in Ituri between the Hema and Lendu. The result is that fighting continues in Ituri. There have been reports of killing, rape, and even cannibalism. Human rights are being trampled and international humanitarian assistance is unable to reach people in need. Thousands of people are seeking refuge in the MONUC headquarters in Bunia. And the echoes of the awful genocide in neighboring Rwanda where 800,000 Tutsis were killed by the Hutus in a matter of weeks rings in the air.

The UN Department of Peacekeeping Operations has briefed the Security Council frequently in recent weeks about the desperate developments in Ituri. DPKO initiated contacts to third countries to seek a lead country that could rapidly deploy a force to Ituri to stop the situation from spinning out of control. On May 10th, Secretary-General Kofi Annan called President Jacques Chirac soliciting a French-led multinational force to go into Ituri. On May 12th in the Security Council, I said the United States Government would support a UN Security Council Presidential Statement authorizing such an initiative and granting Chapter 7 enforcement powers to a French-led multinational force to Ituri. The next day, the French Government issued a statement in Paris saying they were considering leading such a force.

Almost immediately, just with the possibility of a multinational force led by the French going to Ituri, the situation on the ground calmed down. In recent days the United States Government has worked closely with the UN Department of Peacekeeping Operations, in Kinshasa, Kigali, Luanda, Pretoria and other African capitals, and in Paris and other European capitals to make this possibility a reality. As we meet today, a lot of things still have to be worked out, but I am optimistic that a French-led multinational force, with the participation of African and other national troops, will be deployed to Ituri. And for the people of Ituri, when there are "boots on the ground", there will be a real possibility for peace. The danger of inflamed ethnic violence and perhaps even genocide will be much less.

Ultimately, Ituri will know lasting peace and stability only when there is an all-inclusive political process in which the Ituri militias and the people are part. They must have the political will and the sustained commitment to realize this goal. The international community and the United Nations will not impose a solution to their problems. They cannot. But, the good work of the UN is facilitating a multinational force that will help stabilize Ituri and give peace a chance.

I could go on to discuss the United Nations' contribution in Timor Leste, Afghanistan, Kosovo, Abkhazia, Sierra Leone and elsewhere. In each of these local conflicts that threatens regional stability, the UN plays a vital role to help resolve conflicts and rebuild societies. In each of these local conflicts, the United Nations is proving its value and its relevance every day.

To return to the topic on which I was asked to talk; I believe the Security Council members' failure to meet their responsibilities on Iraq has diminished the United Nations. I believe the UN's failures in Rwanda, Kosovo, and Iraq raise serious questions about the institution and point out its limitations. But is the UN relevant? Cote d'Ivoire and the Democratic Republic of the Congo are but two examples of the UN's importance to millions of people every day and the UN's relevance for America and the world.

ISRAEL AND THE UNITED NATIONS

I want to thank the American Jewish Committee for inviting me to visit with you today. And I thank your Board Chairman, Bob Goodkind, for his generous introduction.

Like many Americans, I have an emotional attachment to the State of Israel and a profound respect for its democracy. I am inspired by the strength and courage of the Israeli people. And, I appreciate Israel's loyalty as an important ally to the United States.

As a young Congressional aide just out of law school, I first traveled to Israel more than 25 years ago. It was just weeks after Anwar Sadat's historic visit to Jerusalem. The Congressional delegation met with President Sadat in Aswan, Egypt, and then traveled to Jerusalem to meet with Prime Minister Mehachin Begin. For me it was an unforgettable trip. The atmosphere was charged with great hope. It was a time of enormous promise. Unfortunately, the promise of a lasting peace in the Middle East launched by President Sadat and Prime Minister Begin has not yet been achieved. And, unfortunately, often the United Nations has been an impediment to real progress towards peace in that land.

Later, in the mid-80's, I served as the United States Ambassador to the U.N. Offices in Vienna, Austria. At that time, one of the organizations based in Vienna was the U.N. Relief Works Agency, UNRWA, that provides schools and medical care in the Palestinian Refugee Camps in the Middle East. During those years, I visited Palestinian refugee camps in Gaza, the West Bank, Jordan and Syria. I listened to Palestinians in those camps denounce Israel, but they also denounced Arabs who were exploiting the Palestinian cause for their own gain. I saw how some used the U.N. to support the Palestinian cause and disadvantage Israel. I saw how UNRWA was one of the U.N.'s scaffoldings helping to hold up the Palestinian cause.

Later, while Assistant Secretary of State for International Organization Affairs, I gained a broader, more profound appreciation of how the United Nations is a place often hostile to Israeli interests. During my tenure we fought, unsuccessfully, to repeal the insidious, pernicious U.N. General Assembly Resolution that equated Zionism to racism.

And now I serve as Ambassador and United States Alternate Representative to the United Nations for Special Political Affairs. Most days I sit in the U.N. Security Council representing U.S. interests. And in many of those meetings I see the hostility towards Israel revealed.

Remarks at American Jewish Committee Annual Meeting, Washington, D.C., May 9, 2003.

I remember one meeting of the Security Council that took place right after a meeting of the Quartet. As I'd learned to expect, my Syrian colleague used the meeting to attack Israel. Also as I'd learned to expect, but what nonetheless constantly disappoints me, many other delegations attacked Israel. My British colleague joined in many of the criticisms of Israel, even expressing sentiments that directly undercut the Quartet statement about the peace process made the day before. After the meeting, when I expressed my disappointment at what he had said, British Ambassador Stuart Eldon said, "Oh Rich, this is just politics. You can't take it so seriously."

Ambassador Eldon was right. For him and most of the Security Council members, posturing on the Middle East and attacking Israel is "just politics." It is the accepted norm. It is just what one does on the Middle East issue. When I say to the U.N. Security Council that any reference to excessive Israeli force in the West Bank must be balanced by a condemnation of the terrorist attacks by Hamas, I make my colleagues uncomfortable. However great the merits of my demand, it is socially and politically unacceptable. Invariably, the consequence of my demand is that, rather than mention the Arab terrorist activities, the Security Council then issues no press statement whatsoever.

I believe the United Nations has marginalized itself on the Israeli/Palestinian issue. The U.N. lacks moral authority on this matter. To the extent member states believe their rhetoric and actions on the Middle East in the U.N. are "just politics" that should not be taken seriously, is the extent to which the U.N. itself cannot be taken seriously.

Unfortunately, the bias against Israel in the United Nations is significant.

The Arab bloc within the Non-Alighed Movement and the G-77 has effectively used the General Assembly as a forum for isolating Israel. With their numbers, they have easily passed harsh anti-Israel resolutions in the General Assembly. I already have mentioned the most notorious, U.N. General Assembly Resolution 3379 adopted in 1975 equating Zionism with Racism. It was finally rescinded in 1991 following the Madrid Conference.

Over the past several years an average of 18 resolutions critical of Israel have been adopted by the General Assembly each year. The Arab group and the Non-Alighed Movement often have challenged the credentials of the Israeli delegation at the beginning of General Assembly sessions. The most recent challenge was in May 2002 prior to the U.N. General Assembly Session on Children. No other member state faces such routine attacks.

Of the ten Emergency Special Sessions held by the General Assembly, six have been on the Middle East, four of which have been critical of Israel. Meetings of the tenth Emergency Special Session on Occupied East Jerusalem started in 1997, met most recently in 2002 and remains "suspended" to facilitate the reopening of the issue. Since June 1996, the financing of the United Nations Interim Force in Lebanon, UNIFIL, has become politicized in the Fifth Committee and Plenary as countries hostile to Israel seek to attribute responsibility on Israel for the April 18, 1996, Qana incident and demand Israel's payment for damages.

The U.N. Commission on Human Rights routinely adopts a disproportionate number of resolutions concerning Israel. Over the past three sessions, the Commission on Human Rights resolutions critical of Israel average 6-7% of the total number of resolutions adopted while many rogue states that are among the worst abusers of human rights are not criticized at all. Of all condemnations by the Commission on Human Rights, twenty-six percent refer to Israel alone.

Several divisions of the U.N. Secretariat and U.N. committees established over United State's obligations are critical of Israel. They are discriminatory and one-sided. United States efforts to eliminate them have been unsuccessful. They include the Division for Palestinian Rights of the U.N. Secretariat, the Committee to Investigate Israeli Practices in the Occupied Territories, and the Committee on the Exercise of the Inalienable Rights of the Palestinian People.

President Bush has sought to counter this U.N. bias and hostility against Israel. We have sought to prevent U.N. bodies from unfairly targeting Israel. We are not hesitant to vote against resolutions singling Israel out for criticism. Last summer we announced that the United States would veto any Security Council resolution on the Middle East that did not condemn Palestinian terror attacks and name Hamas, Islamic Jihad and the Al-Aksa Martyrs Brigade as the groups responsible for the attacks. The Bush Administration also has made clear that any U.N. Security Council resolutions must note that any Israeli withdrawal is linked to the security situation, and that both parties must be called upon to pursue a negotiated settlement.

President Bush has demonstrated leadership on the Middle East issue. He has called for reform of Palestinian governance, and some reform has happened. He has developed a Road Map to resolve the conflict that will ensure Israel's security and allow an independent Palestinian state. Working with the Quartet (the U.S., the European Union, Russia and the U.N.) and working directly with the countries in the region, President Bush will continue to provide leadership in trying to resolve this conflict.

However the United Nations, due to its long history of bias against Israel, will not play a central role in these efforts nor can it. The U.N. lacks the moral authority and standing to contribute significantly to the resolution of this conflict.

By distorting the United Nations agenda and using resolutions to relentlessly attack a member state, the majority of U.N. members and the secretariate have contradicted the U.N. Charter, defied its values, and diminished the United Nations as an institution. The United States Government, under the leadership of President Bush, will remain faithful to the high ideals of the U.N. and to our friend and ally, the State of Israel.

Thank you.

LEGITIMACY AND
THE UNITED NATIONS

Thank you for inviting me to join you today to share some thoughts about the United Nations. More particularly, I want to talk about the U.N. and legitimacy.

We are meeting in the days after Operation Iraqi Freedom. Therefore, let me first comment on the United Nations Security Council failure to meet its responsibilities on Iraq.

Last September, Secretary General Kofi Annan said, "I urge Iraq to comply with its obligations – for the sake of its own people, and for the sake of world order. If Iraq's defiance continues, the Security Council must face its responsibilities."[1] Over the next eight weeks there were negotiations on an Iraqi resolution. It would be the Security Council's seventeenth resolution on Iraq. Those exhaustive negotiations resulted in Resolution 1441. It was adopted unanimously and it was well understood by all. It states that Iraq was in material breach of existing U.N. Security Council resolutions, that Iraq must disarm its weapons of mass destruction immediately, that Iraq must provide a full and accurate declaration of all its WMD and must proactively cooperate with U.N. inspectors, and, if Iraq failed to fully and immediately comply, that Saddam Hussein would face "serious consequences" which was well understood to mean that he would face the use of force to make him comply.[2]

By February, Saddam was in material breach of Resolution 1441. Every member of the Security Council understood the terms of the resolution. Every member knew Saddam had weapons of mass destruction.[3] Every member knew that Saddam had not made a full and accurate declaration of his WMD as required. Every member knew that Saddam was not proactively cooperating with United Nations inspectors as required. Every Security Council member knew Iraq's defiance continued. But the Security Council refused to face its responsibilities.

Why? Many considerations lead to this failure. Among the Council members there were economic considerations, member states domestic political considerations, an interest by most of the elected members to avoid tough decisions and accountability, a U.N. institutional bias against armed conflict even in the face of continued Iraqi defiance, different threat assessments, a desire to contain American power,[4] and the willingness of France to unilaterally and pre-emptively threaten a veto in an effort to check U.S. power.[5]

Notwithstanding the failure of the U.N. Security Council to live up to its responsibilities and pass an 18th resolution on Iraq, the United States did act. As

---

Remarks at The Heritage Foundation, Washington, D.C., May 14, 2003.

President Bush consistently and constantly had made clear it would,[6] the United States led a Coalition of the Willing against the brutal tyranny of Saddam Hussein. The Coalition forces advanced in unprecedented speed and Saddam's regime fell. Twenty-five million Iraqis now are free from the terror inflicted by a brutal dictator. Saddam's awful torture, mutilations, and killings are over. The region and the world are no longer threatened by Saddam's weapons of mass destruction. The world is safer and more secure. The world is a better place. Yet, before and after Operation Iraqi Freedom, there have been those who have said that the war to liberate the Iraqi people and to free the world of Saddam's weapons of mass destruction lacked legitimacy because the U.N. Security Council had not passed an 18th resolution on Iraq explicitly authorizing the use of force against Saddam Hussein.

Legitimacy

What do the advocates of a requirement for U.N. Security Council authorization mean by "legitimacy" and can such a requirement be justified?

They seem to believe that the U.N. Security Council is the arbiter of when nations can or cannot use force. The Security Council, they believe, is a "court" where the international community passes judgment on a country's right to use arms in defense of their national interest. Indeed, as one commentator explained, the Kofi Annan doctrine holds that "only the Security Council can legitimately authorize (the) use of force in international affairs. ...(The) Security Council is the sole arbiter of just intervention."[7]

Obviously, no war should be entered into lightly. War is a terrible instrument that has a high cost in death, misery and destruction. Nonetheless, there are times when the terrible cost of war is less than inaction. There are times when a gathering storm must be confronted to avoid even greater devastation later. There are times when armed force is needed and times when it is just.

One strength of a democracy is that the elected leaders must mount the formidable challenge of persuading the people that waging war is necessary. And during the course of war, the elected leaders must continue to make the case that the cause is just and the war's prosecution appropriate. This is not easy, nor should it be. But by what power and by what right does the U.N. Security Council sit in judgment of decisions on war and peace? Who empowered the members of the U.N. Security Council to sit in judgment on the legitimacy of armed action? And what do they mean by legitimacy?

Professor Bryan Hehir has observed, "Legitimacy... implies a shared international conviction that policies and programs affecting individual nations proceeds from international institutions that represent the perspectives and interests of all states."[8] And Professor Thomas M. Frank has written "By 'legitimate' is meant that it must be evident that decisions to deploy (force) are taken in a manner widely perceived to be in accordance with the process of the international system."[9] During the United Nations deliberations on Iraq, Secretary-General Kofi Annan said, "There is no substitute for the unique legitimacy provided by the United Nations Security Council. States and peoples around the world attach fundamental importance to such legitimacy."[10] Mr. Annan went on to say that "the Security Council adopted Resolution 1441... unanimously. That gives it even greater authority based on law, collective effort, and the unique legitimacy of the United Nations."[11]

So, for this school of thought, not only is the United Nations Security Council the sole arbiter of just intervention, the court to decide on the legitimacy or lack of legitimacy of the use of force; but the imprimatur of legitimacy is most authoritative when the Security Council acts unanimously.

Why should we care about the champions of this viewpoint, especially since Kosovo and now Iraq have demonstrated that the failure of the U.N. Security Council to authorize force has not (and will not) prevent the United States from acting to protect its national interests? We should care because this ideology seeks to greatly inhibit the United States ability to use force in order to protect our interests. This expansive view of the U.N. Security Council's role in conferring legitimacy, if embraced, raises the costs of unilateral action and even of action by a large "coalition of the willing" that lacks this Security Council seal of approval.[12]

"Legitimacy": A Wrong Headed Power Grab

While Secretary-General Kofi Annan and others have said that the U.N. Founders sought to ensure that the use of force is the last resort,[13] there is nothing in the 1945 history of the U.N. founding conference in San Francisco to suggest that and it is not reflected in the U.N. Charter.[14] Indeed, the United Nations was intended to be an institution of collective security.[15] And while the culture of non-coercion at the U.N. may have been understandable during the Cold War, it is not so today. As Professor Anne-Marie Slaughter has said, "we are once again in an era in which threats to international peace and security may increasingly require the use of force."[16]

The idea that only the U.N. Security Council can legitimately authorize the use of force was never seriously advanced by the U.N. founders, is not in the four corners of the U.N. Charter, and certainly was not accepted when the U.S. Senate considered the U.N. Charter in 1945. As Michigan Senator Arthur Vandenberg, the "indispensable voice for U.S. ratification of the U.N. Charter, described it, 'this is anything but a wild-eyed internationalist dream of a world state. ...It is based virtually on a four-power alliance.'"[17]

Not only does the founding history and the Charter contradict the argument that only the U.N. Security Council can provide legitimacy for the use of force, so does the Council's make up. The U.N. Security Council is not the representative body of the international community that U.N. maximalists claim it to be. The Security Council has limited membership with the concentration of the pivotal political power, the veto power, in just a few hands.

The permanent members of the Security Council do not have the greatest moral authority, the most military might, the largest economies or the furthest cultural reach. They merely are the victors of World War II plus China. As *The Economist* pointed out during the Iraq deliberations, "Britain and France are well aware of the inappropriateness of their status... (and) Russia should be equally embarrassed but is not."[18] After all, Russia's economy is about the size of Belgium. Based on the size of their population, economic power, and other factors, there are a number of countries that could and often have claimed they deserve permanent seats on the Security Council; among them India, Japan, Germany, Indonesia, Nigeria, Egypt and Brazil.

Looking at the permanent members of the Security Council, Charles Krauthammer wrote, "The idea that legitimacy flows from the blessings of France and Russia, Saddam's lawyers and suppliers, is on its face risible."[19] And should the vote of China, hardly a democracy, alone make the difference between international legality and illegality.[20]

More generally, the U.N. Charter was a manifesto committed to freedom and justice. It promotes self-determination of people and promotes fundamental human rights. Yet many members of the U.N., including many on the Security Council, do not have the consent of their own people and do not honor fundamental human rights.

Furthermore, putting aside the veto power of the small exclusive group of permanent members, should small countries far from the region in question, with no direct stake in the conflict, and often little independent information have the determinative vote on whether or not a war is "legitimate."[21] Does it make sense that the vote of Mauritius, a small island nation with no army, navy or air force could cast a decisive vote on whether or not a war is "legitimate"? For that matter should Guinea or Cameroon?

Despite whatever symbolism and mythology that the United Nations maximalists would like to convey to the Council, it is a highly political arena. It is a place members go to pursue their national self interest. And sitting on the Security Council, I can assure you that it is a contact sport. Whether it is China on Tibet, Russia on Chechnya and on Abkhaza, France pursuing its commercial interests, or Guinea on Liberia, each member state protects its own turf and seeks to advance its broader interests. As the saying goes, "it ain't beanbag." And often the higher the stakes, the more narrow the national self-interest and the more tenacious the fighting to pursue those interests. Votes are bought and sold, deals are made, accommodations reached. President Harry Truman once said that the only statesmen are dead politicians. On the big issues, only politicians have seats at the U.N. Security Council table and their elbows can be sharp. So the suggestion that the Council is a detached, quasi-judicial body deliberating on whether something is legitimate or not, well, that is just hokum.

As Clive Cook wrote not long ago in *The National Journal*, "The U.N. is a place where governments – including many corrupt and tyrannical governments – go to pursue their interests; it is not in its own right a constitutionally well-founded source of law or legitimacy."[22]

Some of those who have attacked the U.S. led coalition against Saddam's Iraqi regime have said that this action flies in the face of the multilateral system of the international rule of law set up in 1945. They suggest that by acting without explicit U.N. Security Council authorization, the coalition action is not only illegitimate but threatens the long-standing and well-established global multilateral system.[23] But, in fact, no such system has ever operated. From its founding throughout the Cold War, the only military actions that received a prior U.N. Security Council resolution authorizing the use of force were in Korea in 1950 and Iraq in 2001.[24] Meanwhile, since the United Nations was established there have been 202 different armed conflicts that have involved 114 countries.[25] These conflicts have killed 29 million people and generated well over 25 million refugees and 41 million internally displaced persons.

128

In fact, it should be noted, that France's armed intervention in Cote d'Ivoire earlier this year did not have prior U.N. Security Council authorization.

Clearly, Security Council prior authorization of armed action is the rare exception, not the rule. There is no long-standing, well-established and widely recognized requirement of council prior authorization to legitimize war. In fact, sometimes the Security Council gives authorizations after the event such as in Sierra Leone in 1997 and in Kosovo.

Another Security Council practice that undermines the claim of council legitimizing power is that it picks and chooses which of its many resolutions it will actively enforce. Selective enforcement of resolutions hardly suggests the gravitas and importance of council action the U.N. maximalists claim. Indeed, until President Bush took the lead by challenging the U.N. members on Iraq, any attempt to disarm Iraq as required by numerous council resolutions had been dropped completely.

The glaring failures of the U.N. further bring into question its own legitimacy. The 1990s demonstrated the inability of the U.N. to act as the sole, primary agent to address crisis. Its supervision of Somalia was botched.[26] In Bosnia the U.N. created 6 safe areas under Security Council mandates. While supposedly under U.N. protection, 7,414 Bosnian Muslims were slaughtered in Srebrenicia, and another 13,000 were killed in the other U.N. enclaves.[27] In Rwanda, as a matter of deliberate policy, the U.N. Security Council took no action to stop the genocidal killing, mostly by machetes, of 800,000 Tutsis by Hutus.[28] As one commentator wrote, "The story of Rwanda offers crushing proof that unity on the Council is no safeguard against cravenness."[29] And, as Slobovan Milosovich committed genocide of Kosovo Albanians, the U.N. Security Council was unable to act due to Russia's veto threat.[30] Somalia, Srebrenicia, Rwanda, Kosovo. It is a litany of U.N. failures, misery and death.

Further undermining the U.N.'s own legitimacy, let alone any claim that it uniquely can grant legitimacy, is the rampant hypocrisy in the United Nations. The distance traveled from the U.N. Charter and the distortion of its ideals is so great that it seems normal for Cuba, Sudan, Vietnam and Zimbabwe to sit on the U.N. Commission on Human Rights while the United States was kept off; and for Libya to chair that body.

The U.N. Charter, the history of the United Nations, the composition of the U.N. Security Council and the way it functions, the failures of the U.N., and its hypocrisy, all undercut the assertion that "only the Security Council can legitimately authorize (the) use of force in international affairs." That view is post-Cold War wishful thinking of U.N. enthusiasts and of those who seek to limit America's freedom to act in pursuit of its vital interests.

America's Reply

How should America respond to this power grab?

America has a unique status in the world. America has unprecedented dominance militarily, economically, technologically and culturally. The unipolar moment seems to have become a unipolar era.[31] Inevitably this causes concern by others. Latent resentments develop over "American power and American willfulness." History shows that inevitably weaker powers will try to create counterbalancing coalitions to contain the great power. And it is now quite clear that one arena in which America will confront efforts to contain its power is the United Nations, not just by the French but others as well. On Iraq, it became evident that some Security Council members saw "America as more of a threat than Iraq."[32]

Throughout the twentieth century and into the new millennium, our foreign policy has been informed by a belief in American exceptionalism.[33] As Ronald Reagan said at Westminster Hall, "Freedom is not the sole prerogative of a lucky few but the inalienable and universal right of all human beings."[34] We recognize that human rights are universal, our values are just, and America fights when required not to build an empire but to make the world safer, more secure, and more free.

The United States cannot afford to be reckless nor careless in advancing our values or protecting our vital interests. No country, not even the world's sole superpower, can afford to unnecessarily irritate or offend others. We benefit by expending effort and, when necessary, compromising to enlist others to our cause. Broadening the risks and sharing the burdens make sense. It is better not to go it alone. But when the issue is grave, the cause just and a gathering danger is great, America cannot hesitate to do that which is necessary.

As in the past, the United States will need friends and allies. America "will need forums within which such alliances can be formed and made reliable."[35] The United Nations is one such forum. We also have an interest in playing by rules that offer predictability and reassurance.[36] But we must be mindful of the ways and means by which U.N. restraints can become constraints.

We should not become so eager for United Nations collaboration that we endow the Security Council with more immediate relevance and authority than it is warranted by history and by the limitations of its membership and procedures. In the end, the United Nations cannot grant legitimacy. We should not shy away from saying this simple fact, even if it makes some uncomfortable. Legitimacy does not come from politicians sitting around the Security Council table working to advance their own nation's interests. Legitimacy comes from the justice of the cause and from the people on the ground.

Secretary of Defense Donald Rumsfeld said in the context of the war on global terrorism, "We will see revolving coalitions that will evolve and change over time depending on the activity and the circumstances of the country. The mission needs to define the coalition, and we ought not to think that a coalition should define the mission."

One approach to the U.N. Security Council when it will not endorse a necessary action is simply to ignore it.[37] During the Iraq debate, President Clinton's U.N. Ambassador Richard Holbrooke said, "Three times Clinton did what many of the Democrats are now saying Bush can't do. He did it in Bosnia in '95, in Iraq with Desert Fox. In December of '98, the U.N. was starting its meeting when they got word that the bombing had begun, and Clinton simply said, 'Well, I'm bombing under U.N. authority because Iraq's in material breach.'"[38]

I believe the United States should actively engage other countries, friends and foes, in the United Nations. We should challenge member states and the Secretariate to act in such a way to be worthy of the aspirations of the U.N. Founders, realists tempered by World War II who sought a means to forge collective security.

As Professor Ed Luck recently wrote: "The United Nations, sadly, has drifted far from its founding vision. Its Charter neither calls for a democratic council nor relegates the collective use of force to a last resort. It was a wartime document of a military alliance, not a universal peace platform."[39]

The United States should challenge the U.N. to take its Charter and its resolutions seriously. Its resolutions are not self-enforcing. Renegade regimes don't care what others think of them. Rogue states will ignore and ridicule a United Nations whose resolutions have no force behind them.[40]

The United States should challenge the United Nations to reclaim its own legitimacy.

---

1.   Kofi Annan, "When Force is Considered, There is No Substitute for Legitimacy Provided by United Nations," address to United Nations General Assembly, New York, New York, September 12, 2002.

2.   SC/RES/1441 (2002).

3.   The universal view was captured in remarks made by Secretary General Kofi Annan a few days after Resolution 1441 was passed, "It's difficult to say what Saddam thinks would be a positive outcome. The only guide I could have is *they keep saying they have no weapons of mass destruction, which nobody believes.*"

4.   "Reactions to the United States' gradual ascent to towering preeminence have been predictable: coalitions of competitors have emerged. Since the end of the Cold War, the French, the Chinese, and the Russians have sought to return the world to a more balanced system. France's former foreign minister Hubert Vedrine openly confessed this goal in 1998: 'We cannot accept... a politically unipolar world,' he said, and 'that is why we are fighting for a multipolar' one. French President Jacques Chirac has battled tirelessly to achieve this end. According to Pierce Lellouche, who was Chirac's foreign policy adviser in the early 1990s, his boss wants a multipolar world in which Europe is the counterweight to American political and military power. Explained Chirac himself, 'any community with only one dominant power is always a dangerous one and provokes reactions.'

"In recent years, Russia and China have displayed a similar preoccupation; indeed, this objective was formalized in a treaty the two countries signed in July 2001, explicitly confirming their commitment to "a multipolar world." President Valimir Putin has declared that Russia will not tolerate a unipolar system, and China's former president Jiang Zemin has said the same. Germany, although it joined the cause late, has recently become a highly visible partner in the effort to confront American hegemony. Foreign minister Joschka Fisher said in 2000 that the 'core concept of Europe after 1945 was and still is rejection of... the hegemonic ambitions of individual states.' " Michael F. Glennon, "Why the Security Council Failed," *Foreign Affairs*, May/June 2003.

5.   "France is not trying to contain Iraq. After all, it spent the 1990's at the U.N. relentlessly trying to undue containment of Iraq. France is trying to contain the U.S." Charles Krauthammer, "France's Game: French Opposition to the U.S. is not about Iraq, but about who runs the world," *Time Magazine*, March 24, 2003.

"The first and last geopolitical truth is that states pursue security by pursuing power. Legalist institutions that manage that pursuit maladroitly are ultimately swept away.

"A corollary of this principle is that, in pursuing power, states use these institutional tools that are available to them. For France, Russia and China, one of those tools is the Security Council and the veto that the charter affords them... During the Security Council debate, the French were candid about their objective. The goal was never to disarm Iraq. Instead, 'the main and constant objective for France throughout the negotiations,' according to its U.N. Ambassador, was to 'strengthen the role and authority of the Security Council' (and, he might have added, of France). France's interest lay in forcing the United States to back down, thus appearing to capitulate in the face of French diplomacy." Michael F. Glennon, *ibid*.

6.   On September 12, 2002, when President Bush first brought the Iraq issue back to the United Nations, he made clear that if the U.N. Security Council did not act to disarm Saddam Hussein that the United States would. He said, "We cannot stand by and do nothing while dangers gather. We must stand up for our security, and for the permanent rights and the hopes of mankind. By heritage and by choice, the United States of America will make that stand. And, delegates to the United Nations, you have the power to make that stand, as well." President George W. Bush, Address to the United Nations General Assembly, New York, New York, September 12, 2002. After Security Council Resolution 1441 was passed, President Bush said, "Saddam Hussein will fully disarm himself of weapons of mass destruction, and if he does not, the United States will lead a coalition to disarm him. President George W. Bush, Remarks of Signing of the National Defense Authorization Act, Washington, D.C., December 2, 2002. In his 2003 State of the Union Address, President Bush said, "The course of this nation does not depend on the decisions of others," President George W. Bush, address to the United States Congress, Washington, D.C., January 28, 2003. Later in January President Bush said, "I call upon the world to come together and insist that this dangerous man disarm. But should they choose not to continue to pressure Saddam, and should he continue to defy the world, for the sake of peace, for the sake of security, this country will lead a coalition of other willing nations and we will disarm Saddam Hussein." President George W. Bush, Remarks for Strengthened and Reformed Medicare Program, Devos Performance Hall, Grand Rapids, Michigan, January 29, 2003.

7.   Philip Gourevitch, *ibid.*

8.   J. Bryan Hehir, "The Limits of Loyalty," *Foreign Policy*, September 1, 2002.

9.   Thomas M. Frank, "The United Nations as Guarantor of International Peace and Security: Past, Present and Future," in Christian Tomuschat, ed., *The United Nations at Age Fifty: A Legal Perspective* (Kluwer Law International; Boston; 1995) p. 35.

10.   Kofi Annan, Address at the College of William and Mary, Williamsburg, Virginia, February 8, 2003.

11.   *Ibid.*

12.   See Ian Hurd, "Legitimacy, Power, and the Symbolic Life of the U.N. Security Council; United Nations," *Global Governance*, January 1, 2002. "The power of social institutions in a society is largely a function of the legitimacy of those institutions. An institution that is perceived as legitimate by an individual is treated with more respect, is endowed with a corporate existence beyond the units that make it up, and finds compliance with its rules more easily secured than in the absence of legitimacy. International organizations seek legitimacy because they have problems in each of these areas."

13.   "Our founders... knew well the terrible devastation and suffering that war brings with it, and they were determined to spare the world from experiencing such agony again. We must never lose sight of that vision. War is always a human catastrophe -- a course that should only be considered when all other possibilities have been exhausted." Kofi Annan, *ibid.*

14.   "As early as 1945, Time magazine reporting from the U.N.'s founding conference in San Francisco, concluded that the U.N. Charter is 'written for a world of power, tempered by a little reason.' " Anne-Marie Slaughter, "Misreading the Record," *Foreign Affairs*, Vol. 82, No. 3, July/August 2003.

15.   See Chapter 7 of the U.N. Charter. "The (U.N.) Charter's provisions limiting the use of force were adopted as part of a large system of collective security that the Security Council was meant to enforce." Edward C. Luck, "The End of an Illusion," *Foreign Affairs*, Vol. 82, No. 3, July/August 2003.

16.   Anne-Marie Slaughter, ibid. See also, Michael Glennon, "Why the Security Council Failed," *Foreign Affairs*, Vol. 82, No. 3, May/June 2003.

17.   Anne-Marie Slaughter, *ibid.*

18.   "Irrelevant, Illegitimate or Indispensable? The United Nations and Iraq," *The Economist*, February 22, 2003.

19.   Charles Krauthammer, "The Critics are Wrong Again," Washington Post, May 2, 2003.

20.   *The Economist, ibid.*

21.   Former Senator Jesse Helms wrote, "The United Nations... complicates matters by giving states with no interest in a particular problem an excuse to meddle without putting anything concrete on the table. Countries that have no natural interest in an issue suddenly want to get involved, and the United Nations gives them the legitimacy to do so without cash or constructive contributions. What, for example, are countries like Togo, Zaire, Panama, or Ireland, or China for that matter, prepared to contribute to

bringing about Middle East peace? They have no legitimate role in the peace process, save that which their U.N. membership (and in some cases seats on the Security Council) gives them. What the United Nations ends up doing is giving lots of countries a seat at the table who bring nothing to the table." Jesse Helms, "Saving the U.N.: A Challenge to the Next Secretary-General," *Foreign Affairs*, September/ October, 1996.

22. Clive Cook, "The U.N. Can Serve the Greater Good, or Undermine It," *The National Journal*, Vol. 35, No. 12, March 22, 2003.

23. "The rupture in the Security Council... could lead to a serious, possibly fatal, breakdown in the system of collective security that was fashioned in the waning days of World War II, a system that finally seemed to be reaching its potential in the years since the end of the Cold War. Whatever comes of the conflict with Iraq, the world will have lost before any fighting begins if the Security Council is ruined as a mechanism for unified international action." Editorial, "The Worst-Case Scenario Arrives," *New York Times*, March 6, 2003.

24. "[I]t was the 1991 (Gulf) War that was the historical oddity, and its aftermath must at least lead to some questioning of whether the model was either realistic or appropriate. Prior to this date, the only war approved by the U.N. was in 1950, and then by a fluke, because the Soviet Union was boycotting the Security Council when the United States gained agreement to push back North Korea's invasion of the South. The U.N. conspicuously failed to condemn Iraq's invasion of Iran in 1980, in a move of unanimous hypocrisy. This was compounded more than a decade later, in changed political circumstances, when the U.N. decided, retrospectively, that this was, after all, aggression...

"By and large, the veto-wielding powers on the Security Council protected themselves and their friends, and so with most armed conflicts little was condemned and even less was approved...

"It was a combination of the unambiguous character of Iraqi aggression against Kuwait and the unprecedented degree of harmony on the Security Council following the end of the Cold War that made possible the series of U.N. resolutions that culminated in resolution 678 of November 1990, allowing member states to use 'all necessary means' to reverse the aggression." Lawrence Freedman, "The Limits of U.N. Power in the New World Order," *The Independent* (London), April 16, 2003.

25. This information is based upon information gathered by the research department of the United States Mission to the United Nations in New York City. Looking at it with a more limited criteria, Professor Michael J. Glennon of Tufts University has determined that since the U.N. was founded there have been more than 100 interstate conflicts without UN. approval. Jonathan Chait, "The Security Council Myth. Power Strip." *New Republic*, March 31, 2003, p. 15.

26. See Robert B. Oakley and John L. Hirsch, *Somalia and Operation Restore Hope: Reflections on Peacemaking and Peacekeeping*, (United States Institute of Peace; Washington; 1995), and Jonathan Moore, ed., Hard Choices: *Moral Dilemmas in Humanitarian Intervention* (Rowman and Littlefield; Lanham, Md.; 1998).

27. "The Bosnian Serbs were entirely to blame for the massacre at Srebrenicia in July 1995. But it could take place only because of the dreadfully flawed decisions made over a number of years by members of the Security Council of the United Nations." William Shawcross, *Deliver Us From Evil: Peacekeepers, Warlords and a World of Endless Conflict* (Simon-Schuster, New York, 2000) p. 161-178, 167. Kofi Annan, then Undersecretary General of the U.N. for Peacekeeping Operations later did a report on Srebrenicia which read in part, "It is with the deepest regret and remorse that we have reviewed our own actions and decisions in the face of the assault on Srebrenicia. Through error, misjudgment and an inability to recognize the scope of the evil confronting us, we failed to do our part to help save the people of Srebrenicia from the Serb campaign of mass murder. ...The tragedy of Srebrenicia will haunt our history forever." See also, Jan Willem Honig and Norbert Both, *Srebrenicia: Record of a War Crime* (Penguin, New York, 1996).

28. "My first images of the Rwandan genocide are now situated alongside those of a U.N. so consumed by fears of its own mortality that it had little evident compassion for those on the ground. When I now think of "Rwanda," I imagine not the country but the U.N. I think of diplomats and U.N. officials hurriedly milling in and out of Security Council meetings. They are reciting their talking points and proclaiming, in the U.N. locution, that they 'remain actively seized of the matter.' And they deliver only rhetoric in the hope that rhetoric represents its own consolation." Michael Barnett, *Eyewitness To A Genocide: The United Nations and Rwanda* (Cornell University Press, Ithaca; New York; 2002) p. xii. See also, Linda Polman, *We Did Nothing: Why The Truth Doesn't Always Come Out When the U.N. Goes In*, (Viking; New York; 2003).

29. Philip Gourevitch, *ibid.*

30.   "The Europeans were taking cover by talking about having a U.N. Security Council Resolution before they acted in Kosovo - an impossibility, as they well knew, since the Russians were bound to veto it." David Halberstam, *War in a Time of Peace: Bush, Clinton and the Generals* (Scribner; New York; 2001).

31.   See Charles Krauthammer, "The Unipolar Moment Revisited," *The National Interest*, 2002/2003 Winter. See also, Charles Krauthammer, "The Unipolar Moment," *Foreign Affairs*, 1990/1991 Winter.

32.   Clive Cook *ibid.*

33.   As Henry Kissinger points out in his book *Diplomacy* in his chapter "The Hinge: Theodore Roosevelt or Woodrow Wilson," it was not Roosevelt's approach of traditional balance of power statecraft that would define U.S. foreign policy, but Wilson's belief in the tradition of American exceptionalism and the universal applicability of American values. Henry Kissinger, *Diplomacy* (Simon & Schuster; New York; 1994).

34.   Ronald Reagan, Address to the British Parliament, London, England, June 8, 1982.

35.   *The Economist*, *ibid.*

36.   Anne Marie Slaughter, *ibid.*

37.   "Consider the Gulf War, usually considered the paradigmatic U.N. operation. President George H. W. Bush admitted in a press conference beforehand that he would drive Saddam out of Kuwait even without the Security Council's permission. Lawrence Eagleburger, Bush pere's deputy secretary of state, foreshadowed the sentiments of the current Bush Administration when he declared, 'It is absolutely essential that the U.S. - collectively if possible but individually if necessary - not only put a stop to this aggression but roll it back.' And the first President Bush was perfectly willing to steamroll his fellow Security Council members." Jonathan Chait, *ibid.*

America is not alone in this view. Note that this French foreign minister Hubert Vedrine wrote in 2001, "We have to keep defending our vital interests just as before; we can say no, alone, to anything that may be unacceptable." And on February 10, 2003, German Chancellor Gerhard Schroder said, "I do not feel obliged to other governments." Michael F. Glennon, *ibid.*

38.   Philip Gourevitch, *ibid.* "After British Foreign Secretary Robin Cook complained that his lawyers told him intervention against Serbia would violate international law, Secretary of State Madeline Albright replied, 'Get new lawyers.' " Jonathan Chait, *ibid.*

39.   Edward C. Luck, "Making the World Safe for Hypocrisy," *New York Times*, March 22, 2003.

40.   Ruth Wedgwood, "Gallant Delusions," *Foreign Policy*, September 1, 2002.

THE GREAT DEBATE: IS THE U.N. RELEVANT?

Is the U.N. relevant to the United States? Yes, and it is important to us. But the U.N. is neither as important nor as central as some argue.

Last September, President Bush came before the U.N. General Assembly and reviewed the 16 U.N. Resolutions on Iraq dealing with human rights violations, the failure to return POWs, terrorism and weapons of mass destruction. In his address, President Bush also reviewed the well-known litany of Saddam Hussein's failure to satisfy the U.N. requirements in each of these areas. And he challenged the United Nations to act to reclaim its legitimacy by taking its own resolutions seriously and forcing Saddam to comply.

That same day, Secretary-General Kofi Annan said to the General Assembly, "If Iraq's defiance continues, the Security Council must face its responsibilities."

Well, Saddam Hussein did continue his defiance of U.N. resolutions and the Security Council members failed in their responsibilities. They failed to pass another U.N. Iraqi resolution. In so doing, they undercut the authority of their own resolutions. They brought into question the Security Council's legitimacy. They diminished the UN as an institution.

And as long as some Security Council members are more concerned about trying to contain United States power than enforcing U.N. resolutions, the United Nations will be diminished. As long as some Security Council members are more concerned about their commercial interests and their domestic politics than upholding U.N. resolutions, the United Nations will be eroded.

In 1999, President Clinton by-passed the U.N. and bombed Kosovo. In 2003, President Bush by-passed the U.N. and launched Operation Iraqi Freedom. In both instances, the U.N. was damaged. In both instances, irresponsible actions by some Security Council members forced the United States President to act outside the U.N. And in both instances, serious structural and procedural weaknesses in the Security Council were revealed.

Nonetheless, the U.N. is relevant and it is important. Just because the U.N. appears unable to face up to all its responsibilities does not mean it doesn't do many good and important things.

Appeared in *The Interdependent* August 29, 2003.

Its central role in humanitarian assistance in many desperate situations is the difference between life and death to countless people. Its contribution in the war against terrorism through establishing norms and curbing terrorists' financial flow is significant. Its contribution in fighting contagious disease such as SARS is notable.

And even in the security area, the United Nations makes a valuable contribution. In East Timor, Afghanistan, Ethiopia/Eritrea and Sierra Leone the U.N. is playing a vital role in peacekeeping, reconstruction and reconciliation. In many local conflicts that threaten regional stability the U.N. is proving its valuable role every day.

THE FUTURE OF INTERNATIONAL REGIMES AND INSTITUTIONS: IS THE U.N. STILL VITAL?

I want to thank the McCormick Tribune Foundation and the Heritage Foundation for organizing and sponsoring this conference on the "Viability of International Regimes and Institutions". I have found the panel presentations to be very interesting and the discussions stimulating. And I want to thank Professor Paul Kennedy[1] for leading off this panel with his presentation.

My premise is simple. The United Nations is important and it often plays a valuable role. But it is less central and less important than many of its friends and supporters believe.

I've been fortunate to go in and out of government a number of times. Three of them have involved the United Nations. I was Ambassador to the U.N. offices in Vienna where nine Specialized Agencies are headquartered, most notably the International Atomic Energy Agency. The IAEA is very professional, generally non-political, fairly efficient and effective. Later I served as Assistant Secretary of State for International Organization Affairs. Among other things, in that post I had to deal with the bloated U.N. budget and reform issues. And most recently as U.S. Ambassador to the United Nations for Special Political Affairs. Among my assignments in the Security Council was working on the issue of Iraq with the French, Russians and Germans. So I've seen the U.N. up close and personal: The good (with the IAEA), the bad (with the U.N. budget) and the ugly (with France on Iraq).

I agree with Assistant Secretary of State Kim Holmes'[2] presentation yesterday that the U.N. Security Council reflects the real world: the divisions, disparities and disputes. But the Security Council has an overlay of that institution's unique structural and procedural weaknesses that create various distortions. Sometimes those distortions contribute to irresponsible behavior and/or gridlock which weaken the institution, diminish it.

A Chinese diplomat once said to me that the permanent five members of the Security Council with their veto powers are composed of the world's sole superpower, the world's major emerging power (since, of course, the Chinese see the 20th century as an historical aberration and their re-emergence as the world's other great power as inevitable), and three collapsed powers. Of course, that characterization is too harsh, but there is some truth to it. The Permanent Five are an historic anachronism.

Remarks at Conference on the Viability of International Organizations and Regimes, Cantigny Conference Series, Wheaton, Illinois, November 7, 2003.

Established in 1945, the five were the victors of World War II and generally seen as the five great powers at that moment in history.[3] But today no one would suggested that the United Kingdom, France and Russia are among the five greatest powers in the world: not by population, by military might or economic reach. Russia's economy is about the size of Belgium and they don't even make good chocolate.

Those countries enjoy a special status as permanent members of the Security Council not justified by their position and power in the real world. As permanent members of the Security Council, they enjoy the power of the veto that commands attention and respect. It is power that is vastly disproportionate to their more modest position in the real world. Understandably they hold their privileges and prerogatives in the Security Council most preciously. If anything, they seek to enhance the power of their special status by building up the jurisdiction, authority and importance of the Security Council. Therefore, France and Russia argue that only the U.N. Security Council can grant "legitimacy" to the use of force. Of course, from their perspective, that would be a very good thing. For while their military capabilities are marginal, if only the Security Council can sanction the "legitimate" use of force, then "a priori" Paris and Moscow would have veto power over the legitimate use of force anywhere in the world at any time. While a good thing for Paris and Moscow, that position is a bit absurd. Nonetheless, their efforts to enhance the prerogatives of the Security Council and to enshrine the institution with even greater power and importance, even as their own wanes, is a dominate dynamic within the U.N. Security Council. Often it is the dominate dynamic.

Today there is a great disparity of power in the real world. What Charles Krauthammer initially labeled the unipolar moment[4] has become the unipolar era. There is only one global superpower. The United States is the world's hyper power, the hegemon. In military might, economic power and cultural reach the United States is unchallenged. Never in history has any country so dominated the world. Far behind are some major powers, smaller powers and LDCs.[5] And within the U.N. Security Council some countries, including some of the permanent five member states, are conflicted. On the one hand they want to maintain and increase the role, influence and power of the Council and on the other, they want to use the Council to restrain (or contain) U.S. power.

On Iraq, part of the division in the Security Council was due to a different assessment of the danger posed by Saddam Hussein's regime. Reasonable people could disagree on how great a threat was posed by Saddam's WMD programs. After all, while Saddam had used his weapons of mass destruction, their use had been against a neighbor, Iran, and a rebellious ethnic group inside Iraq, the Kurds in the north. Would they be used against a target beyond the Middle East? And while the fact of Saddam's WMD programs was well documented, one might read the intelligence differently on how advanced portions of it were such as work on nuclear weapons or delivery systems such as ballistic missiles.

Apparently France had not judged the threat from Saddam to be great since over the years repeatedly and consistently France did not support tougher U.N. Security Council action on Iraq. In 1995, when there was an effort to pass a resolution finding Saddam Hussein in material breach, France opposed it. In 1996, when there was a proposed resolution condemning Saddam Hussein for his genocide of Iraqi Kurds, France opposed it. In 1997, when there was an effort to block travel by Saddam's intelligence and military officials, France opposed it. In 1998, France announced that Iraq was free of all weapons of mass destruction, something that no one believed. And in 1999, France opposed the creation of new, more effective, WMD inspection regime. While undoubtedly France's substantial commercial interests with Saddam Hussein's regime were not irrelevant to this pattern of inaction, also Paris must have viewed the threat posed by Iraq to be less than that which required a robust response.

And one suspects that an element in the different views of Saddam's threat was based on the different power of various Security Council members. As Robert Kagan has written: "Strong powers naturally view the world differently than weaker powers. They measure risks and threats differently, they define security differently, and they have different levels of tolerance for insecurity. Those with great military power are more likely to consider force a useful tool of international relations than those who have less military power... One British critic of America's propensity to military action recalls the old saying 'When you have a hammer, all problems start to look like nails.' This is true. But nations without great military power face the opposite danger: When you don't have a hammer, you don't want anything to look like a nail."[6]

Another part of the division in the Security Council was that some members, including some permanent members, were unsure which posed a "greater danger" - the exercise of United States unilateral power or Saddam's brutal regime. To many of us, this was incredulous and disturbing, but unquestionably it was an unspoken specter that hovered over our Security Council deliberations.

And I believe that the United Nations Security Council's failure to pass an 18th resolution on Iraq weakened the U.N. The institution was diminished.

From 1991 through 2001 there had been 16 U.N. Security Council resolutions on Iraq. They dealt with the Iraq regime's persistent and well documented brutal abuse of human rights, its failure to return POWs or provide information about them after the liberation of Kuwait, cooperation with terrorists and WMD programs. On September 12, 2001, President Bush went before the U.N. General Assembly and challenged its members to take their own resolutions seriously and take action to enforce them.[7]

Eight weeks of incredibly intense negotiations followed. They were painstaking deliberations. Every idea was thoroughly discussed. Every sentence was examined. Every word was carefully calibrated. On November 8th when the Security Council unanimously adopted resolution 1441[8] its language and its intent were well understood by one and all. It clearly states that Saddam Hussein was in "material breach" of the prior U.N. Security Council resolutions. It does not say that the Iraqi regime has to make some progress to come into partial compliance. An effort is not sufficient. Resolution 1441 clearly, directly states that Saddam must proactively cooperate and come into full compliance. And Resolution 1441 does not say that such full compliance should be achieved someday. It must be immediately. That is repeated time and again in resolution 1441: full compliance must be immediate. And the resolution does not say that if Saddam Hussein fails to come into full compliance immediately that then we will see. No. The resolution says that if Saddam continues in material breach, that there will be "serious consequences". And "serious consequences" was well understood by all fifteen members of the Security Council and by Baghdad to mean the use of force. This was clear. It was crystal clear.

Furthermore, when the Security Council began deliberations over a possible 18th resolution on Iraq, no one believed, and no one ever said, that Saddam Hussein was proactively cooperating with U.N. Inspectors. No one. And no one believed and no one ever said that Saddam was in full compliance with U.N. resolutions. No one. No one challenged the basic facts. Saddam was not proactively cooperating with U.N. inspectors and Saddam was not in full compliance with 17 U.N. Security Council resolutions. Nonetheless, the Security Council was unable to act. French President Jacque Chirac issued a unilateral, pre-emptive veto threat. Whatever any 18th Iraq resolution might say, mighty France would veto it. There would be no 18th resolution.

Confronted by the incapacity of the Council to act, just as the Clinton Administration by-passed the United Nations Security Council on Kosovo and began a war, so the Bush Administration by-passed the United Nations Security Council and began combat with Operation Iraqi Freedom.

Canadian Ambassador Paul Heinbekker once said to me that Kosovo taught the Russians that they do not have a veto on things that are of great interest to Washington, and he said that was a good thing. Well, Iraq, in a sense, should have made clear to France that they do not have a veto either.

By failing to act, the Security Council demonstrated that its members do not take their own resolutions seriously. The United States, the United Kingdom and other members of the coalition of the willing were forced to go outside the U.N. Security Council to enforce U.N. resolutions. If the Security Council members do not take their own resolutions seriously, who will? The legitimacy of the Council is undercut by such cavalier disregard of its own resolutions. The United Nations was diminished.

So what does that say about U.N. reform? I believe reform is desirable. And reform is possible on the margins to improve management and budget processes.

The Brahimi Report was a valuable contribution to better U.N. peacekeeping operations.[9] Some of its recommendations have been enacted with respect to forward deployment of equipment and logistics. And these are good things. But the reforms are not profound. They are not revolutionary. And we still have troop contributor countries that make money by contributing their soldiers to U.N. peacekeeping operations and therefore who continue to resist draw downs of U.N. peacekeepers in East Timor and Sierra Leone notwithstanding facts on the ground that should compel such reductions.[10] It still is a constant struggle in the Security Council to craft clear and realistic missions for peacekeeping operations with practical work programs, and to hold missions accountable for their performance.

ECOSOC[11] is too big and unmanageable. And the General Assembly has been marginalized. Increasingly it is not viewed as a serious forum where substantive issues are dealt with in a meaningful manner. The agenda is too big. With the end of the Cold War, the non-aligned movement is no longer able to use the General Assembly as a venue to play off the East and West. It is too politicized on issues like Israel. The various geographic groupings compound the difficulties. The

General Assembly's growing irrelevance has prompted a small group of member states led by Singapore Ambassador Kishorc Mahtubani and Australian Ambassador John Darth to begin a small informal working group of influential member states to consider General Assembly reforms. This is a positive initiative that hopefully will bear fruit.[12] However, on the big issues like U.N. Security Council reform I am not optimistic. I fear, however well intentioned or well conceived, meaningful reforms may prove impossible.

Let me hasten to add that I believe the U.N. does a lot of good. I have seen the value of the United Nations on the ground.

In Mostar, Bosnia-Herzegovina, scene of some of the worst ethnic fighting in that bloody war, I've visited the police headquarters and met with Serb and Bosnian policemen, trained and integrated by the United Nations. They are working together to bring order to their devastated town, to heal ethnic divisions and to repair the torn social fabric.

Visiting an Eritrean refugee camp I've seen a tent city where thousands of innocent displaced people, victims of a senseless war, subsist thanks to United Nations relief efforts as they await the opportunity to return home.

In El Salvador, Jordan and the Democratic Republic of the Congo, I've seen small children inoculated against disease in U.N. health clinics.

In the Siem Reap province of Cambodia, I've observed people who suffered the brutality, pain and anguish of Pol Pot and his reign of terror going to the polls to vote, thanks to the United Nations.

In Burundi, over 200,000 people have been killed and many more raped and mutilated in vicious ethnic fighting. In Bujumbura, I met with President Buyoya to discuss the importance of military reform to achieve stability in that ravaged land. And, in part, thanks to the United Nations, those reforms have begun: Pierre Buyoya, a Tutsi, peacefully turned the Presidency over to Domitien Ndadyizeye, a Hutu, and the country is on track for scheduled elections.

In Mitrovica, Kosovo, I met with a doctor who talked about the importance of the presence of the United Nations in helping her family and others rebuild after genocidal war. "The Balkans have created more history than they can digest."[13] Through helping refugees return, training police and rebuilding schools, the United Nations is giving that doctor's family and others a chance to live normal, productive lives.

In Ethiopia, I visited a U.N. clinic helping equip children with prosthetics for lost limbs due to exploded ordnances. Then I visited a land mine field where United Nations personnel worked to remove the explosives before they could claim more victims.

I've visited with Xanana Gusmao, the former freedom fighter who had been jailed for many years and then was elected the first President of East Timor, the world's newest independent state. He shared with me stories of the U.N.'s invaluable role in monitoring East Timor's referendum for independence, in building schools and municipal buildings, in training teachers and police, and in coordinating donor community assistance for his desperately poor nation.

In Freetown, Sierra Leone, the casualties of war are evident on almost every corner in people who are missing limbs, many of whom also have lost loved ones to their brutal war. The scars of that conflict are deep. The justified bitterness runs strong. Yet in talking to leaders of civil society in Freetown, I heard hope for transitional justice and reconciliation due to the United Nation's Special Court which has indicted and is prosecuting those who committed the worst crimes against humanity during the civil war. Some of the leaders from both the winning and losing sides have been indicted. There will be no impunity. And rising from the ashes of war, these Sierra Leoneans hope to mend their society and move forward.

I've met with Afghanistan President Hamid Karzai and heard him talk about the successful Loya Jirga that selected him and the pride he feels that this United Nations-supported process included women for the first time in his nation's history. He went on to express profound gratitude for the U.N. coordination of reconstruction efforts that have rebuilt hundreds of schools which now welcome girls as students, that have built health clinics throughout Afghanistan, that are helping to train police, and that are helping to draft Afghanistan's first democratic constitution.

And I've been to Israel and Syria and talked to Israelis and Syrians who have told me about the importance of the United Nations Interim Force in Lebanon (UNIFIL) in maintaining the "Blue Line" and helping to prevent the occasional armed clashes from spiraling out of control.

I've also seen the hope people vest in the United Nations to help them improve their circumstances. In Kissangani, in the eastern Congo, I listened to a woman in tears asking the U.N. to help end the cycle of violence that had devastated her family and killed over 3 million people. In Pristina, Kosovo, a Serb councilwoman told me about the desperate need for the U.N. to provide security for her minority community. In Rwanda, I heard a Tutsi who had lost his family in the 1994 genocide beg for justice from the United Nations. And in Sukhumi, Abkhazia, a decorated war veteran told me about the desperation of her children and others trying to find work in an anemic post-conflict economy, and asked the U.N. to help.

The United Nations does help make the world a better place. I know this. I have witnessed it in many corners of the globe. And these good works warrant support.

In Ethiopia/Eritica the U.N. is engaged in a traditional peacekeeping operation. It's interpositional deployment has been critical to build confidence and allow progress toward resolving that border dispute. In Afghanistan the U.N.'s light footprint has helped that country recover from the brutality of the Taliban regime, nurtured the Loya Jorga and helped draft a new constitution. In Bosnia and Kosovo the U.N.'s heavy foot print has contributed to reconstruction and reconciliation. In Sierra Leone a complex U.N. Peacekeeping operation seems to have gotten it right. But in the Democratic Republic of the Congo it is too early to know whether the U.N. will contribute to a durable peace in that country where conflict already has claimed 3-1/2 million lives.

So the list of where the United Nations has made and is making the world a better place is long. But given the gridlock over Kosovo and the recent inability of the Security Council members to meet their responsibilities on Iraq, should the United States go back to the Council on issues of national security that matter to us? Is the U.N. still vital on security issues?

My experience is that when the United States government is willing to lead that we usually can get our way in the U.N. Security Council. It also is my judgment that the structural and procedural weaknesses of the Council won't be reformed. And it is our experience, including most recently on Iraq, that some permanent members will abuse their veto power even at the expense of the very institution that enhances their power.

I believe the United States should engage the U.N. Security Council. We should work that forum. We should show some grace in the day to day work of the Security Council when we do not prevail. However, we should realize that on issues that we believe are in our vital interests that we will not allow the Security Council to restrain us.[14]

It generally is better for the United States not to go it alone. It generally is better to gather support and allies to advance our interests and share our burdens. And the U.N. is an international institution of importance and value; more to others than to the United States. But the U.N. still is a venue that can be used to gain broader support for our cause.

For the United States, the United Nations is not essential. But it can be useful.

1.　J. Richardson Dilworth, Professor of History and Director of International Security Studies, Yale University.

2.　Assistant Secretary for International Organization Affairs..

3.　Initially the Chinese seat was held by nationalist China. And from 1948 to 1971, even after the nationalists were driven into exile on Taiwan and the communists came to power in Beijing, the nationalizes continued to hold the "China" seat in the Security Council. Also, defeated France was not a major power in 1945. But, reportedly Winston Churchill said that France should get a permanent U.N. Security Council seat because it would help them psychologically. In the spring of 2003 after France threatened to veto an 18th resolution on Iraq, columnist George Will suggested that 58 years of psychotherapy was enough and France should be relieved of their permanent seat on the Security Council.

4.　Charles Krauthammer, "The Unipolar Moment", *Foreign Affairs*, 1990/1991 Winter. See also Charles Krauthammer, "The Unipolar Moment Revisited", *The National Interest*, 2002/2003 Winter.

5.　Less Developed Countries

6.　Robert Kagan, *Of Paradise and Power: America and Europe in the New World Order* (New York; Alfred A. Knopf, 2003) pp. 27-28. "More and more over the past decade, the United States and its European allies have had rather substantial disagreements over what constitute intolerable threats to international security and the world order, as the case of Iraq has abundantly shown. And those disagreements reflect, above all, the disparity of power." *Ibid.*, p. 29.

7.　President George W. Bush, Address to the United Nationals General Assembly, September 12, 2002.

8.　SC/RES/1441 (2002).

9.　United Nations, *Report of the Panel on United Nations Peace Operations*.

10.　See, Alix M. Freedman, "Wealthy Countries in Effect Pay Poor Ones to Handle U.N. Missions: The Peacekeeping Allowance Can Add Up to Real Money for Developing Nations," *Wall Street Journal*, October 1, 2003. See also, Robert Block and Alix M. Freedman, "Mission Improbable: U.N. Peacekeeping Is a Troubling Art, Congo Mess Shows", *Wall Street Journal*, October 1, 2003. While at the U.N. Security Council I saw this phenomenon first hand.

11.　The United Nations Economic and Social Council.

12.　There are many interesting ideas about U.N. reform. For one interesting set see Nile Gardner and Baker Spring, "Reform the United Nations", *The Heritage Foundation Backgrounder*, No. 1700, October 27, 2003.

13.　A remark by Bulgarian Ambassador and Permanent Representative to the United Nations Stefan Tavrov during a U.N. Security Council Mission to Kosovo in December, 2002.

14.　Note, Charter of the United Nations, Article 51, "Nothing in the present Charter shall impair the inherent right of individual or collective self-defense…"

How the U.S., as the World's Sole Superpower, Should Deal with Multilateral Organizations and International Regimes

Thank you Professor Ken Lieberthal for that kind introduction. It's a real pleasure for me to be in Ann Arbor this evening to share some observations with you.

The United States is the world's sole superpower. And to the surprise of many academics and other commentators at the end of the Cold War, no one has yet emerged to challenge U.S. supremacy. Japan's economic troubles persist. European spending on military has been reduced significantly even as its economic integration has advanced. And while China continues to make impressive economic gains and some steady military modernization, it does not yet challenge U.S. economic strength, military might or cultural reach.

What Charles Krauthammer labeled America's "unipolar moment" 12 years ago has turned out to be a "unipolar era." And barring some unforeseen major development or catastrophic event, the United States will continue to be the world's sole superpower for many years to come.

This power disparity profoundly impacts international relations today. More than history, sentimentality, values, economic interests, or even geography, the United States supremacy shapes the relations between the states.

Of course, all the considerations that I have mentioned play a role, often an important role in international relations -- as they always have. But in most capitals most of the time, this power disparity is the prism through which foreign policy is developed and actions taken.

As Singapore's UN Ambassador Kishore Mahtubani once said to me, "Rich, you know, in every country of the world, their first concern is their relationship with the United States."

Later Canadian Ambassador Paul Heiniker amended that formulation. He said to me that "(e)very capital's first priority is their relationship to Washington but two. Because of geography and history, the first interest in Paris and Berlin is their relation with one another and then with Washington." This dynamic certainly played out in the UN Security Council during the deliberations on possible 18th resolution on Iraq.

Because of America's size and its power, because of United States pre-eminence in military might, economic strength and cultural reach; America is respected, it is feared, and it is resented.

Remarks at The University of Michigan, Economic Dinner Group, Ann Arbor, Michigan, November 17, 2003.

Understandably, other countries are concerned by the behemoth. And as has been the case throughout history, the less strong and the weak want to restrain the mighty. They do not want to become casualties (directly or indirectly) of what they fear might be the whims or the caprice of the great power.

Similarly in the late 18th century and the 19th century the small and relatively weak United States wanted broadly accepted rules of the sea to constrain the great powers of that time: the United Kingdom and France. Later in the 19th century the rest of Europe sought to constrain the power and actions of Bismark's Austro-Hungarian empire. And the abuse of power in Europe of a strong Germany and the 2 great world wars of the 20th century deepened this inclination and strengthened this desire.

Today, the United States believes its power is well earned, its principles transcendent, and it motives both good and sound. And our history generally supports that perspective. Therefore, we chaff under any effort to harness our exercise of power. We resent it. Confident in the values and performance of "the American experiment," deeply believing in the profound benefits of "American Exceptionalism" for Americans and for others. Confident of our leadership, the United States does not go quietly into a new world of international institutions, regimes, laws and regulations that entangle us, that limit our prerogatives, that constrain our freedom of action, that compromise our power.

Having earned our predominance in the world, having become the world's sole superpower, there is a natural inclination to want to exercise our power to protect our interests, advance our goals, project our values, benefit our people and enhance our position unrestrained by a web of Lilliputian constraints.

Why should American let others tell us what we can or cannot do with our power? Why should America let others dictate the rules of the road? Why should America be dependent on the vote of Guinea, Cameroon or Mauritius in the United Nations Security Council to determine whether the United States can go to war to protect our national security? Why should America accept the legitimacy of and respect the resolutions passed by the UN Human Rights Commission when Libya is the chair and among its members are Cuba and Syria? why should America work with the UN Counterterrorism Committee when Syria is among its members? Why should the U.S. government grant its impremonter of acceptance and its authority to the UN General Assembly which spends more time and effort seeking to delegitimizing Israel than any other global issue? Why should America entrust its security to NATO when last February France, Germany and Belgium seemed more intent in trying to limit U.S. power than help Turkey, a member state, prepare defense plans for an approaching war with Iraq? And why should the United States remain the largest financial contributor to so many international organizations and international bureaucracies that are bloated, wasteful and often seem more intent on constraining the U.S. than advancing freedom, private enterprise or a more secure world? In other words, having achieved its position of pre-eminence in the world, why should America restrain its prerogatives and comprise its sovereignty?

The answer, of course, is that some international organizations and some international regimes serve U.S. interests. Some multilateral organizations benefit us far more than the cost they impose upon us whether financial or by prescribed constraints.

For example, there are a host of multilateral organizations with specific technical missions that create and maintain international regimes that are essential to the daily activities and commerce of the United States.

The *International Civil Aviation Organization (ICAO)* facilitates the safety, regularity, and efficiency of civil air transport and studies the problems of international standards and regulation for civil aviation.

The *International Telecommunication Union (ITU)* was created to maintain and extend international cooperation for the improvement and rational use of telecommunication facilities in order to increase their usefulness and to make them generally available to the public. The ITU harmonizes the actions of nations in telecommunications.

The *World Meteorological Organization (WMO)* helped establish networks of stations and centers to provide meteorological services and observations. WMO maintains systems for the rapid exchange of meteorological and related information and promotes standardization of meteorological observation and ensures the uniform publication of information and statistics.

The *International Maritime Organization (IMO)* facilitates cooperation and exchange of information among governments on technical matters affecting shipping, and works to estimate high standards of maritime safety.

The *World Intellectual Property Organization (WIPO)* promotes the protection of intellectual property throughout the world through cooperation among states. WIPO administers the various "union", each founded on a multilateral treaty and dealing with different aspects of intellectual property.

The *International Atomic Energy Agency (IAEA)* assists developing countries with atomic energy technology. But, far more important to the United States, the IAEA administers an inspection regime to insure that nuclear technology is not diverted to further a military purpose.

The *World Health Organization (WHO)* fights against epidemics and other infectious diseases. for example, WHO played a large role in containing the SARs crisis earlier this year. WHO disseminates information on the effect on health of environmental pollutants. And WHO sets global standards for antibiotics, vaccines, and so on.

These are examples of multilateral organizations and international regimes that are technical in purpose and practice.

While there are competing interests among the member states to some of these multilateral organizations, their deliberations are generally non-political and businesslike. They facilitate global commerce and cooperation. Their work greatly benefits the United States.

Then there are multilateral organizations with humanitarian missions through which the United States can leverage its own aid assistance and, sometimes, can advance requirements upon the recipient that will be better received from an international organization than directly from the world's sole superpower.

For example the Office of the *United Nations High Commissioners for Refugees (UNHCR)* which provides relief to refugees and internally displaced persons. *UNHCR* provides refugees with international protection and seeks permanent solutions for the problems of refugees. I have visited refugee camps in Ethiopia, Eritrea, Burundi, the Democratic Republic of the Congo, Sierra Leone, Syria and elsewhere. The work of the UNHCR on the ground is vital. Often it is the difference between life and death to the innocent victims of war or famine.

The *World Food Program (WFP)* is another U.N. Specialized Agency. It is the world's largest humanitarian agency providing food assistance in Afghanistan, Iraq, Ethiopia, southern African countries and elsewhere.

Of course, there also are *the Bretton Woods organizations*: the *World Bank* and the *International Monetary Fund*. The original purpose of the *IMF* was to promote international monetary cooperation and the expansion of international trade, to promote exchange stability, to maintain orderly exchange arrangements, to avoid competitive exchange depreciations, etc. But, over time the *IMF* and the *World Bank* have been known for their efforts to assist reconstruction and development. In some circles their ways and means are controversial. Both have political and academic critics in the United States. But due to their governing structure which includes a weighted vote, the United States voice is heard and usually its views can prevail.

GATT, and now the World Trade Organization (WTO), have been extremely important and valuable multinational organizations for the United States and the global economy. They have been in the vanguard as multilateral organizations to liberalize trade, open markets and spur economic growth. This, of course, has benefited American business and American consumers enormously. Interestingly, WTO is not only forcing economic reforms in China and elsewhere; but it is helping drive political reforms. These advances will help China and other countries as well -- including the United States. And while WTO does impose constraints on the United States as demonstrated today on U.S. steel tariffs, as an apostle of free trade, even here the WTO is saving us from ourselves and the pressures of U.S. domestic politics.

Now let me turn to areas that are more contentious, where international constraints are more costly, where multilateral organizations play a decidedly secondary role. Let me turn to areas of security.

I believe formal arms control and non-proliferation agreements are fundamentally important. They can and should be improved. But these treaties and international regimes, important as they are, are insufficient by themselves, to contain the growing threat of weapons of mass destruction and the means of delivering them in the hands of rogue states and terrorists.

They are important because they establish a global norm against state possession of weapons of mass destruction (WMD), and form the political and legal rationale for action against violators.

Signatories agree not only that they will not acquire the proscribed weapons themselves, (except, in the case of the NPT, for the five nuclear weapons states), but also that they will not assist others to acquire them. So, for example, it is a violation of the NPT if, say Russia helps Iran acquire nuclear weapons.

In the case of the NPT and the Chemical Weapons Convention, signatories also must agree to declaration and inspection regimes that increase the likelihood that cheaters will be caught.

There are several arguments against these agreements, these international regimes. One is that they lull us into a false sense of security. But if the regimes do anything at all to inhibit WMD, this really comes down to an argument that we should let the threat get worse so we'll be sufficiently alarmed -- hardly a sensible approach.

Another argument is that only the good guys join, so we build up international bureaucracies that mainly police countries that have no intention of acquiring WMD. Actually, under international pressure, countries of concern to us do tend to join -- Iraq, Iran, Libya, North Korea all did. Furthermore, countries change over time so today's good guys could be tomorrow's threats. Better to have them constrained ahead of time.

Moreover, the membership of countries that aren't tempted to acquire WMD is a good thing because it fortifies the global consensus against these weapons. Now all but three countries (Pakistan, India and Israel) are members -- four, if you recognize North Korea's withdrawal earlier this year. And, in fact, the NPT has become a vehicle for a number of countries of concern (so-called "in between" countries) to become non-nuclear: among them South Africa, Brazil, Argentina, Ukraine, Kazakhstan, Belarus, Romania, Algeria, Taiwan and South Korea.

The next concern is that even if the bad guys are members, they can cheat without being caught. Detecting violations is difficult, even more so in the case of biological and chemical weapons, which can be produced in small spaces or concealed in legitimate facilities; and give off fewer tell-tale signatures than nuclear material. The IAEA's enhanced safeguards, allowing environmental samplings and inspections away from declared sites, will be an improvement.

If difficulty in detecting violations were a determinate argument for abandoning the law, much of our domestic criminal code would disappear.

The alternative of not having international non-proliferation regimes is worse than having to work hard and spend money on enforcement and not always succeeding. Fighting proliferation is hard. Without global standards and international non-proliferation regimes it would be harder.

This underscores that WMD non-proliferation regimes, on their own, are not enough. We need diplomacy and collective action that goes beyond the strict terms of non-proliferation regimes. Global agreements against WMD are an important and useful means of notifying countries contemplating such weapons that they may get caught, that they may be politically isolated, and that they could be subject to costly international sanctions, and tougher additional sanctions or worse from individual countries or groups. These international regimes make WMD programs harder to conceal, and create consequences fore those who cheat.

None of that creates a guarantee. But it complicates the planning of our adversaries.

In the end non-proliferation requires a network of activities to stop the spread of WMD: global agreements against WMD, inspections, bilateral and multilateral export controls, effective intelligence, forceful diplomacy, sanctions, denial of technology, deterrence, active defenses, interdiction, and, where warranted as a last resort, pre-emption.

That is a large anti-proliferation tool kit. Given the unacceptable consequences of failure, all these tools should be used. And, WMD agreements, international non-proliferation regimes are an important tool.

Finally, let me turn briefly to the UN Security Council.

The UN Security Council is an interesting multilateral arena. Like others it reflects the real world, more or less. But its peculiar structure and procedures create its own distortions. The five permanent members, who enjoy "veto" power, were selected 58 years ago when the world was a very different place. Looking at the 5 permanent security council members today, no one would argue these five are the world's biggest powers militarily, economically nor in cultural reach. Understandably those whose status and power is much greater in the Security Council than in the real world seek to enhance the Council's power and authority and they hold their P-5 prerogatives most preciously. This is neither a requirement for the United States nor is it necessarily desirable.

On Iraq, the Bush administration saw, as the Clinton administration did on Kosovo in 1999, that the United States cannot let the UN Security Council stop the U.S. from acting to protect its vital interests. In a sense, Kosovo taught the Russians that they do not have a veto over the United States. Similarly, Iraq demonstrated to the French that neither do they.

In the end, the UN Security Council's failure to enforce 17 of its own resolutions on Iraq has diminished the UN Security Council and harmed its legitimacy. The Security Council will survive and it will play a useful role. but it is not, nor should it be, the sole grantor of legitimacy for military force nor a determinative prohibition on the world's sole superpower's use of power.

However, an area where the United Nations Security Council is very valuable to the United States is in helping address the many smaller conflicts where our vital interests are not at stake such as Ethiopia/Eritrea, East Timor, Sierra Leone, Liberia, and the Democratic Republic of the Congo, where 3 ½ million people have died in the past 4 years due to armed conflict and its consequences.

These wars do not threaten United States vital interests. However, they can spread to create regional instability such as in the Balkans, the Mano River region of West Africa and the Central African Great Lakes region. Also, they can result in failed states that can become breeding grounds and safe havens for terrorists. And tragically, these armed conflicts can create terrible humanitarian crisis that morally compel a response to help those innocent victims unable to help themselves.

In these circumstances the collective actions of the United Nations can play a vital role and warrant active and sustained United States support. They deal with real problems. They share the burden. And they allow the United States, as the world's sole superpower, to save its military for those situations of high intensity warfare where we have unique capacity.

The UN Security Council can be a useful multilateral organization for the United States. It deserves our active engagement. It can be an effective instrument of our collective security.

We should not, and can not, let its failure to act, such as in Iraq and Kosovo, limit us from protecting our vital interests. The UN Security Council is not the sole grantor of legitimacy for armed conflict. Legitimacy comes from the values we hold, the facts on the ground and from the people, not from politicians and international bureaucrats around the Security Council table.

So, in conclusion, let me say that the United States gains from working with and through multilateral organizations and international regimes. Even today, as the world's sole superpower, we benefit from collective action whenever possible. We should actively engage in these multilateral fora. We must take into account others views and be willing to compromise. Our view will not always prevail. And we should show grace and humility at all times.

There will be extraordinary times when our vital interests demand action and we must act outside these multilateral organizations. The United States has the power and the resolve to do so when we must. But to the extent possible we should work earnestly and diligently to bring others with us. For us it is not an absolute requirement to work with others, but it certainly is preferable.

Thank you.

THE MIDDLE EAST
AND THE UNITED NATIONS

I thank Congresswomen Ileana Ros-Lehtinen, Chairperson of the Subcommittee on the Middle East and Central Asia, for inviting me to testify on "The Middle East and the United Nations."

<u>The United Nations and Israel</u>

I became engaged in working in the U.N. system 22 years ago when I became U.S. Ambassador to the U.N. offices in Vienna, Austria. Among the first issues that I dealt with was Israeli credentials at the 1983 Conference of the International Atomic Energy Agency. The year before Israeli credentials for the IAEA Conference had been denied. Fortunately, due to vigorous work in Washington, Vienna and in capitals, Israeli credentials were not directly challenged at the 1983 Conference nor have they been subsequently. Some years later, as Assistant Secretary of State for International Organization Affairs I fought the pernicious U.N. resolution that equated Zionism with racism.

As Ambassador to the United Nations for Special Political Affairs in New York, I often confronted double standards in the U.N. Security Council, especially regarding Israel. I remember one meeting of the Security Council that took place right after a meeting of the Quartet. As I'd learned to expect, my Syrian colleague used the meeting to attack Israel. Also as I'd learned to expect, but what nonetheless constantly disappointed me, many other delegations attacked Israel. My British colleague joined in many of the criticisms of Israel, even expressing sentiments that directly undercut the Quartet statement about the peace process made the day before. After the meeting, when I expressed my disappointment at what he had said, British Ambassador Stuart Eldon said, "Oh Rich, this is just politics. You can't take it so seriously."

Ambassador Eldon was right. For him and most of the Security Council members, posturing on the Middle East and attacking Israel is "just politics." It is the accepted norm within the United Nations. It is just what one does on the Middle East issue. When I would say to the U.N. Security Council that any reference to excessive Israeli force in the West Bank must be balanced by a condemnation of the terrorist attacks by Hamas, I made my colleagues uncomfortable. However great the merits of my demand, it was socially and politically unacceptable. Invariably, the consequence of my demand was that, rather than mention the Arab terrorist activities, the Security Council then issued no press statement whatsoever.

Testimony to the Middle East and Central Asia Subcommittee Committee on International Relations, U.S. House of Representatives, Washington, D.C., April 20, 2005.

And just last spring, I served as Ambassador and United States Representative to the U.N. Commission on Human Rights in Geneva, Switzerland. Last year, as in earlier years, the Commission on Human Rights was exploited by some in their relentless campaign to delegitimize Israel, the oldest democracy in the Middle East. While all other country specific concerns are lumped together under UNCHR agenda item 9, Israel is singled out with its own, separate agenda item. The excessive, invective rhetoric assaulting Israel is numbing. The one-sided resolutions are scandalous. On human rights, no nation is blameless. All countries should be vigilant to improve their own human rights records. But the singling out of Israel in this manner reveals more about the double standards and abuse within the U.N. system than it does about alleged human rights failures by the State of Israel.

I believe that over the years the United Nations has marginalized itself in many ways on the Israeli/Palestinian issue. The U.N. lacks moral authority on this matter. To the extent member states believe their rhetoric and actions on the Middle East in the U.N. are "just politics" that should not be taken seriously, is the extent to which the U.N. itself cannot be taken seriously.

Unfortunately, the bias against Israel in the United Nations is significant.

The Arab bloc within the Non-Aligned Movement and the G-77 has effectively used the General Assembly as a forum for isolating Israel. With their numbers, they have easily passed harsh anti-Israel resolutions in the General Assembly. I already have mentioned the most notorious, U.N. General Assembly Resolution 3379 adopted in 1975 equating Zionism with Racism. It was finally rescinded in 1991 following the Madrid Conference.

Over the past several years an average of 18 resolutions critical of Israel have been adopted by the General Assembly each year. The Arab group and the Non-Aligned Movement often have challenged the credentials of the Israeli delegation at the beginning of General Assembly sessions. The most recent challenge was in May 2002 prior to the U.N. General Assembly Session on Children. No other member state faces such routine attacks.

Of the ten Emergency Special Sessions held by the General Assembly, six have been on the Middle East, four of which have been critical of Israel. Meetings of the tenth Emergency Special Session on Occupied East Jerusalem started in 1997, met most recently in 2002 and remains "suspended" to facilitate the reopening of the issue. Since June 1996, the financing of the United Nations Interim Force in Lebanon, UNIFIL, has become politicized in the Fifth Committee and Plenary as countries hostile to Israel seek to attribute responsibility on Israel for the April 18, 1996, Qana incident and demand Israel's payment for damages.

The U.N. Commission on Human Rights routinely adopts a disproportionate number of resolutions concerning Israel. Over the past three sessions, the Commission on Human Rights resolutions critical of Israel average 6-7% of the total number of resolutions adopted while many rogue states that are among the worst abusers of human rights are not criticized at all. Of all condemnations by the Commission on Human Rights, twenty-six percent refer to Israel alone.

Several divisions of the U.N. Secretariat and U.N. committees established over United State's obligations are critical of Israel. They are discriminatory and one-sided. United States efforts to eliminate them have been unsuccessful. They include the Division for Palestinian Rights of the U.N. Secretariat, the Committee to Investigate Israeli Practices in the Occupied Territories, and the Committee on the Exercise of the Inalienable Rights of the Palestinian People.

President Bush has sought to counter this U.N. bias and hostility against Israel. The Administration has sought to prevent U.N. bodies from unfairly targeting Israel. The Bush Administration has not hesitated to vote against resolutions singling Israel out for criticism. In 2002 the Bush Administration announced that the United States would veto any Security Council resolution on the Middle East that did not condemn Palestinian terror attacks and name Hamas, Islamic Jihad and the Al-Aksa Martyrs Brigade as the groups responsible for the attacks. The Bush Administration also has made clear that any U.N. Security Council resolutions must note that any Israeli withdrawal is linked to the security situation, and that both parties must be called upon to pursue a negotiated settlement.

President Bush has demonstrated leadership on the Middle East issue. He has called for reform of Palestinian governance, and some reform has happened. He has developed a Road Map to resolve the conflict that will ensure Israel's security and allow an independent Palestinian state. Working with the Quartet (the U.S., the European Union, Russia and the U.N.) and working directly with the countries in the region, President Bush will continue to provide leadership in trying to resolve this conflict.

However the United Nations, due to its long history of bias against Israel, has limits on how central a role it can play in these efforts. The U.N. moral authority and standing to contribute significantly to the resolution of this conflict has been compromised.

By distorting the United Nations agenda and using resolutions to relentlessly attack a member state, the majority of U.N. members have contradicted the U.N. Charter, defied its values, and diminished the United Nations as an institution.

Having briefly reviewed this litany of assaults on the State of Israel within the United Nations, let me emphasize that it is not exhaustive. There have been other efforts in the U.N. to delegitimize Israel. But the attacks that I have reviewed provide sufficient justification for proposed House Resolution 54. I believe it would be useful to have such an expression of the House of Representatives regarding anti-Semitism at the United Nations. The attacks on Israel are disproportional, one-sided and wrong. They are impediments to progress in resolving the Israeli/Palestinian conflict. And they bring discredit on the United Nations.

The U.N. and other matters in the Middle East

Having discussed the case of efforts within the United Nations to delegitimize Israel, let me briefly touch on a couple of other matters in the Middle East where the U.N. has played a role.

A situation in which the United Nations has been useful has been U.N. Security Council Resolution 1559, adopted on September 2, 2004, and subsequent actions supporting the full sovereignty and independence of Lebanon, free of all foreign.

The Government of Syria had imposed its political will on Lebanon, and compelled the Cabinet and Lebanese National Assembly to amend its constitution and abort the electoral process by extending the term of the Syrian-backed president of Lebanon by three years. This resolution, introduced by the United States and France with the co-sponsorship of Germany and the United Kingdom, supported the extension of control of the Government of Lebanon. This Security Council resolution also made clear that the continued presence of armed Hizballah militia elements, as well as the presence of the Syrian military and Iranian forces in Lebanon, hinders that goal. Through this Security Council resolution in the United Nations, the international community was able to express the view that it was wrong for Syria to continue to maintain its forces in Lebanon in contravention of the spirit and clear intent of the Taif Accord. And it made known its view that it would be wrong of Syria to continue to interfere in the presidential electoral process in Lebanon.

While the situation in Lebanon has not entirely sorted out, Syrian President Asaad has announced that his troops will withdraw from Lebanon and partial withdrawal has begun. Public demonstrations for an independent Lebanon are animating a political transition in Lebanon. And the international community, working through the United Nations, contributed to push for these positive developments.

Finally, let me briefly discuss Iraq. The United nations has a mixed record on dealing with Iraq.

After Saddam Hussein's illegal occupation of Kuwait, the United Nations Security Council passed a series of resolutions condemning the invasion and occupation, and demanding Iraqi withdrawal. When Saddam failed to comply with these U.N. Security Council demands, the use of force was authorized to repel the Iraqi occupying forces. And when Saddam's troops had been defeated, the U.N. Security Council imposed the most intrusive arms inspection in history on Iraq in an effort to dismantle Saddam's weapons of mass destruction. The subsequent arms inspections contributed to substantially dismantling and destroying Saddam's WMD stockpiles and capabilities. In each of these stages, the United Nations played a very useful role.

By the late 1990's, some U.N. Security Council members valued commercial opportunities more highly than continued vigorous monitoring of Iraqi arms. Further U.N. arms inspections were prevented by Saddam with little cost to him, and the United Nations Oil-For-Food program was initiated. We now are learning the extent of the troubling corruption and abuse in the U.N. administration of the Oil-For-Food program. In 2002, President Bush returned the matter of Iraqi non-compliance to U.N. resolutions to center stage. A seventeenth resolution was adopted, U.N.S.C. Resolution 1441, stating Iraq was in violation of prior U.N. resolutions, demanding immediate Iraqi pro-active compliance with the prior arms inspection resolutions, and stating a failure to immediately and fully comply with Resolution 1441 would be met with "serious consequences," which was well understood to be the use of force.

Unfortunately, when Saddam Hussein did not fully comply with U.N.S.C. Resolution 1441, the Security Council was not able to pass an 18th resolution explicitly authorizing the use of force. This demonstrated structural and procedural weaknesses in the U.N. Security Council.

Since the "Coalition of the Willing" led by the United States and the United Kingdom successfully brought down Saddam Hussein's regime, the United Nations has passed a series of resolutions dealing with the occupation, reconstruction and elections. These United Nations actions have contributed to progress in post-conflict Iraq.

So the case of Iraq has demonstrated ways and means where the United Nations has been useful in dealing with a very difficult situation in the Middle East, and instances where the U.N. performance has been disappointing. But going forward in Iraq, the United Nations can play a constructive role. And I anticipate the United States and others will work actively in the U.N. to ensure it does so.

Summary

In the Middle East, the United Nations offers promise and it has displayed disappointment. Like many large institutions, it's a mixed bag. The challenge for the United States Government is to engage the United Nations and work hard to help it realize its promise. If we fail to do so, it will disappoint and opportunities for programs will be missed.

Thank you.

CAN THE U.N. MAKE THE WORLD SAFER?

Thank you Professor Brian Hanson for that kind introduction. It is a pleasure for me to be here this evening at Northwestern University. Northwestern is a great university. I've learned to appreciate it even more during the past two years while my daughter Elisabeth has been earning her Masters in Business Administration at the Kellogg School. You should be proud to be part of the Northwestern University community.

Also, it is a pleasure for me to share this stage with The Honorable Gareth Evans. Gareth has had a distinguished career in Australia, including many years as Foreign Minister. He now serves as President of the International Crisis Group which provides valuable analysis about hot spots around the world. And, he served on the "High Level Panel on Threats, Challenges and Change" created by U.N. Secretary-General Kofi Annan to look at reforms for the U.N. system. The 101 recommendations of the High Level Panel tendered last December were constructive for their insights and for the manner in which they have stimulated greater dialogue about the U.N. and ways and means to strengthen it.

It's been my honor and privilege to represent the United States Government in various capacities in the U.N. system. The United Nations is an important organization with a noble mission. I believe it is very useful to the United States.

I have witnessed the United Nations making the world a better place. In El Salvador, Jordan and the Democratic Republic of the Congo, I've seen children inoculated against disease in United Nations' health clinics.

Visiting an Eritrearean refugee camp, I've seen a tent city where thousands of innocent displaced people, victims of a senseless war, subsist thanks to U.N. relief efforts as they await the opportunity to return to their homes.

In the Siem Reap province of Cambodia, I have observed people who suffered the brutality, pain and anguish of Pol Pot and his reign of terror going to the polls to vote, thanks to the United Nations.

In Mostar, Bosnia-Herzegovina, scene of some of the worst ethnic fighting in that bloody war, I've visited the police headquarters and met with Serb and Bosnian policeman, trained and integrated by the United Nations. They are working together to bring order to their devastated town, to heal ethnic divisions and to repair the torn social fabric.

Remarks at McCormick Tribune Forum, Northwestern University, Evanston, Illinois, April 27, 2005.

In Ethiopia, I visited a U.N. clinic helping equip children with prosthetics for lost limbs due to exploded ordinances. Then I visited a land mine field where U.N. personnel worked to remove the explosives before they could claim more victims.

And just last October, I was in Afghanistan as Head of the American Election Observer Mission. I witnessed brave Afghanis stand up to the Taliban and their threats of violence by going to polling centers for their country's first democratic election. This was an event in which the United Nations played a major role.

So, for me, there is no question the U.N. makes the world a better place. At the same time, the U.N. has problems. There are double standards, ineffectiveness, inefficiencies, and failures. The bureaucracy is bloated and we are learning more about the corruption that lies therein. Countries pursue their national interests within the U.N. in ways that distort the U.N. from its founding mission and purpose. The U.N. faces challenges in the security, development, and management areas.

I applaud the High Level Panel on Threats, Challenges and Change. It was composed to distinguished world statesmen, including my old friend Brent Scowcroft. It accepted a necessary and difficult assignment. Currently I serve on the Panel of Eminent Persons to strengthen the effectiveness of the Organization of Security and Co-operation in Europe formed by the OSCE Chairman in Office, Slovenian Foreign Minister Rupel. As I work on that exercise, I've developed even more respect for the members of the U.N.'s High Level Panel and what they have produced.

I also applaud U.N. Secretary-General Kofi Annan for his reform recommendations released last month in a document entitled "In Larger Freedom."

Today the U.N. is being tested. In some ways it is effective, but in some ways it is wanting

The inability of the U.N. Security Council to enforce 17 prior U.N. Resolutions on Iraq pointed out structural and procedural weaknesses. The unfolding Oil-For-Food scandal is revealing enormous corruption. Just the other day the U.N. Secretary-General's Special Representative for North Korea, Maurice Strong, had to resign his U.N. post when it was revealed that his Canadian company was receiving investments from Tongsun Park, the South Korean businessman who was convicted of felonies for lobbying abuse in the United States. Mr. Park was servicing as an informal advisor to Maurine Strong while he was executing his responsibilities for the Secretary-General. The UNHCR Head faced serious accusations of sexual harassment. For a long period of time this scandal was brushed under the rug. Finally, intense media pressure forced the Secretary-General to re-examine the situation and ask for the UNHCR Head's resignation. United Nations peacekeepers have been accused of rapes and other sexual abuse in the Congo, Haiti and elsewhere. And just the other day the United Nations Commission on Human Rights once again was unable to condemn Zimbabwe for their abysmal record of human rights abuses. All of these developments undermine the reputation and effectiveness of the U.N. They reveal problems which must be addressed. They point to the need for serious reform within the organization.

Some say that today we are witnessing a resurgence of unilateralism; a diminished commitment for international treaty regimes; an increased willingness to bypass the U.N. Security Council; and serious questions about the Preventive Use of Force. I say yes and no. Let's seek some perspective.

For much of the U.N.'s existence its activities were defined by the events of the Cold War. For 45 years the United Nations Security Council was relegated to second tier issues where the United States and the Soviet Union had no direct interest. During the Cold War the only U.N. Security Council prior authorization for the use of force was in Korea. Then, as now, international treaty regimes were spotty. And as demonstrated time and time again, neither Washington nor Moscow felt restricted by the U.N. Where the U.N. did play a role in peacekeeping operations they tended to be conflicts where neither the United States nor the Soviet Union had a strong direct interest.

In other words, for most of the U.N.'s history it was marginalized on security issues.

Today the United Nations and the world face significant new challenges. These challenges are a result of changes in the world, changes in circumstances, and changes in how a number of countries perceive their interests and how to pursue those interests. The Soviet Union collapsed. The Russian Empire imploded. Left standing was one super power with greater military might, economic strength and cultural reach than any other. At the time experts in capitols as well as in academia felt that this would be a temporary situation. We were in a "unipolar moment." They said that soon others would rise to create a new balance of power. Events have proved the experts were wrong. Fifteen years later the United States primacy has grown, not diminished. While China is emerging, it is many decades away from counter-balancing the United States, if it ever does. Similarly Japan and Europe lag far behind. We are not in a unipolar moment, but a "unipolar era." The result is that capitols throughout the world have adjusted how they hope to pursue their foreign policy and strategic interests.

Let me hasten to add that neither the United States Government nor others have managed this new environment as elegantly as one might like. But, the fact is that these realities are creating the strains. The so-called problems in the structures, legalities, and architectures of the international community are symptoms of these new realities, not the cause. And a safer, more secure, more prosperous world will come from developments in the real world. Structures, legalities and architectures in the international system such as the United Nations will play a role on the margins. They are supporting, not creating phenomena.

Nonetheless, let me state clearly that I believe the United States benefits from "Rules for the Road." It benefits because it provides greater predictability for the United States and for others, greater cooperation, and burden sharing. The United States does not have all the answers and often working with others will make us smarter. And the fact that "Rules for the Road" provide greater comfort to others is not irrelevant.

Next I would like to talk about the United Nations and the issue of preventions of violent conflicts. I believe the High Level Panel made an excellent contribution in its proposed definition on terrorism: violent action against civilians for political purposes. This is similar to President Bush's frequent statement that it is never justified to target innocent civilians for violence. If this recommendation is adopted by the United Nations General Assembly, it will be a step forward. It will be creating a norm that is very helpful. Heretofore, it's been impossible to advance such a definition because certain members of the U.N. insist that violent acts against civilians are justified in the situation of national liberation movement. More precisely, they feel it is justified for the Palestinians to commit violence against the civilians of Israel. This has not been the view of the United States. Therefore, again let me note, that if the High Level Panel recommendation is embraced by the U.N. it will be a step forward\.

Also, the High Level Panel makes recommendations about better policing and better intelligence and addressing root causes of violence. All of these deserve careful consideration.

Let me note that after the terrorist attacks on the United States of September 11th, the U.N. did make a valuable contribution by quickly passing a series of resolutions that established international norms on terrorism that were and are quite helpful. Among other things, these resolutions sanctioned the victims of terror to strike back at those who committed terrorist acts and those states that harbor terrorists. This provided further justification for the United States to lead a coalition of the willing against the Taliban regime in Afghanistan. Also, at that time the United Nations passed resolutions dealing with terrorist financing that have created useful instruments to constrict the ease in which the terrorists are able to get funding. This too has been helpful by forcing terrorist networks out of their comfort zone.

Also in the area of terrorism, we have learned that failed states become breeding grounds for terrorists. We saw this in Afghanistan with the Taliban. The United Nations has unique mechanisms to organize the global community to address such trouble spots. We have seen this with United Nations activities to peacekeeping and mediation in Sierra Leone, the Democratic Republic of the Congo, Burundi, Sudan, Afghanistan, and East Timor, among others. These second tier conflicts that are bloody and horrific often do not create an immediate security threat to the United States. Therefore, given the limits of the United States capacity with treasury or blood to wage battle, the U.N. creates a mechanism for other countries to provide troops to U.N. peacekeeping operations, to help stabilize and move these societies toward peace. This has often been effective and is important. It's a way in which the United Nations contributes to preventing a renewal of violence. And it is a U.N. mission that we should seek to strengthen and make more effective.

In the areas of weapons of mass destruction, I would agree that challenges emerge partially due to the demand side and, yes, partially it is the supply side (materials and technology). The demand is created by facts in the real world that push a nation toward the tipping point of nuclear breakout. Nonetheless, the U.N. can make a contribution to nonproliferation. It does this through the International Atomic Energy Agency and its inspection regime. As a former U.S. Ambassador to the IAEA, I have an intimate familiarity with its work and I think it is very useful and often very effective. Nonetheless, we should recognize that there are limits in the capacity of the U.N. to deal with the threat of nuclear proliferation. A prime example has been the unwillingness of the U.N. Security Council to act on North Korea's nuclear breakout due to continued obstruction by China and Russia.

On the question of preventing deadly conflicts, I certainly agree with the various analysis and recommendations that better information and analysis of potential trouble spots and on-going armed conflicts would be very useful. The International

Crisis Group is an example of an NGO that is providing valuable help here. More attention to these efforts should be made. Also, of course, more effective mediation can contribute to preventing deadly conflicts. I know the United States Institute of Peace has engaged in a number of workshops that trying to help develop better mediation techniques, as have others. More experience and more effective mediation in negotiation and diplomacy could contribute to improving prevention of deadly conflicts.

Nonetheless, I am skeptical of the view suggesting that "a better and more effective regulatory framework and legal and judicial regimes" are the solution to conflicts. I have less confidence that such developments will have a substantial impact on making the world safer and more secure. Nonetheless, continued dialogue in this area could well prove useful.

One area of work to prevent deadly conflicts is to avoid the renewal of conflict in war torn countries that have found some semblance of peace. Restorative justice is important to prevent a renewal of conflict. And in this area the U.N. has played a productive role and continues to do so. The best known Truth and Reconciliation Commission was that created in South Africa at the end of apartheid. Many leaders in South Africa and scholars credit the Truth and Reconciliation Commission for providing invaluable assistance in the effort to heal that torn society and avoid a renewal of conflict. Less well known is that the Truth and Reconciliation Commission vehicle has been used with good success in a number of other countries. For example, in East Timor, a conflict in which the Australians took the lead peacekeeping role, the Truth and Reconciliation has made a significant contribution. When the fighting had stopped, the United Nations played a role in establishing the Truth and Reconciliation Commission there and elsewhere.

We also have seen the development of courts to address crimes against humanity. While serious crimes and human rights abuses are dealt with in Truth and Reconciliation Commissions, a more serious accounting and punishment can come from a judicial procedure. The ICTR, the International Criminal Tribunal for Rwanda, in Arusha, Tanzania, and the International Criminal Tribunal for Yugoslavia in the Hague were both well intended. Unfortunately, I think they failed in some aspects of their mission. They have been too slow. They have been seen as one sided. Located far from where the crimes were committed, they have not provided the help in healing the torn societies that they might if the judicial process had been when the evil deeds had been committed. And, as has been noted by so many people, both the ICTR and the ICTY have grown into huge and exceedingly expensive bureaucracies that move at a glacier pace. The international community learned from that experience.

When the civil war ended in Sierra Leone the government in Freetown, in coordination with the United Nations Security Council, created a Special Court. It is located in Freetown, Sierra Leone, so the victims can witness justice being done. Jails and courts were built in order to accommodate this exercise. Also, the Sierra Leone Special Court was given a short timeframe of three years in which to get its work done. Therefore work had to move fast and there have not been the lengthy delays that have plagued the ICTR and the ICTY. Also, and quite importantly, the chief prosecutor for the Sierra Leone Special Court indicted both winners and losers for committing crimes against humanities. One of the sitting ministers of the Sierra

Leone government, a member of the winning side, had led a group that cracked down on rebels. He was indicted for allowing those crackdowns to go beyond the limits of acceptable behavior. He is being held accountable for those atrocities.

The question of restorative justice is important. It contributes to the healing process for societies torn asunder by brutal conflicts. Thereby, it helps prevent a renewal of war. The U.N. has played a useful role. It can play an even greater and more productive role going forward.

On the question of the use of force there is a debate today about the scope of "permissible unilateral self defense." On this there's a fundamental division. The United States should not take this split personally. I believe this is a result in part of where a country sits.

My own view is that legitimacy does not come from politicians sitting around the U.N. Security Council table. Winston Churchill once said you should not watch laws being made because they're like sausage. Not a pretty sight in the making. Well the U.N. Security Council is a sausage factory. Its diplomats represent their country's interests. Its an arena of self-interest, trade offs, compromise and deals. It is not some ivory tower of wise people deliberating justice detached from political inducements.

I share the general view of American exceptionalism which holds that we have values that not only fit in the United States but apply to all mankind. Legitimacy does not come from politicians and political process but from the people on the ground and the morality and the value of the act committed.

I understand why countries that are less strong would like to restrain the United States. They see the sole superpower as a threatening menace even when they agree with her. They recognize that she could turn against them and they wish to constrain her. At the same time the United States understandably wants to avoid such constraints. In the 19th Century there were efforts to develop rules of the sea to regulate sea trade. At that time the United States was less strong, less mighty, and had less reach. Therefore, it's not surprising that at the time the United States supported such international norms to constrain the great powers. At the same time, the United Kingdom and France, who then had the mightiest navies, objected to such constraints. Today the tables are turned. Again, this is understandable. But does that mean the United States needs to constrict its freedom to act when it feels it must to protect its own vital interests? This is a serious issue that needs to be debated. But just as George Bush has said the United States would not ask U.N. Security Council for permission to act to protect our security, so did liberal Democratic Presidential nominee Senator John Kerry. I do not think this is a liberal or conservative issue. It's an issue seen from where one sits, whether in a strong country or a less strong country.

Because it has more military might, greater economic strength, and more cultural reach, the United States has a large foreign policy toolbox. Understandably, the United Nations is useful but certainly not the sole or even the dominant implement to advance U.S. interests and protect our security. Other countries that are less mighty, less strong and have less reach have smaller foreign policy toolboxes. Understandably, for them, the United Nations plays a more prominent role. They have fewer options. This is a difference, in practical politics, not in theology. It should be recognized. Our dialogue should be conducted with an appreciation of this fact.

There are those including the High Level Panel and the Secretary-General, who proposed an expansion of the U.N. Security Council from 15 to 24 members. They have suggested more permanent members. I believe their suggestions don't deal with the root problem in the U.N. Security Council. Ultimately the U.N. Security Council's erosion of authority is a result of a fundamental problem: the Security Council does not reflect power in the real world. It may not have done so accurately in 1945, but certainly it was closer to reality then than it is today. As long as this disconnect exists, the U.N. Security Council will face problems. Furthermore, mere expansion of the Council, as suggested by the High Level Panel and the Secretary-General, may well create a body so large and so unwieldy that the permanent five will consult alone more often and thereby marginalize even more the elected representatives to the Security Council. So this remains an open and difficult issue which warrants discussion and exploration.

I've already touched briefly on the U.N. Commission on Human Rights and its problems of recently having Libya as its chairman and having members such as Sudan, Cuba, and Zimbabwe. The High Level Panel has recommended that it become a universal body like the U.N. General Assembly rather than its current elected membership of 53. I fear if it were to become universal it will have all of the effectiveness and legitimacy of the U.N. General Assembly, which is to say not much at all. The Secretary-General's proposal for abolishing the Commission on Human Rights and creating a smaller human rights council where a two-thirds vote would be required for membership has more appeal. Nonetheless, in a U.N. of 191 countries where only 85 are democracies, the difficulty of having a human rights commission that can enforce the standards encompassed in the U.N. Universal Declaration of Human Rights and other such documents remains questionable.

In the end, the strength of the United Nations is that it has universal membership. And the weakness of the United Nations is that it has universal membership.

The U.N. has 191 members of which only approximately 85 are democracies even though both the U.N. Charter and the U.N. Universal Declaration on Human Rights makes self determination a fundamental value to be embraced by all member states. Three member states have a population that could fit within a sports arena in the United States. At the other extreme you have China and India with populations of over 1 billion. There are imbalances. There are anomalies. And notwithstanding the noble aspirations of the Charter, many of its member states don't even make a passing effort to comply with those standards. This creates the dilemma, not the structures, mechanisms, or architecture.

Some say we must reform and strengthen the United Nations because we have no alternative. Some say that we have run out of choices. I am not so sure. There are other ways for the nations of the world to do business. There are regional organizations. There are bilateral relationships. There are coalitions to deal with specific challenges. Nonetheless, I want to emphasize that I applaud the noble aspirations of the United Nations. I believe the United Nations has done and is doing a lot of good. The United States government should work to reform and improve the United Nations. It is in our interest to do so. There's a lot of work to do. I believe there will be limits to what we can achieve. Nonetheless, it is well worth the effort. So let's work at it.

Thank you.

THE WORLD WITHOUT THE U.N.: COULD THE U.S. TAKE THE LEAD?

For the United States, the United Nations can be a very frustrating place. The rhetoric in the U.N. General Assembly can be unfettered to reality. Some of its resolutions are mischievous at best. The U.N. Commission on Human Rights allows repressive regimes to sit as members, often fails to rebuke the worst human rights abuses such Zimbabwe, and devotes more time seeking to delegitimize Israel (the oldest democracy in the Middle East) then hold to account Fidel Castro for making Cuba an island prison.

The United Nations has waste and inefficiency. The Oil-For-Food program was awash in mismanagement and corruption. The sexual abuse committed by U.N. Peacekeepers in the Congo and elsewhere is abhorrent. And the U.N. Security Council failed to act in Kosovo, failed to enforce its own resolutions in Iraq, and has been slow and anemic in acting to stop the genocide in Darfur, Sudan.

Furthermore, in many ways the United Nations is less central to U.S. foreign policy than for other countries. We live in a time of American primacy. The United States has more military might, economic strength and cultural reach than other nations. We have many implements in our foreign policy toolbox. Countries with less might, strength and reach have fewer options. Therefore, it is understandable that for others the United Nations plays a more central foreign policy role.

And, of course, many countries have greater stature and more power in the U.N. than they have in the real world. They hold their U.N. position and prerogatives most preciously.

Could the United States protect its security and advance its interests without the United Nations? Yes, thank you very much. But it would be more difficult to do so, more expensive, and less comprehensive. The United Nations is very useful for the United States, as it is for others.

In addition to America's great power, the United States has vast interests. The global war on terror has demonstrated that failed states far from home can breed fanatics capable of attacking our homeland. Eruptions in Indonesia, the Middle East and elsewhere can create shocks to America's economy. American values and our humanity compel us to respond to the victims of natural disasters, famine, blight and the tragedy of genocide. And, advancing human rights and liberty are not only the right thing to do, it also is in our interest. As President Bush has said, spreading democracy abroad makes our democracy at home safer and more secure.

Appeared in *The Interdependent*, Vol. 3, No. 2, Summer, 2005.

In the U.N. system are many technical agencies such as the International Civil Aviation Organization and the World Meteorological Organization. If the U.N. were to disappear, such organizations would be reconstituted, albeit with difficulty and cost. And some of the frustrations we have with U.N. technical agencies undoubtedly would reappear. It's the nature of any multinational organization with scores of member states.

In the economic arena, the United Nations has not built a distinguished record of achievement. If the U.N. were to disappear, some useful things would be lost, but undoubtedly the Bretton Woods institutions would continue and, perhaps, even be reinvigorated.

The U.N.'s contribution to humanitarian assistance through UNHCR, the World Food Program and other organs is substantial. Whether helping feed and shelter desperate people driven from their homes in Sudan or helping the tsunami victims , the U.N. is playing a large role. It is one that would be hard if not impossible to duplicate. In the security arena, growing, imminent threats to the United States would be met unilaterally or by a Coalition of the Willing. This is costly and can be cumbersome. But an imminent threat would be confronted and the sacrifice required paid. Regional security organizations such as NATO and ASEAN would continue to play a prominent role.

But recent history has taught us that threats not imminent yet meddlesome such as failed or disintegrating states due to ethnic eruptions, civil wars, resource exploitation, political and civil repression, contagious disease, famine, or other cancers can spread to regional instability and breed terrorists. Restorative justice unaddressed erodes stability. These situations can threaten us. And even the world's superpower lacks the capacity to adequately deal with all these contagions.

Today America's might already is stretched thin due to the on-going challenges in Iraq and Afghanistan. Could the United States alone, or with a Coalition of the Willing, address the on-going conflicts and tenuous post conflict situations in Haiti, Sierra Leone, Liberia, the Democratic Republic of the Congo, and elsewhere? We would ignore them at our peril.

And from human rights to anti-terrorism, the world community has adopted norms through the United Nations. These very useful norms have a reach and acceptability around the globe that could not be duplicated without the U.N.

And as demonstrated recently in pressuring Syria to end its occupation of Lebanon, the United Nations has an imprimatur and force that can be very constructive. It comes from the values in the U.N. Charter, its universal membership, its role as midwife to colonies reborn as new nations, and, in part, because the U.N. is influenced but not dictated by its founding member state.

In both Afghanistan and Iraq, the U.N. played an important role in their recent elections. The OSCE, EU, IRI and NDI also contributed to insuring election legitimacy. But the U.N.'s participation in helping implement the ways and means of free and fair elections and certifying their credibility has an acceptance domestically and internationally that can be decisive.

So the U.N. is a seriously flawed institution in need of significant reform. If the U.N. were to disappear the world would not end. The United States would continue to protect its security and pursue its vital interests. But it would be more costly, more difficult and, in many cases, less effective.

The wise course is to engage the U.N., work with other countries, seek meaningful reform, and pursue our interests. It is not in America's interest for the U.N. to disappear. It is in our interest for the U.N. to be reborn. And we should get at the hard work of doing that.

U.N. SECURITY COUNCIL REFORM: THE NEED, THE PROSPECTS, AND THE CONSEQUENCES

I want to thank Edison Dick for organizing this event. And I want to join with others in congratulating Edison for receiving a lifetime achievement award last night from the American Bar Association's International Law Section. It is an honor well deserved. Also, I thank Ellen Yost, Eddie's co-chair, for helping host this panel. And finally, I want to acknowledge the outstanding contribution to international law given by our moderator, Bruce Rashkow, first in the legal office of the U.S. State Department and for the past ten years as a senior official in the United Nations Office of Legal Affairs.

The United Nations does a great deal of good in the world. It is a valuable instrument of international relations for the United States and others. For example, it provides invaluable humanitarian assistance to people caught in desperate conditions. The U.N.'s World Food Program feeds millions of people every year throughout the world. The U.N. High Commissioner for Refugees is helping shelter, feed, and provide needed medical aid to millions of people in Sudan, Ethiopia, Eritrea, Chad and elsewhere. The U.N. is helping the millions of people in Asia who's lives were devastated by the great tsunami last year.

The United Nations makes a major contribution in setting standards and establishing norms. For example, technical agencies such as the U.N.'s International Civil Aviation Organization and the World Telecommunications Union set standards critical to our modern interconnected world. The U.N.'s Universal Declaration on Human Rights established norms of acceptable behavior that have profoundly effected the constitutions of many countries: norms citizens now expect their governments to honor; norms that challenge repressive regimes and ones that help guide enlightened ones. And the norms set by the U.N. on terrorism are aiding the war on terror.

U.N. peacekeeping operations have helped in the Balkans, East Timor, Sierra Leone, Ethiopia/Eritrea, Haiti, and elsewhere. The U.N.'s International Atomic Energy Agency has safeguards that make it more difficult for nations to divert nuclear technology from civilian to military use.

The United Nations has played a vital role in post-conflict reconstruction and reconciliation in Afghanistan, Sierra Leone and the Balkans, among other places. The U.N. has helped establish law and order in post-conflict societies by training

---

Remarks to Section of International Law, American Bar Association, ABA Annual Meeting, Chicago, Illinois, August 7, 2005.

police and establishing courts. The U.N. has contributed in the area of reconstruction by helping rebuild infrastructures. And the U.N. has furthered restorative justice by helping set up Truth and Reconciliation Commissions and through Special Courts that bring to justice those guilty of the worst crimes against humanity.

At the same time, it is important to acknowledge the United Nations' considerable shortcomings. Like all big organizations, the U.N. has waste, fraud and abuse. The U.N. needs better management procedures, greater transparency and increased accountability. The Oil for Food scandal powerfully points out the need for U.N. management reform.[1] And the grave allegations against U.N. Peacekeepers in the Democratic Republic of the Congo of rape and abuse properly shocks all U.N. member states and requires accountability, new practices and improved procedures.[2] The U.N. Commission on Human Rights is compromised by double standards and a failure to adequately act against some of the world's worst abusers of human rights such as Zimbabwe and Sudan. [3] The horrific failures o he United Nations in Rwanda and Srebrenica echo in Darfur where in the past two years genocide has caused the death of approximately 400,000 people and the displacement of over 2 million people now living in desperate conditions in refugee camps. The U.N. Security Council has been slow and timid in acting to stop the genocide because of China, motivated by oil concessions in Sudan, Russia, due to its sale of MIG fighter jets to Sudan, and Algeria's solidarity with the Islamic government in Khartoum.

For all of these reasons, and the breakdown over Iraq, the United Nations is in desperate need of major reform.[4] Therefore, I applaud the good work of the High Level Panel and its report.[5] I commend Secretary-General Kofi for his recommendations issued last spring.[6] And I encourage interested parties to review the Gingrich-Mitchell report.[7]

Hopefully, at the heads of state summit scheduled at the U.N. headquarters in September, many major reforms can be adopted. If the United Nations is to play a vital role going forward in the 21st century reform is essential.

The strength of the U.N. is that it is a universal organization. And the weakness of the U.N. is that it is a universal organization.

As a universal organization, the United Nations has a special heritage, a unique reach, and an unparalleled acceptability. It provides a forum for 191 countries to gather, exchange views, and conduct multilateral and bilateral business. The United Nations promotes understanding, collaboration and cooperation. All of this is good.

But as a universal organization with institutions and structures; with procedures and practices designed to recognize every member state as sovereign and equal, the reality within the U.N. is distorted from reality outside. Three countries with total populations that would fit in Madison Square Garden are equal, within the U.N., with India and China who have populations of well over 1 billion people. Countries with no army, no navy and no air force such as Mauritius, in the U.N., are equal to countries with great military might such as the United States, the United Kingdom and Russia. Countries in which citizens have no say who governs them or how in the U.N. are equal to democracies where citizens are sovereign. And countries that barely subsist, in the U.N., are equal to those with the largest, most sophisticated and wealthiest economies in the world. Among the United Nations arenas in which those distortions are played out most dramatically and most consequentially is the U.N. Security Council.

In 1945, it was the World War II victors who took the lead in creating the United Nations.[8] Arguably at that time the Security Council they created roughly reflected the real world with permanent seats with veto power bestowed on the United States, the Soviet Union, the U.K., China and France. In addition to the permanent five, initially there were 6 rotating elected seats with no veto. In 1963, the elected seats were expanded to 10, giving the Security Council its current size of 15.

Of course, the U.N. Security Council has never been a perfect reflection of the real world. In 1945, there was some controversy over the status of France as a permanent member with British Prime Minister Winston Churchill pushing for its inclusion. After the communists took over China, the Chinese permanent seat in the Security Council remained with the Nationalist Chinese on Taiwan, not the mainland, for almost 25 years. Nonetheless, during the long Cold War, the Security Council was a rough approximation of the real world with both the Soviet Union and the United States holding their permanent seats with veto power. But today, no one could credibly argue that the U.N.'s permanent five are the world's greatest powers.

A couple of years ago after a Security Council meeting, the Chinese Ambassador and I were visiting. This Chinese diplomat said that today the Security Council's permanent members were composed of the world's sole superpower, the world's emerging power, and three collapsed powers. Of course, that view is too harsh. Nonetheless, there is some truth to it.

Since the Security Council is the forum of greatest power in the United Nations, it is natural that Security Council reform has been the most controversial item on the reform agenda.[9] It has received the most attention from member states and the media. Security Council reform has sucked up almost all of the oxygen from the reform debate.[10]

The High Level Panel Report punted. It suggested two alternatives. One, to add six new permanent members (likely Brazil, Germany, India, Japan, Egypt and either Nigeria or South Africa) plus three new elected members holding two-year terms. The second suggestion was to create a new tier of eight semi-permanent members chosen for renewable four-year seats added to the current ten elected members who are elected to two-year terms. Under this second alternative, the right to cast a veto would be limited to the five original permanent members.[11]

The Gingrich-Mitchell Commission on U.N. reform has a number of thoughtful and provocative suggestions, especially on issues regarding humanitarian intervention.[12] However, this commission did not address Security Council reform at all. It was too controversial.

For approximately ten years, the United States Government has taken the position that it supports Security Council reform in the abstract and in particular the U.S. supports Japan's aspiration for a permanent seat. But the U.S. has not lead on this issue in the past, nor has it taken any leadership on Security Council reform during the current deliberations. And as practitioners, scholars and other U.N. observers know, on controversial issues in the United Nations action very seldom is taken without active U.S. leadership.

Last month United States Ambassador Sharin Tahir-Kheli said to the U.N. General Assembly that "the United States supports expansion of the Security Council. …we recognize that 2005 is not 1945… (However) we will oppose any proposal that would make the Security Council less effective than it is today. And we will oppose calling for votes on proposals that do not command the breadth of support necessary to be put in practice."[13]

For many months the so-called "Group of 4" (Germany, India, Japan and Brazil) have worked energetically, tirelessly, persistently in New York and in capitals around the world pushing their proposal for Security Council reform. They have used persuasion and other inducements. They did pick up some support. But so far they've failed.[14] Why?

First, some countries have greater influence, greater prestige and greater power in the U.N. than they have in the real world. That is true in the U.N. General Assembly and even more so in the Security Council. Those Security Council permanent members who are no longer so consequential in the real world – whose relative economic strength, military might and cultural reach in the world are less dominant than in 1945, hold their prerogatives and power of P-5 status most preciously. Those countries to whom events have circumscribed their capacity to project power relish, depend and sometimes abuse their power in the U.N. Security Council where their veto power ensures that their views will be taken into account. In the Security Council their views matter. In the Security Council they have a say even on matters in which they are insignificant or irrelevant in the real world. Understandably, these countries have no intension of giving up their special status even if real world realities no longer justifies such a status; perhaps, especially if real world realities no longer justify it. Also, understandably, they resist diluting their power and influence by expanding the number of permanent members in the Security Council. However, if in their judgment it becomes necessary to expand the number of permanent members in order to save themselves, to retain their special status, they will do so.

A second challenge to U.N. Security Council expansion is criteria. What should the criteria be for permanent membership? In 1945, it was the victors of World War II. What should it be today: military might, economic strength, cultural reach, geographic balance, population, international engagement, or perhaps, compliance with international norms on human rights, democracy, non-proliferation, trade, etc.? It is unclear. Therefore a natural selection is less clear. And how would such criteria apply to the existing P-5? After all, among the current P-5 are those that fail to respect human rights. And Russia's economy is the size of Belgium's.

Third, just as giving a country permanent membership on the Security Council would enhance its power within the U.N. and in the real world, so it will disadvantage some other significant or major powers not granted this special status.[15] Naturally, these countries violently oppose Security Council expansion; any expansion that would dramatically benefit rival countries and, consequently, disadvantage themselves.[16]

Allow me to quote from Pakistani Ambassador Munir Akram's speech to the U.N. General Assembly on July 11, 2005:

> Regarding U.N. Reform, Ambassador Akram said, "Unfortunately, this important endeavor was, almost from the

outset, hijacked by a 'small group of nations' seeking new and unequal privileges for themselves in an enlarged Security Council. ...During these months, the endeavor by the so-called Group of Four (Germany, Japan, Brazil and India) to secure support and endorsement of their position has taken forms, which if practiced in national elections, would be judged unethical or worse. An outcome for Council reform achieved by such questionable means is unlikely to be sustainable or to strengthen the United Nations. ...To add insult to injury, self-interest has been portrayed as altruism. The seekers of special privileges and power masquerade as the champions of the weak and disadvantaged – asserting that the special privileges they seek will make the Council more 'representative' and neutralize the power of the present permanent members. History has witnessed many such who proclaim that they came 'to bury, not to praise Caesar.' "[17]

For these reasons, Security Council reform is unlikely.[18] The growing problem for the United Nations is that the more the Security Council does not reflect the real world, the less credibility, the less legitimacy, and, therefore, the less authority it will have.

Ultimately the countries most harmed by a diminished Security Council are not the major powers, but the less strong. After the threatened French veto of an eighteenth Iraq resolution and the consequent failure of the Security Council to act, Singapore Ambassador Kishore Mantubani said to me, "How dare France create this train wreak. After all the ones who are hurt are us, the smaller states who need the Security Council. You big boys don't need it. You have the power to act outside the United Nations. But the rest of us, we need it. We need a strong, functioning, effective Security Council."

Do I see a solution to this dilemma? No, I do not. For the immediate future, the Security Council will muddle through. But I fear that in the long term the crisis of credibility will grow and the U.N. Security Council will become less consequential.

---

1.   See, for example, Warren Hoge, "Panel Accuses Former U.N. Aide of Bribe Schemes: Guilty Plea of 2nd Official Details Taking Cash for Information on Bids," *New York Times*, August 8, 2005; Editorial, "Oil for Fraud," *Wall Street Journal*, August 9, 2005; Peter A. McKay, "U.N. Ex-Official Faces Accusations Over Iraq Relief," *Wall Street Journal*, August 9, 2005; Colum Lynch, "Oil-Food Official Pleads Guilty: Graft in U.N. Program Include Ex-Chief," *Washington Post*, August 9, 2005; Betsy Pisib, "Ex-U.N. Officer Pleads Guilty," *Washington Times*, August 9, 2005; Warren Hoge, "Panel Completes Inquiry on U.N. Oil-for-Food Official," *International Herald Tribune*, July 27, 2005; Robert McMahon, "Iraq: U.N.'s Oil-For-Food Audits Suggest Systematic Mismanagement, *RFE/RL, January 11, 2005* Judith Miller, New York *Times, June 14, 2005. and* Mark Hosenball, "Scandals: All in the Family U.N. Practices Under Scrutiny," *Newsweek*, June 27, 2005. Note, for a presentation pointing out the shared responsibility of member states for weak oversight of the Oil-For-Food Program, see, Professor Joy Gordon, Fairfield University, Testimony on the U.N. Oil-For-Food Program, Before the Subcommittee on National Security, Emerging Threats, and International Relations, Committee on Government Reform, U.S. House of Representatives, Washington, D.C., April 12, 2005.

2.   Reuters, "U.N. Council Condemns Sex Abuse by Its Troops," *New York Times*, June 1, 2005.

3.   See, Richard S. Williamson, *Human Rights, Democracy and Restorative Justice* (Chicago, Illinois; The Prairie Institute; 2004), pp. 51-58.

4.   The issue of U.N. reform has been alive since 1945. See Edward C. Luck, *Reforming the United Nations from a History of Progress* (New Haven, Conn.; Academic Council on the U.N. System; 2003), Occasional Paper No. 1.

5.   Report of the Secretary-General's High Level Panel to Study Global Security Threats and Recommend Necessary Challenges, *A More Secure World: Our Shared Responsibility*, 2004. See also, Newt Gingrich and George Mitchell, "U.N.: 60 and at Crossroads, Reform Now to Restore Credibility and Relevancy," *Washington Times*, February 9, 2005. For other useful documents on U.N. Reform, see, Kim R. Holmes, Assistant Secretary of State for International Organization Affairs, Remarks hosted by The U.N. Foundation, Hyatt Regency, Washington, D.C., April 19, 2005; and The Stanley Foundation, "Toward Larger Freedom," Report of the 40th Conference on the United Nations of the New Decade, Vitznau, Switzerland, June 17-22, 2005; available at http://reports.stanleyfoundation.org.

6.   Secretary General Kofi Annan's Report *In Larger Freedom: Towards Security, Development and Human Rights For All*, March 20, 2005. Available at http://www.un.org/largerfreedom/contents.htm.

7.   Report of the Task Force on the United Nations, *American Interests and U.N. Reform* (Washington, D.C.; U.S. Institute of Peace; 2005). The Task Force was co-chaired by former Speaker of the House Newt Gingrich and former Senate Majority Leader George Mitchell.

8.   See generally, Stephen C. Schlesinger, *Act of Creation: The Founding of the United Nations* (New York, N.Y.; Westview Press; 2003).

9.   See also, Thomas G. Weiss, "Security Council Reform: Problems and Prospects in September 2005," UNA-USA Policy Brief No. 9, June 23, 2005; and Warren Hoge, "U.N. Tackles Issue of Imbalance of Power, " *New York Times*, November 28, 2004.

10.   For a thoughtful discussion of this topic see Edward C. Luck, "The U.N. Security Council: Reform or Enlarge?," Paper prepared for the "U.N.: Adapting to the 21st Century" conference, Center for International Governance Innovation, Waterloo, Ontario, April 3-5, 2005.

11.   Report of the Secretary-General's High Level Panel to Study Global Security Threats and Recommend Necessary Challenges, *A More Secure World: Our Shared Responsibility*, 2004.

12.   *Ibid.*, footnote 6.

13.   Statement by Ambassador Sharin Tahir-Kheli, Senior Advisor to the United States Secretary of Sate on U.N. Reform, in the Plenary of the U.N. General Assembly on U.N. Reform, July 12, 2005.

14.   Note: Steven R. Weisman, "U.S. Rebuffs Germans Anew on Bid for Security Council," *New York Times*, June 9, 2005; and James Dobbins, "America is Punishing Germany for Its Iraq Opposition," *Financial Times*, July 13, 2005.

15.   A variation of this theme has been China's actions to keep Japan out of the Security Council. See, for example, Norimitsu Onishi and Howard W. French, "Ill Will Rising Between China and Japanese," *New York Times*, August 3, 2005. See also, Fred Hiatt, "China's Selective Memory," *Washington Post*, April 18, 2005.

16.   See generally, Edward C. Luck, "Tokyo's Quixotic Quest for Acceptance," *The Eastern Economic Review*, May 2005; 168, p. 5.

17.   Statement by Ambassador Munir Akram, Prominent Representative of Pakistan to the United Nations, in the Plenary of the U.N. General Assembly under Agenda Item 53: "Question of equitable representation on and increase in the membership of the Security Council and related matters," July 11, 2005.

18.   See, for example, Warren Hoge, "Plans to Expand Security Council May Be Frustrated for Now," *New York Times*, July 15, 2005.

SINO-U.S. RELATIONS AND THE ROLE OF THE U.N.

I want to thank Ambassador Ma Zhengang and General Brent Scowcroft as they ably preside over our discussions today. It's a pleasure to be back at the China Institute of International Studies to participate in this "Sino-U.S. Dialogue on Global Security."

I have been asked to discuss the role of the United Nations in Sino-U.S. Relations. I believe the work of the U.N. provides an opportunity to deepen America and China's cooperative relationship. It can help us minimize misunderstanding and miscalculations. It can help us expand our friendship.

Today the United States is the world's sole superpower and China is the world's great emerging power. Both have many implements in their foreign policy toolbox due to their military might, economic strength and cultural reach; far more than most nations. One such foreign policy instrument is the United Nations. Understandably for countries that have less military might, economic strength and cultural reach and therefore fewer implements in their foreign policy toolbox than do we, the U.N. plays a more central role. Naturally they seek to bring the U.N. to bare on more issues than do we.

Also it is natural that such countries seek to use the United Nations – and other multilateral fora – to constrain the actions of the hyperpower and other great powers. In the 19th century when America had less might, strength and reach, we supported international regulation of the sealanes. At the time, the great naval powers, France and England, opposed such constraints. Such efforts to tie Gulliver down are not necessarily personal. They are the normal manifestation of nations' constant search to advance their own self-interest. Countries want predictability and the stability it brings. It is true that Gulliver can break the Lilliputians' ropes, it has the capacity to act unilaterally. But that the superpower can act unilaterally does not mean that it should. Rules of the road and the predictability they bring also benefits the strong. So while reserving its capacity to act unilaterally when it must, as a general rule the world's superpower benefits by acting multilaterally. It increases cooperation, is cost-effective by broadening participation and sharing costs, and it provides some stability to the inherent instability of a unipolar world.

As China continues to rise on the back of its expanding economy, the United Nations provides the opportunity for international integration through an organization with universal membership. Within the family of U.N. organizations,

---

Remarks at China Institute of International Studies, Beijing, China, November 17, 2005.

China can engage the entire international community on issues of security, economic development and trade, humanitarian assistance, health, technical standards and other norms, nuclear cooperation, cultural matters, education and many others.

There are new challenges that threaten our way of life from the pandemic of HIV-AIDS to the rise of fundamentalist Islamic Jihad. These emerging threats provide opportunities and responsibilities for both China and the United States.

My friend Singapore Ambassador Kishore Mahbubani once said to me that the war in Afghanistan demonstrated the United States can project its power anywhere in the world and the war in Iraq showed that there is nowhere to hide. Perhaps. But Afghanistan also demonstrated the value of broad support and cooperative action, and Iraq is teaching us the limits of American unilateral action.

On many critical security issues the United Nations is playing an important role. The U.N. establishes norms on terrorism, nuclear proliferation and other sensitive matters. In second tier conflicts that are threatening but may not directly challenge the vital interest of the great powers such as those in West Africa and the African Great Lakes Region, Haiti and East Timor, U.N. Peacekeepers have made an invaluable contribution. The U.N. provides a vehicle to deal with failed states and post-conflict situations. The U.N.'s role was critical to Afghanistan's Loya Jurga and the following elections.

At the same time we should recognize that the U.N. has limits. For example, the Security Council has failed to actively engage the nuclear proliferation challenges of North Korea or Iran. The response to genocide in Sudan has been anemic. And my experience has been that generally on security situations in which any of the Security Council's permanent veto wielding members have a significant interest, the United Nations is "above the battle and beside the point."

Cautiously China has become more active on security matters in the United Nations. In the 1990's, for the first time, China sent participants on a U.N. Peacekeeping mission: the large-scale engagement in Cambodia. More recently China sent engineers as part of the U.N. Peacekeeping Mission in the Democratic Republic of the Congo and last year Chinese "special police" were deployed to the Peacekeeping Mission in Haiti. These developments are positive.

At the same time, recent events may be forcing the United States to confront its own limits, and to become more realistic and humble. Perhaps there will be a broader recognition that just because America can act unilaterally does not mean it always should. This should lead to more constructive multilateral engagement at the United Nations and elsewhere.

More active Chinese and American U.N. engagement also should benefit Sino-U.S. relations. Through working together in the United Nations, we will both broaden and deepen our mutual understanding. Patterns of coordination will develop further. Habits of cooperation will evolve. All of this will be healthy for our two countries individually, to Sino-U.S. relations and to stability in the world.

China and U.S. interests are not coincidental. There are areas of fundamental philosophical and practical divergence. But it is in both of our interests to expand areas of cooperation and deepen understanding of one another. Sino-U.S. relations will continue to be a complex multi-faceted feast. And one vehicle for greater cooperation, understanding and enlightened self-interest lies within the United Nations.

Thank you.

U.N. REFORM FOR U.N. RENEWAL

As we gather this afternoon, there are those who say the United Nations is a morally bankrupt institution due to double standards and broken promises. There are those who charge that U.N. mismanagement is so rampant with fraud, waste and abuse that it cannot be fixed. There are those prepared to turn their backs on the U.N. and cavalierly walk away. I reject such views.

The U.N. is a very useful institution. The U.N. Charter embraces the same values upon which America was founded: human rights, self-determination, the rule of law, opportunity for all. Today and every day millions of people around the world benefit from the U.N.'s many programs and activities: the poor, the sick, the hungry, the weak who are victims of repression, those caught in cycles of senseless violence, those who are victims of ethnic cleansing and genocide.

Having visited U.N. political and peacekeeping missions in Afghanistan, Ethiopia and Eritrea, the Democratic Republic of the Congo, Sierra Leone, Bosnia and Herzegovina, Kosovo, and most recently Liberia – to name but a few – I know first hand that the U.N. is contributing to peace and security around the world.

And now as the international community tries to address the grave and growing danger of Iran's nuclear program, the U.N.'s International Atomic Energy Agency initially, and with last week's referral, the U.N. Security Council, are the instruments of choice for the United States and the world to try to deal diplomatically with this crisis.

Clearly the United Nations is useful. But, like all institutions, the U.N. also has problems, very serious problems. Problems that weaken the U.N. and in some cases cripple it. Some are first and foremost the result of Member State misbehavior. Some are caused by U.N. structures, procedures and process. Some are due to mismanagement, lack of transparency, lack of independent oversight, lack of accountability, lack of management flexibility.

To ignore the desperate need for U.N. reform is to allow the U.N.'s promise to blind you to its debilitating weaknesses. To allow entrenched interests to prevent reform is to allow fear of change to stand in the way of the renewal required for the United Nations to thrive and contribute to a better world. To fail to act on common sense management and budget reforms is to deepen the divide between donor and recipient states, to hamstring the Secretary-General, and to limit the U.N.'s effectiveness and reach. To fail to act boldly to reform the U.N. will relegate this noble institution to a twilight of decline.

Remarks at Dag Hammarskjöld Auditorium, The United Nations Headquarters, New York, New York, February 9, 2006.

No one will benefit from such inaction. Those people who will be harmed most are those who are poor, sick, oppressed and victims of cycles of violence. Those countries who will suffer most are those less mighty, less strong, and with less reach for whom the U.N. is more central to their interests than those with great military might, economic strength, and vast cultural reach for whom the U.N. is less central.

In the area of management reform, the U.N. has taken some worthy steps on accountability, including creating an ethics office, and disclosure requirements covering more people at different levels and more activities and gifts.

Next, the United Nations has to follow through with creating an Independent Audit Advisory Committee to validate the work of the Office of Internal Oversight Services and external auditors, and recommend proper levels of funding and staff for those oversight functions. There needs to be an effective "Whistleblower Protection Policy." The United Nations needs a "control environment." There needs to be an effective "Whistleblower Protection Policy."

The United Nations needs a budget and program assessment and review process. A substantive, exhaustive, and meaningful annual report from the Secretary-General and his top management team should be provided to all stakeholders. These are management tools that will help both the Secretariate and Member States.

Also the Secretary-General should be given management flexibility including more leeway in hiring – to move beyond current restrictions on geographic considerations. The Secretary-General also should be given flexibility to move people and posts.

The United Nations must develop a culture of responsibility. In the past year U.N. scandals have been uncovered in procurement, sexual abuse by U.N. peacekeepers in the Congo, and the "Oil for Food" program. Senior management should be held accountable and pay the price for these failures, not just low level employees.

Regarding mandates, early next month the Secretary-General is scheduled to make a report on mandates 5 years old or more for review. Drawing upon this report, the Member States should make serious, tangible reallocation decisions. Funds should be shifted from lower priorities to higher priorities; for example, from conferences and reports to actual technical assistance to help developing countries.

Let me now turn to Human Rights.

Human rights issues go to the core values of the United Nations; its highest aspirations and greatest opportunities. Human rights go to the heart and soul and mission of the U.N. Respect for human rights is in the Charter to which all Member States subscribe in theory, if not always in practice. The U.N. Universal Declaration on Human Rights and subsequent U.N. documents have established fundamental norms reflected in national constitutions and laws around the world. These rights are fundamental, inalienable and transcendent. Respect for human rights contribute – indeed they are central – to maintaining international peace and security. For, as George Marshall pointed out over 55 years ago, countries that respect the human rights of their own citizens are more likely to respect the rights of other countries. They are less likely to engage in foreign adventurism.

The U.N. Commission on Human Rights has failed in its responsibilities. At that forum many of the world's most brutal oppressors escape rebuke. It is embarrassing. It is shameful. It brings dishonor on the U.N. And most important, it fails the oppressed, the repressed, the victims of human rights abuse to whom we all have a responsibility – particularly the United Nations.

As Mark Malloch Brown, Chief of Staff to U.N. Secretary-General Kofi Annan, has said, "For the great global public, the performance on non-performance of the Human Rights Commission has become the litmus test for U.N. renewal."

The U.N. forum to address human rights is not just another U.N. organ for regional rotation, for business as usual. It is more than that. It is more fundamental. It is loftier than that. It goes to the heart and soul of the United Nations. It goes to U.N. Member States' responsibilities and opportunities to themselves, to the U.N., and to the victims of human rights abuse.

Those countries that fail in their responsibilities to respect the rights of their own citizens should not, can not be allowed to sit in judgment of others.

The time for U.N. reform and renewal is now. Nowhere is it more necessary than in the U.N.'s human rights mechanisms. If not here, where can the U.N. achieve meaningful reform? If not now, when?

The United Nations is a place of promise and of mischief. Shortcomings, disappointments and scandals have led to reflection and re-examination. We ought not wallow in despair but go forward with reform. We ought not let ourselves become discouraged but get at the hard work required for renewal.

To paraphrase George Bernard Shaw: Most men see the world with all its problems and ask why? Some men see a better world and ask why not? For all of us who believe in the values of the U.N. Charter, its mission, its promise, its opportunity, it's time to ask "why not?" It's time to roll up our sleeves and get to work.

U.N.'s Human Rights Commission Will Never Succeed Without Reform

Last year was supposed to be the year of reform at the United Nations. Secretary-General Kofi Annan outlined a broad menu of proposals. The oil-for-food scandal revealed gross U.N. mismanagement. Nonetheless the member states were unable to act.

In September, the largest gathering of world leaders in history met at the U.N. They were unable to approve reform proposals and merely agreed to a package of general principles.

Entrenched narrow interests, recalcitrance and ineffective diplomacy all contributed to this failure. A Peacekeeping Commission has been agreed to, but otherwise nothing. And a deadline to reform the U.N.'s machinery on human rights is fast approaching.

If the member states are unable to agree to reforms this month, the discredited U.N. Human Rights Commission will meet this spring. Undoubtedly, it again will fail in its responsibilities.

As Mark Malloch Brown, Chief of Staff to U.N. Secretary-General Kofi Annan, has said, "For the great global public, the performance or non-performance of the Human Rights Commission has become the litmus test for U.N. renewal."

Establishing important norms on human rights has been an area of United Nations achievement. The U.N. Universal Declaration on Human Rights adopted in 1948 and subsequent U.N. human rights agreements have become standards around the world agreed to by all in name, if not always in practice. The United Nations provides a forum for us to stand up for the fundamental values that have defined American Exceptionalism and are the right of all mankind, not just the lucky few.

It is in America's interest to promote human rights. Nations that respect the rights of their own citizens are less likely to disrespect the rights of other countries and engage in military adventurism. Countries that share our values are our natural friends and allies.

Furthermore, it is America's responsibility and its opportunity to advance those rights which our forefathers fought to secure, from which so many of our blessings flow, in which we live in freedom.

Appeared in the *Chicago Sun Times,* February 16, 2006.

The United Nations should be an instrument through which human rights norms are advanced and individual rights are protected. Unfortunately it is not.

In 2004 I served as U.S. Ambassador to the U.N. Human Rights Commission in Geneva and saw first hand the ways in which it is dysfunctional. I listened to countries defend Fidel Castro's Cuba where political dissent means incarceration. I heard delegations defending the atrocities of Robert Mugabe in Zimbabwe where there is no free press and property is seized arbitrarily for political gain. Even North Korea's Kim Jong-Il was defended by some.

With 54 members, the Commission has proven too large to work effectively. Chronic human rights abusers such as Cuba, Zimbabwe and Sudan are allowed to serve on the Commission. In 2002, Libya chaired the Commission. As Peggy Hicks of Human Rights Watch has said, allowing human rights abusers on the panel has been debilitating. They are there to protect themselves from criticism, not advance human rights.

It is important to name and shame human rights abusers. But in recent years, there has been a growing predisposition among many countries to resist resolutions condemning specific states for their human rights abuses. In 2004 while I served in Geneva, the Commission even failed to condemn the ethnic cleansing going on in Sudan.

In pushing to transform the Commission into a new Human Rights Council, the United States and Europe are seeking to shrink its size, change the membership selection process, affirm the body's responsibility to condemn human rights abusers, and have the council exist year-round so it can act when rights violations are discovered. These are all straightforward, common sense reforms.

Nonetheless, there is strong resistance led by Belarus, Cuba, China, Egypt, Russia and Vietnam.

Human rights are fundamental and they are transcendent. Countries are being tested. The time for action is now. If U.N. members cannot act on Human Rights, what can they do?

U.N. HUMAN RIGHTS COUNCIL: HOPE UNREALIZED

Human Rights are important to Americans. As former Secretary of State George Shultz said, "What unifies us is not a common origin but a common set of ideals: freedom, constitutional democracy, racial and religious tolerance. We Americans thus define ourselves not by where we come from but by where we are headed: our goals, our values, our principles, which made the kind of society we strive to create."[1] I believe in those words. That is one reason I'm delighted to be here today at Northwestern University School of Law to discuss the United Nations Human Rights Council.

Just as human rights are central to the American Experience, so have human rights been enduring values of the United Nations. The U.N. Charter embraces two overriding goals: "to save succeeding generations from the scourge of war" and "to reaffirm faith in fundamental human rights."[2] And as Professor Mary Ann Glendon writes in her comprehensive book on the U.N. Universal Declaration of Human Rights, *A World Made New*, that United Nations declaration is "the parent document of the modern human rights movement."[3]

The United Nations has played a vital role in developing international human rights norms and in getting wide acceptance for these norms rhetorically, if not always in practice. Governments have signed on to the U.N. Universal Declaration of Human Rights and subsequent human rights documents. These commitments provide standards to which people can seek to hold their governments accountable. This is a considerable achievement.

But while the human rights values embraced in these U.N. documents are noble the machinery of the United Nations is imperfect and the behavior often scandalous of member states in implementing these standards and holding fellow member states to account.

The U.N. Commission on Human Rights had 54 member states elected for staggered terms. Unfortunately, over the years it became discredited as repressive regimes successful sought election to the Commission. In 2003, Libya, a routine violator of human rights, was elected Chair of the Commission. At the annual meetings in Geneva, condemnation of democratic Israel was routine while many brutal authoritarian regimes escaped rebuke.

Remarks at Northwestern University School of Law, Chicago, Illinois, October 17, 2006.

185

The litany of double standards exhibited at the UNCHR was long. At times, the flagrant hypocrisy was simply stunning.

In 2004, I went to Geneva as the United States Ambassador to the U.N. Commission on Human Rights. I listened to countries defend Fidel Castro's Cuba where political dissent means incarceration. I heard countries defend Burma's military junta. I heard delegations defending the atrocities of Robert Mugabe in Zimbabwe where there is no free press and property is seized arbitrarily for political gain. Even North Korea's Kim Jung II was defended by some.

The deliberations were an international puzzle palace of mirrors that did not reflect the real world where too many people are denied their basic human rights. In some ways, the UNCHR exhibited the worst distortions and double standards of the entire U.N. system. And it was all the more shameful because the matter at hand was human rights.

Let me review two issues which were particularly egregious. One involved Cuba and the other the performance of the European Union on Darfur.

One of the members of the United States delegation was Luis Zuninga, a Cuban-American. While a senior at the University of Havana, Luis was told he must sign a document to become a member of the Communist Party. He refused. Nineteen years later he was released from a Cuban prison and sent to Miami. He now is a United States citizen.

Early on at the meeting in Geneva when Luis was speaking, the Cubans called for a point of order and in highly personal and abusive language tried to shout him down. Among other things, they called Luis a terrorist. At that point, in my capacity as head of the U.S. delegation, I took the floor and declared: "Mr. Chairman, please remind the Cuban delegations that we are in Geneva and not Havana."

There was much more of this sort of outlandish behavior. During the second week of the meeting, a member of the U.S. delegation was threatened by a member of the Cuban delegation with the words, "You know you will pay a high toll for what you are doing, and we will be the ones to do it." The next week, a U.S. delegate, while distributing copies of a newspaper article to interested attendees of the session, was approached in the Commission chamber by a member of the Cuban delegation who demanded to know what he was distributing and ripped the copies of the article from his hands. A U.N. guard had to restrain the Cuban delegate. In a third incident, a member of our delegation was jogging on the streets of Geneva on a Saturday when a van pulled up and a member of the Cuban delegation leaned out and told the delegate that he "better watch out, we're keeping an eye on you." Other delegations also reported being threatened by members of the Cuban delegation. Just minutes after approval of a resolution critical of the continuing abuse of human rights by Fidel Castro's regime, many people witnessed a member of the Cuban delegation attack from behind a representative of an American-based organization in the lobby just outside the commission chambers. The victim, Frank Calzón, was hit in the head, knocked unconscious and fell to the floor. U.N. security guards had to physically subdue the Cuban delegate. Cuban Ambassador Jorge Mora Godoy's comment on this outrageous behavior was that the victim deserved what he got.

A U.N. spokesman said that the Cuban delegate's behavior was "shocking and unacceptable." Yes, it was unacceptable, but it should not have been shocking. What was on display in Geneva is the way the Cuban government treats its own people. The tactics remain sadly familiar – the insults, the threats, the assault and battery, the attacks on all those who dare disagree. On the island, you are either with the regime or you are against it. There is no middle ground. If you do not agree, you are harassed, detained, or imprisoned. But that such ugly behavior was on display at the 60th Session of the United Nations Commission on Human Rights not only reflects badly on Havana, it also shows Castro's contempt for the Commission and its mission.

While the behavior of the Cuban delegation at the UNCHR was outrageous, we have grown to expect that from Fidel Castro's brutal regime. Far more disheartening was the behavior of the European Union on Sudan.

Early on during the Commission meeting, I met with Irish Ambassador Mary Whelan in her capacity as chair of the European Union. We reviewed the Commission agenda and various initiatives on both thematic and country specific resolutions, comparing notes on strategy and who would take the lead on which resolutions. Among those on which the EU wanted to take the lead was Sudan where the ethnic fighting has reached alarming levels. With many other resolution on which the United States would be taking the lead, I was happy to tell Ambassador Whelan that we'd agree with her suggestions on the division of labor including allowing the European Union to take the lead on Sudan. However, I told her how important the United States viewed the brutal behavior in Sudan and that we would be a co-sponsor on the Sudan resolution. It was vital, I told her, that we condemn the on-going ethnic cleansing in the strongest possible terms.

As the weeks of the Commission session went on, I'd receive reports on those resolutions on which we were not taking the lead including Sudan. The Sudanese Ambassador was taking a rigid stand against any resolution. Even some of the African Commission members were uncomfortable with that.

Then during the third week of the Session, U.N. Secretary General Kofi Annan traveled to Geneva to address the Commission on Human Rights during a Special Day of Remembrance on the tenth anniversary of the genocide in Rwanda when Hutu's killed 800,000 Tutsis, mostly with machetes, during a 100-day rampage of horror. Near the end of his speech, the Secretary General said we must address the "ethnic cleansing" currently going on in Darfur, Sudan where 30,000 blacks already had been killed by the Arab government and Arab militias, and where over 900,000 blacks were internally displaced in desperate conditions due to Arab violence.

The Secretary General's words had a profound affect on the Commission members, especially African states. They began to pressure the Sudanese to accept some sort of a resolution on the situation in Darfur.

During the fifth week of the Commission Session, the EU Chair, Ambassador Whelan, and African representatives began to meet to see if a compromise was possible. At one point near the end of the week I met with a group of Africans and then with the Europeans. I made clear that the draft I had been shown was unacceptable. Any resolution must "condemn" the ethnic cleansing that was going on; must "demand" the violence against the black Sudanese stop immediately; must "require" the Government of Sudan allow international humanitarian assistance to flow to the distressed population; and must "call" on the Government to allow immediate and unrestricted access to Darfur by international observers including a rapporteur from the UNCHR. This was the minimum. The United States would not join in supporting anything less.

Apparently Ambassador Whelan met with African representatives over the weekend. On Tuesday, my delegation was told that negotiations had broken down. The original resolution would come to a vote later in the week. Some countries sympathetic to Sudan, including some Africans, nonetheless felt the Commission could not be silent while ethnic cleansing was going on in Sudan. Therefore a number of African delegations informed us that they would vote to condemn Sudan when the tabled resolution came before the Commission. Our count showed that while it would be a close vote, the Sudan resolution would pass. Human Rights Watch and several other NGOs did their own whip counts and agreed that the resolution would pass.

The delegations gathered in the U.N. chamber on Thursday morning for the 10:00 a.m. opening gavel. The vote on Sudan was scheduled for that morning. Then at 9:45 a.m. a number of African delegations approach Ambassador Whelan on the floor with a last minute proposal for a "Chairman's Statement" on Sudan. In a matter of minutes, without consulting any other delegation, the Irish Ambassador agreed to the deal in her capacity as EU Chair. Delegations were informed that there would be no vote that day on the pending Sudan resolution.

During the lunch break, we saw the proposed compromise. None of the four required elements were contained in the draft accepted by the Irish Ambassador in behalf of the European Union. After consulting with Washington, I went to a 2:00 p.m. meeting hosted by the Irish for non-EU co-sponsors of the original Sudan resolution that had been tabled earlier. The Irish delegation walked through the text, acknowledged that it was far softer than what had been tabled and beyond what many countries had said they could accept, however, it was important to get African "buy in" to any action and this language accomplished that goal. Furthermore, consensus was a vital U.N. principle, and this language could provide consensus.

When the Irish had finished giving their rationale, I took the floor to state clearly and strongly the United States government's position on the "ethnic cleansing" in Sudan. Consequently, there would be no "consensus" on this compromise because my delegation would not support it. And if it were introduced as a resolution, the United States would vote no. I was followed by the Canadian, then the Australian, and then the New Zealander. Each agreed with me and expressed profound disappointment with the Irish for caving to this weak proposal and for failing to consult with the resolutions co-sponsors before committing the European Union to the deal. Then a Czech representative began to make similar remarks. At that the Irish chair of the meeting tapped the table and said to the Czech, "You are out of order. Your comments should be held for a European Union meeting discussion on this topic. They are not appropriate at this meeting or at this time." Signs of things to come as the EU bloc further organizes and disciplines its members within the United Nations.

There followed a frantic flurry of consultations over the next 24 hours. In the end, the United States forced a vote on the original resolution. While it had the votes 48 hours earlier, in the end some fell off because now they could vote for the weaker

EU language. The muscular resolution condemning "ethnic cleansing" in Sudan failed. Later, the emasculated EU language passed which did not "condemn," did not "demand" and did not "call" on the Sudanese Government to do anything; but which noted their cooperation, etc. The United States voted against this retreat.

This little drama is ugly and noteworthy on a number of counts. First and foremost, the 60th Session of the United Nations Commission on Human Rights was unable to demonstrate the political will to condemn ethnic cleansing. After World War II, the world said, "Never Again." Then came the Killing Fields of Cambodia, genocide in Rwanda, ethnic cleansing in Bosnia and then Kosovo. The world said, "Never Again." Yet the atrocities in Darfur are known. Even the Secretary-General labeled these terrible acts as "ethnic cleansing." Nonetheless, the Commission could not bring itself to condemn these monstrous acts. The Commission was unable to keep faith with the Sudanese victims nor have fidelity to the values enshrined in the Universal Declaration of Human Rights. This is profoundly sad. If the Commission would not condemn ethnic cleansing, what moral authority did it have? It dishonored the Commission and its members who failed in their responsibilities.

But, secondly, this is noteworthy because of what it says about the internal dynamics in United Nations fora, including the Commission on Human Rights. There the desire for diplomatic cooperation and consensus decision-making is greater than concern about people being killed and others driven out of their homes due to their ethnicity. Arabs brutalizing blacks. Form over substance. Collegiality over principle. The insular, closed world of U.N. diplomacy eclipsed consideration of real events happening in the real world; even events of horror and death.

I have seen this dynamic many times in many U.N. fora over the past 24 years. But never have I witnessed it to such craven and immoral effect. It never ceases to amaze and to disappoint.

Third, it reminds me that the business of diplomats is to get agreements. Too often diplomats judge their success by whether or not they got the deal; not the benefit or harm of the deal itself.

And fourth, the emerging influence and discipline of the European Union within the United Nations is a force which bears watching and one which is not altogether healthy.

The failure of the Commission on Human Rights to deal with the ethnic cleansing in Sudan in a clear, straightforward, muscular fashion was ugly. Indeed, ten years from now I suspect the failure to act appropriately on genocide in Sudan will be the only thing for which the 60th Session of the U.N. Commission on Human Rights will be remembered.

These stories from the 2004 session of the U.N. Commission on Human Rights show why that body had become discredited and in need of fundamental reform.

Secretary-General Kofi Annan recognized the need to reform the U.N. Commission on Human Rights. When his comprehensive reform proposals, *In Larger Freedom – Towards Development, Security and Human Rights* were issued in the spring of 2005, he stated "I ask member states to create a new Council to fulfill one of the primary purposes of the Organization, which clearly now requires more effective operational structures – the promotion of human rights. This would replace the present Commission on Human Rights, whose capacity to perform its tasks has been undermined by its declining credibility and professionalism. The Human Rights Council, I suggest, should be smaller than the Commission, and elected directly by a two-thirds majority of (the General) Assembly."[4] And Mark Malloch Brown, then chief of staff to the Secretary-General, said, "For the great global public, the performance or non-performance of the Human Rights Commission has become the litmus test for U.N. renewal."[5]

Following months of deliberations, a number of reforms were set out in the 2005 World Summit Outcome Document.[6] At the outset, the United States Government strongly supported the creation of a new Human Rights Council that could better offer rapid attention to urgent or continuing human rights violations and provide technical assistance to countries to strengthen domestic human rights protections. And, as suggested by Kofi Annan, the U.S. wanted a smaller body and one that kept off states that were habitual violators of human rights.[7]

As Secretary of State Condoleezza Rice noted to the U.N. General Assembly, the new Human Rights Council "must have fewer members, less politics, and more credibility. ...It must have the moral authority to condemn all violators of human rights – even those that sit among us in the hall. ...And it should never-never empower brutal dictatorships to sit in judgment of responsible democracies."[8]

The deliberations that followed the World Summit proved very contentious. As Ambassador John Bolton said in December, 2005, "There's a lot of opposition for the same reason that countries like Cuba, Zimbabwe (and) Burma try to get on the Human Rights Commission, to block scrutiny of their existing human rights record. Those countries that are the worst abusers of human rights fear a mechanism that they can't block or pervert to their own ends."[9]

Ultimately efforts to make the new Human Rights Council smaller and its membership more stringent failed. The size went from 53 member states to 47. Election remained by a mere majority not the two thirds suggested by the Secretary-General and championed by the United States. So, when the new U.N. Human Rights Council was overwhelmingly adopted in March, 2006, the United States abstained. In an "explanation of vote," Ambassador Bolton said, "[O]ur preeminent concern was always about the credibility of the body's membership. ...(A)bsent stronger mechanisms for maintaining credible membership, the United States cannot join consensus on this resolution. We did not have sufficient confidence in this text to be able to say that the HRC would be better than its predecessor."[10]

In contrast to the American position, almost all other countries voted for the new U.N. Human Rights Council.[11] Unfortunately, United States skepticism seems warranted by the Council's poor performance so far.

For example, beyond the 47 members of the Human Rights Council, all countries not on the Council are invited to send representatives to speak at meetings, and Iran sent their prosecutor general, Saaed Mortazavi who "has been implicated in torture, illegal detention, and coercing false confessions by numerous former prisoners. Joe Stark, of Human Rights Watch said, "Iran's decision to send Mortazavi to Geneva demonstrates utter contempt for human rights and for the new council."[12]

And the disproportionate attention to Israel and the one-sided, unbalanced resolutions against Israel have continued under the new Human Rights Council. Again let me cite a Human Rights Watch statement. Under the heading "Lebanon/ Israel: U.N. Rights Body Squanders Chance to Help Civilians," Human Rights Watch stated, "By adopting a politicized resolution that looks only at Israeli abuses in the current conflict, the Human Rights Council undermines its credibility and wasted an opportunity to protect civilians in the region. ...The one-sided approach taken by the Human Rights Council is a blow to its credibility and an abdication of its responsibility to protect human rights for all. ...This is a poor way to launch a new institution."[13] At the same time, the Council has failed to address such critical human rights crisis as Darfur, Sri Lanka and Uzbekistan."[14]

After the Human Rights Council's second session ended on October 6th, Amnesty International that had championed this new organization, provided this troubling commentary: "Amnesty International is concerned that the three weeks of the second session were marked by too many vestiges of practices that were responsible for discrediting the Commission on Human Rights. ...Old-fashioned political maneuvering reminiscent of the (old) Commission at its worst prevented the Council from addressing the gross and systematic violations that were taking place in Sudan's Darfur region and Eastern Chad as the Council met."[15]

And the *Washington Post* editorialized last week, "The Council, which completed its second formal session last week in Geneva, has turned out to be far worse than its predecessor – not just a 'shadow' but a travesty that the United Nations can ill afford. ...The ludicrous diplomatic lynch mob has been directed by the Organization of the Islamic Conference, which accounts for 17 governments on the 47-member council and counts on the support of like-minded dictatorships such as Cuba and China. Council rules allow an extraordinary session to be called at the behest of just one-third of the membership, making it easy for the Islamic association to orchestrate anti-Israeli spectacles. ...If there is no turnaround, the Council's performance ought to invite consideration of the measure that was applied to the U.N. cultural organization, UNESCO, when it ran amok in the 1980's: a cutoff of U.S. funding."[16]

In the seven months since the United Nations General Assembly created the new Human Rights Council many serious and disheartening issues have arisen. Under the mechanisms adopted for electing members, will repressive regimes, chronic abusers of human rights, be kept off? Once elected, can countries rise above the pull of region, religion or ideology and act on a commitment to human rights? On complex and difficult issues such as the Middle East, can a responsible even-handedness prevail? And on urgent matters of monstrous abuse such as the "genocide in slow motion" in Darfur, can the Council give a global voice of conscience to the voiceless victims suffering on the ground?

In other words, can the member states in the U.N. Human Rights Council keep faith with the transcendent values of inalienable human rights granted to every person by their creator and reaffirmed in such seminal documents as the U.N. Universal Declaration on Human Rights? That is the promise of the United Nations. That is the hope. Tragically, that ray of hope grows dim.

1.   George P. Shultz, "Human Rights and the Moral Dimension of U.S. Foreign Policy," an address at the 86th Annual Washington Day Banquet at the Creve Coeur Club of Illinois, Peoria, Illinois, February 22, 1984, published as Current Policy No. 551 by the United States Department of State Bureau of Public Affairs, Washington, D.C., 1984.

2.   The U.N. Charter was signed at the United Nations Conference on International Organization in San Francisco on June 26, 1945. See, Stephen C. Schlesinger, *Act of Creation: The Founding of the United Nations* (Boulder, Colorado; Westview Press; 2003).

3.   Mary Ann Glendon, *A World Made New: Eleanor Roosevelt and the Universal Declaration of Human Rights* (New York, N.Y.; Random House; 2001).

4.   The Secretary-General Statement to the General Assembly, New York, March 21, 2005. Available at http://www.un.org/largerfreedom/sg-statement.html. See also Kofi Annan, "In Larger Freedom: Decision Time at the U.N.," *Foreign Affairs*, May/June 2005; and Report of the Secretary-General's High-Level Panel on Threats, Challenges and Change, *A More Secure World: Our Shared Responsibility*, 2004. Available at http://www.un.org/secureworld/. See also, the report of the Gingrich-Mitchell Task Force on the United Nations; United States Institute of Peace," American Interests and U.N. eform: Report of the Task Force on the United Nations," June, 2005. Available at www.usip.org/un/report/usip_un_report.pdf.

5.   Richard S. Williamson, "U.N.'s Human Rights Commission will Never Succeed Without Reform," *Chicago Sun-Times*, February 16, 2006.

6.   Available at http://www.un.org/summit2005/documents.html.

7.   See, Mark Lagon, remarks to the Human Rights Council Working Group, October 18, 2005, USUN Press Release #176(05).

8.   As quoted in the Statement of Ambassador John R. Bolton, "Challenges and Opportunities in Moving Ahead on U.N. Reform," Hearing before the Senate Foreign Relations Committee, U.S. Congress, Washington, D.C., October 18, 2005. See also, Mark P. Lagon statement in the Human Rights Working Group, November 1, 2005, USUN Press Release #196(05).

9 .   Remarks by Ambassador John R. Bolton on Human Rights and U.N. Reform, at the Security Council Stakeout, December 7, 2005, USUN Press Release #235(05).

"We think that the Commission on Human Rights was largely discredited for two major reasons: one is that it was co-opted, in some cases, by some of the worst abusers of human rights -- Libya, Zimbabwe and others -- and so we've said that we need to see some membership improvements in the new Council on Human Rights, that the worst offenders should not be eligible to serve on the Council. So we've proposed that any country that's under sanction for human rights abuses should not be eligible to serve on the Council.

"There is a belief from some countries that we should never exclude a country from membership in anything. We reject that. We think that if you're a country that is going to express views on human rights, that's going to be responsible for providing technical assistance to other countries on human rights, you should have a demonstrated commitment to treat your own people appropriately.

"The second big issue on which there's a disagreement is the mandate. We think that the Council, to do its work effectively, needs to be able to call attention to grave and urgent cases of human rights abuses and Darfur is a perfect example. This goes back very much to our responsibility, our commitment to "responsibility to protect" issues. The Council has to be able to call attention when there is a grave and urgent case emerging.

"There is a view from some countries in New York that this kind of country-specific resolution would embarrass countries. Again, we reject that. We think that it's important to shine a bright light on human rights cases to encourage countries to correct them." Kristen Silverberg, Assistant Secretary of State for International Organization Affairs, On-the-Record-Briefing, Washington, D.C., December 20, 2005.

10.   Explanation of Vote by Ambassador John R. Bolton, on the Human Rights Council Draft Resolution, in the U.N. General Assembly, March 15, 2006, USUN Press Release #51 (06). See also, Secretary Condoleezza Rice, U.S. Pledge on Human Rights Council Membership, Washington, D.C., April 13, 2006. Available at http://www.state.gov/secretary/rm/2006/64594.htm.

11. "In replacing the Commission on Human Rights, the Human Rights Council has the potential to be significantly more effective; it has a clear mandate to address all human rights situations, including gross and systematic violations, and a new universal review mechanism to ensure that all countries' human rights records are addressed periodically. It will meet in more frequent session, at least three times a year for at least ten weeks. The Council will be able to convene more easily in special sessions to respond more effectively to both chronic and urgent human rights situations. Importantly, the rules governing the election to the Human Rights Council require that U.N. member states take account of candidates' human rights record and pledges." Amnesty International, "U.N. Human Rights Council: A new Beginning for Human Rights," Public Statement 5/10/06. Available at http://web.amnesty.org/library/index/engior4001 72006?open&of=ENG-393.

12. Human Rights Watch, "Iran: Remove Rights Abuser From Delegation at U.N.", June 22, 2006. Available at http://hrw.org/english/docs/2006/06/22/iran/3602.htm.

13. Human Rights Watch, "Lebanon/Israel: U.N. Rights Body Squanders Chance to Help Civilians," August 11, 2006. Available at http://hrw.org/english/docs/2006/08/11/lebano13969.htm.

14. 'In the face of atrocities in the Sudan, attacks on civilians in Sri Lanka, and impunity for mass murder in Uzbekistan, this council was largely silent.' Human Rights Watch, "U.N. Rights Council Disappoints Again," October 6, 2006. Available at http://hrw.org/english/docs/2006/10/06/global14354. htm.

15. Amnesty International, Public Statement, "U.N. Human Rights Council: Member Governments Must Do More to Build an Effective Council," October 11, 2006. Available at http://www.amnesty.org/ news/document.do?id=ENGIOR400352006.htm.

16. Editorial, "Reform Run Amok: The U.N.'s New Human Rights Council Makes the Old One Look Good," *Washington Post*, October 12, 2006.

TRANSITIONAL JUSTICE: DARK PAST TO LIBERAL FUTURE

As we see in Iraq, Afghanistan, the Democratic Republic of the Congo and elsewhere, the traumas of post-conflict societies do not end when the killing stops. The process of reconciliation and reconstruction in torn societies is difficult. It can be expensive and it takes time, but, as we have seen in the Balkans and Sierra Leone, it can be done.

The great challenge for transitional justice is what to do about terrible crimes when the killing stops. How can transitional justice address a dark past in a manner that contributes to a future of sustainable peace founded upon a respect for individual rights with a durable rule of law?

Lessons Learned

As post-conflict torn societies deal with the issues of accountability, reconciliation and restoration, some lessons have been learned. There have been a variety of Truth and Reconciliation Commissions in Chile, El Salvador, Ecuador, Nigeria, South Korea, Timor Lestre, Ghana, Morocco, Sierra Leone and elsewhere. The ways and means of informing the public, soliciting and recording personal stories of abuse and making the findings available to the public have varied. Each recognizes the suffering of victims, records the atrocities for history, shames the perpetrators and, thereby, contributes to healing the wounds.

However, when circumstances permit, justice should go beyond recording past atrocities. When the post-conflict government is less fragile, a judicial process of fact-finding, re-affirming the rule of law, and accountability should be pursued.

In 1993, the international community, through the United Nations, set up the international tribunal at the Hague to punish war crimes committed in the Balkans. The next year the U.N. Security Council established its second *ad hoc* tribunal in Arusha, Tanzania, to deal with those who directed the genocide in Rwanda. At the International Criminal Tribunal for the former Yugoslavia (ICTY) strong sentences have been handed down on Serb and Croat generals and concentration camp commanders. At the International Criminal Tribunal for Rwanda (ICTR), the former prime minister of Rwanda, Jean-Paul Kambanda, has been indicted. These are positive developments, but the wheels of justice have moved excruciatingly slow. This past spring, ten years after the Dayton Peace Accords and four years into his trial, former Serbian President Slobodan Milosevic died before the verdict had been rendered on his crimes. As the saying goes, justice delayed is justice denied.

Appeared in *The Interdependent*, Vol. 4, No. 3, Fall, 2006.

The ICTY and ICTR have proven to be very expensive, each costing the international community about $100 million a year. These proceedings are taking place far from the country where the crimes were committed. Consequently, the restorative impact of these tribunals is muted and their contribution easily marginalized.

The Sierra Leone Special Court is an improvement over the ICTY and ICTR. In the 1990's in Sierra Leone, there was a particularly bloody civil war between the Revolutionary United Front rebel group, supported by Liberian President Charles Taylor, and the government. By 2001, the rebels had been defeated. Weary of confronting former insurgents generally who might trigger a new round of violence, a Truth and Reconciliation Commission was established to address most of the atrocities. It was given two years to finish its work, but to deal with the worst crimes, Sierra Leone went further. In January, 2002, the U.N. Security Council and the Sierra Leone Government set up a Special Court, which is a hybrid of both national and international courts.

The chief prosecutor, American David Crane, was selected by U.N. Secretary General Kofi Annan and approved by Sierra Leone President Ahmad Jajan Kabbash. Funding for the court came from voluntary contributions, with the United States and Britain the largest donors. In less than a year the offices for the Special Court were constructed, scores of educational town meetings were held throughout the countryside to inform the people about the court, and the Court indicted 12 persons whom it was alleged bore the greatest responsibility for war crimes, crimes against humanity, and violations of international humanitarian law. That was an unprecedented, breathtaking pace. Significantly, among the 12 indictees, one was a sitting Sierra Leone government minister -- a leader of the winning side -- for using excessive force and abusing the rebels. Also among the indictees was Liberian President Charles Taylor.

When the Sierra Leone Special Court unsealed its 11 count indictment of Charles Taylor in June, 2003, he was the sitting president of Liberia. The former warlord who had incited, fomented and supported rebellion and instability throughout Africa's Mano River Region for his own benefit, was now encircled as bloody fighting closed in upon him. Most felt Taylor would fight until the death of the last of his drugged-up child soldiers and that countless civilians would die. To avoid the senseless bloodbath, Nigeria's President Olusegun Obasanjo offered Taylor asylum if he would promptly leave Monrovia. It was an offer Taylor could not refuse.

With Taylor's departure, Liberia's fighting soon ended. Through the United Nations, the international community supported Liberia's transition from tyranny and bloodshed to democracy and hope. Ellen Johnson Sirleaf was elected president of Linberia in October 2005and several months after she took office, she asked President Obasqanjo to return Taylor to face trial before the Sierra Leone Special Court. Soon Taylor was back in Freetown behind bars.

Because of fears of violence, Taylor has been moved to The Hague for trial in that court with the proceedings still under the direction of the Sierra Leone Special Court. If he ia found guilty, Great Britain has agreed to jail Taylor. The process may not be perfect, but is a powerful contribution to transitional justice nonetheless -- and the message goes beyond Taylor's victims in Sierra Leone.

Perhaps man's continued inhumanity to man today is demonstrated most powerfully by the "genocide in slow motion" that continues in Darfur. As diplomats struggle to buttress a sustainable peace agreement and the international community works to organize and deploy an effective peacekeeping operation to enforce that peace once achieved, the U.N. Security Council – with American support – has given jurisdiction to the International Criminal Court to investigate and prosecute war crimes and crimes against humanity committed in this tragic war.

A Way Forward

Records of past crimes serve as testaments to injustices suffered and provide recognition of the pain, a history that cannot be dismissed nor denied, a measure of justice, a path toward forgiveness.

Whenever possible, when the danger of reigniting the fighting is not prohibitive, those who have committed the worst crimes against humanity should be brought to trial. Consistent with legal principles, the exact modalities will vary due to history, culture, feasibility and other local considerations. The trials should be timely when evidence, memories and wounds are fresh; and when the contribution to reconciliation is greatest. Whenever possible, the trials should take place where the victims can witness justice being done to decrease the possibilities of perceived divisive political manipulation and increase the impact of the message of accountability.

The international community, the U.N., the Council of Europe, non-governmental organizations, academics and others should continue to study the ways and means of transitional justice, develop "best practices," be prepared to provide technical assistance, legitimacy and resources for societies moving from a dark past to a brighter future. The new U.N. Peacebuilding Commission should provide valuable help in this area. For a new, stable, free society under the rule of law to emerge, past injustices must be faced, justice must be done, and a measure of reconciliation achieved.

SECTION IV:
DEMOCRACY

DEMOCRACY FOR IRAQIS
MAKES WORLD SAFER FOR US ALL

For 35 years, Saddam Hussein ruled Iraq with vicious brutality. In a few days, millions of Iraqis will go to polling stations to vote for new leadership. They will be taking an important step in securing their freedom and in assuming the personal responsibility necessary to sustain it.

The United States is the world's oldest democracy. And democracy promotion has long served as part of the moral and strategic foundation of American foreign policy.

Early in the twentieth century President Woodrow Wilson insisted that the United States' role in the world was "not to prove... our selfishness but our greatness." And Wilson led America into World War I to "make the world safe for democracy."

Two decades ago, Ronald Reagan stood at the Berlin Wall and said, "Mr. Gorbachev, tear down this wall." But President Reagan also made clear that America's "crusade for freedom" ought not end with the fall of the Soviet empire.

Reagan said, "The task I've set forth will long outlive our own generation... For the sake of peace and justice, let us move toward a world in which all people are at last free to determine their own destiny."

America promotes democracy because it is the right thing to do, and because the advance of democracy makes the world safer.

Every human being has inherent dignity and worth. Self-determination is a fundamental human right upon which America has prospered. And, as Reagan said, "Freedom is not the prerogative of the lucky few, but the right of all mankind."

Democracy is a rampart against state encroachment on individual rights and liberty. If you can participate in choosing your government through a democratic process, you can protect your interests and rights from abuse by government. It fosters greater political equality.

Democracy is the surest path to a just society because it gives people the opportunity to live under laws of their own choosing. It provides restraints and accountability.

A democracy provides its citizens the freedom to follow their dreams, develop their talents, and reap the reward of their labors. It helps create growth and opportunity.

Appeared in the *Chicago Sun Times*, January 26, 2005.

Among other things, today Americans are threatened by global terrorism.

Dictatorships where there is no hope nor opportunity provide fertile soil to grow terrorists frustrated and bitter by their impotent lot in life, attracted to fanaticism, and willing to strike out in senseless violence against innocent civilians.

Democracy, by empowering its citizens, encouraging personal responsibility, providing opportunity, and allowing hope to flourish crowds out the despair upon which terrorism relies.

And democratic societies with their capacity to adjust and adapt to changing circumstances at home and abroad are inherently more stable than dictatorships unresponsive to the will of the people. Furthermore, democracies are more reluctant to engage in foreign adventurism and begin wars of aggression because they must build and sustain popular support. Whereas dictatorships often capriciously invade neighbors for the vain glory of its ruler such as Saddam's invasions of Iran and Kuwait.

So promoting democracy helps in the war on terrorism, creates a more stable world and is a restraint on wars of aggression. For all these reasons the advance of democracy in Iraq is important for the Iraqi people and for us. And for all these reasons the Saddam loyalists, dead enders and terrorists are committed to derail the upcoming election.

Sadly, therefore, the violence rises in Iraq as these desperate spoilers seek to thwart the march of freedom. Nonetheless, thousands of dedicated Iraqis are risking life and limb to prepare for election day. And millions plan to cast their first meaningful vote.

It has been a difficult, perilous and bloody path from Saddam's brutal reign to this election. The Iraqi people will take an enormous step toward freedom when, in a few days, they cast their votes.

In the face of critics and skeptics, in the past year the march of freedom has advanced through free and fair elections in Afghanistan, Ukraine and among the Palestinians. Different cultures. Difficult circumstances. Yet in each election brave people chose freedom. And in each country those people are taking control of their own destiny.

The run up to the Iraqi election has not been smooth. It seldom is. The election will not be perfect. Elections never are.

But in the end the overwhelming majority of the Iraqi people will go to the polls, they will vote, and they will take a critical step toward freedom, opportunity and hope. And the world will be safer for it.

And we can be sure, as President Bush has said, "Freedom and fear, justice and cruelty, have always been at war, and we know that God is not neutral between them."

REASONS FOR HOPE IN IRAQ'S CRITICAL ELECTION

All people want freedom. They want to live in societies that are secure, just; and where hopes and dreams can be realized. But securing freedom is not easy. It can be dangerous. It is difficult. And it is messy. Yet it is well worth it.

In recent months the march of freedom has advanced. In Afghanistan, millions of Muslims turned out to vote notwithstanding violence and intimidation. In Ukraine, people demonstrated in the streets in protest against an effort to steal the election. They prevailed. Even the Palestinians held free and fair elections.

Now we approach Iraq's election for the Transitional National Assembly. The violence is rising. Saddam loyalists, dead enders and international terrorists are increasing their carnage. Some Sunni leaders are urging an election boycott. What will happen and what will it mean?

For 35 years the Iraqi people lived under Saddam's brutal dictatorship. The violence was capricious and it was vicious. There were no rules but the shifting whims, insecurity, and vain glory of Saddam. Hundreds of thousands of Iraqi Kurds were gassed to death. A hundred thousand Shia in the southern marshland were poisoned. Tens of thousands of people were arbitrarily arrested, tortured, raped and killed.

Judy Van Rest, Executive Vice President of the International Republican Institute, who spent over a year in Baghdad with the Iraqi Provisional Authority working with women to build civil society, told me about visiting one of Saddam's many mass graves. Standing on a small mound, before her the mass grave stretched in every direction as far as the eye could see.

The insecurity imposed by Saddam's reign of terror was wide and it was deep. It will take time for the people victimized by Saddam's brutality to develop confidence in themselves and in the rule of law. Understandably, a sense of insecurity and hesitancy remain. But many Iraqis are finding their voices. And many are active participants in this election process.

A poll conducted by the International Republican Institute indicates that despite the insurgents' threats and Iraq's lack of democratic tradition, 80 percent of Iraqis say they are likely to vote.

Appeared in *Tech Central Station,* January 26, 2005.

With over 50 percent of the population Shia, they will win the majority of seats. Not surprisingly, an overwhelming majority of Shia plan to vote.

Some are concerned that the Iraqi Shiites are too closely aligned with the Iranian Shiites. Some are. But there also is a great deal of friction between the Shiites of Iraq and those of Iran. Of course there's some bad Shiites, but many are good people who want a sovereign Iraq and not three countries. So they will work for compromise with the minority Kurds and Sunnis.

The Kurds represent about 25 percent of the population. The Kurdish area of Iraq has had semi-autonomy for many years. Again, the poll indicates large numbers of Iraqi Kurds plan to vote. They want their interests well represented in the drafting of a new Iraqi constitution.

The Sunni are slightly less than 25 percent of the population. Saddam Hussein was a Sunni and many were favored during Saddam's rule. Many Sunni are concerned they will be disadvantaged in an election where they are so outnumbered by Shia and Kurds. The Sunni community has been targeted for the harshest threats of violence if they vote. And some Sunni leaders have urged an election boycott.

Undoubtedly, this will dampen Sunni voter turnout. Some predict a Sunni turnout of 5-8 percent. It probably will not be that low, but it will be a modest turnout.

Ultimately the Iraqi people must choose democracy. They must take the step to vote. If most Sunnis do not vote, that's their choice. They will learn the costs of not participating. And, I expect, in the fall constitutional referendum more Sunnis will vote; and more still in the assembly election to be held by year's end.

The high level of violence will continue up to and on election day. Undoubtedly some polling stations will be targeted.

Nonetheless, on election day, we can expect that over two-thirds of Iraqis will vote. The 275 member Iraq Transitional National Assembly will be elected and it will have legitimacy. It will not solve the problems in Iraq but it will be an important step forward. Iraqis will have more control over their destiny.

After their election, there will be a lull in violence as the enemies of freedom try to figure out who they now should target. Then the insurgents will continue their violence.

The insecurity in Iraq is bad, and it will continue to be bad. But delaying the election will not help. The overwhelming majority of Iraqis wants to move forward. They have choices to make. And they are prepared to vote.

This election is not the solution to Iraq's problems. But it is a step forward toward a new sovereign Iraq where the people have a say in the constitution that will govern them, where the rule of law will take hold, where the people select their leaders, and where compromise and cooperation will be the rhythm of life.

While their insecurity remains their greatest concern, by a margin of 6 to 1 the Iraqi people believe things will be better one year from now. The democratic election on January 30th will be an important step toward that better future.

UKRAINE:
DEMOCRACY TAKING ROOT

It's a pleasure for me to be in Ukraine, the world's newest democracy.

Last December an "Orange Revolution" nullified a fraudulent election and then, through a free and fair election, the opposition prevailed and an authoritarian government was swept away.

Here in Kiev, where people had gathered to protest the rigged election, now they gathered to cheer their victory. And in the Ukrainian neighborhoods of Chicago and in free societies everywhere, we also cheered.

But the struggle for Ukraine's new democracy did not begin with those crowds protesting in Kiev, nor did it end with that successful election day.

Building a democracy is difficult. It takes time. But even in countries with no history of "free and fair elections", it can be done.

Construction of a sustainable democracy is well worth the effort. For democracy empowers the people, giving them the opportunity to help steer their own destiny. It is a rampart against human rights abuse. Democracies are more stable than authoritarian regimes and less likely to engage in foreign adventurism. Also, democracies are not fertile grounds for producing terrorists.

Democracies tend to share common values with the United States. They are America's natural allies. As President Bush has said, "spreading democracy abroad makes our own democracy more secure."

Ukrainians, like people everywhere, aspired to end authoritarian rule and usher in liberty. Many brave Ukrainians risked much and worked tirelessly for years to realize their dream. And these Ukrainians had help.

Americans with the International Republican Institute (IRI) and the National Democratic Institute (NDI) were on the ground working with civil society and helping the opposition to organize. Over many years, IRI held workshops and training sessions throughout Ukraine on polling, message, media, organizing down to the local neighborhoods, the rule of law, voter identification and voter turn out, among other things.

The Organization for Security and Co-operation in Europe (OSCE), also has been here. A quick review of OSCE programs in Ukraine is illustrative of how wide ranging the work was that led up to that successful election and how much remains to be done to build a sustainable democracy.

Remarks in Kiev, Ukraine, April 1, 2005.

The OSCE had projects on media, the rule of law and election procedures. OSCE helped train journalists and supported 30 two-day events throughout Ukraine on media ethics in election related coverage. It developed and disseminated objective information concerning media coverage of the various candidates during the campaign and helped ensure all candidates were granted national and regional coverage.

OSCE helped develop a manual of updated media legislation and disseminated 15,000 copies. It supported training for media lawyers. The OSCE coordinated seminars for judges and produced and distributed 4,000 manuals focused on the peculiarities of resolving election disputes by courts.

The OSCE supported publication of a journal devoted to election related issues. It worked to clarify issues concerning the legal framework for voting abroad. And the OSCE provided information about citizen's legal rights to vote and how to refer legal issues to existing legal aid structures.

The OSCE conducted 32 training workshops for members of Territorial Election Commissions in all of Ukraine's 25 oblasts.

The OSCE helped in voter education, voter awareness, and updating Voter Lists. It even helped produce 35,000 templates in Braille to enable visually impaired voters to vote at each polling station.

On election day the Ukrainians went to the polls. OSCE, IRI and NDI were among the international observers that day. All reported that election failed to meet minimal acceptable international standards for free and fair elections. This empowered the people to gather in Kiev and launch the Orange Revolution.

A new election was held. Opposition leader Victor Yushchenko was elected Ukraine's new president. And now work must be done for democracy to take root, to flourish, and to be sustainable.

The rule of law must be made unassailable. Corruption must be rooted out. Both commerce and government must be open and transparent. A tolerance for different views and a respect for a free media must be realized. The habits of compromise, civility and coalition building must be developed.

Parliamentary elections approach. They must be free and fair and the results respected.

These things do not happen overnight. IRI, NDI, OSCE and other international organizations will remain active to help the Ukrainian people achieve success. But in the end, it is the Ukrainian people, it is you, who will determine the success of this noble enterprise. I am encouraged by what I have seen. The leaders of civil society in Kiev with whom I have met seem to have the necessary commitment to succeed. In doing so, they will build a better future for their children and a safer world for us all.

Thank you.

UKRAINE:
THE ORANGE REVOLUTION

It's a pleasure to be here at the Kazakhstan International Bureau of Human Rights. I share with you a belief that everyone is entitled to fundamental human rights. And I applaud your efforts to bring such basic rights to the people of Kazakhstan. I recognize that the road can be difficult. Many of you have sacrificed a great deal to advance this cause. The international community supports you. Groups such as the Organization for Security and Cooperation in Europe will continue to champion your cause and progress will be made.

The other day I was in Ukraine. I'd like to share a story with you about the Orange Revolution that speaks to the dream of freedom realized because of the dedication and work of people like you.

In the early evening last Friday at the OSCE offices on Striletska Street in Kiev, I met Vladyslav Kaskiv. A man of medium build in his late 30's, Vlad has a pleasant, if unremarkable face. He had been identified to me as one of the key leaders of the "Orange Revolution" and I was anxious to hear his story.

As we introduced ourselves and exchanged pleasantries, I thanked Vlad for what he had done as a leader in Ukraine's struggle for democracy. I told him that he was a "hero" for what he had done. Vlad turned a bit red and his eyes looked down at the table at which we sat. Vlad said, "You're too kind. I was not a leader. There were no leaders. People love freedom. They love it. They always have loved freedom. Events and their love of freedom drew the people to Maidan Square (Independence Square). My role and the role of a few others was not to lead them, we merely helped coordinate and guide the protesters. Their love of freedom led them. And they would not accept 'no' for an answer. This time they would not be denied."

History of Ukraine

Ukraine has a long history during much of which they were controlled by outsiders. In 1240, Kiev was invaded by the Tatar-Mongols led by the grandson of Genghis Khan. This led to nearly a century-long rule by Tatar-Mongols. There followed many centuries in which Ukraine was attacked and ruled by Poland and Lithuania in the Rzecz Polpolita Commonwealth, Russia, Germany and others.

After the 1917 Russian Revolution, Vladimir Illyich Lenin expanded his power into Ukraine. Ukraine experienced a brief period of independence when the Ukrainian Central Rada – the Council – formally issued a proclamation for Ukrainian

Remarks at the Kazakhstan International Bureau of Human Rights, Almaty, Kazakhstan, April 4, 2005.

independence on January 22, 1918. But in 1919, the Ukrainian National Republic was defeated in a war against Polish expansionists and again overrun.

Eventually Russian forces retook Ukraine. And then as a brutal means to control the population, Josef Stalin caused the Great Famine of 1932-33 by forcibly collecting grain and deliberately starving to death nearly ten million people. Then in September 1941 during the early days of World War II, Nazi Germany entered Kiev and razed the city. In November 1943, Soviet forces retook the city and began their final domination of Ukraine which lasted for almost 50 years.

Given that history, one might think the flame of freedom would not burn in the heart of Ukrainians. After all, they had seldom enjoyed independence let alone democratic freedom. But like all women and men, Ukrainians desired freedom for themselves and their children.

As the political power wielded by the Soviet Union's Communist leaders was fading, in July 1990 the Ukrainian Soviet Socialist Republic proclaimed Ukraine's sovereignty. And then that October tens of thousands of Ukrainians took to the streets of Kiev demonstrating for their independence. It was the largest protest in central Europe in 30 years. During those dramatic days the eyes of the whole world turned to Kiev and people wondered whether Mikhail Gorbachev would send Soviet tanks into Kiev to trample the demonstrators. But unlike Hungary in 1956, and Czechoslovakia in 1967, and Kazakhstan in 1986, no tanks came. The days of the Soviet Empire were drawing to a close and the seeds of Ukraine's Orange Revolution were planted.

New Dawn and the Birth of Revolutionaries

Among those who took to the streets to demonstrate in October 1990 was Vladyslav Kaskiv and thousands of other students. When I asked him why he went into the streets back then, he told me it was simple, "I wanted independence and democracy. And so did the others." Vlad went on to say that "all the PORA's leaders who organized the tent cities in December 2004 had been there in 1990. We were students who believed. We all went on a hunger strike in 1990." But he went on, "Once we received independence and a democratic system, we went on with our lives. Not one of the student leaders who had been in the streets in 1990 became a politician. They were civil activists, but not politicians. Only a few, like me, entered the NGO[1] community. The others went into business or government jobs; but not politics."

At this point my embassy translator, Oksana Sukhina, spoke. She said, "I was a student in 1990. I went into the streets to demonstrate. I wanted freedom. But like others I did not become a politician. The Communist leaders and their children were the privileged ones. They still controlled the levers of power and commerce. I had to get on with my life. I had to earn a living. So I went to work. But this time," Oksana continued, "it was different. (During the Orange Revolution) we had children of regime leaders in our protest tents. It's a new generation with a new ideology."

In a referendum held on December 1, 1991 the people of Ukraine voted for independence and elected Leonid Makarovych Kuchma as Ukraine's first ever democratically elected President. But no political opposition organized. Under

Kuchma the old former communists claimed to be changed, but said Vlad, "they had not changed. They were the same, the same people, the same ideas, the same authoritarian way of doing things. And the political opposition was not strong. The opposition was not sustained. We may have been independent, but we were not free."

In retrospect Vlad clearly is disappointed that he and his fellow student leaders did not seize the moment 15 years ago. They had declared victory and gone on with their lives. They learned the hard way that in a democracy there are "no final victories." The opposition must remain engaged. Because only then can the checks and balances necessary in a democracy effectively work to restrain those in power.

Nonetheless, those years were not wasted. The institutions of a civil society gradually developed. And come the revolution those structures proved invaluable for the march of freedom to prevail.

Early in our conversation, Vlad said to me, "The demonstrations in Maidan Square, the Orange Revolution, were not some spontaneous phenomenon. It wasn't just some impromptu event. It was the culmination of a long process. It would not have happened if there had not been 15 years of work building civil society that promoted human rights, the human rights championed by the demonstrators. There were many players doing the grassroots work. And to a great extent that work depended on the support of donor countries. The United States, international organizations, they were crucial."

"How can you assess even millions of dollars invested into civil society?" Vlad continued, "Without this investment this revolution in Ukraine would not have happened."

In Ukraine, from America the International Republican Institute and the National Democratic Institute had been active for years. Training sessions were held on how to organize political parties down to the neighborhood level, how to conduct polls and interpret the data, how to develop messages and communicate them to the people, how to develop voter lists and get out the vote campaigns, as well as the other practical nuts and bolts mechanics of politics. They also held workshops on human rights and how to use the rule of law to defend those fundamental rights, how to organize non-governmental organizations (NGOs) and coordinate among them. And special meetings were held to recruit women into the process.

In an interview in the *Kyiv Post*, politician and democracy activist Luba Maiborada said that an IRI training session in the early 1990's helped her get elected as a deputy to the Cherkasu oblast council.[2] Ms. Maiborada, in turn, trained others on why they should get involved and how to do it. When asked how effective her training work had been and the work of other organizations involved in raising democracy awareness in Ukraine, she said, "The fact that the Orange Revolution occurred is evidence that work in this area was successful. The awareness of people increased significantly because they believed they were worth more and capable of playing a decisive role in their future. These seminars were held nationwide at all levels. When people first came to these seminars they generally complain about how bad things are, and that they are powerless to change things. Several sessions later, these complaints disappear and attendees are talking more about concrete steps they plan on taking in order to implement changes."

The Organization for Security and Cooperation in Europe (OSCE) also had a very active program in Ukraine. OSCE had projects on media, the rule of law and election procedures. OSCE helped train journalists and supported 30 two-day events throughout Ukraine on media ethics in election related coverage. OSCE helped develop a manual of updated media legislation and disseminated 15,000 copies. It supported training for media lawyers. The OSCE coordinated seminars for Judges and produced and distributed 4,000 manuals focused on the peculiarities of resolving election disputes by courts.

The OSCE worked to clarify issues concerning the legal framework for voting abroad. And OSCE provided information about citizen's legal rights to vote and how to refer legal issues to existing legal aid structures. The OSCE conducted 32 training workshops for members of Territorial Election Commissions in all of Ukraine's 25 oblasts. The OSCE helped in voter education, vote awareness, and updating voter lists. It even helped produce 35,000 templates in Braille to enable visually impaired voters to vote at each polling station.

All these efforts were building blocks for the Orange Revolution. As Vlad said, "The OSCE programs, IRI, Open Society, all these outside donor groups helped prepare the way. The NGOs in Ukraine are small, but there are lots of them. And at a critical moment this civil society played a key role in the Orange Revolution."

Vlad continued, "When we first created a volunteer network for the Revolution, these NGOs already had a network around Ukraine. We combined these small pieces and created a unified infrastructure we lacked. It saved us millions of dollars. It saved us time. We did not have to create a network. We may not have been able to create one. We just coordinated and united the NGOs that already were out there. We developed a scheme. But it only was possible because of years of work by many people supported by many donors to build a Ukrainian civil society. It is those people who led the Revolution. They made it possible."

Mukacheval: Prelude To A Revolution

Vlad talked at length about an election in April, 2004, in a small Ukrainian border town named Mukacheval. I had never even known that town existed, let alone given any thought to its election one year ago.

Vlad explained that during that election in Mukacheval the opposition confronted the government forces. In that contest Kuchma "used all the technologies of falsification: false voter lists, false absentee ballots, false manuals on election day." This forced the opposition to use all the methods they knew, and some that they learned along the way, to fight the regime's election fraud. Vlad said it was a very difficult time. In the end, the opposition in Mukacheval took to the streets to demonstrate against the rigged election with all its skullduggery. Vlad explained that there were "not so many people in the streets. But in a small town like Mukacheval you do not need many people to have a big impact." And to sustain the protest they innovated and pitched a "tent city" so that protesters remained at post around the clock.

The events in Mukacheval caught the attention of the U.S. Embassy in Kiev, the OSCE and others who sent people to observe the unfolding events. And the demonstration worked. The rigged election results that initially had been certified were thrown out. A second vote was taken. The opposition won and took office.

In the small town of Mukacheval there had been a trial run for the approaching presidential election. Vlad called it a "pilot election," in which the opposition learned the regime's tactics to try to steal an election and began to develop their defenses to stop the theft. And, importantly, the United States, OSCE and others had been put on alert. They now knew the extent to which the ruling regime would go to hijack the election process in order to try to insure victory. And they set to work trying to make it harder for such a fraud to occur.

At the U.S. Embassy, Ambassador Herbst began to convene periodic meetings with NGOs to coordinate their election related work. This pattern of coordination among NGOs was then leveraged by opposition leaders in the days leading up to the presidential election and then during the critical days of the Orange Revolution.

In the days after the events in Mukacheval, OSCE was able to identify key problems in the election. They were the first to raise issues of absentee ballots and voter lists. OSCE was the only organization that addressed problems of voters abroad where there was the biggest exposure for fraud. Vlad believes that unaddressed these areas of fraud would have inflated the regime's vote by over 10 percent. "All these anti-fraud efforts were initiated by OSCE," Vlad told me. "OSCE was able to coordinate the activities of other donors and focus attention on all these problems. I give a big thank you to OSCE."

<u>Russia Overplays Its Hand</u>

It is not easy for a fading empire to retain power over its former subjects. Russia is learning that lesson.

First the Soviet Empire that held dominion over the USSR and the Warsaw Pact collapsed as central Europe broke away. Then the Russian Empire imploded into 15 independent nations. Having resigned itself to losing its dominance in central Europe, understandably Moscow wants to keep a tight influence over the Near Abroad, those countries once a part of the USSR who abut the territory of mother Russia. Moscow sees these countries as part of "Russia's Zone of Influence" and resents all real or perceived efforts to dislodge them whether from outsiders or from forces within those Near Abroad. Russia seeks to vigorously oppose all such efforts. But how best to do that is not always clear. And in Ukraine, as in some other cases, Moscow's efforts not only failed to achieve the desired results, they quickened and deepened the separation.

Ukrainian President Leonid Kuchma had proven a very reliable friend to Moscow. His drift toward authoritarian rule caused no disquiet for Vladimir Putin. On matters of importance to Moscow, he was accommodating. And while he sought to build bridges to the West, his eyes and heart seemed comfortably fixed on Moscow. Therefore, Moscow was a strong supporter of Kuchma and his chosen successor, Viktor Yanukovych.

But Vlad told me that Kuchma and Putin made a big mistake leading up to the election. "Violations of human rights and freedom (in Ukraine) had increased dissatisfaction with the regime, but that would not have been enough to ignite the revolution," Vlad said. "But then Ukrainians felt their independence was threatened by Russia. That was enough. That fed the fire of revolution."

Vlad then told me about Russian 2003 plans to build a dam. This would have impacted Tuala Island and had the effect of Ukraine losing property. It would have affected the border. According to Vlad, the controversy became so heated that "it came close to war between Ukraine and Russia." He said that even Ukrainians "loyal to Russia felt it was aggression by Russia and they did not support it." So leading into the presidential election campaign the atmosphere toward Russia had been poisoned.

Nonetheless, caught in the old thinking of Soviet Union days, the regime's candidate, Viktor Yanukovych, ran on his link to Russia. That's right, rather than running on his own merits, or on his status as Kuchma's chosen successor, Yanukovych embraced Vladimir Putin. Putin openly campaigned for him, twice coming to Ukraine during the closing weeks before election day. And it was common knowledge that Putin poured money into Ukraine at the close of the campaign to buy apparatchik and other old style Ukrainian bosses to deliver the vote for his candidate. Some knowledgeable sources estimate that Moscow spent well over $200 million, and perhaps up to $300 million. Talk about old thinking. Of course the former communist bosses were happy to pocket the money, but they were unable to deliver the vote. And the gambit just demonstrated to many voters already dissatisfied by Ukraine's repressive regime that Moscow's heavy hand in Kiev would rule if there was not change.

There is an old saying in politics that the successful politician picks the right opponent. Well in the fall of 2004, events (and luck) had provided Viktor Yushchenko with the right opponent. And Vladyslav Kaskiv and other opposition leaders were intent on denying any victory through fraud by the regime; just as they were confident they would win any free and fair election.

This Fraudulent Election Will Not Stand

The first round of the Presidential election went pretty much as planned. Splinter candidates were eliminated. Yanukovych and Yushchenko were left standing The final results were in doubt. Yanukovych had a following as did Yushchenko. The margin might be close. So a fair election that scrupulously followed the law would be critical to determine the real winner.

On November 20, the date of the second round of voting, Ukraine was flooded by international election observers. Senator Richard Lugar, chairman of the United States Senate Foreign Relations Committee, led the IRI election observer mission. Drawing on lessons learned in the April election in Mukacheval, the election observers knew what fraudulent techniques for which they should be on the lookout. The regime did not disappoint. Again, the regime employed false voter lists, false absentee ballots, false manuals on election day and other such "technologies" to rig the election. But unlike in tiny Muchacheval, this time the world was watching. This time international observers were there to document the abuse and blow the whistle. With the exception of the CIS (Commonwealth of Independent States) observers who were controlled by Russia, the international election observers joined in a common chorus that this vote had failed to meet the recognized international standards of a "free and fair" election. Senator Lugar issued a statement that read in part, "It is now apparent that a concerted and forceful program of election day fraud and abuse was enacted with either the leadership or cooperation of government authorities."[3] The election was a fraud. And the entire world knew it. All the world knew the election had been rigged, that is, but the people of Ukraine. And even if they did know, what could they do about it?

In Ukraine the government controlled the national media. There was no free media. And the regime relentlessly broadcast on television, on radio, and in the newspapers that their candidate, Viktor Yanukovych, had won and won fairly. That was becoming the accepted common wisdom within Ukraine as Vladyslav Kaskiv and others began to gather in Kiev's Maidan Square to protest. In retrospect the outcome of their protest may seem inevitable. Retrospectively we can have 20/20 vision. But at the time, at least for most people, things looked less tidy and the final result did not seem predetermined.

Vlad admitted to me that he and his colleagues had their doubts in the beginning. On the first day a respectable crowd gathered to protest the election skullduggery. It wasn't very large, but big enough to be noticed. On November 22nd, the second day, Vlad came to Maidan Square at about 9:30 a.m. Vlad recalls that "there only were about 450 people there. I was disappointed. Later I learned that at 10:00 a.m. that morning students had gathered at 14 different universities around Kiev to protest the election. And then groups, large groups, of students from each of the 14 sites began to march toward Maidan Square. I did not know this.

"By 11:00 a.m. the numbers at Maidan Square only had grown to 600 or 700. Barely respectable. Certainly not enough to overthrow a government. I was concerned, anxious. And then I heard a faint chant 'You cannot stop the freedom. You cannot stop the freedom.' The sound grew louder and louder. Soon enough 10,000 students from the Polytechnical Institute began to flood into the square. By noon the other students had arrived. We numbered over 30,000. I thought the whole world could now hear our chant, 'You cannot stop the freedom. You cannot stop the freedom.'

"But," Vlad continued, "We still did not have enough people. We did not have critical mass. Then in the afternoon people of Kiev began to join us standing in protest. The numbers grew to 60 to 70,000 people. It was a lot.

"Then we had a third wave. The next morning, the third day, election observers from East Ukraine arrived. They numbered nearly 100,000. They were activists. In the east, a Yanukovych stronghold, they had witnessed some of the worst violations. The word spread. These people, these Ukrainians had witnessed the voter fraud. The television and the radio that continued to say the election had been fair and the victor clear; that was old style Soviet propaganda. These new people, these people from the east had seen the fraud. They knew. 'You cannot stop the freedom.'

"We had truth on our side. We had the people. But these new people that had arrived on the third day, they were from outside Kiev. They had no homes to go to at night. So they stayed in our tent cities. And our tent cities grew.

"We had tried to be organized for protesters staying in the tent cities. We had learned lessons from our relatively small tent city in Mukacheval. But we had not expected such numbers. As the crowds in the square grew to 500,000 to 750,000 at one time, and over one million throughout the city, the numbers staying in the tent cities grew too. We did not expect so many people. We created it to warm protestors, as a service center. But it grew into a real town. In one day it had grown to the maximum amount we had expected. But it continued to grow. We thought 2,500 might live in the tents. It grew to 15,000 at Maidan Square (with 1,700 tents) and there were five other tent cities throughout Kiev. The numbers grew to over 50,000."

All I could think about was the logistical nightmare of accommodating so many people in tents in December in Kiev: the cold, the food and water, the close quarters. But Vlad said the outpouring of support from so many Ukrainians made it possible to succeed. Vlad said, "People brought us so much food, truckloads. We did not know what to do. It was an uncontrolled splash of charity. People came up and asked what do you need?

"At one time, as it was cold and damp, I thought we needed some warm boots. I told a man. He comes back 45 minutes later with 170 pairs of very expensive, warm hiking boots. Each pair cost more than $100. And they were distributed to the people. The next day I went to a store to buy gloves and noticed all the shoes in the store were gone. I asked where they had gone. The salesperson told me a crazy person had come in and bought all of our shoes. A former government official showed up one day and gave me three enormous barrels of honey. It was extraordinary....

"One of the Tent leaders of PORA told me he had to stop asking for money. We had no space to store it, over $1 million was raised. And I can tell you, very little disappeared. It was all used to keep the tent cities alive, to keep the demonstrations going. When PORA opened a bank account and let it be known, more support poured in. $25 million was deposited. $400,000 came from Chicago, your hometown. My mother works in Greece. She organized other poor Ukrainian workers living in Greece. Within hours she raised $15,000.

"Our expenses for food, hot tea, and the rest were huge. But the support was greater. The people came and the people stayed: old people, students, all sorts of people. I am still surprised that 500,000, a million people stayed. They stood in the same spot. And I never saw two people fight the entire time. We were united for freedom....

"I did not expect people to stay so long. I did not think it would be necessary. Three times Yushchenko personally stopped people from attacking government buildings. It was historic."

I asked Vlad, in Maidan Square, when did you know you had won? When did you realize that freedom would prevail?" Vlad smiled, "I knew in April, 2004, in Mukacheval. I knew way back then. The Ukrainian people love freedom. In Mukacheval they learned how to achieve it."

A Different Perspective

I could not help but be inspired by Vladyslav Kaskiv and his story, just as the entire world had been inspired by the Ukrainian people last November and December when they gathered in Maidan Square and proclaimed "You cannot stop the freedom."

Of course, there are many stories of those dramatic days of the Orange Revolution. American Ambassador John Herbst saw the drama unfold from a slightly different vantage point. He had worked with the international donors who helped build up Ukraine's civil society. In the months leading up to the Presidential election, he worked with Ukrainian NGOs. Throughout the days of revolution he talked to senior government officials and leaders of the opposition.

Ambassador Herbst told me that he had not known who would win the election even if the vote had been fair. Both sides had popular support. And he certainly had not anticipated the growth of the demonstrations and the people's staying power. He does not think anyone had expected that.

Ambassador Herbst believes that the government would have cracked down on the demonstrators. They wanted to. But the police would not do it. He told me that the order to crack down had been given, but the police would not carry it out. He also said that from the outset of the demonstrations there were leaks from government intelligence people. In fact the leaks had begun last April, around the time of the events in Mukacheval. The regime simply lost the capacity to control the country.

Looking Forward

The Orange Revolution launched a fragile democracy in Ukraine. It will take time to take root. But unlike the 1990's, this time patriots such as Vladyslav Kaskiv are intent on staying engaged. They intend to continue their hard work to make their democracy work. They are asking the international community to help and they continue to organize civil society at home.

Vlad and others with whom I spoke in Kiev said special attention must be targeted on anti-corruption efforts. Many people told me that Ukraine has no real experience in fighting corruption. Nonetheless corruption must be fought in legislation, execution, administrative reform, raising government salaries and in strengthening the rule of law. An aggressive anti-corruption education campaign must be waged. For, they said, a democratic election is not enough. Fair and effective democratic governance must follow in order to build the trust necessary to sustain the reforms required for democracy to succeed.

And then there are parliamentary elections scheduled for later this year. They must be well run, be free, be fair. Otherwise distrust and apathy will erode the hard won gains achieved in Maidan Square.

I, for one, am optimistic. The international community seems to understand the importance of solidifying the advance of freedom in Ukraine. And leaders of the revolution such as Vlad seem dedicated to staying engaged and to working hard over the long haul to ensure that the democracy they launched succeeds. I think Vlad and others still can hear the chant, "You cannot stop the freedom." And the movement begun in the tiny border town of Mukacheval did not end in Maidan Square. The Orange Revolution was just the end of the beginning of a new democratic Ukraine. And now Ukrainian patriots are engaged in keeping it.

1.   Non-Governmental Organization.

2.   Roman Olearchyk, "Activist: The Revolution Will Keep Spreading," *Kyiv Post*, March 31, 2005.

3.   Elsewhere in Senator Richard Lugar's statement on the Ukrainian Elections, he elaborated on the abuse. He said, "OSCE/ODIHR and other observers mention an extensive list of serious procedural violations including: Illegal expulsions of opposition members of election commissions; Inaccurate voter lists; Evidence of students, government employees and private sector workers being forced by their deans and supervisors to vote for one candidate over another; Busloads of people voting more than once with absentee ballots; Representatives of the media being beaten and their equipment stolen or destroyed; and suspiciously large use of mobile voting."

Democracy:
There Are No Final Victories

Sir Rodric Braithwaite, Dr. Lena Nemirovskaya, it is a pleasure to share the dais with you today. The good work of the Moscow School of Political Studies to promote the development of democratic institutions and civil society in Russia has been consequential. I applaud your accomplishments and I certainly support your continuing efforts. It is an honor to have this opportunity to visit with so many local elected officials from throughout the Russian Federation.

I align myself with Natan Sharansky, who has written in his new book *The Case for Freedom: The Power of Freedom to Overcome Tyranny and Terror*, "I am convinced that all people desire to be free. I am convinced that freedom anywhere will make the world safer everywhere. And I am convinced that democratic nations, led by the United States, have a critical role to play in expanding freedom around the globe."[1]

Or as President Bush said in his 2003 State of the Union Address, "There is a myth that though we love freedom, others don't, that our attachment to freedom is a product of culture; that freedom, democracy, human rights, the rule of law are American values, or Western values. ...Ours are not western values, they are the universal values of the human spirit. And anywhere, any time ordinary people are given the choice to choose, the choice is the same: freedom, not tyranny; democracy, not dictatorship; the rule of law, not the rule of the secret police."[2]

We live in an extraordinary time in which freedom is on the march. Fewer than one-third of the world's nations were democracies in 1947. According to Freedom House's annual surveys, today more than two-thirds are on a democratic path.[3] And you are architects of this sweeping change in the human condition.

You are building the culture of democracy in Russia. As local elected officials you have the opportunity and the responsibility to till the soil and help the institutions and habits of democracy take root. The Moscow School of Political Studies is committed to help you in this noble enterprise. And there are many, like me, anxious to offer you support.

There is no one model for democratic government. One size does not fit all. The unique history, traditions and culture of a society will inform the democratic

---

Remarks to Public Policy Forum, Moscow School of Political Studies, Washington, D.C., April 11, 2005.

institutions of each country. They will vary in structure and function. But certain fundamental things are required for a successful, sustainable democracy. There must be periodic elections that are free and fair. The media must be free and widely available. The right of assembly must exist. And the "rule of law" must prevail. These building blocks establish the foundation of a democratic society. They guarantee citizens the right to select and reject their leaders. They establish accountability. They are ramparts of freedom.

Successful democracies establish checks and balances on the power of government, on those in office. The patterns of democracy and the rhythms of elections result in periodic changes of those in power. There are no final victories. Recognizing that those in office today will be in the opposition on some future day tempers abuse in office. It also helps the election day losers to accept their defeat knowing they can fight another day.

America's democracy has a maze of checks and balances; of power divided among the three branches of the federal government and within our federal system of a national government and our fifty sovereign states. In the United States it is very difficult to get things done, very difficult. And that too is a protection for individual liberty.

The history of the United States, like that of each nation, is unique. Thirteen colonies, each separate, came together to declare their independence in 1776. The various colonies fought together against the British crown. Having achieved their independence after a long and bloody struggle, each colony held its own independence most preciously. The newly independent colonies only grudgingly and cautiously joined together loosely under the Articles of Confederation and lightly wore the yoke of association. As the failings of such loose association became evident, the former colonies, now states, again sent representatives to Philadelphia to wrestle with the challenges of forming a more perfect union: one that safeguarded personal liberty, respected state sovereignty, yet forged a functioning federal government. What emerged in the U.S. Constitution was a design with three equal and separate branches of national government: the Executive branch (the President, the cabinet departments, etc.); the Legislative branch (the Senate and the House of Representatives); and the Judicial branch. And, stated explicitly in the Constitution, those powers not explicitly enumerated for the federal government would reside in the sovereign states. Therefore, power was not only divided, checked and balanced, among the three branches of the federal government; but also power was divided between the center (the national government) and the regions (the state governments).

Even with the drafting of the basic document, the Constitution, the job was not done. Amendments have been passed over the years to adjust and readjust various aspects of our American democratic machinery. A few years after our Constitution was adopted, the United States Supreme Court in *Marbury vs. Madison*[4] asserted the right to review and determine the constitutionality of laws passed by Congress and signed into law by the President. That precedent was accepted. Today that exercise of judicial power has deep grooves in the pattern and habits of American democracy.

Seventy-four years after ratification of the U.S. Constitution, America faced its greatest constitutional crisis and descended into its most bloody conflict, the Civil War. Among other things, that war was about the respective powers of the national government seated in Washington, D.C., and that of the states. When the war ended with the Army of the Confederacy surrendering at the village of Appomattox Court House, the dynamic debate of state powers was far from resolved.

In the 1930's when the United States and the entire world sank into the Great Depression, President Franklin Delano Roosevelt launched The New Deal. FDR's initiatives greatly expanded the federal government's power and prerogatives, often at the expense of the power of state governments. And World War II furthered the growth of power in Washington. Even in the 1950's under the Presidency of Dwight Eisenhower, a Republican, the federal government expanded its reach as the interstate highway system was built.

And from President Lyndon Johnson's "Great Society" in the 1960's[5] to President Ronald Reagan's "New Federalism"[6] in the 1980,'s there has been a creative ebb and flow of concentration and decentralization of power between the federal government and the states. That shifting tide exists to this day. America's democracy is being reinvented as we go along. However, it is a fundamental and irrefutable principle that power comes from the people to the government and not the other way around. The people elect their local, state and national office holders. A president does not appoint America's fifty governments nor can the president dismiss them.[7] They are chosen by the people. And through the ballot box the people can throw them out.

The principles of American democracy are simple. All people are created equal with basic inherent rights, fundamental human rights. Government is the servant of the people. And the powers of governance are divided between three co-equal branches of the national government and between the federal government and the states. This provides a system of checks and balances to curb abuse and deny an unhealthy concentration of power. Laws are clear and the process of governance is transparent. A robust free press, an active civil society, and open debate serve as further checks against government abuse. And ultimately, the American people through the power of their votes in periodic free and fair elections holds to account their government and their leaders.

Yes, the principles are simple. But the practice is complex, untidy, difficult. Democracies are rambunctious. They are constantly in flux. As has been written,

> Dictatorship is like a big proud ship – steaming away across the ocean with a great bulk and powerful engines driving it. It's going fast and strong and looks like nothing could stop it. What happens? Your fine ship strikes something – under the surface. Maybe it's a mine or a reef, maybe it's a torpedo or an iceberg. And your wonderful ship sinks! Now take democracy. It's like riding on a raft, a rickety raft that was put together in a hurry. We get tossed about on the waves, it's bad going, and our feet are always wet. But that raft doesn't sink. …It's the raft that will get to the shore at last.[8]

The habits of democracy: compromise, coalitions and consensus, are not built in a day. They take time.

Natan Sharansky, born in the Soviet Union, a refusnik imprisoned by the U.S.S.R., and today a leading politician in Israel, tells us, "The determination of men and women who are free never to return to a life of fear should never be underestimated."[9] I know that the men and women in this room, elected Russian local leaders, have such determination. Your form of democracy will not be identical to that of America, nor should it be. It will grow from your own history, culture and traditions. You will learn from other democracies that have gone before. Yet your democracy will be uniquely Russian. Make no mistake about it, the Russian people have the right to be free and the determination. As elected leaders, you have the opportunity and the responsibility to nurture Russia's young democracy, to ward off authoritarian tendencies from the center, to ingrain the habits of democracy. This is an opportunity you dare not squander.

Good luck and thank you.

---

1.   Natan Sharansky, *The Case for Democracy: The Power of Freedom to Overcome Tyranny and Terror* (New York, N.Y.; Public Affairs; 2004), p. 17.

2.   President George W. Bush, State of the Union Address, Washington, D.C., January 28, 2003.

3.   Morton H. Halpern, Joseph T. Siegle and Michael M. Weinstein, *The Democracy Advantage: How Democracies Promote Prosperity and Peace* (New York, N.Y.; Rutledge; 2005), pp. 215-16. See also, Larry Diamond and Marc F. Plattner, eds., *The Global Resurgence of Democracy* (Second Edition) (Baltimore, Md.; John Hopkins University Press; 1996).

4.   Marbury v. Madison, 5 US 137 (1803), 5 US137 (Cranch). See, William E. Nelson, *Marbury v. Madison. The Original Legacy of Judicial Review* (Lawrence, KS; University Press of Kansas; 2000).

5.   See, Lyndon B. Johnson, Great Society Speech, Public Papers of the Presidents of the United States, Lyndon B. Johnson, Book I (1963-64), p. 704-707. See also, John A. Andrew, *Lyndon Johnson and the Great Society* (Chicago, Illinois; Ivan R. Dee, Publisher; 1998), and Vaughn Davis Bornot, *The Presidency of Lyndon B. Johnson* (Lawrence, Kansas; University Press of Kansas; 1983).

6.   See generally, Richard S. Williamson, *Reagan's Federalism: His Efforts to Decentralize Government* (Latham, Md.; University Press of America; 1990).

7.   In 2004, Russian President Vladimir Putin abolished the direct election of Russia's regional governors and initiated presidential appointment to those offices.

8.   Roaldus Richmond, ed., "A Yankee Businessman in New Hampshire," *American Life Historic: Manuscripts from the Federal Writers' Project, 1936-1940*, in Morton H. Halperin, et. al., eds., *ibid.*, p. 1.

9.   Natan Sharansky, *ibid.*, p. 62.

DEMOCRACY A TOUGH SELL TO RUSSIANS BUT WORTH THE EFFORT

Earlier this week, President Bush joined over 50 other world leaders in Moscow to celebrate the 60th anniversary of the defeat of Nazi Germany. It was a gala celebration.

The pomp and circumstance of this commemoration, however, could not paper over the major problems facing Russia nor the serious challenges Russian President Vladimir Putin presents to America and the world.

Moscow's domain is a shadow of its former self. The Kremlin's influence is in retreat. Not long ago the Soviet Union stood as the second great superpower locked in a global stand off with the United States. But then the Soviet Union collapsed and the Russian empire imploded. Its military is smaller, with much of its machinery in ill-repair. Its influence in neighboring states, once part of the Soviet Union, is waning. Except for resource extraction, the Russian economy is contracting. Life expectancy in Russia is declining and medical care is in shambles. Its population is shrinking. Pensioners are protesting reduced benefits. And the war in Chechnya rages on.

Despite her much diminished status, Russia remains a major power. Its enormous Eurasia land mass stretches over eleven time zones. One hundred forty eight million people live there. Russia has vast oil and gas reserves. It retains an enormous nuclear arsenal. And with its sale of arms to Syria and nuclear cooperation with Iran, Putin is demonstrating his capacity to influence world events in troubling ways.

Because Russia remains a major power, it is important for the United States to engage Moscow, not isolate her. America will benefit if we can enlist Putin to be more helpful with North Korea and Iran's threatened nuclear breakouts. The entire world, including America, will be safer if we help Russia secure her loose nukes. Moscow has been a partner on the war on terror. If Russia is able to move to a real market economy under the rule of law, her own citizens will benefit but so will the global economy. And a collapsed Russia would create dangerous and unpredictable tremors from which no one will be immune.

However, while America constructively engages Russia, we also cannot ignore Russia's authoritarian drift at home nor the Kremlin's efforts to thwart the march of freedom abroad.

Appeared in the *Chicago Sun-Times,* May 12, 2005.

For our character as a people, it is important for America to keep faith with our fundamental values of freedom and human rights. It is important to act on our understanding that these values are transcendent and precious to every human being by seeking to spread freedom. As we work to spread freedom in Afghanistan, Iraq and elsewhere in the Greater Middle East, consistency requires us to give support to freedom's march elsewhere. And a truly democratic Russia will be more stable and secure, more prosperous and a more dependable ally.

In recent months, Putin has concentrated more power in his hands while weakening the role of the Duma (Russia's parliament) and the judiciary. Putin cancelled gubernatorial elections and changed election laws to lock out grassroots opposition movements. Putin has shut down Russia's last nationwide independent television station. And the Kremlin has arrested independent business executives and de facto expropriated Yukos Oil.

In reaction to the Rose Revolution in Georgia, the Orange Revolution in Ukraine and the ouster of Askar Akayev, Kyrgyzstan's authoritarian leader friendly to Moscow, Putin is trying to gut the Organization of Security and Cooperation in Europe (OSCE). Among other things, the OSCE monitors human rights and democracy.

As one of the 55 member states of the OSCE, Russia has entered into a number of agreements to support basic human rights standards, the rule of law and democracy. As history's march has spread democracy and freedom to Russia's neighboring states, Mr. Putin finds those past commitments inconvenient and OSCE's role in supporting freedom intolerable. Putin has blocked the OSCE budget to force change. He hopes to eviscerate OSCE's role in human rights and democracy.

In the face of these Russian assaults on freedom's march, President Bush is pursuing a two track strategy.

Bush went to the celebration in Moscow and stood next to Putin. But he also traveled to Latvia and Georgia, two new democratic republics once enslaved by the Soviet Union's communist totalitarianism.

Bush continues to engage Putin on the war on terror, North Korea, Iran and other matters. But he also presses Putin to reverse his authoritarian trends at home and his efforts to obstruct freedom's march abroad.

Last month at the dedication of the Abraham Lincoln Presidential Library and Museum in Springfield, President Bush said that Lincoln "did not believe America could surrender its founding commitments and remain the same country."

He went on to say, "Our interests are served when former enemies become democratic partners – because free governments do not support terror or seek to conquer their neighbors. Our interests are served by the spread of democratic societies – because free societies reward the hopes of their citizens, instead of feeding the hatreds that lead to violence. Our deepest values are also served when we take our part in freedom's advance – when the chains of millions are broken and the captives are set free, because we are honored to serve the cause that gave us birth."

In confronting Putin and championing freedom in Russia, President Bush is doing the right thing. As he has said, "Whenever freedom is challenged, the proper response is to go forward with confidence in freedom's power."

THE LIBERIAN
PRESIDENTIAL ELECTION

After 25 years of turmoil and 14 years of civil war, yesterday's election was a victory for the Liberian people and an important step towards finding the reconciliation and opportunity that the Liberian people deserve.[1]

The International Republican Institute (IRI)[2] has a long history of working in Liberia leading up to the 1997 elections, IRI returned in early 2003 and began work to open an office and a political party resource center.[3] IRI's program has been based upon preparing the political parties for this national election and the run-off elections. IRI has provided training to the political parties on grassroots mobilization, platform creation, fundraising, party organization, and the integration of women and youth into Liberia's political activities.[4]

The IRI Liberian election observer delegation collectively has observed more than 50 national elections worldwide.[5] Yesterday IRI deployed observer teams to 10 of Liberia's 15 counties and monitored more than 90 polling sites including one camp for internally displaced persons. While the results of the Liberian elections are still preliminary, IRI observation teams found the October 11 elections to be peaceful, with an overwhelming turnout among Liberian registered voters.

At the Joe B. Tate School in the upper Montserrado area of Monrovia, where I observed the opening of the polling site, I found over one thousand people waiting outside. Some told me they had arrived at midnight, others 2 a.m., in order to be among the first to cast their votes. At that location, as elsewhere we observed, Liberians stood in long lines for hours in an orderly and respectful manner before casting votes for their future. The seriousness in which they took their civic responsibilities and their eagerness to help select their next president was inspirational.

IRI observers witnessed Liberian election officials as well-trained, knowledgeable and serious-minded in the execution of their responsibilities. They took great pride in their role in helping insure the success of this election and were meticulous in their actions.

As happens in every election, some glitches and anomalies occurred over the course of the election day. For example, voting at many sites began late due to a delay in the delivery of ballots and other voting supplies. However, polling station proceedings overall were orderly, methodical and in compliance with election laws.

The National Election Commission (NEC) should be commended for addressing problems by issuing a mid-morning Election Day statement to accommodate the

---

Remarks in Monrovia, Liberia, October 12, 2005.

exceedingly long lines of Liberians patiently waiting to vote, and to alleviate confusion over marking ballots.[6] IRI observers did note, however, that many voters had not been educated about the voting process and that NEC officials at times went behind voting booths to explain the voting process, which runs contrary to election procedure. While voter education in Liberia is made more difficult by the 85% illiteracy rate, NEC should continue to aggressively pursue voter education efforts.

IRI observed that the large number of domestic election observers from political parties and civil society at every polling station wee critical to the transparency and legitimacy of this election and public trust in the process. These observers were at their station prior to the opening of polling sites and remained until the vote tallies were completed, often late into the night.

In particular, the counting process at election stations was done meticulously and adhered to NEC procedures, allowing transparency for the many domestic and international observers. All ballots were counted and recounted and recounted again in front of election observers. Polling site tallies were announced. This contributes to public confidence in the election process and acceptance of results.

The large and very visible presence of the United Nations Mission in Liberia (UNMIL) and Liberian national police, which have contributed substantially to stability nationwide, provided confidence of a secure environment for voters.[7] UNMIL and national police uniformly acted in a non-intrusive, professional and effective manner. IRI election observers witnessed no violence on election day.

Our delegation does express concern, however, regarding reports from civil groups and at least one candidate that money or other inducements had been offered to secure votes prior to Election Day.[8] However, IRI saw no direct evidence of such transactions. Also, concerns were raised by a number of people about difficulties some Muslim Liberians had in registering to vote.

IRI observation teams note that in the coming days during which the tally will be finalized, it is important for all candidates to work towards inclusion and avoid disruption to enable the Liberian people to move towards a possible run-off election.[9] The law provides an adjudication procedure through the NEC whose determination can be appealed to the Liberian Supreme Court. It is important that if grievances arise this established procedure be followed and the results respected.

Everyone with an interest in a brighter future for Liberia should be encouraged by the steps taken yesterday by the Liberian people toward building a sustainable democracy.

At a polling station in Dwahzon Town, Momo Sambole, a 39 year old Liberian, told me that "people feel the best solution is the ballot box, not guns."

After 14 years of civil war and two years of a transitional government under United Nations auspices, yesterday the Liberian people demonstrated that Momo Sambole was right. In overwhelming numbers the people came to choose their new president through the first "free an fair" election in Liberia's history. They have stepped forward to claim their future.

---

1.   For an excellent volume on Liberia's recent history, see, John-Peter Pham, *Liberia: Portrait of a Failed State* (New York, N.Y.; Reed Press; 2004.). See also, Gus J. Liebenow, *Liberia: The Quest for a Democracy* (Bloomington, Ind.; Indiana University Press; 1987); Gabriel I.H. Williams, *Liberia: The*

Heart of Darkness (Victoria, British Columbia; Trafford Publishers; 2002); Adekeye Adebajo, *Liberia's Civil War: Nigeria, ECOMOC, and Regional Security in West Africa* (Boulder, Colo.; Lynne Rienner Publishers; 2002); and Stephen Ellis, *The Mask of Anarchy: The Destruction of Liberia and the Regional Dimension of an African Civil War* (New York, N.Y.; New York University Press; 2001).

2.   The International Republican Institute is a non-profit, non-partisan organization dedicated to advancing democracy worldwide.

3.   When the country's civil war reached Monrovia in May 2003, IRI staff was obliged to leave Liberia. IRI re-opened its office and resource center in Liberia in May 2004.

4.   IRI political party resource center provides the parties with computers, photocopiers, reference materials, and other materials to help parties and civil society organizations to gear up for the elections. IRI also fielded an observation team of experts from the U.S. and Africa to monitor the May, 2005 voter registration process in Liberia.

5.   My co-leader of the IRI election observer mission was former Assistant Secretary of State for African Affairs Constance Berry Newman. Other delegates were The Honorable Maimuna Adaji, member of parliament of Nigeria for Kwara State; Donald Bogue, chairman and chief executive officer, Command Audio Corporation; Geoffrey S. Connor, attorney, Jackson Walker, LLP, and founder, Texas Global, LLP; Nicholas Cook, specialist on African affairs, U.S. Congressional Research Service; Eric Dell, chief of staff and counsel, Office of Congressman Joe Wilson (SC-2); Dr. Kwesi Jonah, acting head, Governance Center at the Institute for Economic Affairs in Ghana; Dr. J. Peter Phan, director, William R. Nelson Institute for Public Affairs, James Madison University; Gregory Simpkins, professional staff member, U.S. House Subcommittee on Africa, Global Human Rights and International Operations; Richard J. Wall, managing partner, O'Donnell Waiss, Wall and Meschke; and The Honorable Noah Wekesa, member of parliament of Kenya for Kwanza constituency.

6.   The Liberian National Election Commission trained and hired to work in voting places 18,573 people.   None are members of political parties.

7 .   "Following the signing of the Comprehensive Peace Agreement on August 18, 2003, between the government of Charles Taylor and the two armed rebel opposition groups, Liberians United for Reconciliation and Democracy (LURD) and the Movement for Democracy in Liberia (MODEL), and Charles Taylor's departure into exile in Nigeria, Liberia became temporary home to the world's largest and most expensive United Nations peacekeeping mission.   With an annual budget of U.S. $846 million, in November, 2004 UNMIL consisted of some 14,100 military personnel from 47 countries, as well as 750 civilian police officers and 607 international civilian staff operating under a robust Chapter VII mandate.   …UNMIL succeeded in disarming and demobilizing more than 100,000 former fighters between December, 2003, and November, 2004.   The disarmament, demobilization, reintegration, and rehabilitation (DDRR) process played an important role in stabilizing Liberia after 15 years of civil war." Wolf-Christian Paes, "Eyewitness: The Challenges of Disarmament, Demobilization and Reintegration in Liberia," *International Peacekeeping*, Vol. 12, No. 2 (Summer 2005), pp. 253-254.

Of particular concern to future stability is the need to reintegrate Liberia's former child-soldiers. "…the lies of children and youth from the infamous "Small Boys Unit." Children who had been turned into killing machines and had become war veterans at ages as tender as seven… Every ounce of their innocence and youthfulness had been drained from them … these kids were desperate for respite, but had known no other way of life, so they saw only a bleak and hopeless future." Christian Udechukwa and Celine Loader, "Liberia's Return to Sanity," *Aspire Magazine*, Oct./Nov. 2005, pp. 16-22.

8.   One leader of civil society told the IRI delegation that it was difficult to determine when traditional Liberian gifts became vote buying.   And one presidential candidate said when he went out campaigning, especially in remote villages up-country, it was expected that he offer a small gratuity to the people who came out to meet him.

Chad Flego, IFAS country director told me on October 7th, "Is it a real campaign? Yes.   Is there bribes, intimidation and vote buying? Yes, absolutely.   I've never seen so many bags of rice.   So don't just look at the procedures of voting.   There are irregularities and they are going on now."

9.   Liberian election law calls for House elections to be determined by whomever wins the plurality of the vote and for Senate by which two candidates win the largest number of votes in each district.   However, the President must receive at least 50% plus one vote.   For this election there were 22 presidential candidates.   In the event that no candidate received a majority of the vote in the first round, a run off of the two leaders would be held on November 8, 2005 (4 weeks after the first vote).

REAL WINNER IN LIBERIA'S VOTE: HOPE DEFEATS DESPAIR

Liberia is a small country in West Africa of about 3 million people that has gone through 25 years of turmoil and misery.

During these years two sitting presidents were brutally killed in office and one was driven from office. There have been 4 transition governments. And there were 14 years of violent civil war in which over a million people were driven from their homes, 200,000 people were killed, many more lost limbs, and torture was common.

Liberia's social fabric has been torn. Life expectancy has fallen 10 years to 47. Unemployment hovers near 75% in the official economy. Illiteracy has risen to 85%. There is no running electricity nor running water even in Monrovia, the capitol. Nonetheless, the Liberian people gave expression to their dreams by flooding to polling stations earlier this month to cast their votes in Liberia's first ever "free and fair" election.

It was inspirational. I witnessed this advance in the march of freedom as a co-leader of the International Republican Institute's Election Observer Mission to Liberia.

Professor Peter Pham has written that "for the last two decades, Liberia has been a failed state where the collapse of government institutions has occasioned one of Africa's longest conflicts and created a complex humanitarian crisis that destabilized an entire region. Not surprisingly, in its Annual Survey of the World, *The Economist*, concluded that Liberia was the worst place to live in 2003."

Liberia's last authoritarian ruler, Charles Taylor, not only terrorized and plundered his own country, but supported rebel movements in neighboring Sierra Leone, Guinea and Cote d'Ivoire. For his misdeeds in Sierra Leone he was indicted by a U.N.-sponsored Special Court on 17 counts of crimes against humanity. Facing rebel advances at home and growing international pressure to account for his crimes, Taylor fled Liberia and sought asylum in Nigeria in August, 2003.

Unfortunately, the transition government created as a result of peace talks in Accra has proven to be corrupt like its predecessors. While office holders grew rich, no progress was made in education nor development. And tens of thousands of former child soldiers exploited in the civil war remain uneducated, untrained and unintegrated into society.

Appeared in the *Chicago Sun-Times*, October 21, 2005.

In such a depressed environment how could anything grow but despair?

The elections scheduled for 2003 were postponed to 2005 so the fighting could end, restructuring could happen, and some sanity could be found.

The international community invested by deploying a 15,000 person United Nations Mission in Liberia (UNMIL) of peacekeepers, police and civilians. Civic education was launched. And the table was set for elections.

Last May, voter registration went well. 1.3 million Liberians registered. During the summer political campaigns were launched. For the first round of the election 22 presidential candidates were on the ballot.

Talking to leaders of civil society, political parties, the National Election Commission, UNMIL and presidential candidates in the days prior to the vote, there was plenty of anxiety mixed in with the cautious hope things would go well.

I began election day at a voting place in Montserrado. When I arrived one hour before the voting was to begin there already were over one thousand people lined up to vote. Patrick Scro, a 20 year old near the front of the line, told me he had shown up at 2 a.m. He was there because his country needed education and housing. Maureen Cloe, a 32 year old and mother of 3, told me she arrived at 3:45 and was voting for education.

Joe Etta, an elderly woman who was stooped over and needed help walking, had arrived at 5:30 a.m. She told me she hoped her vote would "end the sound of guns, end the fighting."

In Dwahzon Town, Tom Gbrngbaro was voting "to end the nightmare once and for all."

Voter turnout was large. There was no violence. People were orderly and took their vote seriously. They were taking a step toward unity, sustainable peace, and, hopefully the opportunity for a better life.

As Momo Sambole, a 39 year old woman at a polling station on the outskirts of Monrovia told me, "People feel the best solution is the ballot box, not guns." And in that there is a ray of hope in this land of so much misery.

LIBERIA:
FROM BARBARITY TO HOPE

Liberia, like too many other African countries, has gone through a long period of violence, mayhem and tragedy. But last month, Liberia held its first free and fair election, which offers the people an opportunity to leave their grisly nightmare behind and begin their long, difficult path to building a sustainable peace where good governance, transparency and accountability supplant cronyism, deception and graft.

As an international election observer to this Liberian vote, I was inspired to see the hope of Liberians casting their votes for a brighter future.

Liberia was founded by freed American slaves in 1847. Liberia continues to be divided by the Americo-Liberian minority comprising only 5% of the people and the overwhelming majority of indigenous Liberians that come from 16 different ethnic groups. For over a century, Liberia was dominated by the Americo-Liberian True Whig Party that directed Liberian politics from 1871 to 1980.

In April, 1980, indigenous Liberian Master Sergeant Samuel K. Doe seized power in a coup d'etat in which President Talbert was butchered in cold blood and 13 ministers were stripped to their underwear, staked to posts on the beach and executed.

A civil crisis flared up and the ensuing 25 years of conflict have led to senseless violence, 4 transitional governments, and a non-functioning state apparatus.

One observer described the past quarter century in Liberia as a period of "public executions on the beach, drug crazed young thugs terrorizing citizens at roadblocks, rampant theft of national resources, corruption, nepotism, abuse of human rights, tribalism, blood diamonds and warlords."

Many indigenous Liberians believe in a spiritual world of unseen forces and the visible world of everyday life. In war when killing occurred, the victor could take on the power of his enemy by ingesting part of his body, his heart or liver, and thus his spirit. During periods of intense violence in Liberia there were regular reports of "ritual killings." Witchdoctors were reported to have scrutinized potential victims prior to ripping their living hearts out of their bodies. Then the person who "commissioned" the deed consumed the heart in whole or in part to gain the power of the victim and to intimidate others.

During this past quarter century the quality of life grew more bleak. Competent civil administration and the rule of law disappeared. The infrastructure deteriorated, the economy collapsed and, today, most of Liberia has no electricity, no running water and no public health services.

Appeared in *Tech Central Station,* November 4, 2005.

Liberia's life expectancy is 47 years. Illiteracy is near 85%. Unemployment in the formal sector is over 70%.

Liberia's last authoritarian leader was the warlord Charles Taylor who not only terrorized his own country but supported rebel activities in the neighboring states of Sierra Leone, Guinea and Cote d'Ivoire. For his misdeeds in Sierra Leone he was indicted by a U.N. sponsored Special Court on 17 counts of "crimes against humanity." Facing rebel advances at home and growing international pressure to account for his crimes, Taylor fled Liberia for asylum in Nigeria in August, 2003.

For over two years the international community through the U.N. Mission in Liberia (UNMIL) has worked to keep peace and support a transitional government in preparations for elections.

Stability in West Africa and the quality of life in Liberia depended on a free and fair election.

The specter of Charles Taylor and the threat of violence hang in the air. As one observer said to me days before the vote, "Many worry about Charles Taylor, but few dare mention his name."

In the run up to election day there were many unanswered questions. Would there be violence? Would the turnout be large enough to give the election legitimacy? Would the mechanical burdens be met for the 10% of polling stations so remote that no cars nor even helicopters could reach them and ballots would be delivered and later retrieved by porters walking four days through the jungle? Would the ballot boxes be secure and would every vote by counted? Would the losers accept the results?

The hopes of many Liberians was captured in Yomitown, a small village of mud huts with 143 voters. In the middle of Yomitown, the villagers came together to build a Palaber Hut, a round structure with a thatched roof and open sides. They built it to be their polling station for election day. It was a source of pride. The chance to vote was a reason for hope.

As Steve McClein, a Liberian policeman told me when I visited the Peynesville Town Hall Center in the outskirts of Monrovia, "We've had a long conflict. We don't want it to happen again. We want peace. Our new president must unify the people by going to their aid: healthcare, education, salaries and roads. This is our dream, to have a new day."

Or, as Bishop David Daniels of the Liberian National Methodist Episcopalian Church told me just before the vote, "Guns will not free you. Lay down guns and go to school. That is the only answer. This election brings hope. The time for hope is now."

By the time polling stations opened there were long lines waiting to vote, some having arrived at two and three in the morning to be among the first to cast their ballots.

Fahnguor Rogers got in line at 5:45 a.m. He told me that he wanted government transparency so the new government would not be corrupt like all the others he had known. And he wanted "education and training for the young people, especially the former child soldiers who hang around with nothing to do and no skills but killing."

In Harbel town the lead election official was Thomas Howard, a 34 year old with four children ages 19, 14, 9 and 2 ½. He told me, "I hope our new President brings real education where people can learn to read."

At a polling site in the Monrovia Free Pentecostal School, Samuel Goweh, 38, told me, "A good result (in the election) will leave us a peaceful country and move us forward. The ex-combatants need to be sent to school, retrained and become useful citizens. We need water, electricity and education."

Prince Jacob, a Nigerian soldier serving as a U.N. Peacekeeper in Liberia who had served in Rwanda after the genocide there, told me, "Even though the genocide in Rwanda was large, Rwanda was a short war. So it was easier to reintegrate (ex-combatants), In Liberia it was a long war. Here it is harder to integrate."

Sumuwoo Harris, a Lutheran minister, said to me, "The warlords like the young people. They only are taught to do violence. They do not have any skills. They are disgruntled people. The politicians have played upon the disgruntled to give themselves power. That must end. We must re-establish institutions to help the youth get out of the streets. They need education. They need training. We must give this to them or they will remain disgruntled to be played upon and used."

About the election, Minister Harris went on to say, "The task is monumental. It will be a difficult and long road forward. It will take cooperation and it will take patience."

The Liberian people, traumatized by 25 years of turmoil, conflict and violence went to the polls in large numbers: casting their votes. Liberians gave voice to their hopes and dreams by engaging in the first "free and fair" election in their nation's history.

I was encouraged by the thoughtful comments of Julliet Cooper, a 22 year old poll watcher at the Wells-Hairton School in Monrovia. I asked her what she thought would come from the vote. She told me, "There is a lot of work for the new President. He must bring water. He must bring light, electricity, roads. …The expectations of the Liberian people are very high so he will have to work fast. In 6 months they expect something. After 6 months there will be a lot of noise." But, she said, "The Liberian mind is mature. If the results are not there in 6 or 12 months, the president will have to explain. He will have to keep the people informed on what progress is being made." That sounds like the prescription for any healthy democracy anywhere in the world. Only time will tell whether the roots of sustainable democracy are taking hold in Liberia.

As Tom Gbrngbara told me, his hope is that this election will "end the nightmare once and for all."

Liberians went to vote in large numbers. Liberian political party, civil society and international observers all declared the voting "free and fair." In a few weeks the two leading presidential contenders, Ellen Johnson Sirleaf and George Weah, will have a run off election. And then the new president must seize the opportunity to form an inclusive government that will work for the Liberian people and not primarily to enrich themselves as so many have done before.

Democracy is not just voting. It is a process. As Sumnwoo Harris told me days before the election, "People who do not win are not losers. They should be partners. It is not the responsibility of one person to deliver the country. We need unity to rebuild the country."

The voters are selecting their new leader. The democratic process provides a legitimacy for the new Liberian president to unify the country and lead. For the sake of the people who have been traumatized by war, live in desperate conditions with no running water, no electricity and few jobs, hopefully the new President will begin to rebuild Liberia's torn society.

That is the hope and that is the opportunity of Liberia's first free and fair elections.

VOTE SIGNALS
HOPE FOR DEMOCRACY
IN LONG BESIEGED CONGO

The Great Lakes Region of Central Africa arguably has been the world's most tragic. Now there is a ray of hope.

Years of French and Belgium colonial rule, often brutally administered, were followed by newly independent countries suffering under a series of corrupt regimes and bloody conflicts.

Twelve years ago in Rwanda the gates of hell opened. In 100 days the Hutu majority killed 800,000 Tutsis, most by machetes. More recently Burundi had a civil war in which 200,000 people died. But these fatalities have been eclipsed by the long and bloody conflict in the Democratic Republic of the Congo. Nearly 4 million people have died there in fighting and by the resulting famine and disease.

A few years ago I traveled to the Congo. In Kinshasa, the capital, I met with President Joseph Kabila in his opulent and well guarded palace; beautiful, serene and far from the daily traumas outside. I also walked Kinshasa's broken streets of poverty, pain and sorrow filled with people living in desperate conditions. In the eastern Congo, deep in the jungle, I stood on the banks of the Congo River where one day in May, 2002, skulls floated following a skirmish where nearly 100 people were beheaded.

While in Kisangani one woman caught the misery and hopelessness of the Congo when she said to me, "This is the land of arbitrary injustice. The judicial system does not work and we do not know what will happen to us tomorrow." And a priest said to me "When will the politicians and military stop talking and start doing? The people desperately need peace."

In this vast chaotic country at the heart of Africa the killing continued. Armed groups looted, plundered, destroyed villages and incited ethnic conflict. In Ituri there wee killings to eradicate rival tribes. In the Kivus there have been reports of cannibalism. And humanitarian workers tell of child soldiers, slavery, torture and rape.

The Congo is about the size of France. Sixty million people live there. One in ten infants die. Life expectancy is 51 years with excess mortality due to AIDS. A mineral rich nation; the diamonds, gold, cobalt, coltan and copper are exploited by corrupt political leaders and foreign mercenaries while the people live in poverty with per capita income of less than $2 a day.

Appeared in the *Chicago Sun-Times*, January 2, 2006.

Atrocities, poverty and death plagued the Congo since this conflict began in 1998. But after five years of civil war, a fragile transition government was formed under U.N. auspices. The uneasy coalition of former belligerents stuck with the help of U.N. Peacekeepers despite aborted rebellions, challenges from armed groups outside the peace process, and interference from the neighboring countries of Rwanda and Uganda.

Then earlier this month the Congo held its first democratic vote since gaining independence in 1960.

There were some violent incidents, but the turn out was large. Janvier Elimwa, a motorbike taxi driver in Goma, in eastern Congo, was reported to have said, "What I know is that today's vote is a vote for peace."

Charles Begi, a 34 year old teacher in Kinshasa, was reported to have said, "We are the small people. We don't eat for days sometimes. I have never voted before, and now we are passing from one era to another. Now the small people of the country are choosing its future."

The people of the Congo voted overwhelmingly to approve their new constitution. It will limit the power of the president, give the country's regions more influence and strengthen the judicial system. The document is not perfect. It has flaws. But for people accustomed to corrupt and violent rule, people too familiar with misery and death, this vote provides the possibility of progress. It begins a process that may lead to an inclusive government that will recalibrate the geopolitical reality in Africa's Great Lakes Region.

This democratic vote provides hope in a land too long shrouded by the heart of darkness.

MONGOLIA'S
DEMOCRATIC ADVANCE

It's a great pleasure for me to be here in Ulaanbaatar, Mongolia. Since I was a boy and heard stories of Genghis Khan and the mighty Mongol warriors riding on horseback across the vast, rolling, grassy steppes of inner Asia, I have dreamed of visiting this land. And these past few days, I have not been disappointed. I have been inspired. The beauty of the Mongolian landscape, the warm welcome of its people, and the advance of freedom here have more than met any expectations I might have had.

Last fall, President George W. Bush became the first sitting American president to visit Mongolia. While at the Government House, President Bush said, "Fifteen years ago Mongolians gathered outside this great hall by the thousands, braving sub-zero temperatures and defying a repressive regime to demand their liberty. The protestors included students and workers and monks, and a group of young democrats on a hunger strike. By the force of their convictions, they drove the communist leadership from power. Within months, free elections were held, and a free Mongolia was born. …You're an example of success for this region and for the world."[22]

It's a particular pleasure to be here as Mongolia celebrates the 800th anniversary of its founding. This land of nomadic horsemen and traditions dating back to the time of Genghis Khan is based on rugged individualism, self-reliance and family.[23] As nomadic families follow their seasonal routine of moving their herds of goats, sheep, cattle, camels and horses to new grazing land based on the time of year, they move their gers and all their earthly possessions. This history and tradition has created a sturdy stock of people who have welcomed freedom after decades of authoritarian rule under the specter of the Soviet Union.[24]

Since 1991, Mongolia has taken many political and economic reforms. As Ambassador Pamela Slutz said the other day, "Since beginning its transition in 1991, Mongolia has achieved remarkable progress in setting the foundations for a democratic, open-minded economy. From this first wave of reforms, Mongolia has much to be proud of."[25] You have successfully held free and fair elections. Twice there have been peaceful transitions of power from one party to the other. And since the early 1990's, the International Republican Institute (IRI) has worked actively to assist the Mongolian people in this transition.

IRI's early programming focused on improving the capabilities of opposition political parties.[26] More recently, in addition to working to develop a more competitive political environment and providing international election observer missions, IRI has

---

Remarks at Ulaanbaatar, Mongolia, June 29, 2006.

worked to advance a more transparent and effective legislature, ethics reform, anti-corruption legislation and to increase public participation in Mongolia's democratic processes and particularly in Parliament. Also in recent years, while continuing to work with the Democratic Coalition, IRI has worked with the MPRP. It has been a privilege for IRI to work to advance freedom in Mongolia.

But let me be clear. IRI can provide technical assistance and support for these reforms, but it is the Mongolian people who must want to advance a democracy agenda and, in fact, it has been the Mongolian people who have embraced this challenge and achieved noteworthy results.

Free and fair elections are critical to a free society. But elections alone do not make a democracy. What happens between elections is as important as the day of voting. Democracy requires sturdy institutions that ensure the rule of law, a free press, a vibrant civil society, and transparent decision-making. It is difficult, sometimes hazardous work to erect these guardrails of a free society.

During the past few days I have met with President Enkhbayar, Prime Minister Enkhold, Speaker Nyamdorj, other leading Parliamentarians, the General Election Commission, members of civil society such as the Women's Forum leaders, and many ordinary Mongolians. I have heard their views, asked questions and replied to their inquires. I am impressed by their resolve to keep working to improve Mongolia's democratic institutions. The people want to get it right. Having experienced freedom, they do not want to retreat. They want freedom to advance.

Yesterday I was about 60 kilometers northeast of Ulaanbaatar in the Terelj National Park. I stopped at a ger.[27] As I've experienced everywhere in Mongolia, I was welcomed and invited in. The entry faced south. I ducked to get through the entry. Inside the ger was like most others. To the right was the kitchen. In the middle was a wood stove. Around the outer ring were three beds, the woodwork painted a colorful orange. Atop two 60 years old chests were arranged 68 family photos, most faded by age. There was a small Buddhist altar atop two ancient suitcases.[28]

Tserenjarga, the husband, and Nansalmaa, his wife, married when they were twenty. Now they are 72. For years, Tserenjarga worked in the mines. Now he and his wife are nomadic herders. They have 120 sheep and 40 cows. They had one horse that was stolen. They milk their livestock every day and make yogurt. They sell the yogurt for about 30¢ a liter and make about $5 a day from selling it plus the cheese they make. Once a year the sheep are shorn and they sell the wool for about $100. Tserenjarga also receives $36 a month in pension. They have three sons, all now live in the cities; two in apartments and one in a house. But Tserenjarga and Nansalmaa said they accept no money from their children who have their own families and their own responsibilities.

Tserenjarga and Nansalmaa have dark leathered skin from lives lived outside, and they walk with the slight stoop of those who have known hard manual labor all their lives. Their clothes are old and worn, their ger modest. Yet their hospitality was warm and generous. Having arrived at their doorstep a complete stranger, they welcomed me in with warm, welcoming smiles. They served me cheese and yogurt. We toasted over milk vodka. We told stories. We laughed.

I asked them about how things had changed since the end of authoritarian rule. They said that their day to day life was the same as it always had been. They awake early, milk the livestock, tend to their herd, make yogurt and cheese. They welcome whomever comes by their ger. In recent years, with so many moving into Ulaambaatar, prices have gone up so their money doesn't go as far as it once did.

Near the end of my visit, I asked them if they were better off with democracy than they had been under the old authoritarian regime. This old, weathered couple at the end of another long day of hard work sat in their modest ger and said without hesitation, "If you work hard you prosper. If you are lazy you do not. We are better off with democracy." As we said good-bye my affection for the welcoming Mongolian people again was reaffirmed, and my confidence in Mongolia's democratic future was strengthened.

A country cannot pick its neighbors. Mongolia is surrounded by two great powers in China and Russia. But a nation can choose its values and its friends. Strategic interests may shift but shared values endure. The United States and Mongolia embrace the enduring values of freedom, democracy and market economics. Democracy is a journey, not an end. We can all improve our bulwarks of democracy. But working together, I believe, we will continue to find common ground and together we can guarantee for our nations the individual freedom our creator intended for all mankind.

Thank you.

---

1.   President George W. Bush, "Remarks at Government House;" Ulaanbaatar, Mongolia; November 21, 2005.

2.   For a wonderful book that provides insight into the sweep of Mongolia's history and culture, see Jack Weatherford, *Genghis Khan and the Making of the Modern World* (New York, N.Y.; Crown Publishers; 2004).

3.   After the death of Genghis Khan, his empire was divided into several powerful Mongol states, but these broke apart in the 14th century. The Mongols eventually retired to their original steppe homelands and later came under Chinese rule. Mongolia won its independence in 1921 with Soviet backing. A Communist regime was installed in 1924 and Mongolia remained a Soviet satellite until 1991. *CIA – The World Factbook – Mongolia.*

4.   Speech by U.S. Ambassador Pamela J. Slutz to The American Center for Mongolian Studies, "Vision 2020: Whither Mongolia?", reprinted in *The UB-Post*, June 15, 2006.

5.   In the early stages of Mongolia's transition to democracy, the Mongolian People's Revolutionary Party (MPRP) – heir to the Communist Party – was dominant, and in the 1992 elections, they won 71 of 76 seats in the Parliament, the State Great Hural (SGH). However by 1993, the opposition parties had organized together and formed the Democratic Coalition, winning the Presidential election that year. In 1996, with IRI's help (the MPRP declined offers for assistance), the Democratic Coalition won 50 of 76 seats in the SGH.

6.   "Traditional gers are the moveable, domed structures used by nomads for centuries. Made of a latticed wood structure covered with layers of felt canvas, each ger is heated by a wood stove and furnished with painted wood-framed beds. The traditional ger has a lattice-work frame of narrow birch and willow boards held together by leather strips. The sections are about 7.5 feet long and are bound together to form a large circular structure. This collapsible lattice is called khana. The average ger uses six to eight khana, with the door frame as a separate unit, and the ceiling formed with an umbrella-like frame-work of slender poles called uni. In the center of the ceiling is a small hole, a toono, which allows smoke to escape and fresh air and light to enter."

7.   "Woven through the nomadic culture is a rich Tibetan-Buddhist tradition which has incorporated some elements of Mongolia's ancient Shamanist practices."

SECTION V:
HUMAN RIGHTS

DARFUR:
THE RESPONSIBILITY TO PROTECT

I thank Professor Doug Cassel for organizing this conference. I found especially interesting the observations of Canadian General Romeo Dallaire who served as United Nations Commander in Rwanda ten years ago during a time of hell.[1]

Unfortunately many countries bear some responsibility for the genocide in Rwanda. As the United Nations Secretary-General's High-Level Panel on Threats, Challenges and Change notes, the United States' intervened to oppose the deployment of international peacekeepers that might have prevented the carnage.[2] And this morning Ambassador John Shattuck, who served in the Clinton Administration at that time, has given us added insights on that moral and political failure.[3]

Professor Benjamin Valento in his important book *Final Solutions: Mass Killing and Genocide in the 20th Century* has written that ethnic hatreds play a much smaller role in mass murder and genocide that most assume.[4] He shows that the impetus for mass killings usually comes from a relatively small group of powerful leaders to counter threats to their power, and to solve their most difficult problems.

Every genocide is unique with singular contributing factors and horrors that are particular. But every ethnic cleansing and each act of genocide is evil.

In Sudan, for 20 years a bloody civil war has raged between the Islamic government in Khartoum and the largely Christian rebels in the south. This north/south conflict revolved around natural resources and political power. Over 2 million people have died due to this fighting and its consequences. Over the past few years serious peace talks took place. As the framework of an agreement developed, there were some in the western Darfur region of Sudan who felt they were being disadvantaged.[5] About eighteen months ago, a small rebel movement began.

Khartoum, already stretched thin to deal with the rebels in the south, armed a nomadic Arab militia in the west known as the janjaweed to put down the small rebellion in Darfur. In the weeks and months that followed government attack helicopters would scraife villages in Darfur. These aerial assaults would be followed by janjaweed riding on horses and camels who would swoop into villages burning homes, killing males including baby boys, raping and pillaging, and driving the survivors out into the vast desert in search of subsistence.[6]

Remarks at the School of Law, Northwestern University, Chicago, Illinois, January 25, 2005. (A version of these remarks appeared in the *Northwestern University Journal of International Human Rights*, Volume 4, Issue 1).

The target of these brutal attacks is not limited to the rebels. Sudan's Arab government and the janjaweed Arab militias are systematically killing and expelling Darfur's non-Arab black population. The reported violence is horrific.

Zahara Abdulkarim told a reporter of warplanes circling her village, gunshots and bombs destroying mud-and-thatch huts. She described how a janjaweed stood over her husband's body while others set fire to her home. Then two men took turns raping her. When they were done they took a knife and slashed across her left thigh to mark her as a slave. By nightfall, Abdulkarim reports that more than 100 women in the town of Ablich had been raped and many killed.[7]

Zahra Abdel Karim tells a similar story. One day the Janjaweed militia swooped into her village. Her husband and two young sons were among the slaughtered. Her two sisters were gang-raped and then killed. She was gang-raped and then slashed with a sword. Naked and bleeding she hobbled across the desert to Chad to save her last child.[8]

Last summer Janjaweed stormed a girls' school, chained students together and set the building on fire. When African Union observers arrived, the charred remains of eight girls were still in shackles.

One woman from the village of Silaya reports having been abducted when she was five months pregnant along with eight other women. She described six days when "five to six men would rape us in rounds, one after the other for hours every night."[9]

Even many of the refugee camps have been attacked. Tamur Bura Idriss recounted how on a Sunday morning janjaweed militia descended on his refugee camp, herded away the cattle the refugees had brought with them, and began killing. He reports that one gunman said, "You blacks, we're going to exterminate you."[10]

The atrocities are horrific and the international communities response has been anemic.

After World War II when the world had learned the full horrors of the Holocaust, the international community said, "Never again."[11]

Then came the killing fields in Cambodia, and the international community said, "Never again."[12]

And then came Rwanda. The mass murder was planned. It was known. Yet, again the international community did nothing! And after 800,000 people (Tutsis and moderate Hutu) had been killed in a matter of 10 weeks, mostly by machetes, neighbors killing neighbors, and the bodies were staked high, the world said, "Never again."[13]

Then came ethnic cleansing in Bosnia and Kosovo, and the world said, "Never again."[14] And now similar atrocities are being committed in Darfur, Sudan. The crimes are known. The terrible human toll is documented. Yet, again, the international community is doing little. Meanwhile the horrors continue, the death toll rises, and the terrible suffering goes on.

Last March, President Bush publicly called for the Sudanese Government in Khartoum to reign in the Janjaweed and stop the razing of villages, the rape and the murder.

Every spring, the United Nations Commission on Human Rights meets in Geneva, Switzerland. Last year I served as the United States Ambassador to that meeting. What happened there on the issue of Darfur speaks volumes about the lack of will on the part of the international community to effectively deal with even the worst atrocities and human rights abuses.

Before the Commission on Human Rights had convened, I held a wide range of bi-lateral consultations on issues of great concern to the United States and others. Among those with whom I met was Ambassador Mary Whelan of Ireland in her capacity as the rotating President of the European Union. We exchanged views on many areas of shared concern. Then we agreed on who would take the lead on this or that agenda item. For example, the United States took the lead on human rights abuses in Cuba, China, Belarus and elsewhere. Ambassador Whelan informed me that the European Union would like to take the lead on the atrocities in Darfur. I agreed to her request, but first made sure we agreed on the minimum required for any final resolution we would take to a vote. The resolution had to condemn the violence. It had to demand the atrocities end. It had to require free access for humanitarian aid to the victims. And it had to insure that international observers would be accepted in Sudan to monitor events on the ground. Ambassador Whelan agreed with all these points. We had a deal.

From the outset of the Commission on Human Rights meeting, many African delegations made known their discomfort at singling out Sudan for condemnation yet they also were uncomfortable with totally ignoring the terrible injustices in Darfur. Sudan, for its part, took a hard line position that, in fact, no atrocities were taking place; and furthermore, if bad things were happening in Darfur, the government in Khartoum had no responsibility.

Then in early April, Secretary-General Kofi Annan traveled to Geneva to give a speech at the U.N. Commission on Human Rights in remembrance of the Rwandan genocide 10th anniversary. In his remarks, the Secretary-General was forthright and forward leaning. He called the atrocities in Darfur "ethnic cleansing" and he called for action to put a stop to these evil acts. Having the U.N.'s first black African Secretary-General starkly lay out the facts and then call for the international community to act dramatically changed the dynamic.

Now most African states accepted that the Commission on Human Rights had to do something. And gradually Sudan recognized that a resolution probably was inevitable.

The African delegations began talks among themselves. Then they initiated discussions with the European Union President. The second to last week of the Commission meeting, I was shown the language tentatively agreed to by the Africans and the E.U. President. I was alarmed. The language was so weak as to be meaningless. It did not condemn, nor demand, nor require, nor even insure international observers. It even expressed appreciation for the Sudanese government for its cooperation with the UNCHR.

This language required no consultation with Washington. It fell so far short of any meaningful content that I immediately rejected it. I told the E.U. President that this was an insult to the victims in Darfur, a rejection of the minimum standards of human rights to which we had all pledged fidelity, a breach of our agreement on the content of any resolution on Darfur, and, therefore, that the United States could not and would not support any such resolution.

The E.U. President, Ambassador Whelan, was well intentioned and a seasoned diplomat. She urged me to reconsider. Of course, she said, we all know how terrible the atrocities on the ground are. She agreed that stronger language would be preferable. But it was important to get the buy-in of sub-Saharan Africa. And the value of consensus was critical.

I replied that since Sudanese Arabs were systematically killing and displacing Sudanese blacks, perhaps it was sub-Saharan Africa that should be concerned about their buying in to condemn the ongoing atrocities. Furthermore, while the broadest possible support and ideally consensus were desirable, our responsibility to the victims and to facts on the ground was a far higher obligation. "No," I said, "I can see no circumstances in which the United States could support such a weak and dishonorable resolution."

After the U.S. position became widely known, negotiations between the Africans and the European Union broke down. I was informed that a vote would proceed on the far sterner draft resolution with which the United States, the Europeans and many others had agreed. As the date for the vote approached, it was clear that it would be close. My political officers from the U.S. Mission to the United Nations Offices in Geneva had a whip count of the 54 UNCHR members that showed passage with only two votes to spare. Human Rights Watch and other NGOs had similar estimates of a close vote tipping slightly for passage. But whether it passed or not, the muscular resolution on Darfur had the appropriate language. It would send a powerful unambiguous message to Khartoum that the carnage must stop and that there would be consequences for their continued atrocities.

Moments before the scheduled vote, some African delegations approached the Irish Ambassador on the floor of the Commission chamber. There was a brief huddled meeting and then the Irish Ambassador asked the chair for a brief recess. I knew this could not be good.

During the recess, Ambassador Whelan informed her European Union colleagues that the Africans had approached her with a last minute compromise resolution. It was far weaker than the text on which we were about to vote, but it had shown some modest movement from the anemic language of the draft to which she had agreed earlier. Then Ambassador Whelan told her E.U. colleagues that she had to make a decision on the spot. And in her capacity as European Union President and consistent with the powers of that office, she had accepted the compromise language and bound all other E.U. member states to that position.

Within moments, all delegations learned what had occurred. I made known that while I would consult with Washington, I saw no circumstances in which the United States could support the new language. Many of my colleagues, including the Irish Ambassador, implored me to reconsider. Of course, they said, you are right about the awful facts on the ground. It is ethnic cleansing, they agreed. And, of course, Khartoum should be condemned and required to end the atrocities at once. But, they said to me, "Mr. Ambassador, you know how valuable consensus is in the

United Nations. By agreeing with this new language the spirit of collegiality and cooperation in the Commission will be upheld. And, after all, this is the best we can do at this time."

I talked with Washington. I was relieved that they agreed with me entirely and gave me latitude to vote "no" on the new soft resolution and to push vigorously for a vote on the original resolution condemning Khartoum and demanding the atrocities stop, which I did.

In the end, the stronger U.S. resolution on Darfur failed. The soft rebuke passed. The message to Khartoum was that to the international community the ethnic cleansing in Darfur was no big deal. And the killing continued.

Consensus and cooperation inside the international communities foremost human rights forum proved more important than the tens of thousands of blacks in Darfur who continued to be killed and the hundreds of thousands more who have been driven from their homes and live in desperate conditions. Today, the best estimates are that over one hundred thousand people have died due to the atrocities in Darfur and more than 1.8 million people have been internally displaced or driven to refugee camps in Chad. It is a humanitarian and human rights disaster.

In July, the United States took this matter to the U.N. Security Council. The U.S. delegation sought sanctions against Khartoum, or at least the threat of sanctions. Again, the international community failed. Certain permanent members of the Security Council with economic interests in Sudan – oil concessions and military sales – opposed any direct reference to sanctions. Also African and Islamic members of the Security Council opposed sanctions. The result was another weak resolution and mixed message to Khartoum.

In fact, there now have been three U.N. Security Council resolutions.[15] More recently the Security Council has threatened sanctions against the Sudanese government and a travel and assets freeze against those suspected of war crimes. Yet, notwithstanding the continued violence, the U.N. has not followed these threats with action. Even Secretary-General Kofi Annan has urged the Security Council members to take tougher steps to stop the deteriorating situation in Darfur.[16]

Yesterday, the United Nations General Assembly devoted the entire day to commemorate the freeing of the Jews at the Auschwitz concentration and extermination camp sixty years ago.[17] But what does any such commemoration mean if the words "never again" are not given meaning by real action?

The Holocaust was preceded by the 1904 genocide of the Harero people by the German army in their African colony now called Namibia.[18] The genocide in Darfur was preceded by Auschwitz, Cambodia, Rwanda, Bosnia and Kosovo. Tragically, there seems to be a great capacity for mass murder. Yet, we do nothing.

Secretary of State Colin Powell labeled the atrocities in Darfur genocide months ago.[19] The U.N. Secretary-General impaneled a group of experts to look at the facts on the ground and render a determination of whether or not the legal threshold has been met to label the ethnic killing in Darfur as genocide.[20]

I doubt that the victims of Darfur care much about whether they are the victims of genocide or of ethnic cleansing. They only know the pain of great loss and suffering due to homes burned to the ground, men slaughtered, women raped, and the desperate life threatening conditions in which they live in IDP or refugee camps. And they live the anguish of a painful and uncertain future.

The African Union has authorized thousands of troops to monitor the situation.[21] The United States and some other donor countries are providing logistical and other support. Yet only a fraction of the authorized forces have been deployed. We must increase the international support to the African Union for this mission.

Hundreds of millions of dollars of humanitarian assistance has flowed to Sudan. The United States is the largest donor country. Again, more is needed.

The U.N. Security Council should impose sanctions on the Sudanese government and others engaged in these terrible crimes against humanity. Political and economic pressure must rise. Concerns about delicate diplomatic minuets and economic self-interest must take a back seat to the urgent need to stop the carnage immediately. Action must be taken.

And it must be made clear to those engaged in these evil acts, to the victims and to others who might contemplate such despicable acts in the future that there is no impunity. A judicial accounting must begin to start down the path of accountability and restorative justice.

There have been too many mass killings, ethnic cleansings and genocide in recent history. We have seen, as Professor Valento points out, that usually mass killings begin due to a relatively small group of leaders trying to hold on to their power and solve their most difficult problems. We must ensure that such "leaders" know that mass killing is not an acceptable solution. It will not be tolerated. And they will be held to account if they unleash such dark forces.

The international community has a responsibility to protect. We do not have the capacity to protect all innocent people everywhere. But that fact does not free us from the responsibility to protect those whom we can.

In Darfur atrocities continue to be committed every day. We know this. Having failed so often to stop mass killings and genocide, it is time for the international community to act now. It is time the international community confronts this evil. The values we subscribe to require it. Our conscience demands it.

Thank you.

---

1.   See, Romeo Dallaire, *Shake Hands With the Devil: The Failure of Humanity in Rwanda* (Toronto; Random House Canada; 2003). See also, Romeo Dallaire, "Looking at Darfur, Securing Rwanda," *New York Times*, October 4, 2004; and Linda Melvern, *A People Betrayed: The Role of the West in Rwanda's Genocide* (London, U.K.; Zed Books, Ltd.; 2000)..

2.   The U.N. Secretary-General's High-Level Panel on Threats, Challenges, and Change, *A More Secure World: Our Shared Responsibility*, December 2, 2004. Available at http://www.un-globalsecurity.org.

3.   See, John Shattuck, *Freedom on Fire: Human Rights Wars and America's Response* (Cambridge, Massachusetts; Harvard University Press; 2003), pp. 51-76.

4.   Benjamin Valento, *Final Solutions: Mass Killing and Genocide in the 20ᵗʰ Century* (Ithaca, New York; Cornell University Press; 2004). Similarly, in Bill Berkeley, *The Graves Are Not Yet Full: Race, Tribe and Power in the Heart of Africa* (New York, N.Y.; Basic Books; 2001), the author shows how "Africa's ruinous conflicts are not the product of age-old hatreds but of calculated tyranny." See also, Eric D. Weitz,

A Century of Genocide: Utopias of Race and Nation (Princeton, New Jersey; Princeton University Press; 2003); Rudolph Rummel, *Death by Government* (New Brunswick, New Jersey; Transaction Press; 1994); and Samuel Totten, William S. Parsons, and Israel W. Charney, eds., *Genocide in the Twentieth Century: Critical Essays and Eyewitness Accounts* (New York, N.Y.; Garland; 1995).

"Abdalla Adam Khator, 50, is from Darfur, in western Sudan. His grandmother was an Arab, her grandfather was a member of an African tribe. He calls himself an African. ...As a student here (Khartoum) in the 1960's, he took up the banner of Arab-Africa unity, led by the Egyptian president Gramal Abdel Nasser. But today, Mr. Khafir finds himself wrestling with the gut-wrenching fact that, in the past two years, 102 of his relatives have been killed in Darfur by those he calls Arabs. Yet in the end Mr. Khatir, a writer and a member of the Darfur Writers and Journalists Association, does not view this as a war between Arabs and Africans. He blames it squarely on the government in Khartoum. Its leader, he says, have deliberately inflamed nascent ethnic divisions in a bid to stay in power." Somini Sengupta, "In Sudan, No Clear Difference Between Arab and African," *New York Times*, October 3, 2004.

5.   See, for example, Somini Sengupta, "War in Western Sudan Overshadows Peace in the South," *New York Times*, January 11, 2005; and Chris Tomlinson, "Sudan, Rebels Finally Make Peace," *Chicago Sun-Times*, January 10, 2005.

6.   See generally, Samantha Power, "Dying In Darfur: Can the Ethnic Cleansing in Sudan be Stopped," *The New Yorker*, August 30, 2004.

7.   Massimo Calabresi, Sam Dealey and Stephen Faris, "The Tragedy of Sudan," *Time Magazine*, October 4, 2004.

8.   Nicholas D. Kristof, "The Dead Walk," *New York Times*, October 16, 2004.

9.   See, Lydia Polgreen, "Civilians Bear Brunt of the Continuing Violence in Darfur," *New York Times*, June 24, 2005. See also, Somini Sengupta, "Despite Pact, New Violence Stymies Aid in Sudan," *New York Times*, November 27, 2004.

10.   Somini Sengupta, "Why in Western Sudan Overshadows Peace in the South," *New York Times*, January 17, 2005.

11.   See, Omar Bartov, *Murder In Our Midst: The Holocaust, Industrial Killing and Representation* (New York, N.Y.; Oxford University Press; 1996); Richard Breitman, *The Architect of Genocide: Himmler and the Final Solution*, (London, U.K.; Bodley Head; 1991); Christopher E. Browning, *Ordinary Men: Reserve Police Battalion 101 and the Final Solution in Poland* (New York, N.Y.; Harper Collins; 1992); Daniel Jonah Goldhagen, *Hitler's Willing Executioners: Ordinary Germans and the Holocaust* (New York, N.Y.; Knopf; 1996); Raul Hilberg, *The Destruction of the European Jews* (New York, N.Y.; Holmes and Meier; 1985); Steven T. Katz, *The Holocaust in Historical Context* (New York, N.Y.; Ozford University Press; 1994); and Paul Weindling, *Health, Race and German Politics between National Unification and Nazism* (Cambridge, U.K.; Cambridge University Press; 1989).

While we are most familiar with the Nazi extermination of 6 million Jews, there was other awful atrocities in that war. For example, in Nanking, China, a city of 1 million, the Japanese army murdered tens of thousands of surrendered Chinese soldiers, and more than 300,000 non-combatants. The Nanking killings continued for seven weeks in front of international witnesses. See Iris Chang, *The Rape of Nanking: The Forgotten Holocaust of World War II* (New York, N.Y.; Viking Penguin, USA; 1998). See also, Lord Russell of Liverpool, *The Knights of Bushido: A Short History of Japanese War Crimes* (London, U.K.; Greenhill Books; 2002).

12.   See, David A. Albin and Marlowe Hood, eds., *The Cambodian Agony* (Armonk, New York; M.E. Sharpe; 1990); Elizabeth Becker, *When the War Was Over: The Voices of Cambodia's Revolution and Its People* (New York, N.Y.; Simon & Schuster; 1986); Dith Pran and Kim DePaul, eds., *Children of Cambodia's Killing Fields: Memoirs by Survivors* (New Haven, Connecticut; Yale University Press; 1997); Ben Kiernan, ed., *Genocide and Democracy in Cambodia: The Khmer Rouge, the United Nations and the International Community* (New Haven, Connecticut; Yale University Southeast Asia Studies; 1993); and Karl D. Jackson, eds., *In Cambodia 1975-1978: Rendezvous with Death* (Princeton, New Jersey; Princeton University Press; 1989). See also, Loung Ung, *They Killed My Father: A Daughter of Cambodia Remembers* (New York, N.Y.; Harper Collins; 2000); and Someth May, *Cambodia Witness: The Autobiography of Someth May* (London, U.K.; Faber and Faber; 1986).

13.   See, Michael Barnett, *Eyewitness to Genocide: The United Nations and Rwanda* (Ithaca, New York; Cornell University: 2002); Alan J. Kuperman, *The Limits of Humanitarian Intervention: Genocide in Rwanda* (Washington, D.C.; Brookings Institution Press; 2001), Philip Gourevitch, *We Wish to Inform You That Tomorrow We Will Be Killed With Our Families: Stories from Rwanda* (New York, N.Y.; Farrar,

Strauss & Giroux; 1998), Samantha Powers, *A Problem From Hell: America and the Age of Genocide* (New York, N.Y.; Basic Books; 2002) Alan Destexhe, *Rwanda and Genocide in the Twentieth Century* (New York, N.Y.; New York University Press; 1995), Elizabeth Neuffer, *The Key to My Neighbor's House: Seeking Justice in Bosnia and Rwanda* (New York, N.Y.; Picador USA; 2001), .Mahmood Mamdani, *When Victims Become Killers: Colonialism, Nativism and the Genocide in Rwanda* (Princeton, New Jersey; Princeton University Press; 2001), and David Rieff, *A Bed for the Night: Humanitarianism in Crisis* (New York, N.Y.; Simon & Schuster; 2002), pp. 155-193.

14.   David Rieff, *Slaughterhouse: Bosnia and the Failure of the West* (New York, N.Y.; Simon and Schuster; 1995).

15.   UNSC Res. 1564; UNSC Res. 1556; UNSC Res. 1574.

16.   Edith M. Lederer, "U.N. Chief Urges Tougher Steps to Quell Sudan," *Chicago Tribune*, December 23, 2004.

17.   Lisa Anderson, "U.N., Survivors Remember Holocaust," *Chicago Tribune*, January 25, 2005.

18.   See, Jeff Kelly Lowenstein, "Our Limitless Capacity for Mass Murder," *Chicago Tribune*, October 24, 2004.

19.   Steven R. Weisman, "Powell Says Rapes and Killings in Sudan Are Genocide," *New York Times*, September 10, 2004. See also, Samantha Power, "It's Not Enough to Call It Genocide," *Time Magazine*, October 4, 2004.

20.   On January 31, 2005, the United Nations Commission investigating the violence in Darfur reported to the U.N. Security Council in a 176 page report that "it had found a pattern of mass killings and forced displacement of civilians that did not constitute genocide, but that represented crimes of similar gravity... The report stated that its findings that genocide had not been committed 'should not be taken in any way as detracting from the gravity of the crimes perpetuated in that region... International offenses such as the crimes against humanity and war crimes that have been committed in Darfur may be no less serious and heinous than genocide." The investigators reported that "indiscriminate attacks by government forces and militias on a widespread basis including the killing of civilians, torture, enforced disappearances, destruction of villages, rapes, and other forms of sexual violence, pillaging and forced displacement." Warren Hoge, "U.N. Finds Crimes, Not Genocide in Darfur," *New York Times*, February 1, 2005. Government leaders in Khartoum and leaders in Darfur condemned the report. However Leslie Lefkow, a Darfur expert at Human Rights Watch put the issue in proper perspective. She said, "I think the whole bickering over genocide or not aside, it is a very strong report. It unequivocally states that there have been crimes against humanity, war crimes and atrocities. The focus on genocide is really a red-herring used by the government of Sudan and others to distract from the larger issue of what has happened in Darfur." Linda Polgreen, "Both Sides of Conflict in Darfur Dispute Findings of U.N. Report," *New York Times*, February 2, 2005.

21.   See, Somini Sengupta, "African Union Strives to End Deadly Cycle in Darfur," *New York Times*, November 29, 2004.

SPEAK OUT AGAINST
OPPRESSION IN ZIMBABWE

In recent months, the march of freedom has advanced through free and fair elections in Afghanistan, Ukraine, Iraq and among the Palestinians. This progress is an enormous achievement for the forces of democracy and, more importantly, for the brave women and men in these countries who defied threats and violence and went to vote.

But the march of freedom is not inevitable. It is difficult, hazardous and fraught with setbacks and disappointments. Recent events in Zimbabwe demonstrate the peril and obstacles to freedom's advancement.

Zimbabwe is rich in natural resources. When it first gained independence from British colonial rule, it stood as a beacon of hope in southern Africa. Elections were held. The rule of law was sustained. And Zimbabwe was Africa's breadbasket.

Today Zimbabwe is ruled by the iron fist of dictator Robert Mugabe. Its last elections were a farce. The rule of law has been hijacked for the arbitrary and capricious use of sustaining Mugabe's rule. And the former breadbasket of Africa has become a basket case. Zimbabwe's inflation rate that was 18% ten years ago now has soared to 400% and its one time food surplus has become famine.

In Zimbabwe people suffer from Mugabe's dictatorship and many seek change. The government knows it cannot prevail in a free and fair election, so again it is moving to rig the parliamentary vote scheduled for next month.`

In Zimbabwe's 2000 parliamentary election and the 2002 presidential election, Mr. Mugabe and his Zimbabwe African National Union-Patriotic Front (ZANU-PF) came close to losing power notwithstanding intimidation and fraud. In the spring of 2002, while on a U.N. Security Council Mission to Central Africa, I met with Mr. Mugabe in his home in Harare. On instructions from Washington, I told him America viewed his election as illegitimate, his suppression of civil society and the media as human rights abuses, and his illegal seizures of farmers' land as unacceptable.

Mr. Mugabe looked at me in shock and white hot rage. He unleashed a loud torrent of accusations and abuse upon me. Clearly, he could not imagine anyone challenging his right to rule no matter how repressive the means he used to sustain himself in power. He wanted to wear the cloak of legitimacy no matter how inappropriate.

Appeared in the *Chicago Sun-Times,* February 21, 2005.

And Mr. Mugabe's pattern of violence, repression and intimidation against his nation's people continues.

Brutal conditions of arrest and detention, characterized by beatings, rape and various forms of torture, are used by government security forces, the so-called war veterans and government run youth militias against political opponents and their supporters, human rights advocates and ordinary citizens.

In the run up to this election, Mugabe has engaged in systematic efforts to silence political opponents and the press. Zimbabwe's government is barring opposition rallies and opposition advertising, refusing to publish voter rolls, intimidating rivals and denying international election observers entry into the country. It is illegal to conduct voter education without government approval, requiring election workers to register and clear electioneering materials with the state. A new law empowers the government to investigate, restrict, and arbitrarily disband nongovernmental groups, churches and charities.

Levenore Matomiulu, the president of the Zimbabwe Congress of Trade Unions, the largest labor organization in Zimbabwe, has said that "it's become practically impossible for civic organizations to assemble."

Albert Nusarurwa, who heads the Legal Resources Foundation, a human rights group in Harare, said, "The government has closed the space for anybody and everybody who opposes it."

In Zimbabwe, a third to a half of all citizens go hungry. The United Nations has warned that Zimbabwe's harvest is almost 60 percent short of what's needed to feed the country. Yet last May Mugabe ordered the World Food Program to cease most emergency deliveries of food. He is using food as a political weapon. Provinces that are opposition strongholds are deprived of grain while swing areas are provided grain for families that hold a ZANU-PF card to prove their loyalty to Mugabe's political power.

Revel Mukowamambe, a chief from the town of Mutare where grain is in short supply, has said, "People are being forced to support ZANU-PF. People are afraid. They're afraid of being beaten, or having their homes burned, or being killed because they support the (opposition party) M.D.C."

Free and fair elections are not about one day's vote. They are about a sustained infrastructure of civil society, freedom to assemble, access to media, and the right of free speech – particularly the freedom to criticize those in power.

Democracy is not easy. It is not dependent upon identical forms of government. Different cultures and various societies will establish their own democracies tailored to their own heritage, habits and aspirations. But democracy does mean the rule of law, free and fair elections, and individual opportunity.

Yes, recently we have witnessed great strides in the march of freedom. But the repression in Zimbabwe reminds us that the path is difficult and progress is not inevitable.

We must give witness to the oppressed people in Zimbabwe who continue to be denied their freedom. We must support their aspirations. And we should call Mugabe to account for his oppression.

The march of freedom requires our support. The people of Zimbabwe deserve it.

HUMAN RIGHTS ABUSE CONTINUES IN VIETNAM

The human rights situation in Vietnam continues to be unacceptable.

Last spring it was my honor and privilege to serve as Ambassador and United States Representative to the United Nations Commission on Human Rights in Geneva, Switzerland. In the Commission Chamber I said, "The Vietnamese Government's intolerance of political dissent, including on the Internet, resulted in the arrest of several democracy activists... Religious freedom problems persist and restrictions are particularly acute for the leadership of the Unified Buddhist Church of Vietnam and for Protestant Christians in the Central and Northwest Highlands." Unfortunately, there has been no real improvement in the situation. There even are signs that it has gotten worse.

In Vietnam, sometimes police beat suspects during arrests, detention and interrogation. Reportedly, security police continue to detain, beat and are responsible for the disappearance of persons. Incidents of arbitrary detention of citizens continues, including detention for the peaceful expression of political and religious views. Prison conditions remain harsh and some persons reportedly have died as a result of abuse while in custody.

In Vietnam, the judiciary is not independent. The Government denies some citizens the right to fair and expeditious trials. And the Vietnam Government continues to hold a number of political prisoners.

In Vietnam, the Government significantly restricts freedom of speech, freedom of the press, freedom of assembly, and freedom of association. The Vietnamese Government does not tolerate most types of public dissent and has stepped up efforts to control dissent on the internet. And security forces continue to enforce restrictions on public gatherings and travel.

The Vietnam Government prohibits independent political, labor and social organizations. Freedom of religion and operation of religious organizations other than those approved by the State are restricted. In particular, Buddhists, Hoa Hao, and Protestants active in unregistered organizations face harassment as well as possible detention by authorities.

Human Rights Watch reports that a few months ago "in the weeks leading up to Christmas, (Vietnamese) police were busy rounding up and arresting dozens of

---

Appeared in *NUOC VIET,* March 7, 2005.

Montagnard Christians and detaining them at district and provincial stations and prisons throughout the region. In Gia Lai province alone – one of the provinces in the Central Highlands – police arrested 129 people between December 12 and 24."

Citizens' privacy rights are restricted. And the Government continues to restrict significantly civil liberties on grounds of national security.

In Vietnam, the Government does not permit human rights organizations to form or operate. Violence and societal discrimination against some ethnic minorities continue. And the Government restricts some core worker rights, such as freedom of association.

There are reports that in Vietnam children work in exploitative conditions. Trafficking in women and children for the purpose of prostitution within Vietnam and abroad continues to be a serious problem. And there are reports of trafficking of women to China for arranged and forced marriages.

In its 2005 World Report, Human Rights Watch states, "Human rights conditions in Vietnam, already dismal, worsened in 2004. The government tolerates little public criticism of the Communist Party or statements calling for pluralism, democracy, or a free press. Dissidents are harassed, isolated, placed under house arrest, and in many cases, charged with crimes and imprisoned. Among those singled out are prominent intellectuals (and) writers."

The oppression is well documented. And it is incumbent on the United States to give a voice for those victims. We must pressure Vietnam to improve its human rights record and to end its campaign of religious persecution. As Professor Viet D. Dinh of Georgetown University told Congress, "This is no longer a war of bullets and bombs, but a battle of ideas and institutions."

In his recent State of the Union Address, President Bush said, "Our aim is to build and preserve a community of free and independent nations with governments that answer to their citizens and reflect their own cultures, and because democracies respect their own people and their neighbors, the advance of freedom will lead to peace."

In the past eighteen months freedom has been on the march. The Rose Revolution in Georgia. Afghanistan. The Orange Revolution in Ukraine. The Palestinians. Iraq. And now the Cedar Revolution in Lebanon has begun.

People throwing off the oppression of authoritarian governments that long abused their own citizens. Brave people realizing free and fair elections to form governments that answer to them, not the other way around.

Free people everywhere must give voice to the voiceless oppressed in their own lands. America must stand by the people of Vietnam in calling for a return of the basic human rights to which every human being is entitled and which will serve as the necessary building blocks to a free society.

It's Time for U.N. Human Rights Panel To Live Up To Its Name

This month the United Nations Commission on Human Rights begins its annual meeting in Geneva.

This U.N. Commission is an imperfect vessel to advance human rights. Its litany of double standards and hypocrisy is long. A few years ago Libya, one of the world's most repressive governments, served as Commission chair. Among its 54 members are such tyrannical regimes as Cuba, Zimbabwe and Sudan.

Each year the Commission devotes time to denounce and try to delegitimize Israel, the oldest democracy in the Middle East. Meanwhile the Commission refuses to rebuke such perennial human rights abuses as Zimbabwe and China.

Nonetheless, the United States goes to Geneva to stand up for the fundamental values that have defined American Exceptionalism and are the right of all mankind.

It is in America's interest to promote human rights and to advance freedom and democracy. So we go to the Commission on Human Rights in Geneva to advance our values, to speak for victims voiceless in their own land, and to name and shame those who deny their citizens the basic human rights to which they are entitled.

This year the Commission must confront a particularly horrific trampling of human rights, the genocide in Darfur, Sudan. It should pass a muscular resolution that condemns the atrocities, demands that they end, guarantees free access for humanitarian assistance to the victims who have been forced to live in life-threatening conditions, and requires accountability from the perpetrators of these terrible transgressions. If the Commission on Human Rights fails to act strongly it will say more about their moral bankruptcy than it will about the tragic events on the ground.

Some 18 months ago the Sudan's Arab government in Khartoum set out to put down a small rebel movement in the western province of Darfur, a large region about the size of France. Rather than launch a surgical attack on the few rebels, Khartoum unleashed the forces of hell.

Khartoum armed an Arab militia named the janjaweed. Then in coordinated attacks led by government attack helicopters followed by janjaweed on camel and horseback, they burned villages of blacks in Darfur, took livestock, killed males from old men to young babies, and often gang raped, disfigured and drove out women and girls.

Appeared in the *Chicago Sun-Times,* March 29, 2005.

The carnage has been widespread. The Sudan government in coordination with the marauding janjaweed Arab militias have destroyed hundreds of villages and driven nearly 2 million people from their homes. They now live in desperate conditions in large camps for internally displaced persons and refugees. And some estimate that the atrocities already may have caused up to 200,000 deaths. It is the largest humanitarian crisis in the world.

Earlier this month, Physicians for Human Rights issued a report that detailed international destruction of community support, economic structures, livestock, food production, wells and farming capacity, as well as, huts and homes that were burned to empty shells.

Human Rights Watch has released a video interview with Musa Hilal, who has admitted committing crimes in Darfur. In it he says that the Sudan government steered the attacks. "These people get their orders from Khartoum," he states.

A document seized from a janjaweed official that the African Union believes is authentic calls for the "execution of all directives from the president of the republic." It goes on to call for the janjaweed to "change the demography of Darfur and make it void of (black) African tribes." It encourages "killing, burning villages and farms, terrorizing people, confiscating property from members of African tribes and forcing them from Darfur."

President Bush has properly labeled these heinous crimes genocide. And for over a year Bush has sought international action to stop the atrocities in Darfur.

Last year at the U.N. Commission on Human Rights, the United States advanced a strong resolution on Darfur. It was opposed from the start by African countries reluctant to condemn one of their own and the usual coalition of repressive regimes. Nonetheless, the vote count seemed close. Several leading human rights groups felt we had the votes to pass our tough resolution condemning Khartoum.

Sadly, at the last minute the European Union, then led by the Irish, agreed to a gentle resolution advanced by Sudan. In the end, they held more precious collegiality in the Commission chamber than those suffering in Darfur.

It was a tragic event. Understandably, Khartoum took the actions of the Commission as evidence that the international community cared little about the victims in Darfur. The carnage continued.

This year will the Commission on Human Rights uphold the values of the Universal Declaration on Human Rights and stand with the victims in Darfur? Or will the members cynically shirk their responsibility?

The United States again will be forward leaning. The credibility and value of the U.N. Commission will be tested. More important, Khartoum will be watching. And the victims hope for relief from their suffering may be in the balance.

THE UNITED NATIONS COMMISSION ON HUMAN RIGHTS: PROTECTOR OR ACCOMPLICE

I want to thank Sub-Committee Chairman, Congressman Christopher Smith, for inviting me to testify today on Human Rights and United Nations reform. The work of this Congressional Committee is important and the topic of today's hearing deserves careful consideration. I hope that my observations can help you in your work.

Human rights matter. They are not values of convenience nor are they merely a fashion of the day. Human rights are inherent, self-evident and transcendent. They are fundamental to what it means to be a human being and working to protect human rights – every man, woman and child's basic human rights – is a noble cause and amongst the foremost responsibilities of government.

Human Rights

Human rights are grounded on the recognition that every human being has "inherent dignity and worth." As Ronald Dworkin has written, "We almost all accept… that human life in all its forms is sacred… For some of us, this is a matter of religious faith, for others, of secular but deep philosophical belief."[1] For me, it is part of my religious faith.[2] But whether the recognition that every human being is "inviolable" and has "inherent dignity" derives from religious faith or philosophical constructs, it compels certain fundamental moral limits on us individually and collectively. It demands that there are things that ought not be done to any human being. And there are things that ought to be done for any human being. Among other requirements, we have a responsibility to give voice to the voiceless victims of human rights abuse and stand for the values we cherish as best we can.[3] No one and no society is faultless. Mistakes are made. But we have an obligation and an opportunity to strive to be faithful to our values and to act so as to project those values as best we are able under the circumstances.

Human rights are not the sole consideration of U.S. foreign policy nor should they be, but neither can human rights be irrelevant.[4] Human rights are fundamental to who we are and human rights properly should animate our actions individually and as a nation. Respecting human rights and defending those values are the right thing to do and it is in our self-interest to do so. Countries that respect human rights

Testimony on Africa, Global Human Rights and International Operations Subcommittee, Committee on International Relations, U.S. House of Representatives, Washington, D.C., April 19, 2005.

under the rule of law are more stable and more prosperous. Spreading democracy and liberty makes the world safer. Democratic nations are less likely to begin armed conflicts. And democratic nations create an environment of opportunity inhospitable to the frustration and fanaticism that breeds terrorists.

The recognition of the inherent dignity of all mankind leads to the acceptance of limits on what we can do. The idea of human rights as enshrined in the United Nations Universal Declaration on Human Rights and other international documents embraces this recognition and seeks to enumerate the rights of all human beings and prescribe the limits of acceptable behavior. And while a broad consensus may be achieved on the ideals contained in such documents, it is less easy to act in strict accordance with such guidelines. And it is harder still to act to condemned such violations and remedy injustices. Furthermore, whether the case be Rwanda, Bosnia, Kosovo or Darfur, man's capacity for inhumanity and terrible transgressions too frequently are revealed and the international community's willingness to act to stop such crimes against humanity too often is anemic.[5]

The American idea is grounded on principles of human rights. As former Secretary of State George Shultz once said, "What unifies us is not a common origin but a common set of ideals: freedom, constitutional democracy, racial and religious tolerance. We Americans thus define ourselves not by where we come from but by where we are headed: our goals, our values, our principles, which make the kind of society we strive to create."[6]

The concern for human rights is interwoven in the national experience and our beliefs as Americans. It is what has differentiated the United States from so many other nations in history. It is fundamental to our character and our values.

Ronald Reagan understood the transcending importance of the American idea, of values, and human rights. At the height of the Cold War when he had labeled the Soviet Union "an evil empire", President Reagan delivered an address at Westminster Hall, London, in which he said, "The ultimate determination in the struggle now going on for the world will not be bombs and rockets, but a test of wills and ideas – a trial of spiritual resolve: the values we hold and the beliefs we cherish, the ideals to which we are dedicated... the great civilized ideas: individual liberty, representative government, and the rules of law under God."[7]

We won the great struggle of the 20th century. Freedom and democracy prevailed over totalitarian communism.

But the struggle for freedom is not over. Brutal authoritarian states continue to enslave people around the world. Basic human rights and personal dignity continue to be denied. This is wrong. Furthermore, these harsh conditions can give root to the frustration and despair that breeds terrorists who lash out at the United States in desperate acts of violence.

Just enumerating the rights of man is not enough. We must act to advance them. It is our responsibility and our opportunity. As President Woodrow Wilson said 91 years ago, "Liberty does not consist in mere declaration of the rights of man. It consists in the translation of those declarations into definite actions."[8]

Democracy

Self-determination is a fundamental human right recognized in the Universal Declaration on Human Rights[9] and by common sense. Furthermore, democracy is the best way to secure sustainable respect for human rights. It is a rampart against state encroachment on individual rights and liberties. As President Bush has said, "[D]emocracy is the surest way to build a society of justice. The best way to prevent corruption and abuse of power is to hold rulers accountable. The best way to insure fairness to all is to establish the rule of law. The best way to honor human dignity is to protect human rights."[10]

Democratic governments around the world do not have identical institutions nor procedures. The particularities will vary from place to place, adopting to history and culture.[11] But all true democracies share certain common characteristics.

Democracy is more than the mechanics of popular elections. A democratic process includes effective participation, equality of voting, an effective opportunity to learn about the alternatives about which one is voting, an open agenda and universal suffrage.[12] Democracy depends on freedom of expression, civil society and the right to dissent.[13] Democracy helps to prevent government by abusive autocracies.[14] Rights are essential building blocks of a democratic process of government so a system of rights are inherent in democratic institutions. Freedoms and opportunities are required for a government to be democratic. Democracy helps people to protect their own interests.[15]

As John Stuart Mill wrote, "[T]he rights and interests of every or any person we secure from being disregarded when the person is himself able, and habitually disposed, to stand up for them... Human beings are only secure from evil at the hands of others in proportion as they have the power of being, and are, self-protecting."[16] Or, as Dr. Kirkpatrick has said, "The reason that popular governments protect human rights best is that people do not impose tyrants upon themselves. Tyrants impose themselves upon people."[17]

If one can participate in determining one's government through a democratic process, you can protect one's interests and rights from abuse by government. Democratic governments give people the opportunity to live under laws of their own choosing. Democratic government provides the opportunity for exercising moral responsibility. Democracy allows human development. Democratic government fosters greater political equality.

The march of freedom is indivisible from the advance of human rights.[18] The spread of democracy is part of the promotion and sustainability of human rights. The spread of democracy deserves our support; it requires our assistance. Our good faith should be buttressed by our actions. As President George W. Bush has said, "The progress of liberty is a powerful trend. Yet, we also know that liberty, if not defended, can be lost. The success of freedom is not determined by some dialectic of history. By definition, the success of freedom rests upon the choices and the courage of free people."[19]

The United Nations

The United Nations has made important contributions to human rights. The horrors of World War II spurred the world community to advance human rights.

257

Among other things, from the ashes of war the United States led the world community to found the United Nations. The U.N. Charter embraces two overriding goals, "to save succeeding generations from the scourge of war" and "to reaffirm faith in fundamental human rights."[20] The words "promoting and encouraging respect for human rights and fundamental freedoms" appear, with slight variations, throughout the U.N. Charter.

As Secretary of State George Marshall observed in remarks before the opening session of the United Nations General Assembly in Paris in 1948, "Systematic and deliberate denials of basic human rights lie at the root of most of our trouble and threaten the work of the United Nations. It is not only fundamentally wrong that millions of men and women live in daily terror of secret police, subject to seizure, imprisonment or forced labor without just cause and without fair trial, but these wrongs have repercussions in the community of nations. Governments which systematically disregard the rights of their own people are not likely to respect the rights of other nations and other people and are likely to seek their objectives by coercion and force in the international field."[21]

But how the general human rights rhetoric in the U.N. Charter might be translated into action was far from clear.

The seminal document in the United Nations pertaining to human rights is the Universal Declaration of Human Rights that was adopted in 1948. The difficult and painstakingly drafting took place in 1947 and 1948.[22]

Eleanor Roosevelt chaired the drafting committee.[23]

The Declaration has a preamble and 30 articles that set forth the human rights and fundamental freedoms to which everyone, everywhere in the world, is entitled. The strongest terms of the Declaration faithfully embrace the values and civil liberties contained in our own Declaration of Independence and Constitution.

While not perfect, the U.N. Universal Declaration of Human Rights was the product of hard work well done. It established important norms on human rights, proclaimed them universal, and called upon all nations to honor and protect them. While not the final resolution of human rights abuses, as William Schulz, Executive Director of Amnesty International USA has written, "The mere articulation of such rights and their near universal acclamation was a formidable achievement."[24]

THE DECLARATION'S IMPACT

Quite properly, many people point out that the world falls short of attaining the Declaration's high aspirations. In fact, in some parts of the world these basic human rights are trampled daily and the people brutalized. Critics charge that these facts not only reveal the hypocrisy and corruption of the United Nations and many of its member states, but also expose the U.N. Universal Declaration of Human Rights as a hollow and meaningless document. I disagree.

As Professor Mary Ann Glendon points out in her excellent book, *A World Made New: Eleanor Roosevelt and the Universal Declaration of Human Rights*:

> [T]he State Department explained the U.S. view of the
> Declaration's nature and purpose by referring to what Abraham
> Lincoln had said about the assertion of human equality in the
> Declaration of Independence:

258

'They (the drafters) did not mean to assert the obvious untruth, that all were then actually enjoying that equality, nor yet, that they were about to confer it immediately upon them. Indeed they had no power to confer such a boon. They meant simply to declare the right so that the enforcement of it might follow as fast as circumstances should permit.

'They meant to set up a standard maxim for free society which should be familiar to all: constantly looked to, constantly labored for, and thereby spreading and deepening its influence and augmenting the happiness and value of life to all people, of all colors, everywhere.[25]

Similarly, prior to the adoption of the U.N. Declaration of Human Rights, Eleanor Roosevelt wrote.

In the first place, we have put into words some inherent rights. Beyond that, we have found that the conditions of our contemporary world require the enumeration of certain protections which the individual must have if he is to acquire a sense of security and dignity in his own person. The effect of this is frankly educational. Indeed, I like to think that the Declaration will help forward very largely the education of the people of the world.[26]

As the U.N. General Assembly neared its final vote on the Declaration, Eleanor Roosevelt as Chairman of the Commission on Human Rights said,

In giving our approval to the declaration today, it is of primary importance to keep clearly in mind the basic character of the document. It is not a treaty; it is not an international agreement. It is not and does not purport to be a statement of law or of legal obligation. It is a declaration of basic principles of human rights and freedoms, to be stamped with the approval of the General Assembly by informed votes of its members, and to save as a common standard of achievement for all people of all nations.[27]

Indeed, "Eleanor Roosevelt expressly campaigned for United States support by arguing that the Declaration would not be legally binding."[28] It stood as a document of basic enumerated rights that's power was in its moral persuasion publicly exercised. It outlined a "common standard of achievement" to which to aspire and it has become the cornerstone of today's international human rights regime. It is the yardstick by which all country's respect for, and compliance with, international human rights standards are measured.

As former Congressman, Father Robert Drinan has written, "The establishment of a catalog of internationally recognized human rights for the first time in the history of the world is a monumental achievement in itself, apart from the enforceability of such rights."[29]

Today the principles set forth in the Declaration have inculcated the modern world; its culture and its politics. No U.N. action before or since has had as profound an effect on contemporary thinking and the lives of as many people throughout the world. As U.N. Secretary General Kofi Annan has written, "The end of the Cold War, the World Conference on Human Rights in Vienna in 1993, and the inception of the United Nations High Commissioner for Human Rights later that year have opened up new avenues for the United Nations to make its work in human rights more meaningful to people throughout the world." But the foundation for that effort is the U.N. Universal Declaration on Human Rights and the principles therein embraced.

The U.N. Commission on Human Rights

Unfortunately, the United Nations Commission on Human Rights often has failed to effectively advance human rights and often has failed to give voice to human rights victims voiceless in their own land. The deteriorating situation is cause for grave concern.

Earlier this month in an address to the U.N. Commission on Human Rights, Secretary-General Kofi Annan stated, "[O]ur responsibility under the Charter is clear: we must do more to promote and protect fundamental rights and freedoms. ...[U]nless we re-make our human rights machinery, we may be unable to renew public confidence in the United Nations."[30]

Last year I served as Ambassador and United States Representative to the U.N. Commission on Human Rights in Geneva. It was an enlightening, if not uplifting, experience. While we successfully pursued resolutions bringing to account the repressive regimes that are denying human rights in North Korea, Cuba, and Burma; we failed to pass important resolutions on the oppressive human rights situation in Zimbabwe, China and elsewhere. It was disheartening to our delegation. It was devastating for those many victims who are denied their inherent human rights in their own lands. It demonstrated structural weaknesses and failures of the Commission on Human Rights. And, unfortunately, it was business as usual at the Commission.

The fact is that repressive regimes seek seats in the 53 member U.N. Commission on Human Rights in order to protect themselves. For example, among the members of the 2005 Commission now sitting in Geneva are such human rights abusers as Cuba, Sudan and Zimbabwe. They form an axes of the repressors, who bind together to try to protect one another. They seek out other delegations concerned about what would be revealed by scrutiny of their own human rights records. They form a powerful bloc within the UNCHR that effectively stops efforts to "name and shame" many repressive regimes. As a senior European diplomat said, "Countries don't want to be named. They want to protect their interests, so they band together."[31]

The United States Ambassador to the U.N. in Geneva, Kevin Moley, an effective diplomat with whom I've had the pleasure of working, is quoted as having said, "The inmates are very close to being in charge of the asylum."[32]

Unfortunately, this group of repressive regimes often receives support even from some of our European friends, who hold human rights in high regard. But they are hesitant to call out abusers. *New York Times* reporter Richard Bernstein reports, "[T]he view is that the U.S. eagerness for what the Europeans call 'name and shame' resolutions might be psychologically satisfying, but they don't bring human rights improvements."[33] I disagree.

The collapse of the Soviet empire and the rush to freedom of central and eastern Europe was instructive on many fronts. Among the lessons we should have learned is that many dissidents behind the Iron Curtain took comfort and subsidence from public expressions by the West that they knew injustices were being committed under communism, they condemned them, and they called for them to end. It was a critical contribution to sustaining the flame of freedom even in the darkest days of Soviet denial and tyranny. As Natan Sharansky has stated, "During my long journey through the world of evil, I had discovered three sources of power: the power of an individual's inner freedom, the power of a free society, and the power of the solidarity of the free world."[34] The free world must stand in solidarity for the values that underpin our just societies. And we must give voice to the human rights victims voiceless in their own lands. That is our responsibility and our opportunity.

The failure of the U.N. Commission on Human Rights to rebuke repressive regimes gives aid and comfort to the repressors. It breaks faith with human rights champions who confront considerable, sometimes unimaginable, hardships at home. It tarnishes the values to which we claim to subscribe. And it diminishes those institutions entrusted to advance human rights, among them the United Nations Commission on Human Rights.

Also, as in earlier years, last spring the Commission on Human Rights was exploited by some in their relentless campaign to delegitimize Israel, the oldest democracy in the Middle East. While all other country specific concerns are lumped together under UNCHR agenda item 9, Israel is singled out with its own, separate agenda item. The excessive, invective rhetoric assaulting Israel is numbing. The one-sided resolutions are scandalous. No nation is blameless. All countries should be vigilant to improve their own human rights records. But the singling out of Israel in this manner reveals more about the double standards and abuse within the U.N. system than it does about alleged human rights failures by the state of Israel.

A further very troubling development last year in the U.N. Commission on Human Rights was the failure of member states to pass a robust resolution on the situation in Darfur. Today the situation in Sudan is the worst humanitarian crisis in the world. Last spring the ethnic cleansing was well underway, and was well known. Nonetheless, the members of the UNCHR lacked the will to condemn the atrocities.

By last spring President Bush had spoken out loudly and clearly, calling on the Sudanese Government to stop the atrocities in Darfur. It was known that a pattern of planned and willful mass slaughter and forced displacement was taking place. The Sudan Government had armed the Arab militias known as Janjaweed. They had coordinated attacks on black villages, killing males from young boys to old men, raping and branding women, killing livestock, burning huts and driving black Africans from their homes. At the time an estimated 30,000 already had been killed and nearly a million people had been displaced.

Nonetheless, the Commission on Human Rights member states, including Europeans, went along with a weak "President's Statement" on the situation in Darfur. Not surprisingly, Khartoum took this as a signal that the international community did not care much about the atrocities. So they continued. Today estimates are that 200,000 have been killed and nearly 2 million people have been driven from their homes. President Bush quite properly has called the atrocities in Darfur genocide.

Many question the value of a Commission on Human Rights that lacks the resolve to condemn ethnic cleansing. A crisis of confidence has developed. What can be done?

Next Steps

Secretary-General Kofi Annan has said, "Human rights are the core of the United Nations' identity. Men and women everywhere expect us to uphold universal ideals. They need us to be their ally and protector. They want to believe we can help unmask bigotry and defend the rights of the weak and voiceless. ...But the gap between what we seem to promise, and what we actually deliver, has grown. The answer is not to draw back from an ambitious human rights agenda, but to make the improvements that will enable our machinery to live up to the world's expectations."[35]

The Secretary-General convened a High Level Panel to consider the entire spectrum of United Nations activities and offer reform proposals. The High Level Panel made many recommendations that warrant careful consideration such as a useful definition of terrorism and support for a democracy fund. However, the Panel's suggestion to "universalize" the UNCHR is ill-advised. If the UNCHR were to enlarge to all 191 U.N. member states it would have the same composition as the U.N. General Assembly. I suspect it would then have all the effectiveness and credibility of the General Assembly, which is to say, not much at all.

Secretary-General Annan drew from the High Level Panel's report in crafting his own reform proposals in his report, "In larger Freedom Towards Development, Security and Human Rights for All." The Secretary-General recommends replacing the Commission of 53 members with a smaller Human Rights Council of 19 members. Rather than meeting for six weeks each year in the spring, he suggests the new Human Rights Council be a standing body. Rather than selection through the regional blocs with a General Assembly ratification by a simple majority, the Secretary-General proposes members to the new Council be limited to countries with solid human rights records and be elected by a two-thirds majority of the General Assembly. This proposed Human Rights Council would review periodically the human rights record of every nation. And the Council would be available to convene on short notice to deal with urgent crisis or gross violations of human rights.

Among the intents of the Secretary-General's proposals is to limit or even eliminate repressive regimes from membership on the Human Rights Council. This is a proper goal. However, given the influence of regional blocs, the political give and take, and general horse trading in the U.N., I am skeptical that this objective will be realized.

Also having served as Ambassador to the United Nations for Special Political Affairs, I have sat through more Security Council meetings than I care to remember. This venue also was designed to meet only as required. Yet in a generation, its meeting frequency has grown from a couple of dozen times a year to over 200 sessions each year. Most are mind-numbingly routine, formalistic and, too often, of marginal value. I foresee this possibility for the proposed Human Rights Council.

The United Nations, its membership, structures and procedures has many purposes. It is an institution that in many ways is very useful to the United States, our values and interests. But it also has challenges. Among them is that while the right to "self-determination" is recognized in the U.N. Charter and the Universal Declaration on Human Rights, many U.N. members are not democracies even in form, let alone in actual practice. Consequently, many U.N. member states do not recognize, let alone practice a form of government that respects the fundamental rights of their people. Nonetheless, undemocratic states have equal standing in the United Nations with those that, while imperfect, nonetheless have vibrant democracies, strong rule of law, and real human rights protections.

That does not mean that we should not engage the United Nations in the area of human rights. We should. But it does mean that we engage the U.N. with our eyes open. We work the issues. And we recognize that while we constantly should seek to improve "U.N. machinery" in the area of human rights and elsewhere, that it will remain an imperfect venue.

The United Nations provides a platform for repressive regimes to have equal standing with the free. It provides venues for oppressors to advance their interests just as it does for those of us that embrace human rights and seek to spread freedom. It is an intensely political arena in which the United States must work tirelessly to champion the values we cherish and to advance the cause of freedom. But, unfortunately, at this time when too many authoritarian and brutal governments sit at the U.N. table, whatever the machinery and whatever the procedures, there will continue to be fundamental clashes in the U.N. on human rights. We should accept this challenge. The victims of human rights abuse are counting on us. And we know that our cause is just and it will prevail.

---

1.   Ronald Dworkin, "Life is Sacred: That's the Easy Part," *New York Times Magazine*, May 16, 1993, p. 36.

    "America's founders began with the premise that man had been created in the image of God and that all were of equal worth and endowed with unalienable rights. In founding the modern world's first democracy, they set out to create a system that would follow this premise and that would suit human nature as they understood it." Joshua Muravchik, *Exporting Democracy: Fulfilling America's Destiny* (Washington, D.C.; The AEI Press; 1991), p. 1.

2.   "The essence of all morality is this: to believe that every human being is of infinite importance and therefore that no consideration of expediency can justify the oppression of one by another. But to believe this it is necessary to believe in God." R. H. Tawney, J. M. Winter and D. M. Joslin, eds., *R. H. Tawney's Commonplace Book*, 67 (1972); as quoted in Michael J. Perry, *The Idea of Human Rights: Four Inquiries* (New York, N.Y.; Oxford University Press, 1998), p. 11. Professor Perry's volume provides an excellent exploration of whether the idea of Human Rights is ineliminably religious.

    "It is often stressed that the idea of human rights is of recent origin, and that this is enough to dismiss its claims to timeless validity. In its contemporary form, the doctrine is certainly new, though it is arguable that it is a modern version of the natural law theory, whose origins we can trace back at least to the Stoic philosophers and, of course, to the Judaic and Christian sources of European culture. There is no substantial difference between proclaiming "the right to life" and stating that natural law forbids killing. Much as the concept may have been elaborated in the philosophy of the Enlightenment in its conflict with Christianity, the notion of the immutable rights of individuals goes back to the Christian belief in the autonomous status and irreplaceable value of the human personality." Leszek Kolakowski, *Modernity on Endless Trial*, 214 (1990), as quoted in Michael J. Perry, *ibid.*, p. 3. See also, Micheline R. Ishey, *The History of Human Rights: From Ancient Times to the Globalization Era* (Berkeley, California; University of California Press; 2004).

3.   For a powerful testament to the importance of giving voice to victims of human rights abuses voiceless in their own land see the book by former Soviet dissident Natan Sharansky, *ibid*. See also, Andrei

263

Sakharov, *Memoirs* (New York, N.Y.; Alfred A. Knopf; 1990); and Robert F. Drinan, *The Mobilization of Shame: A World View of Human Rights* (New Haven, Connecticut; Yale University Press; 2001).

4.   There is a considerable body of work examining United States efforts to execute an effective human rights policy. Sometimes U.S. foreign policy has been successful, sometimes it has not. See generally, Debra Liang-Fenton, ed., *Implementing U.S. Human Rights Policy* (Washington, D.C.; United States Institute of Peace Press; 2004); John Shattuck, *Freedom on Fire: Human Rights Wars and America's Response* (Cambridge, Massachusetts; Harvard University Press; 2003); David P. Forsythe, *Human Rights and U.S. Foreign Policy: Congress Reconsidered* (Gainesville, Florida; University Presses of Florida; 1988); Julie A. Mertus, *Bait and Switch: Human Rights and U.S. Foreign Policy* (New York, N.Y.; Routledge; 2003); David A. Forsythe, *The United States and Human Rights: Looking Inward and Outward* (Lincoln, Nebraska; University of Nebraska Press; 2000); and Tony Evans, *U.S. Hegemony and the Project of Universal Human Rights* (New York, N.Y.; St. Martin's Press; 1996). See also, Eliot Abrams, ed., *Honor Among Nations: Intangible Interests and Foreign Policy* (Washington, D.C.; Ethics and Policy Center; 1998). See also, Leslie H. Gelb and Justine A. Rosenthal, "The Rise of Ethics in Foreign Policy: Reaching a Values Consensus, *Foreign Affairs* (May/June 2003), Vol. 82, No. 3, pp. 2-7, in which the argue that "morality, values, ethics, universal principles," recently have taken on greater centrality in U.S. foreign policy.

5.   Tragically, the failures of the international community to act forcefully to stop the genocide in Darfur is not the first such failure. For example, see Romeo Dallaire, *Shake Hands With The Devil: The Failure of Humanity in Rwanda* (Toronto, Canada; Random House Canada; 2003). See also, Linda Melvern, *A People Betrayed: The Role of The West in Rwanda's Genocide* (London; Zed Books; 2000); Samantha Powers, *A Problem from Hell: America and the Age of Genocide* (New York, N.Y.; Basic Books; 2002); Philip Gourevitch, *We Wish To Inform You That Tomorrow We will Be Killed With Our Families: Stories from Rwanda* (London; Picador; 1999); Michael Barnett, *Eyewitness to a Genocide: The U.N. and Rwanda* (Ithaca, N.Y.; Cornell University Press; 2002); and Alan J. Kuperman, *The Limits of Humanitarian Intervention: Genocide in Rwanda* (Washington, D.C.; Brookings Institute; 2001). Regarding the ethnic cleansing in Bosnia, see Thomas Cushman and Stjepan Mestrovic, eds., *This Time We Knew: Western Responses to Genocide in Bosnia* (New York, N.Y.; New York University Press; 1996).

6.   George P. Shultz, "Human Rights and the Moral Dimension of U.S. Foreign Policy," an address at the 86th Annual Washington Day Banquet at the Creve Coeur Club of Peoria, Illinois, February 22, 1984, published as Current Policy No. 551 by the United States Department of State Bureau of Public Affairs, Washington, D.C., 1984.

7.   Ronald Reagan, Address to the British Parliament, London, England, June 8, 1982. George P. Shultz, Secretary of State for most of the Reagan presidency stated in 1984, "[M]oral values and a commitment to human dignity have been not an appendage to our foreign policy but an essential part of it, and a powerful impulse driving it… There should be no doubt of President Reagan's approach – not isolation or guilt or paralysis but, on the contrary, a commitment to active engagement, confidently working for our values, as well as our interests in the real world, acting proudly as the champion of freedom." Shultz, *ibid.*

8.   Woodrow Wilson, Address, July 4, 1914.

9.   For an excellent examination of the difficult process of drafting the Universal Declaration of Human Rights, see Mary Ann Glendon, *A World Made New: Eleanor Roosevelt and the Universal Declaration of Human Rights* (New York, N.Y.; Random House; 2001).

10.   Remarks by President George W. Bush, Istanbul, Turkey, June 29, 2004.

11.   See, generally, Arend Lijphart, *Patterns of Democracy: Government Forms and Performance in Thirty-Six Countries* (New Haven, Conn.; Yale University Press; 1999). See also Larry Diamond, Juan J. Linz, and Seymour Martin Lipset, eds., *Democracy in Developing Countries: Asia* (Boulder, Colo.; Lynne Rienner; 1989); Larry Diamond, Juan J. Linz, and Seymour Martin Lipset, eds., *Democracy in Developing Countries: Latin America* (Boulder, Colo.; Lynne Rienner; 1989); Larry Diamond, Juan J. Linz,, and Seymour Martin Lipset, eds., *Democracy in Developing Countries: Africa* (Boulder, Colo.; Lynne Rienner; 1988); Jorge I. Dominguez and Abraham F. Lowenthal, eds., *Constructing Democratic Governance: Mexico, Central America, and the Caribbean in the 1990's* (Baltimore, Md.; John Hopkins University Press; 1996); David Beetham, ed., *Defining and Measuring Democracy* (London, U.K.; Sage Publishers; 1994); Alex Inkeles, ed., (New Brunswick, N. J.; Transaction Press; 1991); and Tatu Vanhanen, *The Process of Democratization: A Comparative Study of 147 States* (New York, N.Y.; Crane Russak; 1990).

12.   See, Robert A. Dahl, *On Democracy* (New Haven, Conn.; Yale University Press; 1998), p. 37-43.

As Fared Zakaria has written, "[D]emocracy means liberal democracy: a political system marked not only by free and fair elections but also by the rule of law, a separation of powers, and the protection of basic liberties of speech, assembly, religion, and property... [it] is not about the procedures for selecting government but, rather, government's goals. It refers to the tradition... that seeks to protect an individual's autonomy and dignity against coercion, whatever the source – state, church, or society... It places the rule of law at the center of politics. Fared Zakaria, *The Future of Freedom* (New York, N.Y.; W.W. Norton and Co.; 2003), p. 17 and 19.

13.   See, Seymour Martin Lipset and Jason M. Larkin, *The Democratic Century* (Norman, Oklahoma; University of Oklahoma Press; 2004) in which a lively comparative analysis of democracy is presented including "how institutions that constitute democracy interact with one another, how political parties develop in new democracies, (and) why the quality of civil societies matters more than the mere existence of civil associations."

See also, Morton H. Halperin, "Democracy and Human Rights: An Argument for Convergence," in Samantha Power and Graham Allison, *Realizing Human Rights: Moving From Inspiration to Impact* (New York, N.Y.; St. Martin's Press; 2000), pp. 249-263.

14.   "We believe that the rights of individuals are most effectively promoted and expanded by and through democratic political institutions – where governments are elected through periodic competitive elections, elections that feature freedom to criticize government, to publish criticisms, to organize opposition and compete for power. Human rights violations may occur even in such systems, but they are relatively few and readily corrected." Jeane J. Kirkpatrick, *Legitimacy and Force: Political and Moral Dimensions* (New Brunswick, N.J.; Transaction Books; 1988), p. 85.

15.   "There are, however, essential principles common to every successful society, in every culture. Successful societies limit the power of the state and the power of the military – so that governments respond to the will of the people, and not the will of an elite. Successful societies protect freedom with the consistent and impartial rule of law, instead of selecting applying the law to punish political opponents. Successful societies allow room for healthy civic institutions – for political parties and labor unions and independent newspapers and broadcast media. Successful societies guarantee religious liberty – the right to serve and honor God without fear of persecution. Successful societies privatize their economies, and secure the rights of property. They prohibit and punish official corruption, and invest in the health and education of their people. They recognize the rights of women. And instead of directing hatred and resentment against others, successful societies appeal to the hopes of their own people." President George W. Bush, Freedom in Iraq and Middle East, Remarks at the 20th Anniversary of the National Endowment for Democracy, United States Chamber of Commerce, Washington, D.C., November 6, 2003.

16.   John Stuart Mill, *Considerations of Representative Government* (1861) (New York, N.Y.; Liberal Arts Press; 1958), p. 55.

17.   Jeane J. Kirkpatrick, *ibid.*, p. 85.

18.   While there are some who question whether all people in all cultures seek freedom and can embrace and sustain democracy, the march of freedom in Indonesia, Georgia, Afghanistan and Ukraine suggest otherwise. For a thoughtful exploration of this issue see, Michael Novak, *The Universal Hunger For Liberty: Why the Crash of Civilizations Is Not Inevitable* (New York, N.Y.; Basic Books; 2004). And for an interesting exploration of whether the recent wave of democracy can be sustained, see Larry Diamond and Marc F. Plattner, eds., *The Global Resurgence of Democracy* (Second Edition), (Baltimore, Md.; John Hopkins University Press; 1996).

19.   President George W. Bush, Address to the National Endowment for Democracy, Washington, D.C., November 6, 2003.

20.   Footnote 24/The Universal Declaration of Human Rights.

21.   U.S. Department of State, *Bulletin*, Vol. 19, October 3, 1948), p. 932. For an excellent history of the deliberations and politics of the founding of the U.N., see Stephen C. Schlesinger, *Act of Creation: The Founding of the United Nations* (Boulder, Colorado; Westview Press; 2003). "The importance of that war (World War II) resulted in the widespread conviction that effective international protection of human rights was one of the essential conditions of international peace and progress, and this conviction was set out in a number of statements, declarations and proposals made while the war was still being fought." *The United Nations and Human Rights*, (New York, New York; United Nations, 1984), p. 1.

22.   Cuba and Panama introduced proposals for the preparation of a bill of rights at the first U.N. General Assembly in 1945. In the end the General Assembly transmitted the Panamanian proposal to the Economic and Social Council for consideration by the Commission on Human Rights.

23.   Among the other able public figures on the committee were Peng-chun Chang, a Chinese philosopher and playwright, Rene Cassin, a French Resistance leader, Charles Malik, a Lebanese philosopher, and Carlos Romulo, a Philippean who had won a Pulitzer Prize in 1941.   Other nations represented on the drafting committee were Australia, Chile, the Soviet Union and the United Kingdom.

24.   William F. Schulz, *In Our Own Best Interest: How Defending Human Rights Benefits Us All* (Boston, Massachusetts; Beacon Press; 2001), p. 4.

25.   Mary Ann Glendon, *ibid.*, p. 236.

26.   *Ibid.*

27.   U.S. Department of State, *Bulletin*, Vol. 19 (December 19, 1948), p. 751.

28.   Howard Tolley, Jr., *ibid.*, p. 23.

29.   Robert F. Drinan, S.J., *ibid.*, p. ix.

30.   Secretary-General Kofi Annan, Address to the U.N. Commission on Human Rights, Geneva, Switzerland, April 7, 2005. See also, Mark Turner, "U.N. Overhaul: Annan Confronts Human Rights Commission With Call to Disband and Reform," *Financial Times*, April 8, 2005.

31.   Richard Bernstein, "Are the Foxes Guarding Human Rights at U.N.,?" *International Herald Tribune*, April 1, 2005.

32.   *Ibid.*

33.   *Ibid.*

34.   Natan Sharansky, *The Case for Democracy: The Power of Freedom to Overcome Tyranny and Terror* (New York, N.Y.; Public Affairs; 2004), p. xi.

35.   Kofi Annan, *ibid.*

Trials Can Help Heal a Traumatized, Broken Cambodia

In the past 100 years, there had been a litany of horrific mass killings that will live in infamy.

Stalin's Soviet purges. The Nazi Holocaust. The Cambodian Killing Fields. Rwanda. Ethnic cleansing in Bosnia and Kosovo. And today's genocide in Darfur, Sudan. Grotesquely violent and on a scale that is mind numbing.

Professor Benjamin Valentine of Dartmouth College estimates that between 60 and 150 million people perished in episodes of mass killings during the 20th Century. International and civil wars resulted in about 34 million battle deaths in the same period. That's right, 2 to 5 times more people died from mass killing than on the battlefields.

Societies subjected to such horrific atrocities are torn asunder. These scars from such searing brutality haunt the survivors and continue to tear the social fabric long after the killing stops.

Restorative justice helps bring closure to the violent past and contributes to reconciliation and peace. Establishing an historic record of the atrocities validate the victim's suffering and help free them for forgiveness and progress. Holding to account those who commit the worst crimes against humanity provides justice, strengthens norms of decency and, perhaps, provides some deterrent to those who might contemplate again opening the gates of hell.

In Cambodia from 1975 to 1979, Pol Pot and his Khmer Rouge regime shook hands with the devil in the name of cleansing their society and establishing an egalitarian, communist society. Like other utopian madmen, Pol Pot's distorted vision, for him, justified perverse tactics of unimaginable horror.

In 1975, Pol Pot declared the dawn of a new Marxist utopia. For the next four years, schools and hospitals were emptied, factories destroyed and Khmer Rouge forces sought to purge the country of all external and internal influences. Every fabric of society was scarred or destroyed.

Khmer Rogue forces killed or caused the death of almost 2 million people; about one person in four. And many died horrible deaths.

Appeared in the *Chicago Sun-Times*, May 30, 2005.

They died from hunger, disease, the rigors of mass deportation and acts of genocide committed to cleanse their society of Chinese, Vietnamese, Chams and 17 other ethnic minority groups. The Khmer Rouge sought to eliminate the habits and consciousness of the old society. They sought "purity" and "cleanliness." They sought eradication of "counter revolutionary elements," which, by definition, included all other ethnic groups. Seng Horl, a teacher forced out of Phnom Penh, has said that to survive those gruesome days, "you had to do three things... know nothing, hear nothing, see nothing."

A few years ago while in Phnom Penh, Cambodia I visited Tuol Sleng, a former high school that the Khmer Rouge had turned into an unspeakable chamber of horror. I saw evidence of man's inhumanity to man as I looked at Tuol Sleng's terrible instruments of torture. I looked at photographs of thousands of men, women and children who were imprisoned there before being taken out to the nearby killing fields.

My guide at Tuol Sleng was a middle aged woman who's name is Pha Ka Penn. During the time of Pol Pot, her husband had been beaten to death with bamboo sticks. Her three year old daughter had been imprisoned and starved to death. Her father and two brothers were killed. For years she hid in the countryside. She told me that twenty years later she still awakes in a sweat of fear, feeling she needs to hide.

One Khmer Rouge slogan was "Better to kill ten friends than to leave one enemy alive." And many were killed with searing brutality.

Yale University's Genocide Studies Program has testimony from Denise Affonco that provides a powerful account of the Khmer Rouge's inhumanity to man. She reports about a ceremony she witnessed while hiding in a thicket. She said she was "so frightened by what I saw that I almost fainted.

"The condemned lad was attached, nude from the waist up, to a tree, his eyes bandaged. Using a long knife, Ta Sok, the executioner, made a long incision in the abdomen of the miserable victim, who screamed with pain like a wild beast. I can still hear the cries today. Blood gushed out from all sides and from the intestines also while Ta Sok groped for his liver which he cut out, sliced into pieces, and started to cook in a frying pan.... They shared the cooked liver with a hearty appetite. After having buried the body they left with a satisfied air.... I (could) not sleep a wink and was haunted by these horrors."

Thirty years after the Killing Fields, Cambodia still is haunted by the ghosts of those terrible times. Tens of thousands of skulls are buried in pits or piled in temples, in shrines or in open fields. 19,421 mass graves have been identified. Some have as many as 1,000 bodies. Pol Pot died in 1998. But many Khmer Rouge leaders survived, most live freely. Will they get away with mass murder? There has been no trial, no tribunal, nothing to bring justice. Nothing to ease the nightmares. Nothing to quiet the Devil's cry in the night. Nothing to help heal the torn society.

Justice delayed does not diminish its importance. Last year the United Nations and the Cambodian Government signed a 32 article agreement concerning the prosecution of crimes committed during Pol Pot's reign of terror. The courts will have a mix of international and Cambodian judges.

This spring the United Nations held a donor's conference to raise the money to fund the 3-year judicial process. Most of the money required has been pledged.

Skeptics of the Cambodian Tribunal have legitimate concerns. They fear that strict standards of international justice may not be followed. Others are wary of a process that might provide greater acceptability for Hun Sen, Cambodia's leader who used military force and intimidation to reject the results of a 1993 election and, a year later, used a coup d'etat to oust Cambodia's First Prime Minister. While mindful of these concerns, and vigilant against these possible eventualities, I nonetheless feel the people of Cambodia deserve a measure of justice; a justice the Cambodian Special Courts can provide.

Today Cambodia remains a broken society haunted by the Khmer Rouge. Pha Ka Penn, Denise Affonco, and too many others still suffer nightmares of when Hell's gate was opened. It is time to let the nightmares end. It is time to bring justice so that Cambodia might mend in order that it will know peace, achieve stability and move forward.

ZIMBABWE HAS ENDURED
MUGABE'S WRATH LONG ENOUGH

In late May, Zimbabwe's repressive ruler, Robert Mugabe began another brutal crackdown on his opponents spreading misery, heartache and death.

First, Mugabe rounded up more than 9,000 residents in the capital, Harare, Iden Wetherell, editor of The Zimbabwe Independent, said these arrests were "designed to signal that the government is in control, including in the nation's teeming cities where the government has suffered numerous electoral reversals."

Then, Mugabe launched "Operation Murambatsvina", Drive Out the Rubbish. Helmeted police, backed by paramilitaries carrying assault weapons, began to sworm poor urban neighborhoods torching and bulldozing tens of thousands of shacks and street stalls, as well as vegetable gardens planted by the urban poor. This brutal forced relocation is reminiscent of Pol Pot's "ruralization" in Cambodia.

The assaults were swift, the destruction devastating. One resident of Harare told the BBC, "We were enjoying the winter sun when we heard trucks and bulldozers roll in. There was pandemonium as we rushed to salvage the little we could. In no time my cottage was gone. My life had been shattered before my very own eyes."

For some the loss was even greater. Lavendes Nyika lost her young daughter. She says of the day the riot police arrived, "I didn't even have time to bring Charmaine to safety. She was killed when the walls collapsed on top of her."

Farisai Gatawa escaped with her two week old baby Nyasha before her one-room shack was destroyed. But she had nowhere to go. That night she and her baby slept on cardboard rubble in Zimbabwe's frigid winter air. The next morning Farisai cradled her new born as she died from exposure.

Surely the death toll will rise as hundreds of thousands of impoverished homeless Zimbabweans are on the move.

Roads are congested with people pushing handcarts filled with all their earthly possessions, seeking refuge in rural villages. Others have been dumped in containment areas and left to fend for themselves without clean water, food or sanitation. Some are burning their possessions to keep warm. In these camps, intelligence officers mingle among the dispossessed. The estimated number affected range from 350,000 to 1.5 million people.

Appeared in the *Chicago Sun-Times,* July 8, 2005.

Mugabe is punishing urban voters who sided with the opposition. He is creating a new class of rural poor dependent on government aid. It is calculated. It is brutal. And it is wrong.

Two hundred human rights and civic groups have said Mugabe's crackdown is a "grave violation of international human rights and a disturbing affront to human dignity."

Tragically, these recent atrocities are only the latest example of Mugabe's willingness to employ ruthless tactics to remain in power.

Zimbabwe once was Southern Africa's breadbasket exporting food to neighbors. After Mugabe's illegal land seizures, Zimbabwe is a basket case where nearly half the population goes to bed hungry every night. Last year Mugabe turned down international food aid so he could use scarce food as a political weapon to reward his supporters and deny his opponents. He has cracked down on the free press, jailed political opponents and stolen elections.

While people go hungry and are homeless, Mugabe has the use of two official residences in Herare and others in Bulwavo, Gweru and Mutare. He owns a mansion in Zvimba and the Nyanga highlands. He has just built another palatial mansion with 4 acres of floor-space lined with Italian marble and 25 bedrooms. Meanwhile, the economy has shrunk by 40 percent.

Zimbabwe's courageous Archbishop Pius Neube has said, "Our Government engages in lies, propaganda, the twisting of facts, half-truth, downright untruths and gross misinformation because they are fascists."

The other day President Bush accused Mugabe of "destroying" his country and urged countries in the region to pressure him to change.

The world's most industrialized nations, including the United States, are increasing assistance to Africa to help the world's poorest people. These desperate souls command our compassion and deserve our support. But such aid will be fleeting if countries lack good governance and sensible economic policies. Our humanity and common sense should demand the reforms necessary for these people to have hope for a brighter future. And Zimbabwe is a good place to start.

Saddam Trial Offers Iraqis Closure, Hope for Brighter Future

The other day another important step was taken to bringing a measure of justice and reconciliation in Iraq and to advancing freedom in the greater Middle East.

Almost daily there are stories of horrific violence claiming lives in Iraq. Rebels, dead-enders and foreign terrorists continue their efforts to disrupt the sovereign Iraqi government's move to a new constitution and parliamentary elections later this year. They target innocent civilians, among others. Their ruthless use of violence to disrupt, derail and destroy progress assaults the Iraqi people and tests the resolve of those of us supporting Iraq's democratic process.

Unfortunately, the suicide bombers and terrorist rockets will not end tomorrow, nor the day after tomorrow. It will be a long, tough slog.

But establishing the rule of law, bringing justice and achieving reconciliation will contribute substantially to the stability and peace sought by the Iraqi people and friends of freedom everywhere. And the trial of Saddam Hussein under the rule of law for crimes committed during his reign of terror will help achieve this end.

For over thirty years Saddam ruled Iraq with absolute power. The highest law was not written in statutes but in the whims, paranoia and cruelty of Saddam.

During his reign Saddam used chemical weapons to kill 200,000 Iraqi Kurds. He destroyed the southern marshlands and killed 100,000 Shia from that region. He kept power through the fear he created by summary executions, unspeakable torture and imprisoning all he suspected of disloyalty. Men, women and many children were victims of Saddam's absolute power. Torture chambers, hidden prisons and unmarked mass graves were instruments of Saddam's atrocities, now uncovered. Saddam stood as a mighty Osymandus straddling Iraq and casting a menacing shadow that shrouded the entire Middle East.

Then, last summer, a somewhat disheveled and disoriented Saddam was brought into an Iraqi courtroom before a young Iraqi judge. The once mighty and brutal ruler who held absolute power of life and death over all his people, sat and his rights were read to him, rights he so long denied his own people.

Not only in Iraq, but in Arab streets across the Middle East, people crowded into cafes and shops to watch and marvel at this scene on television showing the once all powerful Saddam being brought before a court of law.

Appeared in the *Chicago Sun-Times,* July 27, 2005.

Societies long torn by tyranny and brutality need to re-establish the rule of law fairly administered and see justice done. It is a testament to injustices suffered. It provides accountability. It presents the promise of a new era where the rule of law replaces the fear of injustice, violence and capricious retribution. Thereby it helps heal sounds and bring reconciliation. It contributes to a new beginning for a society too familiar with terror, tragedy and trauma.

Therefore the trial of Saddam Hussein for his crimes is about more than holding an evil man to account. It creates an opportunity for closure of a dark past and a broader acceptance of a liberal future where the rule of law governs, human rights are respected and fear of secret police knocking at your door at night is a thing of the past.

A few days ago, the first criminal case was filed against Saddam for the 1982 massacre of Shiite villagers in Dujail. There will be more. Separate trials are anticipated for war crime charges from Saddam's Anfal campaign in which about 150,000 Kurds were killed, from his chemical attack on Halabjah and other atrocities.

And if justice is done, and is seen as having been done, it can be a transforming event for Iraq. Throughout the broader Middle East it will be a powerful message of hope to Arabs in the street that rulers can be held to account. And it will be a cautionary message to undemocratic rulers in the broader Middle East that freedom is on the march even in their neighborhood.

Transitional justice in Iraq will help crowd out the violent terrorists. It will demonstrate the new era where laws govern, justice reigns and hope returns. And where hope and opportunity exist, the land is no longer fertile ground to breed terrorists and the violence they bring.

PAST TIME FOR PROMISES
TO END DARFUR VIOLENCE

Sudan is a country where evil has roamed for too long. The man-made devastation is almost incomprehensible. The body count numbingly high.

During a 21-year civil war between the north and the south, over 2 million people died.

President Bush and his special envoy, Ambassador John Danforth, deserve credit for persistent efforts to help mid-wife a peace deal. Earlier this year a fragile peace accord was signed. As part of a power sharing arrangement, on July 9th southern Sudanese rebel leader John Garang was sworn in as vice-president of a new transitional government.

This peace arrangement provided reason for hope.

But on August 1st, Garang was killed in a helicopter crash. Riots followed as thousands of southern Sudanese clashed with police and looted shops in Khartoum. Twenty-four people died in the hours after Garang's death. It is unclear as to whether the peace between the north and south can hold.

Meanwhile devastation continues in the western region of Darfur where forces of the Arab government in Khartoum and the local Arab militia known as the janjaweed, armed by the government, continue to violate the blacks in Darfur.

In the past two years, these forces have engaged in horrific genocide. They have swept into villages in coordinated assaults; government forces in attack helicopters followed by janjaweed riding in on camel and horseback. Villages are burned, livestock slaughtered, women raped and branded, and males from young boys to old men viciously killed.

These assaults have left up to 400,000 dead and driven more than 2 million from their homes. It is the worst humanitarian crisis in the world.

Waves of displaced persons and refugees have walked great distances across desolate deserts. They now live in desperate conditions in temporary camps. Their precarious survival relies on the generosity of the international community. As so often is the case, the most generous donor of relief aid has been America. But more is urgently needed.

Appeared in the *Chicago Sun-Times,* August 6, 2005.

In March, the U.N. Security Council finally overcame resistance from China and Russia and passed a U.S.-drafted resolution to apply some pressure on Khartoum. It imposed a travel ban and asset freeze on those who are committing war crimes in Darfur.

Khartoum said the violence would end. By May there were tentative signs of progress in Darfur. Attacks diminished because government forces and the janjaweed militias have successfully killed or intimidated blacks in Darfur. Almost anyone who might be a target is either dead or has been driven to refugee camps. Some international pressure eased. Media attention shifted to other crises.

But thugs in Sudan continue to act like thugs. We cannot act blasé about this evil.

The Sudanese government still is paying regular salaries to the janjaweed who continue to attack and kill civilians in Darfur.

The other day U.N. High Commissioner on Human Rights, Louise Arbor, reported that "rape and gang rape continue to be perpetrated by armed elements in Darfur, some of whom are members of law enforcement agencies and the armed forces." In Sudan, a climate of impunity continues.

Have they no decency? Have they no shame? They do not.

Last month Secretary Rice traveled to Khartoum for talks with government leaders about the appalling situation in Darfur. When she sat down to meet with Sudanese President el-Bashir to press the case, Sudanese security forces manhandled U.S. officials and reporters traveling with the Secretary.

Scuffling with U.S. Government officials and the media traveling with the Secretary of State is unacceptable. Continued violence in Darfur is intolerable. It must end.

The massacres, atrocities and starvation in Darfur must stop. It's well past time for promises. We must demand performance.

Prodding is no longer sufficient. We now know these thugs will act like thugs as long as they are allowed to do so.

Bilateral and multilateral action must be taken. The United States has been a leader in trying to solve the crisis in Sudan. More can be done. It is time to ratchet up the pressure.

VIOLENCE CONTINUES IN DARFUR

Recent history in Darfur, Sudan, is a sad and gruesome tale. The atrocities have been horrific. The toll of human suffering unimaginable. And the international community's response often has been too little, too late.

After the holocaust in World War II, the world said "Never Again." Then came Cambodia's Killing Fields. Rwanda. Bosnia. Kosovo. And then the killing and anguish in Darfur. When will the moral imperative of "Never Again" be effectively translated into action?

Fortunately, the worst mass killings from large scale organized violence in Darfur have abated, but sustainable peace remains elusive and many continue to die. And despite progress in easing violence and destruction in Darfur, a sense of impunity continues to prevail.

In late September, U.N. Under Secretary-General for Humanitarian Affairs and Emergency Relief Coordinator Jan Egeland had to suspend humanitarian relief in many areas of Darfur because it has become too dangerous. Egeland said that the world has a false impression that things currently are going reasonably well in Darfur. The violence continues. According to Egeland, those responsible for the recent attacks include rebels, splinter groups of the rebels, Janjaweed and the government in Khartoum.

Since its independence in 1956, Sudan has had a long history of violent conflict. The First Sudanese Civil War between the Muslim government in Khartoum and the non-Muslim people of the south began in 1955 and continued until 1972. In 1983, Sudan's president declared Shari'a law in the south and a Second Sudanese Civil War broke out. A ceasefire was reached in 2002 and in 2003 a fragile peace agreement was reached with power-sharing arrangements. During the 21 years of civil war between the north and the south more than 2 million people died.

In 2003, the Sudan's Arab government in Khartoum set out to put down a small rebel movement in the western province of Darfur, a large, poor region of subsistence farming and herding livestock for domestic and export purposes. Rather than reply with a targeted response directed at the few rebels, Khartoum unleashed the forces of hell.

Khartoum armed an Arab militia known as the Janjaweed in Darfur. The militia was drawn from impoverished nomadic Arab ethnic groups in Darfur and Chad.

Appeared in *UNA-USA Newsletter,* October 3, 2005.

More than 20,000 highwaymen and bandits were armed. Then they were unleashed to wage a systematic campaign against black African civilians in the area belonging to the same non-Arab African ethnic groups as the rebels: the Fur, Masaalit and Zaghawa.

In coordinated attacks led by government helicopters followed by janjaweed on camel and horseback, they burned villages of black Africans, looted livestock, killed males and often gang raped, disfigured and drove out women and girls.

These attacks have created havoc and savage mayhem. There has been slaughter, torture and rape. One woman from the village of Silaya reports having been abducted when she was five months pregnant along with eight other women. She described six days when "five to six men would rape us in rounds, one after the other for hours every night."

The ethnic pattern of these atrocities is clear. A United Nations observer team reported that non-Arab black villages were attacked while Arab villages were untouched.

> The 23 Fur villages in the Shattaya Administrative Unite have been completely depopulated, looted and burned to the ground (the team observed several such sites driving through the area for two days). Meanwhile, doted alongside these charred locations are unharmed, populated and functioning Arab settlements. In some locations, the distance between a destroyed Fur village and an Arab village is less than 500 meters.

Eighteen months ago, U.N. Secretary-General Kofi Annan warned of "ethnic cleansing" in Darfur and called on the international community to act. One year ago, then Secretary of State Colin Powell labeled the on-going atrocities in Darfur "genocide." Meanwhile, the violent atrocities continued and the world's response was modest.

In July, 2004, the United States sought a robust U.N. Security Council resolution threatening sanctions unless the violence ended in Darfur. Opposition to firm action was led by Russia, which sells MIGs and other military equipment to Khartoum, China, which gets oil from Sudan, and Pakistan, claiming Islamic solidarity. In the end a weakened Resolution 1556 finally was passed.

In August 2004, the African Union sent 150 Rwandan troops to Darfur to protect ceasefire monitors, but they were not there to protect civilians and the killings continued.

In September 2004, the United States tabled a draft resolution threatening Sudan with sanctions on its oil industry. Again, a weakened Resolution 1564 was adopted.

In November 2004, Khartoum signed two accords with Darfur's two leading rebel groups, the Justice and Equality Movement (JEM) and the Sudanese Liberation Army (SLA). One established a no-fly zone. Nonetheless, the violence continued.

In March 2005, Secretary General Annan sought to increase the peacekeeping force in Darfur. At the end of March, the Security Council passed Resolution 1591 that strengthened the arms embargo, imposed an asset freeze and travel ban on those responsible for atrocities in Darfur, and agreed that war criminals in Darfur would be tried by the International Criminal Court. Still the killing continued.

By July there were 3,000 African Union peacekeepers on the ground in Darfur with thousands more committed. Armored vehicles, training and maintenance assistance, and personal protective equipment had begun to arrive to support the African Union Mission in Sudan (AMIS). And the worst violence abated.

During the genocide in Darfur, 300,000 people have died and nearly two million people have been driven from their homes and live in large internally displaced person camps in southern Sudan or refugee camps in Chad, often in desperate conditions.

Unfortunately, having unleashed the forces of hell, the Sudanese government no longer controls the situation on the ground. Many of the janjaweed who have raped and pillaged Dafur have become accustomed to the spoils of their savagery. While their vicious assaults were launched and flourished in coordinated attacks with government forces, absent such assistance, many of these bandits can continue brutality to which they have grown dependent. And the violence against civilians did not extinguish the rebels but swelled their numbers and fragmented them. So even if Khartoum wanted peace in Darfur, with whom can they negotiate a sustainable peace agreement.

On September 15, African Union mediated peace talks began in Abuja, Nigeria. They are going slowly. The Darfur rebel groups are splintered. It is unclear who can speak for the rebels. Meanwhile the innocent civilians who were victimized by the brutal violence in Darfur tenuously hold on to their shattered lives. The nightmare has not ended.

In late September, both rebels and pro-government militia launched various attacks in Darfur, with casualties reported on all sides. Aid agencies and humanitarian convoys also have been targeted. On September 28th, 250 janjaweed on horseback and camels attacked the Aro Sharow camp for internally displaced persons in northern West Darfur. They destroyed part of the camp, burned some 80 shelters and killed 34 people, seriously wounding another ten.

The genocide in Darfur has created a humanitarian catastrophe. Donor countries must increase aid assistance. NATO and the European Union must increase their logistical support to the African Union peacekeepers in Darfur. The AU security forces number six thousand with plans to deploy another 1,700. The international community's large scale humanitarian assistance must continue while the Sudan Government's harassment of NGO's has decreased, rebel harassment and banditry has increased. This must end. And through on-going attention by the U.N. Security Council, and further action as required, international pressure up to and including further sanctions must be applied to pressure Khartoum and the rebel groups to reach peace agreements.

The immediate tasks are daunting. Stop the scattered violence. Achieve a sustainable peace agreement. Help feed, clothe and shelter the two million people driven from their homes in Darfur.

These immediate tasks must be followed by a return of the displaced people, reconstruction, justice and reconciliation. It will be a long and perilous path in which the United Nations will play a vital role as it has in other post-conflict situations such as East Timor, Sierra Leone and Afghanistan.

The tragedy in Darfur is not over. But a possible path ahead is emerging.

Hopefully the senseless blood and tears of Darfur will stir our conscience and move the international community going forward to finally give meaning to "Never Again."

Surrendering Moral High Ground Would Make Us War Losers

September 11, 2001, was a defining moment. A surprise attack, horrific destruction, innocent deaths ushering America into war. The war on terror is waged to defeat a menacing threat that operates in the shadows and targets innocent civilians to advance its extremist cause.

The terrorists' evil acts have killed innocent civilians not only in America, but in Bali, Spain, Britain, Saudi Arabia and elsewhere.

The "clear and present danger" is real. There can be no substitute for victory. Americans must be protected. Evil must be defeated. And our way of life and our values must prevail.

Yet in confronting the terrorists' evil menace we should not, we cannot, compromise our values so as to tarnish the brave men and women on the frontlines of this war; those serving with honor and sacrificing blood.

We ought not dishonor our heritage. We should not corrode our character. We need not lessen ourselves to prevail. In this great struggle between freedom and extremism, between opportunity and repression, between tolerance and intolerance, it is the values we hold, the rule of law we cherish, the principles to which we subscribe that will sustain us and will determine our victory.

Serious questions have been raised about America's treatment of detainees in the war on terror. Photographs of the abuse of Iraqi prisoners at Abu Ghraib prison shook America's conscience and shocked the world. International observers have raised questions about the treatment of prisoners in Afghanistan. Questions remain unresolved regarding activities in Guantanimo. And now there are reports of secret jails at various undisclosed locations around the world.

At present Congress is considering legislation to ban "cruel, inhumane and degrading" treatment of prisoners. This legislation should pass.

First, experience shows that tortured prisoners do not provide reliable, actionable intelligence. The prisoner says whatever he thinks his captors want to hear to end the punishment.

Two, if America tortures detainees, what standing do we have to demand fair treatment for captured Americans now or in the future?

Appeared in the *Chicago-Sun-Times,* November 9, 2005.

Three, accounts of American abuse of prisoners inflame our enemies and helps al-Qaida recruit more terrorists.

Four, cruel and inhumane treatment of prisoners violates American commitments. The United States has signed the Geneva Convention and the Universal Declaration on Human Rights that outlaw such harsh treatment of prisoners. The Reagan Administration negotiated the Convention Against Torture which was ratified by the Senate and prohibits cruel and inhumane treatment.

Five, according to U.S. military and other investigations, current claimed deviations from the treatment standards set forth in the Geneva Convention creates confusion that contributed to the Abu Ghraib abuse. The American guards on the ground deserve clear rules on what is acceptable behavior and what is not.

Six, the war of ideas is vitally important. Twenty-three years ago, during the height of the Cold War against Moscow's Evil Empire, President Ronald Reagan said, "The ultimate determination in the struggle now going on for the world will not be bombs and rockets, but a test of wills and ideas – a trial of spiritual resolve: the values we hold, the beliefs we cherish, the ideals to which we are dedicated." The Gipper was right then. His words ring true now. Today the struggle is between freedom and democracy and the forces of extremism and intolerance. It is not the time to compromise our fidelity to the rule of law nor our spiritual resolve to the values that make America great.

No country in the world claims a legal right to inflict cruel and inhumane treatment on prisoners. It should be explicitly clear that neither does the United States.

America is the world's oldest democracy. The genius of our founding fathers, the values they employed in launching the American Experiment, generations of Americans rededicated to those ideals and the blood of patriots have built and sustained America's greatness. Now is not the time to stain that greatness.

As Senator John McCain, who served 5 ½ years as a POW at the Hanoi Hilton, said in introducing legislation to ban "cruel, inhumane and degrading" treatment of prisoners, "The enemy we fight has no respect for human life or human rights. They don't deserve our sympathy. But this isn't about who they are. This is about who we are. These are the values that distinguish us from our enemies."

CHINA AND HUMAN RIGHTS NORMS

It's a pleasure to be here at the Chinese Academy of Social Sciences to exchange views on various topics. We have a lot to learn from one another. We all must recognize the importance of continuing a constructive dialogue between the world's sole superpower and the world's great emerging power. We have many common interests where cooperative action can benefit us both.

There is growing economic interdependence between our countries. Both China and the United States benefit from China's dynamic growing economy. America is absorbing a significant portion of China's exports and China is purchasing a substantial amount of America's debt. We have found areas in which we work together in the war on terror. And China's recent more proactive participation in the six party talks about North Korea's nuclear program certainly was welcomed.

Nonetheless there are major points of strain between China and the United States. In the words of Professor Ken Lieberthal, "China remains quietly but seriously worried that the U.S. seeks to contain its rise and to undermine its authoritarian regime. The "color revolutions" over the past year have considerably heightened Beijing's alarm over Washington's intentions and capabilities as has President Bush's post-election focus on democracy promotion as the touchstone of American foreign policy." Meanwhile, the United States has complaints about the trade deficit, China's outward investment strategy in energy, the PRC's military modernization effort and increasing defense spending. Also, the U.S. remains concerned about China's poor human rights record.

To ward off challenges to its poor human rights record, time and again we hear Chinese officials cite the principle of non-interference in their internal affairs. We even hear Chinese scholars refer to the United Nations Charter's recognition of "state sovereignty" as a further bulwark against challenges to China's human rights record. Such an analysis is flawed.

While state to state relations historically have been the organizing principle of modern international law, the United Nations charter to which all member states subscribe, including China, recognizes individual human rights and specifically states the right of self-determination. China also is a signatory to the United Nations Universal Declaration on Human Rights and numerous other U.N. documents and resolutions, as well as other international instruments, that bind it to honoring the human rights of its citizens. Consequently, it is not America that is seeking to project new obligations onto China. Human rights responsibilities are obligations China has freely accepted.

Remarks at the Chinese Academy of Social Sciences, Beijing, China, November 18, 2005.

On September 21st, Deputy Secretary of State Bob Zoellick made remarks in New York City to the National Committee on U.S.-China Relations. He titled his speech "Whither China: From Membership to Responsibility." Secretary Zoellick's thesis was that "all nations conduct diplomacy to promote their national interest. Responsible stakeholders go further. They recognize that the international system sustains their peaceful prosperity, so they work to sustain that system." Zoellick went on to discuss many areas in which China has the opportunity to be a responsible stakeholder: on North Korea and Iran, the global fight against terrorism, Afghanistan, Sudan, Taiwan and Japan.[1] Another area in which China should act responsibly is in human rights.

China as a closed society is not sustainable. As China's dynamic economy continues to grow and to engage the world more, Chinese will seek the rights people enjoy elsewhere. The better off will demand more say in their own lives. And the dislocations and disparities of economic growth will create social unrest best dealt with by an open participatory society rather than a repressive, rigid and therefore fragile regime.

Today's unrest in China is manifest in waves of labor strikes, violent rural protests against corruption, spreading crime and 150 million floating workers. China's official media reported 10,000 incidents of social unrest took place in 1993. Last year there were 74,000.[2] In Hong Kong religious leaders are calling for further democracy demonstrations. Only an open society with a government responsive and accountable to the people can adapt to the rapidly changing circumstances and growing demands of China's 1.3 billion people. Only a China that recognizes and protects the human rights of its citizens can be a responsible global citizen.

Today, free Christian worship is not possible even in state-sponsored churches in China. The government's heavy hand prevents a free media. Self-determination is denied.

As stated in the U.S. Department of State's most recent country report on human rights practices in China, "The People's Republic of China (PRC) is an authoritarian state in which, as specified in the Constitution, the Chinese Communist Party is the paramount source of power... Citizens (lack) the freedom to express opposition to the Party-led political system and the right to change their national leaders or form of government." That report goes on to elaborate on the ways in which the Chinese "Government's human rights record remained poor, and the Government continued to commit numerous and serious abuses." For example, "many who openly expressed dissenting political views were harassed, detained, or imprisoned... Authorities were quick to suppress religious, political, and social groups that they perceived as threatening to government authority... Abuses included instances of extrajudicial killings; torture and mistreatment of prisoners, leading to numerous deaths in custody; coerced confessions; arbitrary arrest and detention; and incommunicado detention. The judiciary was not independent, and the lack of due process remained a serious problem. The lack of due process was especially egregious in death penalty cases... The authorities routinely violated legal protections in the cases of political dissidents and religious figures. They generally attached higher priority to suppressing political opposition and maintaining public order than to enforcing legal norms or protecting individual rights... [M]ore than 250,000 persons were serving sentences in re-education-through-labor camps and other forms of administrative detention not subject to judicial review."[3]

"The number of individuals serving sentences for the now-repeated crime of counterrevolution was estimated at 500 to 600; many of these persons were imprisoned for the non-violent expression of their political views... The Government maintained tight restrictions on freedom of speech and of the press, and a wave of detentions late in the year signaled a new campaign targeting prominent writers and political commentators... During the year, publications were closed and otherwise disciplined for publishing material deemed objectionable by the Government, and journalists, authors, academics, internet writers, and researchers were harassed, detained, and arrested by the authorities... During the year, the Government blocked many websites, began monitoring text messages sent by mobile phones, and pressured internet companies to censor objectionable content. NGOs reported that 43 journalists were imprisoned at year's end."[4] And the list of human rights abuses goes on.

As Human Rights Watch reported, the Chinese "leadership (has) moved unequivocally to limit free expression and build a firewall around the internet, to destroy Falun Gong even beyond China's borders, and to eliminate dissent challenges."[5]

However, as President Bush said the other day while in Japan, "As China reforms its economy, its leaders are finding that once the door to freedom is opened a crack, it cannot be closed. As the people of China grow in prosperity, their demands for political freedom will grow as well."[6]

A responsible China will be one that not only signs international treaties but one that protects and nurtures human rights and participating civil responsibility in which citizens can enjoy real freedom and act to protect their own interests, including protest.

An open, cooperative relationship between China and the United States is in both our interests. And the most enduring relationship will be built on shared values. To forge such a relationship, China must embrace its responsibility to protect the human rights its people deserve and to which China has committed in various international agreements.

Thank you.

---

1.   Robert B. Zoellick, Deputy Secretary of State, "Whither China: From Membership to Responsibility?" Remarks to National Committee on U.S.-China Relations, New York City, September 21, 2005.

2.   Thomas L. Friedman, "How to Look at China," *New York Times*, November 9, 2005.

3.   U.S. Department of State, China (includes Tibet, Hong Kong, and Macau), *Country Reports on Human Rights Practices-2004*, Released by the Bureau of Democracy, Human Rights, and Labor, February 28, 2005. Available at http://www.state.gov/g/drl/rls/hrrpt/2004/41640.htm.

4.   *Ibid.*

5.   *Human Rights Watch World Report 2002*, "China and Tibet," available at http://www.hrw.org/wr2k3/asia4.html.

6.   George W. Bush, President Discusses Freedom and Democracy, November 16, 2005, Kyoto, Japan. Available at http://ww.whitehouse.govnews/releases/2005/11/20051116-6.htm.

African Leaders' Condemnation of Mugabe Erodes His Legitimacy

Robert Mugabe of Zimbabwe is a thug. His repressive regime has long trampled Zimbabwean human rights. Finally events may be tipping against Mugabe and for his long suffering people.

Mugabe has led Zimbabwe since it gained independence in 1980. Never an exemplar of human rights, the situation rapidly deteriorated during the past six years as Mugabe struggled to respond to growing political opposition and a worsening economic crisis.

In Mugabe's campaign of repression the rule of law has been hijacked and recent elections have been a farce. Government supporters have been implicated in assault, arbitrary detention and torture.

Journalists have been arrested and newspapers closed. A new law bans foreign human rights groups and imposes restrictions on local human rights groups.

Eight months ago, Mugabe launched "Operation Marambatavina" – Drive out the Rubbish. Police and paramilitaries stormed poor neighborhoods, torching and bulldozing shakes and street stalls, leaving an estimated one million people homeless. This terrible situation has become more desperate, according to Human Rights Watch, by Mugabe deliberately obstructing efforts by international humanitarian groups to help these victims of forced evictions.

Meanwhile Mugabe's oppressive rule has ravaged Zimbabwe's economy. Once Africa's breadbasket, Zimbabwe now is a basket case where people go to bed hungry. And last month the inflation rate rose to 585%.

Despite his horrific record, Mugabe seeks to wear a cloak of legitimacy. He fights criticism; dismissing charges as lies and assaulting his critics.

He has sought a seat on the U.N. Commission on Human Rights where he has successfully fended off rebuke. When two U.N. humanitarian envoys criticized his brutal forced relocations last year, Mugabe rejected their findings and said they were influenced by Britain to make negative reports.

But now African states, long reluctant to criticize one of their own, have come forward to condemn Mugabe's abhorrent human rights record.

Appeared in the *Chicago Sun-Times,* January 23, 2006.

Last month the African Union Commission on Human Rights issued a report containing unprecedented criticism. The report states concerns over "the continuing violations and the deterioration of the human rights situation in Zimbabwe, the lack of respect for the rule of law and the growing culture of impunity."

Predictably, Mugabe's government dismisses the report as fiction and accuses the commission of "blatantly lying against and vilifying Harare to please the (western) funders." But this time the harsh glare of criticism will not easily be deflected.

As Eleanor Sisulu, director of the Zimbabwe Crisis Coalition's office in South Africa said, "This gives much-needed encouragement to Zimbabweans... Of course the Mugabe government will try to ignore it but this comes from an African institution, run by highly respected Africans."

And Iden Wetherall, an editor with the Zimbabwe independent group of newspapers, said, "This is a highly significant report coming as it does from an affiliate body of the African Union. It will be difficult for the government to counter this. African institutions are holding their leaders accountable. Zimbabwe's delinquency can no longer be swept under the carpet of African solidarity. This is peer review as it should be."

So African leaders, for the first time, have condemned Mugabe's human rights record, significantly increasing pressure to restore the rule of law and stop state-sponsored violence and repression.

Of course, this report alone does not guarantee the end of Mugabe's abuse of human rights. His current term of office runs to 2008 and there are reports he'll seek a constitutional change to extend it to 2010. And Mugabe's record demonstrates that to hold onto power he is willing to tighten his authoritarian grip.

But the ground has shifted and his legitimacy is eroding. As Odindo Ogwen, an African human rights scholar and activist, said, "It is an important step. It shows that the African body is now ready to become serious about correcting the disappointing human rights situation in some African countries." Consequently a ray of hope now shines for the oppressed people of Zimbabwe.

WHY ABUSE IS WRONG

When the photographs of prisoner abuse at Abu Grahb became public, the American people were shocked and tremors were felt beyond our shores. President Bush was correct when he said that these pictures do not represent the "heart" of the American people. Nor did these violations reflect America's traditions.

From our earliest days, the American Experiment has been grounded not on what we could do, but on what we should. During the Revolutionary War, General George Washington told the officer in charge of prisoners, "Treat them with humanity, and let them have no reason to complain of our copying the brutal example of the British army in their treatment of our unfortunate brethren."

It is upon such sentiments that America became a beacon of hope for the world. In talking about America, its values and its promise, Ronald Reagan often spoke of a "shining city upon a hill," an example to the world. We should be true to that light.

The War on Terror will be a long struggle. The Islamic fanatics who have hijacked a great religion to advance their extremist cause target innocent civilians. The horrors of September 11th have been followed by killings of more innocent people in Bali, Saudi Arabia, Spain, Britain, Jordan, and elsewhere. There will be more casualties. Our enemies are vicious. They are not bound by any standard of human decency nor constrained by treaties or international norms. They do not deserve our respect nor our sympathy.

But the debate over how America detainees should be treated is not about them, it is about us: about who we are and our fidelity to those things that have defined America and made it great. It is about those things that have made America "a shining city upon a hill."

America must prosecute the war on terror. American lives must be safeguarded. Our enemy must be defeated. And the full arsenal of American might must be engaged in this great struggle.

But to commit prisoner abuse, to use torture in this campaign against terror is not effective and it is wrong.

Tortured prisoners do not provide reliable, actionable intelligence. As Senator John McCain, who was tortured while a POW in Hanoi, has stated, "In my experience, abuse of prisoners produces bad intelligence because under torture a person will say anything he thinks his captors want to hear – whether it is true or false – if he believes it will relieve his suffering."

Appeared in The Interdependent, Vol. 4, No. 1, Spring 2006.

Such action also endangers Americans. If America tortures detainees, what standing do we have to demand fair treatment for captured Americans now or in the future?

And accounts of U.S. abuse inflame our enemies and help al-Qaida recruit more terrorists. We must shrink the terrorist ranks not swell them.

Ultimately this struggle is a test of wills and ideals. It is between freedom and democracy and forces of coercion and repression; it is between decency and human rights and forces of intolerance and brutality.

Few of those already enlisted as centurions in the terrorist cause can be reclaimed. They are consumed by hatred, committed to brutal violence, and blind to justice. However their numbers are few. Yet many more feel some sympathy to their cause. This multitude must be contested on the battlefield of ideas. They must be persuaded to turn away from theocracy and authoritarian rigidity and to embrace opportunity and choice. They need to see the "shining city upon a hill" and feel its pull.

Brian Michael Jenkins, a terrorist expert at the Rand Corporation, writes in his new book *Unconquerable Nation: Knowing Our Enemy, Strengthening Ourselves*, the real battle against terrorism is ideological. Whatever we do in the war on terror, Jenkins believes, requires a coherent moral dimension. Our strategy must be consistent with fundamental American values. Jenkins argues that this is no matter of "mere morality", it is a strategic calculation.

Americans are not defined by where we came from. Most of us are descendents of immigrants. Our identity and union comes from the ideas we embrace, the ideals we cherish, the values that guide us, and the dreams we share. These are the building blocks of America and we cannot corrode these principles without weakening our very foundation.

Ultimately this struggle will be determined by our fidelity to these ideas, ideals, values and dreams that comprise America. Faith. The rule of law. Limited government accountable to the people. Equality. Tolerance. Freedom and opportunity for all. It is these principles that bind us as a people. It is these principles we've inherited from the generations that have gone before and we are honor bound to pass on.

Breaking international commitments prohibiting cruel and inhumane treatment of prisoners will not advance our cause. Neither will violating U.S. laws and regulations. And disregarding the values that have made America great will diminish the American dream and weaken us.

No country in the world claims a legal right to inflict cruel and inhumane treatment on prisoners. No country admits to sanctioning torture. On this principle America must stand as an example, not an exception. To do otherwise will not help us prevail in the war on terror. To do otherwise will dishonor the patriots who have shed blood for our way of life. To do otherwise will dim the light of the "shining city upon a hill."

HOLD TAYLOR ACCOUNTABLE FOR LIBERIA MAYHEM

Tragically there are monsters who commit terrible crimes to gain and hold onto power. Often they try to put lipstick on the pig; cloaking their brutality with high aspiration or grand design: nationalism, stability, security, defending the true faith, utopian dreams, safeguarding a culture or race. But whatever the rhetorical cosmetic, evil is still evil. And countless victims suffer: death, destruction, displacement and disease.

For victims it doesn't matter whether the crimes are labeled genocide, ethnic cleansing, or savagery. Blood is spilled. People are killed. A way of life is taken. Scars are inflicted. And innocent people are left with haunting nightmares of horrors, a sense of loss, anger, sometimes shame and lingering insecurity. Their lives seem fragile and their future dim.

Slobodan Milosevic fed the Balkans' flames of division: Dubrovnic bombarded, the siege of Sarajevo, the slaughter at Srebrenica, concentration camps and ethnic cleansing.

Saddam Hussein gained power through violence and embraced mayhem, killing and torture to hold it. He invaded neighboring Iran and Kuwait. He gassed and poisoned 300,000 Iraqis. He had people arbitrarily arrested, tortured and killed.

Charles Taylor inflicted ruthless repression at home and fomented civil war in neighboring states. He too used arbitrary arrest, torture and killings. He aided and directed a Sierra Leone rebel group who chopped off victim's arms, legs and ears.

The Balkans, Iraq and Liberia were all torn asunder to sustain these men's rule. The number of victims is mind numbing. The brutality breathtaking. The trauma to victims' psychic tragic. The societal scars substantial.

How do these shattered societies heal and move on?

Post conflict societies face daunting challenges to reconcile, reconstruct and review. It is difficult and it takes time.

One requirement is to reclaim a sense of justice.

Trust and Reconciliation Commissions record testimonials of victims and identify perpetrators so the brutality is documented, the victim's suffering recognized, the perpetrators shamed. This can contribute to healing.

291

But those who commit the worst crimes against humanity, the monsters who unleash the mayhem, should face a court of justice. They should answer for their crimes. Holding these criminals to account through an appropriate judicial process helps heal the wounds.

Milosevic was brought before the International Court in the Hague. But the wheels of justice moved slowly. The trial had gone on for 4 years when the "butcher of the Balkans" died a few weeks ago. There had been no verdict. That Milosevic was indicted and went to trial was helpful. That there was no verdict denied his victims and the Balkans the final justice they deserved.

The ranting and ravings of Saddam during this trial in Baghdad has been disruptive and undignified. Some have said it is a farce. It is not. Evidence has been presented linking Saddam to the 1982 massacre of Shias in Dujail. There will be more charges and the evidence will be laid out, the charges confirmed and justice will be done. There is a saying in the Middle East that while the dogs bark, the caravan moves on. Let Saddam bark. The caravan towards justice is moving on. And justice will be done.

Charles Taylor fled Monrovia for asylum in Nigeria. At the request of Liberia, Taylor finally was returned to Freetown to be held to account. Due to acute security concerns, Taylor was moved out of Sierra Leone to the Hague for trial. He should be held accountable. There should be no impunity. His victims deserve justice to help bring closure to their nightmare. And the norm that began with the Nuremberg trials of bringing monsters to justice will be strengthened.

For the sake of the victims, for the healing of scarred societies, in the name of justice, monsters who commit terrible crimes must be held to account.

DARFUR:
GENOCIDE IN SLOW MOTION

We live in momentous times when the war on terror, the advance of freedom, the spread of weapons of mass destruction and sorting out post-Cold War relationships are only some of the challenges that consume us. History will judge these days on what we do and what we do not do; what we accomplish and what we let languish. And even if we do much, achieve a great deal, but turn our backs on the great moral challenges of our time, history will not be kind to us nor should it be. For even if we accomplish much but lose our souls, we will have failed.

Today the greatest humanitarian crisis in the world is in Darfur, Sudan. It is man made. It is horrific. And it must end.

The international community has the capacity to stop this carnage. Yet it has not done so.

In the days after World War II as the world became fully aware of the Nazis' systematic extermination of the Jews, the civilized world recoiled in horror and shame. Leaders said, "Never again."

Among the measures taken in response to these atrocities were the Nuremberg trials to hold accountable those guilty of the greatest responsibility for the Nazi crimes against humanity. Another step was the creation of the United Nations to help "prevent the scourge of war" and protect the dignity of man. Also, the international community adopted the United Nations Universal Declaration of Human Rights. Respect for and protection of individual rights, among other things, stands as a deterrent to such premeditated slaughter.

Tragically, the rhetoric of "never again" has not been matched by the resolve to stop other mass exterminations.[1] Subsequently genocide took place in the "Killing Fields" of Cambodia and the bloody slayings by machete in Rwanda.[2] Then came gruesome ethnic cleansing in Bosnia and Kosovo. The international community time after time said "never again," and now we have the decimation in Darfur, Sudan. Some have called the ghastly killings in Darfur "Rwanda in slow motion."

This time no one can say that the atrocities are not known. No one can claim innocence. For the pain, suffering and death of innocent people in Darfur is well known. And the inadequacy of the response to this evil is widely recognized.

Brief History of the Conflict

Sudan is a large, diverse and war torn country. About the size of France, Sudan has the largest landmass of any African nation. Sudan sits on the ancient crossroads

---

between Arab North Africa and Sub-Saharan Africa. Sudan's geographic diversity includes desert, jungle, plains and mountains. For countless generations the Arabs of the north and the blacks of the south lived in peace. They intermingled and intermarried. Historically, Sudan was a mosaic of different tribes, various languages, and many religions. More than 150 native languages are spoken in Sudan, including some 20 in the Darfur region. Martin Meredith, in his important book *The Fate of Africa: From the Hopes of Freedom to the Heart of Despair*, writes that in Sudan the British, "used tribal identities to divide their subjects" as a means to keep control of this vast country.[3] The British restricted education in Darfur to the sons of chiefs. In 1935 there was only one elementary school in all of Darfur.[4]

As the British prepared to leave, they began to hand control over to the northern Muslims. In 1954, the British gave all but six of Sudan's 800 senior civil service posts to northerners.[5] This engendered concern and resentment. In August 1955 the Southern Corps of the army mutinied and Khartoum authorities sent 8,000 troops from the north to try to establish order. Leading up to independence, the north offered to consider southern Sudan's demand for semi-autonomy under a federal constitution. However, once the British left in 1956, the north dismissed southern concerns. Then in 1958, when the army took control of the government, General Ibrahim Abboud sought to impose Islam and Arabic in the south. General Abboud "considered Christianity an alien religion, ... expressed contempt for African religions (and) disparaged indigenous languages and customs."[6] He began building Muslim religious schools and mosques in the south. Civil war broke out. The conflict continued as Khartoum tried to repress the south and establish an Islamic republic.

Finally, the government negotiated a peace agreement with the Southern Liberation Movement in 1972. It provided a measure of local autonomy for the south. The constitution adopted in 1973 declared Sudan a secular state with freedom of religion for Christians, Jews and traditional African religions. 500,000 people died in that first civil war. Deep divisions lingered but peace lasted for eleven years.

During this period of peace, friction between the Muslim north and the non-Muslim south continued. Khartoum controlled economic planning in the south and provided limited funds for development there. Khartoum interfered in southern politics. The tension grew further after oil deposits were discovered in southern Sudan in 1978. The south unsuccessfully sought a refinery close to the oilfields. Khartoum ignored this request, and planned a refinery in the north and a pipeline to the Red Sea.

Then in 1983, in Khartoum the head of state, Gaafar Numeiri, declared an "Islamic revolution." He decreed that Sudan would be an Islamic republic governed by traditional Islamic law. Numeiri dissolved the southern regional government and divided the south into three regions. Thousands were arrested. And Sudan again descended into civil war. Thousands of southern troops deserted and formed the Sudan People's Liberation Movement (SPLM) headed by Colonel John Garang de Mabior, a Dinka officer. This civil war lasted for 21 years, claimed the lives of 2 million people, and displaced 4 million people.[7] Throughout this period, Khartoum was stretched thin to deal with the rebellion in the south.

Khartoum's focus on fighting the southern rebellion, the government's limited resources, persistent divisions between Arab and non-Arab, and great poverty were the dry kindling that ignited the awful conflagration of destruction in Darfur.

A large region in western Sudan, Darfur has scarce natural resources and historically has suffered from economic discrimination and neglect.[8] Long on autonomous sultanate, Darfur was conquered by the British in 1916 and merged with Sudan. Professor Gerard Prunier, in his book *Darfur: The Ambiguous Genocide*, traces to British colonial rule policies to keep Darfur backward.[9] They have continued. Khartoum ignored Darfur's infrastructure, rarely paying for road repair, schools or hospitals.

Over time, the deprivation in Darfur has led to fights over land and water between the agriculturalists and nomadic tribes. In the 1980's draught and desertification drove the Arab nomadic pastoralists further south into areas of black agriculturalists. There were occasional violent clashes. Khartoum supported the nomads. In 1985, during a period of famine, Khartoum had Libyan forces deliver food aid in Darfur.[10] The Libyans distributed the aid largely through nomadic tribes they identified as Arabs and armed them. In 1994, Sudan President Omar El Bashir reorganized the administration in Darfur giving members of Arab ethnic groups new positions of power. This accelerated the polarization in Darfur between Arab and non-Arab, which before had been splintered between dozens of tribes, languages and customs. Resentment grew among the "African" agriculturalists toward the Khartoum-backed "Arabs."[11] Also, during this period, the civil war in neighboring Chad spilled over in Darfur and "led some Arab tribes to adopt a supremacist ideology."[12]

In 2003, while Khartoum still was consumed with fighting the rebellion in the south, two insurgences from the "African" agriculturalists engaged in a series of raids and skirmishes killing several hundred government troops.[13] Awful as these casualties were, this small rebel movement posed no serious threat to Khartoum's rule. However, reluctant to divert soldiers from the south, Khartoum opened the gates of hell.

Professor Benjamin Valentino in his book *Final Solutions: Mass Killing and Genocide in the 20th Century* concludes that "(m)ass killing normally is driven by instrumental, strategic calculations. Perpetrators see mass killing as a means to an end, not an end in itself."[14]

Rather than reply with a targeted response directed at a few men of the incipient rebellion, Khartoum further armed the militia in Darfur.[15] More than 20,000 highwaymen and bandits were armed, drawn from impoverished nomadic Arab groups in Darfur and Chad. Then these militia, known as the Janjaweed, were unleashed to wage a systematic campaign of mayhem and destruction against African civilians in the area belonging to the same non-Arab ethnic groups as the rebels: the Fur, Masaalit and Zaghawa. One commentator has written that "(t)he Sudanese government's tactic seems to have been straight from the Maoist theory book. By destroying African villages, the army and their Arab militia allies drained the sea the rebels swim in."[16]

Often the attacks begin with government aerial bombardment of civilians – mainly using Antonov supply planes dropping lethal barrel bombs filled with metal shards, sometimes using helicopter gunships or MIG jet fighters.[17] After the aerial attacks, Janjaweed riding camels and on horseback sweep into villages. They burned huts, destroyed crops, slaughtered or stole livestock, raped and branded women as slaves. African males, infant, men and elderly, have been butchered. And non-Arab Sudanese have been systematically expelled from their homes.

The overwhelming majority of the men, women and children victimized by these merciless atrocities have no relation whatsoever to the insurgents. Their crime is their ethnicity. They are non-Arab and they are defenseless.

Terrible crimes have been committed. Innocent people suffer and many continue to perish. The ethnic cleansing has risen to horrific levels.

The ethnic pattern of these atrocities is clear. A United Nations observer team reported that non-Arab black villages were attacked while Arab villages were untouched.[18]

The 23 Fur villages in the Shattaya Administrative Unite have been completely depopulated, looted and burned to the ground (the team observed several such sites driving through the area for two days). Meanwhile, doted alongside these charred locations are unharmed, populated and functioning Arab settlements. In some locations, the distance between a destroyed Fur village and an Arab village is less than 500 meters.

Following twenty-five days on the ground documenting the situation, Human Rights Watch reported, "Since August 2003, wide swaths of (Fur, Masalit, and Zaghawa) homelands, among the most fertile in the region, have been burned and depopulated. With rare exceptions, the countryside is now emptied of its original Masalit and Fur inhabitants. Everything that can sustain and succor life – livestock, food stores, wells and pumps, blankets and clothing – has been looted or destroyed. Villages have been torched not randomly, but systematically – often not once, but twice."[19]

Twenty-four months ago, U.N. Secretary-General Kofi Annan warned of "ethnic cleansing" in Darfur and called on the international community to act. Eighteen months ago, then Secretary of State Colin Powell labeled the ongoing atrocities in Darfur "genocide."[20] Meanwhile, the violent atrocities continued and the world's response has been modest.

Paul Rosesabagina faced the forces of evil during the genocide in Rwanda and emerged a hero. The film "Hotel Rwanda" was based on his story as a hotel manager in Kigali who saved Tutsis in the midst of the killings by offering them refuge. Not long ago he wrote:

> History shows us that genocides can happen only if four import conditions are in place. There must be the cover of a war. Ethnic grievances must be manipulated and exaggerated. Ordinary citizens must be deputized by their government to become executioners. And the rest of the world must be persuaded to look away and do nothing. The last is the most shameful of all, especially so because genocide is happening again right now in Darfur and the world community has done precious little to stop the killings.[21]

Testimonials of Horror

A numbing number of people have died in Darfur. Estimates range up to 400,000. And more than 2 million Africans have been driven from their homes. Most now live in desperate conditions in refugee camps in southern Sudan and neighboring Chad.[22]

Even while living in these perilous conditions the black Africans from Darfur are not safe. In addition to malnutrition and disease, a number of refugee camps have been attacked by the Janjaweed.[23] When will this nightmare end?

The sheer numbers do not tell the real story. Numbers never do. The stories of the Sudanese army and Janjaweed atrocities are horrific. No mercy has been given. Their ferocious attacks on innocent Africans have left a trail of destruction, death, and misery.

As a consequence of the good work and diligence of journalists, United Nations officials, and human rights and humanitarian workers, the destruction in Darfur has been documented and many of the disturbing stories of horror has been recorded. Nicholas Kristof of *The New York Times* has provided particularly exhaustive and noteworthy coverage on the tragic events in Darfur.[24] It is through the voice of the victims that one can gain some appreciation for the unremitting brutality inflicted upon Darfur.

A 27-year old woman from Amnaty village reported to Amnesty International about the attacks.

> They dropped bombs from Antonovs on our cattle and on our huts. We were hiding near the village and were going back to the village at night to sleep there... Then they attacked the village. It was in the morning. I was preparing breakfast when I saw them coming. They starting shooting. They came with horses and cars and they were all in uniforms. They killed my husband Musa Harum Arba. I ran and left the village. I took my three children and two children of my neighbor and we ran to Hara, the village in the valley. Then we went to Abu Liha where we stayed for two days and from there to Bamina. The Janjaweed found us on the way. Antonovs bombarded us and killed three people. We were many on the run and some people were caught by Janjaweed. Nine girls and two boys were taken by Janjaweed. They took one of my uncles and his son, Khidder Ibrahim. We do not know what happened to these people.[25]

Amina Abakar Mohammed from Furawiyah told her story to award-winning journalist Samantha Power.

> One day "(n)ot long after dawn, when Amina and Mohammed (her 10 year old son) arrived at the wells, they heard the sound of approaching planes. Fifteen minutes later, Amina recalled, the aircraft began bombing... When Amina saw the janjaweed approaching, she hurried the donkeys to a red-rock hillock three hundred yards away. She assumed that Mohammed had fled in another direction, but she turned and saw that he had remained at the wells, with the older boys and the men, in an effort to protect the animals. He and the others were surrounded by several hundred janjaweed. As the circle closed around her son, she ducked behind the hillock and prayed.

By nightfall, the sounds of gunfire and screaming had faded, and Amina furtively returned to the wells. She discovered that they were stuffed with corpses, many of which had been dismembered. She was determined to find her son, but also hoped that she wouldn't. Rummaging frantically around the wells by the moonlight, she saw the bodies of dozens of people she knew, but for a long time she was unable to find her firstborn. Suddenly, she spotted his face – but only his face. Mohammed had been beheaded.[26]

Several months later, Ms. Power visited Furawiyah and went to where the wells in which the Janjaweed had stuffed the bodies of their victims had been. Now there only was desert. The Janjaweed had covered the evidence of their crimes and, in the process, taken away wells that had nourished the people for generations.

Following a visit to the area, Julie Flint testified to the Senate Foreign Relations Committee,

On a hillside in Chad, where a three-month-old refugee baby had just died for reasons that will never be known, I met a 12-year-old survivor of Tullus – a boy called Hussein Dafa'allah. He ran from Tullus with his mother and hid behind a tree with three other children. The youngest of the three, a girl from Fatima, was only seven years old. Hussein said a group of uniformed men approached him as he hid and sat down beside him. These men were not behaving as if they feared attack. Their behavior surely suggests there were no rebels here, nothing that could be considered a military target. The men taunted Hussein, calling him a "Tora Bora" – a rebel, in Darfur-speak. Hussein told me: "There are no Tora Bora in Tullus. It's a village."

One of the men who cornered Hussein was apparently unarmed – a detail that suggests he was not a member of the Janjaweed. He ordered his companions to fire at the children behind the trees and Hussein was hit three times – in the face, a leg and an arm. The three other children were also hit, but no-one could tell me what because of them. When Hussein's father arrived after the attackers left, he strapped his son onto a donkey and took him across Dar Masalit – the Masalit "homeland" – to Chad.[27]

In Terchana, 205 Africans were killed in one day by Janjaweed accompanied by three carloads of soldiers. A forty-two year old from that village, Adam, reported that the dead included twenty-three women and a one hundred-year-old man, Barra Younis. "Barra Younis couldn't walk and the Janjaweed burned him alive in his hut. They saw him there and they burned him." They took the cattle and burned all the village. They took some food for the horses and burned the rest.[28]

A 15-year-old boy from Goz Um Beta has shared his story of abduction and torture:

I was looking after the goats when I was taken by the Janjaweed... Eight other children who were not from my village were also taken, they are still with them, and myself I was able to escape. They took me to a camp in Abu Jidad where there were also many soldiers. They asked me where the goats were and beat me if I wasn't answering. They tied up my sexual organ with a rope and pulled from both sides each time they were asking the questions. They beat me several times a day. ...The other children received the same treatment from the Janjaweed and the soldiers.[29]

Another typical case of torture was reported from the Garsila area. "A Fur man was detained and whipped until all the skin was flayed from his back. The whip handle was then used to gouge holes in his flesh."[30]

And sexual violence is a common crime that accompany Janjaweed attacks.[31] "In the villages of Dingo and Koroma in Dar Masalit, for example, men have reported that the Janjaweed 'took girls into the grass and raped them there.' One of the girls raped was only thirteen-years-old. Near Sissi, three women, aged thirty-two, twenty-two and twenty-five, were abducted at a water hole and taken to Nouri School, which was abandoned, and were raped. In the village of Dureysa, on the Masalit – Fur border, a seventeen-year-old girl who resisted rape was killed and her naked body left on the street."[32]

A 37-year old from Mukjar told Amnesty International how the Janjaweed had raped and humiliated women.

> When we tried to escape they shot more children. They raped women; I saw many cases of Janjaweed raping women and girls. They are happy when they rape. They sing when they rape and they tell us that we are just slaves and that they can do with us how they wish.[33]

A woman from Silaya who was five months pregnant when she was abducted by the Janjaweed with eight other women shared this story.

> After six days, some of the girls were released. But the others, as young as eight years old were kept there. Five to six men would rape us in rounds, one after the other for hours during six days, every night. My husband could not forgive me after this, he disowned me."[34]

And many of the sad stories testify to the strong ethnic and racial component in the horrors of Darfur. A female refugee from Disa was interviewed in Goz Amer camp for Sudanese refugees in Chad and shared her story.

> I was sleeping when the attack on Disa started. I was taken away by the attackers. They were all in uniforms. They took dozens of other girls and made us walk for three hours. During the day we were beaten and they were telling us, "You, the black women, we exterminate you, you have no god." At night we were raped several times. The Arabs guarded us with arms and we were not given food for three days.

A group of Masalit women in Goz Amer refugee camp reported their Janjaweed attackers cried out, "You blacks, you have spoilt the country! We are here to burn you. We will kill your husbands and sons and we will sleep with you!"[35]

A Mesalit chief from the village of Disa reported that during the attack on his village the Janjaweed said:

> You are Blacks, no Blacks can stay here, and no Black can stay in Sudan… The blood of the Blacks runs like water, we take their goods and we chase them from our area and our cattle will be in their land. The power of al-Bashir (president of Sudan) belongs to the Arabs and we will kill you until the end, you Blacks, we have killed your God.[36]

And here are the worlds of a Janjaweed fighter according to a refugee from Kenya.

> Omar al Bashir told us that we should kill all the Nabas. There is no place here for the Negroes anymore.[37]

The testimonies make gruesome reading. And they echo thousands of other stories that have been collected from Darfur. They speak of summarily or indiscriminately killed Africans. They speak of raped, tortured, abducted and forcibly displaced Africans. They give account to how girls and women have been the particular target of sexual crimes. And most of these stories were collected over two years ago. The killings, the atrocities have been known. They continue. Yet the international community has done little. Why?

The International Community's Response

The problems in Darfur began in February, 2003.[38] As the killing of innocent civilians picked up momentum, Khartoum had some discussions with the rebel groups but the peace talks collapsed on December 17, 2003. On January 13, 2004, the World Food Program appealed for $11 million to help the Darfur refugees near the Chad border. On February 17th, the U.N. announces an emergency airlift for 110,000 refugees fleeing the Janjaweed. By March, 2004, the U.N.'s humanitarian coordinator for Sudan, Mukesh Kapila said, "The only difference between Rwanda and Darfur is the numbers involved of dead, tortured, and raped. …This is ethnic cleansing, this is the world's greatest humanitarian crisis, and I don't know why the world is not doing more about it."[39] On April 2nd, United Nations chief humanitarian aid coordinator Jan Egeland said that in Darfur "scorched-earth tactics" have triggered "one of the world's worst humanitarian crises." In a statement on April 7, 2004, President Bush condemned the "atrocities" in Darfur. He said, "The government of Sudan must not remain complicit in the brutalization of Darfur."[40]

Also, in early April on the International Day of Reflection on the 1994 Rwanda Genocide, U.N. Secretary-General Kofi Annan traveled to Geneva to address the U.N. Commission on Human Rights.[41] I was there serving as the U.S. Ambassador to the Commission. At the time negotiations for a resolution on the situation in Darfur seemed dead in the water. Annan talked about the tragic events in Rwanda 10 years earlier when in 100 horrific days the Hutus had slaughtered 800,000 Tutsis, mostly by hand, neighbor wielding machetes against neighbor.[42] Annan outlined his thoughts about how the international community, and in particular the United Nations, might act to avoid a repeat of the terrible slaughter in Rwanda. Then he turned to the gruesome events in Darfur. He called the killings "ethnic cleansing." He demanded "swift and decisive action" from the international community. He even raised the possibility of "military action."

As the first sub-Saharan African ever to serve as U.N. Secretary-General, Annan's words had a powerful impact on all the delegates, especially those from Africa. There was new momentum within the Commission to address the situation in Darfur. In behalf of the United States, I pushed for a resolution that would call on the Sudan government to stop arming those engaged in these terrible acts and stop all other support given to the Janjaweed. I sought a strong and effective mechanism to monitor and report on the events in Darfur. And I sought a guarantee for unfettered access for humanitarian assistance to the displaced people that already numbered some 900,000.[43] From Washington, instructions for demarches seeking support for this resolute position went out to capitals all over the world. For a time there seemed to be reason to hope we would be successful. Unfortunately, we were not.

While following Annan's address most African delegations recognized the need to address the situation in Darfur, regional loyalties made many African states susceptible to Khartoum's enticements for a watered-down resolution. Then in negotiations between the Africans and the European Union, in the end the EU proved more interested in sub-Saharan buy-in to any resolution and the broadest possible consensus than in the people suffering in Darfur. When Irish Ambassador Mary Whelan, then holding the rotating seat of EU president, announced agreement with all the African states on a resolution, it was a disgrace. The final resolution did not condemn the atrocities, nor demand they end, nor require humanitarian access. It even expressed appreciation to the Sudanese government for its cooperation with the UNCHR. The United States could not, in good conscience, support this resolution.[44] The European Union resolution was adopted by the U.N. Commission on Human Rights even though the Member States had the report of the Office of the U.N. High Commissioner on Human Rights' Mission to Darfur that highlighted various terrible acts that were contributing to a reign of terror including, but not limited to, repeated attacks on civilians by the Government of Sudan and its proxy militia forces with a view to their displacement; the use of systematic and indiscriminate aerial bombardments and ground attacks on unarmed civilians; the use of disproportionate force by the Government of Sudan and Janjaweed forces; that the Janjaweed have operated with total impunity and in close coordination with the forces of the Government of Sudan; the attacks appeared to have been ethnically based, and the pattern of attacks on civilians included killing, rape and pillage.[45]

In more than twenty years of multilateral diplomacy, this was one of my greatest disappointments. Well meaning but misguided diplomats had allowed their understandable desire for consensus decision-making or, absent that, the broadest possible support to blind them to the principles of decency and humanity they believed in and they turned their backs on the victims in Darfur. The diplomatic minuet had resulted in a watered-down, weak resolution. The message seemed clear. The international community cared little about the tens of thousands already killed and the hundreds of thousands driven from their homes and living in desperate conditions. Khartoum acted accordingly. The ethnic slaughter continued.

There followed a series of diplomatic milestones, but the relentless violence continued. In April, Khartoum and the two rebel groups[46] agreed to a 95-day ceasefire, but violence continued. On May 28, 2004, Khartoum and the rebels agreed to African ceasefire monitors, but violence continued. On June 3rd, the United Nations gathered donors seeking $236 million in aid for Darfur. Days later, the U.N. said that Khartoum still was blocking humanitarian aid. Diplomacy continued in a parallel universe having little to no impact on the ground.[47] The relentless brutality continued.

In June, the leaders at the Group of 8 Summit joined in calling on the Sudanese government to disarm the militias that "are responsible for massive human rights violations in Darfur."[48] Then the U.N. Security Council passed a resolution calling for an end to fighting in Darfur and urging the creation of a peacekeeping force in southern Sudan.[49]

In July, 2004, former Senator John Danforth became U.S. Ambassador to the United Nations. For over three years he had been President Bush's Special Envoy working to broker a peace agreement in Sudan between the north and south. He brought a keen interest in Sudan and added urgency to the efforts to help end not only the north/south civil war but also the killings in Darfur.

Ambassador Danforth immediately began working on a strong U.N. Security Council resolution that would call for an end to the carnage in Darfur and threaten sanctions. He was met by strong resistance. China has precious oil concessions in Sudan.[50] Russia has large military contracts with Khartoum. And Pakistan sought to provide support for Sudan's Muslim government. With Beijing and Moscow, two veto wielding states, plus Islamabad, and the elected African members of the Security Council all opposed to the U.S. strong language, there was no realistic possibility for the sort of robust Security Council resolution Danforth sought.

After weeks of wavering, the Member States of the Security Council finally passed a resolution condemning the killings in Darfur but stopped short of creating sanctions against the Sudan government is involvement in the atrocities.[51]

In the months that followed the Security Council remained "seized" by the issue. Reports on the events in Darfur were delivered and Security Council meetings were held. With each new deliberation, the language got tougher, but the violence continued. On October 15, 2004, the U.N. World Health Organization estimated that 70,000 already had died in Darfur. And on October 30, Rwandan troops arrived to join Nigerian soldiers in Darfur to monitor another shaky ceasefire. The African Union's decision to deploy monitors to Sudan was a significant step.[52] It was the first commitment to actually do something beyond rhetoric to try to stop the killing. However, the number of A.U. monitors were few, the landmass to watch very large, and the "terms of reference" strictly limited them to monitoring and did not allow them to stop the violence. The killing continued.

In September, President Bush went to the U.N. General Assembly and called the vicious violence in Darfur genocide. He called on the U.N. to act.[53] In November, 2004, it was the United States' turn to assume the rotating seat as President of the U.N. Security Council. Ambassador Danforth sought to take the Security Council on the road to dramatize the international community's concern about Sudan's North/South Civil War and the killings in Darfur. For the first time in more than 30 years, the Council met outside its headquarters in New York City. On November 18, 2004, the Security Council met in Nairobi, Kenya. This increased world attention on the situation and heightened pressure for action. In the run-up to the Security Council's trip to the region, Khartoum felt the mounting pressure and, for the first time, agreed to create "no-fly zones" over Darfur, banning military flights over the region. And on November 27th, Khartoum announced it was lifting all restrictions on aid workers and revoked a state of emergency in North Darfur. On December 19th, Khartoum agreed to stop military operations in Darfur. But the killing continued.

And the victims of the violence have not been limited to Africans from Darfur. International aid workers also have been victims. After the killing of four staffers, on December 21, 2004, the British aid charity Save the Children pulled all 350 of its staff out of Darfur. On March 16, 2005, the U.N. was forced to withdraw all its international staff from areas of Darfur after the Janjaweed said the Arab militias would target foreigners and U.N. convoys.

The devastation continued.[54] By March, 2005, estimates of those who had died in this senseless conflict had risen to over 200,000 and nearly two million people had been driven from their homes and lived in desperate conditions.

In March, Physicians for Human Rights issued a report that detailed destruction of community support, economic structures, livestock, food production, wells and farming capacity as well as huts and homes burned to empty shells.[55] Human Rights Watch released a video interview with Musa Hilal, who admitted committing crimes in Darfur. In the interview he said that the Sudan government steered the attacks. "These people get their orders from Khartoum," he stated.[56]

A document seized from a Janjaweed official that the African Union believed to be authentic calls for the "execution of all directives from the president of the republic." It went on to call for the Janjaweed to "change the demography of Darfur and make it void of (black) African tribes." It encouraged "killing, burning villages and farms, terrorizing people, confiscating property from members of African tribes and forcing them from Darfur."

In the face of continuing ethnic violence and mounting evidence of Khartoum's central role in the on-going carnage, on March 31, the U.N. Security Council voted to refer war crime suspects in Darfur to the International Criminal Court.[57] The ICC launched its formal investigation in June.

By May there were tentative signs of progress. Attacks diminished. Most observers believe the reduced violence was not due to any change of heart but because by then the government forces and the Janjaweed had successfully killed, displaced and intimidated the black Africans in Darfur. Almost anyone who might be a target was either dead or had been driven to refugee camps. Khartoum and their Arab militia allies had "drained the sea the rebels" swam in. But the thugs in Sudan continued to act like thugs.

In July, 2005, the U.N. High Commissioner on Human Rights Louise Arbor reported that "rape and gang rape continue to be perpetrated by armed elements in Darfur, some of whom are members of law enforcement agencies and the armed forces."[58] In Sudan, the climate of impunity continued.

Also in July, Secretary of State Condoleezza Rice traveled to Khartoum for talks with government leaders about the appalling situation in Darfur. When she sat down with Sudanese President el-Bashir to press the case, Sudanese security forces manhandled U.S. officials and reporters traveling with her.[59] Scuffling with U.S. government officials and the media traveling with the Secretary of State, is unacceptable on many levels. But more fundamentally, it demonstrated Khartoum's continued sense of impunity.

By mid-summer, there were 3,000 African Union peacekeepers on the ground in Darfur with thousands more committed. Armored vehicles, training and maintenance assistance, and personal protective equipment had begun to arrive to support the African Union Mission in Sudan. For a time the worst violence abated.

On September 15, a series of African Union mediated talks began in Abuja, Nigeria. The peace talks in Nigeria between Khartoum and the rebel groups sputtered along through the fall. The lack of unity among factions within the rebel groups made progress difficult. The violence continued. There often was a spike in violence before each round of discussions as one group or another sought to enhance their leverage.

During the fall, despite a formal ceasefire of a year's duration between the rebel groups and Khartoum, security in Darfur deteriorated. Much of the violence was directed against internally displaced people and refugees around the refugee camps, but not only them. In the fall there was a wave of violence targeting aid workers.[60] Some of it was "banditing committed by those who have nothing left to live off in a desert region razed by nearly three years of fighting. As a local tribal leader (told *The Economist*) 'There is nothing left to loot apart from the NGO convoys.'"[61] There are many reports of armed gunman ambushing humanitarian aid convoys; beating aid workers; sexually abusing women; and looting supplies.

But even more disturbing are the claims of African Union observers that despite the formal ceasefire that Khartoum's attack helicopters continued to swoop down strafing villages in coordinated attacks with the Janjaweed.[62] In October, the African Union condemned "the government's act of calculated and wanton destruction that had killed at least 44 people and displaced thousands over two weeks."[63]

Relentlessly, the violence continued. In early December, the United Nations Mission in Sudan (UNMIS) reported that in Western Darfur, the Janjaweed attacked Congo Harasa and destroyed the town's wells that humanitarian workers had constructed.[64] United Nations staff and international NGO workers continued to face "harassment, threats and ambushes" in Darfur.[65] Later that month UNICEF reported that 1.25 million children in need were beyond reach of aid in Darfur due to continuing violence. UNICEF country representative Ted Chaiban said, "Persistent instability and political stalemate means that children have little hope for a meaningful future."[66]

In late December, UNMIS reported that both Sudan Government and rebel troops were violating the ceasefire agreement. Banditry and looting continued. Janjaweed activities had increased with fresh attacks on villages and "harassment, beating, (rape) and killing of internally displaced people grazing their cattle outside their camps."[67] The cycle of violence again was escalating. Fighting in the Zalenjei area of west Darfur resulted in 3,800 new arrivals at IDP camps with another 5,000 displaced, reportedly stranded in the conflict area.[68] At the end of 2005, Kofi Annan confirmed that there had been a marked deterioration in Darfur since September "including an increase in ethnic clashes."[69]

Furthermore, by late 2005 the atrocities in Darfur had bled into neighboring Chad. Janjaweed crossed Sudan's border to terrorize displaced blacks from Darfur, marauding near refugee camps, attacking those who traveled out to gather wood, killing men and raping women.[70]

In late January, reacting to growing bloodshed in Darfur, Secretary-General Annan sought to increase the diplomatic pressure. He called on all parties "to immediately stop all hostility, to respect international humanitarian law and resolve their differences at the negotiating table."[71] On the same day, the U.N. Office of the High Commissioner for Human Rights (UNCHR) issued a detailed report portraying dismal human rights conditions in Darfur. The report stated that government forces working with Janjaweed continued to attack camps and villages occupied by IDPs; killing and wounding civilians and destroying homes. OHCHR called on Khartoum to end the prevailing culture of impunity.[72]

In February, 2006, the United States again took the U.N. Security Council's rotating presidency. At the first Council meeting of the month, the United States initiated work on Sudan.[73] And the next day the Security Council unanimously agreed to begin the planning process to send U.N. peacekeepers to Darfur, with a final decision to come later.[74] That planning has begun. However, difficulties are expected in locating countries willing to contribute troops to the U.N. mission.

Meanwhile, the government initiated demonstrations in Khartoum opposing deployment of any U.N. Peacekeeping force in Darfur and sought an extension of the ineffectual African Union presence.[75] The AU did agree to extend its force in Darfur for an additional 6 months. And, despite objections from Khartoum, the AU agreed "in principle" to ask the United Nations to take over in Darfur.[76]

Meanwhile, compounds in Darfur have continued to be attacked and clashes continued between armed groups.[77] There has been an increase in Khartoum's obstruction of humanitarian aid.[78] In late March, Jan Pronk, the U.N. special envoy to Sudan, warned of an upsurge of violence in Darfur.[79] In south Darfur, "militia continue to cleanse village after village," he said. "The government has not disarmed them." Pronk called on the international community to act to augment and assist the 7,000 AU troops that are under funded and poorly equipped. He called for a robust international force.

And in early April, 2006, Manual Aranda da Silva, United Nations humanitarian coordinator in Sudan, reported that about 150,000 people had been driven from their homes in Darfur in February and March and dozens of villages had been burnt to the ground.[80]

Meanwhile the Norwegian Refugee Council, an NGO operating the Kalma refugee camp in Nyala, one of the largest in the region, was ordered to leave Darfur by the Sudanese government.[81] And Khartoum briefly blocked the U.N.'s top emergency aid official, Jan Egeland, from visiting Darfur prompting him to say, "My interpretation is that they don't want me to see what I was planning to witness in South and West Darfur, which is renewed attacks on the civilian population."[82]

And in April, Hedi Annabi, an Assistant Secretary General in the Office of U.N. Peacekeeping told the Security Council that "April seems set to be another month of spiraling violence."[83]

What lies ahead? At the conclusion of his book *Darfur: The Ambiguous Genocide*, Professor Prunier notes, "The Darfur horror is still unfolding... Indignation will be voiced and diplomatic maneuvering will take place while the GoS (Government of Sudan) will continue to procrastinate, lie and obfuscate in its usual fashion. Whatever something practical will be attempted at the international panel level remains to be seen."[84]

With violence still raging in Darfur, indeed an upswing of violence, what should the international community do? What is the responsibility to protect?[85]

Going Forward

Every genocide is unique. Each has singular contributing factors and horrors that are particular. But every ethnic cleansing and each act of genocide is evil. In the face of such evil and as witness to such great suffering, to fail to act is morally inexcusable.

Michael Barnett was a political officer at the U.S. Mission to the United Nations at the time of the genocide in Rwanda. He's written a disturbing book that documents the actions and inactions of the United Nations and its member states during the 100 days of mass slaughter in Rwanda. In *Eyewitness to Genocide*, he writes, "[T]he U.N. preferred talk to action. ...My images of the Rwanda genocide are now situated alongside those of a U.N. so consumed by fears of its own mortality that it had little evident compassion for those on the ground. When I now think of Rwanda... I think of diplomats and U.N. officials hurriedly milling in and out of Security Council meetings. They are reciting their talking points and proclaiming, in the U.N.'s locution, that they 'remain actively seized of the matter.' And they deliver only rhetoric in the hope that rhetoric represents its own consolation."[86] Rhetoric is not sufficient. Action is required. We ought not turn our backs on the moral challenge of Darfur. This tragedy is man made. The carnage is horrific. And it must end.

The United States cannot be the "world's policeman" for every clash and conflict anywhere in the world, nor should it be. There are limits to blood, treasury and reach. The United States must be attentive to national interests: security, economic and otherwise. But, at the same time, the United States cannot turn its back on the principles we hold nor the values we cherish. We cannot deny our humanity. American Exceptionalism is grounded in our morality and driven by a faith in the transcendent value of the great ideas on which our nation was founded: faith, the rule of law, freedom, opportunity and the equal rights of all mankind. Surely ethnic cleansing and genocide so offend our ideals and trample our values that it must stir us to action.

The stain of blood from this killing frenzy in Darfur rests not only on the hands of those in attack helicopters swooping down on defenseless villages and those who ride on camel and horseback to burn dwellings, kill livestock, slay black males and rape women. The taint also rests on those who fail to stop the killing. It scars our time, disfigures the conscience of decency and debases any claim to righteousness.

That we cannot do everything does not mean we should do nothing when we can.

Last year NATO began a fledgling training mission to help better prepare the African Union peacekeepers in Sudan. Lately it has provided some airlifts. On February 12th, President Bush met with Secretary-General Annan in the Oval Office. After their meeting, Annan said, "I'm very happy that we have agreed to work together on the Darfur issue, working with other governments from Europe, from Asia and other regions to ensure that we do have an effective security presence on the ground."[87] And on March 20, 2006, President Bush met with NATO Secretary-General Jaap de Hoop Schaffer and discussed a possible expansion of NATO's role in Sudan.[88] After the meeting, Bush said he would like to see more NATO involvement to "make it clear to the Sudanese government that we're intent upon providing security for the people there, and intent upon helping work toward a lasting peace."[89]

It is important that the United States commit diplomatic and other resources to insure progress at the Darfur peace talks in Abuja. Just as President Bush sent Presidential Special Envoy Jack Danforth to help broker a peace between North and South Sudan, the President should designate a Presidential Special Envoy to the peace talks in Abuja..[90]

The United States should remain actively engaged on the Darfur issue at the U.N. Security Council with other member states and the secretariate working for a comprehensive plan for U.N. Peacekeepers, sufficient resources to get the job done, and early deployment. The United States should continue to push for U.N. Security Council targeted sanctions against individuals responsible for the worst abuses including seizing assets, targeted travel bans and an arms embargo. If we cannot get muscular sanctions through the Security Council, the United States should pursue U.S./European sanctions. The United States, in addition to its own contributions, should actively solicit others to step forward to guarantee success.[91]

The United States, acting with our allies, should push for greater NATO involvement to help stop the killing in Darfur. It is especially important that the United States push France and Germany to support NATO enforcement of a no fly zone over Darfur. President Bush is on the right track. However, the United States must lean forward and redouble our efforts to insure that NATO and the United Nations accomplishes the mission our values require us to accept.

Sixty years ago, the United States joined with others in saying, "Never again." Isn't it time to give meaning to that pledge? Don't we owe that to the innocent, defenseless people of Darfur? Don't we owe that to ourselves?

---

1.   See generally, Peter Ronayne, *Never Again? The United States and The Prevention and Punishment of Genocide Since the Holocaust* (New York, N.Y.; Rowman & Littlefield Publishers, Inc.; 2001); and Linda Polman, *We Did Nothing* (New York, N.Y.; Penguin Putnam Inc.; 2003).

2.   "Rwanda Genocide Failure Berated," *BBC News*, April 5, 2004. Rwandan President Paul Kagame said, "We should always bear in mind that genocide, wherever it happens, represents the international community's failure, which I would in fact characterize as deliberate, a convenient failure. …How could a million lives of the Rwandan people be regarded as so insignificant." See also, "Rwanda: How the Genocide Happened," *BBC News*, April 1, 2004.

3. Martin Meredith, *The Fate of Africa: From the Hopes of Freedom to the Heart of Despair* (New York; Public Affairs; 2005).

4. See, Julie Flint and Alex de Waal, *Darfur: A Short History to a Long War* (London; Zed Books; 2006). See also, Douglas Hamilton Johnson, *The Root Causes of Sudan's Civil Wars* (Bloomington, Indiana; Indiana University Press; 2003).

5. Meredith, *ibid.,* p. 144-5.

6. Meredith, *ibid.,* p. 145.

7. The Sudanese government and the SPLM peace agreement, called the Machakos Protocol, was finalized in 2004. It gives the south the right to self-determination. After a six-year interim period beginning in January 2005 southerners will choose in a referendum whether to remain in a united Sudan or set up an independent state. Sharia was confirmed as the source of law in the northern two thirds of the country, outside Khartoum, while the south is free to be run as a secular part of Sudan.

8. The commerce of the ancient Darfur sultanate had been trade in elephant tusks, ostrich feathers and slaves. In the twentieth century this commerce had become unacceptable and there was little else for the people to draw upon in this largely desolate region of Sudan.

9. Gerard Prunier, *Darfur: The Ambiguous Genocide,* (Ithaca, New York; Cornell University Press; 2005).

10. See generally Alex de Waal, *Famine That Kills* (Oxford, U.K.; Oxford University Press; 1989).

11. Prunier, *ibid.*

12. Julie Flint and Alex de Waal, *ibid.*.

13. The two rebel groups are the Sudan Liberation Army/Movement (SLA/M) and the Justice and Equality Movement (JEM).

14. Benjamin A. Valentino, *Final Solutions: Mass Killing and Genocide in the 20th Century* (Ithaca, New York; Cornell University Press; 2004), p. 235. See also, Eric D. Weitz, *A Century of Genocide: Utopias of Race and Nation* (Princeton, New Jersey; Princeton University Press; 2003).

15. Khartoum had similarly enlisted militia supported by the Sudan military to attack incipient rebellion in Bahr el Ghazal in 1986-88, in the Nuba Mountains in 1992-95 and in the Upper Nile in 1998-2003.

16. Mark Doyle, "Darfur Misery Has Complex Roots," *BBC News*, September 9, 2004.

17. The close coordination between the Sudanese Government in Khartoum and the Janjaweed militia is well documented. See generally, Koert Lindijer, "Analysis: Reining in the Militia," *BBC News*, October 25, 2004.

18. See, U.N. Interagency Report, April 25, 2004, as cited in Wikipedia, "Darfur Conflict". Available at http://en.wikipedia.org/wiki/Darfur_conflict.

19. Human Rights Watch, "Darfur Destroyed: Ethnic Cleansing by Government and Militia Forces in Western Sudan," May 7, 2004. Available at http://hrw.org/reports/2004/Sudan0504/. See also, The World Medical Association, "Genocide Unfolding in Sudan," August, 2004. Available at http://www.wma.net/e/humanrights/phr.htm.

20. U.N. Secretary-General Kofi Annan, Remarks at the day of Remembrance of the 10th Anniversary of the Genocide in Rwanda, Geneva, Switzerland, April 7, 2004. See also, Glenn Kessler and Colum Lynch, "U.S. Calls Killings in Sudan Genocide: Khartoum and Arab Militias Are Responsible, Powell Says," *Washington Post*, September 10, 2004.

21. Paul Rusesabagina, "Darfur," *The Wall Street Journal*, April 5, 2006.

22. "I'm sitting in the dark on the edge of a camp for displaced people in Darfur. …You can see it coming in the afternoons. The sky begins to darken and the horizon goes an ominous brown shade of yellow. Then the wind starts and the dust of the Sahara desert whips up, blasting whirling sands in all directions. The people start to run in their long rags, hands bowed against the wind. Then, the heavens simply open, the wind ferociously hurls drenching curtains of water at everything around. Mothers with their children, whose faces are twisted up in misery, squat grasping the sides of their makeshift shelters – which do almost nothing to keep them dry. The torn plastic bags that make up the walls of their twig shelters slap madly in the wind. The ground turns into a mire of mud. …This is what it is like most nights for them. In the morning we wake up to hear the children crying. In the makeshift hospital here, set up by foreign aid workers, it is so crowded with the sick that some are sleeping on the floors. Among the stench and flies, the children lie wasted, starting into space. Tiny human beings, who were born into the madness of man's inhumanity to man, into the madness of a spate of killing that has left many of their fathers, brothers, grandparents and uncles dead. And now they face starvation which is cruel and

slow. Most of the children are too far gone to eat. Some have the peeling skin and lesions that come with advanced starvation – their skin is wrinkled, loose around their bones. The mothers sit by powerless. ..." Hilary Andersson, "Sudan's Cruel and Slow Starvation," *BBC News*, July 24, 2004. See also, "Darfur Aid Worker's Diary XXI", *BBC News*, September 27, 2004.

23.   See, for example, "Eyewitness: Terror in Darfur," *BBC News*, November 10, 2004.

24.   The following columns by Nicholas Kristof on Darfur have appeared in *The New York Times*: "The Silence of Bystanders," March 19, 2006; "Africa's Brutal Lebenstraum," March 14, 2006; "A Village Waiting for Rape and Murder," March 12, 2006; "Where Killers Roam, the Poison Spreads," March 7, 2006; "What's to be Done About   Plenty?," November 29, 2005; "A Tolerable Genocide," November 27, 2005; "Sudan's Department of Gang Rape," November 22, 2005; "Never Again, Again?" November 20, 2005; "A Wimp On Genocide," September 18, 2005; "Bush, A Friend of Africa," July 5, 2005; "Uncover Your Eyes," June 7, 2005; "A Policy of Rape," June 5, 2005; "Day 141 of Bush's Silence," May a31, 2005; "Mr. Bush, Take a Look At MTV," April 17, 2005; "The Pope and Hypocrisy," April 5, 2005; "The American Witness," March 2, 2005; "The Secret Genocide Archive," February 23, 2005; "He Ain't Heavy," October 20, 2004; "The Dead Walk," October 16, 2004; "As Humans Are Hunted," October 13, 2004; "Reign of Terror," September 11, 2004; "Saying No To Killers," July 21, 2004; "Dithering As Others Die," June 25, 2004; "Magboula's Brush With Genocide," June 23, 2004; "Sudan's Final Solution," June 19, 2004; "Dare We Call It Genocide," June 16, 2004; "Bush Points the Way," May 29, 2004; "Cruel Choices," April 14, 2004; "Starved For Safety," March 31, 2004; "Will We Say 'Never Again' Yet Again?" March 27, 2004; and "Ethnic Cleansing, Again," March 24, 2004. See also, Nicholas D. Kristof, "Genocide in Slow Motion," *The New York Review of Books*, February 9, 2006.

25.   Amnesty International, "Darfur: Rape as a Weapon of War: Sexual Violence and its Consequences," July 19, 2004. Available at http://web.amnesty.org/library/index/engafr540762004.

26.   Samantha Power, "Dying in Darfur: Can the Ethnic Cleansing in Sudan be Stopped," *The New Yorker*, August 30, 2004.

27.   Julie Flint, "Sudan: Peace, but at What Price?", Testimony before the Foreign Relations Committee, United States Senate, June 15, 2004. Available at http://hrw.org/english/docs/2004/06/15/darfur8850.htm.

28.   Human Rights Watch interview, Ahmad, Chad, April 6, 2004.   Available at http://hrw.org/reports/2004/sudan0504/5.htm.

29.   Amnesty International, *ibid.*

30.   Human Rights Watch interview, Darfur, April, 2004.   Available at http://hrw.org/reports/2004/sudan0504/5.htm.

31.   See generally, Human Rights Watch, "Sexual Violence and its Consequences among Displaced Persons in Darfur and Chad," April, 2005. Available at http://hrw.org/backgrounder/africa/darfur0505/.

Nicholas Kristof has written, "[T]he mass rapes in Darfur have been among the most effective means for the government to terrorize tribal populations, break their will and drive them away. Rape is feared all the more in Darfur for two reasons. Most important, a woman who has been raped is ruined; in some cases, she is evicted by her family and forced to build her own hut and live there on her own. And not only is the woman shamed for life, but so is her entire extended family. The second reason is that the people in the region practice an extreme form of female genital cutting, called infibulation, in which a girl's vagina is sewn shut until marriage. Thus when an unmarried girl is raped, the act leads to additional painful physical injuries; and the risk of HIV transmission increases. From the government's point of view, rape is a successful method of control because it sows terror among the victimized population, and yet it initially attracted relatively little attention from foreign observers, because women are too ashamed to complain." Nicholas D. Kristof, "Genocide in Slow Motion," *The New York Review of Books*, February 9, 2006.

32.   Human Rights Watch interview, Feisal, Darfur, April 5, 2004.   Available at http://hrw.org/reports/2004/sudan0504/5.htm.

33.   Amnesty International, *ibid.*

34.   Amnesty International, *ibid.*

35.   Amnesty International, *ibid.*

36.   Amnesty International, *ibid.*

37.   Amnesty International, *ibid.*

38. On April 23, 2003 two hundred and sixty men from the rebel group Sudanese Liberation Army attacked a small airport in El Fasher. Five Antonov airplanes and two helicopter gunships were destroyed and about one hundred Sudanese soldiers were killed. This was the first significant violence committed by the still obscure SLA.

Much of this reconstruction of events was drawn from Reuters Foundation, "Chronology of Darfur's Humanitarian Crisis. Available at http://www.alertnet.org/thenews/newsdest/L10769995.htm.

39 . Samantha Power, "Dying In Darfur: Can the Ethnic Cleansing in Sudan be Stopped?" *The New Yorker*, August 30, 2004.

40. *Ibid.*

41. See generally, "Rwanda Remembers Genocide Victims," *BBC News*, April 7, 2004; "Rwanda Marks Genocide Anniversary," *BBC News*, April 6, 2004. See also, "U.N. Chief's Rwanda Genocide Regret," *BBC News*, March 26, 2004.

42. See generally, Romeo Dallaire, *Shake Hands With the Devil: The Failure of Humanity in Rwanda* (Toronto; Random House Canada; 2003); Linda Melvern, *Conspiracy to Murder: The Rwandan* (New York; Verso; 2004); Philip Gourevitch, *We Wish to Inform You that Tomorrow We Will Be Killed With Our Families: Stories From Rwanda* (New York; Picador; 1998); Samantha Power, *A Problem From Hell: America and the Age of Genocide* (New York; Basic Books; 2002); and Elizabeth Neaffer, *The Key to My Neighbor's House: Seeking Justice in Bosnia and Rwanda* (New York; Reader USA; 2001). And for a volume that offers a ray of hope out of the terrible darkness of Rwanda's genocide, see Immaculee Ilibagizo, *Left to Tell: Discovering God Amidst the Rwandan Holocaust* (Carlsbad, California; Hay House; 2006).

43   Richard S. Williamson, *Human Rights, Democracy and Restorative Justice* (Chicago, Illinois; Prairie Institute; 2004), pp. 125-7.

44. The United States introduced its own robust resolution. But with a softer option now introduced by the European Union, the U.S. resolution failed.

45. Report of the Acting Commissioner for Human Rights on Sudan. E/CN.4/2005/27.

46. The Sudan Liberation Army (SLA) and the Justice and Equity Movement (JEM).

47 . "Transcript of Press Conference by Secretary-General Kofi Annan at United Nations Headquarters, 25 June 2004," Press Release SG/SM/9388. Available at http://www.un.org//News/Press/docs/204/sgsm9388.doc.htm. See also, "Greatest Humanitarian Crisis Today in Southern Africa, World Food Program Head Tells Security Council," United Nations Press Release SC/8933; June 30, 2005; and "United Nations Humanitarian Assistance Transition From Relief to Development," United Nations Press Release IHA/1071; August 8, 2005.

48. G-8 Statement on Sudan, Sea Island, Georgia, June 10, 2004. Available at http://www.g7.utorontsummit/2004seaissudan.html.

49. Security Council Resolution 1547 (2004).

50. "China has invested some $10 billion in Sudan. The state-owned China National Petroleum Corp. owns 40%, the largest share, in the Greater Nile Petroleum Co. (GNPOC). State-owned China Petroleum Engineering and Construction (CPEC) has built a pipeline from the GNPOC fields to the Red Sea, and a refinery complex outside Khartoum.

"China owns most of an oil field in Darfur and 41 percent of a field in the Melut Basin. Another Chinese firm, Sinopec, is building a tanker terminal. About 70 percent of Sudan's oil exports go to China, and account for 10 percent of China's oil imports. In exchange for oil, Beijing provides weapons and diplomatic support. China has supplied Sudan with tanks, artillery, helicopters and fighter aircraft. China has flooded Darfur with antipersonnel mines. It is estimated as much as 80 percent of Sudan's oil revenue goes to buy arms...

"Beijing has also helped Sudan build its own factories to manufacture small arms and ammunitions, the real weapons of mass destruction in Khartoum's campaign of ethnic cleansing." William Hawkins, "China's Role in Genocide," *Washington Times*, March 27, 2006.

51. Security Council Resolution 1556 (2004). The resolution was passed by a vote of 13-0 with China and Pakistan abstaining. See, Paul Reynolds, "Sudan: Step by Step Pressure," *BBC News*, August 4, 2004. "The United Nations is still reluctant to intervene with force in Darfur and a strategy of pressure on the government of Sudan is being tried first."

52. "The African Union Mission in Sudan (AMIS) originated in early July, 2004, when both the African Union and European Union sent monitors to monitor the Darfur crisis ceasefire signed in April 2004. In

August 2004, the African Union sent 150 Rwandan troops in to protect the ceasefire monitors. However, it soon became apparent that 150 troops would not be enough, so they were joined by 150 Nigerian troops." http://en.wikipedia.org/wiki/African.UnionMission_in_Sudan.

53.   President George W. Bush, Address to the United Nations General Assembly, The United Nations, New York, New York, September 23, 2004. There has been controversy on whether or not the atrocities in Darfur have reached a large enough scale to properly be labeled "genocide." Raphael Lemkin, a Polish lawyer coined the word in 1943. He combined the Greek word "genos" – race – with the Latin word "cide." See generally, "Analysis: Defining Genocide," *BBC News*, February 1, 2005.

54.   See, "Egeland: New Famine Threat Faces Darfur," *Aljazeera.com*, February 19, 2005.

55.   See "Sudan: Organized Campaign Against Non-Arabs in Darfur, Says Rights Group," *IRIN News. Org* (U.N. Office for the Coordination of Humanitarian Affairs), June 24, 2004.

56.   "Darfur: Militia Leader Implicates Khartoum," *Human Rights Watch*, Available at http://hrw. org/video/2005/musa. See also, "Video Transcript: Exclusive Video Interview with Alleged Janjaweed Leader," *Human Rights Watch*, March 2, 2005. Available at http://hrw.org/english/docs/2005/03/02/ darfur10225.htm.

57.   UNSC Res. 1593 (2005). Due to the United States objections to the International Criminal Court, the U.S. abstained on this resolution. See also Human Rights Watch, "U.N. Security Council Refers Darfur to the ICC: Historic Step Toward Justice; Further Protection Measures Needed," March 31, 2005. Available at http://hrw.org/english/docs/2005/03/31/sudan10408.htm. At a February 16, 2005 meeting of the U.N. Security Council, Louise Arbor, U.N. High Commissioner for Human Rights, said a referral to the ICC is "the only credible way" to bring the perpetrators of the crimes in Darfur to justice.

For a thoughtful review of ICC prosecutor Luis Moreno-Ocampo's work building a case against the perpetrators of crimes in Darfur, see Elizabeth Rubin, "If Not Peace, Then Justice," *New York Times Magazine*, April 2, 2006. See also, Amnesty International, "Sudan" Who Will Answer for the Crimes?," January 18, 2005. Available at http://web.amnesty.org/library/index/ENGAFR540062005?op en&of=ENG-SDN; Human Rights Watch, "Darfur: ICC Prosecutor Briefs Security Council," June 29, 2005. Available at httpo://hrw.org/english/docs/2005/06/29/sudan11233htm; and Human Rights Watch, "Entrenched Impunity: Government Responsibility for International Crimes in Darfur," December 2005. Available at http://hrw.org/reports/2005/darfur1205/.

58.   See also, "Report of the United Nations High Commissioner for Human Rights and Follow-Up to the World Conference on Human Rights: Situation of Human Rights in the Darfur Region of the Sudan," May 7, 2004; E/CN.4/2005/3.

59.   "U.S.: Sudan Apologize to Rice Over Rough-up. Guards Manhandled Secretary of State's Delegation, NBC Reporter," *MSNBC*, July 21, 2005.

60.   See generally, "Sudan: Darfur's Despair," *The Economist*, October 15, 2005, pp. 47-9. See also, U.N. News Center, "Annan Condemns 'Vicious Attack,' that Killed 20 in Darfur Village," December 20, 2005.

61.   *Ibid*.

62.   *Ibid*. After a government-supported Arab militia attacked the Aro Sharow refugee village on September 28, killing at least 32, the African Union accused both Khartoum and rebels of violating the ceasefire agreement. Available at http://news.bbc.co.uk/2/hi/africa/4300526.htm.

63.   Associated Press, available at http://news.yahoo.com/s/ap/20051002/ap_re_mi_ea/sudan.darfur.com. In December, an attack on the town of Adre, Chad, near the Sudan border led to the death of 300 rebels. Khartoum was blamed for the attack. Available at http://news.bbc.co.uk.l/hi/world/africa/4544352.stm.

64.   U.N. News Center, "U.N. Mission in Sudan Reports Continued Insecurity in troubled Darfur Region," December 7, 2005.

65.   *Ibid*.

66.   U.N. News Center, "1.25 Million Children Beyond Reach of Aid in Sudan's Darfur Region, U.N. Warns," December 20, 2005.

"John Hefferman, the lead researcher and author of the report, 'Darfur: Assault on Survival – A Call for Security, Justice and Restitution," said Khartoum and its militia, the Janjaweed, 'have in a systematic way attacked the very survival of a people by destroying property, livestock, communities and families.' Refugees interviewed by the researchers spoke of early morning attacks by armed men on horseback or in pick-up trucks, backed up by Sudanese military aircraft. The attackers killed and raped villagers, then looted and burned houses and shops, poisoned wells, stole livestock and torched prime farmland. One such testimony was given by a 33-year-old mother from Furawiya Village, who said she traveled for five days, through which she lived off berries and a little food supplied by the international organizations. "Sometimes, I would have to wait in line all day just for one bucket of water. After two months, my donkey died from not having enough food. And then my youngest child, a three-year-old girl got sick. There were no medicines to help her. She died." Stephen Mbogo, "Human Rights Group Call For More Action on Darfur," *CNS.News.com*, January 13, 2006.

67. U.N. News Center, "Western Sudan's Darfur Area is still Scene of Rape and Banditry, U.N. Mission Says," December 27, 2005. "Eleven vehicles of the rebel Sudanese Liberation Army (SLA) reportedly attacked South Darfur's Marla last week Monday and Tuesday, leaving five people dead and four wounded in what was perceived by some to be retaliation for Sudanese Government attacks on Bajo on 13 December and on Duwana on 18 December, UNMIS said."

68. U.N. News Center, "Strife Drives More Sudanese in Darfur from their Homes," U.N. Reports," December 28, 2005.

69. U.N. News Center, "Despite Forceful Security Council Moves, Atrocities Continue in Sudan's Darfur Region – U.N. Report," December 29, 2005.

70. See Nicholas Kristof, "Africa's Brutal Lebenstraum," *New York Times*, March 14, 2006; and Nicholas Kristof, :A Village Waiting for Rape and Murder," *New York Times*, March 12, 2006. See also, Editorial, "Spreading Genocide to Chad," *New York Times*, March 30, 2006.

71. U.N. News Center, "Sudan: Concerned at Rising Violence in Darfur, Annan Calls on Parties to Halt Attacks," January 27, 2006. "The Secretary-General is seriously concerned by the major escalation of violence in the Jebel Marra region of Darfur, particularly the heavy fighting in the Golo and Shearia areas that have forced humanitarian agencies to evacuate," a spokesman for Mr. Annan said in a statement issued in New York."

72. Office of the United Nations High Commissioner for Human Rights. E/CN.4/2005/72/Add.5.

73. See, United States Mission to the United Nations, Press Release #14(06), February 2, 2006.

74. UNSC Presidential Statement, "Reports of the Secretary-General on the Sudan," S/PRST/2006/5 of 3, February 2006.. The resolution called for a 12,000 to 20,000 troop presence in Darfur with the 7,000 African Union troops already there being given new weapons and being incorporated into the U.N. mission. The U.N. peacekeepers would have a greater mandate to protect civilians.

75. Warren Hoge, "Envoy Says Sudan Doesn't Want U.N. Force in Darfur," *New York Times*, February 28, 2006. See also, "U.N. Peacekeeping Plan Stirs Protest," *Chicago Tribune*, March 10, 2003 and Stephen Mbogo, "As Darfur Aid Efforts Struggle, Sudden Rejects Foreign Intervention." *CBSNEWS.COM*, March 22, 2006.

76. "Africa Extends Darfur Peace Force," *BBC News*, March 10, 2006. "Sudan had threatened to leave the AU if it asked the U.N. to take over. ...(However) the government realizes that it would be very difficult to reject a U.N. offer, if it followed a formal request from the AU." See also, Associated Press, "African Troops Extend Darfur Mission, March 11, 2006; Jonah Fisher, "Darfur's Doomed Peacekeeping Mission," *BBC News*, March 9, 2006. See also, "Sudan Rebukes U.N. Plan for Quick Darfur Takeover," *Reuters*, March 25, 2006; and "Sudan Rejects U.N. Darfur Force," *Aljazeera*, March 25, 2006.

77. See, for example, World Food Program, "Violence Along Chad/Sudan Border Threatens Thousands," Press Release, March 24, 2006.

78. "Sudan: U.N. Humanitarian Envoy Criticizes Obstruction by Government, *Reuters*, April 5, 2006; and Eric Reeves, "Khartoum Sharply Accelerates Its War on Humanitarian Aid in Darfur," *Sudan Tribune*, April 7, 2006.

79. Warren Hoge, "Darfur Attacks Overwhelm Peace Force, U.N. Reports," *New York Times*, March 22, 2006.

80. "U.N. Concerned Over Security Situation in Darfur," *China View*, April 7, 2006. Available at www.chinaview.cn.

81. Joe De Capua, "Sudan Orders Norwegian NGO to Leave Darfur, *Voice of America News*, April 4, 2006.

82. Marc Lacey, "Sudan Blocks U.N. Official From Visiting Darfur Region," *New York Times*, April 4, 2006.

83.   Bradley Graham and Colum Lynch, "NATO Role in Darfur on Table," *Washington Post*, April 10, 2006.

84.   Gerard Prunier, *ibid.*, p. 159.

85.   Generally, see Gareth J. Evans, *The Responsibility to Protect: Report of the International Commission on Intervention and State Sovereignty*, January, 2002. See also, Ramesh Takur, *The United Nations, Peace and Security: From Collective Security to the Responsibility to Protect* (Cambridge, U.K.; Cambridge University Press; 2006); Ted Lundberg, "Protect the People," *Washington Times*, September 27, 2005; and United Nations General Assembly, *2005 World Summit Outcome*, September 20, 2005 (Doc. A/60/L.1).

86.   Michael Barnett, *Eyewitness to Genocide: The United Nations and Rwanda* (Ithaca, New York; Cornell University Press; 2002), pp. x-xiii.

87.   U.N. News Center, "Annan and President Bush Agree to Work Together in Darfur," February 13, 2006. See also, "Darfur Peacekeeping Force Tops Bush-Annan Talks," *Associated Press*, February 13, 2006.

88.   Paula Wolfson, "Bush, NATO Leader Discuss Darfur," *Voice of America*, March 20, 2006.

89.   NATO Secretary-General de Hoop Scheffer said if the African Union asks for U.N. assistance, "the NATO allies will be ready to do more in enabling a United Nations force in Darfur." See also, Bradley Graham and Colum Lynch, *ibid.*

90.   In April, 2006, the Abuja negotiations were not moving forward. See generally, "Darfur Peace Efforts Failing," *The Scotsman*, April 10, 2006; and "Nigeria-Sudan: AU Mediators Fail to Move Darfur Talks Forward," *IRIN*, April 10, 2006. See also, Edith M. Lederer, "Council Wants Deal on Darfur Conflict," *Associated Press*, April 11, 2006.

91.   The United States has contributed over $750 million in aid for Darfur for food, shelter, access to clean water, and basic health services. USAID "Darfur Humanitarian Emergency." Available at http://www.usaid.gov//locations/sub.saharan_africa/sudan/darfur.html. The USG has been the largest contributor to Darfur relief by far.

HUMAN RIGHTS,
THE UNITED STATES AND THE U.N.

In the 21st century, man's inhumanity to man continues. Abuse of human rights are taking place and fundamental standards of decency are being trampled. Troubling questions have been raised about the United States' handling of prisoners at Abu Ghraib prison in Iraq and detainees at Guantanemo.

In such a world, what is the meaning of human rights and what is the role of the United Nations?

UNIVERSALITY

Western thought and tradition contributed substantially to the modern concept of human rights.[1] John Locke's *Two Treatises of Government* published in 1689 underlies a great deal of our modern rationale and rhetoric on human rights.[2] Locke's philosophy held that individuals along with others transfer to a public authority their individual right to enforce the law of nature. However, the transfer is not absolute. It is limited by the requirement that the authority, the government, "protect individual rights and freedoms from invasion and to secure their effective guarantee."[3] Consequently, a government that violates this obligation loses its right to govern. In the first instance the rights are those of the individual ceded to the state, not the right of the state bestowed upon the individual however and to whatever extent the state deems convenient.[4]

While acknowledging these antecedents in the Western Age of Enlightenment, the roots of modern views of "human rights" run deeper and wider than Western heritage. While the idea of democracy, political freedom and human rights in the modern sense first found expression during the Age of Enlightenment, the constituent parts to which these ideas gave expression had a powerful presence in non-Western as well as Western societies.

For example, Amartya Sen points out that "[i]n Buddhist tradition, great importance is attached to freedom, and the traditions of earlier Indian thinking to which Buddhist thoughts relate allow much room for volition and free choice. Nobility of conduct has to be achieved in freedom."[5]

Furthermore, even Confucius did not advise blind loyalty to the state. Again, quoting Amartya Sen, "When Zilu asks (Confucius) 'how to serve a prince,' Confucius replies: 'Tell him the truth even if it offends him.'

Lecture delivered at the Whitehead School of Diplomacy and International Relations, Seton Hall University, April 17, 2006.

The censors in Singapore or Beijing would take a very different view. Confucius is not adverse to political caution and tact, but he does not forgo the recommendation to oppose a bad government. 'When the (good) way prevails in the state, speak boldly and act boldly. When the state has lost the way, act boldly and speak softly'."[6] Indeed, every great religion embraces certain fundamental truths appropriate for all people: "justice, truth, mercy, compassion – though the details of their interpretation vary."[7]

Culture is not Sacrosanct

Those critical of the universality of human rights on cultural grounds are suggesting that there are "sharply defined, self-contained, fixed and unified cultural units."[8] And, they argue, that since all values and rights are defined by culture, human rights necessarily differ from one culture to another. In other words, cultural differences make human rights standards relative from one culture to the next. There is no universality. However, not only are the underlying principles upon which modern human rights are built common across cultural lines and drawn from various histories and heritages, the assertion that cultures are inviolable is incorrect.

The perimeter and reach of cultures are difficult to determine. Cultures overlap and evolve. They grow and change. Cultures are not neatly defined and self-contained. Within Asia, for example, there are enormous differences in religion, in economic circumstances and political systems. The majority of India is Hindu; of Pakistan Muslim, of China Confucian; of Japan Buddhist. And within some Asian countries there are followers of these various faiths plus Christianity. Economically Japan and Singapore are prosperous while Bangladesh is desperately poor. Politically, China, North Korea and Vietnam are Communist; Singapore is a one-party regime; while India and Japan are well-established democracies. Even within many Asian countries there are significant ethnic minorities, large economically dislocated and disadvantaged populations, and different tribal heritages.[9]

Cultures are not static. They adapt to changing circumstances. They cross pollinate, absorbing new ideas and new practices while leaving behind others they've outgrown. While modern travel, global telecommunications and instant worldwide news reporting may have accelerated this process of cultural evolution, it is as ancient as culture itself.

There are no quintessential values that separate Asia from the West, that separate one culture from another. Cultures are dynamic, fluid, and inconsistent. They are adapting and adjusting.

Economic Development and Human Rights

Another objection to applying universal human rights invoked by some is that developing countries cannot afford human rights since economic development and nation-building are their first priorities. A derivative of this argument is the assertion by proponents of "Asian values:" that the economic growth of Southeast Asia is attributable to Confucian virtues of obedience, order, and respect for authority. Asian authoritarian governments say that by limiting "western" human rights, their culture embraces the sacrifice of the few for the benefit of the many. The result has been rapid economic growth that benefits all.

This "Asian values" argument had more traction during the unprecedented three decades of unbroken rapid economic growth in the region than it has today. The Asian economic crisis that began in mid-1997 crippled some Asian economies, slowed others and had global repercussions.[10] As one scholar wrote, "The crisis has given rise to questions of the extent to which so-called Asian ways of managing economies and businesses contributed to the situation and must change as a result. The change would be both implicitly and explicitly, toward the universalist free-market capitalism preached by Western economics textbooks."[11] The social costs in Asia have been substantial.[12]

More fundamentally, the very premise that authoritarianism advances economic development is ill conceived.[13] No, what authoritarianism promotes is repression. Economic development is about change. Repression prevents change.

Amartya Sen, winner of the Nobel Prize in Economics, has written that there is little evidence to support the view that authoritarianism and suppression of political and civil rights encourage economic development. "Systematic empirical studies give no real support to the claim that there is a general conflict between political rights and economic performance... (Rather), there is by now a fairly agreed-upon list of 'helpful policies,' and they include openness to competition, the use of international markets, a high level of literacy and education, successful land reforms, and public provision of incentives for investment, exporting, and industrialization. There is nothing whatsoever to indicate that any of these policies is inconsistent with greater democracy."[14]

On the contrary, there is growing evidence of the relationship between economic growth and political freedom. For eleven years the Heritage Foundation and *The Wall Street Journal* have published an annual index of Economic freedom. It empirically demonstrates that countries that embrace economic freedom realize long-term benefits in expanding economic growth and the ability "to weather economic storms." As that study states, "Economic freedom enables a country to utilize its resources efficiently. Economically free countries tend to have higher per capita income than less free countries. ...The level of economic freedom in a country determines whether its fate will be one of prosperity or one of poverty."[15] And the report provides a country by country analysis to support that conclusion.

Furthermore, Amartya Sen has done work that has established that "no famine has ever occurred in any independent and democratic country with a relatively free press."[16] In a free and open society, there is political pressure to get the government to respond to acute suffering. The people can exercise political rights. In China from 1958 to 1961, at the failure of the Great Leap Forward, between 23 and 30 million people died of famine. And the current famine in North Korea is devastating.[17] In neither case did authoritarian governments or "Asian values" protect the suffering people.

Facts are stubborn things. And the facts do not support the proposition that respect for human rights must be sacrificed for economic development. Quite the contrary, freedom and human rights contribute to economic development.

Authoritarian Governments Seek To Retain Power

Many authoritarian regimes and power elites that claim human rights are not universal are anxious to rationalize their own violations of human rights; violations that they commit in order to keep themselves in power. They robustly make the case for resisting Western hegemony to press the "argument of Asian particularity."

However, as I already have discussed, no culture is sacrosanct. Cultures are constantly changing. Furthermore, the same regimes that resist "Western hegemony" by denying universal human rights have no difficulty embracing other "western" ideas that serve their purposes such as market economies and free trade. Their selectivity of which aspects of "foreign" cultures can encroach on their own and which they reject says more about the authoritarian regimes than it says about the legitimacy of universal human rights.

Some authoritarian regimes that reject universal human rights as a Western trespass on their culture, such as the one in power in Burma today, are willing to crush domestic cultures when it suits them to do so. To these regimes and power elites the goal is to sustain their power; the means are whatever is required to do so; and in order to keep power they reject any infringement on their exercise of that requisite coercion.[18]

As Secretary-General Kofi Annan asked in a speech at Tehran University in 1997: "When have you heard a free voice demand an end to freedom? Where have you heard a slave argue for slavery? When have you heard a victim endorse the ways of the torturer? Where have you head the tolerant cry out for intolerance?"[19]

Evil Deeds

As is often pointed out, human rights are the central legacy of World War II. There was widespread and profound moral revulsion over the Nazi holocaust; the massacre in Nanking, China; the Baton Death March; and other monstrous acts committed in that war. The preamble of the Universal Declaration of Human Rights called them "barbarous acts which have outraged the conscience" of humankind. Among other things, these atrocities demonstrated that evil is not the province of any one people.[20] Any culture under the "wrong" circumstances is capable of heinous acts.[21] That is one reason Human Rights must be recognized as universal.

Unfortunately the atrocities of World War II are not unique. There are wicked and unjust acts throughout history. In recent years cruel and inhuman acts including ethnic cleansing have taken place in Cambodia,[22] Rwanda,[23] Bosnia,[24] Kosovo,[25] and currently in Sudan to name just a few.

Since any culture appears capable of such crimes, all cultures must have a minimum standard of behavior with which they must seek to comply and by which they can be judged. While cultures vary from place to place, no culture is "above the law."

Therefore, claims of cultural relativists that seek to carve out safe havens from the reach of basic human rights standards cannot be accepted. Since the potential of such evil acts reaches across cultural boundaries, so must the basic standards of human rights that seek to restrain them.

If we fail to act and do not clearly declare the universality of human rights, we "risk giving oppressive governments the intellectual justification for the morally indefensible."[26]

318

At our most fundamental and profound level, we are all the same. We all desire to chart the course of our own lives, find happiness and redemption according to our own will. Human rights are built upon our shared humanity. They are not derived from citizenship in any country. Human rights are entitlements of every human being. They are universal. And since human rights values transcend the citizenship of any individual, the support for human rights can come from anyone. That is our responsibility and it is our opportunity.

The American Idea and Human Rights

The American idea is grounded on principles of human rights. As former Secretary of State George Shultz once said, "What unifies us is not a common origin but a common set of ideals: freedom, constitutional democracy, racial and religious tolerance. We Americans thus define ourselves not by where we come from but by where we are headed: our goals, our values, our principles, which make the kind of society we strive to create."[27]

It was a belief in human rights that Thomas Jefferson drew upon to justify the American colonies break from the British Crown when he wrote, "We hold these truths to be self evident that all men are created equal and endowed by their creator with certain inalienable rights to life, liberty and the pursuit of happiness."

Early in the 20th century as the United States was drawn onto the world stage, President Woodrow Wilson's belief in the tradition of American exceptionalism and the universal applicability of American values defined U.S. foreign policy. In his first State of the Union Address, President Wilson said

> There is only one possible standard by which to determine controversies between the United States and other nations, and that is compounded of these two elements: our own honor and our obligations to the peace of the world.[28]

Wilson insisted that the United States' role was not to prove our selfishness, but our greatness.[29] And it was on a moral foundation, with the primary objective of a new and more just international order, that Wilson justified the United States entry into the war and not on specific grievances.[30]

In 1917, President Wilson attacked the old, crumbling international order.

> The question upon which the whole future peace and policy of the world depends is this: Is the present war a struggle for a just and secure peace, or only for a new balance of power? ...There must be, not a balance of power, not organized rivalries but an organized common peace.[31]

It was this American idealism and Wilson's belief in the universal applicability of American values that informed his vision of the League of Nations. While, in the end, the Senate refused to ratify U.S. participation in the League, Wilson's view that the United States must help spread democratic governments throughout the world and his belief that the world must develop a "new and more wholesome diplomacy" based on "the same high code of honor that we demand of individuals"[185] has informed U.S. foreign policy ever since. Every American president from Wilson to George W. Bush has preceded on some variation of that vision.

319

Carrying on this tradition, President Bush observed in 2003 in a speech at Whitehall Palace in London, "The deepest beliefs of our nations set the direction of our foreign policy. We value our own civil rights, so we stand for the human rights of others. We affirm the God-given dignity of every person, so we are moved to action by poverty and oppression and famine and disease. The United States and Great Britain share a mission in the world beyond the balance of power or the simple pursuit of interest. We seek the advance of freedom and the peace that freedom brings."[33]

As Richard Schifter, a former Assistant Secretary of State for Human Rights, has written: "[T]he great majority of Americans will at all times support the proposition that our concern for human rights must and should be an important factor in our relations with other countries. Americans are compassionate. We, as a people, care about human rights and human dignity. We object to and disapprove of violations of human rights, wherever they might occur."[34]

U.N. UNIVERSAL DECLARATION OF HUMAN RIGHTS

The horrors of World War II spurred the world community to advance human rights.

From the outset, President Franklin Roosevelt described the war as a fight for freedom. In 1941, he had set out the Four Freedoms - freedom of speech and expression, freedom of worship, freedom from want, and freedom from fear.[35] Freedom from want and freedom from fear as British and American goals were reaffirmed in the Atlantic Charter press statement issued by Prime Minister Churchill and President Roosevelt in August 1941. The Atlantic Charter also recognized the right to self-determination as the United States and the United Kingdom agreed to "respect the right of all peoples to choose the form of government under which they will live." And in 1942, the Allies declared that victory was necessary "to defend life, liberty, independence and religious freedom and to preserve human rights and justice in their own lands as well as other lands."[36]

World War II produced great devastation on the battlefield and large numbers of civilian casualties. However, the full extent of the barbaric horrors of that war were not fully known until near its end as the Nazi concentration camps were liberated. The German's orderly, efficient, systematic program to exterminate the Jews that claimed the lives of 6 million shocked and horrified the world. And there were other awful atrocities in the war. In Nanking, China, a city of 1 million, the Japanese army murdered tens of thousands of surrendering Chinese soldiers, and more than 300,000 noncombatants. The Nanking killings continued for seven weeks in front of international witnesses.[37]

To address the worst war criminals, the Allies issued guidelines known as the Nuremberg Principles[38] and proceeded with the Nuremberg trials. Driven in horror by the holocaust and hopeful of setting a foundation for lasting peace, the great powers also set out to create the United Nations.

CREATING THE UNITED NATIONS

Early on during the war President Roosevelt had begun laying a foundation with the American people for the need for an international organization to help keep peace once the war was over. At the signing of the United States Relief and Rehabilitation

Administration Act on November 9, 1943, he said, "Nations will learn to work together only by actually working together."[39] And on Christmas Eve that year in a radio address, President Roosevelt made clear his vision that such an organization's main purpose would be to keep the peace.[40]

During the summer and fall of 1944, delegations from the U.K., China, the U.S.S.R. and the United States did preparatory work on the United Nations Charter in Dumbarton Oaks.[41] And in early 1945, President Roosevelt told Congress that he hoped to replace "exclusive alliances and spheres of influence" with a "universal organization in which all peace loving nations will finally have a chance to join."[42]

There were many obstacles to establishing the United Nations.[43] For various and differing reasons each of the great powers were wary of a new international organization.[44]

When the delegations gathered in San Francisco a lot of hard work remained to be done to draft an acceptable charter for the new organization. What prominence, if any, would be given to human rights was not yet determined. The issue of the extent to which an international organization could and should assume responsibility for promoting and encouraging respect for the rights of the individual was hotly debated as the U.N. Charter was drafted and approved.[45] The Covenant of the League of Nations had not mentioned "human rights and fundamental freedoms."[46]

Early on, some in the State Department wanted a bill of rights incorporated into the U.N. Charter.[47] At the conference in San Francisco, Cuba and Mexico and Panama actually introduced a Declaration on the Essential Rights of Man.[48] Prior to the United Nations, international law between states "was not generally concerned with basic individual rights such as freedom of worship and of assembly, freedom from arbitrary arrest and detention, the right to a fair trial and freedom from cruel and unusual punishment."[49] The individual was not a subject of international law.

In the end, the United Nations Charter embraces two overriding goals: "to save succeeding generations from the scourge of war" and "to reaffirm faith in fundamental human rights."[50] The words "promoting and encouraging respect for human rights and fundamental freedoms" appear, with slight variations, throughout the U.N. Charter. For example, Article 1 of the Charter states that among the purposes of the United Nations is respect for the "self-determination of peoples" and for "human rights and for fundamental freedoms for all without distinction as to race, sex, language or religion." And, in Article 56, the members pledge themselves to promote those rights and freedoms.

As Secretary of State George Marshall observed in remarks before the opening session of the United Nations General Assembly in Paris in 1948, "Systematic and deliberate denials of basic human rights lie at the root of most of our trouble and threaten the work of the United Nations. It is not only fundamentally wrong that millions of men and women live in daily terror of secret police, subject to seizure, imprisonment or forced labor without just cause and without fair trial, but these wrongs have repercussions in the community of nations. Governments which systematically disregard the rights of their own people are not likely to respect the rights of other nations and other people and are likely to seek their objectives by coercion and force in the international field."[51]

But how the general human rights rhetoric in the U.N. Charter might be translated into action was far from clear. For while the Charter nodded to fundamental human rights it also protected member states' national sovereignty.[52] The Charter reads, "Nothing contained in the present Charter shall authorize the United Nations to intervene in matters which are essentially within the domestic jurisdiction of any State, or shall require the Members to submit such matters to settlement under the present Charter, but this principle shall not prejudice the application of enforcement measures under Chapter VII."[53]

But the United States had made the critical decision to support a United Nations Human Rights Commission.[54] In the end, Article 56 of the Charter directs the U.N. Economic and Social Council to establish "commissions in economic and social fields for the promotion of human rights."[55] And on signing the U.N. Charter in San Francisco on June 26, 1945, President Harry Truman said, "Experience has shown how deeply the seeds of war are planted by economic rivalry and by social injustices."[56] Furthermore, he said that he was looking forward to the drafting of an "International Bill of Rights."

The new U.N. Economic and Social Council set up a small contact group to develop recommendations on the form and functions of a Commission on Human Rights as called for in Article 56 of the U.N. Charter. Eleanor Roosevelt, a member of the United States delegation to the first meeting of the U.N. General Assembly,[57] was asked to serve on this group and she was elected that body's chair. This group recommended that the new Commission on Human Rights first assignment be to write a bill of human rights.[58]

The U.N. Commission on Human Rights was set up in 1946 and has met annually ever since. It is the main body dealing with human rights, though today there are a wide variety of other U.N. bodies that also address human rights concerns.[59]

THE UNIVERSAL DECLARATION OF HUMAN RIGHTS

The seminal document in the United Nations pertaining to human rights is the Universal Declaration of Human Rights that was adopted in 1948. The difficult and painstakingly drafting took place in 1947 and 1948.[60] During deliberations it was far from certain that the work would bear fruit.

Eleanor Roosevelt chaired the drafting committee. Among the other able public figures on the committee were Peng-chun Chang, a Chinese philosopher and playwright, Rene Cassin, a French Resistance leader, Charles Malik, a Lebanese philosopher, and Carlos Romulo, a Philippean who had won a Pulitzer Prize in 1941. Other nations represented on the drafting committee were Australia, Chile, the Soviet Union and the United Kingdom.[61]

The drafting committee had to address many difficult issues. From the outset the group debated how to "implement" any human rights declaration that eventually would be adopted. Should they establish some sort of international tribunal or amend the U.N. Charter to include binding human rights commitments or otherwise make the declaration legally enforceable?[62] What would the "normative weight and practical force" be of this new document?"[63] Should the declaration pronounce that the enumerated rights were "endowed by God" or "endowed by nature"? Should the document explicitly enumerate women's rights? Are human rights indivisible or must political liberties be sacrificed for economic development? How precisely should economic and social "rights" be framed in the declaration?[64] Are individual freedoms inviolable or can the "collective needs" of society override them?

The United States had been among those countries that stressed the preeminence of individual freedoms; political and civil liberties such as freedom of expression, freedom of association, freedom of religion, and due process under the rule of law.[65] The Soviet Union led others who sought to give the priority to economic and social rights such as the right to a job, to education and to health care. Some sought group rights for minorities above and beyond the right of nondiscrimination.[66]

Deliberations continued throughout 1947 and into 1948.[67] Eleanor Roosevelt worked hard to steer the drafting committee towards a declaration that could pass muster in the U.N. General Assembly. It was something new. It was exciting, hopeful, and, to some, threatening.

Even after the long work and hard won compromises in the drafting committee, the declaration had to pass the gauntlet of the U.N. Economic and Social Commission, the General Assembly's Third Committee and finally the U.N. General Assembly. In the Third Committee alone, sixty-eight amendments were proposed. Nonetheless, the Declaration of Human Rights survived largely as the drafting committee had proposed it, and on December 10, 1948 it was adopted by the U.N. General Assembly without a dissenting vote.[68]

The Declaration has a preamble and 30 articles that set forth the human rights and fundamental freedoms to which everyone, everywhere in the world, is entitled. The strongest terms of the Declaration faithfully embrace the values and civil liberties contained in our own Declaration of Independence and Constitution. The U.N. Universal Declaration of Human Rights proclaims that every individual has the right to "life, liberty and security of person,"[69] to "recognition everywhere as a person before the law,"[70] to "freedom of movement... to leave any country, including his own,"[71] to "a nationality,"[72] to "freedom of thought, conscience and religion,"[73] to "freedom of peaceful assembly and association,"[74] and to "take part in the government of his country."[75] Furthermore, it states that no one shall be "held in slavery,"[76] "subjected to torture,"[77] or "subjected to arbitrary arrest, detention or exile."[78] However, while everyone's freedom of expression is affirmed,[79] it is qualified by the Declaration's anti-discrimination provision which reads: "All are entitled to equal protection against any discrimination in violation of this Declaration and against any incitement to such discrimination."[80]

While not perfect, the U.N. Universal Declaration of Human Rights was the product of hard work well done. It established important norms on human rights, proclaimed them universal, and called upon all nations to honor and protect them. While not the final resolution of human rights abuses, as William Schulz, Executive Director of Amnesty International USA has written, "The mere articulation of such rights and their near universal acclamation was a formidable achievement."[81]

As Professor Mary Ann Glendon points out in her excellent book, *A World Made New: Eleanor Roosevelt and the Universal Declaration of Human Rights*:

> [T]he State Department explained the U.S. view of the Declaration's nature and purpose by referring to what Abraham Lincoln had

said about the assertion of human equality in the Declaration of Independence:

'They (the drafters) did not mean to assert the obvious untruth, that all were then actually enjoying that equality, nor yet, that they were about to confer it immediately upon them. Indeed they had no power to confer such a boon. They meant simply to declare the right so that the enforcement of it might follow as fast as circumstances should permit.

'They meant to set up a standard maxim for free society which should be familiar to all: constantly looked to, constantly labored for, and thereby spreading and deepening its influence and augmenting the happiness and value of life to all people, of all colors, everywhere.'[82]

Similarly, prior to the adoption of the U.N. Declaration of Human Rights, Eleanor Roosevelt wrote.

In the first place, we have put into words some inherent rights. Beyond that, we have found that the conditions of our contemporary world require the enumeration of certain protections which the individual must have if he is to acquire a sense of security and dignity in his own person. The effect of this is frankly educational. Indeed, I like to think that the Declaration will help forward very largely the education of the people of the world.[83]

The U.N. Universal Declaration of Human Rights elevated to the international level the most cherished principles and ideals enshrined in America's Declaration of Independence and Bill of Rights. As the President of the U.N. General Assembly, Ambassador Evatt of Australia said of the Declaration after its adoption on December 10, 1948, "It is the first occasion on which the organized community of nations has made a declaration of human rights and fundamental freedoms, and it has the authority of the body of opinion of the United Nations as a whole, and millions of men, women and children all over the world, many miles from Paris and New York, will turn for help, guidance and inspiration to this document."[84] Within a few years, it had influence on the constitutions of the Federal Republic of Germany, Indonesia, Costa Rica, Syria, El Salvador, Haiti and Jordan.

In the end, the U.N. Declaration of Human Rights did not include enforcement provisions. The Declaration of Human Rights key words are "promoting," "encouraging," "assisting in the realization of."

As the U.N. General Assembly neared its final vote on the Declaration, Eleanor Roosevelt as Chairman of the Commission on Human Rights said,

In giving our approval to the declaration today, it is of primary importance to keep clearly in mind the basic character of the document. It is not a treaty; it is not an international agreement. It is not and does not purport to be a statement of law or of legal obligation. It is a declaration of basic principles of human rights and freedoms, to be stamped with the approval of the General Assembly by formal votes of its members, and to serve as a common standard of achievement for all people of all nations.[85]

Indeed, "Eleanor Roosevelt expressly campaigned for United States support by arguing that the Declaration would not be legally binding."[86] It stood as a document of basic enumerated rights that's power was in its moral persuasion publicly exercised. It outlined a "common standard of achievement" to which to aspire and it has become the cornerstone of today's international human rights regime. It is the yardstick by which all country's respect for, and compliance with, international human rights standards are measured.

As former Congressman, Father Robert Drinan has written, "The establishment of a catalog of internationally recognized human rights for the first time in the history of the world is a monumental achievement in itself, apart from the enforceability of such rights."[87]

Today the principles set forth in the Declaration have inculcated the modern world; its culture and its politics. No U.N. action before or since has had as profound an effect on contemporary thinking and the lives of as many people throughout the world. As U.N. Secretary General Kofi Annan has written, "The end of the Cold War, the World Conference on Human Rights in Vienna in 1993, and the inception of the United Nations High Commissioner for Human Rights later that year have opened up new avenues for the United Nations to make its work in human rights more meaningful to people throughout the world." But the foundation for that effort is the U.N. Universal Declaration on Human Rights and the principles therein embraced.

Today the U.N.'s human rights machinery is broad and varied. The creation of the U.N. Commissioner on Human Rights and its Geneva-based secretariat certainly enhanced the U.N.'s capabilities. Personally, as I've referenced in my discussion on the Universal Declaration of Human Rights, I believe the U.N.'s contribution to human rights norm setting has been invaluable. But the most controversial activities, the arena of greatest disappointment, has been the United Nations Commission on Human Rights. I've witnessed the double standards and hypocrisy of that body from many perspectives including in 2004 serving as U.S. Ambassador to the Commission in Geneva.

The litany of double standards exhibited at the U.N. Commission on Human Rights is long. At times, the flagrant hypocrisy is simply stunning.

In Geneva, I listened to countries defend Fidel Castro's Cuba where political dissent means incarceration. I hard countries defend Burma's military junta. I heard delegations defending the atrocities of Robert Mugabe in Zimbabwe where there is no free press and property is seized arbitrarily for political gain. Even North Korea's Kim Jong Il was defended by some.

The deliberations and the Commission on Human Rights were an international puzzle palace of mirrors that did not reflect the real world where too many people are denied their basic human rights. In some ways the UNCHR, year after year, exhibited the worst distortions and double standards of the entire U.N. system.

The UNCHR had 54 members elected by regional groups. Oppressive regimes aggressively sought seats on the Commission. Once on they formed a coalition of similar governments that violated human rights. Together they formed an axis of the oppressors, a coalition of bad actors intent on protecting one another. This group, coupled by neighboring states and those who oppose any naming and shaming, often could form sufficient numbers to stop resolutions that highlighted abuse and held the abusers to some account. Therefore Mugabe's Zimbabwe, Moscow's actions in Chechnya, Beijing's religious persecution and censorship, and many others escaped rebuke year after year. But to capture the parallel reality at the U.N. Commission on Human Rights, I will review in some detail the cases of Cuba and of Sudan at the 2004 meeting in Geneva.

The 60th Session of the U.N. Commission on Human Rights, witnessed outrageous acts of intimidation, threats and aggression on the part of the Cuban delegation.

Early on, when a member of the U.S. delegation, Luis Zùniga, was speaking, the Cubans called for a point of order and in highly personal and abusive language tried to shout him down. At that point, in my capacity as head of the U.S. delegation, I took the floor and declared "Mr. Chairman, please remind the Cuban delegations that we are in Geneva and not Havana."

There was much more of this sort of outlandish behavior.

During the second week of the meeting, a member of the U.S. delegation was threatened by a member of the Cuban delegation with the words, "You know you will pay a high toll for what you are doing, and we will be the ones to do it."

The next week, a U.S. delegate, while distributing copies of a newspaper article to interested attendees of the Commission, was approached in the commission chamber by a member of the Cuban delegation who demanded to know what he was distributing and ripped the copies of the article from his hands. A U.N. guard had to restrain the Cuban delegate.

In a third incident, a member of our delegation was jogging on the streets of Geneva on a Saturday when a van pulled up and a member of the Cuban delegation leaned out and told the delegate that he "better watch out, we're keeping an eye on you." Others also reported being threatened by members of the Cuban delegation.

Just minutes after approval of a resolution critical of the continuing abuse of human rights by Fidel Castro's regime, many people witnessed a member of the Cuban delegation attack from behind a representative of an American-based organization in the lobby just outside the commission chambers. The victim, Frank Calzón, was hit in the head and knocked to the floor. U.N. security guards had to physically subdue the Cuban delegate. Cuban Ambassador Jorge Mora Godoy's comment on this outrageous behavior was that the victim deserved what he got.

A U.N. spokesman said that the Cuban delegate's behavior was "shocking and unacceptable." Yes, it was unacceptable, but it should not be shocking.

But even more disheartening was the failure of the Commission to adequately address the vicious ethnic violence and abuse in Darfur, Sudan.

Early on during the Commission meeting, I met with Irish Ambassador Mary Whelan in her capacity as chair of the European Union. We reviewed the Commission agenda and various initiatives on both thematic and country specific resolutions, comparing notes on strategy and who would take the lead on which resolutions. Among those on which the EU wanted to take the lead was Sudan where the ethnic fighting has reached alarming levels. With many other resolution on which the United States would be taking the lead, I was happy to tell Ambassador Whelan that we'd agree with her suggestions on the division of labor including allowing the European Union to take the lead on Sudan. However, I told her how important the United States viewed the brutal behavior in Sudan and that we would be a co-sponsor on the Sudan resolution. It was vital, I told her, that we condemn the on-going ethnic cleansing in the strongest possible terms.

As the weeks of the Commission session went on, I'd receive reports on those resolutions on which we were not taking the lead including Sudan. The Sudanese Ambassador was taking a rigid stand against any resolution. Even some of the African Commission members were uncomfortable with that.

Then during the third week of the Session, U.N. Secretary General Kofi Annan traveled to Geneva to address the Commission on Human Rights during a Special Day of Remembrance on the tenth anniversary of the genocide in Rwanda when Hutu's killed 800,000 Tutsis, mostly with machetes, during a 100-day rampage of horror. Near the end of his speech, the Secretary General said we must address the "ethnic cleansing" currently going on in Darfur, Sudan where 30,000 blacks already had been killed by the Arab government and Arab militias and where over 900,000 blacks were internally displaced in desperate conditions due to Arab violence.

The Secretary General's words had a profound affect on the Commission members, especially African states. They began to pressure the Sudanese to accept some sort of a resolution on the situation on Darfur.

During the fifth week of the Commission Session, the EU Chair, Ambassador Whelan, and African representatives began to meet to see if a compromise was possible. At one point near the end of the week I met with a group of Africans and then with the Europeans. I made clear that the draft I had been shown was unacceptable. Any resolution must "condemn" the ethnic cleansing that was going on; must "demand" the violence against the black Sudanese stop immediately; must "require" the Government of Sudan allow international humanitarian assistance to flow to the distressed population; and must "call" on the Government to allow immediate and unrestricted access to Darfur by international observers including a rapporteur from the UNCHR. This was the minimum. The United States would not join in supporting anything less.

Apparently Ambassador Whelan met with African representatives over the weekend. On Tuesday, my delegation was told that negotiations had broken down. The original resolution would come to a vote later in the week. Some countries sympathetic to Sudan, including some Africans, nonetheless felt the Commission could not be silent while ethnic cleansing was going on in Sudan. Therefore a number of African delegations informed us that they would vote to condemn Sudan when the tabled resolution came before the Commission. Our count showed that while it would be a close vote, the Sudan resolution would pass. Human Rights Watch and several other NGOs did their own whip counts and agreed that the resolution would pass.

The delegations gathered in the U.N. chamber on Thursday morning for the 10:00 a.m. opening gavel. The vote on Sudan was scheduled for that morning. Then at 9:45 a.m. a number of African delegations approach Ambassador Whelan on the floor with a last minute proposal for a "Chairman's Statement" on Sudan. In a matter of minutes, without consulting any other delegation, the Irish Ambassador agreed to the deal in her capacity as EU Chair. Delegations were informed that there would be no vote that day on the pending Sudan resolution.

During the lunch break, we saw the proposed compromise. None of the four required elements were contained in the draft accepted by the Irish Ambassador in behalf of the European Union. After consulting with Washington, I went to a 2:00 p.m. meeting hosted by the Irish for non-EU co-sponsors of the original Sudan resolution that had been tabled earlier. The Irish delegation walked through the text, acknowledged that it was far softer than what had been tabled and beyond what many countries had said they could accept, however, it was important to get African "buy in" to any action and this language accomplished that goal. Furthermore, consensus was a vital U.N. principle, and this language could provide consensus.

When the Irish had finished giving their rationale, I took the floor to state clearly and strongly the United States government's position on the "ethnic cleansing" in Sudan. Consequently, there would be no "consensus" on this compromise because my delegation would not support it. And if it were introduced as a resolution, the United States would vote no. I was followed by the Canadian, then the Australian, and then the New Zealander. Each agreed with me and expressed profound disappointment with the Irish for caving to this weak proposal and for failing to consult with the resolutions co-sponsors before committing the European Union to the deal. Then a Czech representative began to make similar remarks. At that the Irish chair of the meeting tapped the table and said to the Czech, "You are out of order. Your comments should be held for a European Union meeting and discussion on this topic. They are not appropriate at this meeting or at this time." Signs of things to come as the EU bloc further organizes and disciplines its members within the United Nations.

There followed a frantic flurry of consultations over the next 24 hours. In the end, the United States forced a vote on the original resolution. While it had the votes 48 hours earlier, in the end some fell off because now they could vote for the weaker EU language. The muscular resolution condemning "ethnic cleansing" in Sudan failed. Later, the emasculated EU language passed which did not "condemn," did not "demand" and did not "call" on the Sudanese Government to do anything; but which noted their cooperation, etc. The United States voted against this retreat.

So the failure of the Commission on Human Rights to deal with the ethnic cleansing in Sudan in a clear, straightforward, muscular fashion was ugly. Indeed, ten years from now I suspect the failure to act appropriately on genocide in Sudan will be the only thing for which the 60th Session of the U.N. Commission on Human Rights will be remembered.

REFORM

So while the United Nations has demonstrated a unique capacity to legitimize human rights norms, its performance at rebuking abusers of human rights has been sketchy at best. It has brought dishonor onto the U.N. and eroded its standing. As Mark Mallock Brown, the new United Nations Deputy Secretary-General, has said, "For the great global public, the performance or non-performance of the Human Rights Commission has become the litmus test for U.N. renewal."

The High Level Panel established by Kofi Annan in 2004 to offer reform proposals suggested sweeping changes, among them abolishing of the Commission and creation of a U.N. Human Rights Council with a dramatic reduction in membership and minimal criteria to help keep off states that trample human rights.[88] In the spring of 2005, the Secretary-General offered his own thoughts on U.N. reform including an endorsement for the sort of changes in the Human Rights machinery outlined in the High Level Panel report.[89]

Many months of negotiations followed. In the end the human rights reforms were far more modest than the Secretary-General had called for and that the United States and many others had hoped for. The Commission was abolished and a new Human Rights Council was created. It will exist year round rather than just a spring session, enabling it to address gross human rights violations when they arise. Membership elections will be in the General Assembly, no longer solely by regional groups therefore making it marginally more difficult for repressive regimes to get elected. The size has been cut slightly, from a 54 member Commission to a 47 member Council. And the Council has the responsibility to monitor member states' human rights records and kick-off abusers.

The newly constituted U.N. Human Rights Council is an improvement over the discredited Commission. Are the reforms adopted adequate to guarantee significant improvement? No. It will be a work in progress, an evolving and difficult process. The United States Government was one of only four countries to vote against final passage. Furthermore, the United States recently announced it will not be a candidate for the new Council. This will mark only the second time in the 57 years since adoption of the U.N. Universal Declaration on Human Rights that the United States will be on the sidelines of the U.N.'s premier human rights body.[90] Is that wise? I think not.

The United States should seek to serve on the Human Rights Council because, as I've said, human rights are central to the American idea. Second, advancing those inalienable rights to all mankind is our opportunity and our responsibility. Third, advancing human rights – including democracy – are in America's self-interest. Countries that share our values are our natural friends and allies. Fourth, it is not in the U.S. interest to isolate itself whether in the U.N. or more generally. Fifth, by shunning this new effort to promote human rights we have needlessly offended friends, allies and others truly committed to making it work. And sixth, despite the contrary views of some, my experience teaches me that the United States would have been best able to influence the course of the new Human Rights Council as a full, active member totally engaged in fashioning its new processes, procedures and precedents rather than as an aloof critic outside. This is an opportunity missed; a responsibility not met.

CONCLUSION

In conclusion, let me state that human rights are inalienable and profoundly important. The United Nations, especially in the area of norm setting, has contributed substantially in advancing human rights in the modern world despite many setbacks. And the United States, founded on principles of fundamental freedoms and self-evident rights, and for whom values and ideals are central to our national identity, has a responsibility to advance human rights. The United Nations, among other things, provides America with an opportunity to do so.

1.   "Centuries of Western reforms advancing individual rights in the national level preceded the first international human rights initiatives.. The English Magna Carta and Bill of Rights, the United States Declaration of Independence and Constitution, and the French Declaration of the Rights of Man and the Citizens all contributed to the Western tradition of individual civil and political rights. Shamed by their own violations of these rights in Africa, Europeans convened meetings and drafted conventions to suppress the slave trade. Mistreatment of Christians in Turkey, programs against Jews in Russia, and violations of religious liberties in Spain generated increasing pressure for humanitarian intervention and improved forms of international protection. European wars produced the most important efforts to safeguard individual rights. Following the Napoleonic wars, the Treaty of Vienna guaranteed religious liberties and civil rights for citizens of the projected union between Belgium and Holland. In 1878 The Treaty of Berlin recognized the rights of certain minorities. Various Geneva Conventions adopted after 1863 authorized the Red Cross to provide humanitarian relief to combatants and civilians during war.

"The 1919 Versailles Treaty concluding World War I created the first permanent mechanisms for international supervision of human rights violations. The 1919 Treaty established a mandates system for governing territories taken from the German and Ottoman Empires. Administering powers accepted, as a "sacred trust," responsibility for the well-being and development of subject peoples. Individuals both within and without the trust territories could petition the League Council to redress grievances through a Permanent Mandates Commission. For the first time some nation states became regularly accountable for an international body for mistreatment of individuals subject to their rule. The Treaty also established the International Labour Organization (ILO), a tripartite body of government, employer, and worker representatives. The ILO was empowered to draft conventions protecting specific worker rights, such as minimum age and maximum hours, for implementation by the permanent staff of The International Labour Office. Under Treaty provisions comprising the League of Nations Covenant states promised 'to endeavor to secure and maintain fair and humane conditions of labor for men, women and children." Howard Tolley, Jr.; *The U.N. Commission on Human Rights*, (Boulder, Colorado; Westview Press; 1987), pp. 1-2.

Note also: "The fundamental elements of what today are seen as human rights were given essential and lasting impetus by the growth of the common law and English democratic institutions, the American Revolution and the French Revolution. It was not until the anti-slavery movement of the 19th Century gathered strength, and the beginnings of the law of war were introduced by The Hague Conventions as that century closed that concerns for human rights moved on to the international plane. The introduction of an international law of human rights was a 20th Century innovation." Stephen M. Schwebel, Forward to Anne F. Bayefsky, *How to Complain to the U.N. Human Rights Treaty System* (Ardsley; New York; Transnational Publishers, Inc.; 2002), p. xi.

2.   C.P. McPherson, ed., *John Locke Second Treatise of Government* (Indianapolis, Indiana; Hackett Publishing Co.; 1980).

3.   Jack Donnelly, *Universal Human Rights* (Ithaca, New York; Cornell University Press; 1989), p. 64.

4.   "In *Two Treatises of Government* (John Locke) has two purposes in view: to refute the doctrine of the divine and absolute right of the Monarch, as it had been put forward by Robert Filmer's *Patriarcha*, and to establish a theory which would reconcile the liberty of the citizen with political order... Behind (Locke's) doctrines lies the idea of the independence of the individual person. The state of nature knows no government; but in it, as in political society, men are subject to the moral law, which is the law of God. Men are born free and equal in rights. Whatever a man 'mixes his labor with' is his to use. Or, at least, this was so in the primitive condition of human life in which there was enough for all and "the whole earth was beyond those which the moral law or law of nature supplies. But the origin of government is traced not to this economic necessity, but to another cause. The moral law is always valid, but it is not always kept. In the state of nature all men equally have the right to punish transgressors: civil society originates when, for the better administration of the law, men agree to delegate this function to certain officers. Thus government is instituted by a "social contract"; its powers are limited, and they involve reciprocal obligations; moreover, they can be modified or rescinded by the authority which conferred them." "John Locke (1632-1704)," *The Internet Encyclopedia of Philosophy*, available at http://www.utm.edu/research/iep/l/locke.htm.

5.   Amartya Sen, "Human Rights and Asian Values," *The New Republic*, July 14-21, 1997.

6.   *Ibid.* Note also, Confucius said that "an oppressive government is worse than a tiger." Robert Traer,

Faith in Human Rights (Washington, D.C.; Georgetown University Press, 1991), p. 160.

7.   Shasi Tharoor, "Are Human Rights Universal?" *World Policy Journal*, Vol. XVI, No. 4 (Winter 1999/2000).

8.   Susan Waltz, "On the Universality of Human Rights," *The Journal of the International Institute* (The University of Michigan) available at http://www.umich.edu/-iinet/journal/vol6no3/waltz.htm.

9.   David Little, *ibid.*

10.   See, Wing Thye Wood, Jeffrey D. Sachs and Klaus Schwab, ed., *The Asian Financial Crisis: Lessons for a Resilient Asia* (Cambridge, Mass.; The MIT Press; 2000).

11.   Linda Y. C. Lim, "The Asian Economic Crisis: The Challenges for Government Policy Business Practices," The Asian Society, February 1999.   Available at http://www.asiasociety.org/publications/update_crisis_lim.html.

12.   See, Frank Ching, "The Asian Economic Crisis: Social Impact of the Regional Financial Crisis," *ibid.*   "[E]ven while the social impact of the financial crisis thus far has already been huge, it is likely to increase even greater social costs, in terms of unemployment and, potentially, social instability."

13.   See, for example, Amy Waldman, "In India, Economic Growth and Democracy Do Mix," *New York Times*, May 23, 2004.

14.   Amarty Sen, *ibid.*   See also, Amartya Sen, *Development as Freedom* (New York, New York; Anchor Books; 1999).

15.   Gerald P. O'Driscoll, Jr., Edwin J. Feulner and Mary Anastasia O'Grady, *2003 Index of Economic Freedom* (Washington, D.C.; The Heritage Foundation and The Wall Street Journal; 2004), pp. 2-3.

16.   Amarty Sen, *ibid.*

17.   See, Andrew S. Natsios, *The Great North Korean Famine: Famine, Politics, and Foreign Policy* (Washington, D.C.; United States Institute of Peace Press; 2001).   North Korea's "devastating famine threatens millions with starvation. Severe restriction on public debate within the country led to disastrous economic policies, precluded a clear understanding of the extent of the problem and undermined effective international and national responses." Human Rights Watch, *World Report 1998*.

18.   "The universality of human rights came under sustained attack… governments seeking to justify their authoritarian conduct found it convenient to challenge universality, usually in circumstances in which their repression precluded rebuttal by the people in whose name they claimed to speak." Human Rights Watch, *World Report 1998*.

19.   Shashi Tharoor, *ibid.*

20.   See generally, Eric D. Weitz, *A Century of Genocide: Utopias of Race and Nation* (Princeton, N. J.; Princeton University Press; 2003); and Jonathan Glover, *Humanity: A Moral History of the Twentieth Century* (New Haven, Conn.; Yale University Press; 1999).

21.   "The 'human rights revolution,' which occurred after World War II with the adoption of the human rights documents and instruments, came about not primarily as the result of a new enthusiasm for Western liberal philosophy, or even of Western international hegemony at the time.   It came about primarily as a widespread, profound and indubitable moral revulsion to what the preamble of the Universal Declaration calls, "barbarous acts which have outraged the conscience" of humankind.   These were, of course, the atrocities committed systematically in the name of Japanese and German fascism. The assumption is that any self-respecting human being would be similarly shocked and revolted by such a spectacle. Indeed, such a reaction becomes a mark of what it means to be a self-respecting human being." David Little, *ibid.*.

22.   See, David P. Chandler, *The Tragedy of Cambodian History: Politics, War and Revolution since 1945* (New Haven, Conn.; Yale University Press; 1991), and Ben Kiernan, *The Pol Pot Regime: Race, Power; and Genocide in Cambodia under the Khmer Rouge, 1975-79* (New Haven, Conn.; Yale University Press; 1996).

23.   "Ten years ago this April, the most focused, intense and efficient campaign of genocide in modern history took place in Rwanda.   In the space of a few months, 800,000 Tutsis and tens of thousands of Hutus died in an orchestrated campaign of violence organized by Hutu extremists. Everyone from church workers to children became murderers.   The killings even pitted members of the same family against one another." Lyle Rexer, "My Nightmare, My Neighbor," *New York Times*, May 23, 2004. See, Bill Berkeley, "Road to Genocide," in Nicholas Mills and Kira Brunner, eds., *The New Killing Fields: Massacre and the Politics of Intervention*; (New York, New York; Basic Books; 2002), pp. 103-116; Michael Barnett,

Eyewitness to a Genocide: The United Nations and Rwanda (Ithaca, New York; Cornell University Press; 2002); Linda McIvern, *A People Betrayed: The Role of the West in Rwanda's Genocide* (New York, New York; Zed Books; 2000); Philip Gourevitch, *We Wish to Inform You That Tomorrow We Will Be Killed with Our Families* (New York, New York; Farrar, Straus, and Giroux; 1998); Alex Destexhe, *Rwanda and Genocide in the Twentieth Century* (New York, New York; New York University Press; 1995); and Samantha Powers, *A Problem from Hell: America and the Age of Genocide* (New York, New York; Basic Books; 2002).

24.   See David Rieff, *Slaughterhouse: Bosnia and the Failure of the West* (New York, New York; Simon and Schuster; 1995); Jan Willem Honig and Norbert Both, *Srebrenica* (Harmondsworth, U.K.; Penguin; 1996); Elizabeth Neuffer, *The Key to My Neighbor's House: Seeking Justice in Bosnia and Rwanda* (New York; New York; Picador USA; 2001); and David Rohde, *Endgame, The Betrayal and Fall of Srebrenica, Europe's Worst Massacre since World War II* (New York, New York; Farrar, Straus & Giroux; 1997).

25.   See, William Shawcross, *Deliver Us From Evil: Peacekeepers, Warlords and a World of Endless Conflict* (New York, New York; Simon & Schuster; 2000), and David Halberstam, *War in a Time of Peace: Bush, Clinton, and the Generals* (New York, New York; Scribner; 2001).

26.   Okey Ejidike, "Universality and Relativity in the African Human Rights Discourse," *Student Human Rights Law Centre* (Nottingham University), Vol. 1, No. 3, June 20, 1996. Available at http://www.nottingham.ac.uk/law/hrlc/hrnews/june96/okey.htm.

27.   George P. Shultz, "Human Rights and the Moral Dimension of U.S. Foreign Policy," an address at the 86th Annual Washington Day Banquet at the Creve Coeur Club of Illinois, Peoria, Illinois, February 22, 1984, published as Current Policy No. 551 by the United States Department of State Bureau of Public Affairs, Washington, D.C. 1984.

28.   Woodrow Wilson, Annual Message to Congress on the State of the Union, December 2, 1913, in Arthur S. Link, ed., *The Papers of Woodrow Wilson* (Princeton, N.J.; Princeton University Press; 1966), Vol. 29, p. 4.

29.   Woodrow Wilson, Remarks to Confederate Veterans in Washington, June 5, 1917, in *ibid*, Vol. 42, p. 453. Later President Wilson said, "[B]ecause we demand unmolested development and the undisturbed government of our own lives upon our own principles of right and liberty, we resent, from whatever quarter it may come, the aggression we ourselves will not practice. We insist upon security in prosecuting our self-chosen line of national development. We do more than that. We demand it also for others. We do not confine our enthusiasm for individual liberty and the free national development to the incidents and movements of affairs which affect only ourselves. We feel it wherever there is a people that tries to walk in these difficult paths of independence and right." Woodrow Wilson, Annual Message to Congress on the State of the Union, December 7, 1915, in *ibid*., Vol. 35, p. 297.

30.   In his speech asking Congress for a declaration of war, Wilson said, "It is a fearful thing to lead this great peaceful people into war, into the most terrible and disastrous of all wars, civilization itself seems to be in the balance. But right is more precious than peace and we shall fight for the things which we have always carried nearest our hearts, for democracy, for the right of those who submit to authority to have a voice in their own governments, for the rights and liberties of small nations, for a universal dominion of rights by such a concert of free peoples as shall bring peace and safety to all nations and make the world itself at last free." Woodrow Wilson, An Address to a Joint Session of Congress, April 2, 1917, in *ibid*., Vol. 41, pp. 526-27.

31.   Woodrow Wilson, An Address to the Senate, January 22, 1917, in *ibid*., Vol. 40, pp. 536-37.

32.   Woodrow Wilson, An Address Before the League to Enforce Peace, May 27, 1916, in *ibid*., Vol. 37, pp. 113. See also, Arthur Walworth, *Wilson and the Peacemakers: American Diplomacy at the Peace Conference*, 1919 (New York; W.W. Norton & Company; 1986).

33.   President George W. Bush, Remarks at Whitehall Palace, Royal Banqueting House-Whitehall Palace, London, England, November 19, 2003.

34.   Richard Schifter, "The United States Government's Commitment to Human Rights," in Howard J. Wiarda, ed., *Human Rights and U.S. Human Rights Policy*, (Washington, D.C.; American Enterprise Institute; 1982), p. 53.

35.   *The Public Papers and Addresses of Franklin D. Roosevelt*, 1938-1940, Vol. 9 (Washington, D.C.; 1969), p. 672.

36.   As quoted in Mary Ann Glendon, *A World Made New: Eleanor Roosevelt and the Universal Declaration of Human Rights* (New York; Random House; 2001), pp. 10-11.

37. Iris Chang, *The Rape of Nanking: The Forgotten Holocaust of World War II* (New York; Viking Penguin, USA; 1998).

38. Issued in August 1945, the Nuremberg Principles state that "to wage a war of aggression was a crime against international society and that to persecute, oppress, or do violence to individuals or minorities on political, racial, or religious grounds in connection with such a war, or to exterminate, enslave, or deport civilian populations, was a crime against humanity."

39. *The Public Papers and Addresses of Franklin D. Roosevelt*, 1943 (New York; Random House; 1950), p. 503.

40. Radio Address of December 24, 1945, quoted in Townsend Hoope and Douglas Brinkley, *FDR and the Creation of the U.N.* (New Haven, Conn.; Yale University Press; 1997), p. 108.

41. See, Robert C. Hildebrand, *Dumbarton Oaks: The Origins the United Nations and the Search for Postwar Security* (Chapel Hill, N.C.; University of North Carolina Press; 1990). The Dumbarton Oakes Proposals only a brief reference to the promotion of human rights as one of the General Assembly's activities. It read, "With a view to the creation of conditions of stability and well-being which are necessary for peaceful and friendly relations among nations, the Organization should facilitate solutions of international economic, social, and other humanitarian problems and promote respect for human rights and fundamental freedoms." Chapter IX, Sec. A(1) of the Dumbarton Oaks Proposals, U.S. Department of State, *Dumbarton Oaks Documents on International Organization*, Publication 2192 (1944), p. 19. In contrast the political and security purposes of the new organization were stressed with careful particularity.

42. Edward R. Stettinias, Jr., *Roosevelt and the Russians* (New York; Doubleday; 1949), p. 321.

43. See generally, Stephen C. Schlesinger, *Act of Creation: The Founding of the United Nations* (Boulder, Colo.; Westview Press; 2003).

44. For example, eventually the Soviets agreed to the United Nations reluctantly. At the time George F. Kennan served in the U.S. Embassy in Moscow. Later he wrote, "Insofar as Stalin attached importance to the concept of a future international organization, he did so in the expectation that the organization would serve as the instrument for maintenance of a U.S.-U.K.-Soviet hegemony in international affairs." George F. Kennan *Memoirs 1925 - 1950* (Boston; Little, Brown; 1967), p. 216-17.

45. See generally, Mary Ann Glendon, *ibid.*, pp. 2-20.

46. "The Covenant of the League of Nations reflected the very limited international concern with human rights… The drafters of the Covenant were preoccupied with the maintenance of security, the pacific settlement of disputes, the establishment of a mandates system for former German and Ottoman territories, and the protection of minorities in Central Europe. …It would appear from the records of the Paris Peace Conference and of the League of Nations that member governments continued to feel that international law covered relations between states and not the relation of the citizen to the state." James Frederick Green, *The United Nations and Human Rights* (Washington, D.C.; Brookings Institution Press; 1956), pp. 8-9.

It is noteworthy that the U.S. Senate Foreign Relations Committee's fourth reservation to the Covenant of the League of Nations, read "The United States reserves to itself exclusively the right to decide what questions are within its domestic jurisdiction and declares that all domestic and political questions relating wholly or in part to its internal affairs, including immigration, labor, coastwise traffic, the tariff, commerce, the suppression of traffic in women and children and in opium and other dangerous drugs, and all other domestic questions, are solely within the jurisdiction of the United States and are not under this treaty to be submitted in any way either to arbitration or to the consideration of the Council or of the Assembly of the League of Nations, or any agency thereof, or to the decision or recommendation of any other power." President Wilson refused to accept this reservation. *Congressional Record*, Vol. 59, Pt. 5, 66 Cong. 2 sess., p. 4599.

47. Ruth B. Russell, *A History of the United Nations Charter: The Role of the United States 1940 - 1945* (Washington, D.C.; The Brookings Institution Press; 1958), pp. 326-327.

48. *United Nations Actions in the Field of Human Rights*, U.N. publication, No. E.83.XIV.2, p. 8. "Chile suggested that Chapter I of the Charter include a provision that every state must guarantee: complete protection of individual freedom; the right to live and work; freedom of religion, profession, science, and art; and freedom of the press and information. Cuba proposed that Chapter II of the Charter provide that the Members conform their acts to the principles contained in a Declaration of Rights and Duties of Nations" and "Declaration of the International Duties and Rights of the individual, which the General Assembly should adopt… Panama went even further by suggesting that a 'Declaration of Essential Human

Rights' be appended as an integral of the Charter. The draft declaration... provided for such matters as: freedom of religion, opinion, speech, assembly and association; freedom from wrongful interference with person, home, reputation, privacy, activities, and property; freedom from arbitrary detention and retroactive laws," the right to a fair trial and the right to own property; the right to education; and the right to work, to reasonable conditions of work, and to social security. Each article provided, correspondingly, that the state had an obligation to assure the right or freedom." James Frederick Green, *ibid*, pp. 16-17; citing U.N. Information Organization and U.S. Library of Congress, *Documents of the United Nations Conference on International Organization*, Vol. 6 (1945), pp. 545-49, p. 560.

49.   "In earlier usage, the word 'right' had a legal connotation: the individual had an 'inalienable' right to life, for example, and he could not be deprived of that right by the state without due process of law. Today, the word 'right' also has the connotation of a goal: for example, the individual has the right to a free education, which the state is expected to provide." James Frederick Green, *The United Nations and Human Rights* (Washington, D.C.; Brookings Institute Press; 1956), p. 3.

50.   Preamble, U.N. Charter: "...to save succeeding generations from the scourge of war, which twice in our lifetime has brought untold sorrow to mankind, and to reaffirm our faith in fundamental human rights, in the dignity and worth of the human person, in the equal rights of men and women and of nations large and small, and to establish conditions under which justice and respect for the obligations arising under treaties and other sources of international law can be maintained..."

51.   U.S. Department of State, *Bulletin*, Vol. 19 (October 3, 1948), p. 432.

52.   The question of "state sovereignty" still is a topic of keen interest and debate.   In discussing international interventions in Kosovo and East Timor, in 1999 UN Secretary General Kofi Annan said, "state sovereignty, in its most basic sense, is being redefined... States are now widely understood to be instruments at the service of their people, and not vice versa... [while] individual sovereignty -- by which I mean the fundamental freedom of each individual, enshrined in the Charter of the United Nations and subsequent international treaties -- has been enhanced by a renewed and spreading consciousness of individual rights." Kofi Annan, "Two Concepts of Sovereignty," *The Economist*, September 18, 1999.

Along the same lines, Professors Michael Doyle and Anne-Marie Gardner have written, there is "a serious tension between increasingly influential global principles, on the one hand, and the practical difficulty, on the other hand, of implementing them in the face of states reluctant either to abide by the principles of human rights or to commit the resources needed to give those principles impartial and general effect when they are violated." Michael W. Doyle and Anne-Marie Gardner, "Introduction: Human Rights and International Order," in Jean-Marc Coicaud, Michael W. Doyle and Anne-Marie Gardner, ed.s, *The Globalization of Human Rights* (New York, New York; United nations University Press; 2003), p. 1.

And, in 2000, Kofi Annan wrote, "Emerging slowly, but, I believe, surely, is an international norm against gross violations of human rights that will and must take precedence over concerns of state sovereignty. It is a principle that protects minorities -- and majorities -- from gross violations... No government has the right to hide behind national sovereignty in order to violate the human rights or fundamental freedoms of its peoples. Whether a person belongs to the minority or the majority, that person's human rights and fundamental freedoms are sacred." Kofi Annan "Human Rights and Humanitarian Intervention in the Twenty-First Century," in Samantha Power and Graham Allison, eds., *Realizing Human Rights: Moving from Inspiration to Impact* (New York, New York; St. Martin's Press, 2000), pp. 309, 310-311. See also Robert F. Drinan, *The Mobilization of Shame: A World View of Human Rights* (West Haven, Conn.); Yale University Press, 2001), pp. 3-121.

53.   United Nations Charter, Article 2(7).   The Chapter VII exception permitting U.N. intervention requires a Security Council resolution determining that international peace and security are threatened. Since the five permanent members have the power to veto any proposed Security Council measure, they were protected from any U.N. infringement of their sovereignty.

54.   Secretary of State Edward Stettinus held a meeting with several American NGOs shortly before final negotiations on the U.N. Charter in which the Joint Committee for Religious Liberty, the American Jewish Committee, the NAACP and others pleaded their case for elaboration of human rights. At the end of the meeting, Secretary Stettinus agreed to a Human Rights Commission. This pivotal meeting is discussed in a number of books including O. Frederick Nolde, *Free and Equal: Human Rights in Ecumenical Perspective* (Geneva; World Council of Churches; 1968), pp. 22-24; M. Glen Johnson, "The Contributions of Eleanor and Franklin Roosevelt to the Development of International Protection for Human Rights," 9 *Human Rights Quarterly* 26 (1987), p. 26; and Glendon, *ibid*., p. 17.

55.   United Nations Charter, Article 68.

56.   Harry Truman, *Truman Speaks*, Cyril Clemens, ed. (New York; Kraus Reprint, 1969), p. 56.

57.   Among the prominent Americans on the first U.S. delegation to the U.N. were Senators Thomas Connelly and Arthur Vandenberg, respectively the chairman and ranking minority member of the Senate Foreign Relations Committee, Secretary of State James F. Byrnes, and Edward Stettinius, the former Secretary of State who played such a major role in launching the U.N. and would be the first U.S. ambassador to the United Nations. See Stephen C. Schlesinger, *Act of Creation: The Founding of the United Nations* (Boulder, Colorado, Westview Press, 2003). Republican lawyer John Foster Dulles who had served as Thomas E. Dewey's foreign policy advisor and later would serve as President Eisenhower's Secretary of State was an Alternate Delegate.

58.   At the first meeting of the United Nations General Assembly, Panama had sought immediate passage of a declaration on human rights. Eleanor Roosevelt had it referred to the new Human Rights Commission. Howard Tolley, Jr., *The U.N. Commission on Human Rights* (Boulder, Colorado; Westview Press; 1987), p. 19.

59.   Among the United Nations fora addressing human rights issues are the General Assembly, the Economic and Social Council and subsidiary bodies, the Commission on Human Rights, the Sub-Commission on Prevention of Discrimination and Protection of Minorities, the Commission on the Status of Women, the Committee on the Elimination of Racial Discrimination, the Human Rights Committee, the Committee on Economic, Social and Cultural Rights, the Committee on the Elimination of Discrimination Against Women and the Committee Against Torture.

60.   Cuba and Panama introduced proposals for the preparation of a bill of rights at the first U.N. General Assembly in 1945. In the end the General Assembly transmitted the Panamanian proposal to the Economic and Social Council for consideration by the Commission on Human Rights.

61.   Mrs. Roosevelt, as chairperson, appointed the member of the Committee with the approval of the U.N. Economic and Social Council.

62.   See generally, Glendon, *ibid.* The United Kingdom proposed a convention and introduced a draft text. The Indians advocated protection for individual victims. Australia proposed creating an International Court of Human Rights. Meanwhile, the Soviet Union took the position that only sovereign national institutions could enforce the enumerated rights. And the Chinese delegate suggested a three stage approach: first a declaration, then a convention, and third implementation measures. See Howard Tolley, Jr., *ibid.*, p. 21. See also, John Humphrey, *ibid.*, pp. 27, 40.

63.   Since adoption of the Universal Declaration of Human Rights there have been more than 50 other detailed documents, declarations and conventions that further elaborate international human rights principles.

64.   While the British had proposed only civil and political rights in their daft convention, the United States was willing to consider going further. President Roosevelt had advocated the "freedom of want" in his 1941 State of the Union address that identified the four basic freedoms.

    On January 11, 1944, President Roosevelt further elaborated his view in a message he sent to Congress that stated in part, "We have come to a clear realization of the fact that true individual freedom cannot exist without economic security and independence... In our day those economic truths have become accepted as self-evident. We have accepted, so to speak, a second Bill of Rights under which a new basis of security and prosperity can be established for all regardless of station, race, or creed. Among these are: The right to a useful and remunerative job in the industries, or shops, or farms, or mines of the Nation; The right to earn enough to provide adequate food and clothing and recreation; The right of every farmer to raise and sell his products at a return which will give him and his family a decent living; The right of every businessman, large and small, to trade in an atmosphere of freedom from unfair competition and domination by monopolies at home or abroad; The right of every family to a decent home; The right to adequate medical care and the opportunity to achieve and enjoy good health; The right to adequate protection from the economic fears of old age, sickness, accident and unemployment; The right to a good education." *Congressional Record*, Vol. 90, Pt. 1, 78 Cong. 2 sess., p. 57.

    Furthermore, it was reasoned, "since the Declaration would not have the same legal effect as a convention, the drafters could include provisions for economic., social and cultural rights of a non-justicable character. ...Of the twenty-five articles in the final Declaration, only six refer to economic, social and cultural rights." Howard Tolley, Jr., *ibid.*, p. 21-22. In the end, the U.N. Universal Declaration of Human Rights does include free public education (Article 26); food, clothing, housing, medical care and necessary social services (Article 25); the right to work (Article 23); and to paid holidays (Article 24).

65.   Principles of civil and political rights of the individual were well established in the Western world. The English Magna Carta and Bill of Rights of 1689, the American Declaration of Independence, the French Declaration of the Rights of Man and other bills of rights and constitutional provisions had secured

basic rights of the civilian.

66.   See, Howard Tolley, Jr., *ibid.*, p. 21. Note, as a result of the clash on individual property rights versus community needs, the American Bar Association raised concerns about state socialism and urged delay of adopting the declaration of human rights. American Bar Association, "Declaration on Human Rights: Canadian, American Bars Ask for Delay of Action," *ABA Journal* 34 (October, 1948), pp. 881, 885.

67.   Giving further impetus to the U.N.'s work, the American Declaration of the Rights and Duties of Man was adopted by the Ninth International Conference of American States, held at Bogotá in March-May 1948.

68.   However, eight member states abstained including the Soviet Union and South Africa.

69.   Article 3.

70.   Article 6.

71.   Article 13.

72.   Article 15.

73.   Article 18.

74.   Article 20.

75.   Article 21.

76.   Article 4.

77.   Article 5.

78.   Article 4.

79.   Article 19.

80.   Article 7.

81.   William F. Schulz, *In Our Own Best Interest: How Defending Human Rights Benefits Us All* (Boston Massachusetts; Beacon Press; 2001), p. 4.

82.   Mary Ann Glendon, *ibid.*, p. 236.

83.   *Ibid.*

84.   Quoted in U.N. Department of Social Affairs, *The Impact of the Universal Declaration of Human Rights*, Dec. ST/SOA/5/Rev. 1 (June 29, 1953), p.7.

85.   U.S. Department of State, *Bulletin*, Vol. 19 (December 19, 1948), p. 751.

86.   Howard Tolley, Jr., *ibid.*, p. 23.

87.   Robert F. Drinan, S.J., *ibid.*, p. ix.

88.   Report of the Secretary-General's High-Level Panel on Threats, Challenges and Change, *A More Secure World: Our Shared Responsibility* (2004).

89.   Kofi Annan, *In Larger Freedom – Towards Development Security and Human Rights* (2005).

90.   In 2002 the United States was limited to observer status at the UNCHR, having lost election for membership in an embarrassing diplomatic debacle.

It's Not Too Late To Stop 'Slow Motion' Genocide

More than three years ago, to deal with a small, incipient rebellion in Darfur, the Arab Sudanese government in Khartoum opened the gates of hell.

They armed Arab highwaymen and bandits known as the janjaweed. Then, in coordinated assaults led by government attack helicopters followed by janjaweed on camel and horseback, black villages were burned to the ground, crops destroyed, men killed, and women raped and branded. The violence was vicious, merciless and devastating.

Upwards to 400,000 blacks in Darfur have died. Some 2.3 million have been driven from their homes and live in desperate conditions in refugee camps in Southern Darfur and neighboring Chad. More recently the violence has bled into Chad claiming new victims and further destabilizing that nation.

This humanitarian disaster is man made. It continues, and it must end. Our humanity compels us to act. Yet as this "genocide in slow motion" has taken place, the international community has done little.

At last there has been a breakthrough. It represents the last, best hope to end the carnage. Yet the opportunity teeters on the brink of collapse unless robust action is taken now to sustain the momentum for peace.

In early May, a peace agreement on Darfur was hammered out in talks in Abuja, Nigeria. The African Union worked to midwife the deal. U.S. Deputy Secretary of State Bob Zoellick provided critical last minute negotiating, cajoling and pressure to bring the parties together.

Khartoum and the largest rebel group, the Sudan Liberation Army, agreed to a ceasefire and disarming the Janjaweed militias. Like most agreements to end fighting, this deal is imperfect. It is fragile. It may not hold. But it provides a ray of hope that this terrible torrent of tragedy finally might end.

The two smaller rebel groups have not signed the agreement. While the pact provides for Darfur to have greater political representation, Khartoum has broken similar commitments in the past. The deal calls for disarming the Janjaweed, but accomplishing this necessary step will prove very difficult if not impossible. And since the deal was signed, the horror has continued in Darfur. Blacks from Darfur continue to be killed. Women continued to be gang raped.

Appeared in the *Chicago Sun Times*, June 6, 2006.

Hussein Ahmed Abdulla's cooking wood was stolen and she was repeatedly raped 4 days after the cease-fire officially went into effect. As she was victimized, she reports that the janjaweed assailants cried out "You are slaves, we will finish you."

While these brutal assaults continue, there are mixed signals from government officials in Khartoum. For example, the government agreed to U.N. peacekeepers when they signed the treaty. But there already are reports of splits in the Barshir government with some saying that allowing U.N. peacekeepers will compromise Sudan's sovereignty.

Time is of the essence. Action is required to give momentum to this opportunity to end the carnage.

In February, the U.N. Security Council requested planning to begin for a U.N. Peacekeeping Mission to Darfur. That planning should be accelerated. A robust mandate to deal with any violent violations of the treaty must be adopted by the Council. And deployment of U.N. Peacekeepers must move swiftly.

To its credit, some time ago the African Union sent peacekeepers to Darfur to monitor events on the ground. But their number were few, their equipment limited and their mandate tightly limited to observe and report on violence, not stop it. To translate the words of the new peace accord into action on the ground, U.N. peacekeeper boots on the ground are required.

In March President Bush discussed a possible expansion of NATO's role in Sudan. If needed, NATO should be prepared to enforce a no-fly zone over Darfur to ensure that attack-helicopters no longer strafe villages and kill innocent civilians.

President Bush also has called for increased emergency humanitarian assistance for Darfur to alleviate the dreadful death, destruction and distress that continues.

Having again failed to meet our collective responsibilities to "never again" allow genocide to plague our planet, at least we should act now to seize this last best hope to end the killing in Darfur.

RESTORATIVE JUSTICE WHEN THE KILLING STOPS

As we see in Iraq, Afghanistan, the Democratic Republic of the Congo and elsewhere, the trials, tribulations and traumas of post-conflict societies do not end when the killing stops. Reconciliation, reconstruction and rejuvenation of torn societies is difficult. It can be expensive. It takes time. But, as we've seen in the Balkans, Sierra Leone and elsewhere, it can be done.

Rebels and militia must demobilize and disarm. Security and the rule of law must be re-established.[1] Infrastructures must be rebuilt, jobs created and economies reconstructed. And torn societies must begin the arduous task of reconciliation. Searing scars must be healed. Justice must be done.

Warfare continues to be too familiar. The horrors are ravaging. From genocide in Rwanda and Darfur, to ethnic cleansing in Bosnia and Kosovo; from mutilations in Sierra Leone to cannibalism in the eastern Democratic Republic of the Congo, the crimes are unimaginable. And brutal authoritarian regimes such as Saddam Hussein's in Iraq and the military juanta in Burma have committed massacres, torture and arbitrary arrest of their own people. The crimes are horrific. The human misery incomprehensible. And the legacy of devastation, destruction, and despair long lingers on.

For the victims, it doesn't matter whether the crimes are labeled genocide, ethnic cleansing or savagery. Blood is spilled. People are killed. Loved ones disappear in the dark of night. A way of life is taken. Scars are inflicted. Bitterness, rage and the seeds of revenge are sown. Innocent people are left with nightmares of horror, a sense of loss, anger, sometimes shame and lingering insecurity. Their lives seem fragile and their future dim. The divisions and despair run deep.

Bosnia is only one of the many societies torn asunder by brutal violence since the end of the Cold War. For too long the world stood by and watched during the "Siege of Sarajevo."[2] In Sarajevo, even today, everywhere you see the damage caused by the bullets and shrapnel from the shelling that rained down onto the city during the three-year siege. While most of the city has been rebuilt, the pockmarks are on every street and many buildings, churches and mosques. Twenty thousand people out of a population of 400,000 died in the siege. But, of course, statistics do not tell the real story, statistics never do.[3]

In June, 2002, my embassy driver, Milenko Milinovic, who is Croatian and was a policeman before the war, told me that his five year old son became so hungry

---

UNA-USA Occasional Paper No. 1, August 2, 2006.

during the siege that he ate grass. In 2002, he was 11 years old. When you ask him about the war he can remember very little, but most nights the boy wakes up screaming from nightmares.

Manal Becrirbegovic-Al Share, a Bosniac who is manager of the KPMG office in Sarajevo, was there with her husband during the siege. She told me that in 1992, when the war started, someone wrote on a building in her neighborhood, "This is Serbia." Someone wrote below, "No stupid, this is a post office." At first things were confusing, but rising violence focused the mind.

When I asked Manal what it was like with sniper fire and mortar shells exploding for three years, no electricity, no heat, little water or food, she told me people fought for normalcy. "We went to work," she said. "We found routes down narrow back streets that were safer, where snipers on the hill did not have a clear shot." She told me that while she and her husband worked near to one another, each morning at home they would say good-bye and then take different routes to their respective offices. They never said it but both understood that way there was less chance they both would be killed that day.

When friends came to their apartment to visit, Manal told me, no matter how late the hour they never told the guest it was late and they should be on their way. They would wait and allow their guests to decide when they would depart. That way, she told me, if a sniper killed them on their way home they had chosen their time, not she.

Manal told me that growing up her best friend was a Serb who lived nearby. She still is her friend. But, she told me, during the war she hated Serbs; not the ones who stayed in the neighborhood, not those in Sarajevo. No, she hated the faceless, nameless Serbs on the hills around Sarajevo who fired hell down upon those, mostly Bosniac Muslims, in the city. She went on to say that since no one in her family was killed, it is easier for her not to hate anymore. But she did admit that if one who had lived in her neighborhood and had moved out during the siege to join the Serbs shelling the city were to move back, well that would be different. She said, "That would be impossible."

One day Manal saw a woman carrying her baby down a street in Sarajevo. "The child was killed by a Serbian sniper. The woman sat down on that spot and cried and cried. The sniper could have killed the mother too. He did not. Why? He wanted to create hatred so Serbia would be let go."

The hatred created by such vicious violence violates any sense of decency. It does not easily wash away when the killing stops. It lingers. Sometimes it grows. It wants revenge. It's a cancer eating away at a torn society. A malignancy that is hard to extract.

Manal told me that she had a five year old son born after the war. He asks her what happened to the buildings as he points to where bullets and shrapnel gouged the walls. Manal said, "I tell him. He should know. But I worry. What am I passing on?"

In Kosovo too, there were large scale ethnic killings.[4]

When I first visited Pristino, Kosovo, I spent time with Agron Ramaj, a Kosovan. During Slobodan Milosevic's ten year reign of terror, men in masks, probably Serbian neighbors, broke into his home and they beat his aunt, a woman in her late 60's, near to death.

My driver, Afrim Vitija, had his home broken into. His elderly father was taken away. He was not heard from. Seven years later, a year after the killing stopped, his father's remains were found in a mass grave.

Recent accounts of man's inhumanity to man do not end here. In recent years there have been many horrors: mutilations, massacres and mass murders.

Driving down the streets of Freetown, Sierra Leone, on almost every block I've seen evidence of that country's bloody civil war in the men, women and children who are missing limbs.[5] In Kissingani, the Democratic Republic of the Congo, I've listened to women in tears who told me how their lives were shattered during the ethnic fighting when their husbands were killed and their decapitated bodies sent down the Congo River. In the eastern Congo over the past seven years, some 3.5 million people have died due to their war.[6] In Kabul, an old man told me how his wife was butchered by the Taliban. And the on-going genocide in Darfur provides testimonials of ethnic carnage in which government attack helicopters followed by Arab Janjaweed riding camels and on horseback burn villages, destroy crops, steal livestock, kill males from old men to young children, and rape and brand women.[7]

These grizzly tales properly shock and disgust us. They are vile and unconscionable. They are stories of how societies are shattered, rage is created, and the desire for revenge is sown. No wonder reconciliation is so difficult. No wonder moving from a dark past to a liberal future is so hard.

The great challenge for transitional justice is what to do about terrible crimes after the killing stops.[8] How should the past be dealt with during a transition from an awful, perhaps repressive, past to a more liberal future? How can transitional justice address a dark past in a manner that contributes to a future of sustainable peace founded upon a respect for individual rights with a durable rule of law?[9]

As Professor Ruti Teitel has written, "In these times of massive political movement from illiberal rule, one burning question recurs. How should societies deal with their evil pasts?... How is the social understanding behind a new regime committed to the rule of law created? What legal acts have transformative significance? What, if any, is the relation between a state's response to its repressive past and its prospects for creating a liberal order? What is law's potential for ushering in liberalization?"[10]

Sometimes, how the issue of accountability for war crimes is handled after the end of a conflict can contribute to reconciliation or resumed fighting. Should a government that succeeds a corrupt and repressive predecessor allow the worst criminals in that government to escape punishment if they confess?[11] Some states face a choice of peace or justice.[12] Justice may have to be postponed until democratic institutions strengthen. No one size fits all.[13]

Richard Goldstone, former Chief Prosecutor of the United Nations International Criminal Tribunals for the former Yugoslavia and Rwanda, has written, "The question of how an oppressed or traumatized people should treat its recent past is a difficult and perplexing one. There are no obvious answers or easy solutions. Certainly there is no one simple solution capable of addressing the complexities and subtleties inherent in a range of difficult factual situations. The peculiar history, politics, and social structure of a society will always inform the appropriate approach to these questions in any given context."[14]

Lessons Learned

As post-conflict torn societies have dealt with the issues of accountability, reconciliation and restoration, some lessons have been learned. Some milestones should be met while climbing the steep slope of renewal.

It is necessary to record the abuses that took place, to provide a written record of the crimes committed. By interviewing victims and recording their testimonials, the process provides victims recognition of their suffering. That alone can be cathartic and contribute to healing. It also provides a history of atrocities so in the future they cannot be denied. And by identifying wrongdoers the consequent irrepute and shame provides a measure of justice.

If creating and maintaining such a history is the sole act of transitional justice, it is only a partial contribution to restoration. Amnesty is a last resort. Crimes should be punished if at all feasible. But sometimes it is not. Sometimes a new government emerging from conflict "lacks the power to bring" past malefactors to justice because attempts to do so might provide the overthrow of a "fragile democratic government."[15] While the power realities may compel amnesty, nonetheless amnesty can contribute to forgiveness. And forgiveness can break the recriminations of past violence and contribute to political reconstitution.

In 1993, the South African Peace Agreement would not have been possible without granting conditional amnesty.[16] The white apartheid regime could have held onto power for years. Before Nelson Mandela's release from prison, the likeliest scenario was civil war, not a peaceful black revolution. On becoming the first president of the new democratic South Africa, President Nelson Mandela said that amnesty is bound up in the "renewal of our country," as an integral aspect of the effort to "act together as a united people for national reconciliation, for nation building, for the birth of a new world."[17]

There have been a variety of Truth and Reconciliations Commissions in Chile,[18] El Salvador,[19] Ecuador, Nigeria, South Korea, Timor-Leste, Ghana, Morocco, Sierra Leone,[20] and elsewhere. The precise ways and means have varied of informing the public, soliciting personal stories of abuse, recording the testimonials, and making the findings available to all. But each recognizes the suffering of victims, records the atrocities for history, shames the perpetrators and, thereby, contributes to healing the wounds.

However, when circumstances permit, justice should go beyond recording past atrocities. When the post-conflict government is less fragile, a judicial process of fact-finding, re-affirming the rule of law, and accountability should be pursued. Such an exercise provides justice. It is important that justice be done, but it also is valuable that it be seen to have been done by the parties to the conflict.

As written by Kingsley Chiedu Moghalu, former Special Advisor to the Registrar of the International Criminal Tribunal for Rwanda,

> Precisely because international criminal justice addresses mass crimes, which inevitably dislocate societies, its ultimate aim is to

heal fractured societies and help establish peace and reconciliation by addressing the root cause of such destabilization – impunity ….. If impunity is the absence of accountability, then it follows that the establishment of a culture of accountability is necessary to eradicate it …. Accountability … means legal responsibility and punishment for criminal illegal acts or omissions. It does not mean "truth-telling" for mass atrocities without the consequence of responsibility."[21]

Over sixty years ago, in response to the horrors of the Holocaust, the Allied Forces created the Nuremberg Court that brought the worst Nazi criminals to justice after World War II.[22] It provided accountability for the worst war crimes that had been committed. Sovereign immunity did not protect those who committed the worst crimes against humanity. The principle Nazi leaders were put on trial at Nuremburg while similar proceedings were conducted in Tokyo against Japanese war criminals.[23] It was a dramatic and powerful demonstration that the rule of law, definitive legal findings of guilt, fairly arrived at, would end impunity for war crimes. After Nuremberg, it was widely assumed that international criminal law would be used against those who practiced genocide, mass murdered civilians or systematically tortured prisoners. But for a long time it was not. However, in the past 15 years the same principles that animated the Nuremburg Trials have informed various Tribunals and Special Courts established in different post-conflict transitional societies to bring the worst criminals to justice.[24]

In 1993, the international community, through the United Nations, set up the international tribunal at the Hague to punish war crimes committed in the Balkans.[25] The next year the U.N. Security Council set up its second 'ad hoc' tribunal in Arusha, Tanzania, to deal with those who directed the genocide in Rwanda.[26] At the International Court for the former Yugoslavia (ICTY) some strong sentences have been handed down on Serb and Croat generals and concentration camp commanders. In Arusha, the former prime minister of Rwanda, Jean-Paul Kambanda, has been indicted. These are positive developments.[27] But the wheels of justice have moved excruciatingly slowly. This past spring, ten years after the Dayton Peace Accords and four years into his trial, former Serbian President Slobodan Milosevic died before any verdict had been rendered on his terrible crimes.[28] As the saying goes, justice delayed is justice denied.

The *Chicago Tribune* editorialized at the time of Milosevic's death from natural causes:

> (T)he frustrating story of his final years likely will surface again and again – wherever advocates of multilateral tribunals gather. Milosevic went on trial four long years ago, indicted on 66 counts that soon were encapsulated in legal shorthand. He was charged with genocide and crimes against humanity – the first head of state ever to face those charges.
>
> But the International Criminal Tribunal for the Former Yugoslavia at The Hague had only limited success in making Milosevic's trial something other than the noisy circus he desired. …

Four years of trial with no verdict? This is international justice?

> There has never been real justice for the victims of the Balkan wars. Many Serbians continue to deny the atrocities committed on their behalf by the Butcher of the Balkans.[29]

The ICTY and ICTR have proven to be very expensive, each costing the international community about $100 million a year. Also, these judicial proceedings are taking place far from the country where the crimes were committed. Neither those living in the Balkans nor those in Rwanda who were victims of these awful crimes against humanity can see the wheels of justice move. They get reports of doings far away. But the reports are easily manipulated for various political gains: clouded by allegations of manipulation and malfeasance. Consequently, the restorative impact of these tribunals is muted; their contribution easily marginalized.

The Sierra Leone Special Court, I believe, is an improvement over the ICTY and ICTR.

In the 1990's in Sierra Leone, there was a particularly bloody civil war between the Revolutionary United Front rebel group, supported by Liberian President Charles Taylor, and the government.[30] By 2001, the rebels had been defeated. Understandably, Sierra Leoneans were concerned about maintaining their fragile stability. Weary of confronting former insurgents generally who might trigger a new round of violence, a Truth and Reconciliation Commission was established to address most of the atrocities.[31] It was given two years to finish its work. But to deal with the worst crimes, Sierra Leone went further. In January, 2002, the U.N. Security Council and the Sierra Leone Government set up a Special Court, which is a hybrid of both national and international courts.[32] The Special Court was given a limited budget, a mandate to investigate and prosecute only those who committed the worst crimes against humanity, and it was to complete its work within three years.[33]

The chief prosecutor, American David Crane, was selected by U.N. Secretary General Kofi Annan and approved by Sierra Leone President Ahmad Jajan Kabbash. Funding for the court came from voluntary contributions, with the United States and Britain the largest donors. In less than a year the Chief Prosecutor, Deputy Prosecutor and Registar arrived in Freetown; the offices for the Special Court were constructed; Trial Chambers were being built; scores of educational town meetings were held in cities and villages throughout the countryside to inform the people about the court; its mandate, its procedures and its activities; and the Court indicted 12 persons whom they alleged bore the greatest responsibility for war crimes, crimes against humanity, and violations of International Humanitarian Law.[34] That was an unprecedented, breathtaking pace. Significantly, among the 12 indictees one was a sitting Sierra Leone government minister, a leader of the winning side, for using excessive force and abusing the rebels.[35] Also among the indictees was Liberian President Charles Taylor.[36] This has helped reinforce the message to the Sierra Leone people that justice is even-handed and that no one is above the law. And since the Sierra Leone Special Court is located in Freetown, Sierra Leone, the trials have been accessible to the people. One commentator has written that the "Sierra Leone Court may offer (a) model for war crimes cases," and that other countries have studied it "as a model for dealing quickly and fairly with war crimes."[37]

When the Sierra Leone Special Court unsealed its 11 count indictment of Charles Taylor in June, 2003, he was the sitting President of Liberia defending its capital, Monrovia, from rebel attacks.[38] The former warlord who had incited, fomented and supported rebellion and instability throughout Africa's Mano River Region for his own benefit was now encircled as bloody fighting closed in upon him. Most felt Taylor would fight until the death of the last of his drugged-up child soldiers. Countless civilians also would die. To avoid the senseless bloodbath, Nigeria's President Olusegun Obasanjo offered Taylor asylum if he would promptly leave Monrovia. It was an offer Taylor could not refuse.

With Taylor's departure, Liberia's fighting soon ended. Through the United Nations,[39] the international community supported Liberia's transition from tyranny and bloodshed to democracy and hope. In October, 2005, I was co-leader of the IRI election observer team during Liberia's first free and fair election in which the people choose Ellen Johnson Sirleaf as their President, Africa's first elected female President. She is very impressive. The day before the first round of voting, I met with Ellen in the garden of her home outside Monrovia. I asked about Charles Taylor. She said that Taylor, even from Nigeria, still had influence in Liberia. Many still feared to whisper his name. But if she were elected, as stability took deeper root in Liberia, she would ask President Obasqanjo to return Taylor to face trial before the Sierra Leone Special Court. Therefore, several months after she took office, I was not surprised but nonetheless pleased when President Johnson Sirleaf requested Taylor be returned to Freetown to face trial.[40]

Soon Taylor was back in Freetown behind bars. Let me quote from the *BCC News* about Taylor's arraignment for crimes against humanity.

> Outside the special war crimes court, members of civil society in their Sunday best and war victims with amputated limbs queued up to watch Charles Taylor come face-to-face with justice.
>
> Then the blue-helmeted U.N. soldiers from Mongolia sprinted to take up their places and the armored car that glittered in the sun revved its engine nervously.
>
> A white car with smoke-tinted windows pulled out of the prison gates and slowly drove the short distance to the courtroom. ...He listened, betraying little emotion, as the 11 charges were read out against him...
>
> The charges were detailed, and the detail was terrifying as places and times of murder and rape were read out to the hushed court. ...His long-awaited day in court had in fact lasted little more than an hour.
>
> But for many Sierra Leoneans it seemed a miracle that the man they accuse of concocting the brutal civil war, that all but destroyed their country, had been dragged before a court at all.[41]

Yes, transitional justice for a scared society can bring the miracle of closure and contribute to reconciliation. Because of fears of violence, Taylor has been moved to The Hague for trial "in that court with the proceedings still under the direction of the Sierra Leone Special Court." And, if found guilty, Great Britain has agreed to jail

Taylor. The process may not be perfect. But is a powerful contribution to transitional justice nonetheless; and the message goes beyond Charles Taylor's victims in Sierra Leone. In a June commentary on *SW Radio Africa Zimbabwe News*, Tererai Karimawendo said, "If nothing else, Taylor's trial signals the vulnerability of modern day dictators and should send a strong message to leaders violating human rights. The days of impunity are over."[42]

> Karimawenda went on, "In the Zimbabwe context many organizations have called for the prosecution of Robert Mugabe and ZANU-PF officials for violations of human rights ranging from the massacre of thousands of the so-called Gukurahundi murders in Matabeleland in the 1980's to the demolition of homes and businesses which displaced nearly a million people in 2005. Many anti-government activists have been tortured by state agents and several opposition supporters were murdered by government sponsored thugs and youth militia during various elections.

> "Events in Zimbabwe are being well documented by many civic groups in the country and the United Nations sent its own envoy Anna Tibaijuka last year to assess the effects of the Operation Murambatsvina demolitions. It is widely believed Mugabe will ask for immunity from prosecution as part of any exit deal that seeks to resolve the on-going political and economic crisis.

> "Lawyer Tafadzwa Mugabe of The Zimbabwe lawyers for human rights said this is the dawn of a new era for the enforcement of human right law. He believes much credit needs to be accorded to those who spoke out in the Charles Taylor case because without them there would be no evidence. Tafadzwa also told us when information is documented well as in Zimbabwe, it is bound to be cause for concern for those responsible for abuses because it can always be used for their prosecution."[43]

Saddam Hussein's brutal reign of terror was long, hideous, and merciless. [44] He used chemical weapons in his war against Iran, the first use of such awful weapons on the battlefield since World War II. He directed an invasion and brutal occupation of Kuwait. He shot missiles into innocent civilian populations in Iran, Israel and other neighboring states. He gassed over 200,000 Iraqi Kurds, the first leader to use such terrible weapons to commit such ethnic genocide on his own people since Adolf Hitler's extermination of the Jews. In southern Iraq he drained the marshlands and poisoned 100,000 Iraqi Shia because he questioned their loyalty. He used torture chambers, summary executions, and rape as everyday tools to control his people. And since his fall, the many mass graves that have been uncovered are grim testimonials to Saddam's crimes against humanity.[45]

The post-Saddam Iraqi Government has prosecuted him for his crimes. The first criminal case against Saddam was filed in July, 2005. It charged him for the 1982 massacre of Shiite villagers in Dujail.[46] There will be more. Separate trials are anticipated for war crime charges for Saddam's Anfal campaign, his chemical attack on Halabjah and other atrocities. Rejecting international supervision, the Iraqi court has struggled since the trial began in October. Outsiders have questioned its legitimacy. Saddam has sought to discredit, disparage and destroy the proceedings. In court, Saddam denounced the trial as "the daughter of a whore" and attacked the judge. He has attacked Iraq's occupation by "foreign invaders."[47] Saddam has demanded adjournments, engaged in hunger strikes, and consistently shown contempt for the proceedings. Some have called this trial a farce.[48]

Of course, the trial could have gone better. Perhaps greater international support would have helped. Perhaps other modalities could have encouraged more decorum. The ways and means could have been improved. However, while his trial at times has been undignified, it is not a farce.

For thirty years Saddam was a mighty and brutal leader who held absolute power of life and death over all his people. He abused his power and randomly terrorized, tortured and terminated any targeted by his paranoia or whim. Now, for all his people to see, he has been brought into a court of law, sat while his rights were read to him – rights he so long could deny his people, listened to the charges against him, heard evidence of his crimes presented and has been afforded the opportunity for his lawyers to reply. Despite his trial room shenanigans, this is an extraordinary event.

Not only in Iraq, but across the Middle East, people have followed the once all powerful and feared Saddam Hussein being held to account by the rule of law. If justice is done, and is seen as having been done, it can be a transforming event for the Iraqi people. It will create an opportunity for some closure of the dark past and a broader acceptance of a liberal future where the rule of law governs, human rights are respected and fear of secret police knocking at your door at night is a thing of the past. Beyond Iraq, throughout the broader Middle East, it will be a powerful message to Arabs in the street that rulers can be held to account. And it will be a cautionary message to undemocratic rulers in the broader Middle East that the advance of human rights, justice and the rule of law is on the march even in their neighborhood.

Perhaps man's continued inhumanity to man today is demonstrated most powerfully by the "genocide in slow motion" that continues in Darfur. As diplomats struggle to buttress a sustainable peace agreement and the international community works to organize and deploy an effective Peacekeeping Operation to enforce that peace once achieved,[49] the U.N. Security Council – with American support – has given jurisdiction to the International Criminal Court to investigate and prosecute war crimes and crimes against humanity committed in this tragic war. On March 31, 2005, the United Nation's Security Council adopted Resolution 1593 (2005) in which it decided "to refer the situation in Darfur since 1 July 2002 to the Prosecutor of the International Criminal Court." The ICC's prosecutor, Luis Moreno Ocampo, has embraced this grave responsibility with the intent of holding to account those most responsible and, in his view, to prevent future crimes in Sudan.[50]

Conclusion

When the killing stops, when tyrannical and brutal regimes fall, when war's carnage ends, societies need to re-establish the rule of law fairly administered and see justice done. Records of past crimes should be recorded as testaments to injustices suffered. It provides a recognition o the pain, a history that cannot be dismissed nor denied, a measure of justice, a path toward forgiveness. Truth and Reconciliation Commissions contribute to the healing required to mend traumatized, torn societies.

Whenever possible, when the danger of reigniting the fighting is not prohibitive, those who have committed the worst crimes against humanity should be brought to trial. Consistent with legal principles and a sense of fairness, the exact modalities will vary due to history, culture, feasibility and other local considerations. But the trials should be timely when evidence, memories and wounds are fresh; and when the contribution to reconciliation is greatest. Whenever possible, the trials should take place where the victims can witness justice being done to decrease the possibilities of perceived divisive political manipulation and increase the impact of the message of accountability.

The international community, the United Nations, the Council of Europe, Non-governmental organizations, academics and others should continue to study the ways and means of transitional justice, develop "best practices," be prepared to provide technical assistance, legitimacy and resources for societies moving from a dark past to a brighter future. The new U.N. Peacebuilding Commission should provide valuable help in this area.[51] For a new, stable, free society under the rule of law to emerge, past injustices must be faced, justice must be done, and a measure of reconciliation achieved.

---

1.   See Neil J. Kritz, "The Rule of Law in the Post-conflict Phase: Building a Stable Peace," in Chester A. Crocker, Fen Osler Hampson, and Pamela Aall, eds., *Turbulent Peace: The Challenges of Managing International Conflict* (Washington, D.C.; U.S. Institute of Peace; 2001), pp. 801-820.

2.   See, David Halberstam, *War in a Time of Peace* (New York, N.Y.; Scribner; 2001); Allan Little, *The Death of Yugoslavia* (London, U.K.; Penguin; 1995); Steven Burg and Paul Shoop, *The War in Bosnia-Herzegovina: Ethnic Conflict and International Intervention* (Armonk, N.Y.; Sharp; 1999); Elizabeth Neuffer, *The Key to My Neighbor's House: Seeking Justice in Bosnia and Rwanda* (New York; N.Y.; Praeder; 2001); and William Shaucross, *Deliver Us From Evil: Peacekeepers, Warlords in a World of Endless Conflict* (New York, N.Y.; Simon and Schuster; 2000).

3.   See, David Rieff, "Murder in the Neighborhood," in Nicholaus Mills and Kera Bruner, eds., *The New Killing Fields: Massacre and the Politics of Intervention* (New York, N.Y.; Basic Books; 2002), pp. 55-70.

4.   See David Rieff, *A Bed For The Night: Humanitarianism in Crisis* (New York, N.Y.; Simon & Schuster; 2002), pp. 197-229; and Kirk Brunner, "A Drive in Globarc," in Nicholas Mills and Kira Brunner, eds.; *ibid.*; pp. 89-97.

5.   For an eyewitness account of the bloody civil war in Sierra Leone, see, Phil Ashby; *Unscathed* (London; Pan McMillian Publishing Ltd.; 2002).

6.   See Simon Robinson and Vivienne Walt; "The Deadliest War in the World," *Time Magazine*, June 5, 2006, See also, "Democratic Republic of Congo: Children at War, "*Amnesty International*, September 9, 2003. Available at http://web.amnesty.org/library/index/engafr620342003; and "D.R. Congo: Mai Mai Warlord Must Face Justice," *Human Rights Watch*, May 18, 2006. Available at http://hrw.org/english/docs/2006/05/17/congo13381.htm

7.   See, Julie Flint and Alex de Waal, *Darfur: A Short History of a Long War* (London; Zed books; 2006), and Gerard Prunier, *Darfur: The Ambiguous Genocide* (Ithaca, N.Y.; Cornell University Press; 2005) See also, Nicholas D. Kristof, "Genocide in Slow Motion," *The New York Review of Books*, February 9, 2006.

8.   See, Aryeh Neier, "What Should be Done About the Guilty?," *The New York Review of Books*, 1990. See also, Alice H. Henkin, "Conference Report," in *State Crimes: Punishment or Pardon* (Washington, D.C.; The Aspen Institute; 1989); and Dorothy V. Jones, *Toward a Just World: The Critical Years in the Search for International Justice* (Chicago, Illinois; University of Chicago Press; 2002). And for a useful analysis of who is responsible for the terror, atrocities and violations of human rights that occur in civil wars, See, Neil J. Mitchell, *Agents of Atrocity: Leaders, Followers, and the Violation of Human Rights in Civil War* (New York, N.Y.; Palgrave MacMillan; 2004).

9. "Institutional disapproval of the previous official policies which resulted in the violation of human rights makes a clear distinction between the transitional government and the previous regime. In cases where transgressions were associated with the highest government spheres, the imposition of a criminal sentence against high-ranking perpetrators dilutes any suspicion of continuity." Jaime Malamud-Goti, "Transitional Governments in the Breach: Why Punish State Criminals?" *Human Rights Quarterly*, Vol. 12, No. 1 (1990), pp. 1, 10. See also, Geoffrey Robertson, *Crimes Against Humanity: The Struggle For Global Justice* (New York, N.Y.; The New Press; 1999).

10. Ruti G. Teitel, *Transitional Justice* (Oxford, UK; Oxford University Press; 2000), p. 3.

11. See, Mike Tucker, *Hell is Over: Voices of the Kurds After Saddam.* (Guilford, Conn.; The Lyons Press; 2004), and Lawrence F. Kaplan and William Kristol, *The War Ores Iraq: Saddam's Tyranny and America's Mission.* (San Francisco, Calif.; Encounter Books; 2003). In some countries, "amnesties" haunt the people for decades. See, for example, Larry Rohter, "Argentine Congress Likely to Void 'Dirty War' Amnesties," *New York Times*, August 21, 2003; and Larry Rohter, "30 Years Later, a Coup's Scars Have Been Masked," *New York Times*, September 7, 2003. Kingsley Chiedu Moghalu. "Reconciling Fractured Societies: An African Perspective on the Role of Judicial Prosecutions," in Ramesh Thakur and Peter Malcontent, eds., *ibid.*, pp. 197, 198.

12. See Guillermo O'Donnell and Philippe C. Schmitter, "Transitions from Authoritarian Rule: Tentative Conclusions About Uncertain Democracies," in Neil J. Kritz, ed., *Transitional Justice: How Emerging Democracies Reckon With Former Regimes* (Washington, D.C.; United States Institute of Peace; 1995), pp. 55-64; David Pion-Berlin, "To Prosecute or to Pardon? Human Rights Decisions in the Latin American Southern Cone, *ibid.*, pp. 82-103; and José Zalquett, "Balancing Ethical Imperatives and Political Constraints: The Dilemma of New Democracies Confronting Past Human Rights Violations," *ibid.*, pp. 203-206. See also, Jose Zalaquett, "Balancing Ethical Imperatives and Political Constraints: The Dilemma of New Democracies Confronting Past Human Rights Violations," *Hastings Law Journal*, Vol. 41, No. 6 (August 1992), p. 1426. Professor Timothy William Waters of the University of Mississippi, who worked in the Office of the Prosecutor at the ICTY from 1999-2000, has raised interesting issues regarding whether Serbia's entry into the European Union should be linked to the arrest of General Ratko Mladic for alleged war crimes. He asks, "Is one war criminal's arrest really worth pushing Serbia back into the dark" by denying EU entry and the integration and stability that offers. Timothy William Waters, "Why Insist on the Surrender of Ratko Mladic?" *New York Times*, May 12, 2006.

13. Alex Boraine, President of the International Center for Transitional Justice, has written, "[P]olitical transitions are invariably messy, ambiguous, contradictory, and fragile… The mechanisms and options that may apply in each case are informed by a country's history and culture, the extent of the conflict, and the nature of the transition itself. However, it has become equally obvious that there are lessons to be learned from experiences, the successes, and the mistakes of countries that have undergone earlier transitions. While we must never lose sight of the overarching demand for accountability, the sociopolitical climate will present certain priorities." Alex Boraine, International Center for Transitional Justice, Annual Report 2001/2002.

14. Richard Gladstone, "Preface," Carla Hesse and Robert Post, eds., *Human Rights in Political Transition Gettysburg to Bosnia* (New York, N.Y.; Zone Books; 1990), p. 9.

15. Diane F. Orentlicher, "Settling Accounts: The Duty to Prosecute Human Rights Violations of a Prior Regime," *Yale Law Review*, 100 (1991), p. 2537, 2546. Professor Orentlicher argues that a successful government cannot act in accordance with international law and grant wholesale immunity to atrocious crimes committed by a previous government. It is noteworthy that as the new Iraqi government continues to seek firm footing and secure a measure of stability to that post-conflict society, ideas about amnesty for the insurgents have arisen. See, for example, Qassim Abdul-Zahra, "Amnesty May Be Part of Iraq Reconciliation," *Associated Press*, June 23, 2006; and Ned Parker and Tom Baldwin, "Peace Deal Offers Iraq Insurgents an Amnesty," *Times*, June 23, 2006.

16. There are many, including in South Africa, who reject the view that it was sufficient justice to allow all sides to confess their misdeeds and thereby acquire a form of reconciliation. The survivors of Steve Biko, the black activist who was tortured and killed by government forces, filed a lawsuit challenging the existence of the Commission on Truth and Reconciliation. They claimed that amnesty violated the rights of survivors to seek redress. The South Africa constitutional court rejected their claim.

17. Nelson Mandela, "Glory and Hope: Let There Be Work, Bread, Water and Salt for All," *Vital Speeches of the Day*, 60 (June 1, 1994), p. 486. See also, Alex Boraine, *A Country Unmasked: Inside South Africa's Truth and Reconciliation Commission* (Oxford, England; Oxford University Press; 2000) and Desmond Tutu, *No Freedom Without Forgiveness* (New York, N.Y.; Doubleday, 1999). But there should be no illusion that a Truth or Reconciliation Commission or transitional justice more generally is

a cure for past traumas. Pain and agony and the costs of traumas past may be mitigated, but they do not end. Nora Kenworthy, after "a year spent providing field-based and administrative assistance to an HIV-AIDS organization from Cape Town, South Africa," wrote movingly about the rampant crime, "a plague... whose infection rates are just as rampant (as HIV-AIDS) and for which there is... no cure in sight." She attributes South Africa's high incidence of violent crime in part to the lingering affects of apartheid's injustice. "Apartheid left an interminably long legacy of social trauma – a constant devaluation of what it is to be human, a ruthlessly planned decimation of family and community." Nora Kenworthy, "A Scream of South Africa's Pain," *Washington Post*, March 19, 2006. See also, Nelson Mandela, *Long Walk to Freedom* (New York, N.Y.; Little, Brown and Company; 1994)

It is noteworthy that Nelson Mandela's decision to "forgive" the white racist oppressors who had imprisoned him for years had a precedent in Africa. In Kenya, Jomo Kenyatta had been imprisoned by the British colonial rulers for his leadership of the Mau Mau. "He emerged from detention preaching forgiveness," and became Kenya's first president. For a powerful account of the British brutalization of thousands of Kikhyu, Kenya's largest ethnic group, see Caroline Elkins, *Imperial Reckoning: The Untold Story of Britain's Gulag in Kenya* (New York, N.Y.; Owl Books; 2005).

18.   On the thirty year anniversary of Argentina's last military coup d'etat, Juan E. Mendez wrote about Argentina, Chile, and Uruguay's journey toward transitional justice. "Going against conventional advice to look forward and forget old enmities and past crimes, Argentina in 1983 and Chile in 1990 established truth commissions to investigate and reveal the truth about the crimes committed under past regimes. ...Southern Cone societies are far from perfect democracies But their choice to confront the past honestly has proven to be an invaluable and indispensable blueprint for dealing with today's human rights abuses. ...As the examples of Argentina, Chile, and Uruguay illustrate, dealing with the past is far from easy. But attempting to sweep the past under the rug and forget is a recipe for disaster." Juan E. Mendez, "Key to Future is in Confronting the Past," *International Center for Transitional Justice*, March 24, 2006. Available at http://www.ictj.org/en/news/features/896.html.

19.   See, Margaret Popkin and Naomi Roht-Arriaza, "Truth as Justice: Investigatory Commissions in Latin America," in Neil J. Kritz, ed., *ibid.*, pp. 262-289; and Thomas Buergenthal, "The United Nations Truth Commission for El Salvador," *ibid.*, pp. 292-325.

20.   See, Official Website of Sierra Leone's Truth and Reconciliation Commission Report. Available at http://www.tresierralconc.org/drwebsite/publish/index.shtml. See also, "Sierra Leone: Truth and Reconciliation Report, African Focus Bulletin, October 31, 2004; and "Sierra Leone's Truth and Reconciliation Commission: A Fresh Start?" *International Crisis Group*, December 20, 2002.

21.   Kingsley Chiedu Moghalu, "Reconciling Fractured Societies: An African Perspective on the Role of Judicial Prosecutions," in Ramesh Thakur and Peter Malcontent, eds., *ibid.*, pp. 197, 198.

22.   See generally, Joseph Persico, *Nuremberg: Infamy on Trial* (New York, N.Y.; Random House; 1994); and John H. Herz, "Prosecution of Nazi Criminality," in Neil J. Kritz, ed., *ibid.*, pp. 4-19. See also, however, studies of the feeble response to the Holocaust; Richard Breitman, *Official Secrets: What the Nazis Planned, What the British and Americans Knew* (New York, N.Y.; Hill and Wang; 1999), David Wyman, *The Abandonment of the Jews: America and the Holocaust 1941-1945* (New York, N.Y.; Pantheon Books; 1984); and Raul Hilberg, *Perpetrators, Victims, Bystanders: The Jewish Catastrophe* (New York, N.Y.; Harper Collins; 1992). Furthermore, disturbing new evidence recently has become public that the United States Government had information about the whereabouts of several Nazi war criminals after the war and kept that information secret. See, Scott Shane, "C.I.A. Knew Where Eichman was Hiding, Documents Show," *New York Times*, June 7, 2006.

Note, however, the post-World War II "demand for international accountability (was) not new. Article 227 of the Versailles Peace Treaty famously indicted William II for a supreme offense against international morality and the security of treaties; Under Article 228, the German Supreme Court in Leipzig was called upon to try those accused of war crimes. In the end, William found refuge in The Netherlands and the Leipzig trials led to minor sentences for a handful of lesser offenders, Allied efforts to bring the perpetrators of the Armenian genocide of 1915 to justice ended in a fiasco: the British occupation forces had to free the main suspects in exchange for 29 British soldiers captured by Kemal Ataturk's Turkish nationalists. Maiti Ahtisaari, "Justice and Accountability: Local/or International?" in Ramesh Thakur and Peter Malcontent, eds., *From Sovereign Impunity to International Accountability: The Search for Justice in a World of States* (New York, N.Y.; United Nations University Press; 2004), pp. xii, xiii.

23. Timothy P. Maga, *Judgment at Tokyo: The Japanese War Crimes Trials* (Lexington, KY; University Press of Kentucky; 2001); Arnold C. Brackman, *The Other Nuremberg: The Untold Story of the Tokyo War Crimes* (New York, N.Y.; Morrow; 1987); and Philip R. Piccigallo, *The Japanese on Trial: Allied War Crimes Operations in the East, 1945-1951* (Austin, Texas; University of Texas Press, 1980).

24. See, for example, Tom Hundley, "War Crimes Prosecutions Gain Steam," *Chicago Tribune*, June 10, 2005.

25. U.N. Security Council 827 (1993). For a discussion of the Balkan Wars see David Halberstam, *War in a Time of Peace: Bush, Clinton, and the Generals* (New York, N.Y.; Scribner; 2001). See also, Aryeh Neier, "Rethinking Truth, Justice, and Guilt After Bosnia and Rwanda," in Carla Hesse and Robert Post, eds., *ibid.*, pp. 39-52; and David Rieff, "Murder in the Neighborhood," in Nicolaus Mills and Kira Brumner, eds., *ibid.*, pp. 55-69. And for more information on the ICTY see generally, John Hagan, *Justice In the Balkans: Prosecuting War Crimes in the Hague Tribunal* (Chicago, Ill.; University of Chicago Press; 2003); Michael Scharf, *Balkan Justice: The Story Behind The First International War Crimes Trial Since Nuremberg* (Durham, N.C.; Carolina Academic Press; 1997); and Richard Goldstone, *For Humanity: Reflections of a War Crimes Investigator* (New Haven, Conn.: Yale University Press; 2000).

Note: the full scale of the atrocities in Bosnia still are being uncovered. In October, 2005, a forensic team in Bosnia found the remains of another 482 victims of the Srebrenica Massacre. "New Srebrenica Mass Grave Found," *BBC News*, October 17, 2005.

26. U.N. Sec. Res. 955 (1994). See generally, Elizabeth Neuffer, *ibid.*; Bill Berkley, "Road to a Genocide," in Nicolaus Mills and Kira Brunner, eds., *ibid.*, pp. 103-116; and Linda Melvern, *To Murder: The Rwanda Genocide* (New York, N.Y.; Verso; 2004).

27. See, Virginia Morris and Michael P. Scharf, *The International Criminal Tribunal for Rwanda* (Ardsley, N.Y.; Transnational Publishers, Inc.; 1998); and Dina Temple-Raston, *Justice On The Grass: Three Rwandan Journalists, Their Trial for War Crimes, and a Nations' Quest for Redemption* (New York, N.Y.; Free Press; 2005).

28. But some felt that despite Slobodan Milosevic's death in jail prior to a final decision by the ICTY that "a verdict was denied but justice was not." Richard Holbrooke, "Rough Justice for Milosevic is as fitting as a Tribunal Verdict," *Financial Times*, March 14, 2006.

29. Editorial, "The Butcher of the Balkans," *Chicago Tribune*, March 13, 2006.

30. "Most conflicts, especially third-world civil ones, are marked by atrocities. But the wanton cruelty of Sierra Leone's 11-year bloodbath was particularly barbaric. Although hacking off limbs became the special trademark of the Revolutionary United Front (RUF), the main rebel group, all sides were guilty. Child soldiers, some not yet in their teens, would rip open pregnant women's stomachs after taking bets on the sex of the fetus. Women's vaginas were sewn up with fishing line. Mouths were clamped shut with padlocks. Children were forced to batter their parents to death and then eat their brains. One man was skinned alive before having his flesh picked off and eaten. Another had his heart torn out and stuffed into the mouth of his 87-year old mother. Thousands were burned alive in their homes. In all, some 50,000 – 200,000 people were killed (there is no accurate count) and three-quarters of the country's 6 million inhabitants were forced to flee their homes." "Bringing the Wicked to the Dock," *The Economist*, March 11, 2006.

31. See, Paul James-Allen, Sheku B.S. Lahai, Jamie O'Connell, "Sierra Leone's Truth & Reconciliation Commission and Special Court: A Citizen's Handbook;" National Forum for Human Rights (Freetown, Sierra Leone) and International Center for Transitional Justice (New York); March, 2003.

32. S/2003/321. The Sierra Leone Special Court was established by an agreement between the United Nations and the Sierra Leone Government pursuant to Security Council Resolution 1315 (2000). It is to investigate and prosecute those who committed the worst crimes against humanity during the civil war.

33. See generally, Richard S. Williamson, "Transitional Justice: The U.N. and the Sierra Leone Special Court," *Cardoza Public Law, Policy and Ethics Law Journal*, Vol. 2, No. 1, December, 2003, pp. 1-11. See also, Michael P. Scharf, "The Special Court for Sierra Leone," *"The American Society of International Law,"* October, 2000; and "Special Court for Sierra Leone: Denial of Right to Appeal and Prohibition of Amnesties for Crimes under International Law, "Amnesty International, November 1, 2003. Available at http://web.amnesty.org/library/index/engafr50122003

34. See Special Court for Sierra Leone Press Release 3-10-03, Special Court for Sierra Leone Office of the Prosecutor. Statement by David M. Crane, The Prosecutor.

35.   On March 10, 2003, the Chief Prosecutor of the Sierra Leone Special Court handed down his first series of indictments. Among the eight individuals indicted were Foday Sankoh, the political and military leader of the Revolutionary United Front rebel group and the principal architect of the RUF's "terror" policy, as well as Hinga Norman, the sitting Sierra Leone Minister of Internal Security and Defense, who formerly commanded the Civil Defense Forces, the irregular militia forces that fought the RUF during the war.

36.   On June 4, 2003, Liberian President Charles Taylor was in Accra, Ghana, for the beginning of peace talks on Liberia organized by the Economic Community of West Africa. On that morning, Sierra Leone Chief Prosecutor David Crane unsealed a 17 count indictment of Charles Taylor for war crimes. The Ghana authorities did not arrest Taylor and he returned to Monrovia. ...

37.   Douglas Fabah, "Sierra Leone Court May Offer Modal for War Crimes Cases: Hybrid Tribunal, With Limited Lifespan, Focuses on Higher Ups," *Washington Post*, April 15, 2003. See also, J. Peter Pham, "A Viable Model for International Criminal Justice: The Special Court for Sierra Leone," *New York International Law Review*, Vol. 19, No. 1, Winter 2006, pp. 37-109.

38.   For more background on Charles Taylor's alleged crimes and the trial see "The Charges Against Charles Taylor," *BBC News*, April 3, 2006; and "Q&A: Trying Charles Taylor," *BBC News*, June 20, 2006.

39.   "The United Nations Mission in Liberia (UNMIL) was established by Security Council Resolution 1509 (2003) to support the implementation of the ceasefire agreement and the peace process; protect United Nations staff, facilities and civilians; support humanitarian and human rights activities; as well as assist in national security reform, including national police training and formation of a new, restructured military."

40.   On March 25, 2006, the Nigerian Government stated that Liberia was free to take Charles Taylor back to Freetown so that he could face war crimes charges in Liberian courts. On March 28, the Nigerian Government announced that Taylor had disappeared from his residence in Calabar. On March 29, Taylor was arrested near Nigeria's northeastern border with Cameroon. Nigerian authorities put him on a plane bound to Liberia and then handed him to the U.N. in Sierra Leone, "Charles Taylor," *Wikipedia*, at http://en.wikipedia.org/wiki/Charles_Taylor.html.

See also, "A Close Escape: A Thug on the Run Nearly Messes Up One of the Few Examples of Moral Diplomacy," *The Economist*, April 1, 2006; and Simon Robinson, "Snaring a Strongman," *Time Magazine*, April 2, 2006.

"Despite mounting international pressure for (Charles Taylor's) transfer to the court, Mr. Obasanjo has always refused to hand him over unless specifically requested to do so by a democratically elected Liberian government. This, Ellen Johnson-Sirleaf, Liberia's newly elected president, has now asked him to do. It is a brave move. While desperate for international aid to support the reconstruction of her devastated country, she knows that Liberia's fragile peace could be shattered by the thousands of Taylor supporters still in the country." "War Crimes: Bad News for Africa's Warlords," *The Economist*, March 25, 2006. See also, Zoom Dosso, "Taylor's Hopes of Returning Home May Be Dashed," *Mail & Guardian*, October 18, 2005; and Colum Lynch, "Britain to Imprison Liberia's Taylor if He's Convicted," *Washington Post*, June 16, 2006.

41.   "A Sombre Charles Taylor Faces Court," *BBC News*, April 3, 2006. See also, "Prosecutors Seek Quick Start to Taylor Trial, *CNN.com*, June 21, 2006.

42.   Tererai Karimawenda, "Charles Taylor's Trial Signals Vulnerability of African Dictators," *SW Radio Africa Ness*, June 20, 2006.

43.   *Ibid.*

44.   *Ibid.* See also, Craig Timberg, "Impunity on Trial in Africa: In Cases of Ex-Leaders, Justice Shifts From Soldiers to Courts," *Washington Post*, May 2, 2006.

45.   See, Mike Tucker, *Hell is Over: Voices of the Kurds After Saddam* (Guilford, Conn.; The Lyons Press; 2004), and Lawrence F. Kaplan and William Kristol, *The War Over Iraq: Saddam's Tyranny and America's Mission* (San Francisco, CA; Encounter Books; 2003).

46.   See, for example, John F. Burns, "In Desert Graves, Unearthing Iraq's Horrors," *New York Times*, June 5, 2006.

47.   See, John F. Burns, "First Court Case of Hussein Stems From '82 Deaths: Iraqis Seek to Limit Delay by Focusing in Killings in a Shiite Village," *New York Times*, June 6, 2005.

48.   Typical of Saddam's rantings in the courtroom was in May, 2006, "when Chief Judge Raouf Abdel-Rahman read the charges (against Saddam), which stem from a crackdown against Shiites in the 1980's. 'I can't just say yes or no to this. You read all this for the sake of public consumption, and I can't answer it in brief. ...This will never shake one hair of my head. You are before Saddam Hussein, president of Iraq. I am president of Iraq according to the will of Iraqis and I am still the president up to this moment,' Saddam said." "Saddam's Trial Enters New Phase With Official Charges," *CBS News*, May 15, 2006. See also, Andrew North, "A Day in Court at Saddam's Trial," *BBC News*, May 15, 2006; "Saddam Defendant Ejected by Judge," *BBC News*; May 31, 2006; and "Timeline: Saddam Hussein Trial," *BBC News*, May 31, 2006. See also, for example, Richard Cohen, "Trial and Errors in Iraq", *Washington Post,* May 28, 2006; and George P. Fletcher, "Milosevic and Hussein: Trial by Force," *Korean Times*, March 17, 2006. See also, John F. Burns, "Hussein's Former Envoy Gushes With Adulation on Witness Stand," *New York Times*, May 25, 2005.

49.   See Nicholas Kristof, *ibid.*

50.   See, Sunghee Song, "International Criminal Court Prosecutor Calls for "Unconditional Cooperation" from the International Community to Prevent Future Crimes in Sudan," *UNA-USA E-Newsletter*, June 20, 2006. Available at http://www.unausa.org/site/pp.asp?c=fvKRI8MPJp&6=1790847 See also, Elizabeth Rubin, "If Not Peace, Then Justice," *New York Times Magazine*, April 2, 2006.

51.   See U.N. General Assembly Resolution A/RES/60/180 (2003), and Security Council Resolutions S/RES/1645 (2005) and S/RES/1646 (2005). See also United Nations PBC/OC/l/l and PBC/OC/1/2.

U.N. MUST ADD TO PRESSURE BURMA'S REPRESSIVE JUNTA

Something important happened last month in Kuala Lumpur. Finally, the Association of Southeast Asian Nations (ASEAN) took a stand for human rights. For the first time, at their annual meeting, ASEAN expressed concerns over Burma's lack of democratic reform and called for the release of all political prisoners.

Pascal Khoo Thwe is a Burmese human rights activist now living in exile in England. He has written a powerful memoir, *From the Land of Green Ghosts*, that documents the brutality inflicted by Burma's repressive regime.

In his memoir, Thwe writes about his fiancée, Moe. She was a freedom advocate in the city of Mandalay. She was arrested and tortured. Moe received a savage beating and gang rape. She was told, "This is what you get if you ask for democracy."

Following her release, Thwe tried to nurse Moe back to health. Two weeks later she disappeared. Her body was never found. Eventually Moe's mother was told by the government that she had died "from natural causes" while in prison. Tragically, in Burma such incidents continue to be all too common.

In 1988, a military junta crushed a pro-democracy movement in Burma and seized power. Under international pressure, the regime called elections in 1990. But when the National League of Democracy won the vote, opposition leader Aung San Suu Kyi was put under house arrest and the election nullified.

As Tom Malinowski of *Human Rights Watch* said earlier this year, "[T]he situation in Burma is as bleak today as at any point in (its) sad recent history. The Burmese government's repression, paranoia and mismanagement continue to cause misery and suffering inside Burma and pose a growing threat to the stability and well-being in Burma's neighbors."

Burma's military government, the State Peace and Development Council (SPDC), is one of the most repressive in the world. It severely restricts basic rights and freedoms. It continues to ban opposition political activity and persecute democracy and human rights activists. It has more than 1,100 political prisoners. It recruits child soldiers and commits extrajudicial executions, rape of women and girls, torture and forced relocation.

Appeared in *Chicago Sun Times*, August 19, 2006.

The SPDC has devastated ethnic minority areas. While forcibly relocating minority ethnic groups, it has destroyed 3,000 villages. More than 2 million have fled to Thailand and other neighboring countries. Hundreds of thousands are now internally displaced living in desperate conditions. And Burma's military government has cut off assistance to the internally displaced people.

For years, the United States unsuccessfully has sought to condemn Burma's activities at the U.N. Commission for Human Rights. But despite its record of abuse, Burma has escaped rebuke.

But last month when the ASEAN nations gathered in Malaysia for their annual meetings, an important step was taken. ASEAN has committed itself to democracy, human rights and the rule of law. As Malaysian foreign minister Syed Hamid Albar wrote, "There is genuine concern among the majority of ASEAN members that (Burma) is putting into question ASEAN's credibility and image." So in its joint communiqué the ASEAN nations finally criticized Burma.

It now is important to build international pressure on Burma's military junta to ease its repressive grip and restore respect for human rights.

Vaclav Havel and Archbishop Desmond Tutu commissioned a recent report that calls for "an urgent, new and multilateral diplomatic initiative" on Burma's human rights crisis and U.N. Security Council action.

The recent reforms of the U.N. human rights machinery were only partial and have raised questions about the capacity of the international community to seriously deal with human rights abuses. The U.N. Security Council taking robust action on Burma would be a positive response to such skepticism. More importantly, it would provide support and hope to the Burmese people who have suffered long enough.

The matter deserves attention. A first step has been taken. Our common humanity should require the U.N. now to increase the pressure for human rights in Burma.

HUMAN RIGHTS
AT THE CROSSROADS

Good morning. It's an honor and pleasure to be with the World Conference of Bar Leaders and have this opportunity to speak with you about Human Rights at the Crossroads.

I speak to you as an American proud of the principles upon which the United States was founded, proud of America's historical commitment to human rights, the values that have animated our history. I speak to you as someone who believes in those values and believes America's commitment to these values will long endure.

Nonetheless, human rights are at a crossroads globally and in the United States. Despite the increasing body of international law and growing global norms, human rights abuses – and even genocide -- are all too common. Despite America's heritage and commitment to the rule of law, the war on terror has created new challenges for America still unmet.

Human Rights matter. They are central to the American idea, our history and our aspirations for all mankind. It is in America's interest to promote these values and to advance freedom and democracy. Free and democratic states are more stable than oppressive and authoritarian regimes. Free societies are not fertile breeding grounds for terrorists. And nations that respect the rights of their own citizens are less likely to disrespect the rights of other countries and engage in military adventurism. Countries that share our values – that respect human rights – are our natural friends and allies. The larger the community of freedom, the safer and more secure America will be.

Today, human rights abuses abound. In *Zimbabwe*, Robert Mugabe's regime continues to conduct a campaign of violence, repression and intimidation against the people. In *Belarus*, Alexander Lukashenko, Europe's Last Dictator, denied his people the right to "free and fair" elections. In *China*, religious persecution, censorship and arbitrary imprisonment continues. Nobel Peace Prize winner and opposition leader Aung San Su Kyi is under house arrest in *Burma*. Women are still denied the right to an education in some parts of the world. *Cuba* remains an island prison where the judiciary is not independent nor due process respected. In *North Korea* forced labor camps and famine are tools of political control. In *Vietnam* security police beat suspects during arrests, detention, and interrogation. In *Syria* the government uses its vast powers to prevent any organized opposition activities. The list goes on.

Remarks at World Conference of Bar Leaders, Chicago Bar Association, Chicago, Illinois, September 15, 2006.

But this long litany of abuse pales in comparison to the world's greatest humanitarian crisis; the result of genocide in Darfur: a terrible, turbulent, tortured tale of wretched misery. This "genocide in slow motion" continues. It is a scar upon humanity. That the violence continues, the body count still rises, the rape and mayhem persist is a sad commentary about the international community, human rights and the mechanisms to promote and sustain the rule of law. We must do better or the noble words of our time will ring hollow in the corridors of history.

But let's take a step back. For despite these on-going human rights abuses, progress has been made.

After the horrors of World War II – the great destruction and particularly the holocaust's incomprehensible crimes against humanity, the victorious allied forces sought to avoid a repeat of such nightmares.

Early on President Franklin Roosevelt raised the possibility of a new international organization to advance fundamental values. Due to the success of the Allied coordinated prosecution of the war against the Axis powers, the concept of collective security gained currency. FDR had a vision of a new multilateral organization in which the lessons and habits of collective security would continue. President Truman embraced this vision and helped lead the launch of the United Nations in San Francisco in 1945.

It is important that in addition to the structures and governing mechanisms for the new organization, the U.N. Charter also commits member states to self-determination and human rights.

Soon thereafter a U.N. committee was formed to examine issues of human rights. I find it noteworthy that this committee was chaired by lifelong Democrat Eleanor Roosevelt and among its members was Republican John Foster Dulles, who would later serve as President Dwight Eisenhower's Secretary of State. Also among its members were representatives from Great Britain, the Philippines, Lebanon and the Soviet Union. After lengthy deliberations, this group proposed the U.N. Universal Declaration of Human Rights, which was adopted.

The Declaration is not perfect, but it is the result of hard work well done. As William Shultz, Executive Director or Amnesty International USA has written, "The mere articulation of such rights and their universal acclamation was a formidable achievement."

And, of course, other human rights instruments have followed: U.N. resolutions, treaties and conventions. Human rights norms have been established and recognized. They have been embraced in words, if not always in practice. These have become standards to which oppressed people can turn and seek to hold their governments to account. They are agreed standards that can guide the international community and to which the international community can hold rogue regimes that deny such rights. This advance is consequential.

While the rise of broad based human rights norms has been considerable, the machinery to translate the rhetoric to realities on the ground has had an uneven record at best.

The discredited U.N. Commission on Human Rights is but one example. In 2004, I served as U.S. Ambassador to the Commission in Geneva. The killing in

Darfur, Sudan already had begun. The Arab government in Khartoum had armed and unleashed the Arab janjaweed in Darfur against the civilian population of black farmers as a means to counter a small band of rebels in that region. Government attack helicopters fire down on villages followed by hordes of janjaweed on camel and horseback. Villages were burned, crops destroyed, wells poisoned, livestock stolen, men killed and women raped and branded. The atrocities were horrific, they were known, yet the U.N. Human Rights Commission seemed paralyzed.

In behalf of the United States, I tabled a resolution condemning the atrocities, demanding they stop and requiring Khartoum to allow international observers into Darfur to monitor the situation. Whatever chance such a muscular resolution had disappeared when the European Union cut a deal with African states for a weak resolution on Darfur that did not condemn, demand nor require. Indeed, it even commended Khartoum for its cooperation. The Europeans, like America, were horrified by the atrocities in Darfur, but in the diplomatic minuete and their desire for consensus, they had lost their way. The tougher United States resolution failed. The weaker EU-African resolution passed but without United States support.

Predictably Khartoum read this weak gesture as a reflection that the international community cared little about the atrocities being committed in Darfur, a distant little known area of sub-Saharan Africa. So the crimes against humanity continued and the body count grew. At the time of the 2004 UNCHR meeting in Geneva, the estimated deaths in Darfur were 20,000 and the number of displaced persons was a couple of hundred thousand. Today the deaths number up to 400,000 and the civilians whose villages and homes have been destroyed and who today live in desperate conditions in IDP and refugee camps number over 2.5 million.

The U.N. has long said that Darfur is the worst humanitarian crisis in the world. Yet the atrocities continue.

U.N. Security Council resolutions have been circumscribed and action limited. This is an affront to the standards of human rights to which the civilized world has subscribed and a scar upon humanity.

After World War II as the horrors of the holocaust became well known, the world said "Never again." Then came the Cambodian Killing Fields,. Rwanda. Bosnia. Kosovo. And now Darfur. The words "never again" have not been enforced with the bold action required to stop ethnic cleansing nor, in the case of Darfur, genocide. The international community must do better to stop the slaughter and mayhem in Darfur and where required in the future.

In another area of human rights machinery, restorative justice, the record also is uneven but steady progress has been made. After World War II, the Nuremburg trials were an unprecedented effort to exact a measure of accountability from Nazi leadership for their worst crimes against humanity. It was an extraordinary exercise of justice. When I first joined Mayer, Brown & Platt in the mid-80's, an older gentleman Roger Barrett had been head of the form's litigation department for years. A legendary trial lawyer, he had won numerous complex and significant trials. Mr. Barrett was a legend in the Chicago legal community. Yet he told me as he told others that the most important legal work he had ever done was as a young, junior staff lawyer supporting the Nuremburg trials. I suspect it was.

Many expected that such war crimes trials would continue as required by circumstances. Yet decades passed during which atrocities were, indeed, committed yet no such trials were held. But in the past decade or so the precedent established in Nuremburg has been resurrected with the creation of the International Criminal Tribunal for Yugoslavia in the Hague and the International Criminal Tribunal for Rwanda in Arusha. These have been imperfect mechanisms. Both the ICTY and the ICTR are too expensive and too slow. Last spring, ten years after the Dayton Peace Accords ending the fighting in Bosnia, Sloban Milosevic died in his sleep with no judgment yet rendered on his monstrous deeds. And the fact that the trials are being conducted far from where the crimes were committed means victims cannot witness justice being done and the proceedings are easily susceptible to political manipulation. Nonetheless, the ICTY and ICTR are important milestones on the road to restorative justice.

The Sierra Leone Special Court, part international and part national, has had a much shorter time frame and more disciplined budget. More important, the trials are taking place in Freetown, at the scene of the crimes. And, perhaps, most important, the Sierra Leone Special Court has indicted winners and losers. A sitting Minister was indicted as well as leaders of the rebels.

As for the situation in Darfur, the U.N. Security Council has voted for the International Criminal Court to have jurisdiction and ICC prosecutor Luis Moreno Ocampo has begun to gather evidence for the eventual trials.

And, as you know, the trials against Saddam Hussein and his colleagues have begun in Baghdad. While Saddam has tried to make a mockery of these proceedings, they are not. The once all powerful ruler who cavalierly exercised the power of life and death throughout Iraq, today sits in the dock. Charges of genocide against the Iraqi Kurds have been made and the evidence will be laid before the court for all to see. I believe justice will be done. Thereby the suffering of the Iraqi people will be recorded for history, there will be accountability, a legal line will be drawn between the lawless past and a future under the rule of law, and in this there will be a measure of renewal for Iraqis.

So there has been progress and setbacks in the advance of human rights. There are reasons for hope and cause for despair. Among the immediate challenges at the crossroads are the following.

Earlier this year the discredited U.N. Commission on Human Rights was abolished. Only partial reforms were passed as the U.N. General Assembly inaugurated the new Human Rights Council. Can this new organ rise above its structural weakness and avoid the pitfalls and disappointment of its predecessors?

Will Saddam Hussein's trial meet acceptable judicial standards in procedure, performance and outcome?

Can the international community finally act to end the "genocide in slow motion" that continues in Darfur?

And another matter of human rights at the crossroads is to find the wherewithal to respect human rights even as we prosecute the War on Terror. To paraphrase Bob Herbert of the *New York Times*, we cannot sacrifice the rule of law to the tyranny of fear.

The abuse at Abu Ghraid shocked the world. It did not reflect American morality. It did not reflect America's heart nor soul. It was a disgrace. But it revealed what can happen when inadequate training, insufficient oversight, and the passions of combat collide. Trials were held. A measure of accountability achieved through court martials and reports that condemned not only the soldiers at Abu Ghraib but higher ups who created an atmosphere of permissibility and a failure of command, Should those higher up the chain of command have paid a greater price? I suspect so.

I personally support wiretaps of terror suspects. But I do not endorse the Executive Branch making the decisions to wiretap unchecked by a court of law. That program must be fixed.

And now we are confronted by issues related to detainees and whether Article 3 of the Geneva Conventions should be respected or narrowed through new definitions that would allow various forms of inhuman treatment and torture.

Torture does not produce reliable, actionable intelligence. Trampling accepted standards of Article 3 will put our own military in greater danger if captured by the enemy. And by sacrificing human rights we weaken ourselves in the larger war on terror. Earlier today a letter was released from former Secretary of State Colin Powell, who also is a former Chairman of the Joint Chiefs of Staff, in which he writes, "The world is beginning to doubt the moral basis of our fight against terrorism. To redefine Common Article 3 would add to those doubts. Furthermore, it would put our own troops at risk."

Senator Lindsay Graham of South Carolina has been an Air Force prosecutor for over 20 years. About these matters, he has said, "The rules we set up speak more about us than it does the enemy. The enemy has no rules. They don't give people trials, they summarily execute them and they're brutal, inhuman creatures. But when we capture one of them, what we do is about us, not about them. Do they deserve, the bad ones, all the rights they are afforded? No. But are we required to do it because of what we believe? Yes."

In 1918, the world was ablaze with World War I's brutal fighting. Trench warfare and mustard gas had killed millions. British casualties were very high, as they were for the French, Italians and Russians. There was reason for grave anxiety and despair. The situation seemed in peril, but events took a turn with America's entry into the war. On July 4, 1918, Winston Churchill spoke at a meeting of the Anglo-Saxon Fellowship, an annual event marking the anniversary of the signing of America's Declaration of Independence. While he called for Germany's decisive defeat, he also spoke against vengeance. He spoke against the sort of atrocities committed by the Germans. "We cannot treat them… as they would treat us if they had the power," he said. "We are bound by the principles for which we are fighting. Whatever the extent of our victory, the German people will be protected by these principles. The Declaration of Independence, and all that it implies, must cover them."

Extremism versus moderation. Religious authoritarianism versus pluralism. Regression to the Middle Ages versus modernization. Barbarism versus the rule of law. We are engaged in a struggle. Our enemies know no mercy nor do they deserve it. We must safeguard the homeland. But ultimately the power of ideas, the strength of our morality and the pull of freedom are what will win this war; not weapons, nor fighting on the field of combat, nor sacrificing the fundamental human rights upon which America was founded and upon which justice relies.

America has long been a shining city on the hill, an example to the world. It is our heritage. It is our responsibility. It is our opportunity. To sacrifice our moral values and to circumscribe human rights in the prosecution of the war on terror will compromise our character, hurt our cause, and dim that light.

If we become like them, like the terrorists who neither respect innocent human life, fundamental standards of decency nor the rule of law, we will hurt our cause. By torturing our foes we will not help America and freedom prevail in the war on terror nor keep faith with the brave men and women who have sacrificed their lives so that America might be free.

Here too we are at a crossroads. And here we should take our stand with our better selves, with human rights, with the power of moral rectitude in prosecuting the war on terror. In this way we will prevail against terror and in this way we will be true to our heritage and our humanity.

Thank you.

Darfur:

For the Sake of Our Humanity, Action is Required to Stop the Mayhem Now

This horrific story is not new. The Holocaust. Cambodian Killing Fields. Rwanda. Bosnia. Kosovo. And now Darfur. A long litany of man's inhumanity to man. Apocalyptic scenes of mass murder, brutality and suffering known. Preventable. Yet this "genocide in slow motion" continues unchecked. Where is the outrage? Where is the political will to act? When will the savage slaughter end?

Canadian General Romeo Dallaire was force commander of the U.N. Assistance Mission for Rwanda. He writes of these turbulent times in his book *Shake Hands With The Devil: The Failure of Humanity in Rwanda.* "What happened in Rwanda in 1994 (is) a story of betrayal, failure, naiveté, indifference, hatred, genocide, war, inhumanity and evil. ...The Rwandan story is the story of the failure of humanity to heed a call for help from an endangered people."

In Darfur evil again stalks the earth. A desperate call for help has been made. But despite the humanitarian aid and the diplomatic posturing, humanity is failing to heed the call. The violence continues, the victims suffer, and the international community vacillates. It is well past the time when robust action should have been taken to end this crisis.

As Nobel laureate Elie Wiesel told the U.N. Security Council last week, "passivity helps the oppressor and not the oppressed." Wiesel went on to urge the Security Council members to remember the Rwandan genocide. "I do," he said. "Eight hundred thousand human beings were murdered. We knew then as we know now they could have been saved, and they were not."

Three years ago a small band of Darfur rebels attacked a government airfield. In response, the Arab government in Khartoum opened the gates of hell. They armed Arab militiamen known as the janjaweed and unleashed a scorched-earth campaign in the region targeting the black farming population. Government attack helicopters scrafed villages followed by hoards of janjaweed on horseback and camel swooping in to burn homes, destroy crops, kill or steal livestock, poison wells, kill the men and then rape and scare the women.

The atrocities have been ghastly and the consequences horrendous. The U.N. has long labeled Darfur the worst humanitarian crisis in the world.

Up to 400,000 people have died. Over 2.5 million people have been driven from their homes and live in desperate conditions in IDP and refugee camps. The

---

Appeared in *UNA-USA Newsletter*, September 19, 2006.

janjaweed even stalk those camps, sometimes killing males or raping women who venture out to gather firewood.

In 2004, as Ambassador to the U.N. Commission on Human Rights in Geneva, I tabled a U.S. resolution condemning the killing in Darfur, demanding it end and requiring Khartoum to admit U.N. observers to monitor the situation on the ground. That resolution failed. Instead a weak resolution was adopted by the member states noting the situation on the ground but not condemning, demanding nor requiring. It even commended Khartoum for its cooperation.

Before the vote I addressed my colleagues on the Commission on Human Rights. I said that in the future we "will be remembered for one thing and one thing alone: Did we have the courage and strength to take strong action against the ethnic cleansing in Darfur? We will be asked, 'Where were you at the time of the ethnic cleansing?' 'What did you do?'"

Two and a half years later, the killing continues and those questions still hang above us.

During this time, in fits and starts, the international community has addressed the mayhem and suffering in Darfur. A large humanitarian effort has been made to alleviate the suffering. The United States has been the most generous nation, giving more than $1.6 billion in humanitarian aid and peacekeeping assistance. Brave humanitarian workers on the ground have provided aid in perilous conditions. This past July alone there were 36 attacks on aid workers and in the past two months a dozen have been killed.

The United Nations and other international organizations have passed resolutions condemning what is going on. But Khartoum, reading the language of these declarations as weak and the international community's political will as halting, has not been detoured. A small African Union peacekeeping force was deployed to the region. While courageous, they are undermanned, ill-equipped, and have a limited mandate. The carnage has continued.

In May, the United States played a leading role in brokering a peace agreement between Khartoum and one of the rebel groups in Darfur. While imperfect, the deal seemed to offer a brief window of hope. It appears to have closed.

Today, in Darfur, people are being displaced, killed, violated and terrorized. John Prendergast of the International Crisis group just returned from Darfur. He has stated that he "found that the crisis is spiraling out of control: violence is increasing, malnutrition is soaring, and access to life-saving aid is shrinking."

The other day Secretary-General Kofi Annan said about Darfur, "Can the international community, having not done enough for the people of Rwanda in their time of need, just watch as this tragedy deepens? Can we contemplate failing yet another test? Lessons are either learned or not; principles are either upheld or scorned. This is no time for the middle ground of half measures or further debate."

The United States has been among those pressing for more robust action. This summer America introduced a U.N. Security Council resolution for U.N. Peacekeepers for Darfur and promised logistical assistance. While the resolution passed, Khartoum has refused to accept U.N. peacekeepers. The U.S. has called on allies to join Washington in pressing Sudan to accept the U.N. peacekeepers deployment. And last Friday, President Bush expressed frustrations with the situation and said it is time for the U.N. to act, with or without Khartoum's consent.

This month world leaders gather in New York City to address the opening of the U.N. General Assembly. There will be countless bi-lateral and group meetings on the margins of the General Assembly formal sessions. This moment should be seized by the international community finally to act to end the genocide in Darfur.

The United States and others must demand that the African Union peacekeepers remain on the ground and that they soon be replaced by robust U.N. peacekeepers. Beyond "the responsibility to protect" the innocent people who continue to be victimized within Darfur, the situation is a threat to international peace and security. It already has contributed to instability and violence in neighboring Chad.

NATO should enforce a no fly zone over Darfur and provide the intelligence assets to help the peacekeepers. ICC Prosecutor Luis Moreno Ocampo should be supported in his continuing work to acquire evidence of the atrocities for later prosecutions. And sanctions restricting travel of Khartoum leaders and freezing assets should be imposed.

Peter Ronayne, in his powerful book *Never Again?* writes about the tragic genocide in Rwanda twelve years ago, "Rwanda dared the outside world to act against a heinous international crime it had pledged to arrest. ...The tragedy of Rwanda is particularly dramatic because the opportunity clearly existed in the United States and its partners to intervene effectively, save hundreds of thousands of lives, and invigorate as never before the ethical vision embedded in the U.N. Convention on the Prevention and Punishment of the Crime of Genocide."

In Darfur, the international community has failed to live up to its pledge of "Never again." Incomprehensible violence has been committed and innocent lives have been lost. This "genocide in slow motion" continues. Too little has been done.

In the future we will be asked, "Where were you at the time of genocide in Darfur? What did you do?"

As the U.N. General Assembly convenes this month, world leaders should seize this moment to act to end this carnage. If not now, when?

SADDAM'S TRIAL GIVES COMFORT TO HIS VICTIMS

For decades Saddam Hussein's brutal regime held power through intimidation, arbitrary arrest, torture, killing and mass murder. Every Iraqi lived in fear of Saddam's paranoia and cruelty.

Since Saddam's fall, Iraqis have been free from fear of that tyrant, but they have been confronted by other dangers. Iraq has been engulfed in sectarian violence as the struggle for advantage, position and power has not been contained within the legitimate political process, but exploded into on-going bloodshed. .

Yet in the midst of this river of death and destruction, a significant step is being made to achieve restorative justice. A trial has begun to bring accountability, and a measure of healing.

Saddam Hussein is standing trial for genocide in the Anfal military campaign against Iraqi Kurds in the 1980's.

Saddam, the once all-powerful ruler who cavalierly controlled life and death in Iraq sits in the dock.

One of the Kurdish prosecutors, Jiyan Aziz, said "When I first entered the court, I felt that the time of judgment had arrived. To see Saddam and his gang there, so powerless now, and how they had hurt so many people in the past, it gave me comfort."

Saddam is accused of ordering the killing of nearly 200,000 Kurds in a targeted reign of terror.

With brutal efficiency Saddam sought to eradicate the Iraqi Kurds. Saddam ordered the use of chemical weapons against his own people. Thousands of Kurdish villagers were destroyed. Many of those that escaped death by chemical weapons were sent to prisons and tortured.

Mike Tucker has interviewed victims of Saddam's unrelenting savagery and published the chilling testimonials in his book, *Hell is Over: Voices of the Kurds After Saddam*. Amin Ismail told him: "The torture in Kirkuk was the worst. ...There the secret police used heavy steel fan blades, electricity on your private parts, and there was a deep dungeon. In the dungeon, the Iraqis put snakes near us. ...(They) had no dignity or sympathy toward us – they were far from humanity."

Appeared in *UNA-USA Newsletter*, September 19, 2006.

And Jemil Mahmoud Suleiyman Besefky said, "Horror is not just a word, it is real as the hawk in the sky and the wind on a river. ...What Hitler wanted to do to the Jews, Saddam wanted to do to us, to exterminate us as a race, as a people, as a culture. Never again will we see the chemical attacks and the mass graves. ...Never again."

The evidence of these atrocities is considerable, the chain of responsibility to Saddam inescapable. There are remains from mass graves, countless testimonials from survivors and official documents ordering the eradication of Iraqi Kurds.

As a society struggles to emerge from a dark past and move forward to a liberal future, restorative justice is important. It creates a record of the past misdeeds and suffering that cannot be denied at some future date. It provides accountability and a measure of justice. It demonstrates the power of the rule of law and signifies its arrival. And through justice being done, it can contribute to healing.

The Iraqi people have suffered greatly for too long. Unfortunately, their travails are not over. But the trial of Saddam Hussein for crimes against humanity is consequential for the rule of law, for international norms against genocide; but most importantly, for the Iraqi people.

Genocide in Darfur: The U.S. Role in Protecting Human Rights

The greatest humanitarian crisis in the world is in Darfur, Sudan. It is manmade. It is horrific. And it must end.

The international community has the capacity to stop this carnage. Yet it has not done so. And now while the vicious violence continues in Darfur, the horrors, mayhem and slaughter have bled over into neighboring Chad.

Just last week in the *New York Times,* Nicholas Kristof reported another story of unspeakable sorrow. He wrote:

> "In isolated villages, everything is more straightforward – like the men on Tuesday who captured Abdullah Idris, a 27-year old father of two, in the fields as he was farming. They tried to shoot him in the chest, but the gun misfired.

> "So they beat him to the ground, explained Osman Omar, a nephew of Mr. Abdullah who was one of several neighbors who recounted the events in the same way. And then they used their bayonets to gouge out his eyes.

> "Mr. Abdullah lay on his back on a hospital bed, his eye sockets swathed in bandages soaked in blood and pus. A sister sat on the floor beside him, crying; his wife and small children stood nearby, looking overwhelmed and bewildered. He was so traumatized in the incident that he has been unable to speak since, but he constantly reaches out to hold the hands of his family members.

> "Three men and two women were killed in that attack by the janjaweed, the militias of Arab nomad that have been slaughtering black African farmers for more than three years now. A 25-year old woman was kidnapped, and nobody has seen her since.

> "The janjaweed even explained themselves to the people they were attacking. Survivors quoted them as shouting racial epithets against blacks and yelling, 'We are going to kill you, and we are going to take your land.'

Remarks at Benedictine University, Lisle, Illinois, November 20, 2006.

"Mr. Abdullah's eyes were gouged out as part of a wave of recent attacks here in southeastern Chad. Officials from the U.N. refugee agency counted at least 220 people killed in the last week in this area near Goz Beida.

"We're used to seeing brutal janjaweed attacks in Darfur itself and along the border with Chad, but now they have reached 60 miles and more inside Chad, and Chadian Arab groups are joining in the attacks on black African tribes."[1]

Paul Salopek is a journalist who was on assignment for *National Geographic* in East Africa earlier this autumn. He was captured in Darfur by a pro-government militia, beaten, his car and equipment stolen. He was held behind bars for 34 days by Sudanese military intelligence. His crime, as best he could determine, was "reporting on a humanitarian catastrophe that is largely invisible to the outside world, and that is poised to grow worse in the weeks ahead."[2]

Mr. Salopek wrote upon his release that "(t)housands of villages will likely die soon in Darfur, the arid homeland of millions of farmers and herders who have been targeted in a ruthless civil war. ...Their torched huts, seen from the air, look like cigarette burns on a torture victim's skin."[3]

The moral terrain of international relations is not simple, nor is it easy. The moral dilemmas with which we are confronted are complex and they are difficult. Nonetheless, to deny our moral responsibility is to deny our humanity. We cannot do everything. Resources, reach and resolve have limits. But there are some atrocities so horrendous, some suffering so great, some values so fundamental that mere rhetoric and condemnation is inadequate.

After the Holocaust, the world said "Never Again." Then came the Cambodian Killing Fields. Rwanda. Bosnia. Kosovo. Each time the world said "Never Again," as the innocent suffered, bloodshed and mayhem ran wild and bodies were piled high. Now the world watches the "genocide in slow motion" in Darfur. Again the list of ethnic cleansing and genocide is being extended. Again words of outrage and condemnation are spoken. Again too little, too late, is being done to stop the vicious violence.

Human Rights Matter

Human Rights matter. They are central to the American idea, our history and our aspirations for all mankind. As American diplomat and scholar Dr. Jeane J. Kirkpatrick has written, "The fact that Americans do not share common history, race, language, or religion gives added centrality to American values, beliefs, and goals, making them the key element of our national identity. The American people are defined by the American creed. The vision of the public which defines us is and always has been a commitment to individual freedom and a conviction that government exists, above all, for the purpose of protecting individual rights."[4]

Human rights are grounded on the recognition that every human being has "inherent dignity and worth."

The concern for human rights is interwoven in our national experience and our beliefs as Americans. It is what has differentiated the United States from so many other nations in history. It is fundamental to our character and our values.

As Joshua Muravchik wrote in his book *Exporting Democracy: Fulfilling America's Destiny*, "America's founders began with the premise that man had been created in the image of God and that all were of equal worth and endowed with inalienable rights. In founding the modern world's first democracy, they set out to create a system that would follow this premise and that would suit human nature as they understood it."[5]

From early in the Twentieth century when the United States thrust itself onto the world stage as a major, and eventually the major, global power, the tradition of American Exceptionalism and the universality of American values have informed U.S. foreign policy.

President Woodrow Wilson insisted that the United States' role was "not to prove; ...our selfishness but our greatness."[6] And it was on a moral foundation, with the primary objective of a new and more just international order, that Wilson justified the United States entry into the war and not on any specific grievances.[7]

At the outset of World War II, President Franklin Roosevelt described the war as a fight for freedom.[8] And, led by the United States, in 1942, the Allies declared that victory was necessary "to defend life, liberty, independence and religious freedom and to preserve human rights and justice in their own lands as well as other lands."[9]

The United States included human rights in its planning for the post war order. "With active United States support, (human rights) appeared in the Nuremburg Charter, in the United Nations Charter, and in the Charter of the Organization of American States."[10] President Truman reaffirmed America's commitment to freedom and democracy in launching the Marshall Plan to rebuild European democracies devastated by World War II.[11] And it was during Truman's Presidency that Eleanor Roosevelt chaired the committee that drafted the U.N. Universal Declaration on Human Rights.[12]

In his inaugural address, President Kennedy made clear America's continued commitment to human rights at home and abroad when he said, "[T]he torch has been passed to a new generation of Americans, born to this century, tempered by war, disciplined by a hard and bitter peace, proud of our ancient heritage, and unwilling to witness or permit the slow undoing of those *human rights* to which this nation has always been committed, and *to which we are committed today at home and around the world*."[13]

President Ford's administration negotiated the Helsinki agreement that, among other things, committed the Soviet Union and other "closed and controlled countries to permit greater freedom of movement for individuals and freer flow of information and ideas."[14] At the European Security Conference in Finland at which the Accord was signed, President Ford said, "[I]t is important that you realize the deep devotion of the American people and their government to human rights and fundamental freedoms and thus to the pledges that this conference has made regarding the freer movement of people, ideas, information."[15]

In his inaugural address, President Jimmy Carter said, "Because we are all free, we can never be indifferent to the fate of freedom elsewhere... Our commitment to human rights must be absolute."[16]

We won the great struggle of the 20th century. Freedom and democracy prevailed over totalitarian communism.

But the struggle for freedom is not over. Brutal authoritarian states continue to enslave people around the world. Basic human rights and personal dignity continue to be denied. This is wrong. Furthermore, these harsh conditions can give root to the frustration and despair that breeds terrorists who lash out at the United States in desperate acts of violence.

It is in America's interest to promote human rights and to advance freedom and democracy.[17] Free and democratic states are more stable than oppressive and authoritarian regimes.[18] Free societies are not fertile breeding grounds for terrorists. And nations that respect the rights of their own citizens are less likely to disrespect the rights of other countries and engage in military adventurism.[19]

Countries that share our values are our natural friends and allies. The larger the community of freedom, the safer and more secure America will be.

As President Bush has said, "The advance of freedom is the calling of our time, it is the calling of our country... We believe that liberty is the design of nature, we believe that liberty is the direction of history... And we believe that freedom – the freedom we prize – is not for us alone, it is the right and the capacity of all mankind."[20]

Human rights are not the sole consideration of U.S. foreign policy nor should they be, but neither can human rights be irrelevant.[21] Human rights are fundamental to who we are and human rights properly should animate our actions individually and as a nation. Respecting human rights and defending those values are the right thing to do and it is in our self-interest to do so. Countries that respect human rights under the rule of law are more stable and more prosperous. As Winston Churchill said, "Justice knows no frontiers."[22]

Humanitarian Intervention

However, accepting that human rights properly should enliven U.S. foreign policy, does not mean America should engage in humanitarian interventions willy-nilly whether unilaterally, as part of a coalition of the willing, or as part of a broad international mission sanctioned by a multilateral institution such as NATO or the United Nations.

America must strive to be faithful to our fundamental values at home. America should project those values by example, by embracing and advancing important international moral norm setting such as the U.N. Universal Declaration on Human Rights, and by being willing to give voice to voiceless victims of human rights abuse through naming and shaming abusers. But the issue of humanitarian intervention must meet a higher test.

Intervention can be relatively benign or robust. It can take the form of episodic or sustained diplomacy, whether unilateral or multilateral. Intervention can be made through incentives such as economic assistance[23] or trade benefits or disincentives such as curbing aid or imposing sanctions.[24] And in the most acute situations, intervention can take the form of peacekeepers or peacemakers. While military intervention is the last resort, it nonetheless may be the only choice.

We cannot intervene everywhere. Every conflict and every humanitarian crisis cannot be met. Resources are finite.[25] Political will is limited. And capacity, even for the world's sole superpower, even for donor nations collectively, can stretch only so far.[26] But just because we cannot do everything does not mean we should do nothing.

Any decision to make an intervention must recognize that conflicts within countries are inherently messy. There are no clear battlefields and no sharp line between combatants and civilians. Often there are many parties to the conflict with shifting alliances and uneven discipline.[27] Guerilla movements have little understanding of norms and poor command and control mechanics.[28] Agreements are rarely absolute. In such an environment, armed bandits with no political agenda often operate.[29] And however committed the external interveners, it is extremely difficult and dangerous if local combatants are prepared to fight to the end and, as in Iraq, kill themselves to inflict casualties on the outsiders.[30]

At best, humanitarian interventions are partial solutions. They seek to relieve suffering but may not address the conflict itself nor its underlying causes. Sometimes the target population for humanitarian relief is a community which a combatant is trying to displace through terror and deprivation. There is a danger that peacekeepers may be drawn into the conflict. While the primary purpose is to relieve the suffering, not to maintain peace and security, alleviating the suffering itself might tip the balance of a conflict politically or militarily.[31]

The burden for possible humanitarian interventions, as in so many crises around the world, falls heaviest upon the United States. Often we are the only country with the economic, logistical, intelligence and military capabilities to lead a large scale humanitarian operation in remote corners of the world. Nonetheless, the United States military is not trained to be, nor should it become, "international social workers."[32] Humanitarian missions do not exploit the unique capabilities of United States armed forces for high intensity combats.[33] Many functions of humanitarian interventions can be competently handled by other countries.[34] This invites multilateral responses to humanitarian crisis. Sometimes this may be through a coalition of the willing, sometimes through regional organizations[35] and often through the United Nations.

Genocide provides a particularly compelling case for intervention.

Even skeptics of humanitarian intervention often support military action to stop genocide. Columnist Charles Krauthammer has written, "At what point does a violation of humanitarian norms become so extraordinary as to justify, indeed morally compel, military intervention? At the point of genocide … [l]esser crimes have a claim on our sympathies but not our soldiers."[36] Henry Kissinger has said that in the case of genocide, "the moral outrage has to predominate over any considerations of power politics," and that in Rwanda he "personally would have supported an intervention."[37] And President George W. Bush's desire to prevent genocide before it starts guided policy and diplomacy at the US Mission to the United Nations to be forward-leaning on Burundi and the eastern Democratic Republic of the Congo.[38]

This leads me back to the particulars of the "genocide in slow motion" in Darfur.

A large region in western Sudan, Darfur has scarce natural resources and historically has suffered from economic discrimination and neglect.[39] Long an autonomous sultanate, Darfur was conquered by the British in 1916 and merged with Sudan. Professor Gerard Prunier, in his book *Darfur: The Ambiguous Genocide*, traces to British colonial rule policies to keep Darfur backward.[40] They have continued. The Arab government in Khartoum ignored Darfur's infrastructure, rarely paying for road repair, schools or hospitals.

Over time, the deprivation in Darfur has led to fights over land and water between the agriculturalists and nomadic tribes. In the 1980's draught and desertification drove the Arab nomadic pastoralists further south into areas of black agriculturalists. There were occasional violent clashes. Khartoum supported the nomads. In 1985, during a period of famine, Khartoum had Libyan forces deliver food aid in Darfur.[41] This accelerated the polarization in Darfur between Arab and non-Arab, which before had been splintered between dozens of tribes, languages and customs. Resentment grew among the "African" agriculturalists toward the Khartoum-backed "Arabs."[42] Also, during this period, the civil war in neighboring Chad spilled over in Darfur and "led some Arab tribes to adopt a supremacist ideology."[43]

In 2003, while Khartoum was consumed with fighting a major rebellion in the south, two small insurgences from the "African" agriculturalists engaged in a series of raids and skirmishes killing several government troops in Darfur.[44] Awful as these casualties were, this small rebel movement posed no serious threat to Khartoum's rule. However, reluctant to divert soldiers from the south, Khartoum opened the gates of hell.

Professor Benjamin Valentino in his book *Final Solutions: Mass Killing and Genocide in the 20th Century* concludes that "(m)ass killing normally is driven by instrumental, strategic calculations. Perpetrators see mass killing as a means to an end, not an end in itself."[45]

Rather than reply with a targeted response directed at a few men of the incipient rebellion, Khartoum further armed the militia in Darfur.[46] More than 20,000 highwaymen and bandits were armed, drawn from impoverished nomadic Arab groups in Darfur and Chad. Then these militia, known as the Janjaweed, were unleashed to wage a systematic campaign of mayhem and destruction against African civilians in the area belonging to the same non-Arab ethnic groups as the rebels: the Fur, Masaalit and Zaghawa. One commentator has written that "(t)he Sudanese government's tactic seems to have been straight from the Maoist theory book. By destroying African villages, the army and their Arab militia allies drained the sea the rebels swim in."[47]

Often the attacks begin with government aerial bombardment of civilians – mainly using Antonov supply planes dropping lethal barrel bombs filled with metal shards, sometimes using helicopter gunships or MIG jet fighters.[48] After the aerial attacks, Janjaweed riding camels and on horseback sweep into villages. They burn huts, destroy crops, slaughter or steal livestock, rape and brand women as slaves. African males, infant, men and elderly, have been butchered. And non-Arab Sudanese have been systematically expelled from their homes.

The overwhelming majority of the men, women and children victimized by these merciless atrocities have no relation whatsoever to the insurgents. Their crime is their ethnicity. They are non-Arab and they are defenseless.

Terrible crimes have been committed. Innocent people suffer and many continue to perish. The ethnic cleansing has risen to horrific levels.

The ethnic pattern of these atrocities is clear. A United Nations observer team reported that non-Arab black villages were attacked while Arab villages were untouched.[49]

Two and a half years ago, U.N. Secretary-General Kofi Annan warned of "ethnic cleansing" in Darfur and called on the international community to act. Twenty-eight months ago, then Secretary of State Colin Powell labeled the ongoing atrocities in Darfur "genocide." [50] Meanwhile, the violent atrocities continued and the world's response has been modest.

Paul Rosesabagina faced the forces of evil during the genocide in Rwanda and emerged a hero. The film "Hotel Rwanda" was based on his story as a hotel manager in Kigali who saved Tutsis in the midst of the killings by offering them refuge. Not long ago he wrote:

> History shows us that genocides can happen only if four import conditions are in place. There must be the cover of a war. Ethnic grievances must be manipulated and exaggerated. Ordinary citizens must be deputized by their government to become executioners. And the rest of the world must be persuaded to look away and do nothing. The last is the most shameful of all, especially so because genocide is happening again right now in Darfur and the world community has done precious little to stop the killings.[51]

Testimonials of Horror

A numbing number of people have died in Darfur. Estimates range up to 400,000. And more than 2.5 million Africans have been driven from their homes. Most now live in desperate conditions in refugee camps in southern Sudan and neighboring Chad.[52] Even while living in these perilous conditions the black Africans from Darfur are not safe. In addition to malnutrition and disease, a number of refugee camps have been attacked by the Janjaweed.[53] When will this nightmare end?

The sheer numbers do not tell the real story. Numbers never do. The stories of the Sudanese army and Janjaweed atrocities are horrific. No mercy has been given. Their ferocious attacks on innocent Africans have left a trail of destruction, death, and misery.

As a consequence of the good work and diligence of journalists, United Nations officials, and human rights and humanitarian workers, the destruction in Darfur has been documented and many of the disturbing stories of horror has been recorded. It is through the voice of the victims that one can gain some appreciation for the unremitting brutality inflicted upon Darfur.

Amina Abakar Mohammed from Furawiyah told her story to award-winning journalist Samantha Power.

> One day "(n)ot long after dawn, when Amina and Mohammed (her 10 year old son) arrived at the wells, they heard the sound of approaching planes. Fifteen minutes later, Amina recalled, the aircraft began bombing... When Amina saw the janjaweed approaching, she hurried the donkeys to a red-rock hillock three hundred yards away. She assumed that Mohammed had fled in another direction, but she turned and saw that he had remained at the wells, with the older boys and the men, in an effort to protect the animals. He and the others were surrounded by several hundred janjaweed. As the circle closed around her son, she ducked behind the hillock and prayed.
>
> By nightfall, the sounds of gunfire and screaming had faded, and Amina furtively returned to the wells. She discovered that they were stuffed with corpses, many of which had been dismembered. She was determined to find her son, but also hoped that she wouldn't. Rummaging frantically around the wells by the moonlight, she saw the bodies of dozens of people she knew, but for a long time she was unable to find her firstborn. Suddenly, she spotted his face – but only his face. Mohammed had been beheaded.[54]

Several months later, Ms. Power visited Furawiyah and went to where the wells in which the Janjaweed had stuffed the bodies of their victims had been. Now there only was desert. The Janjaweed had covered the evidence of their crimes and, in the process, taken away wells that had nourished the people for generations.

In Terchana, 205 Africans were killed in one day by Janjaweed accompanied by three carloads of soldiers. A forty-two year old from that village, Adam, reported that the dead included twenty-three women and a one hundred-year-old man, Barra Younis. "Barra Younis couldn't walk and the Janjaweed burned him alive in his hut. They saw him there and they burned him." They took the cattle and burned all the village. They took some food for the horses and burned the rest.[55]

Another typical case of torture was reported from the Garsila area. "A Fur man was detained and whipped until all the skin was flayed from his back. The whip handle was then used to gouge holes in his flesh."[56]

And sexual violence is a common crime that accompany Janjaweed attacks.[57] "In the villages of Dingo and Koroma in Dar Masalit, for example, men have reported that the Janjaweed 'took girls into the grass and raped them there.' One of the girls raped was only thirteen-years-old. Near Sissi, three women, aged thirty-two, twenty-two and twenty-five, were abducted at a water hole and taken to Nouri School, which was abandoned, and were raped. In the village of Dureysa, on the Masalit – Fur border, a seventeen-year-old girl who resisted rape was killed and her naked body left on the street."[58]

A 37-year old from Mukjar told Amnesty International how the Janjaweed had raped and humiliated women.

When we tried to escape they shot more children. They raped women; I saw many cases of Janjaweed raping women and girls. They are happy when they rape. They sing when they rape and they tell us that we are just slaves and that they can do with us how they wish.[59]

A woman from Silaya who was five months pregnant when she was abducted by the Janjaweed with eight other women shared this story.

After six days, some of the girls were released. But the others, as young as eight years old were kept there. Five to six men would rape us in rounds, one after the other for hours during six days, every night. My husband could not forgive me after this, he disowned me."[60]

A group of Masalit women in Goz Amer refugee camp reported their Janjaweed attackers cried out, "You blacks, you have spoilt the country! We are here to burn you. We will kill your husbands and sons and we will sleep with you!"[61]

A Mesalit chief from the village of Disa reported that during the attack on his village the Janjaweed said:

You are Blacks, no Blacks can stay here, and no Black can stay in Sudan… The blood of the Blacks runs like water, we take their goods and we chase them from our area and our cattle will be in their land. The power of al-Bashir (president of Sudan) belongs to the Arabs and we will kill you until the end, you Blacks, we have killed your God.[62]

The testimonies are gruesome. And they echo thousands of other stories that have been collected from Darfur. They speak of summarily or indiscriminately killed Africans. They speak of raped, tortured, abducted and forcibly displaced Africans. They give account to how girls and women have been the particular target of sexual crimes. The killings, the atrocities have been known. They continue. Yet the international community has done little. Why?

The Response

The problems in Darfur began in February 2003.[63] In April 2004, on the International Day of Reflection on the 1994 Rwanda Genocide, U.N. Secretary-General Kofi Annan traveled to Geneva to address the U.N. Commission on Human Rights. Turning to the gruesome events in Darfur, he called the killings "ethnic cleansing." He demanded "swift and decisive action" from the international community. He even raised the possibility of "military action."[64] But rather than strong action, the Commission passed a weak resolution that did not condemn the atrocities, nor demand they end, nor require humanitarian access.[65] The message to Khartoum was clear: the international community cared little about carnage in a far away land. The killings continued.

Over the next months, as the body count rose, the United States sought robust resolutions in the U.N. Security Council condemning the violence and applying sanctions on the perpetrators. And repeatedly these initiatives failed. China and Russia joined African states and Islamic nations in resisting muscular action. Why?

Economic interests, regional loyalty and religious solidarity.[66] It has been multilateral diplomacy at its cynical worst and the U.N. as feckless, unctuous and shameful.

As the months went by, the U.N. Security Council remained "seized" by the issue. The body count continued to rise.

Eventually the African Union sent a contingent to monitor one shaky ceasefire after another.[67] Today the AU troops in Sudan number 7,000. But it is impossible for them to cover an area about the size of Texas, with poor equipment and little support. And with a mandate to monitor but not protect, the AU troops are merely witnesses to the on-going atrocities and not a protection for the innocent people. The mayhem, mass displacement, rape and killings continue.

These dreadful crimes against humanity have not gone on in the dark of night. They are known. For example, in July 2005, U.N. High Commissioner for Human Rights Louise Arbor reported that "rape and gang rape continue to be perpetrated by armed elements in Darfur, some of whom are members of law enforcement agencies and the armed forces."[68]

Relentlessly, the violence has continued. In December, 2005, the U.N. mission in Sudan (UNMIS) reported that in Western Darfur, the Janjaweed attacked Congo Herasa and destroyed the town's wells that humanitarian workers had constructed.[69] U.N. staff and international NGO workers continued to face "harassment, threats and ambushes in Darfur.[70] In December, 2005, the U.N. Children's Fund reported that 1.25 million children in need were beyond reach of aid in Darfur due to continued violence.[71]

By last spring, the atrocities in Darfur had bled into neighboring Chad. Janjaweed crossed Sudan's border to terrorize displaced blacks from Darfur, marauding near refugee camps, attacking those who traveled out to gather wood, killing men and raping women.[72]

In February, 2006, the U.N. Security Council agreed to begin the planning process to send U.N. peacekeepers to Darfur with a final decision to come later.[73] In early May, a peace agreement on Darfur was hammered out in talks in Abuja, Nigeria.[74] Khartoum and the largest rebel group, the Sudan Liberation Army, agreed to a cease-fire and disarming the Janjaweed militias. But there has been no cease fire. The Janjaweed have not been disarmed. Due to objections from the Sudanese government in Khartoum, there are no U.N. peacekeeper boots on the ground.[75] By the estimate of some observers, the human rights situation in Darfur has deteriorated further.[76] The tragic river of blood in Darfur continues to flow.

This past weekend, the *New York Times* reported the story of Halima Abdelkarim.

> "Last spring, Janjaweed militia attacked her village. They killed many men and seized 10 women and girls, including Halima and her little sister, Sadia.

> "Halima says that the janjaweed, many of them wearing Sudanese military uniforms, mocked the women with racial epithets against blacks, beat them with sticks, and gang-raped them all. Halima, who was then four months pregnant, says she was raped by three men and saw two rape Sadia – who was just 10 years old.

"After two days of torment, the janjaweed released them. But Sadia refused to give up her donkey, and so they shot her, Halima recalled. 'I was with her. She died right away.'

"The survivors trekked to a shanty-town outside Goz Beida. At first they were safe, and Halima gave birth to a baby daughter. But a couple of months ago the janjaweed began to attack them when they left the camp to get firewood.

"So last month, the janjaweed caught Halima again. …

"Halima was gathering firewood with a large group of women, who were hoping for safety in numbers. But raiders with guns suddenly appeared and caught seven of them.

"The men asked what tribe they belonged to, and upon learning that they were Dajo who had already fled their villages, said, 'We're looking for you.' Halima was carrying her infant girl, Noorelayn, and she says the janjaweed threw the baby to the ground.

"'You blacks are not human,' she quoted them as yelling. 'We can do anything we want to you. You cannot live here.'

"Finally, she says, three men raped her, beat her and stole her clothes. Another of the seven who were caught, Aziza Yakuh, 17, confirmed Halima's story, and added that the janjaweed told her while raping her: 'You blacks are like monkeys. You are not human.'

"The only way for these women to survive is to gather firewood to sell or exchange for food. Only women collect firewood, because, as they themselves say: 'The men are killed; the women are 'only' raped.'

"Halima's husband doesn't know about the latest attack. She didn't tell him about the first one, but he figured out what must have happened during the two days she disappeared. Although he didn't blame her, he left her for a few months partly to work out his anger at the janjaweed, and partly to cultivate crops to feed his family. The area he went to was attacked this month, with the janjaweed killing many men or occasionally gouging out their eyes with bayonets. There has been no word from him."[77]

What Should We Do?

A few days ago, Khartoum bowed to outside pressure and agreed in principle to accept some U.N. peacekeepers in Darfur.[78] Given Khartoum's history of deceit, delay and denial, we should take this most recent gambit with a grain of salt. Already there are conflicting reports out of Khartoum on whether or not the Government has, in fact, agreed to a U.N. presence. [79] This weekend, Jan Egeland, U.N. Under-Secretary General for humanitarian affairs said, "This is the moment of truth for Darfur. We are playing with a powder keg. It could get infinitely worse."[80]

The United States must have high level engagement on Darfur.[81] The recent appointment of Andrew Natsios, former director of USAID, as President Bush's personal envoy on this matter is a positive step.[82]

The United States should increase its intelligence gathering in the area, so we have a better sense of what is happening on the ground.

President Bush should make Darfur a higher priority in direct talks with China and Russia, particularly Beijing for whom oil has trumped stopping the carnage.

The U.S. must use this moment for robust engagement on Darfur at the U.N. Security Council with other member states and the Secretariate to insure sufficient political support for U.N. Peacekeepers to Darfur, adequate resources to get the job done and early deployment. The U.S. should help provide the necessary logistical support for the U.N. Peacekeeping mission. The U.S. should continue to push for Security Council targeted sanctions against individuals responsible for the worst abuses, including seizing assets, targeted travel bans and an arms embargo.

As a fall back, if we cannot secure requisite targeted sanctions in the U.N. Security Council, we should pursue U.S.-European sanctions.

Acting with our allies, the U.S. should push for greater NATO involvement to help stop the killing in Darfur. It is especially important that Washington push France and Germany to support NTO enforcement of a no-fly zone over Darfur.

And finally, if, despite recent signals from Khartoum that they may accept U.N. Peacekeepers, the Sudanese Government reverses itself and again opposes U.N. Peacekeepers, the United States should be prepared to consider a Chapter VII deployment with or without Khartoum's acquiescence.

Sixty years ago, the United States joined with others in saying, "Never again." Is it not time to give meaning to that pledge?

Close

Today we live in an era of American Primacy in which we stand with unparalleled military might, economic strength and cultural reach. We live in a time when our ideas, values and way of life are challenged by Islamic extremists who target innocent people for death and destruction. We face growing dangers from the spread of weapons of mass destruction in the hands of rogue regimes in North Korea, Iran and elsewhere. And today our best and most noble patriots serve in uniform and shed blood in Iraq and Afghanistan.

This is not a time of discretionary foreign policy. It is not a time when America's focus can be lost. But it also is a time when we can ill afford to lose our moral compass. It is a time when we must stay true to our values and call on our better selves.

At the death of President Franklin Delano Roosevelt in April, 1945, Winston Churchill said of the President and America's military might in World War II, "[T]his was no more than worldly power and grandeur, had it not been that the cause of human freedom and of social justice, to which so much of his life had been given, added a luster to this power and pomp and warlike might, which will long be discernable among men."[83]

It is our challenge, opportunity and responsibility to make sure "the cause of human freedom and social justice" adds luster to America's power today. That cause must animate our actions. We must give voice to the voiceless victims of abuse. And, when confronted by the evils of ethnic cleansing or genocide we must go beyond mere rhetoric to provide humanitarian assistance and to act to end the carnage. The "genocide in slow motion" in Darfur has gone on too long, claimed too many innocent people, scared our time too deeply. America, our allies, the civilized world must act.

Twenty-five years ago, President Ronald Reagan said, "We have a decision to make. Will we continue with yesterday's agenda and yesterday's failures, or will we reassert our ideals and our standards, will we reaffirm our faith, and renew our purpose? This is a time for choosing."[84] Let us choose to act to stop the mayhem, torture and genocide in Darfur.

Thank you.

---

1.   Nicholas D. Kristof, "Bandages and Bayonets," *New York Times*, November 12, 2006.

2.   Paul Salopek, "Humanitarian Catastrophe Unfolds in the Troubled Region of Sudan," *Chicago Tribune*, October 8, 2006.

3.   *Ibid.* See also, Katharine Houreld, "Sudan Closing Off Darfur to Outside World," *Christian Science Monitor*, November 17, 2006.

4.   Jeane J. Kirkpatrick, *Legitimacy and Force: Political and Moral Dimensions* (New Brunswick, N.J.; Transaction Books, 1988), p. 135.

5.   Joshua Muravchik, *Exporting Democracy: Fulfilling America's Destiny* (Washington, D.C.; AEI Press; 1991), p. 1.

6.   Woodrow Wilson, Remarks to Confederate Veterans in Washington, June 5, 1917, in Arthur S. Link, ed., *The Papers of Woodrow Wilson* (Princeton, N.J.; Princeton University Press; 1966), Vol. 42, p. 453.

On another occasion, President Wilson said, "[B]ecause we demand unmolested development and the undisturbed government of our own lives upon our own principles of right and liberty, we resent, from whatever quarter it may come, the aggression we ourselves will not practice. We insist upon *secretly* in prosecuting our self-chosen *liners* of national development. We do more than that. We demand it also for others. We do not confine our enthusiasm for individual liberty and the free national development to the incidents and movements of affairs which affect only ourselves. We feel it wherever there is a people that tries to walk in those difficult paths of independence and right." Woodrow Wilson, Annual Message to Congress on the State of the Union, December 7, 1915, in *ibid.*, Vol. 35, p. 297.

7.   In his speech asking Congress for a declaration of war, Wilson said, "It is a fearful thing to lead this great peaceful people into war, into the most terrible and disastrous of all wars, civilization itself seems to be in the balance. But right is more precious than peace and we shall fight for the things which we have always carried nearest our hearts, for democracy, for the right of those who submit to authority to have a voice in their own governments, for the rights and liberties of small nations, for a universal dominion of rights by such a concert of free peoples as shall bring peace and safety to all nations and make the world itself at last free." Woodrow Wilson, An Address to a Joint Session of Congress, April 2, 1917, in *ibid.*, vol. 41, pp. 526-27.

8.   In 1941, President Roosevelt set out the Four Freedoms – freedom of speech and expression, freedom of worship, freedom from want, and freedom from fear. (*The Public Papers and Addresses of Franklin D. Roosevelt*, 1938-1940, (Washington, D.C.; 1969), Vol. 9, p. 672.) Freedom from want and freedom from fear as British and American goals were reaffirmed in the Atlantic Charter press statement issued by Prime Minister Churchill and President Roosevelt in August 1941. The Atlantic Charter also recognized the right to self-determination as the United States and the United Kingdom agreed to "respect the right of all peoples to choose the form of government under which they will live.

9.   As quoted in Mary Ann Glendon, *A World Made New: Eleanor Roosevelt and the Universal Declaration of Human Rights* (New York, N.Y.; Random House; 2001), pp. 10-11.

10. Louis Henkin, *The Age of Rights* (New York, N.Y.; Columbia University Press; 1990), p. 66.

11. See generally, David McCullough, *Truman* (New York; Simon & Schuster; 1992), p. 562-65. See also, Leonard Mosley, *Marshall: Hero For Our Times,* (New York, N.Y.; Hearst Books; 1982), pp. 401-411.

12. See generally, Mary Ann Glendon., *ibid.*

13. Theodore C. Sorensen, *Kennedy* (New York; Harper & Row, Publishers; 1965), pp. 245-48.

14. Gerald R. Ford, *A Time To Heal: The Autobiography of Gerald R. Ford* (New York; Harper & Row, Publishers; 1979), p. 301.

15. *Ibid.*, p. 305.

16. President Jimmy Carter Inaugural Address, January 20, 1977, *Public Papers of the Presidents of the United States, Jimmy Carter, 1977* (Washington, D.C.; Government Printing Office, 1978), Vol. 1, 2F. See also, Jimmy Carter, *Keeping Faith: Memoirs of a President* (New York, N.Y.; Bantan Books; 1982).

As stated by Cyrus Vance, Secretary of State during most of the Carter Presidency, in the early months of the Carter Administration, "[T]he resolve of this Administration is to make the advancement of human rights a central part of our foreign policy... America fought for freedom in 1776 and in two World Wars. We have offered haven to the oppressed. Millions have come to our shores in times of trouble. In times of devastation we have shared our resources. Our encouragement and inspiration to other peoples have never been limited to the power of our military or the bounty of our economy. They have been lifted up by the message of our Revolution, the message of individual human freedom. The message has been our great national asset in times past. So it should be again." Cyrus R. Vance, address at Law Day ceremonies at the University of Georgia School of Law at Athens, Georgia, April 30, 1977, Department of State Bulletin, May 23, 1977, pp. 505-8.

In his memoirs of his years as President Carter's Secretary of State, Vance wrote, "The fourth element of a new American approach should be the harnessing of the basic values of the Founding Fathers to our foreign policy. Historically, our country had been a force for progress in human affairs. A nation that saw itself as a 'beacon on the hill' for the rest of mankind could not content itself with power politics alone. It could not properly ignore the growing demands of individuals around the world for the fulfillment of their rights. I believed that these aspirations were producing new or strengthened democratic institutions in many nations, and that America would flourish in a world where freedom flourishes. Cyrus Vance, *Hard Choices: Critical Years in American Foreign Policy* (New York, N.Y.; Simon and Schuste;, 1983), p. 29. Elsewhere Vance writes, "In fact, championing human rights is a national requirement for a nation with our heritage... Without this moral strength it would be impossible for any president to call upon the American people for the sacrifice which from time to time must be made." *Ibid.*, p. 421.

17. See, William F. Schulz, *In Our Own Best Interest: How Defending Human Rights Benefits Us All* (Boston, Massachusetts; Beacon Press; 2001).

18. One reason that democracies are more stable than authoritarian regimes is that freedom is an effective means of sustaining economic growth and countering poverty. See, Amartya Sen, *Development as Freedom* (New York, N.Y.; Anchor Books; 2000). See also, John Shattuck and J. Brian Atwood, "Defending Democracy: Why Democrats Trump Autocrats," *Foreign Affairs*, Vol. 77, No. 2 (March/April 1998).

19. As the father of the Soviet hydrogen bomb and later the foremost Soviet dissident and human rights advocate Andrei Sakharov said, "A country that does not respect the rights of its own people will not respect the rights of its neighbors." Quoted in Natan Sharansky, *The Case For Democracy: The Power of Freedom to Overcome Tyranny and Terror* (New York, N.Y.; Public Affairs; 2004), p. 3.

20. President George W. Bush, Freedom in Iraq and the Middle East, Remarks at the 20th Anniversary of The National Endowment for Democracy, United States Chamber of Commerce, Washington, D.C., November 6, 2003.

21. There is a considerable body of work examining United States efforts to execute an effective human rights policy. Sometimes U.S. foreign policy has been successful, sometimes it has not. See generally, Debra Liang-Fenton, ed., *Implementing U.S. Human Rights Policy* (Washington, D.C.; United States Institute of Peace Press; 2004); John Shattuck, *Freedom on Fire: Human Rights Wars and America's Response* (Cambridge, Massachusetts; Harvard University Press; 2003); David P. Forsythe, *Human Rights and U.S. Foreign Policy: Congress Reconsidered* (Gainesville, Florida; University Presses of Florida; 1988); Julie A. Mertus, *Bait and Switch: Human Rights and U.S. Foreign Policy* (New York, N.Y.; Routledge; 2003); David A. Forsythe, *The United States and Human Rights: Looking Inward and*

Outward (Lincoln, Nebraska; University of Nebraska Press; 2000); and Tony Evans, *U.S. Hegemony and the Project of Universal Human Rights* (New York, N.Y.; St. Martin's Press; 1996). See also, Eliot Abrams, ed., *Honor Among Nations: Intangible Interests and Foreign Policy* (Washington, D.C.; Ethics and Policy Center; 1998). See also, Leslie H. Gelb and Justine A. Rosenthal, "The Rise of Ethics in Foreign Policy: Reaching a Values Consensus; *Foreign Affairs* (May/June 2003), Vol. 82, No. 3, pp. 2-7, in which the argue that "morality, values, ethics, universal principles," recently have taken on greater centrality in U.S. foreign policy.

22.   Winston Churchill, "Liberty and the Law," Remarks to Law Society Dinner to the American Bar Association," The Guildhall, London, U.K., July 31, 1957. Available in Robert Rhodes James, M.P., ed., *Churchill Speaks: 1897-1963* (New York, N.Y.; Barnes & Noble Books; 1980), p. 972, 974.

23.   Economic assistance can be bilateral or multilateral, given with or without conditions. The two largest multilateral donors are the International Monetary Fund and the World Bank. There are a number of commentators who believe IMF and World Bank intervention in developing countries with its extensive conditionality is "far from being the solution to global economic instability and poverty, (but that) these two international institutions are a major problem." Ana I. Eiras, "IMF and World Bank Intervention: A Problem, Not a Solution," *Heritage Foundation Backgrounder*, No. 1689, September 17, 2003. For a more varied review of incentives and disincentives, see Richard N. Haass and Meghan L. O'Sullivan, eds., *Honey and Vinegar: Incentives, Sanctions and Foreign Policy* (Washington, D.C.; Brookings Institution Press, 2000).

     Note also that economic intervention need not be state intervention. For an interesting study of American private equity fund, takeover of Japan's Long-Term Credit Bank, see Gillian Tett, *Saving the Sun: A Wall Street Gamble to Rescue Japan From Its Trillion-Dollar Meltdown* (New York; Harper Business; 2003).

24.   Most often sanctions take the form of economic restrictions such as the economic sanctions placed on the apartheid regime in South Africa. The UN Security Council sometimes also imposes an embargo on arms trade such as those applied to Charles Taylor's government in Liberia in 2002-03. In both the case of South Africa and Liberia sanctions provided great pressure on the targeted governments and, I believe, contributed to necessary changes. For an interesting article about economic forces such as trade in natural resources fueling civil wars even more than ethnic feuds in countries such as Sierra Leone, see Paul Collier, "The Market for Civil War," *Foreign Policy*, May/June, 2003, p. 38. However, there are some commentators who believe that sanctions are too blunt and inflict too much collateral damage on innocent civilians. For example, see Marrack Goulding, *Peacemonger* (London; John Murray Publishers; 2002) p. 19. Sanctions "are regarded as a blunt instrument which rarely causes a government to change its policies. They usually result in disproportionate suffering to the civilians who have the misfortune to live under that government's misrule; they give the governing class unmatched opportunity to amass illegal wealth; and they can inflict collateral damage on the neighbors of the sanctioned state."

     For a discussion of the general impact of economic sanctions on Haiti and their severe impact on the general population while the elite may actually have benefited, see, David Malone, *UN Decision-Making in Haiti* (Oxford, England; Oxford University Press; 1998).

25.   The United States pays 25 percent of the costs of UN peacekeeping operations. OECD member states, which includes the US and the other Western industrialized democracies, South Korea, Japan, Mexico, the Czech Republic, Hungary, Poland and Turkey, pay 93.7 percent of the costs of UN peacekeeping operations. (The UN assessments were revised in 2000. Previously the OECD paid 82.9 percent of UN peacekeeping operations.)

26.   See E.W. Chamberlain III, "Wanted: 20 Divisions; US is Underprepared to Manage Conflicts in a Dangerous World," *Chicago Tribune*, October 19, 2003, Sec. 2, p. 1l.

27.   This is an ongoing problem in the eastern Democratic Republic of the Congo where neighboring states have armed proxy rebel groups.

28.   In Burundi, international assistance was necessary to help rebel groups who wanted to negotiate a cease-fire learn how to set an agenda for meetings and prepare their positions.

29.   In December, 2002 and January, 2003, armed bandits in East Timor endangered the UN peacekeeping/ nation-building mission.

30.   The "long slog" in post-war Iraq is demonstrating once again the effectiveness of guerillas and terrorists willing to kill themselves in order to kill members of the "coalition of the willing" and the humanitarian workers such as the UN and the Red Cross; and the consequent pressure on Washington. See, for example, Charles Krauthammer, "War by Car Bomb," *Washington Post*, October 31, 2003;

editorial, "Fickle Interventionists," *Wall Street Journal*, October 31, 2003; Alex Berenson, "The Art of War vs. the Craft of Occupation," *New York Times*, November 2, 2003; William Safire, "Iraq War III," *New York Times*, November 3, 2003; Richard Cohen, "From Bosnia to Baghdad," *Washington Post*, November 4, 2003; and editorial, "A Lonely Fight," *Washington Post*, November 4, 2003. See also, David Rieff, "Who Botched the Occupation?" *New York Times Magazine*, November 2, 2003.

31. "Even when a third-party intervention force is recognized as neutral, turning that status into a military advantage can be extremely problematic. An effort to appear neutral may actually prolong the conflict, preventing either side from defeating the other. Neutral intervention might mean little more than abetting 'slow-motion savagery.'" James Jay Carafano, "The U.S. Rule in Peace Operations: Past, Perspective, and Prescriptions for the Future," Heritage Lectures, No. 795, The Heritage Foundation, July 24, 2003. See also, Richard K. Betts, "The Delusion of Impartial Intervention," in Chester A. Crocker and Fen Osler Hampson, eds., *Managing Global Chaos: Sources of and Responses to Global Conflict* (Washington, D.C.; United States Institute of Peace Press, 1996), p. 335.

32. Michael Mandelbaum, "Foreign Policy as Social Work," *Foreign Affairs*, Vol. 75, No. 1, pp. 16-32, Jan./Feb. 1996. In this article, Professor Mandelbaum argued that "President Clinton's foreign policy, rather than protecting American interests, has pursued social work worldwide. Three failed interventions in 1993 – in Russia, in Somalia, and the first try in Haiti – illustrate this dramatically. Preoccupied with 'helping the helpless,' the administration alienated vital allies, changed direction repeatedly to repair Clinton's sagging image, and let special interest groups harm US policy toward Japan and Russia."

33. James Jay Carafano of The Heritage Foundation sets out this view as follows, "The need to conduct other peace operations is a matter of strategic judgment. The United States is engaged in a global war on terrorism, a war that may take many years, and require the extensive use of our troops. The armed forces are already straining to meet the demands of global conflict. America needs to pace itself and reserve its military instruments for advancing vital national interests. In that regard, peacemaking operations should be avoided, as they could well embroil the United States in conflicts that would require substantial military resources.

"America should also refrain from taking on major roles in peace enforcement operations. These activities offer substantially fewer risks than peacemaking, but that means *many nations with only a modicum of military capability and some outside support can also perform them. The United States should reserve its forces for the great power missions that require the preponderance of military power that only the United States can provide.*" (italics added) James Jay Carafano, "The U.S. Role in Peace Operations: Past, Perspective, and Prescriptions for the Future," Heritage Lectures, No. 795, The Heritage Foundation, Washington, D.C., July 24, 2003. And Alex Berenson writes, "[T]he Army's dislike of peacekeeping operations had deepened over time, because they detracted from the primary mission of defending the United States." Alex Berenson, "The Art of War vs. the Craft of Occupation," *New York Times*, November 2, 2003.

34. See generally, Michael E. O'Hanlon, *Expanding Global Military Capacity for Humanitarian Intervention* (Washington, D.C.; Brookings Institution Press; 2003). See also, Watanabe Koji, ed., *Humanitarian Intervention: The Evolving Asian Debate* (Tokyo, Japan; Japan Center for International Exchange; 2003).

35. In fact, almost all interventions need the assistance of other countries for base rights, overflights, economic help, political support, intelligence and combat forces. Regarding regional organizations, only NATO has real capacity to project power. But other regional organizations, with the active support of major powers, can be useful. For example the Economic Community for West African States (ECOWAS) has played a helpful role in Côte d'Ivoire with French and US support and in Liberia, primarily with US help.

36. Charles Krauthammer, *Washington Post*, December 11, 1992, quoted in Alan J. Kupperman, *The Limits of Humanitarian Intervention: Genocide in Rwanda* (Washington, D.C.; Brookings Institution Press; 2001), p.1.

37. Henry Kissinger quoted in Charlie Rose Show, Transcript 2140, April 16, 1998; as quoted in Kupperman, *ibid.*, p. 4.

38. The conflict in the eastern Democratic Republic of the Congo is estimated to have claimed the lives of 3½ million people due to fighting and the consequences of war such as disease and malnutrition. And much of the fighting has had a disturbing ethnic element. This became acute in April-July 2003 when the Lendu and Hema tribes in the Ituri District engaged in large scale ethnic killings. See generally, Arthur Asiimwe, "More Dead in Congo as Leaders Hold Crisis Talks, *Reuters*, May 14, 2003; Rodrique Ngowi, "UN Beefs Up Forces in Troubled Congolese Town as Thousands Flee," *Associated Press*, May 16, 2003;

and Will Ross, "Fleeing DR Congo With Tales of Horror," *BBC News*, May 22, 2003. Furthermore, the eastern DRC has been the scene of some of the most gruesome atrocities from beheadings in Kissanjani in May, 2002, to cannibalism in a number of areas. See, Daniel Bergner, "The Most Unconventional Weapon: Soldiers in Congo are Resorting to the Practice of Cannibalism," *New York Times Magazine*, October 20, 2003.

39.   The commerce of the ancient Darfur sultanate had been trade in elephant tusks, ostrich feathers and slaves. In the twentieth century this commerce had become unacceptable and there was little else for the people to draw upon in this largely desolate region of Sudan.

40.   Gerard Prunier, *Darfur: The Ambiguous Genocide,* (Ithaca, New York; Cornell University Press; 2005).

41.   See generally Alex de Waal, *Famine That Kills* (Oxford, U.K.; Oxford University Press; 1989).

42.   Prunier, *ibid.*

43.   Julie Flint and Alex de Waal, *ibid.*.

44.   The two rebel groups are the Sudan Liberation Army/Movement (SLA/M) and the Justice and Equality Movement (JEM).

45.   Benjamin A. Valentino, *Final Solutions: Mass Killing and Genocide in the 20th Century* (Ithaca, New York; Cornell University Press; 2004), p. 235. See also, Eric D. Weitz, *A Century of Genocide: Utopias of Race and Nation* (Princeton, New Jersey; Princeton University Press; 2003).

46.   Khartoum had similarly enlisted militia supported by the Sudan military to attack incipient rebellion in Bahr el Ghazal in 1986-88, in the Nuba Mountains in 1992-95 and in the Upper Nile in 1998-2003.

47.   Mark Doyle, "Darfur Misery Has Complex Roots," *BBC News*, September 9, 2004.

48.   The close coordination between the Sudanese Government in Khartoum and the Janjaweed militia is well documented. See generally, Koert Lindijer, "Analysis: Reining in the Militia," *BBC News*, October 25, 2004.

49.   See, U.N. Interagency Report, April 25, 2004, as cited in Wikipedia, "Darfur Conflict". Available at http://en.wikipedia.org/wiki/Darfur_conflict.

50.   U.N. Secretary-General Kofi Annan, Remarks at the day of Remembrance of the 10th Anniversary of the Genocide in Rwanda, Geneva, Switzerland, April 7, 2004. See also, Glenn Kessler and Colum Lynch, "U.S. Calls Killings in Sudan Genocide: Khartoum and Arab Militias Are Responsible, Powell Says," *Washington Post*, September 10, 2004.

51.   Paul Rusesabagina, "Darfur," *The Wall Street Journal*, April 5, 2006.

52.   "I'm sitting in the dark on the edge of a camp for displaced people in Darfur. …You can see it coming in the afternoons. The sky begins to darken and the horizon goes an ominous brown shade of yellow. Then the wind starts and the dust of the Sahara desert whips up, blasting whirling sands in all directions. The people start to run in their long rags, hands bowed against the wind. Then, the heavens simply open, the wind ferociously hurls drenching curtains of water at everything around. Mothers with their children, whose faces are twisted up in misery, squat grasping the sides of their makeshift shelters – which do almost nothing to keep them dry. The torn plastic bags that make up the walls of their twig shelters slap madly in the wind. The ground turns into a mire of mud. …This is what it is like most nights for them. In the morning we wake up to hear the children crying. In the makeshift hospital here, set up by foreign aid workers, it is so crowded with the sick that some are sleeping on the floors. Among the stench and flies, the children lie wasted, starting into space. Tiny human beings, who were born into the madness of man's inhumanity to man, into the madness of a spate of killing that has left many of their fathers, brothers, grandparents and uncles dead. And now they face starvation which is cruel and slow. Most of the children are too far gone to eat. Some have the peeling skin and lesions that come with advanced starvation – their skin is wrinkled, loose around their bones. The mothers sit by powerless. …" Hilary Andersson, "Sudan's Cruel and Slow Starvation," *BBC News*, July 24, 2004. See also, "Darfur Aid Worker's Diary XXI", *BBC News*, September 27, 2004.

53.   See, for example, "Eyewitness: Terror in Darfur," *BBC News*, November 10, 2004.

54.   Samantha Power, "Dying in Darfur: Can the Ethnic Cleansing in Sudan be Stopped," *The New Yorker*, August 30, 2004.

55.   Human Rights Watch interview, Ahmad, Chad, April 6, 2004. Available at http://hrw.org/reports/2004/sudan0504/5.htm.

56. Human Rights Watch interview, Darfur, April, 2004. Available at http://hrw.org/reports/2004/sudan0504/5.htm.

57. See generally, Human Rights Watch, "Sexual Violence and its Consequences among Displaced Persons in Darfur and Chad," April, 2005. Available at http://hrw.org/backgrounder/africa/darfur0505/.

Nicholas Kristof has written, "[T]he mass rapes in Darfur have been among the most effective means for the government to terrorize tribal populations, break their will and drive them away. Rape is feared all the more in Darfur for two reasons. Most important, a woman who has been raped is ruined; in some cases, she is evicted by her family and forced to build her own hut and live there on her own. And not only is the woman shamed for life, but so is her entire extended family. The second reason is that the people in the region practice an extreme form of female genital cutting, called infibulation, in which a girl's vagina is sewn shut until marriage. Thus when an unmarried girl is raped, the act leads to additional painful physical injuries; and the risk of HIV transmission increases. From the government's point of view, rape is a successful method of control because it sows terror among the victimized population, and yet it initially attracted relatively little attention from foreign observers, because women are too ashamed to complain." Nicholas D. Kristof, "Genocide in Slow Motion," *The New York Review of Books*, February 9, 2006.

58. Human Rights Watch interview, Feisal, Darfur, April 5, 2004. Available at http://hrw.org/reports/2004/sudan0504/5.htm.

59. Amnesty International, *ibid.*

60. Amnesty International, *ibid.*

61. Amnesty International, *ibid.*

62. Amnesty International, *ibid.*

63. Samantha Power, "Dying in Darfur: Cant he Ethnic Cleansing in Sudan be Stopped?" *The New Yorker*, August 30, 2004.

64. Kofi Annan, "Secretary-General Observes International Day of Reflection on 1994 Rwanda Genocide," April 7, 2004. Available at http://www2.unorg.ch/news2/documents/newsen/sg64003e.htm.

65. Richard S. Williamson, *Human Rights, Democracy and Restorative Justice* (Chicago, Illinois; Prairie Institute; 2004), pp. 125-7.

66. See, for example, James Traub, "China's African Adventures Where the West Sees a Need for Reform, Beijing Sees Nothing But Resources and Opportunity," *New York Times Magazine*, November 19, 2006, pp. 74-79; Andrew Batson, "China and Africa Strengthen Ties With $1.9 Billion in Deals," *Wall Street Journal*, November 6, 2006; and Chen Aizzhu, "Beijing Pledges Aid, Loans to Africa," *Washington Times*, November 6, 2006.

67. "The African Union mission in Sudan (AMIS) originated in July, 2004, when both the African Union and the European Union sent monitors to monitor the Darfur crisis ceasefire signed in April 2004. In August 2004, the African Union sent 150 Rwandan troops in to protect the ceasefire monitors. However, it soon became apparent that 150 troops would not be enough, so they were joined by 150 Nigerian troops." http://en.wikipedia.org/wiki/AfricanUnionMissioninSudan.

68. See, "Report of the United Nations High Commissioner for Human Rights and Follow-Up to the World Conference on Human Rights: Situation of Human Rights in the Darfur Region of the Sudan," May 7, 2004; E/CN.4/2005/3.

69. U.N. News Center, "U.N. Mission in Sudan Reports Continued Insecurity in Troubled Darfur Region," December 7, 2005.

70. *Ibid.*

71. U.N. News Center, "1.25 Million Children beyond Reach of Aid in Sudan's Darfur Region, U.N. Warns," December 20, 2005.

72. See Nicholas Kristof, "Africa's Brutal Lebenstraum," *New York Times*, March 14, 2006, and Nicholas Kristof, "A Village Waiting for Rape and Murder," *New York Times*, March 12, 2006. See also, Editorial, "Spreading Genocide to Chad," *New York Times*, March 30, 2006.

73. UNSC Presidential Statement, "Reports of the Secretary-General on the Sudan." S/PRST/2006/5 of 3, February 2006. The resolution called for a 12,000 to 20,000 troop presence in Darfur with the 7,000 AU troops already there being given new weapons and being incorporated into the U.N. mission. The U.N. peacekeepers would have a greater mandate to protect civilians.

74.   See, Darfur Peace Agreement, available at http://allafrica.com/peaceafrica/resources/view/00010926. pdf. See also, Robert B. Zoellick, Deputy Secretary of State, "Briefing on Abuja Peace Agreement for Darfur," Abuja, Nigeria, May 5, 2006. Available at http://www.state.gov/s/d/former/zoellick/rem/2006/65933.htm.

75.   Ophecra McDoom, "Sudan Rejects U.N. Troops for Darfur: Minister," *Reuters*, February 22, 2006; "Sudan Has Begun Campaign to Keep U.N. From Taking Over Peacekeeping in Darfur," *ABC News*, March 1, 2006; Louis Oelofse, "Darfur Protesters Condemn U.N. Plan," *BBC News*, March 8, 2006; "Protests Over Darfur U.N. Troops," *BBC News*, March 8, 2006; Anne Penketh, "Sudan Blocks U.N. Troops in Fear Darfur Could Become Graveyard," *The Independent*, March 11, 2006; Colum Lynch, "Sudan Rejects Request to Allow U.N. Troops," *Washington Post*, September 20, 2006; U.N. Troops in Darfur Remain Taboo," *Afrol News/IRIN*, September 25, 2006; "Sudan's President Reiterates Rejection of U.N. Troops in Darfur," *Reuters*, September 25, 2006; Paul Reynolds, "Western Pressure Fails to Move Sudan," *BBC News*, October 23, 2006; Michele Kelemen, "Darfur Violence Pits Sudan Against the U.N.," *NPR*, November 3, 2006; Audra Ang, "Sudan Leader: No U.N. Troops for Darfur," *Associated Press*, November 3, 2006; Frehlwot Shlfrewaw, "Sudan Stands Firm on Rejection of U.N. Troops After Annan Meet," *Africa News*, November 16, 2006.

76 .   Amnesty International, "Sudan" Human Rights Situation Deteriorating in Darfur Five Months After Peace Agreement," News Service No. 257, October 5, 2006. See also, "U.S.: New Offensives in Darfur and Chad Threaten Civilians," *Human Rights Watch*, October 23, 2006.

77.   See, Alfred De Montesquiou, "Sudanese Army, Militia Reportedly Raid Villages in North Darfur, *Washington Post*, November 20, 2006; "New Offense in North Darfur," *Times OnLine*, November 20, 2006; "Offense by Sudan in Darfur is Reported," *International Herald Tribune*, November 19, 2006; Nicholas D. Kristof, "The Face of Genocide," *New York Times,* November 19, 2006; "Sudanese Troops, Militia Accused of New Attacks," *CBS News*, November 18, 2006; "African Union Says Militia Attacks on Civilians Continue in Darfur," *Voice of America,* November 14, 2006; Nicholas D. Kristof, "Poisoned Arrows vs. Machine Guns," *New York Times,* November 14, 2006; "Darfur Militias in Deadly Attacks," *BBC News*, November 12, 2006; and Nicholas D. Kristof, "Bandages and Bayonets," *New York Times*, November 12, 2006..

78.   Robert F. Worth, "Sudan Says It Will Accept U.N. African Peace Force in Darfur," *New York Times*, November 17, 2006; and Alfred de Montesquiou, "Sudan Indicates Approval of U.N. Forces to 'Assist' in Darfur," *Washington Post*, November 18, 2006.

79.   See, Mohamed Osman and Salah Nasrawi, "Sudan Hails Deal on Mixed U.N. and African Force in Darfur as a Diplomatic Victory, *International Herald Tribune*, November 20, 2006; Noel King, "Sudanese Official Says Disagreement Continue Over Proposed Darfur Force," *Voice of America*, November 19, 2006; and "Sudan Denies Agreement on Mixed U.N.-AU Peacekeeping Force in Darfur," *Peoples Daily Online*, November 19, 2006.

80.   Associated Press, "U.N. Humanitarian Official Says Darfur Crisis is at Crucial Moment," *New York Times*, November 19, 2006.

81.   See, J. Stephen Morrison and Chester A. Crocker, "Time to Focus on the Real Choices in Darfur," *Washingtonpost.com*, November 7, 2006.

82.   Colum Lynch and Glenn Kessler, "Bush to Name Envoy for Darfur: Natsios Will Lead U.S. Effort to Quell the Violence in Sudan," *Washington Post*, September 19, 2006; and, President George W. Bush, "President Meets with Andrew Natsios, Special Envoy for Sudan," Oval Office, White House Office of the Press Secretary, October 2, 2006. See also, "U.S. Envoy to Sudan to Join a Fast For Darfur," *Reuters*, October 4, 2006.

83.   Winston Churchill, "The Death of President Roosevelt," Address in the House of Commons, London, United Kingdom, April 17, 1945. Available in Robert Rhodes James, M.P., ed., *Churchill Speaks: 1897-1963* (New York, N.Y.; Barnes & Noble Books; 1980), p. 856, 859.

84.   President Ronald Reagan, "Remarks at the Conservative Political Action Committee," Washington, D.C., March 20, 1981. Available in Ronald Reagan, *Speaking My Mind: Selected Speeches* (New York, N.Y.; Simon and Schuster; 1989), p. 93, 99.

Darfur:
How Much More Destruction, Despair and Death?

During nearly three and a half years of mayhem and carnage in Darfur, devastation and death have scarred this large arid region of western Sudan. The Arab government in Khartoum in concert with Janjaweed militiamen on camel and horseback have swept through villages showing no mercy. Up to 400,000 black Africans have died. Over 2.5 million blacks have been driven from their homes and now live in desperate conditions in IDP and refugee camps. Atrocities have been common such as girls and women raped and branded, people burned alive, and boys tortured. And their suffering has been met by "the sounds of silence." Its past time for action to end this river of blood.

From time to time there have been rays of hope. And time after time the glimmer has been extinguished by a new rise of vicious violence against innocent civilians.

Last month, not withstanding a litany of peace agreements, Khartoum launched yet another offensive in Darfur. Government soldiers and Janjaweed militia are looting, poisoning wells, burning villages and killing innocent civilians.

The diplomatic minuet to end this catastrophe has been long. The resolve insufficient. The results anemic.

In 2004, soon after the killings began, President Bush condemned the violence and called for it to end. In April, 2004, Secretary-General Kofi Annan showed leadership by calling the killings in Darfur "ethnic cleansing," raising the possibility of a humanitarian intervention, and challenging the international community to act to avoid a repeat of the Rwandan genocide. But that spring the UN Commission on Human Rights was unable to pass a resolution condemning the violence, demanding it end, and requiring access for humanitarian aid. Tragically, the message to the Sudanese government was that the international community cared little about the bloodletting in an African country little known and far away. Not surprisingly, the carnage continued.

Since then the international community consistently has lacked the political will to act decisively with unity and purpose to end the bloodshed. For years now, the combination of Islamic religious solidarity, African regional loyalty and the strong economic interests in Sudan of China and Russia have successfully prevented muscular diplomatic action against Khartoum. The killing has continued.

Appeared in *UNA-USA Newsletter*, December 5, 2006.

Efforts to impose effective sanctions against Khartoum and Janjaweed leaders have been thwarted. Peace agreements have not held. And while the African Union has deployed 7,000 peacekeepers to Darfur with logistical support from the west, their number is too few to cover such a vast area, their equipment insufficient, and their mandate limited to observe and report, not to stop the carnage.

The United States has introduced Security Council resolutions to plan and deploy United Nations Peacekeepers to Darfur. While in August, finally, a resolution passed to send UN Peacekeepers, Khartoum has refused to accept them. So there are no UN boots on the ground.

Meanwhile the violence and bloodshed in Darfur has bled over to neighboring Chad. The other day UN High Commissioner for Refugees Antonio Guterres said, "There is an earthquake in the area. The epicenter is Darfur but the effects can be felt quite far away." Mahemal Nimir Hamata, a Chadian general, says, "We risk a conflagration that will consumer the entire region. We'll be another Congo." More than 4 million people have died in the Congo conflict, 4 million!

Just last week the United Nations High Commissioner for Human Rights Louise Arbour reported that in Darfur on a daily basis atrocities, rape and pillage against civilians are at "a horrific level." She also said that the Sudanese government and the Janjaweed militias supported by the government were "responsible for the most serious violations of international human rights and humanitarian law." Monitors are reporting that the Janjaweed militias are "consolidating in government-controlled areas where they were receiving more weapons." And African Union observers in Darfur reported deadly Janjaweed militia attacks on civilians continue and the Sudanese air force is bombing villages.

Also last week, the head of the UN Office for Coordination of Humanitarian Affairs Jan Egeland said that 4 million victims of the ethnic carnage in Darfur and Chad need emergency assistance and that thousands are dying from hunger and disease.

Khartoum's response is to deny, delay and obstruct. Sudan President Omar al-Bashir dismisses the casualty counts of the UN, AU, humanitarian workers and journalists. He claims fewer than 9,000 people have died during the Darfur conflict. He says, "All the figures have been falsified."

Last week Sudan's representative Farah Mustafa told the UN Human Rights Council that "there is an international campaign to offer false data to international public opinion." He said, "The information about hundreds of thousands killed is untrue." And Sudan Ministry of Humanitarian Aid Commissioner Hassabu Mohammed Abdella said that Egeland's statements were "a pure political act." Humanitarian aid to Darfur is deliberately hindered. Attacks on humanitarian aid groups are growing. UN Peacekeepers are denied. And the mayhem, atrocities and carnage continue.

Earlier this year, UN Security Council Resolution 1706 was passed authorizing a UN mission of 20,000 peacekeepers to Sudan "to use all necessary means" to pacify Darfur. Even as the violence escalates, Bashir continues to oppose deployment and he has powerful allies.

Last month Russian Deputy Foreign Minister Alexander Saltanov said Russia rejects deployment of UN troops. He said Russia supports "the efforts of the Sudanese government to solve the crisis internally or in the African context.," And Libyan leader Moammer Gadhafi has said that "(t)he presence of international forces in Darfur would be a return to colonialism." But the tragic fact is that the Sudanese government is part of the problem and, despite good intentions, the African Union has been inadequate to the task at hand.

Secretary-General Kofi Annan has called for high-level meetings to address the deteriorating situation in Darfur. In September, President Bush appointed former director of U.S. AID Andrew Natsios as Presidential Envoy to Sudan, guaranteeing sustained high level engagement on Darfur. Natsios, who has dealt with humanitarian issues in Darfur for decades, has had intensive discussions in Sudan and elsewhere on this issue. And while he has reported that his discussions have been constructive, Natsios also has said that "either we see a change" by January 1st or we will take a "different approach."

There have been too many horrific stories from Darfur: too much destruction, too many atrocities, too much death, and the "genocide in slow motion" has gone on too long.

The United States and other capable countries should increase intelligence gathering in Darfur and Chad. We need better, more timely information about what is going on.

President Bush and other world leaders should make Darfur a higher priority in discussions with Beijing and Moscow.

NATO should consider enforcing a no fly zone. Sudanese government airplanes and attack helicopters should not be allowed to continue to kill innocent civilians.

In September, Secretary of State Condoleezza Rice warned that Khartoum faces "a choice between cooperation or confrontation." Khartoum is not cooperating. Patience has meant the river of blood continues to flow. If the diligent efforts of Presidential Envoy Natsios cannot make a breakthrough this month; it may be time for the UN Security Council to pass a Chapter VII resolution and deploy UN Peacekeepers with or without Khartoum's acquiescence.

The world cannot idly stand by as yet again Darfur suffers a dramatic escalation of violence, insecurity, and death. The firestorm of genocide must end. We should be haunted by the unimaginable toll of Darfur's destruction, despair and death. Some meaning must be given to the promise made after World War II, and too frequently broken since, of "Never Again."

SECTION VI:

SECURITY

THE IRAN NUCLEAR CHALLENGE

It is a pleasure to participate in this "Dialogue on Multilateral Diplomacy and the Management of Global Issues." I have found the presentations and interventions by our Iranian colleagues to be extremely interesting. I have been asked to discuss Iran's nuclear challenge.

The Danger

The danger of nuclear proliferation is grave. In addition to the five declared nuclear weapons states recognized by the Nuclear Non-Proliferation Treaty (China, France, Russia, U.K. and U.S.), in recent years India and Pakistan have become declared nuclear weapon states. North Korea has sent a letter stating its intent to leave the NPT. North Korea has "developed the equipment and technical expertise necessary to extract plutonium for use in nuclear weapons" according to Siegfried Hecker, former head of the Los Alamos National Laboratory.[1] And the probe of Libya's nuclear activities is revealing a significant global black market in nuclear technology.[2]

Furthermore, if Iran were to acquire nuclear weapons, it could propel a nuclear break-out of the region in Egypt, Turkey and Saudi Arabia. Such a massive hemorrhage could endanger the entire nuclear non-proliferation regime. Furthermore, since Iran already has developed the Shahab-3 long-range missile as a possible delivery system, Iran going nuclear would be all the more menacing to Israel and others.[3]

Consequently, addressing the Iranian nuclear challenge has far flung repercussions. Success in containing this problem is critical.

History

Iran has had a nuclear program for a long time. In 1959, Iran purchased a research reactor from the United States. In the 1970s the Shah announced plans to build 23 nuclear power reactors. At the time, despite some mischief, the Iranian nuclear power program was not seen as a step toward a nuclear weapons program because Iran did not seek the technology to enrich its own fuel or reprocess its own spent fuel.[4] While the Shah's grand plans were not realized, Iran continued to devote resources to its nuclear program.

For a long time, the United States government has expressed concerns about Iran's nuclear intentions. These concerns have grown more acute over the past three

Remarks at Conference Dialogue on Multilateral Diplomacy and the Management of Global Issues, Stockholm International Peace Research Institute, Stockholm, Sweden, January 23, 2004.

years as its nuclear program has advanced.[5] Iran has gained expertise through its Bushehr nuclear reactor project with Russia.[6] There are concerns Russia also may have been cooperating in laser uranium enrichment technology. And the NCR has held press conferences exposing alleged nuclear facilities in Iran.[7]

In 2003, International Atomic Energy Agency inspectors (IAEA) made several visits to Iranian nuclear facilities. The IAEA released a report, *Implementation of the NPT Safeguards Agreement in the Islamic Republic of Iran, Report by the Director General*,[8] which identified three areas of concern: Iran's failure to report uranium imported from China in 1991, questions about the centrifuge enrichment program, and questions about the heavy water program. Among other things, the IAEA inspectors found considerable amounts of highly-enriched uranium (HEU) in environmental samples taken at Natanz and elsewhere.[9] This IAEA report concluded that "Iran failed to meet its obligations under its Safeguards Agreement with respect to reporting of nuclear material, the subsequent processing and use of that material and the declaration of facilities where the material was stored and processed."[10]

As we heard again today, Iran continues to claim that its nuclear power is for peaceful purposes to free up oil and natural gas resources for exports to generate hard-currency revenues. Its stated goal is to have 7,000 MW of nuclear power online by 2020 which would account for 10% of the country's power generating capacity.

In September 2003, the IAEA gave Iran until October 31 to provide guarantees that its nuclear program was for peaceful purposes and to open the country to snap inspections by the IAEA. Iran responded by threatening to withdraw from the Nuclear Nonproliferation Treaty (NPT).[11]

Then on October 21, 2003, Iran and the foreign ministers of France, Germany and Britain issued a declaration in which Iran accepted a number of the demands of the international community with respect to its nuclear program.[12] President Bush called this "a very positive development."

In the declaration, Iran pledges "through full transparency" to meet all of the IAEA demands and "correct any possible failures and deficiencies." It agrees to sign and ratify the Additional Protocol[13] and to act in accordance with the Protocol pending its ratification. And Iran committed "voluntarily to suspend all uranium enrichment and reprocessing activities as defined by the IAEA." The Europeans said that once the concerns about the nuclear matters were fully resolved, "Iran could expect easier access to modern technology and supplies in a range of areas."

Fix Iran

Like others, I appreciated hearing Mr. Straus Nassari's presentation on Iran's thinking about this issue and his report on the on-going negotiations in which Iran is engaged with France, Germany and the U.K. on this delicate matter.[14] I certainly agree with Mr. Nassari that "the situation is volatile and very fragile."

The October declaration was a very positive step. Mr. Nassari's statement of Iran's desire to reach a satisfactory solution also is encouraging. However, there are two points I must make. First, Iran should not be too confident that Germany and France can "deliver" the United States to embrace whatever agreement they might make with Tehran. While President Bush said the October Declaration was a positive step, he did not go further. And while the United States believes "a united international front is especially critical in dealing with Iran's (nuclear program),"[15] in Iraq we saw the inability of Paris and Berlin to bridge the gap with Washington between their views and those of the United States. While hopeful for a united international community, the United States will not sacrifice its international security interests for the sake of "unity."

Second, the issue of the suspension of all "enrichment-related activities" and "any reprocessing activities" is central. The IAEA Board of Governors resolution used this language which, I presume, covers not just the actual enrichment of uranium but also further construction at Natanz or any other enrichment facilities, manufacture of additional centrifuges and related equipment, processing of uranium to make feedstock for enrichment, and other fuel-cycle activities. However, today Mr. Nassari has said that "we agreed to suspend enrichment activities... not to suspend enrichment related activities." Of course, I cannot speak for the Bush Administration, but I cannot conceive of the Bush Administration or any American Administration accepting anything less than a permanent, durable, verifiable cessation of enrichment.

The value of the October declaration will depend on its implementation. It is not a substitute for Iran satisfying the demands of the September IAEA Board resolution. Iran must resolve the outstanding questions about its nuclear program.

In how Iran complies with its existing IAEA obligations and how the issue of enrichment is resolved, Tehran will demonstrate whether or not it has made a fundamental decision not to acquire nuclear weapons or whether it has not done so.

Continuing efforts to acquire nuclear weapons is a very risky course of action. Continued efforts to do so will be detected. The damage to Iran's reputation would be significant. And the damage would be great to many broader interests from Iran's own security to its integration into the global community of nations to its economic welfare. Iran has a great deal to lose if it continues to try to acquire nuclear weapons and it has a great deal to gain by not doing so. Hopefully in the weeks and months ahead this difficult issue can be dealt with to the satisfaction of the entire international community.

A Bigger Fix

Finally, let me just briefly touch upon the larger issue raised by the Iran nuclear matter and by India, Pakistan and North Korea. The Nuclear Non-Proliferation Treaty allows non-nuclear weapon states to acquire nuclear technology that not only can create the component for civilian nuclear reactors but also for nuclear weapons.[16] The NPT requires that produced or processed uranium or plutonium be accounted for and placed under IAEA safeguards. However, states can use peaceful nuclear programs as a cover for nuclear weapons programs. Furthermore, having acquired the ways and means to build a nuclear bomb under the cover of a peaceful nuclear program and in compliance with the NPT, a signatory state can withdraw from the NPT with 90 days notice. Then, after leaving the NPT, proceed to construct a nuclear weapon. This is no longer an abstract question, but an immediate danger. Therefore, long-term, whether within the NPT or outside of that treaty, we should develop other mechanisms to reduce national control by non-weapon states of materials and facilities that can be used to advance nuclear weapons capabilities.

I recognize that this would take time and be difficult. But the question of whether to internationalize the fuel cycle and fuel supply or to create other management guarantees to address this problem warrants serious consideration.

Thank you.

---

1.   Demetri Sevastopula and Peter Spiegel, "North Korea able to make Plutonium for Weapons," *Financial Times* (London), January 22, 2004. Note also, "North Korea could be producing nuclear weapons at the rate of eight to 13 a year in the next year or two, the International Institute of Strategic Studies predicted yesterday." Ewen MacAskill, "North Korea Soon Be Making 10 Nuclear Bombs A Year," *The Guardian*, (London), January 22, 2004.

2.   Mark Huband, Roula Khalaf and Stephen Fidler, "Global Black Market Revealed by Libya's Decision To Come Clean on its N-Weapons, *Financial Times* (London), January 22, 2004 and Mark Huband, Roula Khalaf and Stephen Fidler, "Probe Reveals Huge Libya Procurement Effort," *Financial Times* (London), January 22, 2004.

3.   See, International Crisis Group, "Dealing With Iran's Nuclear Program," ICG Middle East Report No. 18, October 27, 2003.

4.   Iran's AEOI sought laser enrichment technology in the United States in the late 1970s, and the former head of the AEOI states that reprocessing-related experiments were conducted. Also there were intelligence reports that the Shah had a secret group to work on nuclear weapons. See, Leonard S. Spector, *Nuclear Ambitions* (Colorado; Westview Press; 1990), p. 204.

5.   See, Leonard S. Spector "Iran's Secret Quest for the Bomb," *Yale Global*, May 16, 2003.

6.   In December 2002, Iran and Russia signed a protocol for peaceful cooperation in nuclear power. Russia had been assisting Iran on the Bushehr nuclear power facility, work on which first began in 1974 by West Germany, but was halted following the 1978/1979 revolution. In 1995, Russia began work under a $800 million contract to complete a 1,000-MW pressurized-light water reactor, as well as to supply two modern VVER-440 units. The United States strongly opposed Russian assistance for the Bushehr project.

7.   "The National Council of Resistance of Iran (NCR) held a press conference on August 14, 2002, at which it unveiled satellite photographs of nuclear sites at Natanz and Arak. On May 27, 2003, the NCXR revealed sites that might be used for uranium enrichment to complement Natanz: the Lashkar-Abad site near Itashtgeret and a site near Ramandeh village. On July 8, 2003, the NRC revealed two more sites,, including the Kolahdouz Complex (related to centrifuge enrichment) and Ardekan nuclear fuel site." Sharon Squassoni, "Iran's Nuclear Program: Recent Developments," CRS Report R521592, August 15, 2003. The NRC is an umbrella for other Iranian resistance groups, including the Muhahedin-e Khalg organization (MEK). The NCR has been on the U.S. Department list of foreign terrorist organizations since 1997.

8.   GOV/2003/40, June 6, 2003.

9.   The Iranians claimed that their enrichment equipment had been contaminated with HEU before Iran imported it from foreign brokers.

10.   *Ibid.*

11.   On October 6, Iran's envoy to the IAEA, Ali Akbar Salehi, said that Iran would withdraw from the NPT if Western pressure continued.

12.   Apparently the Europeans made a pending European Union trade and cooperation agreement with Iran contingent on resolving the nuclear issue.

13.   The Additional Protocol (INFCIRC/540) was developed in response to the failure of nuclear safeguards in Iraq. It is designed to strengthen the IAEA's ability to detect undeclared nuclear activities.

14.   Sirous Nassari is Chief Executive Officer of ICT Services Corporation in Tehran. A former Iranian diplomat, he served as Iran's Ambassador to the U.N., was involved in negotiations to end the Iran/Iraq War, and is currently a negotiator for Iran with the European countries on the nuclear issue.

15.   See Richard L. Armitage, Deputy Secretary of State, Testimony before the Senate Foreign Relations Committee, Washington, D.C., October 28, 2003.

16.   Highly enriched uranium and plutonium.

REST OF WORLD NEEDS TO PRESSURE IRAN ON NUKES NOW

The spread of nuclear weapons is a great and growing danger. This is especially true in a world of rogue regimes and global terror networks.

Therefore Iran's nuclear program is a subject of great and growing concern. It is especially disturbing because of its destabilizing impact in the dangerous and precarious Middle East already embroiled by violence in post-conflict Iraq and Afghanistan. Iran's possible nuclear breakout requires muscular action by the international community to ensure that Iran's Mullahs do not acquire the bomb.

Iran's new president, Mahmoud Ahmadingad, is a former member of the Revolutionary Guards who rolled back reforms while mayor of Tehran. He was elected president with the backing of powerful Islamic conservatives who used their network of mosques to mobilize support. And under his presidency, Iran continues to aid insurgents in Iraq.

For nearly two decades, Iran hid critical parts of its nuclear program from the world. Like North Korea, Iran had joined the Nuclear Nonproliferation regime as a long-term political deception. Having publicly forsworn efforts to build nuclear weapons, Iran received aid and technology for their "peaceful" atomic energy program while pursuing a secret program to build nuclear weapons.

In 2003, Iran's covert nuclear activities were discovered. For years Iran had secretly been engaged in constructing a facility near Natanz to enrich uranium, a key component of advanced nuclear weapons. The plant was extremely advanced and there were hundreds of gas centrifuges ready to produce nuclear uranium.

For some time Britain, France and Germany, with U.S. support, have been involved in efforts to coax a recalcitrant Iran to circumscribe its nuclear program. Economic and other incentives have been offered to Tehran, including less proliferation-prone technologies, in exchange for accepting limits that would ensure Iran does not build a nuclear weapon.

A condition for these negotiations has been that Iran suspend enrichment while this diplomatic dialogue sought solution. Then last month Iran unsealed their nuclear conversion plant near Isfahan and indicated they will resume full-scale enrichment work.

Appeared in the *Chicago Sun-Times,* September 29, 2005.

A few weeks ago the International Atomic Energy Agency (IAEA) again documented Iran's past nuclear infractions including such things as failing to account properly for importing enrichment equipment and materials from the nuclear black market, secretly enriching uranium and separating plutonium, and attempting to import beryllium.

The suspicions about Iran's nuclear ambitions continue. Iran's recent derailment of negotiations with the Europeans are troublesome. During the recent U.N. World Summit Iranian President Ahmadinejad delivered a defiant speech in which he refused to end Iran's nuclear program, rejected the Europeans' compromise proposal and railed against the United States. Last month, Gary Milhollin, director of the Wisconsin Project on Nuclear Arms, stated categorically, "Iran is determined to get the bomb."

It is time for the international community to act to ratchet up the pressure on Tehran to abandon any ambitions for nuclear weapons and agree to safeguards adequate to provide transparency and comfort that past nuclear shenanigans have ended.

This is an instance in which the United Nations could and should prove its value.

The final "outcomes document" at the U.N. World Summit was thin gruel. Those who hoped for sweeping new commitments on fighting global poverty, non-proliferation and terrorism were disappointed with the Summit's meager agreements, as were those hoping for necessary institutional reforms.

The best way for the United Nations to demonstrate its usefulness is not in grand pronouncements but in the hard work of diplomacy by addressing specific dangers as they emerge. Iran's nuclear threat is such a menacing development. It should be dealt with.

After Iran's most recent acts of defiance, even French Prime Minister Dominique de Villepin said, "The proliferation of weapons of mass destruction... calls for a determined response on our part. ...It is legitimate, once dialogue has been exhausted, to refer (Iran) to the Security Council."

Britain and the United States are working in capitals and in Vienna to get the IAEA to formerly refer the Iran nuclear issue to the U.N. Security Council which has the power to impose sanctions on the Islamic Republic.

Russia has built a nuclear power station in Iran and recently announced a further commercial contract to provide them with nuclear technology. Experts estimate that China soon will be getting at least 12 percent of its energy from Iran. In the past, Tehran has relied on Russian and/or China to threaten a veto of any U.N. sanctions. And some large developing countries that sit on the IAEA Board of Governors also have reservations about referring this matter to the U.N. Security Council.

This diplomatic dance has gone on long enough. Iran's nuclear program is a menace to the broader Middle East and to the world. The danger is growing.

Russia, China and the entire international community are being tested.

The international community, using the IAEA and the U.N. Security Council, must increase pressure on Tehran to do the right thing. The time to act is now.

A Nuclear Iran is a Danger We Must Prevent

Iran's nuclear ambitions are a clear and growing danger. President Bush's effort to ratchet up the diplomatic pressure, for now, is the correct strategy.

The United States is requesting that the International Atomic Energy Agency (IAEA) refer the issue to the U.N. Security Council, which can impose targeted sanctions on Tehran.

To achieve even this modest increase of diplomatic pressure is not easy. The path forward is buffeted by strong crosswinds of differing risk assessments and conflicting self-interest. Miscalculation could lead to disaster.

As a former Ambassador to the IAEA in Vienna, I have some appreciation of the perilous path ahead.

The crisis is a result of Tehran's relentless push to acquire nuclear weapons technology. In 2003, Iran's covert nuclear program was discovered. Iran admitted hiding its military-run program for 18 years. As IAEA inspectors began their work in Iran, Tehran engaged in a pattern of obstruction. Then, in early January, Iran broke the IAEA seals on the Natanz enrichment facility and two related sites.

Iran's president Mohmoud Ahmadinejad is a maholaviat with a totalitarian ideology and, apparently, a mystical belief in his own mission. He says the holocaust never happened and threatens Israel's existence. Iran's improved version of the Shahaf-3 missile has a range of more than 1,300 miles, making Israel and U.S. forces in the Middle East in easy range. And as the international community considers a response to its latest provocation, Iran is defiant.

It appears Iran believes it is in a strong position and is calculating on a weak response. Once menaced by Saddam Hussein to its west and the Taliban to its east, today Iran is free from those encumbrances.

Tehran agreed to IAEA inspectors and a nuclear dialogue with France, Germany and the U.K. in 2003 when over 150,000 U.S. troops had landed in Iraq and just taken down Saddam. The situation on the ground has changed dramatically. U.S. troops are tied down by an insurgency in Iraq and the on-going mop up in Afghanistan. Even General George Casey, U.S. Commander in Iraq, has acknowledged that American troops are "stretched."

Appeared in the *Chicago Sun Times*, February 5, 2006.

And Iran has leverage. It has the capacity to further disrupt the U.S. missions in neighboring Iraq and Afghanistan. Furthermore, Iran is the world's 4th largest oil supplier with the capability to drive up oil prices.

No one will be safer if Tehran acquires nuclear weapons. No one. The Middle East is a tough and precarious neighborhood. Nukes in the hands of a radical regime in Tehran further destabilizes the Muslim world. Israel will face an imminent danger. And the industrial world's oil supply will be exposed to a new, unpredictable threat.

Nonetheless, for various reasons, many other leading nations are reluctant to confront this growing danger. Some see a nuclear Iran as 5 to 10 years down the road. Why deal with a difficult problem now if you don't have to? Furthermore, other countries, even major powers, are willing to let storms gather because they believe, in the end, the U.S., as the world's sole superpower, will deal with any danger before it is too late. So why should they risk their equities?

The Europeans, having engaged in 2 ½ years of good faith, if naïve, negotiations with Tehran, now are standing with the U.S. in calling for a Security Council referral. But others hesitate.

China's energy demand to fuel its growing economy has become a transcending priority for Beijing, and Iran is an important supplier. Russia has a nuclear deal with Iran worth billions. And Moscow is mindful of any unrest among Muslims in its southern caucus region and central Asia.

India, a leading member of the IAEA Board of Governors, also depends on Iranian oil for its growing economy. And India's left parties, which provide key support to the government, are demanding that New Delhi abstain in any IAEA vote. And Arab states are mindful of Tehran's capacity to incite problems for them at home.

So the Iran nuclear crisis is complex. Yet a unified international community confronting Tehran is the best, perhaps the only way, to effectively deal diplomatically with this crisis. The Bush Administration is right to seek robust diplomatic pressure on Tehran. But our patience cannot be limitless. The danger will grow. And no option to deal with this nuclear threat can be taken off the table. None.

IRAN:
THE NUCLEAR CHALLENGE:
IRAQ AND THE TICKING CLOCK

We gather to discuss U.S.-Iran relations at a critical time when the pace of events seems to be accelerating; alarm over Iran's nuclear program is growing, the diplomatic train is moving, events in Iraq may be reaching a tipping point, military options are being discussed and a window for dialogue has opened. There are many issues, many difficult questions, many possibilities, and little time to sort this out. All of this is unfolding while Washington-Tehran relations remain in stalemate.

The United States Government's official position was summed up by Under Secretary of State Nick Burns in his recent Congressional testimony, "Successive U.S. administrations have recognized that Iran's regime poses a profound threat to U.S. interests in the Middle East and more broadly across the globe. Over the past six months, however, since the August, 2005, inauguration of President Mahmoud Ahmadinejad, the threat has intensified as Iran's approach to the world has become even more radical. Today, the Iranian leadership is actively working against all that the U.S. and our allies desire for the region – peace in Lebanon, peace between Israel and the Palestinians, and an end to terrorism. In fact, no country stands more resolutely opposed to our hope for peace and freedom in the Middle East and Iran.

"Iran's leadership directly threatens vital American interests in four distinct and grave areas: its pursuit of nuclear weapons capability; its role as the "Central Banker" in directing and funding terror; its determination to dominate the Middle East as the most powerful state in the Persian Gulf region; and finally, its repression of the democratic hopes of the Iranian people." [1]

Receiving the greatest attention in Washington and around the world is grave concern over Iran's nuclear program. Richard Lugar, Chairman of the Senate Committee on Foreign Affairs has said, "Iran's recent decisions to limit International Atomic Energy Agency inspections and restart uranium enrichment represent a fundamental challenge to global stability and efforts to prevent nuclear proliferation. If the international community cannot muster the cohesiveness and determination to stop the Iranian nuclear drive, we will have undermined the international non-proliferation regime, risked igniting a regional arms race in the Middle East, and allowed a government with close links to terrorist organizations to acquire nuclear weapons." [2] Robert Joseph, Under Secretary of State for Arms Control and International Security, was even more to the point when he said, "[A] nuclear-armed Iran is intolerable." [3]

Remarks at Dialogue on Multilateral Diplomacy and the Management of Global Issues, Stockholm, Sweden, April 22, 2006.

Iran's known oil reserves rank it second in the world only to Saudi Arabia and, today, Iran provides about 5% of the world's oil. Nonetheless, over 20 years ago Tehran embarked on a secret program to produce fissile material.[4] This covert program was uncovered in 2003. That year, after several visits to Iranian nuclear sites, the International Atomic Energy Agency issued a report titled, *Implementation of the NPT Safeguards Agreement in the Islamic Republic of Iran, Report by the Director General* which identified three areas of concern and concluded that "Iran failed to meet its obligations under its Safeguards Agreement with respect to reporting its nuclear material, the subsequent processing and use of that material and the declaration of facilities where the material was stored and processed."[5]

In October of that year, Iran and the foreign ministers of France, Germany and Britain issued a declaration in which Iran accepted a number of the international community's demands with respect to its nuclear program including a pledge "through full transparency" to meet all the IAEA demands and "correct any possible failures and deficiencies." Iran also agreed to sign and ratify the Additional Protocol and to act in accordance with the Protocol pending its ratification. And Iran committed "voluntarily to suspend all uranium enrichment and reprocessing activities defined by the IAEA." The Europeans then began discussions with Iran to resolve the various concerns about nuclear matters. However, in the summer of 2005 these discussions broke down when Iran announced its intentions to restart its enrichment program.[6]

Having rejected France, Germany and Britain's efforts to avert a crisis, Iran then was given a Russian proposal to shift Iran's nuclear enrichment work to Russian soil. In December, Tehran formally rejected the Russian offer.[7] Since then France, Germany, Britain, China, Russia, the United States and the IAEA have repeatedly requested Iran suspend work on uranium enrichment. And repeatedly, Tehran has rejected those requests.

In January Tehran resumed its research.[8] Reportedly Iran is operating a small centrifuge cascade. It is conducting research and development on a pilot facility in Natanz. Iran has notified the IAEA that in the fall it will begin installing the first 3,000 centrifuges at an industrial enrichment plant at Natanz. Iran is producing feedstock for centrifuges at a uranium facility in Isfahan. Reportedly, Iran already has produced 85 tons of uranium hexafluoride at Isfahan. It has constructed an underground tunnel for storing uranium hexafluoride. The Isfahan facility is capable of converting uranium hexafluoride to uranium metal.[9]

The consensus view in the United States and among experts in Europe and elsewhere is that "(t)he only plausible explanation for the urgency of the Iranian enrichment program is to produce fissile material that can be used in nuclear weapons."[10]

At the very least, as stated in a recent report of the International Crisis Group, most countries have the "concern – reinforced by Iran's lack of transparency in the past, continuing support of militant Middle East groups and incendiary presidential rhetoric – that once able to highly enrich uranium, (Iran) will be both able and tempted to build nuclear weapons."[11] And that is an unacceptable threat.

Let me note that concerns which would have been grave anyway given the nature of the Iranian regime, the past deceptions of Iran's nuclear program, the current facts on the ground and Iranian statements about the program, and the support of terror groups are heightened further by the extreme statements of President Ahmadinejad. His statements that the Holocaust never happened and his pledge to eliminate the State of Israel are delusional, reckless and dangerous.[12]

The IAEA Board of Governors referral of the matter to the U.N. Security Council,[13] the Council's subsequent unanimous Presidential Statement on the matter,[14] and the Council's referral back to the IAEA Board has begun the diplomatic process that will lead to sanctions.[15] How comprehensive and how punishing such sanctions ultimately will be is unknown.[16] A great deal of diplomatic work lies ahead. But, unless there is a change in course, some sanctions seem inevitable.[17] They will be painful, they will be costly on all sides, and they will further isolate Iran from the international community.[18]

There has been a great deal of speculation about the so-called military option since Seymour Hersh's recent article in *The New Yorker* about Pentagon contingency planning for a U.S. military strike on Iran to eliminate Iran's nuclear program.[19] That Pentagon contingency planning is going on should be no surprise. It is only prudent to develop a full range of options. President Bush has repeatedly and clearly stated that, in dealing with the escalating Iran nuclear crisis, no option is off the table.[20] But the administration also has been clear that it wants to seek a diplomatic solution to this challenge and that it does not want to act alone.[21] Furthermore well understood are the known costs, risks and danger of unknowable consequences from military action.[22] So is military action possible? Absolutely. Is it likely at this time? No. Is it to be avoided? Yes, if possible.

Now during our exchanges with our Iranian interlocutors at this conference it has been clearly stated that Iran's nuclear program is a matter of great national pride for both the nation's leadership and the people.[23] It also has been noted that under the Nuclear Non-Proliferation Treaty to which Iran is a signatory that members have the right to the full nuclear fuel cycle, including enrichment capability, so long as it is not diverted to a weapons program.

However, given Iran's long covert nuclear program, the unresolved anomalies uncovered by the IAEA, and the rhetoric of President Ahmadinejad, the international community's deep suspicions of Iran's ultimate intentions are only reasonable. And Iran's rejection of repeated diplomatic overtures, the rejection of Russia's offer to reprocess uranium for Iran on its soil, and the fact that Iran has no immediate need for the capacity to enrich uranium for its peaceful nuclear energy production heightens these grave concerns.

However, there is another path worth pursuing to try to resolve this crisis. Direct talks with Tehran in which the United States participates is an option well worth pursuing. While there are many who have a legitimate concern that any such direct talks will legitimize the Iranian regime, given the great importance of this mater, the apparent inability to defuse this crisis and the enormous costs – known and unknown – of a military option; every diplomatic avenue should be pursued up to and including direct talks.

The Iraq situation continues to be very troublesome. Since the Iraqi people adopted a constitution last fall and the parliamentary election in December, a new government has been unable to form and sectarian violence has been on the rise. While America remains hopeful, indeed is deeply committed, to holding Iraq together and avoiding all-out civil war, possible dismemberment and all the spreading traumas such developments could cause the Iraqi people and the entire region remain a possibility. That is why Ambassador Zal Khalilzad raised the unprecedented possibility of direct talks with Iran about the situation in Iraq. Such an invitation was not tendered lightly. It was offered with the recognition that Shia are a majority of the people in Iraq and that Iran, as the largest Shia nation in the world, is not without influence with the Iraqi Shia community. It was offered with the knowledge and approval of President Bush and Secretary of State Rice. It was offered with the conviction that it is in the best interest not only of Iraqis, but also Iran and the United States that Iraq become a stable and secure society.[24]

All thoughtful observers knew that it might not be an easy invitation for Iran to accept. During our discussions here in Stockholm, our Iranian colleagues have shared insights with us about the careful deliberations at all levels in Iran of whether to accept this offer. And our Iranian colleagues have impressed upon us how monumental it was that the Supreme leader Ayatollah Seyed Ali Khamenei publicly spoke in support of such direct discussions. Unfortunately, soon after the Iranians accepted the invitation to direct talks, the United States suspended any commencement of such a conversation until such time as the new Iraqi government is formed.[25] Understandably, this diplomatic two-step has raised concerns and created doubts in Tehran about Washington's sincerity in first making the request for direct talks.

This interregnum ultimately should not sidetrack direct talks. It is in the interests of resolving the serious questions and rising threat of Iran's nuclear program and for peace and stability in the broader Middle East for such talks to proceed.[26]

For over two years the United States left it to the European three (Germany, France and Britain) to negotiate directly with Iran on the nuclear issue. Some progress was made. But Tehran knows that only the United States (or Israel with the aid of the U.S.) can project military power to threaten Iran. Tehran realizes that the United States will be indispensable to implementing any future agreement. And recent events have demonstrated the limits to the diplomatic space of Russia, India and even China on this matter.

Russia and China are reluctant to advance a U.N. Security Council sanctions regime.[27] They have their own important equities with Iran.[28] Furthermore, they are concerned that any Security Council resolutions imposing sanctions would provide the legal basis for military action. They fear a repeat of what happened in Iraq. Understandably, Russia, China and many others, including America's closest allies in Europe , want to avoid the military option if at all possible. They will demand that all diplomatic opportunities are exhausted including direct United States talks with Iran.[29]

The known costs of a military strike are high.[30] Due to the scattered sites of Iran's nuclear program and the location of many of them in highly populated areas, the likelihood of destroying all of Iran's nuclear program is slight and the assurance of killing many innocent civilians certain.[31] It would be seen by many as a unilateral, illegitimate, act of war. U.S. difficulties in Iraq and Afghanistan would increase greatly. The chance of new violence by Hezbollah in Lebanon and, perhaps, in the West Bank would rise. Oil prices would go up further. And there is a real risk of rising terrorist attacks on American targets.[32]

So while the danger of Iran armed with nuclear weapons is unacceptable, the cost of military action is steep indeed. This too argues for taking the chance to talk directly with Tehran.[33]

And, as anyone knows who has engaged in high stakes international negotiations; despite the best intelligence, most thoughtful preparations, and skilled game playing prior to talks; once direct negotiations begin new possibilities often are presented and unforeseen movement can be found. There is a large basket of issues in which both Washington and Tehran have keen interests. First and foremost the nuclear issue; but also Iraq, Afghanistan, Lebanon, the Palestinians, and oil supplies to name just a few.

There may come a time for military steps. No option can be taken off the table. But before that question must be confronted; all reasonable opportunities should be explored, not limited to but including direct talks whether multilateral negotiations or bilateral conversations.

---

1. Nicholas Burns, "United States Policy Toward Iran," Statement Before the International Relations Committee, U.S. Congress, Washington, D.C., March 8, 2006. See also, U.S. Department of Defense, "The National Defense Strategy of the United States of America," March, 2005.

2. Senator Richard G. Lugar, Opening Statement for Hearing on "A Nuclear Iran: Challenges and Responses," Foreign Relations Committee, U.S. Senate, March 2, 2006, Washington, D.C.

3. Robert G. Joseph, "Iran's Nuclear Program," Statement Before the International Relations Committee, U.S. Congress, March 8, 2006, Washington, D.C.

4. See, Leonard S. Spector, "Iran's Secret Quest for the Bomb," Yale Global, May 16, 2003. Revenue from oil experts fund about 50% of Iran's annual budget. Nonetheless, because of limited refining capacity, Iran imports about $4.5 billion of gasoline. See, "Iran: Energy Overview," BBC News, February 15, 2006.

5. IAEA GOV/2003/40, June 6, 2003. The three areas of concern identified by the IAEA were Iran's failure to report uranium imported from China in 1991, questions about the centrifuge enrichment program, and questions about the heavy water program. Among other things, the IAEA inspectors found considerable amounts of highly-enriched uranium (HEU) in environmental samples taken at Natanz and elsewhere.

In February, 2004, the father of Pakistan's nuclear program, Abdul Qadeer Khan, says that he had provided atomic secrets to Iran – as well as Libya and North Korea – beginning in the late 1980s. IAEA inspectors report similarities in design and components for the advanced P-2 centrifuge.

6. See generally, "Fact box: Timeline Of The Iranian Nuclear Crisis," Radio Free Europe, April 19, 2006.

7. On December 25, 2005, "Tehran formally rejected an offer from Moscow to enrich uranium for its nuclear program in Russia. Iranian officials insist upon Iran's right to enrich uranium on its own soil." Ibid.

8. On January 3, 2006, "Iranian Atomic Energy Organization deputy head Mohammad Saidi told state television that Tehran will resume its nuclear-fuel research. The Iranian government confirmed the report on 9, January. ...10 January 2006: Iran resumes nuclear research, triggering Western condemnation. Mohammad Saidi ... says that Iran agreed with the IAE on 9 January for IAEA inspectors in Iran to 'reopen those places on which we agreed.' Resumed activities, he said, are merely in 'research, and nothing more. We distinguish between fuel-related research and the production of fuel.' On the same day, IAEA Director-General Muhammad el-Baradei informed the IAEA governing board that Iran intends to begin small-scale uranium enrichment at its Natanz facility." Ibid.

9. Robert G. Joseph, ibid.

10.   Robert G. Joseph, *ibid.* Mr. Joseph notes that "Iran claims that this program is entirely peaceful, for production of fuel for power reactors. (But) the only power reactor Iran will have for at least ten years is the one being built by Russia at Bushehr, the fuel for which Russia is obligated to provide for the first ten years."

11.   International Crisis Group, *Iran: Is There A Way Out of the Nuclear Impasse?* Middle East Report No. 51, p. 2, February 23, 2006.

12.   See, Tom Baldwin, "The State of Israel will soon be History, says Iran's President," *The Times* (of London), April 15, 2006; Arli Akbar Dareini, "Israel 'Heading Toward Annihilation'," *Chicago Sun-Times*, April 15, 2006; "Iran Says Jews Must Go Back to Europe," *Iran News*, April 24, 2006; "Israel's Jews Should Go Home: Ahmadinejad," *Expatica*, April 24, 2006. "The fact is that Israel can ultimately not continue its existence," (Ahmadinejad) said." See also, "Iranian President: Israel Cannot Continue to Exist," *People's Daily*, April 25, 2006; and "Israel Won't Ignore Iran Threat," *Jerusalem Post*, April 25, 2006. Note, on April 14-16, 2006, Tehran hosted a conference entitled "Support for the Palestinian Intifada Conference." This was the third time Tehran had organized such a conference. Bill Samii, "Iran: Intifada Conference in Tehran Has Multiple Objectives," *Radio Free Europe*, April 14, 2006.

"The Israeli defense minister (Shaul Mofaz) today said Iran's nuclear programme was the biggest threat to Jews 'since Hitler'... 'Of all the threats we face, Iran is the biggest... Since Hitler we have not faced such a threat.'" "Iran Greatest Threat to Jews," *Guardian*, April 24, 2006.

Note, however, Oxford Analytica, "Iran President Has Little Impact on Foreign Policy," *Forbes*, May 4, 2006.

13.   On February 4, 2006, "IAEA governing board votes overwhelmingly to report Iran to the U.N. Security Council over its nuclear activities. ...Ten days after the IAEA voted to report it to the U.N. Security Council over its nuclear activities, Iran confirms that it has resumed work on uranium enrichment. "Factbox: Timeline of the Iranian Nuclear Crisis," *Ibid.*

14.   UNSC/8679 (March 29, 2006).

15.   SC/8679, Security Council, in Presidential Statement Underlines Importance of Iran's re-establishing Full, Sustained Suspension of Uranium-Enrichment Activities, March 26, 2006.

16.   At the time these remarks were delivered there was support for requiring Iran to halt its enrichment program. See for example, "Iran Given Stark Nuclear Choice," *BBC News*, March 30, 2006; "Iran Urged to Stop Nuclear Work," *BBC News*, April 12, 2006; Jim Hoagland, "Iran's Gift New Unity In the West," *Washington Post*, February 23, 2006; "Key Nations' Stances on Iran," *BBC News*, March 30, 2006; Bill Gasperini "Russia Joins Call for Iran to Halt Nuclear Program," *Voice of America*, April 12, 2006; "U.K. Concern At Iran Nuclear Claim," *BBC News*, April 12, 2006. See also, "U.N. Presses Iran on Nuclear Plans," *CNN*, April 13, 2006.

17.   At a time these remarks were delivered there was no consensus within the U.N. Security Council or more generally on whether sanctions would be imposed on Iran. But, if unable to get U.N. sanctions, it is likely the U.S., Europe and like-minded states will apply some sanction regime at lest as to the supply of nuclear technology. See generally, "The Security Council and Iran: Diplomacy Drags," *The Economist*, April 1, 2006; Mark Turner and Guy Dinsmore, "U.S. Plan Seeks Allies for Sanctions on Iran," *Financial Times*, March 9, 2006; David Crawford, "Divide Over Iran Likely to Impede Security Council," *Wall Street Journal*, March 9, 2006; Carne Ross, "Could Sanctions Stop Iran?" *Washington Post*, March 30, 2006; Senator Sam Brownback, "Preventing a Nuclear-Armed Iran: Will China and Russia Help, Heritage Lecture #934; The Heritage Foundation, April 17, 2006 (Available at www.heritage.org); Simon Freeman, "U.S. Renews Push for Sanctions Against Iran," *The Times* (of London), April 14, 2006; and Neil King, Jr., "Hu Doesn't Bend on Iran, Yuan," *Wall Street Journal*, April 21-23, 2006.

18.   In addition to burdens on Iran, imposition of further sanctions on Iran, at the very least, would increase market concerns about the reliability of oil supply and drive up the cost of oil.

19.   Seymour M. Hersh, "The Iran Plans: Would President Bush Go To War To Stop Tehran From Getting the Bomb?" *The New Yorker*, April 17, 2006. See, for example, Reuel Marc Gerecht, "To Bomb, or Not to Bomb: That Is the Iran Question," *The Weekly Standard*, Vol. 11, Issue 30, April 24, 2006; Thomas McInerney, "Target Iran: Yes, There is a Feasible Military Option Against the Mullah's Nuclear Program" *The Weekly Standard*, Vol. 11, Issue 30, April 24, 2006; William M. Arkin, "The Pentagon Preps for Iran," *Washington Post, April 16. 2006;* Peter Baker, "Bush Dismisses Talk of Using Force Against Iran," *Washington Post*, April 11, 2006; "U.S. Could Attack Iran Next Year, Russian Expert," *RIAS Novosti*, April 17, 2006; Nedra Pickler, "Top Brit: Nuking Iran is Completely Nuts," *Chicago Sun-Times*, April 10, 2006; Paul Reynolds, "Iran Attack Debate Raises Nuclear Prospect," *BBC News*, April 10, 2006; "Gulf

States Won't Help U.S. If It Attacks Iran," *Associated Press*, April 17, 2006; "U.K. Dismisses Talk of Iran Attack," *BBC News*, April 9, 2006; Stefan Smith, "Tehran Mocks U.S. Ability to Win Military Action," *Agence France-Presse*, April 15, 2006; "Tehran Accuses U.S. of Mind Games," *BBC News*, April 10, 2006; and Garth Smyth, "Iran Shrugs Off Risk of U.S. Strikes on Nuclear Plants," *Financial Times*, April 17, 2006. See also, Paul Kerr, "Reports Grow That U.S. Plots Strike Against Iran," *Arms Control Today*, May, 2006.

See also, "Blair Refuses to Rule Out Iran Force," *UPI*, April 24, 2006; and "British PM Denies Discussing Military Action Against Iran with U.S.," *China View*, April 24, 2006.

20. "Bush Keeps Iran Military Option," *BBC News*, April 18, 2006; and Peter Baker, Defna Linzer and Thomas E. Ricks, "U.S. Is Studying Military Strike Option on Iran," *Washington Post*, April 19, 2006.

21. See, for example, "U.S. Does Not Want to Act Unilaterally on Iran," *Interfax News Agency*, April 14, 2006; and "Diplomacy is First Tactic Over Iran, Says U.S.," *The Scotsman*, April 10, 2006.

22. See for example, Andrew Sullivan, "General Bush's Lose-Lose Iranian War Options," *The Times* (of London), April 14, 2006; Richard Clarke and Steven Simon, "Bombs That Would Backfire," *New York Times*, April 16, 2006; and Editorial, "Military Fantasies on Iran," *New York Times*, April 11, 2006.

23. See, for example, "Pakistan, Father of Mullahs' Nuke Pride in Iran," *Iran News*, April 22, 2006.

24. See, Michael Slackman, "Iran and U.S. Agree to Talks About Iraq," *International Herald Tribune*, March 17, 2006; and Associated Press, "U.S., Iran Willing to Talk About Iraq," *CBS News*, March 16, 2006.

25. On April 21, 2006, the political log jam in Iraq was broken and Jawad al-Maliki emerged as the consensus Prime Minister. See, Lee Keath, "Shite Alliance Nominates New Iraqi Prime Minister," *Mail and Guardian*, April 22, 2006; Jim Muir, "Shias Agree on Nominee for Iraq's Prime Minister, *News Telegraph*, April 22, 2006. Unfortunately, by then the ground had shifted and the United States announced it would not hold direct talks with Iran. See, Michele Kelemen, "U.S. Dismisses Notion of Direct Talks with Iran," *NFR*, May 4, 2006; "White House Rejects Direct Talks with Iran," *Agence France Presse*, May 4, 2006; "U.S. Dismisses Idea of Directly Talking to Iran," *Xinhau*, May 4, 2006.

26. See, Melinda Smith, "U.S. Senators Call for Direct Talks with Iran," *Voice of Amrica*, April 18, 2006.

27. See, for example, "Security Council Divisions on Iran," *International Herald Tribune*, April 22-3, 2006; "Key Nations' Stances on Iran," *BBC News*, March 30, 2006; "Russia: Analyst Says Moscow Will Not Follow West's Cue on Iran," *Radio Free Europe*, January 16, 2006; Robert Parsons, "Russia: Is Moscow Changing Course on Iran?" *RFE/RL*, January 17, 2006; "Russia, China Urge Caution on Iran Nuclear Dispute," *Radio Free Europe*, January 17, 2005; "Iran Sanctions Depend on Proof: Russia has Ruled Out Sanction Against Iran Unless There is Proof that its Nuclear Programme is Not Peaceful," *BBC News*, April 21, 2006; and "Russia Warns on Aggravating Iran Standoff," Associated Press; April 23, 2006.

28. Among other interests in the region, China has large contracts for Iranian oil and Russia has commercial interests in Iran plus concerns about Tehran's capacity to cause unrest among Russia's Muslim population. See for example, Rupert Wingfield-Hayes, "Satisfying China's Demand for Energy," *BBC News*, February 16, 2006.

29. See, Carol Giacomo, "New Push for Direct Talks Between U.S. and Iran," *Reuters*, May 4, 2006; Guy Dinmore, "U.S. Allies Urge Direct Dialogue with Iran," *Financial Times*, May 3, 2006; "Former Foreign Ministers Urge Direct Talks With Iran," *RFE/RL*, April 26, 2006; Andre de Nesnera, "Experts Urge Direct U.S.-Iranian Talks to Resolve Nuclear Issue," *Voice of America*, April 28, 2006; "Former Iran Diplomat Urges Direct Talks with U.S.," *Iran Mania*, April 27, 2006.

30. See, Edward N. Luttwak, "Three Reasons Not to Bomb Iran – Yet," *Commentary*, April, 2006. Note: British Prime Minister Tony Blair, "There may be a military option but the impact could be catastrophic," Seymour M. Hersh, *ibid*.

31. See, "Iran's Key Nuclear Sites," *BBC News*, January 16, 2006.

32. See generally, "Iran Will Harm U.S. interests If Attacked: Leader," *Reuters*, April 26, 2006; and "Iran Threatens Global Retaliation if U.S. Attacks," *Iran Mania*, April 26, 2006.

33. See generally, Ray Takeyh and James Dobbins, "Dialogue Can Stop Iran at the Nuclear Threshold," *Financial Times*, April 4, 2006. In contrast see, Kenneth R. Timmerman, "Negotiating With Evil," *Front Page Magazine.com*, May 4, 2006.

Iran's Nuclear Issue:
Is It Time To Dance?

Our discussions these past two days have been fascinating. We gather at a time of growing anxiety over Iran's nuclear program due to Tehran's decision to proceed with uranium enrichment, defiance of the international community, including the International Atomic Energy Agency (IAEA), and President Mahmoud Ahmadinejad's heated rhetoric. The matter again has been under discussion at the United Nations Security Council and the specter of sanctions has been raised.[1] The United States, the Europeans, Russia and China all have said that an Iran with nuclear weapons is unacceptable. Various proposals have been offered. Most recently the United States has said it is prepared to join multilateral negotiations on this issue. Nonetheless, articles continue to be published about U.S. preparations for the military option to deal with this crisis.[2] And as tensions rise, Tehran has said it will take until August 22nd before it will reply. In light of these many developments and the continued confusion and uncertainty about various parties' intentions,[3] the candor of our Iranian interlocutors during our discussions is valued and appreciated. Our talks have been very useful.

Now I'd like to recap where I think we are and raise possibilities for a path forward.[4] More specifically, I want to discuss whether it is time to dance. That is, is it time to get serious about the diplomatic option? Can engagement be worthwhile for Tehran, Washington and other interested parties?

By spring the game was afoot. There had been a lopsided vote by the IAEA Board of Governors referring the Iran nuclear issue to the U.N. Security Council.[5] Iran had removed IAEA seals from its nuclear facilities and announced it would not comply with the Additional Protocol. Iran announced it had 164 cascades and it would start reprocessing.[6] The Security Council had issued a Presidential Statement.[7] And there was some hope that the Russian proposal to guarantee fuel for Iran peaceful nuclear facilities and to take spent fuel from Iran might provide a way out of the dilemma.

Unfortunately, Tehran rejected the Russian proposal. Tensions rose.

Then, on May 31st, Secretary Rice issued a statement that the United States was prepared to join multilateral negotiations with Iran to resolve the nuclear issues if Tehran suspended its reprocessing.[8] In June the IAEA issued a report on Iran's

---

Remarks at Dialogue on Multilateral Diplomacy and the Management of Global Issues, Saltsjobad, Sweden, July 14, 2006.

nuclear program that was highly critical.[9] On June 6th, European Union's foreign policy chief Javier Solana flew to Tehran to present a new negotiating package.[10]

The P5 plus 1 package reaffirms Iran's inalienable right to peaceful nuclear energy; supports building a light water reactor; agrees to suspend Iran's file at the U.N. Security Council; offers a Euratom/Iran nuclear cooperation agreement; offers WTO membership; lifts restrictions on the export of civilian aircraft to Iran; offers a Trade and Economic Cooperation Agreement with the European Union; presents a long-term strategic energy partnership with the European Union; offers extension and modernization of Iran's oil and gas sectors; provides fuel guarantees and a fuel bank; raises the possibility of an intergovernmental regional forum on security and, in the context of regional security, offers recognition of territorial integrity and sovereignty.

In exchange, the P-5 plus 1 asks for Iran to suspend enrichment and reprocessing during negotiations; address outstanding issues with the IAEA; resume implementation of the Additional Protocol; demonstrate that its new nuclear activities are linked to credible and coherent economic rationales; and agree to a long term suspension of enrichment.

The so-called sticks mentioned included a U.N. Security Council Chapter VII, article 41 resolution; an embargo of Iranian goods and technology; freezing assets and a ban on financial transactions; a travel visa ban; suspension of technology cooperation with the IAEA; a ban on investment against Iranian entities; a reduction – or freeze – of bilateral contacts; ending support for Iran's WTO membership, an arms embargo; and reduced government support for trade and export credit insurance.

Meanwhile, since April, there has been a shift in tone and tactics by the United States. While President Bush has said that no option is off the table and military contingency planning proceeds, there has been greater emphasis on diplomacy. In Secretary Rice's May 31st statement, she said that the United States recognizes Iran's right to civilian nuclear power. That is a change. She made no immediate demand on centrifuges other than a suspension of reprocessing while negotiations take place. And, most significantly, Secretary Rice said that the United States is prepared to participate in the European negotiations with Iran.[11] This is a big step. Our Iranian interlocutors have raised questions about whether the Rice offer is serious or is it just a ploy to allow the United States to check the box that it tried diplomacy before going forward with the military option. They are skeptical.

While I understand the Iranian suspicion and caution regarding whether or not the United States offer to talk is sincere – especially in light of the past U.S./Iranian stop and go trail of disappointments, I believe the offer is genuine. I believe the United States Government is prepared to talk. I believe President Bush wants the diplomatic route to resolve the thorny issues. I believe it is in Iran's self-interest to accept the offer for multilateral talks and constructively explore whether we can agree on how to move forward.

I recognize that Iran feels embolden and more confident by its current situation. High oil prices certainly are benefiting the Iranian economy. President Ahmadinejad has the confidence of a fervent true believer. You see America still entangled in Afghanistan and bogged down in Iraq. You know American diplomatic ties – even with our good friends – are frayed after the failure of diplomacy in the run up to

Operation Iraqi Freedom. You re aware of President Bush's low approval ratings at home. You feel more confident in your role in the greater Middle East. You believe Russia will forestall any U.N. sanctions on Iran.[12] And you are mindful of how popular the nuclear program is among the Iranian people.[13]

Fair enough. But one lesson over the past six years is the strong resolve of President George W. Bush, even in the face of broad criticism. President Bush certainly has proven his willingness to act and act decisively when he feels America is endangered. It is clear the military option is not completely off the table.[14] It is clear American military might has the reach and fire power to inflict great damage on Iran. It is known that U.S. military planning is going on. It is suspected that there are some voices in the Administration, and it is known that some of the Administration's strongest supporters outside government, feel that military action against Iran is inevitable and should be taken. As Senator John McCain has said, "There is only one thing worse than the U.S. exercising a military option, and that is a nuclear armed Iran."[15]

Also, I would suggest that relying on Moscow to save Iran from crippling economic sanctions, perhaps, should give Iran little comfort. First, Russia has a large basket of interests and concerns. Many of them are with the United States, many are with Europe. Some are of greater priority to Moscow than Iran. And, of course, Moscow will act in its own best self-interest. Are you certain Moscow will be your firm protector in the U.N. Security Council come what may? Perhaps. Perhaps not.

Furthermore there are a range of penalties that might be imposed on Iran outside of the United Nations. A coalition of the willing composed of the United States and major European economies alone certainly could inflict damage on Iran's economy. And a range of other steps short of military action could be disruptive and harmful to Iran.

But, I believe, the better next step, the preferred option now available is to talk. We should look past the inartful language and insults of President Ahmadinejad's May 9th letter to President Bush and the apparent (perceived) slight that President Bush did not reply to it. We should be mindful of President Ahmadinejad's inflammatory and utterly unacceptable threats to the sovereign state of Israel but not allow these reckless words to prohibit sincere efforts to resolve this rising nuclear crisis.[16] America will continue to condemn Iran's support for terrorist groups such as Hezbollah and seek their end. America will continue to express great concern about human rights abuses in Iran, Nonetheless, the Bush Administration's offer to join multilateral talks with Iran on the nuclear issue is sincere. It is an offer supported by both senior Republicans and senior Democrats in Congress.[17] It is in both the interest of the Iranian people and the American people to resolve this matter diplomatically, to say nothing about others in the greater Middle East.

Let me return to Secretary Rice's May 31st statement and her answers to questions on this matter. She said, "The Iranian people believe they have a right to civil nuclear energy. We acknowledge that right." She went on to say, "President Bush has consistently emphasized that the United States is committed to a diplomatic solution to the nuclear challenges posed by the Iranian regime. ... Thus, to underscore our commitment to a diplomatic solution and to enhance the prospects for success, as soon as Iran fully and verifiably suspends its enrichment and reprocessing activities, the United States will come to the table with our EU-3 colleagues and meet with Iran's representatives."

Then, in answers to questions from reporters, Dr. Rice repeatedly returned to the Administration's commitment to negotiations, to a diplomatic resolution. She said, "What we are talking about here is an effort to enhance the chances for a successful negotiated solution to the Iranian nuclear problem, something President Bush has said that he very much wanted to do. ... We now believe in that the United States might be able now to add weight to the negotiating track by joining these discussions." Later Dr. Rice said, "The President made very clear that we are going to do everything we can to find a diplomatic solution to the nuclear problem." "It is our view," she said, "that a diplomatic solution to the nuclear program is necessary."

"This is an effort to reinforce diplomatic negotiations that we believe should succeed and have a chance to succeed with the strongest possible way," said Dr. Rice. And she again repeated, "The President has said that we are committed to a diplomatic solution to this problem."

Near the end of her "question and answer" period with the press, Secretary Rice again returned to America's desire to negotiate. She said, "We cannot allow Iran to get a nuclear weapon. That everybody has agreed to. Therefore, our choice is to provide an atmosphere in which Iran comes back to negotiations and we solve this by a negotiated track – we're trying to give that the very best chance. ... I want to emphasize the diplomacy again here. This is a real opportunity. It is an opportunity for the world to clarify Iran's intentions and it is an opportunity for Iran to make its intentions clear."[18]

And just today there are press reports that despite the complications due to Hezbollah's kidnapping of Israeli soldiers and the response with military strikes by Israel against the Iranian-backed Hezbollah,[19] that President Bush said while visiting German Chancellor Angela Merkel in Stralsund, Germany, "(T)heir deadline passed" but the Iranians "can show up anytime and say 'Wait a minute, now we'd like to go back and negotiate.'"[20]

The United States wants to pursue the diplomatic track in good faith. We all know the issues are difficult and the talks will be tough. But a negotiated settlement of this problem certainly is better than the alternative. All parties should try to resolve this problem peacefully. This will best serve the interests of the Iranian people and of the American people.

Therefore, I urge our Iranian interlocutors, when they return to Tehran, to urge their colleagues to provide a positive response to this invitation to talk. On August 22nd Iran should answer the pending proposal in the affirmative. Let's exhaust all reasonable options before fateful red lines are crossed. It's time for the diplomatic dance to begin.

---

1.   Cam Simpson, "World Powers Refer Iran to U.N. Council," *Chicago Tribune*, June 12, 2006; and Helene Cooper, "Russia and China, in Shift, Inch Toward Iran Sanctions: Willing to Press Case at Security Council," *New York Times*, July 13, 2006.

2.   See, for example, "What Are U.S. Military Options in Iran?" *Fox News*, April 24, 2005; and Kelley Beaucar Vlahos, "Bush Critics Want Tougher U.S. Approach to Iran," *Fox News*, June 21, 2006; and Jonathan Karl, "What Are the U.S. Military Options Against Iran? Military Analysts Believe Air Strikes May Force Iran's Hand," *ABC News*, March 9, 2006.

3.   For various analysis of Iran's nuclear ambitions see statements by Kenneth M. Pollack, "The Iranian Nuclear Program: Motivation and Priorities," Karen Sadjadpour, "Iran's Political/Nuclear Ambitions and U.S. Policy Options," Patrick Clawson, "Iran's Motives and Strategies: The Role of the Economy," and Geoffrey Kemp, "Iranian Nuclear Ambitions: Motives and Strategies," U.S. Senate Committee on Foreign Relations; Hearing: "Iran's Political/Nuclear Ambitions and U.S. Policy Options," Washington, D.C.; May 17, 2006. See also, Chen Kane, "Nuclear Decision Making in Iran: A Rare Glimpse," *Middle East Brief*, Crown Center for Middle East Studies, Brandeis University, No. 5, May 2006.

4.   For various perspectives on the options available to the United States to deal with the Iranian nuclear issue see statements by Ambassador Frank G. Wisner, "Iran, the United States and the International Community: The Time is Right to Engage," James Phillips, "U.S. Policy and Iran's Nuclear Challenge," Vali Nasr, "Iran's Nuclear Program," and Julia Nancy, "U.S. Policy Options: Iran's Oil and Gas Sector," U.S. Senate Committee on Foreign Relations; Hearing: "Iran's Political/Nuclear Ambitions and U.S. Policy Options," Washington, D.C.; May 18, 2006. See also, Kenneth Katzman, "Iran" U.S. Concerns and Policy Options," Congressional Research Service Report RL 32048, June 2, 2006.

5.   Report by the IAEA Director General, "Implementation of the NPT Safeguards Agreement in the Islamic Republic of Iran," GOV/2006/38, June 8, 2006. See also, the IAEA Staff Report, "Report on Iran Nuclear Safeguards Sent to Agency's Board and U.N. Security Council," April 28, 2006. Available at http://www.iaea.org/NewsCenter/News/2006/iranreport_sg.html.

6.   For excellent description and analysis of the current status of the Iran nuclear program, see, Robert J. Einhorn," Statement on The Nuclear Issue" and David Albright, Statement on "Iran's Nuclear Program: Prediction and Potential," before the U.S. Senate Committee on Foreign Relations, Hearing: "Iran's Political/Nuclear Ambition: U.S. Policy Options;" Washington, D.C.; May 17, 2006.

7.   United Nations Security Council Presidential Statement, "Call on Iran to Take Steps Required by IAEA Board of Governors; Requests Report from IAEA Director General in 30 Days," March 29, 2006. S/PRST/2006/155.

8.   Secretary Condoleezza Rice, Press Conference on Iran, U.S. Department of State; Washington, D.C.; May 31, 2006.

9.   Dr. Mohamed El Baradei, Introductory Statement to the Board of Governors, Vienna, Austria, June 12, 2006. See also, Elaine Sciolino, "Iran Resumes Uranium Enrichment Work," *New York Times*, June 9, 2006; and Elaine Sciolino, "Nuclear Monitor Says Iran Fails to Provide Data," *New York Times*, June 13, 2006.

10.   "EU's Solana to present Iran with Nuclear Proposal," *CNN.com*, June 5, 2006; and "Iran Rejects Early Nuclear Reply," *BBC News*, June 29, 2006.

11.   At the May 31, 2006 Press Conference, Secretary Rice, however, did say the U.S. would not participate in bilateral negotiations with Iran and that this initiative was not about a "Good Bargain" that would head to normalization.

12.   During our two days of discussions, our Iranian colleagues repeatedly expressed a high degree of confidence that Russia would prevent imposition of U.N. sanctions on Iran for three to four years.

13.   See, for example, Mahan Abedin, "Iranian Public Opinion and the Nuclear Stand-Off," *Mideast Monitor*; April/May 2006; Vol. 1, No. 2.

14.   See, for example, Seymour M. Hersh, "Last Stand: The Military's Problem with the President's Iran Policy," *The New Yorker*, July 10, 2006.

15.   Senator John McCain, Speech at the Munich Security Conference; Munich, Germany; February 4, 2006.

16.   "On April 14, 2006 President Mahmud Ahmadinejad called Israel 'a Zionist regime' that 'is on the road to being eliminated.' This comment was only the latest in a series of events... His October 2005 call for the elimination of Israel and his December 2005 comments denying the Holocaust..." Naghmeh Sohrabi, "Conservatives, Neoconservatives and Reformists: Iran After the Election of Mahmud Ahmadinejad," *Middle East Brief*, Crown Center for Middle East Studies, Brandeis University, No. 4,

April 2006. Note, however, at a meeting of the Shanghai Cooperation Organization on June 16th, President Ahmadinejad ratcheted down the rhetoric. See, Howard W. French, "Iran's President Hints at Hope for Defusing Nuclear Crisis," *New York Times*, June 17, 2003.

17.   See, for example, the statements of Senator Richard Lugar and Senator Joseph Biden at U.S. Senate Committee on Foreign Relations, Hearing on "Iran's Political/Nuclear Ambition and U.S. Policy Options," Washington, D.C., May 17, 2006.

18.   Secretary Condoleezza Rice, *ibid*.

19.   See, for example, "U.S. Blames Iran, Syria for Hezbollah Capture," *Reuters*, July 12, 2006; Greg Myre and Steven Erlanger, "Clashes Spread to Lebanon as Hezbollah Raids Israel," *New York Times*, July 13, 2006; Hassan M. Fattah and Steven Erlanger, "Israel Pumps Up Pressure on Lebanon: Airstrikes Hit at Hezbollah Near Beirut," *International Herald Tribune*, July 15-16, 2006.

20.   David Jackson, "Bush Holds Out Possibility of Talks With Iran," *USA Today*, July 14, 2006.

U.S. Can't Just Talk While Iran Builds Nuclear Weapon

The Middle East has long been a troublesome neighborhood. But now the dangers are rising.

Post-Saddam Iraq remains in turmoil claiming Iraqi and American casualties. The clash between Iraqi Shia and Sunni could spread beyond its borders to threaten moderate Arab regimes and international oil supplies. Israel's armed clash last summer left Hezbollah degraded, civilian devastation, fresh bitterness, and Israeli military invincibility in question. Syria remains a renegade state that sponsors instability. Iran's President Ahmadinejad denies the Holocaust and calls for the elimination of Israel while pursuing advanced nuclear technology and, presumably, a nuclear weapon.

Of all these, the looming threat of an Iran Nuclear Bomb is most alarming.

There is no reservoir of good will between the United States and Iran. Shortly after the Revolution, Iran took Americans hostage. Iran provides support to Hezbollah and Hamas. Iran is playing an unhelpful role within Iraq. And Ahmadinejad's rhetoric confirms the West's worst suspicions.

Despite Tehran's assurances that its nuclear program is intended solely for peaceful purposes, there is ample evidence to expect the worst. For 18 years Iran had a covert nuclear program. When discovered, Tehran denied the facts and sought to destroy evidence. It kicked out international inspectors. It appears to have negotiated in bad faith with the Europeans. And it refuses to stop its program to enrich uranium.

Nuclear weapons in the hands of an extremist regime that supports terrorist groups, sows seeds of unrest in neighboring Iraq, and threatens the existence of democratic Israel is absolutely unacceptable. And so far neither American actions nor those of the international community have deterred Tehran.

The United States has imposed a wide range of sanctions on Iran and calls for regime change in Tehran. The U.N. Security Council is considering imposing sanctions, but Russia and China are watering down proposals from America and Europe. And Tehran threatens retaliatory action if Security Council sanctions are imposed.

Appeared in *Chicago Sun Times*, November 20, 2006.

The crisis is escalating. Is military action inevitable? Despite the challenges and costs to America in Iraq and Afghanistan, it is important that no option be off the table. Tehran should understand America's power to mobilize its military might.

Logistical challenges and limited intelligence mean military action, while able to degrade Iran's nuclear program and set it back many years, would not be conclusive. Given the location of Iran's nuclear sites, civilian casualties are unavoidable. And the repercussions are not easily assessed nor contained.

Given these ominous developments, is it possible to avoid confrontation? Perhaps not. But if there is any prospect of finding a solution to this issue, direct discussions on a variety of matters will be required. But to get talks going neither side can feel that negotiations seriously prejudice their interests.

The United States requires centrifuge spinning to stop so Iran doesn't drag out talks merely to buy time to advance a weapons program. Iran fears U.S. intentions and further international isolation. Consequently, the most promising way forward may be a temporary, mutual suspension to be proposed for a finite, but renewable, period of time.

The United States would suspend certain sanctions and Iran would suspend enrichment.

This would test whether there is any desire by Tehran to reach a negotiated agreement to avoid a crisis and, if not, strengthen international resolve to pursue punitive measures to thwart Iran's nuclear ambitions.

SECTION VII: REGIONAL

THE ECONOMIC COMMUNITY
OF WEST AFRICAN STATES

It is important symbolically and substantively that this U.N. Security Council Mission to West Africa makes an early stop here at the ECOWAS headquarters in Abuja.[1] On this trip, United Nations Security Council members are looking at sites of regional instability in West Africa.

Guinea-Bissau is struggling to recover from conflict.[2] Unfortunately, its economic conditions are desperate and its democratic institutions are in decay. As Secretary-General Kofi Annan wrote not long ago, "The situation in Guinea-Bissau has worsened. There is now a consensus that Guinea-Bissau, which had seemed so promising following the ending of the 1998-1999 armed conflict ... is now once again embarked on a downward course."[3] Indeed, after visiting Bissau, both I and many of my Security Council colleagues are concerned that Guinea-Bissau has slipped into a pre-conflict situation. It's downward course creates misery and instability that invites more potential conflict.

Last fall armed conflict broke out in Cote d'Ivoire. After many killings, pillage and rape, a peace agreement was reached in January[4] and a transition government is in place. This is encouraging. The eventual success of the fragile transition government will depend in large part on the substantial peacekeeping forces there. The 4,000 French troops of Operation Licorme are playing an important peacekeeping role.[5] But even more critical is the ECOWAS peacekeeping force in Cote d'Ivoire, MICECI.[6] There are many reasons to be hopeful about developments in Cote d'Ivoire, including the appointment of Prime Minister Diarra.[7] But there also are matters of concern such as the failure to fill the critical Ministries of Defense and of National Security in the transitional government of National Reconciliation, the question of how deeply committed President Gbagbo is to the Linas-Marcoussis Agreement, and the government's recent purchases of sophisticated weapons for the army.[8] When our Security Council Mission visits Cote d'Ivoire, we will discuss these issues with our interlocutors.

In Liberia, the civil war rages on. In recent years more than 200,000 Liberians have been killed in armed conflict and close to 1 million Liberians are now displaced persons, many of them are refugees. The rebel group LURD,[9] controls approximately 60 percent of the country. The rebel group MODEL[10] is gaining on the government in the east. And last week, for the second time, the LURD stormed the Liberian capital

---

Remarks at ECOWAS Headquarters, Abuja, Nigferia, June 30, 2003.

of Monrovia causing bloodshed and death. President Charles Taylor, the former warlord, has brought misery and death to too many Liberians[11] and he has exported conflict to Sierra Leone, Guinea and Cote d'Ivoire. The Sierra Leone Special Court has issued a 17 count indictment of Mr. Taylor for his central role in the atrocities committed against the people of Sierra Leone during the war.[12] And President Bush has called for Mr. Taylor to leave the country.

Of course, ECOWAS is deeply involved in trying to resolve this conflict through negotiations. We appreciate the briefing Dr. Mohamed Ibn Chambas[13] has given us this morning on the status of those negotiations. And the United States appreciates the on-going efforts to organize an ECOWAS peacekeeping force to go to Liberia to help keep peace after a negotiated settlement has been achieved. As you know, the United States Government has pledged to support this effort.

Yet another trouble spot in West Africa is Sierra Leone which our Mission also will visit. Following their devastating civil war,[14] Sierra Leone appears to be getting it right. Sierra Leone seems to have emerged from its conflict and put in place the institutions of transitional justice[15] and of democracy,[16] and built the foundation for a stable society and sustainable peace. We hope the positive momentum in Sierra Leone will continue. And we will look for lessons from the Sierra Leone experience when we visit there.

So here in West Africa, there are many challenges to establishing and maintaining peace and security. While ECOWAS initially was established as a economic union in West Africa to raise the living standards of its people,[17] over time it has recognized that robust economic development cannot be achieved without peace. The United States supported ECOWAS when it adopted the Mechanism for Conflict Prevention, Management and Resolution, Peace and Security. The United States supported ECOWAS when it adopted the Protocol on Democracy and Good Governance. And the United States has been the largest contributor to MICECI, the ECOWAS peacekeeping force in Cote d'Ivoire.

We believe in the importance of regional organizations. We believe ECOWAS has an important role to play in West Africa in achieving and consolidating peace and security; and in consolidating democracy and good governance. And, of course, the United States supports ECOWAS' contribution to eradicating poverty, increasing the involvement of the private sector, and promoting sustainable economic development in West Africa.

A few days ago President Bush made a major address in which he laid out his vision and detailed his agenda for relations between the United States and Africa.[18] He began by saying that "[a]ll of us… share some basic beliefs. We believe that growth and prosperity in Africa will contribute to the growth and prosperity of the world. We believe that human suffering in Africa creates moral responsibilities for people everywhere. We believe that this can be a decade of unprecedented advancement for freedom and hope and healing and peace across the African continent. That's what we believe."[19]

President Bush went on to say that "[t]he first great goal in our partnership with Africa is to help establish peace and security across the continent."[20] He then reviewed U.S. support for the peace process in the Democratic Republic of the Congo, his determination "to help the people of Liberia find the path to peace," and the work the United States is engaged in to help end the long civil war in Sudan. President Bush reaffirmed United States support for African peacekeeping forces, such as the ECOWAS force in Cote d'Ivoire. And the President announced that "the United States will devote a $100 million over the next 15 months to help countries in the region increase their own counter-terror efforts."[21]

The second great goal is to help Africa achieve better health care and higher literacy. In his State of the Union address last January, President Bush asked Congress to commit $15 billion over the next five years to fight AIDS abroad, especially focusing on African and Caribbean countries where the crisis is most severe.[22] And since health depends on defeating hunger, this year the United States will give more than $800 million to cope with food emergencies in Africa.[23] To advance literacy in Africa, President Bush has committed to spend $200 million to train more than 420,000 teachers in Africa and provide scholarships for 250,000 African girls.

The third great goal is to help Africa's economies through "aid and trade." The cornerstone of President Bush's initiative here is the Millennium Challenge Account that will provide a 50 percent increase in America's core development assistance over the next three years for countries that embrace reform and freedom.[24] And to help African trade, President Bush has asked Congress to extend to 2008 the African Growth and Opportunity Act, which gives greater access to American markets for African products.[25]

President Bush has an ambitious agenda to advance his bold vision. The other day the President said, "America is committed to the success of Africa because we recognize a moral duty to bring hope where there is despair, and relief where there's suffering. America is committed to the success of Africa because we understand failed states spread instability and terror that threatens us all. America is committed to the success of Africa because the peoples of Africa have every right to live in freedom and dignity, and to share in the progress of our times."[26]

In a few days President Bush will begin a five nation trip to Africa. It will begin in West Africa when he visits Senegal. It also will end in West Africa with a visit by President Bush here in Nigeria. The United States is committed to a safer, more secure and more prosperous Africa. And we recognize the critical role of regional organizations such as ECOWAS. I am delighted to participate in this U.N. Security Council Mission to West Africa to learn about the challenges ahead. I am delighted to be here at the ECOWAS Headquarters to learn more about your good work and how we can support you. And I can assure you that when I return to New York better informed about your issues, I will remain dedicated to help support your efforts for a better life for the people of West Africa.

---

1. The Economic Community of West African States, ECOWAS, was established on May 28, 1975, in Lagos, Nigeria. It is composed of the following West African countires: Benin, Bukina Faso, Cape Verde, Cote d'Ivoire, the Gambia, Ghana, Guinea, Guinea-Bissau, Liberia, Mali, Niger, Nigeria, Senegal, Sierra Leone and Togo. ECOWAS headquarters is in Abuja, Nigeria.

2. Civil War raged in Guinea-Bissau in 1998-99.

3.   S/2003/621, para. 25.

4.   The Linas-Marcoussis Agreement between the various warring factions established a cease-fire and a transition government leading up to national elections in 2005.

5.   There are approximately 20,000 French citizens in Cote d'Ivoire and France has large commercial interests in their former colony.

6.   Mission de la CEDEAO en Cote d'Ivoire. CEDEAO is ECOWAS translated into French, Communaute Economique Des Estats de l'Afrique de l'Quest.

7.   Mr. Seydon Diarra is a seasoned civil servant and experienced diplomat. 72 years of age, he has no political history nor apparent political ambitions which made him an acceptable and qualified Prime Minister for Cote d'Ivoire's transitional government of National Reconciliation.

8.   In recent months President Gbagbo purchased fixed wing aircraft, five attack helicopters and either 2 or 4 drones.

9.   Liberians United for Reconciliation and Democracy.

10.   Movement for Democracy in Liberia.

11.   On December 24, 1989, rebels led by Charles Taylor invaded Liberia from Cote d'Ivoire. The Civil War was one of Africa's bloodiest; more than 200,000 Liberians died and more than a million displaced Liberians became refugees in neighboring countries. In October 1990 an Interim Government of National Unity was formed in Gambia under the auspices of ECOWAS. But Charles Taylor refused to work with the interim government and continued the war.

After several peace accords and declining military power, Mr. Taylor agreed to the formation of a 5 man transitional government in 1993. Disarmament and demobilization of warring factions were carried out hastily and special elections were held on July 19, 1997. As the dominant Liberian warlord, Charles Taylor won the election by a large majority. Most commentators believe he won primarily because Liberians feared a return to war if he lost.

In 1999, in response to the oppression of the Taylor government, a rebel group called Liberians United for Reconciliation and Democracy (LURD) began fighting government security forces in Lofa County along Liberia's border with Guinea. The fighting spread into western and central Liberia. More recently a second rebel group, the Movement for Democracy in Liberia (MODEL) began to fight in eastern Liberia. An estimated 200,000 Liberians have died during this most recent civil war and 700,000 have been displaced.

12.   On June 4, 2003, Liberian President Charles Taylor was in Accra, Ghana, for the beginning of Liberian peace talks organized by ECOWAS. On that morning, Sierra Leone Special Court Chief Prosecutor David Crane unsealed a 17 count indictment of Charles Taylor for war crimes.

13.   Dr. Chambas is Executive Secretary of ECOWAS.

14.   In 1997, Major Johnny Paul Koroma overthrew Sierra Leone's elected President Ahmad Tejan Kabbah. After 10 months in office the junta was ousted by Nigerian-led ECOMOG forces, and the democratically elected government of President Kabbah was reinstated. But in 1999, Captain Foday Sankoh and his Revolutionary United Front (RUF) tried to take power by force. The ensuing war left over 50,000 dead and countless victims of mutilation, rape, looting and abuse. Over 2 million of Sierra Leone's 4.2 million people were displaced.

15. In 2002, the Special Court of Sierra Leone was created to try those who "bear the greatest responsibility for the commission of crimes against humanity (and) war crimes. The Court has indicted 12 individuals from both sides of the fighting. In 2002, the Sierra Leone Truth and Reconciliation Commission began taking testimony in order to "create an impartial historical record... (and) to address impunity."

16. Elections were organized and held in the spring of 2002 for the parliament and presidency.

17. The ECOWAS objectives are "[t]o promote cooperation and integration, leading to the establishment of an economic union in West Africa in order to raise the living standards of its peoples, and to ensure economic growth, foster relations among Member States and contribute to the progress and development of the African continent."

18. Remarks by President George W. Bush to the Corporate Counsel on Africa's U.S.-Africa Business Summit, Washington Hilton Hotel, Washington, D.C., June 26, 2003.

19. *Ibid.*

20. *Ibid.*

21. *Ibid.*

22. President George W. Bush, "State of the Union" Address, the U.S. Capitol, Washington, D.C., January 28, 2003.

23. Remarks by President George W. Bush to the Corporate Council on Africa's U.S.-Africa Business Summit, Washington Hilton Hotel, Washington, D.C., June 26, 2003.

24. The criteria President Bush has established for countries to qualify for Millennium Challenge Account funds are one, to rule justly; two to invest in the health and education of their people; and three, to have policies that encourage economic freedom.

25. The African Growth and Opportunity Act became law in 2000. While Sub-Sahara Africa has 11 percent of the world's population, it has less than 2 percent of the world's trade. AGDA has helped increase African exports to the United States 10 percent.

26. Remarks by President George W. Bush to the Corporate Council on Africa's U.S.-Africa Business Summit, Washington Hilton Hotel, Washington, D.C., June 26, 2003.

BUSH WON'T LET RUSSIA STOP FREEDOM'S MARCH

Today there is a gathering tide of history; freedom is on the march.

Georgia. Afghanistan. Ukraine. The Palestinians. Iraq. People empowered, seizing their destiny, and choosing their leaders through the ballot box.

Even in tiny Togo, a small African nation ruled by an authoritarian military dictator for 38 years, freedom is stirring. After the death of President Gnassingbe Eyadema four weeks ago, the military installed his son Faure Gnassingbe as Togo's new president. But intense international pressure, most notably from other African states, and, even more important, by the people of Togo, led to his stepping down. Togo's Parliament has chosen one of its own, Abass Boufo, to be interim president with elections within 60 days.

Egypt's Hosni Mubarak has announced that after 50 years of one party rule he will seek to amend the constitution to allow the first direct multi-party presidential race in Egypt's history.

In Lebanon, the people are in the streets demanding Syrian occupation end so they can work toward self-determination.

Throughout the Middle East people are seeing this tide of freedom. They are inspired. And they are asking themselves why can't they too have a say in their own future. The oppressive boots of despots are feeling the ground move beneath them.

Millions of people from Asia to West Africa, from the Caucasus to the West Bank are experiencing the freedom we take for granted. Many risking their lives to vote. All investing their dreams in democracy.

In this tide of history we see hope. But there are those who view it with fear.

We see freedom's march as a cause to support, nurture and advance. But there are those who see it as a threat to constrain, deny and roll back.

There are those who stand against freedom's march. Authoritarian governments desperate to hold on to their power and prerogatives. Even some in fledgling democracies who seek to roll back freedom's hard earned advance.

For America's forward strategy of freedom to succeed and for oppressed people to secure their liberties, among other things, America must speak out for freedom movements and rebuke those who would deny freedom's progress.

Appeared in the *Chicago Sun-Times,* March 12, 2005.

President Bush clearly has reaffirmed our nation's course. He has said America will stand tall for freedom's march. That is America's tradition, values, responsibility and opportunity. For, among other things, a freer world is a safer world.

Therefore President Bush's recent meeting with Russian President Vladimir Putin in Bratislava, Slovakia, was consequential.

America's basket of interests with every nation are varied. Perhaps that is especially true with Russia, a nuclear power facing the internal dangers of a weak economy, internal rebellion, declining life expectancy and pensioners' unrest.

The threat of nuclear proliferation in North Korea and Iran, cooperation in Iraq, and loose nukes on Russian soil are only a few of the issues that Washington and Moscow must work on together. The agenda is long. It is important. And it is difficult.

Therefore it is even more noteworthy that President Bush took the occasion to push back on Russia's recent retrenchment from acceptable democratic practices.

In recent years Putin, a former KGB colonel, has tightened his grip on power. He shut down the Duma investigation of the suspicious 2000 Moscow Apartment explosion that killed scores of people and boosted Putin's election campaign. He has shut down the independent national TV station. Governors throughout Russia had been elected. Putin has eliminated those elections. All now are appointed by Putin. By eliminating local leaders, Putin has cut off feedback from the people to Moscow's leaders who are increasingly disconnected from them. Putin has led a brutal crackdown in Chechnya. And now people are talking about changing the constitution to prolong Putin's power.

In Ukraine, Putin sought to interfere with the election and initially proclaimed the first fraudulent vote to have been fair. Moscow sought to interfere in the recent election in Moldova. And Putin seeks to eviscerate the Organization of Security and Cooperation in Europe because of its role in exposing electoral fraud in post-Communist states of Georgia, Ukraine and elsewhere.

In his inaugural address President Bush pledged to promote freedom throughout the world. And in Bratislava, Bush again demonstrated that he is good to his word.

In a private meeting and then in public with Putin standing beside him, President Bush made clear that Russia's authoritarian drift is unacceptable and that the United States expects that trend to reverse and shift toward more freedom and real democracy.

The United States has many issues on which we should and we will work with Russia. But only a democratic Russia will be a reliable partner.

As President Bush said in his inaugural address, "The survival of liberty in our land increasingly depends on the success of liberty in other lands. The best hope for peace in our world is the expansion of freedom in all the world."

So we must support new democracies in Georgia and Ukraine. We must nurture freedom's progress in Togo and Lebanon. And as President Bush did in Bratislava, we must be forward leaning against backsliding in Russia.

Freedom is on the march. We can ill afford to leave the Russian people behind.

A Strong, Engaged Europe is Required

I am delighted to be in Zagreb to participate in this conference. I thank the Bertelsmann Foundation for sponsoring the event. Also, I thank Croatian President Stjepan Mesic and Prime Minister Ivo Sanader for their presentations; as well as the other speakers.

The subject of this conference, "Southeast Europe on the Way Into the European Union," is especially timely due to the issues raised by the referenda earlier this week in France and the Netherlands in which the people overwhelmingly rejected the proposed European constitution.[1] This rebuff has shaken confidence within the EU, caused the value of the Euro to fall, challenged the pace of European integration, and raised questions about future expansion of the European Union in southeast Europe.[2] What next?

Historic Divisions

Robert Kaplan, in his important book *Balkan Ghosts*,[3] wrote about the difficult history of this region; a history of deep cultural, religious and ethnic divisions that has led to tragic violence not only in the Balkans but also violence that began here and become a contagion engulfing all of Europe and beyond in World War I. Not long after the fall of the Berlin Wall, Kaplan wrote, "Here the battle between Communism and capitalism is merely one dimension of a struggle that pits Catholicism against Orthodoxy, Rome against Constantinople, the legacy of Hapsburg Austria-Hungary against that of Ottoman Turkey – in other words, West against East, the ultimate historical and cultural conflict."[4] My friend Stephan Taurov, Bulgarian Ambassador to the United Nations, once said to me that the Balkans has more history than it can digest.

Yugoslav Nobel laureate Ivo Andric, in his short story "A Letter from 1920," wrote about an invisible border between love and hate in Bosnia, and how beneath "so much tenderness and loving passion" sometimes lie "entire hurricanes of tethered and compressed hatreds maturing and awaiting their hour."[5] In the 1990's that hour came with horrific consequences: the siege of Sarajevo, Srebrenica; ethnic cleansing in Bosnia and Kosovo; mass murder and bloody battles.[6] All of Europe and ultimately NATO were drawn into the conflict. And within the United Nations Security Council, East and West clashed over how to deal with the conflict in Kosovo.[7] These recent violent years in Southeast Europe left fresh scares, deepened divisions,

---

Remarks at Conference: Southeast Europe on the Way into the European Union, Zagreb, Croatia, June 4, 2005.

demonstrated the manner in which disputes here can involve those beyond the immediate area, and reminded us about the dangers of a divided Europe (dangers which have not been fully addressed).

As one commentator wrote in *The New York Times* 10 years after the Berlin Wall had fallen, "When the East-West division of Europe was erased in 1989 with the collapse of the Berlin Wall, a new division immediately began forming: that between Central Europe and the Balkans. Even before the outbreak of fighting in Yugoslavia in 1991, the Central European states of Poland, Hungary, and Czechoslovakia were pulling dramatically ahead of Balkan countries like Romania and Bulgaria in terms of progress toward stable, democratic rule.

"These northerly states of the former Warsaw Pact had several advantages: they were heirs to the tradition of the Hapsburg Empire, and they had sizeable middle classes prior to World War II and Communist rule. The Balkan states were burdened by centuries of Byzantine and Turkish absolutism, and even before the Communist takeovers their middle classes had been mere specks amid vast seas of peasantries.

"The admission of Poland, the Czech Republic, and Hungary into the North Atlantic Treaty Organization has formalized this dangerous historical and religious division of Europe between a Roman Catholic and Protestant West and an Orthodox Christian and Muslim East."[8]

In recent years there has been progress in Southeast Europe. In many countries, including here in Croatia, democratic institutions have developed and greater stability has been achieved. Yet destabilizing conditions remain with struggling economies and high unemployment, the unresolved final status of Kosovo, indicted war criminals still at large, continued ethnic tensions and organized crime. Instituting the reforms required to achieve progress in these areas will benefit the people of Southeast Europe. And advancing integration into Europe, including entry into the European Union, will help sustain a more stable region and diminish the dangers of a deepened East/West divide.

As David Kaplan wrote in the *Washington Post*, "(T)here are two Europes now. There is a western Catholic-Protestant Europe and an Eastern Orthodox Europe, which is poorer, more politically unsettled and more ridden with organized crime... Healing the emerging divide in Europe – one that is potentially worse than the division of the Cold War because it is based on religion and culture-means" expanding NATO (and the European Union).[9]

NATO has begun its expansion into Southeastern Europe with Bulgaria's recent membership.[10] And both Bulgaria and Romania have begun their accession into the European Union.[11] Most have assumed that the EU's integration and its expansion inevitably would continue. But this week's votes in France and the Netherlands have shaken those assumptions.

The EU Votes

Three years ago the Villa Faber Group on the Future of the EU reflected common wisdom about the European Union at that time. Its report stated that the debate within accession countries and between applicants and the European Union was not about whether there would be expansion, but "the when and how of enlargement."[12] Nonetheless, at the time Ulrika Guerot, the Head of the EU – Unit of the German

Council on Foreign Relations in Bonn, noted that the question of "which Europe do we actually want?" had been raised since the beginning of European integration and continued to be raised. As one commentator had written, "While the institutional framework of a united Europe inexorably marches on, the fabric of a shared supranational European identity lags behind. ...A European identity that transcends the national identities of Europe's member states is still a distant dream. But Europe's rapidly changing demographics cannot wait for this dream to come true. Identity is a crucial component of social cohesion, and the rapid influx of immigrants, mainly from the Muslim world, demands a choice: Should immigrants be encouraged to integrate into the national cultures and identities of the EU member states? Or should Europe instead pursue a multicultural model, in which patriotism is discouraged in favor of a society divided by different identities, values, and historical narratives, but united by abstract rights and duties under EU treaties and regulations?"[13]

However comfortable EU political elites might feel about the inexorable march of a united Europe, many Europeans remain uncertain. And this uncertainty was exacerbated by the economic malaise of low productivity and high unemployment in many countries within the EU. Many who voted "No," undoubtedly, are angry about their troubled economy.[14] Some fear economic competition, especially cheaper labor, from Eastern and Southeastern Europe.[15] Some fear Brussels with more power and Paris and The Hague with less. Some do not want to lose national control over such things as immigration policy; especially when faced with the continued influx of Muslim immigrants. They are anxious about the future. And many fear the EU treaty "would erode France's generous cradle-to-grave social safety net."[16] As British Prime Minister Tony Blair said after the French vote, "Underneath all of this there is a more profound question, which is about the future of Europe and, in particular, the European economy."[17] And central to all these matters is the relationship between the European Union and national governments.[18]

The European Union was conceived when memories of World War I and World War II were fresh and raw. The EU was conceived to ensure an end of war on the European continent. But memories have faded. The threat of intra-European war enflaming the entire continent seems distant to many. Europeans have new worries, new concerns and "fresh battle lines have been formed."[19] In the face of this popular anger and anxiety, clearly the champions of a further integrated Europe have failed to make their case. As one analyst wrote, the French "result suggests a disconnect between ordinary people and France's political, business, and media establishment, where support was strong."[20] Ulrika Guerot, like many others, had thought the question of which Europe the people wanted would be determined by an EU constitution.[21] However, Guerot wrote, "(T)he EU will not take a 'constitutional quantum leap' without acceptance from the EU's population. This is to say, not without a voting procedure that offers the political legitimacy the Union needs. If change cannot gain support from each and every country," he wrote, "the EU will face a situation where it will only be able to follow through with the 'constitutional quantum leap' towards a political Union with the countries that are disposed to do so."[22] The geostrategic situation, the need to achieve economic and political stability in Central and Eastern Europe, seemed to be a determinative winds advancing inevitable EU enlargement and tighter integration. But then came this week's events.

This week's unexpectedly robust rejection of the EU constitution by voters in France and the Netherlands has prompted a period of reexamination of the path ahead. Last Sunday by a vote of 55% the French said "No" to the proposed EU constitution on a 70% turnout.[23] Days later the Dutch voted "No" by a margin of better than 62%. Two founding states of the European Union. Two rejections by the people. Elie Cohen, director of research at the National Center for Scientific Research in France said the referendum result was "an earthquake, a major historical event."[24] Writing in the *Financial Times*, Jacob Arfwedson and Sylvain Charat stated, "Never before has the French electorate rejected both its leadership and Europe to this extent."[25] *The International Herald Tribune* stated that "(t)he French no, the first by a founding member of the EU, represents one of the biggest reversals in the 50-year history of European integration."[26]

When the Netherlands delivered a second blow to the EU Constitution, the *Wall Street Journal Europe* stated, "The emphatic results from two of the EU's founding members will further heighten concerns over the political stability of the 25-nation union. Though the EU's existence isn't threatened, concern over the deep internal conflicts exposed by the votes have already helped drive the euro down by three cents against the U.S. dollar."[27] Meanwhile the *Financial Times* reported, "Europe's political crisis deepened yesterday as Dutch voters followed the French by resoundingly rejecting the proposed European Union constitutional treaty... The result means that citizens of two of the six founding nations of the EU have opposed plans to deepen political integration."[28]

These events prompted European Union president Claude Junker, prime minister of Luxembourg, to declare, "The treaty is not dead... The European process does not come to an end today."[29] And most certainly Mr. Junker is correct. But, it also is true that these votes "will raise questions about the pace of future economic change across the continent, as championed by the Union, and the expansion of the EU to take in new members."[30] Inevitably there will be a period of self-examination, inward thinking and political recalculation across the European Union.

As EU President Juncker said, " 'We who lead Europe, we have lost the power to make Europeans proud of themselves. Europe is not just for itself. It is also for others in the rest of the world. We are too modest, too timid. We are lacking in the determination and courage that are needed.' In particular Juncker admitted that Europe's leaders had failed to persuade the European electorate of the virtues of enlargement."[31]

The French and Dutch "No" votes are having a significant affect on voters in other European Union countries and forcing political leaders to put on hold their own countries referendums on the EU constitution. While the French and Dutch political leadership struggle to bridge their internal political divide, the United Kingdom has "called on France and the Netherlands to state publicly whether there (is) any future in the new European constitution after the resounding No votes in both their countries' referendums this week."[32] "Denmark and Portugal have signaled that if the U.K. delayed its referendum they too could put their votes on hold."[33] Reportedly "Ireland is wavering" in its commitment to hold a referendum. ...Yesterday, the Estonian parliament also said it needed more time to proceed with the ratification and to decide whether to hold a referendum. ...Polish plans to hold a referendum in October are also likely to be delayed."[34]

Unquestionably, there will be a pause in the ratification process. There will be calls for a new balance in Europe. The French-German hegemony within the EU will be challenged. As Pawel Swieboda, head of the European department in Poland's Foreign Ministry said yesterday, "If there is anything I would like from the summit between Chirac and Schroeder, it is that the relationship should be less open to each other and rather more inclusive when it comes to dealing with other member states."[35] The economic implications of the proposed EU constitution are unclear. "EU members have been split sharply between advocates of freer markets with fewer regulations, and protectors of social welfare. In France, fear of losing the 35-hour workweek and other benefits figured strongly in the campaign. Among the Dutch, a common complaint was that bigger countries like France and Germany demanded discipline of the small nations, but themselves showed contempt for EU spending rules."[36] Perhaps these issues will need to be addressed, especially during this time of economic uncertainty in Europe.[37] The EU's revised stability and growth pact may be subject to even further recalibration. Other issues will be reexamined. If the proposed EU constitution dies, perhaps parts of it will be added to the Treaty of Nice.[38] Whether this period of Europe's internal focus will be relatively brief or prolonged, modest or dramatic, is yet unknown. We will begin to know more from the EU Summit scheduled for June 16th.

EU Enlargement

As Professor Werner Weidenfeld has written, "Since the signing of the Treaties of Rome in 1957, Western European history has been an on-going process integrating and enlarging European institutions. Over the course of that time, the institutions now known as the European Union have become a major pillar for the security and stability for Europe as a whole."[39] As French political scientist, philosopher, and historian Raymond Aron wrote, "Europeans would like to exit from history, from la grande histoire, from the history that is written in letters of blood."[40] The European Union's most recent enlargement, the fifth, reached eastward to former Warsaw Pact nations. This process has enhanced economic and social progress in Europe while providing broader stability.

"Enlargement has been easily the most successful EU policy of all," states *The Economist*. "Taking in ten members last May has helped to create a zone of peace and growing prosperity on the EU's borders, and also imported much-needed economic dynamism into the old continent. Similar points can be made in respect of the Balkan countries – and for Turkey."[41]

As Prime Minister Sanader said, "For Europe it is a genuine political and geostrategic interest to be whole and united and the European Union is the vehicle for the realization of this goal. Therefore, the EU must continue on its set course, despite certain voices which speak about 'enlargement fatigue' and are not in favor of further EU enlargement."[42]

If the established conditions set forth in the Accession Treaty with Bulgaria and Romania are met, another EU enlargement should happen in 2007.[43] The European Union will have expanded to the Balkans, and the states of the former Yugoslavia, possibly, along with Turkey, are poised to be the next wave of European Union enlargement.

"Croatia's progress towards the European Union is grounded within the Stabilization and Association Process and the SAP instruments (are the) basis for integration preparation. The Stabilization and Association Agreement (SAA) between Croatia and the EU and its member states was signed in October 2001, while the process of ratification in member states was concluded in September 2004. The SAA entered into force on 1 February 2005, together with the Protocol 7 on enlargement."[44]

In February, 2003, Croatia completed its application for membership in the European Union and, subsequently sought a European Commission opinion (avis) on Croatia's application. The response was encouraging. The main findings of the avias finalized in April 2002 "underlined that Croatia was a functioning democracy with stable institutions guaranteeing the rule of law, (a) functioning market economy which should be able to cope with competitive pressure within the Union in the medium term, with a precondition that continues implementing reforms. It was also noted that Croatia should be in the position to take the other obligations of the membership in the medium term, if considerable efforts are made to align its legislation with the acquis and ensure the implementation and enforcement."[45]

As President Mesic[46] said this morning, these reforms are taken freely by Croatia because, first and foremost, they are in the interest of the Croatian people. But surely the possibility of EU ascension is an impetus for these reforms. That is good for Croatia and for all of Europe.

The disintegration of Yugoslavia led to a period of bloody conflict with ethnic cleansing, genocide and war crimes. After the war, various stability initiatives for the region were undertaken by NATO, the United Nations, the Organization of Security and Cooperation in Europe and the European Union. Over time the EU assumed the role of primary regional stabilizer.[47] And the possibility of gradual EU accession clearly has contributed to internal reforms within and to closer cooperation among the countries of southeastern Europe.[48] "Offering the prospects for membership in the EU has been a successful instrument for helping shape the transition to East Central Europe."[49]

Democratic institutions, transparency, the rule of law, market economies, and vibrant civil societies contribute to freer, more prosperous societies that are stable and less menacing to neighbors. Again, these reforms within the countries of Southeastern Europe are good for the people in these new nations and are undertaken by their governments primarily to benefit their citizens. But the requirements for EU accession, the expertise, and the assistance of the European Union reinforce and, perhaps, facilitate, discipline and hasten along these transformations. As Iris Kempe and Wim van Meurs have written, "(T)he level and intensity of EU assistance, and the pull of EU integration, are key factors in any post-communist transition process toward democracy and a market economy. The agenda the EU defines for its relations with a certain country, as well as the forms and intensity of assistance linked to this agenda, are the determinants of the relationship."[50]

So the reforms induced by offering European Union membership are good for the people. And expanding the EU into Southeastern Europe expands the community of interest and shared concerns. It expands "to the region the area of peace, stability, prosperity and freedom established over the last 50 years by the EU and its member states."[51]

Even before the developments of this past week, many recognized that "the duration of the integration process of association and pre-accession to the EU will be much longer and more protracted for Southeastern Europe than in any previous round of enlargement."[52] And now even the possibility of further EU enlargement has been brought into question by the French and Dutch "No" votes on the EU constitution.

The *Financial Times* has reported that "(f)uture enlargement of the European Union to include Turkey, the Balkan states and even Ukraine could become the highest profile casualty of France's No vote to the EU constitutional treaty, according to political and diplomatic observers in several member states. Doubts about the enlargement process emerged as a central theme fueling opposition to the treaty in both France and the Netherlands in recent weeks. ...As a result, the EU's plans for accession negotiations with Croatia, Turkey, Albania and the rest of the former Yugoslavia have been thrown into varying degrees of doubt."[53] While others at this Conference have not raised this unfortunate, even dangerous possibility, I believe this development must be addressed since such a development could be devastating to Southeastern Europe.

Let there be no mistake about it, the risk is real. Right after the French vote, Polish Prime Minister Merck Belka said that now "it would be difficult in the near future to conceive of any EU expansion. 'This is so obvious,' (he said), 'you do not need diplomatic language to say so.'"[54]

Given the strong, clear results of the French and Dutch referenda, a pause in the enlargement process is required. But for the United States, a strong integrated Europe is in our interest. We need a vibrant, stable Europe, not as a counterweight to American power, but as a partner prepared to proactively engage the world and to contribute to solving global problems such as confronting terrorist networks, containing the spread of weapons of mass destruction and advancing democracy, economic liberalization and stability around the world.[55]

So I am concerned by this pause in the progress of the European Union. I trust this period will be used well to make changes that will earn the support of the European people that is required for the EU to be sustainable and strong.

I also am concerned by this pause because I recognize that bringing Southeastern Europe more fully into Europe, including membership in the European Union, will help bridge the east/west divide, help replace ethnic conflict with multiethnic cooperation, and provide a better platform for progress in the Balkans in growing economically, in rooting out organized crime, in establishing transparency and the rule of law, and strengthening the institutions and values of democracy. All these things will benefit the people of Southeastern Europe. And they will bring a stability that is sustainable.

For 50 years now, with many stops and starts, the expansion and integration of the European Union has progressed. This week's votes in France and the Netherlands cannot be ignored. The political class must consider the message sent. Adjustments would seem to be required. But the vision of an expanded European Union that includes Southeastern Europe, with integrated markets, within which war has become "unthinkable" and which actively engages global challenges is a vision that should continue to compel Europe towards its realization. Such an enlarged Europe will benefit its people, change historic paradigms that too often led to armed conflict, and provide the United States not with a counterweight to American power, but with a stronger partner to engage the world.

---

1. "Turning its back on half a century of European history, France decisively rejected a Constitution for Europe on Sunday, plunging the country into political disarray and jeopardizing the cause of European unity. ...The rejection could signal an abrupt halt to the expansion and unification of Europe, a process that has been met with growing disillusionment among the wealthier European Union members as needier countries like Bulgaria and Poland have negotiated their entry." Elaine Sciolino, "French Voters Soundly Reject European Pact: Deal Setback to Union," *New York Times*, May 30, 2005. See also, John Leicester, "French Say No to EU Constitution: 55-45 Rejection Could Set Europe's Plans Back By Years," *Chicago Sun Times*, May 20, 2005.

2. See, Philip Webster, David Charter and Anthony Browne, "Europe Turmoil as Treaty Collapses,": *The Times* (London), June 14, 2005.

"Everything that seemed to be understood about how the European Union functions is now shaken,' said Gunter Verheugen, a vice president of the European Commission. ...'They had referendums in France and Netherlands and now we are seeing the same wave of popular mistrust in other countries. In my view, earthquake is an appropriate description.' " Elaine Sciolino, "Europe's Next Problem Is All About Money," *New York Times*, June 16, 2005.

"The European Union risks 'permanent crisis and paralysis' unless it can persuade member nations to adopt a constitution, the bloc's top official warned... 'The results of the referendum in the Netherlands and France have plunged the European Union into doubt,' Barroso said, adding it had raised the question, 'What is the point of the European project?' " Robert Wielaard, "EU Chief Sees Crisis If Charter Not Passed: Rifts Abound on Eve of 25-Nation Summit, *Chicago Tribune*, June 16, 2005.

"Europe 'is at a crossroads,' said Jose Manuel Barroso. President of the executive European Commission. Failure to recover momentum will plunge the EU into permanent crisis and paralysis,' he warned." Tracy Wilkinson, "Turmoil in Full View at EU Summit," *Chicago Tribune*,. June 17, 2005.

" 'Europe is not in a state of crisis, it is in a state of profound crisis,' said Jean-Claude Juncker." Tracy Wilkinson, "Budget Wrangling Adds to Disharmony Among EU Nations," *Chicago Tribune*, June 18, 2005.

"Reflecting the turmoil after a series of political setbacks in recent weeks, leaders of the European Union lashed out at one another, reinforcing the view that the half-century process of European integration may be over. 'My enthusiasm for Europe has suffered a profound shock,' said Jean-Claude Juncker... France's president, Jacques Chirac, '... Europe is in serious crisis.'... (T)he European Union is likely to enter into a period of paralysis and self-doubt as member countries decide to what extent they must put national interests and domestic politics before common goals." Elaine Sciolino, "European Union's Heated Budget Negotiations Collapse," *New York Times*, June 18, 2005.

3. Robert D. Kaplan, *Balkan Ghosts: A Journey Through History* (New York, N.Y.; St. Martin's Press; 1993).

4. *Ibid*, p. 7.

5. As cited by Kaplan, *ibid*., p. xi.

6. See generally, David Halberstam, *War in a Time of Peace* (New York, N.Y.; Scribner; 2001), and Richard Holbrooke, *To End a War* (New York, N.Y.; Random House; 1998).

7. In 1999, on the eve of NATO's aerial bombing campaign over Kosovo, a resolution had been tabled at the United Nations Security Council authorizing the use of force to stop the Serbian ethnic killing of Albanian Muslims. Confronted by this draft resolution, Russia made clear its intention to exercise its veto power to deny passage. Faced with this confrontation, the United States withdrew the resolution and the NATO bombing commenced.

8. David D. Kaplan, "In the Balkans, No Wars Are Local," *New York Times*, April 7, 1999.

9. David D. Kaplan, "Why the Balkans Demand Amorality," *Washington Post*, February 28, 1999.

10. Of course, Greece and Turkey long have been members of NATO.

11. Again, Greece long has been a member of the European Union.

12. Martin Brusis and Janis A. Emmanouilidis, eds., *Thinking Enlarged: The Accession Countries and the Future of the European Union* (Bonn, Germany; Europa Union Verlag; 2002), p. 117. The Villa Faber Group "originates from a project on issues and consequences of EU enlargement the Bertelsmann Foundation jointly manages with The Bertelsman Group for Policy Research at the Center for Applied Policy Research, Munich. Both organizations worked with a group of 18 experts from the current and future member states to write a joint memorandum on the accession countries perspective concerning future reforms of the European Union."

In France, the European Coal and Steel Community was launched in 1951 as the precursor to the modern European Union.

13. Emanuele Ottolenghi, "Can Europe Do Away with Nationalism?" *New Atlantic Initiative* (Washington, D.C.; American Enterprise Institute; May-June 2005). See also, Helle Dale, "Finding European Identity," *Washington Times*, June 14, 2005.

"(T)he question of whether human beings will preferably cling to their historical and emotional homelands over such created unity has not been answered." Georgia Anne Geyer, "Cold Feet May Leave EU in Hot Water," *Chicago Tribune*, May 27, 2006.

"(W)ith the setback on the constitution, new emotion has replaced the politesse that normally surrounds (EU summits). Leaders have already begun to posture and position themselves for the maximum benefit of their own constituencies, not the common good." Elaine Sciolino, "Europe's Next Problem Is All About Money," *New York Times*, June 16, 2003.

14. The "months of debate (about the European Constitution) have become as much a funnel of discontent over (Chirac's) government as a debate about the European Union. ...(Chirac) has seen his approval rating nose dive to 32 percent, tying his record low." Katrin Bennold, "Chirac and Socialists Reel After a Debate on Europe," *New York Times*, May 29, 2005.

15. See, for example, Noelle Knox, "French Gripes Over EU Focus on Town Hall," *USA Today*, May 27, 2005.

16. Elaine Sciolino, *ibid*. French commentator Dominique Moisi said that in voting No on the EU constitution the "French people were expressing their anger at their government's failure to create jobs, and their fear that the European Union can no longer shelter them from the harsh winds of globalized competition." Peter Ford, "French Vote Turns Clock Back on EU: Constitution Opposed Because of Fear of Greater Capitalism," *Chicago Sun-Times*, May 31, 2005.

17. *Ibid.*

18. See, Derek Beach, *The Dynamics of European Integration: Why and When EU Institutions Matter* (London, U.K.; Palgrave Macmillan; 2005).

19. "Max Kohnstamm, 91, one of the founding fathers of what has become the European Union, remembers when all the bitter memories were still fresh. 'There was an enormously strong feeling after 1945: This cannot happen again,' he said from his home in Belgium's Ardennes forest. And for 60 years that sentiment helped drive Europe toward ever-closer cooperation and unity. But last week it was suddenly obvious that as the bad old memories have faded, no clear vision of the future has taken their place." Christopher Dickey, "Europe's Dream Deferred," *Newsweek*, June 13, 2005.

20. John Leicester, "Fear of Free-Market Capitalism, Loss of Jobs Did In Treaty," *Chicago Sun Times*, May 30, 2005.

"Instead of a rubber stamp that leaders expected, the two referendums morphed into a popular debate over where Europe is headed. ...Politicians failed to explain clearly how the constitution would benefit average people. ...The process forward will be slow, painful and humbling. It is called democracy." Editorial, "Old-Fashioned Democracy Thwarts EU's Grand Plan," *USA Today*, June 3, 2005.

"The EU has long been a reserve for professional politicians. Dramatic changes – the euro, the accession of ten new members, the decision to start entry talks with Turkey – were made at the top and presented *faits accomplis*. The Dutch no vote seems to have been more about this way of doing business than about hostility to the European project as such." "The Referendum in the Netherlands: Dutch Mess Up," *The Economist*, June 4, 2005.

Some two weeks after the vote, former French President Valery Giscard d'Estaing, the architect of the EU constitution, gave an interview in which he blamed French President Jacques Chirac for the treaty's rejection. "This was not a vote on the constitution," Mr. Giscard d'Estaing said... 'That is the key point that has been missed by the political leaders... The French message was we want change in our political leadership.' " Mr. Giscard d'Estaing said the blame spreads further. He said "that, had the European

Union leaders not left open the possibility of full membership for Turkey in their bloc, the constitution probably would have passed in France." Elaine Sciolino, "European Charter's Architect Faults Chirac for Its Demise," *New York Times*, June 13, 2005. See also, Larry Elliott, "The Week the Monster Turned on Its Creators," *The Guardian*, June 6, 2005; Timothy Garton Ash, "Decadent Europe," *The Guardian*, June 9, 2005; and David A. Bell, "Class Conflict," *The Nest Republic Online*, June 1, 2005..

21. The 448 –article European "Constitution is essentially a vehicle to streamline decision-making in the expanded 25-member bloc and a blueprint for the next stage of its growth and unification. It eliminates the six-month rotating European Union presidency, creating a president with a maximum five-year term; details a list of basic rights; and determines what functions, such as issuing visas or rules on immigration will be governed by the European Union headquarters in Brussels and what others, such as foreign policy and defense, will remain with member states." Sciolino, *ibid*. The nine nations that have ratified the treaty are Austria, Hungary, Italy, Germany, Greece, Lithuania, Slovakia, Slovenia and Spain. See also, Peter Norman, *The Accidental Constitution: The Story of the European Constitution* (London, U.K.; Euro Comment; 2003).

22. Ulrike Guerot, "The Debate on the 'Finalite' of the EU – From Delors and Fisher to Blair," in Martin Brusis and Janis A. Emmanouilidis, eds., *ibid*, p. 47, 50.

23. "In considering the draft European constitution, the French took their responsibilities seriously. Leading upto Sunday's referendum, a poll found that 83 percent had discussed the constitution in the previous week, and five of the top 10 sellers on the French nonfiction list were about the treaty. When voting came, almost 70 percent voted. The convincing victory for the No camp – 55 percent voted to reject the constitution and only 45 percent voted in support – demonstrates profound misgivings about the European project in the country most responsible for launching it." Editorial, "The French Rejection," *Washington Post*, May 31, 2005.

24. John Thornhill and Martin Arnold, "Chirac to Announce New Strategy as He Seeks to Recover From Stunning Setback," *Financial Times*, May 31, 2005.

25. Jacob Arfwedson and Sylvain Charat, "A New Mandate for Losership," *Financial Times*, May 31, 2005.

26. Graham Bowley, "Europe Lurches Toward a Period of Crisis: Dutch Expected to Hand Union the Next Blow," *International Herald Tribune*, May 31, 2005. See also, Elaine Sciolino, "French No Vote on Constitution Rattles Europe: Other Beliefs in Doubt: Naysayers Gain Ground in Netherlands – Chirac in Crisis," *New York Times*, May 31, 2005. See also, Editorial, "Fiddling While Paris Burns," *Wall Street Journal Europe*, June 1, 2004; Noelle Knox, "European Union Struggles With Constitution Rejection," *USA Today*, May 31, 2005; and Craig Whitlock, "Circumspect EU Turns To Dutch on Constitution: Referendum Defeat Could Deal Plan a Fatal Setback," *Washington Post*, May 31, 2005.

27. Dan Bilefsky, "Dutch Deliver Second Blow To EU Constitution Hopes," *International Herald Tribune*, June 2, 2005.

28. "Europe in Turmoil as the Dutch Vote No: Euro Tumbles Amid Political Uncertainty in EU," *Financial Times*, June 2, 2005. See also, Nicholas Watt, Luke Harding and Michael White, "Crisis Talks as Treaty Nears Collapse," *The Guardian*, June 3, 2005. It is noteworthy that notwithstanding the French and Dutch no votes, on June 2nd, Latvia ratified the EU constitution. Arthur May, "Defying a Trend, Latvia Ratifies EU Constitution," *Washington Post*, June 3, 2005. "The 71-5 vote in Latvia's 100-member Parliament was widely expected. Latvian lawmakers ratified the treaty to show the rest of Europe the way ahead, said lawmaker Janis Lagzdins, a member of the People's Party." This was a symbolic step. ...It was also a gesture of good will and a symbolic invitation to other countries to follow Latvia's example, and not France's." "Latvia: EU Constitution Ratified in Symbolic Step," *Chicago Tribune*, June 3, 2005.

29. Graham Bowley, *ibid*. See also, Richard Bernstein, "Europe is Still Europe: Charter's No Can't Undo Legal Realities," *New York Times*, June 7, 2005; and Editorial, "No Votes Are Not the End of Europe," *Washington Times*, June 7, 2005. However, for the perspective that says that "voters have clearly rejected closer union and Europe will start to unravel," see Larry Elliott, "What Do No Votes Mean for the Union?" *The Guardian*, June 3, 2005.

After the No votes, Frits Bolkestein, a former member of the European Commission, stated that the European Union "should now restrict itself to its core activities: to smooth the path for economic exchange between member states, to solve common problems and to create advantages of scale. ...Those activities should respect the principle of subsidiary, which means that whatever member states can do equally well or better should not be undertaken by the Union. ...The error that is steadfastly made is to think that because some cause is worthy, it must be done by Brussels." George Anne Geyer, "No Vote Don't Mean the End of the EU," *Chicago Tribune*, July 10, 2005.

30. *Ibid.*

31. Graham Bowley, *Ibid.* "Referendums have proven to be the only effective discipline to force Europe's leaders to make the case for Europe... Direct democracy is awkward, unpredictable and easily exploited by opportunists, but for a political entity that is so disconnected from voters, it has proven to be the only effective way to give voters a say. Two cheers for referendums." Dan O'Brien, "The EU Constitution: The Silver Linings of Defeat," *International Herald Tribune*, May 231, 2005. "France has spoken and it is not a pretty sound. Sunday's rejection of the European Union's constitutional treaty amounted to a cry of rage and fear. It has exposed crises of leadership and reform in France and the wider EU. At one level, it is difficult to argue with a 56 percent vote on a high turnout of 70 percent. And if there is any comfort to be drawn from this seismic event, it is that the French NO vote may force the EU political class to pay attention at least to the views of electors and abandon the top-down elitism on which the European project has moved forward." Editorial, "From Sunday's No to Economic Reform," *Financial Times*, May 31, 2005. See also, Lorne Cook, "EU Elites Staggered; KO from Dutch Likely," *Washington Times*, May 31, 2005.

"Will May 2005 go down in history as a turning point for democracy in Europe. The disconnect between European votes and their leaders that was so starkly highlighted over the past two weeks both in state elections in Germany and the referendums on the European constitution in France and the Netherlands is hardly new. But if in recent decades disillusionment with politics has tended to translate into growing apathy, today the disenchanted electorate is returning to the ballot box in droves. Voter power, it seems, is making a comeback. ...For the first time since May 1968, a general sense of frustration has resulted in rebellion against political institutions, (Hubert) Vedrine (a former Socialist foreign minister who heads the Francois Mitterrand Institute) said, 'Voters are using whatever electoral contest (that) presents itself to say no to their leaders." Katrin Bennhoild, "Voters to the Barricades: Power of 'no' Could Herald Era of Change," *International Herald Tribune*, June 4/5, 2005. See also, Bijorn Khezri, "The End of an Age in Europe," *Wall Street Journal Europe*, June 1, 2005.

"French democracy has blundered its way to the right result. ...The French, the Dutch, and other European's have lost patience with political systems that seem increasingly remote and political elites that seem increasingly disdainful of the interests and values of the people they claim to represent." Jeffrey Cimbalo and David Frum, "Marianne Unfaithful," *Wall Street Journal*, June 1, 2005. See also, Slavoj Zizek, "The Constitution is Dead, Long Live Proper Politics," *The Guardian*, June 4, 2005.

32. James Blitz, "Europe Turmoil Over Constitution: U.K. Urges French and Dutch to Outline Plans," *Financial Times*, June 3, 2005. On June 6, 2005, Britain suspended its Referendum on the European Constitution. In announcing the indefinite delay, UK foreign secretary Jack Straw said, "Until the consequences of France and the Netherlands being unable to ratify the treaty are clarified, it would not in our judgment now be possible to set a date" for a UK referendum on the EU constitution. He continued, "These referendum results raise profound questions about the future direction of Europe. ...The European Union does now face a period of difficulty." And opposition Conservative member of the parliament Liam Fox said, "This constitution is a case for the morgue if ever I saw one." Alan Cowell, "Britain Suspends Referendum on Europe Constitution," *New York Times*, June 7, 2005. "Speaking in the House of Commons, Mr. Straw painted the debate over the proposed constitution as a struggle over what economic direction the EU takes – with Britain on one side, leading some countries in Eastern Europe, and some less market-oriented economies on the Continent on the other." "U.K. Postpones EU Constitution Vote," *Wall Street Journal*, June 7, 2005. Note that "Britain's decision to abandon its referendum ignores the appeals of French President Jacque Chirac, German Chancellor Gerhard Schroeder and Senior EU officials to allow the ratification process to proceed." Tom Hundley, "Britain Retreats on EU Charter Vote," *Chicago Tribune*, June 7, 2005. In an interview with the *Financial Times*, Prime Minister Tony Blair said that "French and Dutch voters did not dismiss European integration but needed to be convinced. They are simply saying: We have got immediate problems on jobs, on the impact of globalization, on security, on immigration, and on organized crime – and what do you the leadership of Europe say to us? I think in order to make progress we have to answer in a clear way. And in particular ...we have got to show how you can have a new European social model for today's world." Gemma Loughead, "Blair Calls for Debate on Future EU Model." *Financial Times*, June 7, 2005. See also, Matthew Tempest, "British Vote on Constitution Shelved," *The Guardian*, June 6, 2005.

"(A)t a news conference after Thursday's meetings, Prime Minister Jiri Paroubek of the Czech Republic announced that his country would indefinitely postpone ratification. Prime Minister Anders Fogh Rasmussen of Denmark made a similar declaration, saying a referendum 'makes no sense,' and adding, "We will postpone a vote until there is sufficient clarity.' " Elaine Sciolino, "European Leaders Give Up on Ratifying Charter by 2006," *New York Times*, June 17, 2005.

33. "Opposition Widens: European Constitution Facing Oblivion," *Financial Times*, June 4/5, 2005.

34. *Ibid*. See also, Georgia Parker and Ian Bickerton, "Rejection in Netherlands Could Trigger Messy Wave of Poll Postponements," *Financial Times*, June 1, 2005.

35. Judy Dempsey, "Calls Grow For a New Balance in Europe: French-German Role 'must be Inclusive,'Officials Assert," *International Herald Tribune*, June 4/5, 2005. See also, Marc Champion and Dan Bilefsky, "Blair-Chirac Could Paralyze EU: Disputes on Budget, Charter May Undermine UK's Bid to Steer Bloc in Its Direction," *Wall Street Journal*, June 15, 2005.

36. Editorial, "Building a Better Europe," *International Herald Tribune*, June 4/5, 2005.

37. See, for example, Editorial, "The Union Faces a Fresh Crisis: Debate Over the British Rebate and the French Agricultural Subsidies Heats Up," *Wall Street Journal Europe*, June 13, 2005; John W. Miller and Marc Champion, "EU Tackles Budget Amid Turmoil Over Constitution," *Wall Street Journal*, June 13, 2005; Philippe Naughton, "Anglo-French Showdown Threatens Summit," *The Times*, June 14, 2005; and Simon Freeman, "Farm Subsidies 'on the Agenda' for EU Summit," *The Times*, June 15, 2005. See also, Tobias Buck, "A Recipe for Jobs or a Race to the Bottom? The EU Debates a Single Market in Services," *Financial Times*, March 15, 2005..

38. See, Quentin Peel, "Parts of Constitution Might Be Added to Treaty of Nice," *Financial Times*, June 1, 2005.

39. Werner Weidenfeld, Preface, Wim van Meurs, ed., *Prospects and Risks Beyond EU Enlargement: Southeastern Europe: Weak States and Strong International Support* (Opladen; Germany; Leske & Budrich; 2003), p. 7.

40. As quoted by Christopher Caldwell, "Raymond Aron and the End of Europe," 2004-2005 Bradley Lectures, American Enterprise Institute, Washington, D.C., April 7, 2005. The European Union is to be the vehicle by which Europe will "exit from history."

41. Editorial, "The Europe that Died," *The Economist*, June 4, 2005.

42. Ivo Sanader (Prime Minister of the Republic of Croatia), Welcoming Address, *Croatian International Relations Review*, Volume X, No. 36/37, July/December 2004, p. 96.

43. "Even Bulgaria and Romania, which have signed accession treaties, could find the doors bolted at the last moment – the French parliament still has to ratify Bulgarian and Romanian membership. The omens are worse for Turkey." "The European Constitution: Dead But Not Yet Buried," *The Economist*, June 4, 2005.

44. Visnja Samardzija, Mladen Stanicic, "Croatia on Path Towards the EU: Conditionality and Challenge of Negotiations," *ibid.*, p. 97, 98.

The Protocol 7 extended the concessions that were given to the new candidates bilaterally on the EU 25 and thus the SAA became applicable to the enlarged EU.

Trade and transport provisions of the SAA have been applied as of January 1, 2002, through the interim Agreement on trade and related issues and came officially into force on March 1, 2002.

45. *Ibid*. "The Opinion was accompanied by the European Partnership for Croatia (Council Discision on the principles and conditions in the European Partnership with Croatia. COM (2004) 275 final.) which identified the short and medium term priorities during the preparation for accession. In June 2004, the European Council confirmed the status of Croatia as a candidate country for membership and brought a decision on opening negotiations on full membership."

46. Stjepan Mesic, the President of the Republic of Croatia.

47. A number of diverse reasons thrust the European Union to play the dominate role as regional stabilizer, including: "the speeding up of the gradual withdrawal of American and NATO troops from the Balkans; the on-going devolution to the EU of full responsibilities for the region; the probable forging of a new security and defense "division of labor" between NATO and the EU; the American fight against Taliban and Al-Qaeda cells, which led to the redeployment of important American troops previously stationed in the Balkans to Afghanistan; the return of the Russian Federation as a crucial security partner in the international arena, particularly in Central Asia; and the return of the Middle East to the international security agenda." Adrian Pop, "Security: From Powder Keg to Cooperation," in Wim van Meurs, ed., *ibid.*, p. 117.

48.   "Due to different historical legacy those (southeast European) countries had completely different geostrategic goals and (the Stabilization and Association Agreement with the EU) was their first common goal. For political leaders of the region, and more importantly, for the people in general, Europe is a syntagm without an alternative and the vast majority of citizens are aware that it is the future for this area." Sandra Knezovic, "The South Eastern Europe Security Dysfunctions and the EU Response: From Pacification to Integration," *Croatian International Relations Review*, Vol. X, No. 36/37, July/December 2004, p. 167.

49.   Werner Weidenfeld, *ibid*.

50.   Iris Kempe and Wim van Mewurs, "Europe Beyond EU Enlargement," in Wim van Meurs, ed., *ibid*, p. 11, 22-3.

51.   Werner Weidenfeld, *ibid*.

52.   Iria Kempe and Wim van Meurs, *ibid*., p. 65. "Some countries in the region have better potential for political, administrative and economic reform than others. Some have a relatively straightforward and shorter road toward EU membership,, some a correspondingly limited inclination toward regional cooperation. Other states and state-like entities have to cope with major modernization problems and weak state institutions, face a long and arduous road towards EU membership, need to depend more on regional cooperation, and face major burdens in terms of sovereignty status, inter-ethnic relations and state consolidation."

53.   Daniel Dombey, "Accession Talks: Further Enlargement Risks Being Biggest Casualty of Referendum," *Financial Times*, May 31, 2005.

Fareed's analysis of the No vote is that three signals were sent by the voters: "First, it's a signal against economic reform. ...The second signal that this vote sends is against immigration and labor mobility. ...Finally and related to these first two: the most emphatic signal from last week is about Turkey. Turkish membership in Europe has suffered a mortal blow." Fareed Zakaria, "What's Wrong With Europe," *Newsweek*, June 13, 2005.

54.   "(T)he European Commission tried desperately to disentangle worries about enlargement and the constitution. The ratification of the constitution and future steps to enlargement policy are two separate procedures," said a spokeswomen for Jose Manuel Barroso, Commission president. But officials acknowledge the prospects for the continued expansion of the Union are looking poor." Daniel Dombey, *Ibid*.

"European leaders will not discuss expansion of the EU to include Turkey or other countries at this week's EU summit, it was confirmed today. Senior officials stressed that previous agreements with Turkey and Croatia were still valid and that earlier EU decisions to expand to Romania and Bulgaria remain on track, but it will be the first time in many years that the issue has been dropped from an EU summit declaration." "Expansion Off the Agenda at EU Summit," *The Guardian*, June 13, 2005.

"Opposition to Turkish membership of the EU, which boosted the no votes in France and Holland, is eroding enthusiasm among Turks for a 40-year European dream. Warnings that Turkey will be the main casualty of the double no vote have alarmed business leaders who question whether it is worth embarking on years of membership talks," Helena Smith and Nicholas Watt, "Enthusiasm for 40-Year Dream Begins to Wane," *The Guardian, June 3, 2005.*

French foreign minister Philippe Douste-Blazy told the French daily *Le Figaro*: 'Without the treaty, it seems to me difficult to add more countries when the rules of communal living between us are not clearly defined. It is one of the elements of the absorption capacity of the European Union. After the French referendum, we must reflect on this type of thing." Nicholas Watt, "France Blocks Turkey's Path," *The Guardian*, June 14, 2005.

"Reflecting the turmoil... President Jacque Chirac of France for the first time threw into doubt what had been a given – the continuing enlargement of the European Union. 'In this situation, can the union continue to expand without the institutions capable of making this expanded union function efficiently? Mr. Chirac said." Elaine Sciolino, "European Leaders Give Up on Ratifying Charter by 2006," *New York Times*, June 17, 2005.

"Charles Grant, director of the Center for European Reform, a London think tank, said, "... It is up to political leaders to explain why enlargement is good for Europe, and if they cannot do that, enlargement will not happen,'" Tom Hundley, "Amid Crisis, EU Leaders Bicker," *Chicago Tribune*, June 19, 2005.

55.   French President Chirac, and others, speak of a united Europe serving as a counterweight to America, as a constraint on United States power, a way to contain the "hyperpower." Such a development would not

be in the U.S. interest. It is to be guarded against. But a strong Europe able to proactively join in causes of joint interest such as the war on terror is very useful.

"The problem has been more recently that a more integrated Europe with stronger common political institutions has not necessarily made for a stronger partnership with the United States, as some like to argue. In fact, precisely the opposite has happened. The trans-Atlantic crisis of the last few years goes beyond disagreements over American policy in Iraq to the very heart of European identity and to nature of the EU project." Helle Dale, "Finding European Identity," *Washington Times*, June 8, 2005. See also, Irwin M. Stelzer, "Afternoon Delight," *The Weekly Standard*, June 14, 2005.

Note: "For many, the dream of creating a European superpower built from peace, not war, seems seriously dented, making it increasingly unlikely Europe can one day become an effective counterweight to the United States" Thomas Wegner, "Europe In a Deep Crisis Over Unity," *Chicago Sun Times*, June 19, 2005.

Note also: "The leaders of the 25 European Union nations went home after a failed two-day summit meeting in anger and in shame, as domestic politic and national interests defeated lofty nations of sacrifice and solidarity for the benefit of all. The battle over money and the shelving of the bloc's historic constitution, after the crushing no votes in France and the Netherlands, stripped away all pretense of an organization with a common vision and reflected the fears of many leaders in the face of rising popular opposition to the project called Europe." Elaine Sciolino, "Summit Fight Shakes Europe: Failed Talks Expose Problems in Union," *New York Times*, June 19, 2005.

CHINA'S MIRACLE BOOM SEEING SIGNS OF UNREST

For over 20 years I have been traveling to Beijing. During that time the economic growth has been phenomenal. When I first visited, the streets were packed with people on black bicycles, thousands as far as the eye could see, with only occasional automobiles. Today Beijing is a busy metropolis with automobile congestion similar to New York City or Chicago. Twenty years ago most of Beijing contained one story dwellings. The Beijing Hotel, standing nine stories, towered over the landscape. Today there are hundreds of skyscrapers: modern business offices, hotels and apartment buildings. The change is dazzling.

China has transformed itself from a closed, backward, largely agrarian society to a dynamic industrial power. China is the world's great emerging power.

In the process, China has begun to play a more active role on the world stage that extends beyond its economic reach. China is more active in the United Nations. To deal with its energy shortages at home, China is purchasing oil reserves in Central Asia, Africa and increasing its diplomatic and commercial activities with such oil producers as Sudan, Venezuela and Iran.

China sells technology for ballistic missiles. Its defense budget is growing rapidly. And through various alliances and maneuvers, Beijing is trying to curb America's influence in Asia and Central Asia.

Consequently, American policymakers quite properly are focusing on dealing with China's growing economic, military and diplomatic power. We must.

But earlier this month while in Beijing for meetings with senior Chinese officials and scholars another set of issues came into focus.

At a meeting at the Chinese Academy of Social Science, I asked what was China's greatest security risk. Professor Tao Wewzhao replied, "Social unrest." I heard variations of that theme throughout my meetings.

Chinese have proven to be smart, entrepreneurial and hard working. But the great engine of China's rapid economic growth is cheap labor. With 1.3 billion Chinese there is a near limitless supply of workers. As the economy grows in China the gap between rich and poor grows too. Up to 150 million Chinese workers earn less than $1 a day. And except for the deep countryside, 700 million poor peasants on

---

Appeared in the *Chicago Sun-Times*, December 4, 2005.

small plots of land living at subsistence levels have access to television and therefore know not only how Chinese are living in cosmopolitan Beijing, Shanghai and other coastal cities, but how people live in New York and Paris. Of course, this disparity causes unrest.

Over dinner Professor Yuan Jian, of the Chinese Institute of International Studies, discussed the great social dislocation caused by China's rapid economic growth. Today there are up to 150 million Chinese "floating workers," migrant workers from rural villages that have moved to cities. While their wife or elderly parents cultivate their small plot of land, they have moved to cities in an attempt to become part of modern China. They live on the outskirts of cities in miserable conditions working long hours for little pay. Increasingly jobs are taken. With less job availability, there is more competition for what jobs are to be had thus driving wages even lower.

There are another 150 million Chinese living in rugged hills and mountains. Dr. Yuan has studied these people. On visits to remote areas she finds most totally out of touch with modern China. They want to know "Who is our Emperor?" They live on small terraced land and goats. They are desperately poor and lack decent education. Inbreeding in small remote villages creates problems including lower life expectancy. Dr. Yuan believes social unrest also is growing in these remote areas.

The combustibility of social unrest is heightened in China by a system with few legitimate outlets to express dissent or choose their leaders. There is no real free media, religious freedom, nor any right to organize to be heard. While there has been some progress in local village elections, provincial and national leaders are chosen by a small elite. And having secured power, leaders hold on for many years. While economic change is rapid, political change is glacial. Such a system is ill-equipped to adapt and adjust to rapidly changing social and political needs. Echoes of the disruption and instability of the Cultural Revolution still can be heard.

Today's China continues to be an economic miracle. But it also is a country of 1.3 billion people with rising unrest and limited capacity to deal with the need for change. China's official media reported 74,000 incidents of social unrest last year. There will be more.

PUTIN FEARS HUE AND CRY
OF ORANGE REVOLUTION

Concerned by the spread of democracy and the contagion of color revolutions, Vladimir Putin, a former KGB officer, is moving to restrict Russian Civil Society.

The March of Freedom has advanced in Georgia, Ukraine, Afghanistan, Lebanon, Iraq and Kyrgyzstan. But the spread of democracy is not inevitable. There have been set backs in Kazakhstan, Azerbaijan and elsewhere. President Putin fears the challenge from pluralism and democracy at home. Therefore, since the Orange Revolution in Ukraine, Putin has rolled back freedoms in Russia.

Putin's government has launched a broad campaign to ensure that Russia's corrupt autocracy survives. Independent national television stations have been taken over. Pro-western parties have been driven out of parliament. Business magnates who challenged Putin are prosecuted. And the popular election of governors have been eliminated. Now in a step to further consolidate Putin's power at home, an assault has been launched on Russia's fragile civil society.

Putin's allies are advancing a law in the Russian Dumas that would restrict activities of human rights groups, organizations that promote democracy, and all other independent organizations in Russian civil society. The bill would force all foreign and domestic non-governmental organizations (NGOs) regardless of their funding source to re-register with the authorities, inviting greater scrutiny and possible abolition of any group deemed threatening to the Kremlin's interests.

Alexi Ostrovsky, a sponsor of the legislation, clearly stated the bill's intent. He told the newspaper *Nezarismaya Gazeta*, that the new law "should help the government crack down on politically active NGOs that… might promote an Orange Revolution."

The proposed law would drive most foreign NGOs out of Russia. It would be impossible for foundations such as the National Endowment on Democracy and the International Republican Institute to operate in Russia. And all Russian civic groups deemed suspicious by the authorities for any reason could be denied registration.

As recognized in various Human Rights documents and numerous international treaties to which Russia is a party, people have a right to associate with whomever they please, to organize, and express their views. This is fundamental to a free,

---

Appeared in the *Chicago Sun-Times*, December 19, 2005.

vibrant society. As Secretary of State Condoleezza Rice said the other day while in Kiev, Nongovernmental organizations in Russia "are simply trying to help citizens to organize themselves better, to petition their government to make changes in the policies that affect their very lives. That is the essence of democracy."

But it is that very "power to the people" that Putin's Kremlin fears. The Kremlin is stripping away the peoples' capacity to seek changes that affect their very lives. It appears the goal is not to threaten Russian democracy but to end it except for some hollow trappings in an effort to retain legitimacy for a Soviet style autocracy.

Moscow no longer is capitol of the other global superpower. It's power has declined, its reach receded, its influence waned. Nonetheless it is a country of 145 million people with a vast Eurasian landmass, great reserves of oil and gas, a decaying but nonetheless threatening nuclear arsenal, and continuing aspirations to be a major global force. We ignore the retreat of freedom in Russia at our own peril.

The United States must stand with the people and against Putin's latest assault on Russian freedoms. Faced with criticisms from America and Europe, Putin has said he'll relax the planned crackdown on NGOs. Now is the time to re-double our efforts to support Russia's civil society.

Russians living in freedom, in a pluralistic society, and sharing our values are our natural friends and enduring allies. A corrupt autocracy seeking to roll back freedom, retrench and reestablish authoritarian rule will not be able to sustain stability at home nor be a friend on whom we can depend.

OLD ALLIANCE HAS NEW ROLE IN GLOBAL DIPLOMACY (NATO)

The Atlantic Alliance has been the bedrock of America's Security since World War II. However, just a couple of years ago it seemed in tatters. Commentaries and books such as Laurent Cohen-Tanugi's *An Alliance At Risk* spoke of acrimony, bitter rhetoric and an "ideological divide" between the United States and Europe precipitated by the Iraq War but due to deeper and more fundamental divisions.

The gravitational pull of the Cold War was gone and the imminent threat of nuclear Armageddon no longer focused the mind. Events seemed to accentuate the divisions more than the common interests between America and Europe. A shroud of doom, gloom and doubt fell upon NATO and the Atlantic dialogue.

But earlier this month at the 42nd Munich Conference on Security, I heard a more robust and hopeful tone. As NATO Secretary General Jaap de Hoop Scheffer said, "The state of the transatlantic alliance is good... NATO is in demand and it is delivering." Why have things changed?

First, rumors of NATO's death were premature. Even at the height of acrimony over Iraq, NATO was successfully helping in Afghanistan.

Second, the brazen unilateralism some heard in American pronouncements about Iraq have quieted down. In Munich, even Secretary Rumsfeld seemed to strike a more diplomatic tone saying, "No nation can succeed in the war on terror without the cooperation of others."

Third, Europe is less confident. The European Union constitution was defeated. New fears about their energy supply have emerged. There are concerns about Islam at home fed by the riots in France last summer and Muslims virulent protest of Dutch caricatures depicting the Prophet Muhammad. Balkan integration is going slowly. And European diplomacy has failed so far to contain Iran's nuclear threat.

Four, threats of growing concern invite cooperation: global terrorism, the spread of weapons of mass destruction, and energy reliability, to name a few.

Five, NATO is showing the capacity to transform to meet emerging threats. In part that required a recognition that NATO must go outside its area to protect those within it. The new NATO Response Force (NRF) provides the means to respond

Appeared in the *Chicago Sun-Times,* March 14, 2006.

swiftly to crisis as demonstrated in getting humanitarian relief to victims of Pakistan's earthquake last fall. NATO has increased its footprint in Afghanistan. In Darfur, NATO has a fledgling training mission for the African Union forces trying to stop the ethnic carnage. NATO's campaign on terror now includes maritime surveillance and escort operations in the Mediterranean. And, perhaps most important, NATO increasingly is engaged as a political instrument to find the shared response demanded by shared threats.

In Munich, UK Defense Minister John Reid said, "The value of NATO is not only a sentiment of the past, but a history of common values and common history that holds commonality to deal with new threats."

The Transatlantic Alliance certainly has its problems. Integration of new members is a challenge. Burden sharing issues remain as too many Europeans continue to fail to pay their fair share for the common defense. Standing the NRF to full strength is still a promise, not a reality. How to address issues of reliable energy supplies is unresolved now that Moscow has made abundantly clear its willingness to interrupt supply to achieve political gain. France's inevitable petulance. Then there is Iran's nuclear threat.

But the spirit in Munich reflected a sober recognition that it is in all our interests to put practical benefit above differences. The shared values and interrelated threats across the Atlantic make the hard work of forging a shared plan well worth the effort.

In Munich, Senator John McCain was awarded the annual Medal "Peace through Dialogue." He said, "As history's pace quickens, and with some difficult times ahead, the members of NATO will need to rely on each other more often in the future than in the past. The world will rely on NATO to a greater degree as well – as a security guarantor, as a peacekeeper, and as diplomatic leverage."

BUSH SHOULD USE G-8 FORUM TO PROMOTE FREEDOM IN RUSSIA

Next month President Bush and his colleagues from the world's most industrial nations will travel to St. Petersburg for the annual meeting of the G-8 to be hosted by Russian President Vladimir Putin. This presents a dilemma and an opportunity.

After the collapse of the Soviet empire, the leaders of the world's most industrial nations agreed to expand their number to include Russia even though Russia's economy did not warrant membership. Even today, despite its robust oil and gas industry, Russia's economy pales in comparison to the rest of the G-8.

Nonetheless, Russia was invited into the club as a means to encourage the Soviet Union's successor state to embrace democratic reforms and international norms. For a time, it seemed that Moscow was holding up its end of the bargain. But recently Putin has reversed that trend. In Russia, there has been a decisive anti-democratic, authoritarian drift.

Putin eliminated direct election of governors. He shut down the only independent national TV station. Oil and gas resources have been consolidated under Kremlin control. Nongovernmental organizations have been restricted. Putin supports the authoritarian governments of Uzbekistan and Belarus while using energy supplies and other means to try to destabilize democratic Ukraine and Georgia.

The dilemma is that President Bush's travel to St. Petersburg for the G-8 summit would seem to legitimize Putin's authoritarian drift and sanction his international misbehavior.

Last month in Vilnius Vice President Dick Cheney delivered a strong speech condemning Russia's backsliding on democracy, human rights and foreign affairs. Cheney pointed out that "the (Russian) government has unfairly and improperly restricted the rights of her own people." And in reference to Russian actions last winter, he said, "No legitimate interest is served when oil and gas become tools of intimidation or blackmail."

Cheney's speech drew sharp rebukes from Russian officials. While declaratory policy has a short shelf life, it is important to give expression to the values we cherish and to provide solidarity and encouragement to those within Russia dedicated to the struggle for enduring freedom against considerable odds. But more can and should be done to give greater substance to Cheney's words.

Appeared in the *Chicago Sun-Times,* July 3, 2006.

President Bush has made the keystone of his presidency the advance of freedom. He correctly has observed, "The work of democracy is larger than holding a fair election, it requires building the institutions that sustain freedom." This moment requires President Bush to stand up for the Russian "institutions that sustain freedom."

The upcoming G-8 meeting in St. Petersburg also provides an opportunity to advance the march of freedom.

The weekend before the G-8 meeting, several hundred leaders of besieged independent Russian NGOs are meeting in Moscow. President Bush, through teleconference, should address that gathering to reiterate America's commitment to them, their work to build a vibrant civil society, and the values of pluralism to which they are dedicated.

The freedom agenda should be raised during the G-8 meeting in St. Petersburg. And, importantly, German Chancellor Angela Merkel should make clear that issues of human rights, free markets, the rule of law, and international norms will be on the G-8 agenda when they meet next year in Germany. Russia will not be let off the hook.

And, finally, America should increase its support for Russian civil society. Putin, by means of his new laws restricting NGOs, has impeded their work. But while this is an obstacle it need not be a prohibition.

America has led efforts to nurture indigenous elements of civil society in areas of the former Soviet Union. In the Baltics, Georgia, Ukraine and elsewhere this has helped the advance of freedom. Putin's authoritarian drift should not deter continued support for Russian civil society but be cause to redouble these efforts.

As Ronald Reagan said, "Freedom is not the sole prerogative of a lucky few but the inalienable and universal right of all human beings." That includes the Russian people. It is to our shared values and to them we owe our allegiance.

RUSSIA IS PUTTING SCREWS ON GEORGIA TO PREVENT WESTERN TILT

Vladimir Putin's heavy handed reprisals against Georgia are part of Moscow's determination to keep as much as possible of the former Soviet Union under its tight sphere of influence, preventing any Western tilt.

The most recent clash came when Georgia arrested, then released, four Russian spies. Moscow was incensed. Having imposed a boycott of Georgian wine and mineral water earlier this year, Moscow turned the economic screws tighter by halting all transportation links between the two countries. Russia recalled its diplomats. Putin deported hundreds of Georgians, closed Georgian businesses in Russia and gathered names of all Georgian students and their parents. This specter of a major purge has been accompanied by the Duma's consideration of banning all money transfers to Georgia, effectively stopping the remittances from one million Georgians living and working in Russia. Some estimate this represents about 10% of Georgia's GNP.

For 200 years there have been problems between Georgia and Russia. For 70 years, Georgia was part of the Soviet Union. When the Soviet empire collapsed, Georgia gained independence. And since the Rose Revolution elected Mikhail Saakashvili president 3 years ago, Georgia has become a staunch U.S. ally, sought integration with Europe and pursued membership in NATO.

In a sense, Moscow refuses to accept the reality of sovereign and independent states that had been part of its domain. It already has lost sway of the Baltic states. But the Caucuses and Central Asia are areas Putin believes are inextricably bound to Russia by shared history and geographic proximity.

Moscow believes the United States is intent on weakening Russia and sees Georgia as a stalking horse for the West. It is too independent. Commencing "intense negotiations" to join NATO too threatening. Russia suspects Georgia cooperates with terrorists crossing into Chechnya.

Meanwhile Tblisi has legitimate concerns about Russia infringing on its independence.

Russia supports two break-away regions in Georgia, Abkhazia and South Ossetia. Moscow has issued Russian passports to Abkhazians. Russia has disrupted international frameworks to resolve these issues.

Appeared in the *Chicago Sun-Times,* October 17, 2006.

Meanwhile, Shaavashvili, from time to time, has needlessly provoked Russia. Many believe it was not coincidental that Tblisi arrested the four Russian spies the day after more intense talks on NATO began.

The conditions are ripe for an unintentional war. Neither side wants it, but the situation could spin out of control. Both sides feel aggrieved. The dispute has become too personal with both Putin and Saakashvili on television using heated rhetoric. Both countries are becoming more nationalistic. By linking the possible independence of Kosovo to the status of Abkhazia, Moscow lays the foundation for a declaration of Abkhazia independence.

Georgia shares America's values of democracy, the rule of law and market economics. It has sought our friendship and strategic alliance. America should welcome this ally in freedom's march and help Georgia sink roots for democratic institutions and build the guardrails of freedom.

At the same time, however, we should urge prudence over provocation and that heated rhetoric cool.

The Georgian people are free and independent. They have the sovereign right to chart their own course. And Russia must learn to accept and respect their sovereignty.

However, while you can pick your friends you cannot pick your neighbors. Russia is a reality in their neighborhood: a large, threatening and dangerous bear. Not only is Georgia's history intertwined with Russia, so is its future.

Section VIII:
MISCELLANEOUS

ECONOMIC DEVELOPMENT IN AFRICA

Thank you, Mr. Chairman.

President George Bush and Secretary of State Powell have made clear that the United States is committed in supporting African efforts to improve the lives of African people through lasting economic growth and development. We have demonstrated that commitment each day through our efforts to end conflict in Africa, through our leadership in the fight against HIV/AIDS, through our support for food security and agricultural development, and through opening our markets to more of Africa's products.

The United States supports the principles of the New Partnership for Africa's Development, NePAD, as a solid basis for African-led development. As President Bush and his G-8 partners noted in the G-8 Africa Action Plan, "The NePAD offers an historic opportunity to overcome obstacles to development in Africa." We hope that its bold rhetoric and commitments are reflected in concrete action for change and greater well-being.

At the heart of NePAD's vision is the understanding that development begins at home. We will be strong and willing partners in support of that vision. With our G-8 partners in Kananaskis, we have already pledged to develop deeper partnerships with countries whose actions and policies reflect the commitments in NePAD, including by providing enhanced assistance to those that do so.

The challenge we face today is to consider how the United Nations and its Funds and Programs can best support Africa's development goals and the efforts of African nations to accelerate growth. The U.S. should learn lessons from its experiences with the U.N.'s New Agenda for the Development of Africa to best support NePAD.

Consistent with the Millennium Declaration and the Monterrey Consensus, the U.N. should concentrate on the most effective use of its resources to achieve concrete results. As President Bush said in Monterrey, "Our new approach for development places responsibility on developing nations and on all nations. We must build the institutions of freedom, not subsidize the failures of the past. We must do more than feel good about what we are doing, we must do good." In that regard, we are heartened by the Secretary General's call to streamline and focus the U.N.'s work in Africa to make it more effective.

Although it has become a cliché to call for a coordinated, coherent approach in which all stakeholders focus on their comparative advantages, nevertheless,

---

Remarks at United Nations Security Council Open Meeting, December 3, 2002.

this truth remains a formidable challenge to realize. Development partners can all improve their efforts in this regard. Such a focus will maximize the impact of aid resources, make development programs more effective, and limit the burden placed on recipient countries – an issue highlighted by the expert report.

But coherence is not a donor preference, it is a development imperative. It rests heavily upon the establishment of clear, sound development priorities by the countries themselves. Therefore, one specific area where the U.N. can support increased coherence is through continued emphasis on cooperating with African governments, civil society and the Bretton Woods Institutions in the Poverty Reductions Strategy Paper process. This will not only build capacity to Africa, it also will help identify appropriate divisions of labor in the context of a country-led process.

Mr. Chairman,

As several speakers have stressed during this debate, the most fundamental requirement for realization of Africa's development goals is peace. Over the past decade too much of Africa has been essentially off limits to the development process due to civil war and other conflicts. It is here that the U.N. system has and should continue to make a vital contribution.

Peace throughout the continent is crucial for development of regional markets and infrastructure, which are essential for Africa's sustainable development. Regional development simply can't happen if large portions of the region are in conflict and cannot participate.

Therefore, the real progress in Sierra Leone, from years of civil war to free and fair elections, thanks to the commitment of the Sierra Leone people and, in part, due to the continuing contribution of UNAMSIL, is extremely encouraging. Also encouraging are recent developments in the Democratic Republic of the Congo, including, but not limited to the Sun City Agreement, the Pretoria Agreement and the current withdrawal of Rwandan armed forces from the eastern Congo. These are reasons for hope, and the United States remains a committed partner with our African friends to find real, sustainable peace wherever conflicts rage. This, in turn, sets a necessary precondition for economic growth and progress.

We welcome and will support work being done by the Economic Commission of Africa to assist African efforts on governance and peer review, both centerpieces of NePAD. This work will represent a strong base on which to energize efforts by African countries to achieve the higher standards of political and economic governance outlined in NePAD as critical to development success. The ECA also is making strong analytical contributions on economic development.

We also recognize the strong catalytic role and leadership the United Nations is playing in the fight against HIV/AIDS around the globe, but in particular in Africa. The United States will continue to make fighting the epidemic a major foreign policy priority, and we shall wage this war through bilateral, regional and multilateral partnerships.

Similarly, we welcome U.N. action on food security and agricultural development and productivity being carried out by the WFP, FAO, IFAD, and UNDP. Even more needs to be done. Agriculture is the bedrock of the African economy and the growth rates necessary to meet poverty reduction goals cannot be met without strong sustained growth in African agricultural productivity. This growth can be achieved through investment in rural development, including extension services, research, and biotechnology development, as well as a sound policy environment such as land tenure policies that respect the rule of law to enable farmers to reap the rewards of their work. The U.S. initiative announced to support African agricultural development and productivity will complement these efforts.

More generally, the U.N. has a far broader presence in Africa than any single bilateral or multilateral donor. It is therefore able to reach and help build capacity in places that may otherwise fall through the cracks of other donor mechanisms. As noted in the experts' report, capacity building is essential and is an area that we and G-8 partners are devoting increasing attention.

Mr. Chairman,

The United States encourages the U.N. to focus its support for NePAD on achieving results at national and regional levels to achieve the international development goals of the Millennium Declaration, and we welcome the Secretary-General's call for stronger regional cooperation. NePAD provides a framework and an approach for development but it needs to be translated into action at the national and regional levels, not by building an unwieldy NePAD bureaucracy.

Mr. Chairman,

NePAD represents an African-developed vision of that great continent's future. We urge the United Nations to work to help Africans transform their vision into an early reality. President Bush reminded us in Monterrey that "We fight against poverty because opportunity is a fundamental right to human dignity. We fight against poverty because faith requires it and conscience demands it. And we fight against poverty with a growing conviction that major progress is within our reach."

SMALL ARMS AND LIGHT WEAPONS

I want to thank the Colombian Permanent Representative for drafting the non-paper on the subject of arms embargoes, which has informed our current discussion. Ambassador Valdeiveso's Chairmanship of the 1267 Committee which, among other things, deals with arms embargoes, has been exemplary. He has been fair, businesslike, effective and the 1267 Committee has made a significant contribution to the war against terrorism in curbing the financing of terrorists and in working on arms embargoes. Sadly, these weapons are contributing to violence and suffering around the world.

The United States recognizes the agonizing consequences of illicit trade in small arms and light weapons, especially in areas of conflict where the problem is most acute. These weapons are contributing to violence and suffering around the world. Such agonizing consequences exist in Sierra Leone, the Central African Republic, where there are three guns for every citizen, and Guinea Bissau, among other countries.

The United States believes that solutions to the problem of the illicit trade in small arms and light weapons must be practical and effective. The most effective way to prevent small arms and light weight weapons from getting into the hands of those who will misuse them is through strict export and import controls, strong brokering laws, ensuring the security of small arms and light weapons stockpiles and destroying excess.

The United States has one of the strongest systems in the world for regulating the export of arms. These are extremely rigorous procedures. All commercial exporters and brokers of significant military equipment, including small arms and light weapons, must be licensed and submit each transaction for approval by the Department of State. This includes automatic rifles, machine guns, shoulder – fired missile and rocket systems as well as light mortars. All transactions are conditioned on U.S. authorization for re-export. We rigorously monitor arms transfers and routinely investigate suspicious activities. In the past six years, we have interdicted thousands of illicit arms and cut-off exports to countries that failed to comply with U.S. law. Individuals convicted of violating our export control laws are subject to statutory debarment, fines up to $1 million and/or incarceration for up to 10 years.

The United States also has been active internationally in stemming the illicit trade in small arms and light weapons. We offer bilateral financial and technical assistance to help countries develop national export and import controls, improve

Statement at United Nations Security Council Open/Formal Session, New York, N.Y., October 11, 2002.

border security against arms smugglers, and to secure and destroy illicit stocks of small arms and light weapons in conflict-prone regions. The U.S. has contributed approximately $100 million in assistance to improve small arms controls in Russia, the Caucasus, Central Asian and Eastern European states, the United Arab Emirates, Sierra Leone, Uganda, Liberia, Rwanda, Ethiopia, DR/Congo, Angola, Sri Lanka, East Timor, the Philippines and Columbia. We remain ready to continue this support.

The United States strongly supports effective export and import controls, restraint in trade to regions of conflict, strict observance and enforcement of Security Council embargoes, strict regulation of arms brokers, transparency in exports, and improving security of arms stockpiles and destruction of excess.

The paper submitted by the Government of Colombia in advance of this session thoughtfully focused on the issue of arms embargoes. The United States supports almost all of the recommendations by the monitoring group established by Resolution 1373, political and financial. Exchanging information on the status of existing arms embargoes is of great value to the Security Council in deciding how best to establish and enforce Security Council embargoes.

The lack of success of some of these embargoes is due to porous borders, weak enforcement, and a lack of political will by national governments. Just this week the Report to the Security Council of the Panel of Experts on Liberian Sanctions confirmed that the Government of Charles Taylor continues, in flagrant abuse of the Security Council's arms embargo, to procure weapons, including machine guns, missile launchers, mines, and small arms through black market, illegal arms deals. This continued influx of weapons threatens the tentative stability that has been achieved in Sierra Leone.

The Panel's Report notes that in many cases of illegal imports to Liberia, the End-User certificates used as cover for weapons diverted to Liberia, were all from ECOWAS Member States. It is crucial that ECOWAS Members themselves take the necessary steps to effectively enforce their own Moratorium on the Import, Export, and Manufacture of Light Weapons. It is disappointing that only half of the Member States have created Moratoriums.

The crisis in Cote d'Ivoire is an example of the bleeding of the supply of weapons between military and civilian populations, which is exacerbating divisions within society. The United States urges parties in Cote d'Ivoire to negotiate a peaceful solution to the current crisis. Yet, the responsibility to control small arms cannot be placed on a single state alone. Cote d'Ivoire's neighboring states, some of which also are unstable because of their own inability to control the flow of small arms, are contributing to instability by allowing the illicit trade and passage of small arms across their borders.

The view of the United States is that DDR (Disarmament, Demobilization, Reintegration) provisions are an important element of negotiated Peace Settlements, such as we are seeing in Sierra Leone, DRC, and Angola.

Mr. President,

The United States has a history of demonstrated commitment to finding practical and effective ways of curbing the illicit trade in small arms and light weapons such as our own strict export/import controls on small arms and the significant financial support we have given to other states. We look forward to working with other states in continuing to fulfill and enforce all Security Council created small arms embargoes.

Thank you, Mr. President.

AFRICA'S FOOD CRISIS AS A THREAT TO INTERNATIONAL PEACE AND SECURITY

Congratulations to our Colombian Security Council President.

Introduction

We would like to thank World Food Program Executive Director Jim Morris both for his presentation and for his efforts over these last months to avert famine and starvation in Africa.

The situation in southern Africa and the Horn is grave, with some 30 million people at risk of starvation. Drought is one cause of the crisis but poor government policies are as much to blame. Indeed, there is scholarship that concludes the vast majority of all famines in recorded history have resulted from government policies, not natural causes.

Famine is not a natural occurrence and is not inevitable. Where famine takes hold, we must look for the failures of governance, of development and of assistance.

Clearly, productive investment in agriculture and rural development to boost agricultural productivity is essential. Science and technology, including biotechnology have great promise for allowing African agriculture to keep pace with gains in the rest of the world, and to contribute to Africa's development.

However, if widespread famine is to be averted in Africa, the international community must act immediately to mobilize adequate levels of assistance.

U.S. Efforts

The United States began to react to the crisis in southern Africa early this year and to the Horn in September. In southern Africa we have tried to provide sufficient food assistance early on in order to prevent a famine, not respond to one. The United States Government has provided or pledged half a million metric tons of food to the southern African region, with a total value of approximately $266 million dollars.

In addition to food assistance, the United States Government has provided more than $10 million in non-food assistance to the affected countries for regional management and logistics, agriculture, supplementary and therapeutic feeding, emergency health, and cholera response and prevention.

Remarks at United Nations Security Council Open Meeting, New York, N. Y., December 3, 2002.

In the Horn of Africa food aid requirements are projected to range between 1.5 and 2.5 million metric tons to meet the needs of 11 to 15 million people. Experts fear a repeat of the horrendous events of the 1980's. The U.S. Government often has been able to meet up to half of food aid requirements for the Horn of Africa during times of crisis. However, drought in the United States and a corresponding rise in food grain prices will reduce the availability of U.S. food assistance worldwide this year. At best, we will be able to supply only about one-third of what the Horn Africa countries will need during this crisis.

Despite our efforts, much more needs to be done. We strongly encourage other donors to find the resources to respond to this urgent situation in Africa. We urge others as well to help settle unwarranted fears about available food supplies and keep the focus on getting safe, nutritious food to the hungry.

Southern Africa, Zimbabwe and Zambia

In southern Africa, the crisis is most dire in Zimbabwe and Zambia. Even with 100 percent funding of the World Food Program appeal and if government and commercial import predictions are fully realized, there will be a significant cereal deficit. Commercial markets, however, have not functioned well due to centralized marketing and foreign exchange issues.

Governments' policies on genetically modified food aid also have hindered the food aid distribution process.

Biotech Food Aid

We are deeply concerned that our efforts to provide desperately needed assistance could be delayed, if not derailed, by the confusion that prevails over biotechnology food issues.

The whole kernel maize being provided by the United States Government as part of our relief assistance is the same as that eaten by millions of Americans daily. It is safe, wholesome, and can make the difference between life and death for millions of southern Africans.

Many governments in the region already recognized this and are distributing United States Government-provided maize or maize flour to their people. The United States Government is firmly committed to materially aiding the nations of southern Africa and has been first among international donors to recognize the scale of problem and dedicate resources toward meeting the need.

However, some recipient and/or transit countries continue to have concerns about accepting whole-kernel biotech maize. We respect these governments' decisions and our goal is to work with those countries in an effort to help them better understand the facts and science of biotech foods so that their concerns do not lead to delays that risk endangering the well-being of millions of people.

We are consulting with the affected states to adopt an agreement to allow the unrestricted import and distribution of food aid, including biotech produce, on an emergency basis for the duration of this crisis.

At the same time, the United States Government is concerned that food aid and the crisis in southern Africa is being used as a tool to inflame the debate about biotechnology. It is important that decisions about food aid that may contain biotech products be based on sound science.

Given the urgency of the circumstances and availability of safe U.S. food, we urge those countries with concerns to reconsider their restrictions on U.S. maize. The United States Government remains concerned about starvation among the people in the region and continues to stand ready to provide our food assistance.

We do not believe there are food safety problems with biotech food. The United States Government does not segregate maize by seed origin, and we buy the commodities on the open market. This food is the same as the food eaten by Americans and has passed the regulatory process of the United States Environmental Protection Agency, the Food and Drug Administration, and the United States Department of Agriculture.

Commissioner Byrne from the European Union (EU) also has issued a statement that recognizes biotech varieties of maize to be safe for human consumption.

We also believe potential environmental problems, such as cross-pollination with local varieties, are not significant.

A number of countries have approved biotech maize varieties, including South Africa, Argentina, and several European states, following economic, environmental, and health safety reviews.

The United States Government has a seven-year track record of consuming biotech commodities that speaks to their food safety and environmental benefits for producers and consumers. The biotech corn provided by the United States is exactly the same corn eaten by millions of Americans and others daily.

Severe food shortages have resulted in abnormally high prices, making food unaffordable to many rural and urban families. Particularly in Zimbabwe, Malawi, and Zambia.

The high prevalence of HIV/AIDS in the region has left large portions of the population increasingly vulnerable to health problems associated with a lack of food.

Zimbabwe

Detrimental policies, particularly in Zimbabwe, have aggravated the effects of lower than average rainfall.

Since January 2002, the United States, through the World Food Program and World Vision, has programmed 210,000 metric tons of food assistance to Zimbabwe. Of this total, nearly 150,000 metric tons have arrived in the region. Much of this is currently stored in the region due to delays caused by Zimbabwe's recent decision to insist that all biotech corn be milled prior to importation. This requirement substantially raises costs, hastens storage losses, and reduces the amount of food available for emergency relief.

Zimbabwe has traditionally been a food exporter, supplying much of the food imports taken in by other countries in the region. The Government of Zimbabwe's violent and chaotic seizure of land from commercial farmers has decimated the most productive component of Zimbabwe's agricultural sector, reducing agricultural production by nearly 70 percent in the last two years, crippling its ability to feed not only its own population, but neighboring countries.

Further, Zimbabwe's economic policies have exacerbated agricultural conditions. Zimbabwe's economic disruption is typical of an economy in the midst of a devastating war. In 2001 and 2002 Zimbabwe has been the poorest performing economy in Africa with negative growth rates of 8.5% and 10.6% respectively. But in Zimbabwe there is no invading militaries, no domestic rebellions, and, except for the current drought, no significant natural disasters to blame. This threat of calamitous famine is, in large part, a consequence of misguided government policies. Price controls inhibit production and trade of food staples. The continuing monopoly of the Government of Zimbabwe's Grain Marketing Board on commercial imports of grain combined with foreign exchange restrictions make agricultural inputs such as tractors and fertilizer, unavailable or prohibitively expensive. Production estimates in the agricultural industry indicate 26% negative growth this year.

There also have been numerous reports of the Zimbabwean Government using food as a political tool and denying it to opposition areas. For example, in the Insiza District, WFP suspended food distributions after ruling party Zanu-PF activists and officials intimidated its implementing partner and distributed three metric tons of food commodities to its supporters. To date, the issue has been unresolved. U.S. Embassy and United Nations personnel looking into the hunger issue among displaced farm workers were attacked by "war veterans."

The United States cannot accept any act of politicization of food aid. These actions must be investigated and we believe that the Secretary General and the international community should consider how best to ensure that food is not used as a weapon, or a political instrument in the region.

Conclusion

Southern Africa and the Horn face the real possibility of mass starvation. Hunger is already severe in many areas. Averting a catastrophe requires broad and urgent international support, increased resources, new tools and better use of existing ones, resolution of concerns over biotech food and real reform in crisis countries. We will do our part and we will work with the World Food Programme to support it in this vital task.

Famine should not happen in the 21st century. If we can avert disaster this time, we should look much harder at how to help create conditions that will make the chance of it happening again, especially on this scale, much smaller.

In summary, I have four questions: one, what is the contribution of government policy to the threat of famine in southern Africa? Two, what is the role of food import policies to the threat of famine? Three, what is the role of government food distribution mechanisms on the threat of famine? And four, what is the impact of theft and corruption on the threat of famine?

Thank you.

CHILDREN AND ARMED CONFLICT

My delegation wants to thank the Security Council President for putting this important topic on our agenda. We also thank the Secretary-General for his very useful report on Children and Armed Conflict and his statement this morning. And we thank the Secretary-General's Special Representative on Children and Armed Conflict, Olara Otunnu, for his important work and the progress he has helped achieve in this area.

The use of children as combatants is one of the worst aspects of contemporary warfare. Young girls and boys are especially vulnerable to exploitation during warfare and its aftermath. They are unable to protect themselves, and they are stripped of their opportunity for better lives. Over 300,000 children are used in government or rebel forces in over 30 armed conflicts around the world. These children serve as soldiers, runners, guards, sex slaves and spies.

Our children are our future. Allowing their exploitation in armed conflicts does irrevocable harm to them and it diminishes the future for all, robbing a people of the future leaders they will need to reconstruct their society when the conflict ends, scarring the next generation that a society needs to reconcile and find justice when the killing stops, distorting the next generation's perspectives, diminishing the contribution they can make to rebuild the economy and social structures and irreparably harming the child's opportunity for a healthy, productive, normal life. Therefore, we have a special responsibility to make extra efforts to protect the children caught in the destructive cauldron of armed conflicts.

On December 23, 2002, the United States formally ratified the two Optional Protocols to the Convention on the Rights of the Child on the involvement of children in armed conflict. The United States has been and wants to continue to support the important efforts to end the use of child soldiers contrary to international law. We want to support efforts to end the exploitation of girls and boys in armed conflict.

In his report, the Secretary-General touches upon a number of areas in which today children tragically suffer as a consequence of their exploitation in armed conflicts. As noted in the Secretary-General's report, when war displaces families and communities, children often spend their entire childhood in camps where they are at risk of exploitation and forcible recruitment by armed groups. In armed conflicts, girls and young women are present in many of today's fighting forces. These child soldiers, boys and girls, are a cynical exploitation that exacerbates the violence and

Statement at United Nations Security Council Formal Chamber, New York, N.Y.; January 14, 2003.

great suffering endemic in any conflict. We must do better to protect the human rights of children caught in armed conflict. We must do better to protect our future.

The United States strongly supports setting 18 as the minimum age for compulsory recruitment by state actors and for recruitment or use in hostilities by non-state actors. We also support having states take all feasible measures to ensure that members of their armed forces below 18 years of age do not take a direct part in hostilities. And we support the Special Representative of the Secretary-General for Children and Armed Conflict as he works to obtain commitments for the protection and well being of children in conflict and post-conflict situations.

The United States supports the principle that child protection should be an explicit feature in peacekeeping mandates and, where appropriate, that child protection advisors be part of United Nations peace operations.

The United States supports the working group on child protection training for peace personnel in developing training materials that can be adapted to the mandate of peace operations and employed to train military, police and civilian personnel.

My delegation was pleased to learn of the progress that is being made to implement various United Nations Security Council resolutions to protect children in armed conflicts. As the Security Council discussed during deliberations last fall on the conflict in the Democratic Republic of the Congo, it is especially important that humanitarian access be available in zones of conflict. Arbitrary and capricious denial of humanitarian access by state or non-state actors is inconsistent with humanitarian law.

The United States joins others in opposing the illicit commercial exploitation of natural resources in conflict zones. We must be mindful to mitigate the adverse impact on children. In the Interlaken Declaration of November 5, 2002, the United States joined 47 other governments pledging to eliminate conflict diamonds from international trade through the implementation of a global rough diamond certification system.

And, the United States applauds the progress by regional and subregional organizations in making children and armed conflict a priority concern in their policies and programs.

Now I turn to one of the most important aspects of the Secretary-General's report. For the first time, in response to a Security Council request (resolution 1379 (2001)), this report from the Secretary-General explicitly names governments and armed groups that recruit or use child soldiers in violation of their international obligations. Such public exposure can be a powerful tool to expose violators, hold them to account, and, hopefully, better protect children in armed conflicts. The list names twenty-three armed parties to conflicts in five countries: Afghanistan, Burundi, Democratic Republic of the Congo, Liberia, and Somalia. Let me comment briefly about each of these.

Significant positive progress has been made in Afghanistan since the inception of the Bonn Process just over one year ago. As the Secretary-General's report notes, the Afghan National Army will not recruit underage soldiers. Despite the use of child soldiers by factions, the lives of Afghan children have improved markedly. Since October 2001, America's Fund for Afghan Children has raised $11.4 million, including more than $1 million in the past three months. Refugee and internally displaced children are perhaps Afghanistan's most vulnerable, and the United States has donated more than $145 million over the past year to assist in resettlement.

Although Burundi has not received the same attention as Afghanistan, the situation there is extremely volatile and the international community must be vigilant in preventing a catastrophe on the scale witnessed by Burundi's neighbors in the recent past. There have been encouraging developments, but circumstances in Burundi are still such that children continue to be exploited as combatants. Our work towards any peace agreement, to prevent inherent instability and danger, should prohibit the use of children in armed conflict.

In the Democratic Republic of Congo, we have witnessed the sad exploitation of children in war over the past few years. Human Rights Watch reports that official communications from the government have called on children between 12 and 20 years old to enlist. Meanwhile, rebel groups have habitually recruited children to aid their causes. While the task before us is difficult, it is important. There are ways to help these victims. There are ways to improve opportunities for exploited children. For instance, the United States continues to support the work of the Displaced Children and Orphans Fund and the Patrick J. Leahy Victims Fund, both of which offer grants to rehabilitate child soldiers in the region of the DRC and around the world.

The government of Liberia's flagrant failure to adhere to international law is a major contributing factor to the ongoing instability in West Africa. The armed forces of Charles Taylor, the President of Liberia, and the militias he has backed, have a record of recruiting underage children. As long as his government continues to support civil strife in West Africa, the threat to the region's children is real, the damage is great. The international community must be vigilant.

In Somalia, the situation is just as grave. Reports have indicated that boys as young as 14 and 15 years old have participated in militia attacks. Faction leaders recruit young boys to serve as personal bodyguards. Yet, the situation could get worse, if the international community does not take extra efforts to protect these children. Some recent estimates suggest that there are at least 175,000 internally displaced children in Somalia. This ongoing tragedy can not be tolerated. We must do better to ensure that these children are not subject to exploitation.

As I noted, explicitly naming governments and armed groups that recruit or use child soldiers in violation of their international obligations can be a powerful tool in our efforts to protect children in armed conflict. These obnoxious practices cannot stand the light of public scrutiny. The perpetuators of the abuse of children in armed conflict want to remain in the shadows, hidden from scrutiny, protected from accountability. Our oral and legal obligations compel us to force these harmful practices, these damaging activities, into the light of day. Impunity in this area is unacceptable.

The crushing consequences on the children in armed conflict must be ameliorated. A better future depends on it. A society's reconciliation, justice and opportunity after the killing stops require it. The Secretary-General's report is a good start. It responds to the Security Council's request for a list drawn from countries currently on the Security Council's active agenda. However, some of the worst violations of children on armed conflict are not included on the list, even though they are mentioned in the report.

For example, Burma is an area of concern. It is thought to have the largest number of child soldiers in the world. Human Rights Watch recently reported that there is the widespread forced recruitment of boys as young as eleven in Burma. Reportedly, children are routinely picked up off the streets, forced into the army, and never see their families again. According to Human Rights Watch, many children are forced to fight against armed ethnic opposition groups and carry out human rights abuses such as rounding up villagers for forced labor, burning houses and even massacring civilians. Armed opposition groups forcibly recruit young children.

In Uganda, the Lord's Resistance Army (LRA) has waged a civil war against the government of Uganda since the mid-1980's and has abducted between 10,000 and 16,000 children from Northern Uganda to serve as soldiers. Children are forced to participate in acts of extreme violence. Girls as young as twelve are given to commanders as "wives." Some abducted children have managed to escape, while others have died from disease, mistreatment or combat wounds. In recent months, reports of abductions have risen, and one NGO estimates that 4,000 children have been abducted just since June, 2002.

Colombia's children have long been caught up in that country's devastating conflict, including some 6,000 to 14,000 who are currently being used as soldiers by armed groups, paramilitaries and militias. Boys and girls, some as young as eight years old, are often recruited forcibly and used as combatants, spies, human shields, messengers, porters, kidnappers, guards, cooks, sexual companions or slaves, or for placing and/or removing bombs. Girls in armed groups and paramilitaries are particularly at risk of sexual abuse.

Clearly, the abuse of children in armed conflict goes beyond the scope of the Secretary-General's current report. And clearly, we have a moral responsibility, a moral imperative, to leave no child behind. We cannot ignore the damage to children in armed conflict wherever that devastation occurs.

Therefore, the United States would like to see the Secretary-General submit a list to the Security Council next year of the worst abusers of children in armed conflict not limited to countries currently on the Security Council's agenda. And, the United States would like to see active monitoring of those that have already been named.

In conclusion, let me again thank the Secretary-General and Olara Otunnu for their good work and contributions in this area. It is extremely important. Our children are our future. We must be more vigorous and more vigilant in working to protect children in armed conflict.

Thank you.

THE IMPORTANCE OF MULTILATERAL DIPLOMACY

It's a pleasure for me to have this chance to visit with students from Georgetown University's School of Foreign Service. I am a great admirer of Georgetown University where I have a son who is a senior. He has had a marvelous time there.

Many of you, perhaps most, are considering a career in the United States Foreign Service. I recommend it to you. It will provide a challenging career full of excitement and reward. You will enter an institution with a long and distinguished tradition. You will serve your country and contribute to its continued success. You will dedicate your career to a cause greater than your own self-interest, and in that comes great satisfaction.

America needs talented men and women to serve. As President John F. Kennedy said, "Ask not what your country can do for you, but what you can do for your country."

Beyond my importation for public service and my recommendation that you consider becoming United States Foreign Service Officers, I want to ask you to reflect on the growing importance of multilateral diplomacy to advancing U.S. interests and urge you to consider developing an expertise as multilateral diplomats.

Importance of Multilateral Venues

Multilateral venues such as the United Nations, NATO, the Organization of American States and others are important to the United States. They are even more important to most other countries.

While the United States diplomatic tradition, infrastructure, reach and experience is built upon a vast network of bilateral relationships, with embassies in most capitals around the world, that is not the case for most countries. Most nations lack military might. They have limited economic strength. And they have little political reach beyond their immediate neighbors. This especially is true for the scores of former colonies who have gained independent statehood following World War II.

Most countries do not have the resources to enable them to have bilateral embassies everywhere. They are limited to having embassies in neighboring states and in a few major countries that have direct or regional influence on their interests.

Remarks at the School of Foreign Service, Georgetown University, January 30, 2003.

Consequently, most of their diplomatic activity with most other countries takes place in major multilateral venues; and in particular in the United Nations in New York City and Geneva.

In the U.N. corridors many countries engage in an array of bilateral diplomacy. U.N. meetings are where most countries seek to protect their interests, advance their agendas and express their sovereign independence. By taking them seriously in the venue they hold most precious, we demonstrate respect for them. By taking seriously the issues they raise in their preferred forum, we engage them and their interests in a serious and respectful manner. And if it is in our interests to be treated with respect and not just with fearful trepidation, we must give that respect to others.

The phenomenon of European integration also has increased the preference of multilateral venues among some of our strongest allies. While European nations have traditions and experience in bilateral diplomacy as long or longer than our own, none have bilateral embassies in all the nearly 200 independent countries around the world. The cost is prohibitive.

Furthermore, in the past 50 years the integration of European nation states economically and their increased political coordination have been successful from many perspectives. Mighty Germany that twice in the 20th century lit the continent into a war conflagration has been tamed and integrated into the European Union. Wars of aggression against neighbors, a common European phenomenon over the centuries, have been forestalled. And economic integration has helped European countries compete with America. It is little wonder that our European allies have a growing faith in multilateral institutions and international law. It has worked successfully for them in Europe, why shouldn't it work globally?

Consequently, whether the United States likes it or not, our European friends, including some of our strongest bilateral allies, by experience, habit and preference are taking more issues to multilateral organizations, including issues in which the United States has a vital interest.

Also the profound global power imbalance today has made multilateralism more attractive for the rest of the world.

With the collapse of the Soviet empire and the implosion of the Russian empire, America stood as the world's sole superpower. Never before had any nation had so much preeminence in the world economically, culturally and militarily. As Charles Krauthammer wrote at the end of the Cold War, the world stood in a "unipolar moment".

At the time, most experts predicted that the United States dominance soon would be balanced by the growing power of Europe and the emergence of China. The unipolar moment would pass and the ballast of a balance of powers would reemerge. But that has not happened.

While Europe has grown economically, the countries of Europe seem to have accepted a more modest, secondary role militarily. Their defense budgets have not been robust, but decreased as a percent of their GNP. Technologically their weapon systems fall farther and farther behind. And while China's growth to greater economic strength and military might continues, it remains very far behind America. It will be decades, if even then, before China the emerging power will become China the superpower able to balance America's strength. America's unipolar moment has become our unipolar era.

Given America's preeminence as the world's sole superpower, it is natural that other countries want to influence and contain the exercise of American power. However benevolent America might be, however responsible we might act, others are concerned about – even resentful and fearful of – American power and the prerogatives that power bestows upon us.

Unable to compete economically or militarily, other countries seek other ways and means to level the playing field. They seek to restrain American unilateralism. They seek to influence our decisions. They try to drive issues into multilateral fora where they have a say. And they are particularly attracted to venues such as the United Nations in which they have power much greater than they have in the real world. Thus the adamancy of France and Russia to designate the U.N. Security Council as the sole body empowered to "legitimize" the use of force (except for French troops sent into the Ivory Coast). For in the U.N. Security Council they too have "veto power", a 58 year old anachronism. In the U.N. Security Council, the structure and procedures untethered to the real world, empower France and Russia to rough equivalence with America. Through the distorted prism of the U.N. Security Council, Russia (a collapsed power) and France (a declining, middling power) are superpowers too.

Whether America likes it or not, Russia, France and other countries will continue to take issues to the United Nations. And some of those issues will matter to America. Some of those issues will impact United States vital interests.

Ultimately, as in Kosovo and with Operation Iraqi Freedom, America may choose to ignore the U.N. America has the power to do that. But doing so may be costly.

Our recent diplomatic efforts in the United Nations on Iraq, the success in passing Security Council resolution 1441 last November and our efforts to pass an 18th Iraq resolution now demonstrate this dynamic.

Finally, multilateral venues matter because some of the greatest threats to our interests, the spread of weapons of mass destruction and global terrorism, are best dealt with multilaterally. And while ad hoc coalitions of the willing can be gathered when required, containing WMD and combating terrorism will require long, sustained campaigns. And multilateral organizations engaged in support of these efforts provide institutional advantages.

All these considerations argue for the importance of multilateralism. And this proposition, in turn, argues for the importance of multilateral diplomacy.

Multilateral Diplomacy Differs From Bilateral Diplomacy

Former Senator Claiborne Pell wrote, "As a former career diplomat, I would like to see the Foreign Service give greater attention to developing and rewarding skills in multilateral diplomacy. It ought to be regarded as a national disgrace when others outperform us in the multilateral arena." But outperform us they do.

This is my third time working in the State Department. As an Assistant Secretary of State and during both of my ambassadorial tours, I consistently have been impressed with the high intelligence and work ethic of the foreign service officers

471

with whom I have worked. They are among the best and brightest. And most have developed excellent skills for bilateral diplomacy. But most have little experience in multilateral diplomacy, or none at all. Therefore, it is not surprising that the United States is often outperformed in the multilateral arena.

In pointing out most FSOs' weakness in multilateral diplomacy, I do not suggest that they are not good diplomats. Most are. But multilateral diplomacy is different than bilateral diplomacy. To point out that the world's greatest basketball player Michael Jordan failed as a professional baseball player because he could not hit a curve ball does not diminish his athletic prowess. Rather it demonstrates that the skills of a basketball player are different than those of a baseball player. Similarly, multilateral diplomacy is different than bilateral diplomacy. This fact should be acknowledged and if, as I suggest, multilateralism is of growing importance to American interests, we should encourage new, bright FSO's to engage in multilateral diplomacy and develop and reward their progress.

Among other things, good bilateral diplomats must develop skills for keen observation, analysis and writing since a great deal of their job is to report back to Washington on what is going on in a foreign country and why; to anticipate what might happen in the future; and to suggest who and how events might be shaped. Wide sources of information must be cultivated. Those sources of information must be protected. Policies consistent with United States interests are encouraged and those inconsistent discouraged. Occasionally agreements are gingerly negotiated to mutual satisfaction. The host countries' sovereignty is respected.

Multilateral arenas are political bodies, more like legislatures or city councils than diplomatic drawing rooms. They are places for brinkmanship, lobbying, logrolling, energetic persuasion, coalition building, isolating opponents, rewarding friends and punishing opponents. It is energetic, constantly challenging and invigorating. It is about rounding up support and counting votes, hard counts. Often it is about getting sovereign states to do things they do not want to do. All in all, multilateral diplomacy is far more rough and tumble than the delicate minuet of bilateral diplomacy. It can be faster. It is negotiating with many interlocutors simultaneously. And when the vote is taken it is about winning or losing.

Multilateral diplomacy is not about "useful discussions". It is not about "constructive dialogue". It is not about winning a "sympathetic hearing" for U.S. concerns. Multilateral diplomacy is about the vote. Other delegations are with us or against us. The vote is taken. Did the U.S. position prevail or was it defeated? Did the U.S. deliver or were we "outperformed"?

For some, a very few, the politics of multilateral diplomacy are second nature, they have an instinct for it. For most, it takes time and training and experience to develop the skill set to master the politics of multilateral diplomacy.

We need bright FSOs willing to work in different multilateral venues as they go through their career: Geneva, Vienna, Rome, Brussels, New York and elsewhere. We need FSOs who will master the skills of multilateral diplomacy in order that the United States not be "outperformed".

Conclusion

As I have said, I believe whether America likes it or not, multilateral institutions will play an increasingly important role in the years ahead. Interesting and important issues affecting the United States will be addressed in multilateral arenas. The challenges will be significant and the consequences will be profound. The diplomatic skills required to represent America and advance U.S. interests will be considerable. And participating in that diplomatic effort will be invigorating and rewarding.

Therefore, in addition to my earlier suggestion that you seriously consider public service by joining the foreign service, I further hope that you will consider working in multilateral diplomacy. Our country needs you. And, I believe, you will find it rewarding.

THE NEED TO ADDRESS THE PROBLEM OF CHILD SOLDIERS, "CHILDREN IN THE CROSSFIRE: PREVENTION AND REHABILITATION OF CHILD SOLDIERS"

Thank you very much for those kind words of introduction. It's a pleasure to be with you this afternoon.

I would like to begin by thanking Secretary Chao and the Department of Labor for hosting this conference and World Vision for sponsoring our luncheon discussion. I also want to acknowledge each of you in the audience because all of you have taken to heart a cause which desperately needs fervent advocates in every corner of the globe.

The topic we are here to address requires as much courage, faith, and determination as any issue facing the world community today. That being the case, I am particularly gratified that we are joined by representatives from several governments who are prepared to address this issue in their own countries: El Salvador, the Philippines, Colombia, Burundi, Sierra Leone, Sri Lanka and Uganda. I am particularly heartened that the Government of Burundi has agreed to be an active participant in this event. As you know, Burundi was one of the five countries named in the United Nations Secretary-General's report on children and armed conflict. To face up to this fact is to take the first difficult step towards progress. Shame lies in inaction, shame lies in indifference, but there is no shame whatever in facing a crisis openly and welcoming assistance and support from others.

The very fact that we must gather to discuss child soldiers trapped in the toils of war in the early days of the 21st century should shock the conscience of the world. Our children are our future. Allowing their exploitation in armed conflicts does irrevocable harm to them and it diminishes the future for all, robbing a people of the future leaders they will need to reconstruct their society when the conflict ends, scarring the next generation that a society needs to reconcile and find justice when the killing stops, and often irreparably harming the child's opportunity for a healthy, productive, normal life. Therefore, we have a special responsibility to make extra efforts to protect the children caught in the destructive cauldron of armed conflicts. Comb through President Bush's speeches and public statements and you will find a recurrent, sharply worded theme: it is our duty to make sure that no child is left behind. The president emphasizes that word "duty," as he should. There is no better platform upon which to build a just world than the obligation of adults to serve their children...and serve them well.

Remarks at Conference on Child Soldiers, Washington, D.C., May 8, 2003.

So to stand here today and acknowledge that over 300,000 children are currently being used in armed conflict as soldiers, messengers, guards, runners, bearers, spies, cooks, and sex slaves is almost to speak the unspeakable. The problem is most critical in Africa and Asia, but we know it exists in Latin America, Europe, and the Middle East. Children as young as ten years old have been abducted from their homes and forced into situations where they witness, and sometimes perpetrate, violence against their own families and communities.

And once these children have escaped the toils of war—or been discarded because they have been so badly wounded, physically and mentally, that they can no longer function as the tools of tyrants—their situation hardly improves. Lacking education, guidance, and a sense of how an orderly world operates, they have few opportunities for hope. The number of children trafficked or exploited for sexual purposes has grown dramatically in recent years. Political conflict, poverty, transnational criminal rings, and the cynical exploitation of the power of the Internet all play a part in the sordid destruction of human dignity.

In the Mano River Region of West Africa, the use of child soldiers perpetuates violence across borders. For many children, the only life known is one of violence and bloodshed, as rebels and mercenaries prowl for new recruits. Child soldiers who cannot reintegrate into society have hampered efforts for peace in Sierra Leone, which cannot escape the instability in neighboring Liberia. Ongoing conflict in Western Cote d'Ivoire has wreaked havoc on the younger generation, pulled into a fight they did not start. As the New York Times reported just this past Monday, "Every-growing numbers of youths from Sierra Leone, Liberia, Guinea and Ivory Coast are now schooled in nothing but the art of destruction."

The international community has taken some important steps in responding to these abuses, steps the United States has strongly supported. The First Optional Protocol on the Involvement of Children in Armed Conflict to the Convention on the Rights of the Child was adopted by the United Nations General Assembly on May 25, 2000 and came into force on February 12, 2002. Over one hundred and eleven countries have signed and over 52 (including the United States) have ratified it. *Inter alia,* the first Optional Protocol confirms that the minimum age is 18 years for compulsory recruitment into the armed forces of a State Party or other "armed group." In addition, State parties must take "all feasible measures" to ensure that members of their armed forces who are under 18 years old do not take a "direct part" in hostilities and that "armed groups" do not recruit or deploy in hostilities persons under 18.

The second Optional Protocol to the Convention on the Rights of the Child, also ratified by the United States, addresses the sale of children, child pornography, and child prostitution. It is the first instrument of international law to define these terms legally and it is essential in our efforts to combat trafficking for forced commercial sexual exploitation. The Protocol requires State Parties to protect children up to the age of 18 by treating the actions of exploiters as criminal acts that merit serious punishment. In the global arena, the Optional Protocol promotes international law enforcement cooperation.

These two Protocols are important commitments and emblems of an emerging international consensus. The United States also supports the working group on child protection training for peace personnel and the principle that child protection should be an explicit feature of peacekeeping mandates. The United States has welcomed the report of the Secretary General on Children in Armed Conflict, published in November

2002, that I mentioned earlier. As mandated by Security Council resolution 1379 of 2001, this report included an annex that lists parties to armed conflict that recruit or use children in violation of relevant international obligations. As a consequence, the report cites 23 parties, including governments and/or rebel groups in Afghanistan, Burundi, the Democratic Republic of the Congo, Liberia and Somalia that recruit and use child soldiers in violation of international obligations applicable to them. This list has focused world attention on situations that need immediate attention, and it sends a clear political signal to the implicated states of their need to comply with their international obligations.

Such public exposure can be a powerful tool to expose violators, hold them to account, and, hopefully, better protect children exposed to armed conflicts. To keep up the pressure, Security Council Resolution 1460 calls for the submission of a follow-on report in 2003 on the status of Children in Armed Conflict in the states listed in the 2002 report. The United States would like to see the Secretary-General go further than this, actually, and submit a list of the worst abusers of children in armed conflict not limited to countries currently on the Security Council's agenda. Some of the worst violators of children in armed conflict do not appear on the list, countries such as Burma, Uganda, and Colombia, even though they are mentioned in the report. The United States also would like to see active monitoring of those that have already been named. In this case, more is better. Much better. The obnoxious use of children in armed conflict cannot stand the light of scrutiny. The perpetuators of the abuse of children in armed conflict want to remain in the shadows, hidden from scrutiny, protected from accountability. We need to know, the world needs to know, what is happening to our children.

I am pleased to report that significant positive progress has been made in Afghanistan since the inception of the Bonn Process just over one year ago. As the Secretary-General's report notes, the Afghan National Army will not recruit underage soldiers. Despite the use of child soldiers by factions, the lives of Afghan children have improved markedly. Since October 2001, America's Fund for Afghan Children has raised $11.5 million, including more than $1 million in the past few months. Further, the United States Government has donated more than $185 million since September 2001 to assist in general resettlement efforts in Afghanistan, especially efforts affecting refugee and internally displaced children.

Although Burundi has not received the same attention as Afghanistan, the situation there is extremely volatile and the international community must be vigilant in preventing a catastrophe on the scale witnessed by Burundi's neighbors in the recent past. There have been encouraging developments, but circumstances in Burundi are still such that children continue to be exploited as combatants. Our support for the Burundi transition government is consistent with our calls to prohibit the use of children in armed conflict.

In the Democratic Republic of the Congo, we have witnessed the sad exploitation of children in war over the past few years. Human Rights Watch reports that the government has called on children between 12 and 20 years old to enlist. Meanwhile, rebel groups have habitually recruited children to aid their causes. Here too there is progress toward a transition government. Here too we are working in the Security Council to eliminate the use of child soldiers. But the recent increased violence in the Ituri Province in the Eastern Congo is a cause of intense concern.

The government of Liberia's flagrant failure to adhere to international law is a major contributing factor to the ongoing instability in West Africa. The armed forces of Charles Taylor, the President of Liberia, and the militias he has backed, have a record of recruiting underage children. As long as Taylor's government continues to support civil strife in West Africa, the threat to the region's children is real; the damage is great. Reform of the Liberian Government; electoral, judicial and respect for human rights continue to be principle goals of United States policy in Western Africa.

Sadly, the situation is just as grave in Somalia. Reports have indicated that boys as young as 14 and 15 years old have participated in militia attacks while faction leaders recruit young boys to serve as personal bodyguards. If the international community does not make extra efforts to protect these children, the situation could get worse. Some recent estimates suggest that there are at least 175,000 internally displaced children in Somalia.

In light of these ongoing tragedies, we recognize the contributions and dogged efforts of the United Nations Secretary-General, the Security Council, the Secretary-General's Special Representative on Children in Armed Conflict, the United Nations Children's Fund (UNICEF), the Office of the United Nations High Commissioner for Refugees (UNHCR), the International Committee for the Red Cross (ICRC), and non-governmental organizations. Working with governments and armed groups in the field, they have demobilized children and provided them with access to education, social services, and alternative employment to facilitate their reintegration into society.

But the magnitude of the problems that confront these children is such that the United Nations cannot act alone. Responsible governments must use the United Nations as a tool to eliminate children and armed conflict, but must supplement that effort elsewhere. Therefore, the United States supports programs to assist in the rehabilitation of child soldiers through grants and cooperative agreements, including the Displaced Children and Orphans Fund and the Patrick J. Leahy War Victims Fund.

- The Displaced Children and Orphans Fund focuses on developing and supporting programs that relate to children affected by war; it also supports children orphaned by AIDS, street children, and children with disabilities. Since 1989, the Displaced Children and Orphans Fund has contributed more than $74,000,000 to programs in 28 countries. Administered by USAID and carried out by nongovernmental organizations, the fund has programs in Angola, Brazil, Democratic Republic of the Congo, Croatia, Eritrea, Ethiopia, Indonesia, Kenya, Kosovo, Liberia, Malawi, Peru, Rwanda, Sierra Leone, South Africa, Sri Lanka, Uganda, Vietnam, and Zambia.

- Also in place since 1989, the Patrick J. Leahy War Victims Fund works in war-affected countries to provide a dedicated source of financial and technical assistance for civilian victims of war. The Leahy War Victims Fund supports programs that provide prosthetic services and programs that follow up such services with patient monitoring. The fund has provided over $60 million in more than 16 countries.

Exploited and scarred by war or the sex trade, hundreds of thousands of children around the world virtually define the word "victim." They are being maimed and through them, we are being maimed, despoiled of our future and subject to the worst kinds of cynical brutality.

In Washington, at the United Nations, in national capitals around the globe and in gatherings like this one of public officials and private citizens, the time has come to turn back this flood tide of barbarity. We, the civilized world, face many tests—terrorism, the HIV/AIDS crisis, the scourge of drugs, to name only a few—but no test is more threatening to our moral integrity than the enslavement and exploitation of children. How can we create a better world if we do not first insist on keeping our children safe? The answer to this question is obvious. The term "child soldier" must be banished from the vocabulary of humankind. We can no longer permit or tolerate the reality to which it refers.

Once again, let me say how much I appreciate your dedicated efforts.

Thank you very much.

A New World, Old Institutions and Rules of the Road

It's a pleasure for me to be here today. I'm a big fan of the work done by the U.S. Institute of Peace. Their books on negotiating with various countries are insightful. I have found the USIP publications on Transitional Justice very useful. Andrew Natsios' volume on the humanitarian crisis in North Korea is the best thing I've read on that important topic. And I could go on.

Also, I count the Institute's President, Richard Solomon, as a good friend. We've worked together on various matters for many years. And I recognize that Dick has been a very successful "institution builder" at the helm of the U.S. Institute of Peace. So thank you for inviting me to be here today.

Global dynamics are constantly changing. Part of the challenge of power, politics and diplomacy is to try to understand the currents of change, to reassess existing paradigms and re-evaluate established institutions, to recalibrate your interests and adjust your behavior in the hopes of guiding those changes. I'd like to spend a few minutes reviewing the United Nations failure to act on Iraq, to look at some of the lessons we might learn from these events, and to raise some broader issues suggested by this episode.

The UN and Iraq

By the summer of 2002, there was a great deal of speculation about Iraq. In June, at the Graduation Ceremony at the U.S. Military Academy at West Point, President Bush had laid out his strategy of pre-emption.[1] He said, in part, "We will not leave the safety of America and the peace of the planet at the mercy of a few mad terrorists and tyrants...We must take the battle to the enemy, disrupt its plans, and confront the worst threats before they emerge...[Americans should] be ready for pre-emptive actions, when necessary to defend our liberty and to defend our lives."[2]

That summer, Secretary of Defense Donald Rumsfeld said, "Defending against terrorism and other emerging 21st century threats may well require that we take the war to the enemy. The best, and in some cases the only defense is a good offense."[3]

And, speaking about Iraq, Secretary of State Powell had said, "Inspections aren't the issue: disarmament is the issue. Making sure they have no weapons of mass destruction and they did what they said they were supposed to do, but we know that they haven't...So the issue is (the) removal of all weapons of mass destruction.[4]

Remarks at United States Institute of Peace, Washington, D.C., May 14, 2003.

Then in August, Vice President Dick Cheney gave two forceful speeches that addressed Saddam Hussein, Iraq's weapons of mass destruction, and the growing threat posed by Saddam's brutal regime.[5] And, in both speeches, the Vice President raised questions about the effectiveness and reliability of any UN inspection regime. He said, "One must keep in mind the history of the UN inspection teams in Iraq... Against that background, a person would be right to question any suggestion that we should just get inspectors back into Iraq, and then our worries will be over. Saddam has perfected the game of cheat and retreat, and is very skilled in the art of denial and deception."[6]

Consequently, when the United Nations General Assembly opened in September, there was a great deal of anticipation for what President Bush would say. Would President Bush by-pass the UN, or would he engage the UN on the issue of Iraq?

Speaking just before President Bush, UN Secretary-General Kofi Annan said, "I urge Iraq to comply with its obligations – for the sake of its own people, and for the sake of world order. If Iraq's defiance continues, the Security Council must face its responsibilities."[7]

In his address, President Bush methodically reviewed the 16 UN resolutions on Iraq dealing with human rights abuses, terrorism,[8] the return of POWs and Saddam's weapons of mass destruction.[9] He reviewed the sad history of Saddam's refusal to comply with these UN resolutions. He laid out the growing threat to international peace and security from the Iraqi regime. And, President Bush challenged the United Nations Security Council to meet its responsibilities, to address this threat, to prove its relevance by taking action against Saddam Hussein.[10]

The next day, work on another Iraq resolution began. It would be the UN Security Council's 17th Iraq resolution.

At the outset, France and Russia said that any Security Council resolution must explicitly require that if Iraq failed to comply, before any action would be taken against Iraq, that the Security Council would have to pass an 18th resolution explicitly authorizing the use of force. That issue was hotly debated. The other key points of contention were whether the resolution would state Iraq already was in material breach of prior UN resolutions, what would be the modalities of the arms inspection regime, would Iraq be required to make a declaration of its weapons of mass destruction, what would the time line be.

For eight weeks there were intense negotiations at the UN and in capitals; negotiations at the level of experts, ambassadors, foreign ministers and heads of state; every idea was discussed, every sentence was deliberated, every phrase was examined, every word turned this way and that. People who have been at the UN far longer than I said the length and intensity of the negotiations were unprecedented. By the time the Security Council came together on November 8th to vote on Resolution 1441, the substance of the 17th Iraqi Resolution was well understood by each Security Council member. And Resolution 1441 passed unanimously.

Resolution 1441 was not about arms inspections, it was about disarmament. It was not about progress towards disarmament, it was about total disarmament of all Saddam's weapons of mass destruction. It was not about disarmament someday. It called for disarmament immediately. The resolution uses the world "immediate" more than half-a-dozen times. And the resolution did not say that if Saddam fails to comply with its requirements, well then we'll see what we are going to do. No. Resolution 1441 states that if Saddam did not comply he would face "serious consequences," a term well understood by all 15 members of the Security Council and by Secretary-General Kofi Annan to mean the "use of force."

Resolution 1441 was clear. It was well understood. Yet, when Saddam Hussein did not comply with the requirements of 1441, when he was in material breach of the resolution, the Security Council was unable to act.

Remember that on September 12, 2002, Secretary-General Kofi Annan said that "if Iraq's defiance continues, the Security Council must face its responsibilities."[11] Iraq's defiance did continue. The Security Council did not face its responsibilities. And the Secretary-General's resolve last September had withered to a whimper by February and March, 2003.

A number of factors contributed to this failure. Certainly the economic interests of some countries argued against war; especially Russia, France and Germany.[12] Also, in several countries domestic politics made it difficult for them to face their responsibilities regarding Iraq's continuing defiance of UN resolutions,[13] Syria, as an Arab neighbor to Iraq, faced political and security constraints.

Also, a number of the elected-1O on the Security Council wanted to avoid the responsibility of making this difficult decision.[14] An Ambassador from a large elected-10 nation said to me, "Richard, we ran for the Security Council to be important, to play a role. We did not run in order to decide questions of war and peace. You are asking too much of us."

The UN Secretariat, including Secretary-General Kofi Annan and Chief UN Arms Inspector Hans Blix sought to avoid war. As I've noted, Kofi Annan's bold challenge in September that Security Council members must meet their responsibilities by February had eroded to saying that if the Security Council did not have unanimity on an 18th Iraq resolution, it would lack legitimacy.[15] In other words, if Syria was not prepared to vote to compel Iraq compliance with UN Security Council resolutions, then notwithstanding the fact of Iraqi defiance and even if the other 14 supported action consistent with 17 previous UN resolutions, that action would not be legitimate. Quite a profound re-interpretation of the UN Charter. A view practically guaranteed to result in gridlock, inaction, and UN irrelevancy.

In December, Hans Blix reported that Saddam Hussein's weapons declaration had not been complete and accurate as required in Resolution 1441. In other words, Saddam was in material breach of 1441. In January, Dr. Blix told the Security Council that Saddam Hussein was not pro-actively cooperating with UN arms inspectors as required in Resolution 1441. In other words, Saddam was in further material breach of the UN resolution. Dr. Blix saw that the United States and some countries took the words of Resolution 1441 seriously, and said that this continued defiance by Saddam Hussein would force the Security Council to "face its responsibilities," he became spooked.

Subsequently, Dr. Blix seldom spoke a declarative sentence. His circumlocutions and balancing qualifiers were a study in equivocation. He was to present the facts. The Security Council had the responsibility to make the decisions based on the facts as known. But, Dr. Blix is a diplomat who believes that, whatever the facts, war is bad and more diplomacy is good. He struggled to ensure that despite Saddam's continued defiance of Resolution 1441 and despite UN inspectors consequent inability to fulfill their responsibilities under Resolution 1441, that he made no statement that could provide firm footing for Security Council action. Thereby, Hans Blix failed in his responsibilities. He pulled his punches. He did his very best to obviate, divert and confuse. In the end, this contributed to Security Council divisions. Therefore, Hans Blix's irresolve helped make war inevitable.

Also contributing to the UN's failure to act were fundamentally different "threat assessments" among the Security Council members. The United States viewed Saddam's brutal past, his adventurism, his WMD program and his support of terrorists as a "gathering storm." France, however, did not see Saddam Hussein's regime as a great danger. Rather, to Paris, the Baghdad regime was a land of commercial opportunity. Other Security Council members lined up in various positions in between those two views. Those who did not view Iraq as a growing danger tended to excuse Saddam's defiance of UN resolutions. They tended to be satisfied with halting progress in arms inspections even if there was no progress in disarmament.

The final and determinative factor that led to UN inaction on Iraq was the decision of France to seize this issue and exploit the Security Council venue to try to balance U.S. power. President Jacques Chirac has made it clear that he seeks a "multipolar world" to counterbalance U.S. hegemony. He embraced this opportunity to use the Security Council in an effort to contain U.S. power.[16] This dynamic has been much discussed and extensively analyzed, so I will not rehash this subject. But whatever possibility the UN Security Council had to meet its responsibilities on Iraq ended by President Chirac's declaration of a pre-emptive, unilateral veto of any 18th Iraqi resolution whatever it said.

The UN provides France a permanent seat on the Security Council with the power to veto resolutions. This special status is a relic of 1945. It no longer makes sense. It grants France influence in the United Nations far greater than its power or influence in the real world. On Iraq, France recklessly wielded this power. Ironically, in so doing, France diminished the very institution which affords it a status far above its station in the real world. One Ambassador from a leading nation of the Non-Aligned Movement said to me, "Who gave France the right to try to check United States power at the United Nations? We're the countries that are harmed (by the UN being diminished) and we don't like it."

So a number of factors contributed to the UN's failure on Iraq: economic considerations, Member States domestic political considerations, an interest by some to avoid tough decisions and accountability, a UN institutional bias against armed conflict even in the face of continued defiance, different threat assessments, and the willingness of a permanent member of the Security Council to unilaterally wield a pre-emptive veto in an effort to check U.S. power. These events point out problems in the structure, procedures and process of UN Security Council deliberations; problems that contributed to the UN's failure to act; and problems that will impede UN effectiveness going forward.

After the UN's failure in Rwanda, Kosovo and Iraq, we cannot ignore the problems of the UN. They limit this institution.

But the United Nations is not the only institution formed after World War II and developed during the Cold War that is showing its age. During the ramp up to Iraq, for the first time NATO denied defensive planning to a Member State when requested. Turkey, a NATO member, asked for NATO to help plan its defense in the event of a war in Iraq.[17] But France, Germany and Belgium joined together to deny that request. Apparently they denied Turkey's request not because they felt it lacked merit, but because they did not want to imply that war was inevitable. Of course it was easier to take that position when sitting in Paris, Berlin or Brussels than if they sat in Ankara, next door to Iraq. This position, of course, undermines the very foundation of NATO, a mutual defense organization. Eventually a procedural gimmick was used to circumvent this impediment.[18] But it reveals strains in NATO.

New World

The fact is that the world is dramatically different than it was. Some major nations are relatively weaker than they were, while others are stronger. With the collapse of the Soviet Union, the bipolar world is gone. We live during a unipolar moment.[19] The United States has unparalleled military might, economic strength and cultural reach. The quick war in Iraq just reinforces that reality.[20] There is nowhere to hide from American power.

Understandably, other nations are conflicted by these new realities. They may embrace our values, appreciate the benefits they gain from freer trade, respect our military power, and value our disinterest in empire; but they nonetheless are concerned by America's unchecked power and sensitive to any sign that we might act as a rogue elephant. When the United States is seen walking away from the Kyoto Treaty and rejecting the International Criminal Court, other nations fear U.S. unilateralism that leaves them marginalized, impotent, and vulnerable.

Going Forward

The United States, like every nation, reserves the right to act if its vital interests are threatened. I believe other countries understand and accept that. But what about the rest of the time? Does the United States reject any restraints on its prerogatives and power? Admittedly, some of the Cold War institutions are showing their age and do not reflect today's world. They have not adapted to new realities and are less effective as time goes on. But does that mean that the world's sole superpower rejects their relevance and goes its own way?

I'd suggest that it is in the interest of the United States to make clear that we accept "rules of the road" as a general proposition. It is in our interest to initiate a dialogue with our friends, our allies, and the international community more generally about the need to review international organizations founded during a different time that may need reform to meet the new realities. There is a broad spectrum of multilateral institutions: the United Nations, NATO, WTO, and the G-8, to name a few. What are the competitive advantages and disadvantages of each? What are their limitations? What is their potential? Should and can some be reformed? Are new structures necessary? Predictability can be a good thing. Inviting a constructive dialogue with the rest of the world will reassure them that we do not intend to act on a whim or in defiance of established procedures just because we can. And, if we make the "rules of the road" better, we will benefit too.

Again, the United States is the world's sole superpower. We have that status due to our military might, economic strength and cultural reach. And, I believe, we have achieved this position not due to some historical fluke, or chance. We stand in this position because of the values embraced in our Declaration of Independence and in our Constitution. We stand tall because of the recognition of and respect for individual liberty and the rule of law. We stand today on the shoulders of American patriots, entrepreneurs and civic leaders who have gone before. And, we hold this unique status because of our fidelity to those values and our commitment to support our country in treasury, blood and love. It is a position earned. I believe in American exceptionalism and therefore I believe the rest of the world benefits from our leadership and generosity. And, if America's vital interests are at stake, we can and we must act to protect them.

However, to me, this does not mean that in most things broadly accepted "rules of the road" are not in our interest as it is in the interests of others. So, going forward, we should reach out to others and enlist them in a new dialogue about "rules of the road" and about institutions that better fit the new world in which we live.

Thank you.

---

1. President George W. Bush, Remarks at the Graduation Ceremony at the U.S. Military Academy, West Point, New York, June 1, 2002. "The gravest danger of freedom lies at the perilous crossroads of radicalism and technology. When the spread of chemical and biological and nuclear weapons, along with ballistic missile technology, when that occurs, even weak states and small groups could attain a catastrophic power to strike at great nations.

2. *Ibid.* See also, President George W. Bush, Remarks at the National Defense University, Washington, DC, May 1, 2001. See also, Robert L. Bartley's "At Dawn in a New Diplomatic Era," *Wall Street Journal*, June 17, 2002. In his essay, Mr. Bartley concludes, "We can expect President Bush's doctrine of preemption against terrorist gangs and terrorist states will set the diplomatic tone of the next half-century."

3. Secretary of Defense Donald Rumsfeld, Remarks to the National Defense University, Washington, DC, June 3, 2003.

4. Secretary of State Colin L. Powell, Press Briefing, Manila, Philippines, August 3, 2002.

5. Vice President Dick Cheney, Remarks to the Veterans of Foreign Wars 103rd National Convention, Nashville, Tennessee, August 26, 2002, and Remarks Honoring Veterans of the Korean War, San Antonio, Texas, August 29, 2002.

6. Vice President Cheney went on to say, "A return of inspectors would provide no assurance whatsoever of his compliance with UN resolutions. On the contrary, there is a great danger that it would provide false comfort that Saddam was somehow 'back in his box.'" Vice President Dick Cheney, Remarks to the Veterans of Foreign Wars 103rd National Convention, Nashville, Tennessee, August 26, 2002. And on September 3, 2002, Secretary of Defense Rumsfeld said, "I think that the intrusiveness of any inspection regime that would be sufficiently permissive to enable the rest of the world to know that in fact the UN resolutions were being fulfilled and lived up to would be such that its unlikely (Baghdad would) agree to it," Secretary of Defense Donald Rumsfeld, Department of Defense News Briefing, September 3, 2002.

7. Kofi Annan, "When Force Is Considered, There Is No Substitute For Legitimacy Provided By The United Nations," Address to the United Nations General Assembly, New York, NY, September 12, 2002.

8. For a fascinating investigation of the evidence of Saddam Hussein's involvement in the 1993 bombing of New York's World Trade Center and Ramzi Yousef, the mastermind of that terrorist act, see Laurie Mylroie, *Study of Revenge: The First World Trade Center Attack and Saddam Hussein's War Against America* (Washington, DC, The AEI Press; 2001).

9. President George W. Bush, Address to the United Nations General Assembly, New York, NY, September 12, 2002.

10. For a provocative review of U.S. history and policy on Saddam Hussein's Iraqi regime, see David Wurmser, *Tyranny's Ally: America's Failure to Defeat Saddam Hussein* (Washington, DC, The AEI Press, 1999).

11. Kofi Annan, "When Force is Considered, There is No Substitute for Legitimacy Provided by the United Nations," Address to the United Nations General Assembly, New York, NY, September 12, 2002.

12. Saddam Hussein's Iraq regime's debt to Russia is over $16 billion, France over $9 billion and Germany over $6.5 billion.

13. See Peter Finn, "U.S.-Style Campaign With Anti-U.S. Theme; German Gains by Opposing Iraq Attack," *Washington Post*, September 19, 2002; Peter Finn, "Ruling Coalition Wins Narrowly in German Vote; Strong Anti-War Stance Helps Schroeder Defeat Conservatives," *Washington Post*, September 23, 2003; Vivienne Walt, "Chirac Plays to France's Powerful Past, *USA Today*, February 27, 2003.

14. Among the elected-10, the following Security Council members never publicly declared whether or not they would support an 18th resolution on Iraq: Angola, Cameroon, Chile, Guinea, Mexico and Pakistan.

15. UN Secretary-General Kofi Annan, Remarks at the College of William and Mary, February 8, 2003, Williamsburg, Virginia.

16. See Charles Krauthammer, "France's Game: French Opposition to the U.S. is Not About Iraq But About Who "Runs the World," *Time Magazine*, March 24, 2003.

17. See Thomas Fuller, "Threats and Responses: NATO is Torn Over Weapons For the Turks," *New York Times*, February 7, 2003; Peter Finn, "Belgium to Block NATO Military Aid for Turkey," *Washington Post*, February 10, 2003; Craig S. Smith and Richard Bernstein, "3 Members of NATO and Russia Resist U.S. on Iraq Plans," *New York Times*, February 11, 2003; Judy Dempsey, Robert Graham and James Harding, "NATO is Plunged Into Crisis Over Block on Turkish Defense: France, Belgium and Germany Deepen Split With U.S. Over Action on Iraq," *Financial Times* (London), February 11, 2003; and Editorial, "The Alliance Comes Apart at the Seams: The Iraq Crisis is Causing Wider Collateral Damage to NATO," *Financial Times* (London), February 11, 2003.

18. "NATO agreed late tonight to begin military planning for the defense of Turkey in the event of a U.S.-led war with Iraq…The impasse was broken when the issue was taken to NATO's Defense Planning Committee. France does not have a seat on the body, and the two other holdouts, Germany and Belgium, eventually gave in to pressure to accede to the formal Turkish request for help." Keith B. Richburg, "NATO Agrees to Begin Aid to Turkey; Germany, Belgium Stand Down As Deadlock Ends," *Washington Post*, February 17, 2003. See also, Richard Bernstein and Steven R. Weisman, "NATO Settles Rift Over Aid to Turks in Case of a War," *New York Times*, February 17, 2003, and Henry Chu and Sebastian Rotella, "NATO Agrees to Assist Turkey," *Los Angeles Times*, February 17, 2003.

19. Charles Krauthammer, "The Unipolar Moment," *Foreign Affairs*, Vol.70, Issue 1, Winter 1990-91. See also Charles Krauthammer, "The Unipolar Moment Revisited," *The National Interest*, 2002/2003 Winter.

20. See Ediorial, "Power & Duty; U.S. Action is Crucial to Maintaining World Order," *Los Angeles Times*, March 23, 2003. See also, Max Boot, "Power Resentment Comes With the Territory," *Washington Post*, March 23, 2003; Ivo H. Daalder and James M. Lindsay, "American Empire, Not 'If' but 'What Kind,'", *New York Times*, May 10, 2003; and Richard Bernstein, "Europe Seems to Hear Echoes of Empires Past," *New York Times*, April 14, 2003.

WHO REBUILDS AFTER CONFLICT?

The topic for this conference, post-conflict reconstruction, is both a timely subject and a daunting challenge. In recent years the United Nations and the larger international community have been involved in Haiti, Bosnia, Rwanda, Kosovo, East Timor, Sierra Leone and Afghanistan, to name just the most prominent. Some have been more successful than others. And, as we gather here in Loch Lomand, Scotland, the work of rebuilding Iraq has begun. The Coalition Forces, as the occupying power, exerts effective authority over Iraq's territory and has the principle responsibility for rebuilding Iraq as assigned by the laws of war and the 1907 Hague Convention. The United States, United Kingdom and other members of the Coalition Forces sponsored UN Security Council Resolution 1483 inviting allies and partners to contribute to the rebuilding of Iraq and establishing a role for the United Nations.

The exact roles in post-conflict Iraq are not yet well defined. But one thing is known, post-conflict reconstruction takes time. It takes commitment and it takes stamina. As Senate Foreign Relations Committee Chairman Dick Lugar wrote in a recent *Washington Post* op-ed essay, "The days when Americans could win battles and then come home quickly for a parade are over."

My remarks are not focused on the difficult and challenging situation in Iraq. Rather, my observations are intended to draw on some of the recent post-conflict experiences and to suggest some general considerations for post-conflict reconstruction.

As set out in a recent Stanley Foundation Policy Bulletin, "The complexity of post-conflict reconstruction has threatened to overwhelm traditional humanitarian and development assistance mechanisms. Post-conflict societies often lack workable governance, suffer from heavy penetration by external actors, are threatened by massive security problems, and face tremendous development challenges," Who rebuilds after conflict?

Earlier in this conference, Jim Dobbins made an amusing and useful observation. He said that when it comes to post-conflict reconstruction there are three categories of experts. There are those who are intimately familiar with the local situation and who have been involved in it for a long time. Often they say that rebuilding the society and a durable peace are impossible. The second group of experts are those who have worked in previous reconstruction efforts but are unfamiliar with the particulars of the country where rebuilding must now begin. Usually they say it will

---

Remarks at the Stanley Foundation Conference, Cameron House, Loch Lomond, Scotland, June 20, 2003.

be difficult, it will take time, but it can be done. Then there are those experts who neither have prior experience in reconstruction nor know much about the country that now must be rebuilt. Invariably, they think reconstruction will be easy and it will be quick. Unfortunately, Jim pointed out, often it is the third category that are the policy makers who are making the decisions both about the initial intervention and on reconstruction plans.

First, we should recognize the root causes of the conflict. Perhaps it is a long history of ethnic hatred such as in Rwanda, Bosnia and Kosovo. Perhaps it is legitimate security concerns such as those contributing to the conflict in the Democratic Republic of the Congo. Perhaps it is resource exploitation, territorial dispute, terrorism or the threat from weapons of mass destruction.

To rebuild a society, the facts must change on the ground. And often the warring parties will not come to terms themselves. Often they will not voluntarily seek outside help to resolve the dispute, separate the fighting forces, and implement a peace agreement like the Ethiopia and Eritrea border dispute. Often today's conflicts are far messier than that.

The United Nations has pretty much decided not to do peace making or peace enforcement. Therefore, in many situations, the UN is limited in its capacity to change facts on the ground. The UN is limited in its ability to establish the foundation for sustainable reconstruction.

There are only about twenty countries that can do peace enforcement. And only the United States Government can do large-scale peace enforcement such as in Afghanistan. Maybe someday a European force will be able to do large-scale peace enforcement, but not today. Consequently, resources become skewed where the United States does large-scale peace enforcement operations such as Iraq and others pick up other aspects of reconstruction. Also, it means, that certain capitals, and often in particular Washington, must be persuaded to invest to change "facts on the ground" or no sustainable reconstruction will take place. Of course, as Ed Luck has pointed out, this can be a problem not just because of the United States Government's ambivalence toward the United Nations, but also because of the world's ambivalence and even hostility towards United States power. But when military action is required, clarity of mission is necessary.

And when military intervention is initiated, there should be a plan for continuity between the military action and the post-conflict phase. This is especially necessary in the area of security and transition to civilian authority. There needs to be a blend of military requirements and the police function; moving to a non-military police force.

Sometimes military force is not necessary. Sometimes diplomatic force, economic sanctions and incentives and other tools can change facts on the ground. Here better cooperation and coordination between major powers, regional powers and the United Nations would be helpful. Unfortunately, in New York I have seen the UN Secretariat often more interested in its own position, prerogatives and perspectives than in getting the job done. In the game of power politics globally, regionally and locally, the United Nations is, at best, a supporting player and coordinator not a leader. A bit more humility, proportion and cooperation by the UN Secretariat might help better effect changes on the ground in some places in order that real reconstruction can begin.

Also, we must appreciate that, however good our intentions may be, sometimes we cannot eliminate the root causes of conflict, rather we must seek to manage them. We will not eliminate poverty in the foreseeable future, but we can try to create the opportunity for economic growth in a post-conflict society and alleviate life-threatening devastation due to food and medical shortages. We will not eliminate ethnic hatreds developed through generations and well founded on past transgressions, but we can help develop the rule of law, justice and other institutions to protect ethnic groups from capricious violations from other ethnic groups. We cannot eliminate the legitimate security concerns of neighboring states that have lost blood and treasury due to violent trespass, but we may be able to create buffer zones to help build confidence and lower the threat level. My point is simply that often the challenge in rebuilding after a conflict requires an honest appraisal of the root causes of the conflict and, where they cannot be "solved", at least we should try to manage them so as to contain and alleviate the danger that they again will enflame the society. We should try to establish institutions to deal with the root causes.

Next, it is necessary that the local people take initiative and, ultimately, take ownership of rebuilding after the conflict. Too often the international community is confronted by a country that seems to say, "I have a problem. What are you going to do about it?" The international community cannot be paternalistic in its reconstruction efforts and the indigenous community cannot become mere recipients of assistance. The venture must be cooperative. It must be a partnership. And over time the local actors must become the senior partners, success in rebuilding after a conflict is not in the eyes of the international community, but in the eyes of the people within the country.

Today in Kosovo, the Special Representative of the Secretary-General is failing. He is authoritarian. He does not trust the elected members of the Kosovo Interim Governmental Institutions and he treats them accordingly. He proposes an idea, and if the Kosovars don't accept it in 10 second, he imposes it by edict under his reserve powers. This is a pattern guaranteed to fail. When the UN leaves, which it will one day soon, all those things imposed by the SRSG will disappear too. He should invest the time and effort, the patience and persuasion, the flexibility and nuance to work with the elected Kosovars, to get them to embrace reforms (even if they are not perfect or exactly the preferred reforms envisioned by the SRSG). Local people and their chosen leaders must take ownership of reconstruction or it will not be sustained as the international community departs, as it surely will.

In post-conflict reconstruction, the international community has a tendency to pick local leaders who say what we want them to say, not those with constituencies and interests behind them. We must guard against this tendency. Leaders anointed by outsiders are seldom effective and rarely long endure.

Once security is achieved, I agree with Jim Dobbins' hierarchy of tasks. Let me be clear, they all must be dealt with early, but there should be a priority among them for resource allocation; political and monetary. One, establish a functioning civil authority. Two, create an environment for economic activity to begin, free the regulatory environment. Three, establish civil institutions, the political framework. And four, initiate traditional development tasks such as poverty alleviation.

Now let me elaborate on part of establishing the transition from military to civilian administration: justice and reconciliation. Without that it is hard to build an enduring peace. Often there are different rules if a conflict ends with clear winners and losers rather than a negotiated settlement. Especially where there has been a negotiated settlement for the arrangements of the post-conflict society. As Kieran Prendergast said, in these cases the international community should be cautious. The international community should approach this matter with a good deal of humility. There is a tension between wanting to punish the perpetrators of abuses and the desire to move on. A tension between accountability and reconciliation. The people on the ground have worked out what is possible. Of course, there should be no impunity, especially for the worst crimes against humanity. But sometimes it may be better to let the local people work out accountability on their own terms and in their own time.

And the devise of a Truth and Reconciliation Commission has proven effective in El Salvador, South Africa and elsewhere. It records the misdeeds. It names names. It can be a transitional justice vehicle for an accounting, forgiveness and reconciliation.

Regarding the United Nations, I agree with other participants at this conference that the UN can play a useful and significant role in rebuilding after a conflict. It has comparative advantages, especially in the area of humanitarian assistance. It's universality and its experience gives the United Nations an acceptability and reach in the post-conflict society and in the donor community that can be extremely helpful. The UN is especially well situated to coordinate humanitarian assistance.

Sometimes, like in East Timor, the United Nations can play the role of the leader in post-conflict reconstruction. It can be in charge. But in other situations, such as in post-conflict Iraq, the UN will not be in charge. In those cases the UN can decide not to contribute. But if the United Nations does decide to participate, it should accept the hierarchy that exists. Someone must be in charge of rebuilding after a conflict.

Rebuilding after conflict is a long and difficult process. In this post-Cold War era, we are gaining experience and, hopefully, learning lessons. Conferences such as this one that brings together scholars, NGOs and diplomats are very useful. I appreciate this opportunity to exchange views with you. Thank you.

U.S. Interests and International Organizations

With the collapse of the Soviet empire and the implosion of the Russian empire, the United States became the world's sole superpower. With Soviet tanks no longer threatening them, Europe decreased their level of defense spending and fell further behind U.S. military might. And China, while an emerging power, still lags far behind. The post Cold War "unipolar moment" has become the "unipolar era."

The United States is unchallenged in military might, cultural reach and economic power. The United States has the capacity to act alone to protect its vital interests when it must. But it is better to work with others when possible to spread the burden and, in some cases, to increase the likelihood of success.

Throughout the 20th century and into the new millennium, our foreign policy has been informed by a belief in American exceptionalism. As Ronald Reagan said at Westminster Hall, "Freedom is not the sole prerogative of a lucky few but the inalienable and universal right of all human beings." We recognize that human rights are universal, our values are just, and America fights when required not to build an empire but to make the world safer, more secure and more free.

However, the United States cannot afford to be reckless nor careless in advancing our values or protecting our vital interests. No country, not even the world's sole superpower, can afford to unnecessarily irritate or offend others. While America may have the capacity to go it alone, to always do so would be neither prudent nor wise.

As in the case of Operation Iraqi Freedom, a coalition of the willing can be formed with like-minded states to advance important security interests. However, enduring international organizations also are valuable vehicles in which and through which to take action. As permanent institutions they offer structured gathering places, a venue to exchange views, predictable ways and means to reach consensus when possible, mechanism to implement decisions, and the "indicia of legitimacy" to give those decisions broader acceptability.

The United Nations, with all its contradictions and disappointments, has been important in establishing international norms on human rights and against global terrorism. Its universal membership and acceptance in far flung corners of the globe give UN action a reach and bona fide that is valuable to us in advancing freedom and fighting evil fanatics who, to advance their twisted political cause, would target innocent civilians for harm.

Appeared in *National Security Forum Review*, Spring, 2004.

The works of the U.N. system to provide humanitarian relief in war-torn countries or places devastated by natural catastrophes is valuable and important. U.N. peacekeeping missions in Africa, Afghanistan and East Timor have advanced peace, reconciliation and justice. In these areas, it is in the U.S. interest to support and contribute to U.N. efforts.

And the U.N. helped sanction an international coalition in the first Gulf War which, in turn, helped other countries join with America to repel Saddam Hussein's illegal occupation.

But the U.N. Security Council's anachronistic structure and procedures make it susceptible to abuse. America must be prepared to act without U.N. Security Council sanction when required as President Clinton did in Kosovo and President Bush in Iraq. U.S. sovereignty cannot be sacrificed.

Some global challenges are better suited to multilateral response such as the proliferation of weapons of mass destruction. The U.N., the International Atomic Energy Agency, the London Suppliers Group and other international institutions have helped deal with the dangers of WMD proliferation. Similarly the World Trade Organization has been an extremely useful vehicle to lower trade barriers, which, in turn, benefits the United States and the entire global economy. The World Health Organization helps contain contagious disease such as SARs. And the United Nations Environmental Program helps address pollution issues that know no borders.

NATO has been a valuable linchpin of the U.S./European relationship for over 50 years, helping address grave security issues and usefully providing a foothold for America in Europe. NATO made a vital contribution to containing the Soviet Union during the long Cold War. Today NATO is playing an important role in helping central and eastern Europe move from the dark past of Soviet domination to enduring freedom and security.

So while the United States is the world's sole superpower and consequently has the capacity to act alone if it must, America benefits from international organizations. America, founders of the United Nations, the North Atlantic Treaty Organization and other international institutions, has benefited from them and will continue to do so. Ultimately the mission must define the coalition (or the international organization) and not the other way around. But often the mission can and should be advanced within and through an international organization.

AMERICA UNBOUND AND MULTILATERALISM

Is America unbound? Are there reasons to accept the challenges, frustrations, compromises and occasional limitations of multilateralism?

During the "long twilight struggle" of the Cold War the rules of the game were known and they were accepted. We lived in a bi-polar world. There was a fundamental clash of values, systems, and aspirations. Washington and Moscow were adversaries. The specter of possible nuclear armageddon focused the mind. And while there was active competition to advance sphere's of influence, generally it was waged on the margins. In Angola, Vietnam, Afghanistan and elsewhere political and occasional hot wars were waged. Often proxy's were used. Sometimes the big boys directly engaged. There were ebbs and flaws. Generally there was checkmate.

For a variety of reasons, in the 1980's the dynamic shifted. In 1989 the Berlin Wall came down. The Soviet Empire collapsed. In December, 1991, the Russian Empire imploded. The Cold War was over. Freedom had triumphed over Communist totalitarianism. Market economies had prevailed over controlled economies.

The threat of nuclear annihilation receded. Other nations no longer were compelled to take sides. Unshackled from the security threat of Soviet tanks lined up across the Iron Curtain, our European allies were free to resort priorities in order to address other interests. Understandably, defense spending declined.

It no longer was a bi-polar world. America stood as the world's sole superpower. Militarily, economically and culturally, America was the global goliath. It was a unipolar moment.

Soon, however, commentators, politicians and policy analysts began to predict the imminent end of American dominance. Pointing to history, they said a unipolar world was inherently unstable. Other power centers in Europe, Japan and China would quickly rise up to challenge American preeminence. Others would grow to fear America unbound. Citing historical precedents, they predicted that soon countries would form alliances to counter American power and check its freedom of action. A new global multi-polarity would emerge. But this did not happen. No balancing power has emerged. The unipolar moment has become a unipolar era.

Lecture delivered at the Whitehead School of Diplomacy and International Relations, Seton Hall University, March 28, 2006.

Japan confronted problems in the 1990's that slowed its economic growth. Its military remained relatively weak as Japan struggled to break out of its post-World War II anti-military laws and cultural habits.

China, unquestionably, is an emerging great power. However, Beijing has a long-term horizon. They are confident China will reclaim its rightful status as the great Asian power it had been for thousands of years. Fueled by unprecedented economic growth, Beijing cautiously plans and patiently executes its emergence economically, diplomatically, culturally and militarily. Beijing is not constrained by a requirement for yearly or biannual transformation, but rather it looks to generational progress. It may take 20, 40 or 60 years to achieve its rightful place, but it will happen.

Among the significant impediments to China's emergence are the challenges and dislocations of uneven rapid economic growth and consequent social problems. Many are benefiting from new opportunities, new wealth, and new lives. But the economic boom remains principally in coastal cities. The 950 million Chinese living inland in rural areas and remote mountains have been left behind. They have inferior health care, education and welfare. They remain tied to small plots of land with few economic options. And aware of the disparity between their lot in life and the promise in coastal cities, inevitably discontent is on the rise. There are increasing incidents of social unrest. The need for oil, gas and other raw materials required to expand economic growth inland steer China's foreign policy. And the individual empowerment due to China's new market economy inevitably leads to personal habits and expectations that stress one-party rule. So while China will continue to emerge as a great power, it faces internal challenges with a cautious, patient approach. That means its day of superpower status to check America, if that day does come, is down the road awhile, not tomorrow.

The anticipated rise of Europe to counterbalance America also has hit bumps along the road Without the specter of the Soviet Union, Europe is less compelled to defer to the United States. It seeks its own identity. EU integration continues. There is a single currency. EU enlargement has been a powerful propeller for political reform and economic liberalization in central and eastern Europe. Unquestionably, Europe has cultural and political reach. Europeans are clever and able diplomats. This population is well educated and skilled. The combined European economy is enormous. But Europe continues to struggle to speak with one voice; competitive tensions among Britain, France, Germany and Italy break out frequently. And Europe face numerous obstacles in its path to pre-eminence.

Defense budgets have shrunk. Over the past 15 years, Europe has fallen further and further behind America militarily. Technologically, Europe's military is generations behind. The size of their armed forces have decreased. And Europe's ability to project their military might is sorely circumscribed. Europe also is experiencing enormous demographic challenges. Birth rates are in decline. No European nation has a birthrate adequate to sustain current population levels. The power of unions, various regulatory barriers, and high taxation all dampen Europe's economic engine. Work weeks have become shorter. Productivity has not kept pace. Wages and benefits have increased. And as the "baby boom" generation nears retirement, Europe's social contract is strained to the breaking point. Absorbing central and eastern European countries' economies into the European community has been a drag on growth. While there has been progress in the Balkans, Kosovo's final status remains unresolved. And with the June, 2005, Dutch and French rejection of the European Union constitution, integration has suffered a major setback. The idea of a unified Europe to balance America has promise, but that promise is far from realized. And Russia, while enjoying an economic rebirth fueled by extraction of its vast oil and gas reserves, lags far behind. Rusian life expectancy continues to fall, birth rates continue to decline, and its health services remain in shambles, Russia's population continues to decrease. And while the energy business booms, fueling growth of a middle class and expansion of consumer goods, Russia has no broader modern industrial base. The commercial rule of law is corrupted by crony capitalism and political agendas. Russia's military equipment is old and in decay and its army shrinking. Russia continues to be threatened by ethnic unrest at home and perceived challenges by the near abroad. So while Russia's energy business is creating renewed confidence and assertiveness in the Kremlin and a rebounding economy, this rejuvenation is from a Russia that had been greatly diminished. Russia is a world power that must be taken into account, especially in the energy sector; but Russia is no longer a great power.

So while there are global shifts occurring, and areas that might emerge to check America, for now, and seemingly for many years to come, American primacy will be a defining reality.

However, American global preeminence has not made the world more stable nor created a sustainable world order. The East-West bipolar ballast is gone. The discipline created by the imminent fear of nuclear armageddon has receded. Things are messier. Admittedly, to some extent the Cold War world seems simpler and more orderly due to the rose-colored glass of a rear view mirror. Nonetheless, countries now feel less restraint in pursuing narrow national interests and new threats have emerged. As former CIA Director James Woolsey famously said, we have slayed a terrible dragon but now find ourselves in a jungle with a vast array of venomous serpents. There has been an eruption of ethnic conflicts, uncivil civil wars, failed states, ethnic cleansing and genocide, proliferation of weapons of mass destruction, the emergence of terrorist networks of global reach, to say nothing of environmental degradation and pandemic disease that know no borders.

Also, other countries, even longtime allies and friends of the United States, are uneasy with the imbalance of power. They are anxious about the unchecked capacity of the global hegemon to act as it sees fit. At some level they fear the "hyper power."

These national concerns are fanned by America's continued heavy investment in its military and, at times, America's apparent disregard for others views.

Why does the United States devote nearly 4% of its GNP to defense spending compared to Europe's far less than 2%? First, America with its far flung economic and cultural reach, with its great power, also has far flung interests: economic, political, cultural. Therefore America seeks the capacity to protect those interests. Second, America seeks to project its values and ideals. Founded on the concept of universal, inalienable human rights, embracing the idea of "American Exceptionalism," and having prevailed over the totalitarianism of Nazis, fascists and communists, America answers to the opportunity and responsibility to have these values animate its foreign policy.

At the height of the Cold War, President Ronald Reagan said, "The ultimate determination in the struggle now going on for the world will not be bombs and rockets, but a test of wills and ideals – a trial of spiritual resolve: the values we hold, the beliefs we cherish, the ideals to which we are dedicated... the great civilized ideas: individual liberty, representative government and the rule of law under God." These sentiments are echoed by President Bush's policies and rhetoric regarding the "Advance of Freedom" around the world.

For many – the cynical, the "hard-headed realists," those without the capacity to project power so as to give meaning to such aspirations – these sentiments by one more powerful, one with the capacity to act on such sentiments (if not guarantee success by such action) is unnerving at best, if not reckless, destabilizing, dangerous.

Having prevailed over fascism, Nazism and Soviet communism, America is wary of allowing any new threat to emerge. There is concern about "Gathering Storms." These concerns – real and imagined – contribute to the United States' large defense budget. And given the sense of deep "insecurity" seared in Americans by the terrible terrorist attacks of 9/11, the political, as well as the geopolitical imperative of large military spending is likely to continue for years to come.

America's forward leaning approach to expand its influence has not been limited to military hardware. It has not been limited to ever more accurate smart bombs, more maneuverable aircraft, and missile defense technology. It also has been political.

As Robert Kagan wrote in his provocative book *Of Paradise and Power*:

> The end of the Cold War was taken by Americans as an opportunity not to retract but to expand their reach, to expand the (Atlantic) alliance they lead eastward toward Russia, to strengthen their relations among the increasingly democratic powers of East Asia, to stake out interests in parts of the world, like Central Asia, that most Americans never knew existed before.

But just as it is understandable – perhaps natural and unavoidable – that America would seek to solidify its preeminence (to entrench its hegemony), so too, it is understandable, natural and perhaps unavoidable that others wish to restrain goliath.

Without the threat of the mighty Soviet Union on the other side, they feel no need for an equally – or more powerful – ally on their side to protect them. To some extent their world view is shaped by the reality of their capacity to act. Again turning to Kagan:

> Europeans' repeated dissent from the harder American approach to the Cold War reflected Europe's fundamental and enduring weakness relative to the United States... Europe simply had fewer military options at its disposal, and it was more vulnerable to a powerful Soviet Union. ...During the Cold War... these (differences) were more tactical than philosophical disagreements. They were not arguments about the purposes of power, since both sides of the Atlantic clearly relied on their pooled military power to deter any possible Soviet attack, no matter how remote the chances of such an attack might seem. The end of the Cold War, which both

widened the power gap and removed the common Soviet enemy, not only exacerbated the differences in strategic perspectives but also changed the nature of the argument... More and more over the past decade, the United States and its European allies have had rather substantial disagreements over what constitutes intolerable threats to international security and the world order, as the case of Iraq has abundantly shown. And, (according to Kagan), these disagreements reflect, above all, the disparity of power.

And the less strong, to a greater or lesser degree, fear the more strong. They feel – and to some extent certainly are – vulnerable to the interests and caprice of the greater power. And in a world where there is no adequate counterweight in the hard power of military might, nor in economic muscle, to the world's sole superpower, that anxiety is high. It is not comfortable to feel such insecurity even if the greater Power is seen as benign; even if there is no clear and present danger posed by the hyperpower. For even if there are shared values, shared history, and substantial intermingling of interests, that "the lion sleeps tonight "is no guarantee that he will not awake, and stirred by an interest, a concern, a threat that is not shared, act alone in a way detrimental to some or all lesser powers.

Such concerns grew in the late 1990's when the Clinton Administration bombed Iraq, Afghanistan and Sudan. Then all the fears seemed realized when the Bush Administration announced its withdrawal from the Kyoto Treaty on climate control and the International Criminal Court. These international instruments had gestated for a long time. The United States actively participated in the treaty negotiations. Other countries, in good faith, had taken U.S. concerns into account and sought to accommodate them over long and often contentious negotiations. In the end broad consensus was achieved. Appropriate U.S. government officials had signed the documents. Celebratory ceremonies had been held. The hard work of implementation had begun. Notwithstanding all that had gone before, the Bush Administration said no and defiantly walked away from these treaties. Frankly, on the substance, on the merits, I believe these two agreements are in fact seriously flawed and, as agreed to, were unacceptable. But there were other options to address the legitimate outstanding problems in the treaty documents.

And not only did America walk away from these two widely accepted agreements, it did so in a manner that many felt was high-handed, disrespectful and offensive. This heightened concerns in the international community about American power. It gave alarm that the lion had awaken and was trampling the high grass that nurtured others. What else others held dear might now be endangered?

Given these concerns, of course, the many will seek to constrain the unchecked ability of the superpower to act unilaterally. Of course, they will seek indirectly to constrain the more powerful whom they cannot constrain directly. This is not personal. It is business: the quite serious business of world affairs; the sometimes deadly business of war and peace.

As an aside, let me note that these days too often America takes as very personal efforts to constrain its power. That is an unfortunate mistake. One, it's not personal, it's business – except perhaps for the French. Two, by taking it as a personal affront, an insult, Washington's view can become clouded and that can contribute to miscalculation. And three, it will only be through having a bit of cold detachment, understanding others' views, and reflecting on our own enlightened self-interest in the long run (not in the heat of the moment) that American policy makers will gain the perspective required for sound judgments.

Turning to Kagan one last time,

> American statesmen of the late eighteenth century, like the European statesmen of today, extolled the virtues of commerce as the soothing balm of international strife and appealed to international law and international opinion over brute force. ...[T]hey were realistic enough to know that they were weak, and both consciously and unconsciously they used the strategies of the weak to try to get their way in the world. They denigrated power politics and claimed an aversion to war and military power, all realms in which they were far inferior to the European great powers. They extolled the virtues and ameliorating effects of comments, where Americans competed on a more equal plane. They appealed to international law as the best means of regulating the behavior of nations, knowing well they had few other means of constraining Great Britain and France. ...In the eighteenth and early nineteenth centuries, it was the great European powers that did not always want to be constrained.

It is not personal. It is business. And it depends upon where you sit. It is the way in which a country plays the cards which they are dealt. Weak. Less weak. Less powerful. Powerful. Mighty. All quite properly seek to advance their interests as they see those interests with the various tools available to them.

For America, for the world's sole superpower, the question becomes – given our capacity to act alone, given our power to act unilaterally when we must, is it nonetheless in our interest in various circumstances to forfeit some of that freedom of action?

Because we can act alone, should we? To what extent is it in America's interest to recognize and empower other stakeholders? And if and when it is in America's interest to act with others – be it their consent, their financial support, their collective allegiance to agreed rules of the road, or joint military action – what is the best means to do so? Coalitions of the willing? Loose confederations of like-minded states? Alliances based on treaty agreements? Particularized special international agencies such as the World Trade Organization with membership requirements and submission to negotiated rules of commerce? Geographic groupings? Which leads us also to the United Nations: an organization of universal membership? The U.N. has a charter all states subscribe to in the abstract, but many violently trespass in practice. The U.N. has machinery and procedures that enhance the influence of the weak. It gives the veto to four countries that empowers them in ways that vastly exceeds their power in the real world. Within the U.N. America's power is greatly limited to that it holds in the outside. In short, is multilateral cooperation in U.S. interests? I'd suggest it most certainly is in our interests.

There are various reasons why multilateral cooperation is in America's interest. One, in a world in which the United States has such a vast array of interests, there also are limits to treasury, limits to blood, and limits to the domestic political support for foreign engagement. Multilateralism provides a useful means for burden sharing. Two, predictability. It is easier to navigate the sea of international relations, to protect American commerce, valves and security interests if there are "Rules of the Road" that provide predictability. Established procedures for problem solving, agreed norms for acceptable behavior, and buy-in on conflict resolution help America as well as others. Three, multilateralism provides reach. It provides a presumption of "buy in" to norms established, rules agreed to. Unilateral decisions and bilateral actions do not. Four, participation does have a value in and of itself. Broad exchange of views encourages collegiality and a sense of shared ownership. Broad participation develops a deeper vesting in decisions made because you have had a say even if your views did not prevail in part, or in totality. Five, multilateralism can improve the quality of decision-making. Despite the occasional frustrations with the lengthy, sometimes circumlocutos, and often painful process of multilateral decision-making, the process provides valuable insights. The exchange of views and the back and forth of multilateral negotiations teases out the various vantage points, interests and perspectives of others. It can lead to better decisions. Sixth, some argue that multilateral cooperation is a prerequisite for legitimacy. On this point there is a fundamental split between America and many of our friends. This division pre-dates the emergence of American primacy. American Exceptionalism has been a faith in the transcendence of our values, of our ideals. It has been an unshakable belief in the American idea. Equal rights, democracy and the rule of law were not only the founding principles upon which the United States was founded, but "the inalienable rights of all mankind."

American Exceptionalism preceded the wave of new democracies in the past 100 years. And it certainly preceded America's rise to global preeminence. There is a deep and abiding faith in the values upon which an action is taken, a confidence in the merits of the case both moral and practical, and a belief that the practical results on the ground are what give and sustain the legitimacy of any act. Whereas the Europeans, coming from a different tradition and embracing their experience with the European Union, find legitimacy in process. It's a view others have grown to embrace for reasons principled and pragmatic.

While multilateral cooperation, in our view, may not be required for "legitimacy," it certainly does provide broader acceptability. And notwithstanding this chasm, it would be reckless for America not to consider in weighing its own actions the process and value of "legitimacy" to which others subscribe. The value of broader buy-in by others in difficult decisions, and in particular the use of force, is powerfully demonstrated by the events unfolding in Iraq.

Having argued for multilateral cooperation, let me nonetheless make clear that there are limits to it. Buying into the various institutions, procedures and process of multilateral cooperation, are restraints not prohibitions.

When there is a clear and present danger America must act, multilaterally if possible, but unilaterally if necessary. Presented with an immediate threat, no country, in fact, sacrifices its capacity to act alone if it must. Of course, perspectives on when a gathering storm has become a clear and present danger will vary. I do not intend to explore the vital issue in detail today. There long will be heated debate about when such action outside the accepted procedures of multilateral deliberations is appropriate and required. But such decisions should not be made in the shadows nor irrespective of others. The debates must be joined. Each case must be vigorously advanced. Patience and respect for others must be afforded. Violence to institutions ignored that are otherwise valuable must be considered. Similarly damage to important bilateral relations must be weighed. Ignoring the guide rails of the rules of the road is not cost free.

There are reasons to accept the limitations of multilateralism. America should embrace multilateral cooperation when it is in our interest, which is often. While America can, and sometimes must, act unilaterally, America should seek out multilateral cooperation as a way and means to enhance our power, project our values, and protect our interests.